Peter Norton's
Guide to
Access 97
Programming

Peter Norton
and Virginia
Andersen

SAMS
PUBLISHING
201 West 103rd Street
Indianapolis, Indiana 46290

Copyright © 1997 by Peter Norton

FIRST EDITION

International Standard Book Number: 0-672-31050-3

Library of Congress Catalog Card Number: 96-72077

2000   7 6 5

Interpretation of the printing code: the rightmost double-digit number is the year of the book's printing; the rightmost single-digit, the number of the book's printing. For example, a printing code of 97-1 shows that the first printing of the book occurred in 1997.

Composed in Goudy and MCPdigital by Macmillan Computer Publishing

Printed in the United States of America

President, Sams Publishing	*Richard K. Swadley*
Publishing Manager	*Rosemarie Graham*
Director of Editorial Services	*Cindy Morrow*
Managing Editor	*Jodi Jensen*
Director of Marketing	*Kelli Spencer*
Product Marketing Manager	*Wendy Gilbride*
Assistant Marketing Managers	*Jen Pock*
	Rachel Wolfe

Acquisitions Editor
Elaine Brush

Development Editor
Marla Reece

Software Development Specialist
John Warriner

Production Editor
Tonya Simpson

Copy Editor
Bart Reed

Indexer
Benjamin Slen

Technical Reviewer
Angela Murdock

Editorial Coordinators
Mandi Rouell
Katie Wise

Technical Edit Coordinator
Lorraine Schaffer

Editorial Assistants
Carol Ackerman
Andi Richter
Rhonda Tinch-Mize

Cover Designer
Jay Corpus

Book Designer
Anne Jones

Copy Writer
David Reichwein

Production Team Supervisors
Brad Chinn
Charlotte Clapp

Production
Michael Dietsch
Brad Lenser
Paula Lowell
Carl Pierce

Overview

Contents

Acknowledgments

No one ever writes a book alone. I have been so very fortunate to have the help of many talented and patient people to whom I owe a sincere debt of thanks.

First, it has been a real pleasure to work with Elaine Brush, my Acquisitions Editor for this book. She was so calm and understanding through the always hectic schedule required by computer books. I also want to thank Marla Reece, my Development Editor, whose gentle guidance through the process and clear knowledge of the subject were so much appreciated. Many thanks also go to Bart Reed and Angela Murdock, the copy and technical editors who so carefully worked out the bugs in my manuscript and VBA code.

Being mostly left-brain, I owe a definite debt of gratitude to the Sams art department for their handsome artistic contributions to this book.

I would also like to thank Matt Wagner, my agent at Waterside Productions, who found this very special opportunity for me.

Heartfelt thanks pour out to Don Kiely for helping me out with the chapter about publishing on the Web; and to Michael Groh, who took time out from his busy life as Editor of the Access-Visual Basic Advisor publication to write the chapters about working in a multiuser environment. Not only are the chapters well-written and informative, but my colleagues managed to complete them on a tight schedule.

My friend Pat Starr was the inspiration for the Pat's Pets application. She and her daughter Barbara were very helpful in gathering the material for the pet store inventory database. Mary Sue and Merv, both experienced in real estate, were the ready and willing source for the Elgin Enterprises information.

My patient husband, Jack, has not only been tolerant of my hours at the computer every day but also helped by acquiring and entering much of the data you see in the databases in this book. Thanks, Jack!

The ultimate thanks should go to the late Dr. Grace Hopper, who told me in 1948 that there would be a future for women in "high-speed digital computers." She was right.

—*Virginia Andersen*

About the Authors

Computer software entrepreneur and writer **Peter Norton** established his technical expertise and accessible style from the earliest days of the PC. His *Norton Utilities* was the first product of its kind, giving early computer owners control over their hardware and protection against myriad problems. His flagship titles, *Peter Norton's DOS Guide* and *Peter Norton's Inside the PC* (Sams Publishing) have provided the same insight and education to computer users worldwide for nearly two decades. Peter's books, like his many software products, are among the best-selling and most-respected in the history of personal computing.

Peter Norton's former column in *PC Week* was among the highest-regarded in that magazine's history. His expanding series of computer books continues to bring superior education to users, always in Peter's trademark style, which is never condescending nor pedantic. From their earliest days, changing the "black box" into a "glass box," Peter's books, like his software, remain among the most powerful tools available to beginners and experienced users alike.

In 1990, Peter sold his software development business to Symantec Corporation, allowing him to devote more time to his family, civic affairs, philanthropy, and art collecting. He lives with his wife, Eileen, and two children in Santa Monica, California.

Virginia Andersen has written or significantly contributed to more than 20 books about computer-based applications, including Microsoft's Access, Word, and Office, Borland's dBASE and Paradox, Corel's WordPerfect, and Lotus 1-2-3. She has also written text books and instructor's manuals, as well as the computer-related definitions for a scientific dictionary. She taught courses in computer science, information management, and mathematics at the University of Southern California graduate school and other universities for over 15 years. She concurrently spent over 25 years applying computers to such projects as mapping the surface of the moon for the Apollo landing site, estimating the reliability of the Apollo parachute system, and detecting submarines with computerized undersea surveillance tools.

Her years of practical experience made good use of her bachelor's degree in mathematics from Stanford University and her two Master's degrees from the University of Southern California, one in Computer Science and the other in Systems Management.

She lives in Southern California with her husband, Jack, three computers, 49 rose bushes, and two cats.

Tell Us What You Think!

As a reader, you are the most important critic and commentator of our books. We value your opinion and want to know what we're doing right, what we could do better, what areas you'd like to see us publish in, and any other words of wisdom you're willing to pass our way. You can help us make strong books that meet your needs and give you the computer guidance you require.

Do you have access to CompuServe or the World Wide Web? Then check out our CompuServe forum by typing GO SAMS at any prompt. If you prefer the World Wide Web, check out our site at http://www.mcp.com.

 Note: If you have a technical question about this book, call the technical support line at 317-581-4669.

As the team leader of the group that created this book, I welcome your comments. You can fax, e-mail, or write me directly to let me know what you did or didn't like about this book—as well as what we can do to make our books stronger. Here's the information:

Fax: 317-581-4669

E-mail: Rosemarie Graham

            enterprise_mgr@sams.mcp.com

Mail: Rosemarie Graham
            Comments Department
            Sams Publishing
            201 W. 103rd Street
            Indianapolis, IN 46290

Introduction

During my years teaching computer science and information management for the University of Southern California, I was continually amazed at the variety of ways my students applied relational database and spreadsheet tools to practical problems. They proved to me that a database is not some inert pile of data to be shoveled clumsily about, but instead is a sensitive information source that can be carefully manipulated to suit almost any requirement. I have always wanted to show my readers that Access, my personal favorite among database management systems, can be used not only for traditional information storage and retrieval but for real-time decision making, as well.

As the lines between Microsoft programs blur, Access can take advantage of its Office companions' new features as well as its own. I hope that as you work with this book to program Access applications, you will see what I saw—Access truly is the information management tool for the next century.

Finishing a book and seeing it on the shelf of the local bookstore is not the end of the story. During my years as a university instructor, I found that the student critiques submitted at the end of each term were a rich source of ideas for improving the course material and the approach to the subject. If you have any comments or suggestions about this book, either the text or the material on the accompanying CD, please contact me via CompuServe at 110074,1217.

Conventions Used in This Book

Note: Notes tell you interesting facts or important points that relate to the surrounding text. Notes can even help you keep out of trouble.

Technical Note: Technical details provide background information or explanations for how Access works. The Technical icon can help you learn more about the reasons why.

Tip: Tips tell you new ways of doing things that you might not have thought about before. Tip boxes also provide an alternative way of doing something that you might like better than the first approach.

Warning: The Warning icon alerts you to potential hazards that can cause serious problems with your application, with data, or with your hardware or network system. Be sure you understand a warning thoroughly before you carry out the instructions that follow it.

Peter's Principle: The Peter's Principle sets off text that will help you with some basic tenets you'll find useful as you work with Access and databases. You'll also find some interesting facts and experiences that will enrich your knowledge and maybe make you smile.

The Analysis icon indicates text that explains the meaning of code segments or describes the behind-the-scenes actions that have occurred.

Knowing how something works or how it is structured gives you a broader understanding of the details you work with in your programs. The architecture icon denotes the internal structure of the Access model or of hardware components in a network environment.

Whenever you upgrade from one version of an application such as Access or use Access with other software components, you must know whether or not the components are compatible. The Compatibility icon clues you in to tips, techniques, and notes that will make you aware of these issues.

Watch for the development icon to show you points you should keep in mind while developing your database. Many of these cases are ways to avoid problems later or to create a better overall system.

These sections point to cross references to future sections where you'll gain a better understanding of the current topic or to future chapters where you'll see how the smaller pieces work together to form a smooth-flowing bigger picture.

Because of the importance of sharing information from a database, you'll often find Access working across a network or on the Internet. The networking icon points to problems, tips, or explanations related to networking issues.

With the large size of many databases and the traffic in network connections, performance is an important factor for all database users. The performance icon shows you problems or points you should consider regarding performance and ways to make your system work more quickly.

Finding problems or knowing in advance what might cause a problem is an important way to avoid a programmer's frustration. The troubleshooting icon points to clues to finding problems or tells how to avoid future problems.

I

Getting Your Bearings

1

Why
Program
Access?

As the premiere database management system, Microsoft Access is used by millions all over the world. If it is so good at storing and retrieving information, why would anyone want to go to the trouble of programming an application created by Access? Although Access, with all its wizards and other versatile tools, can produce an amazingly complete and detailed finished application, it cannot provide all necessary capabilities and services to all users without some help.

By design, Access is meant to provide the most universally useful database features, which it does with remarkable thoroughness. However, each user or organization is bound to have special needs and processes that require enhancing the Access database tables, forms, reports, and queries. As a bonus, programming Access can create a foolproof user interface and significant error-trapping procedures that can ensure vital database validity. The following are some things you can do with Access:

- Suppose your database is quite large and you need to make the same change to a lot of records at once. With VBA, you can run through the entire recordset very efficiently in one operation rather than change the values one-by-one in a form.

- If you were operating a mail-order book business and needed to add state tax to the orders within your own state, you would need to look at the value in the State field of the customer's address. A program can do that for you and add the tax if the customer is in your home state or omit it, if not.

- The validity of your database is very important. You can add procedures that catch errors in data entry and display meaningful messages to the user. If the error is not significant, you can display a reminder to return and complete the data entry at a later date or refuse to move on until the error is corrected.

- Suppose you want to extract certain records, such as those for customers from a particular state, but each time you run the program you might want to see the list of customers from a different state. Using VBA code, you can prompt the user to enter the desired value when they run the program.

These are only a few of the cases in which you can benefit by programming Access.

Access As a Front-End Development Tool

Back in the old days, if a noncomputer person wanted a system to manage an important database, he or she had to hire an expensive programmer/consultant. With the advent of tools such as Access and Excel, someone with little programming expertise, but a clear picture of the requirements, can create a sophisticated application in a short amount of time. Access replaces the high-priced programmer who sat between the end user and the computer.

A Short History Lesson

The growth of computer hardware and software has evolved through several generations since the early 1950s, when Honeywell introduced the first truly electronic computers. The transition from one generation to the next was clearly defined in the early years. For example, the step from vacuum tubes to transistors and then the next step to integrated circuits were quite distinct and dramatic.

Programming technology was no less evolutionary. In the first generation, programmers were forced to write instructions in machine code consisting solely of numbers. At least they were permitted to use decimal numbers rather than the binary code the computer understands. The second generation opened up the world of assembly languages, which were different for each model of computer. Numeric machine code had been replaced by three-letter codes that were a little easier for humans to keep track of.

In the early 1950s, the third generation of programming languages was born. Thanks to the late Dr. Grace Hopper, the concept of a language translator made programming possible in plain language. FORTRAN (FORmula TRANslation), COBOL (COmmon Business Oriented Language), BASIC (Beginners All-purpose Symbolic Instruction Code) and many others became quite popular in the 1950s and 1960s. The compilers and interpreters translated the high-level code into binary for machine consumption.

The early BASIC, developed at Dartmouth College in the early 1960s for instructional use, was a conversational procedural language. Each instruction the student entered was immediately interpreted and executed. The object-oriented Visual Basic of today is quite different. Programs written in VB are first compiled, and then executed as a package.

The fourth-generation languages, often referred to as 4GLs, brought forth many front-end applications that served as intermediaries between the user and the program generator. Access is an example of a fourth-generation language. It creates code in the background to carry out what you tell it, interactively, to do. The code that is produced is event-driven; that is, nothing will happen while the program is running unless something happens: the user clicks a button, presses a key, moves the mouse pointer, or takes some other action.

The fifth generation is a bit fuzzier. It includes expert and knowledge-based systems, artificial intelligence, and language translation machines. Many expert systems such as programs for medical diagnosis or oil exploration were quite successful because their scope was extremely limited.

Much research has been poured into creating computers and programs that can think and reason as well as humans. In 1981, Japan announced its plan to capture and store all human knowledge by developing the fifth generation of computers. These intelligent supercomputers would be able to learn, reason, and make decisions. They also would be able to converse with humans in natural languages and understand pictures. Their natural language capabilities would even accurately translate idiomatic phrases into other languages. Naysayers and skeptics had a good time making jokes about trying to translate English to Russian and back. One such joke had the computer translate the saying "out of sight, out of mind" to Russian and back. When returned to English, it became "an invisible maniac."

It seems unlikely that anyone will ever be able to store all human knowledge into one machine, as the Japanese planned, and expect it to be able to reason using that body of knowledge. But, who knows?

As versatile as Access is, building a well-suited, totally responsive and integrated application for a specific use still requires some customization through additional programming. Access employs three programming languages to enable you to add the fine-tuning to an application.

Creating End-User Applications

End user is a term often used to describe someone who has the need to use the computer for database management or other intricate efforts but who lacks the time or training to learn all the nuances and complexities of the system. Therefore, a *developer*, the one who does have the time and training, creates a system that is simple on the outside but quite complex on the inside.

An end-user application provides smooth movement through all the computerized activities of the supported organization and responds quickly and appropriately to user actions. The developer also attempts to program responses to all foreseeable error conditions, whether caused by the user, by invalid data, or by the system itself.

Displaying Information

Message boxes, such as the one shown in Figure 1.1, are an important part of any application. Although the message in the figure is just for fun, message boxes provide relevant and helpful information about current activity or explain the reason for an error condition. In cases in which the user tries to delete a record or a value, a message might ask him to confirm the deletion. Message boxes do not require input from the user, only that the box be closed before proceeding.

A message box might contain up to three command buttons with various labels such as OK, Cancel, Retry, and so on. Message boxes can display a choice of icons and also have a custom caption in the title bar.

Figure 1.1.
A typical message box.

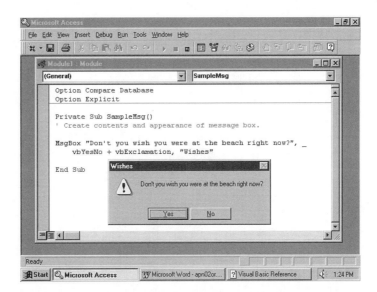

Responding to User Actions and Input

The Access Command Button Wizard attaches actions to a command button's OnClick event property. This results in a procedure that is executed when the user clicks the button. One example is a command button on a form that closes the form and returns to the main window.

Another important aspect of user interaction is requesting information from the user (for example, a query that extracts records meeting a certain condition, such as customers whose addresses are in California). The procedure displays a dialog box and asks the user to enter the state code, which is then used as the selection criterion in the query.

Dialog boxes differ from message boxes in that they require a user response. Dialog boxes ask questions, offer options, and acquire additional information. You are certainly familiar with Access's dialog boxes, and now you'll get a chance to create your own with Access programming.

Trapping Errors

In addition to the data validation rules you specify in the table definition, you can create procedures that alert the user to data errors such as conflicts between two values. For example, the user checks the Paid check box on a customer form and then enters a value in the Amount Due field. The procedure could test the value in the Paid field (Yes or No) and, if Yes, set the GotFocus property of the Amount Due text box to No. This would prevent the user from even reaching the Amount Due field. The procedure also could set the Amount Due to zero when the Paid field is checked.

The user cannot always interpret the cryptic error messages that Access displays. In trying to make the application foolproof, it helps to intercept these error messages and substitute a more helpful message. Access assigns a code number to each type of trappable error, which your procedure can decode to select a more appropriate custom message. For example, user errors on data entry cause form errors. Forms have an OnError event property to which you can attach the substitute message procedure.

Frustrating system and runtime errors are less predictable, but just as disabling for the user. With programming, you can create error-handling procedures to help solve the problem that caused the error, or at least give the user some information about why the error occurred and how to respond to it.

Peter's Principle: You and your users will be a lot happier if you get in the habit of building error traps throughout the application. As you create the application, make mental notes about all the places in the system where the user or the system could possibly make an error. Then add code that executes in the event of an error, even though it is just to stop the procedure and display an error message to the puzzled user. You'll notice when you examine the procedures the wizards have created that they abound in error contingency plans.

Returning Results of Calculations and Comparisons

With the Access Expression Builder, you can specify some rather complex expressions as the source of the data for a text box, the box's control source property. Using a function is a shortcut to creating the expression. After you have built the function, you can refer to it by name from other forms and reports in the database.

Most functions also will accept arguments in place of actual values, so they can be used to calculate the result based on a value specified by the user. For example, you have built a function to compute the annual income from a bond after the user has entered the annual rate. The annual rate is the argument of the function. When the user enters a rate, the function calculates the resulting income.

Following Conditional Branching and Loops

Conditional branching and looping procedures are a very important part of programming an application. Figure 1.2 illustrates three popular branching techniques. *Conditional branching* refers to determining the next course of action based on the outcome of a comparison. For example, if the

Balance Due field contains a positive value greater than zero, go to the procedure that prints invoices; if not, go on to the next step in the regular path.

Figure 1.2.
Three popular branching techniques.

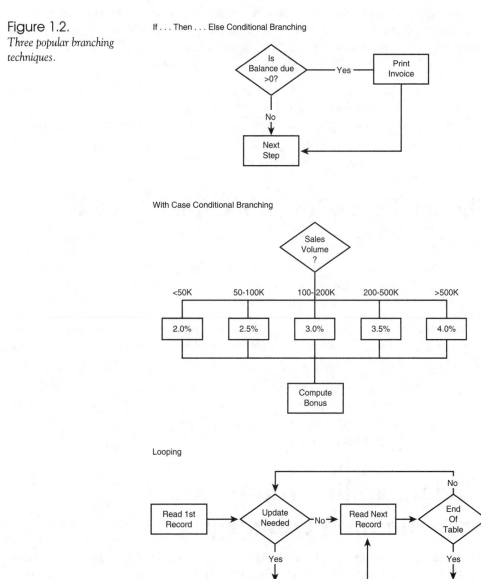

If . . . Then . . . Else Conditional Branching

With Case Conditional Branching

Looping

Another case of conditional branching is accomplished with the Select Case statement. When you have a list of several alternatives, the Select Case statement specifies what action to take with each of the different values. For example, salesmen have a graduated scale of commission depending on their sales volume. Each sales volume interval would have its own Case statement to compute the amount of commission. When computing the amount of commission a salesman has earned, the procedure reads the total sales and jumps to the matching Case statement.

Looping procedures enable you to perform a series of operations on an entire recordset. For example, to update the current inventory in a retail store, you process the transaction against the master list, one record at a time. Items sold are subtracted from the number in stock and items received are added. After the loop is begun, it continues until the end of the recordset, updating where necessary and skipping the records with no matching transactions.

Sharing Data with Other Applications and the Web

The boundaries between Microsoft Office 97 applications have dimmed almost to the point of being invisible. For example, Access can easily import charts and graphs from Excel, and Word can use an Access database as a data source for mail merge.

New features enable you to send a database via e-mail and to create hyperlinks that you can click to jump to another location. The destination might be in another file in your system, or as far away as the World Wide Web.

Chapter 17, "Linking with Other Office Applications," describes exchanging data with other Microsoft applications. Chapter 18, "Working in a Multiuser Environment," discusses sharing and controlling databases in a workgroup setting. Chapter 20, "Posting Your Database to the Web," gives more information about HTML and publishing on the Web.

Understanding the Access Programming Languages

Access speaks three programming languages fluently: Structured Query Language (SQL), macros, and Visual Basic for Applications (VBA). SQL is the language that Access uses behind the scenes in query design. Macros are lists of actions that are to be followed when the user clicks a button or some other specific event occurs.

VBA is a much more comprehensive and complex language that can be used to do almost anything while the application is running. It consists of objects, collections, events, methods, procedures, statements, and properties.

Chapter 9, "Writing VBA Procedures," presents more details about VBA program structure and syntax. Appendix A, "What's New in Programming Access 97?," highlights the new programming and application development features and capabilities that appear in Access 97.

Structured Query Language (SQL)

The queries you create in the Access Design View grid are implemented in SQL code. While you are building a query, you can look at the SQL code any time by switching to SQL view. To switch the view, select it from the View menu or click Design View, and then choose SQL View from the pull-down menu.

Figure 1.3 shows a relatively simple select query in the query design window. The query concerns the decision to reorder certain products. When the In Stock amount falls below the reorder level, the product is placed on order. The query is based on two related tables: the list of products in the Products table and the supplier information in the Suppliers table. The tables are linked by the Supplier ID.

Figure 1.3.
A select query that extracts information for reordering.

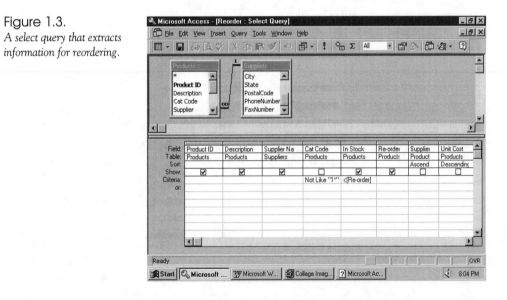

The query extracts relevant data from records matching the selection criteria but does not include any product whose category code (Cat Code) begins with 1, which is the major level code for fish-related products. Figure 1.4 shows the SQL code that was generated from the settings in the Design View grid.

Figure 1.4.
*The SQL code generated by
the query in Figure 1.3.*

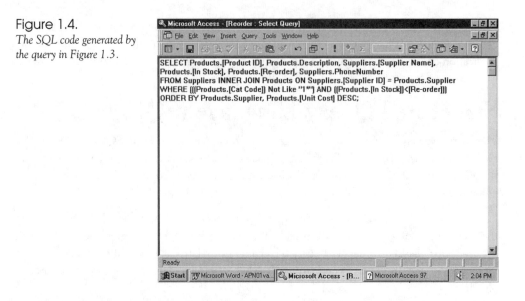

The complete SQL statement is as follows:

```
SELECT Products.[Product ID], Products.Description, Suppliers.[Supplier Name],
Products.[In Stock], Products.[Re-order], Suppliers.PhoneNumber
FROM Suppliers INNER JOIN Products ON Suppliers.[Supplier ID] = Products.Supplier
WHERE (((Products.[Cat Code]) Not Like "1*") AND ((Products.[In Stock])<[Re-order]))
ORDER BY Products.Supplier, Products.[Unit Cost] DESC;
```

In the first section of the SQL code, the SELECT operator lists which fields are to be included in the query result. The fields are named using both the table and field names with the dot operator between them. In the expression SELECT Products.[Product ID], the operator tells Access to look in the Products table for the Product ID field. Field names that contain a space or a dash must be enclosed in square brackets.

See Chapter 2, "Reviewing Access Database Elements," for more information about the naming conventions used in Access.

The FROM and INNER JOIN operators specify the relationship between the two tables: Suppliers is the parent table, which has a one-to-many relationship with the Products table. The linking fields are specified by the ON operator: The SuppliersID field in the Suppliers table is linked to the Supplier field in the Products table. In other words, you can look up supplier information for a product by finding a record in the Suppliers table that has the same supplier code as the record in the Products table.

The WHERE operator lists the selection criteria specified in the criteria row of the Design View grid. This shows that the answer table should include records for all the products that need to be reordered (except fish products).

The final operator, ORDER BY, specifies the sort order: in ascending order by supplier and, secondarily, in descending order of unit cost.

Chapter 7, "Programming with SQL," takes a closer look at the SQL language, its uses, and its components.

Macro Coding

Unlike macros found in other applications, Access macros are not merely recordings of keystrokes. An Access macro consists of a list of actions that are carried out, step by step, in response to an event. For example, a macro can run when the user presses a command button, when a form closes, or when a text box control gets focus. A macro also can execute when a specific condition occurs. Such a conditional macro might display a message box when data entered into a field has a certain value.

Macros are created in a special macro grid in the Macro Builder window. To begin a new macro, use one of the following methods:

- Choose New in the Macros tab of the Database window.
- Click Build (...) next to one of the properties on the property sheet, and then choose Macro Builder in the Choose Builder dialog box.

If you start a macro from the Macro Builder, you are asked to name the macro before proceeding. The macro grid (see Figure 1.5) displays at least two columns with two optional columns available, as needed. The default columns are Action and Comment. To add the Macro Name and Condition columns, choose Macro Names or Conditions from the View menu.

Figure 1.5.
The macro grid can consist of up to four columns.

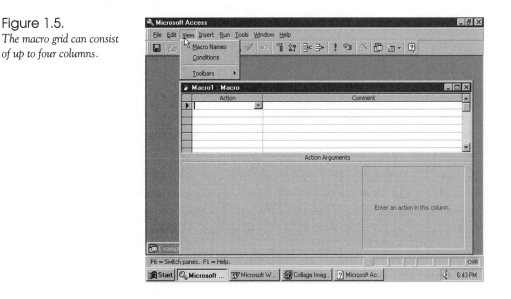

To enter the action that is to take place when the macro runs, choose from the Action pull-down menu. ApplyFilter, Beep, CancelEvent, GoToPage, Maximize, and ShowAllRecords are just a few of the nearly 50 macro actions in the list. Many of the actions have additional arguments that can be specified in a pane that opens below the grid.

Figure 1.6 shows three windows: a form with a macro attached to one of its text boxes, the Macro Builder window, and the result of running the macro. The active window, the message box in the upper-right corner, is displayed when the word Dog is entered in the Type field of the MacroEx form shown in the upper-left window. The macro condition tells Access to carry out the specified action if the value Dog is entered in the Type field. The large bottom window shows the macro code in the macro design window. The macro is named DogMacro, and the action is the command MsgBox, which displays a message box. The action arguments below the grid pane specify the text of the message box and whether to beep when the message appears.

Figure 1.6.
A macro that displays a message box.

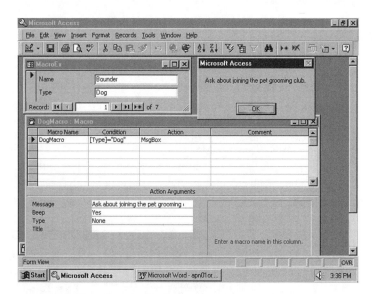

The last two lines in the Action Arguments pane, Type and Title, specify what kind of icon you want displayed in the message box and enable you to add a custom title, respectively. You can choose to display no icon or the Critical, Warning?, Warning!, or Information icon. The default for Type is None, and the default for Title is Microsoft Access.

After you have built the macro, you attach it to the event property of the button or other control. To attach a macro, set the event property the macro is meant to respond to, such as OnClick or OnGotFocus, to the macro. The names of all the macros in the database appear in the control's property pull-down menu. Conditional macros can be attached to a text box in a form and respond to one or more specific values.

Macros are useful for straightforward responses to events, but they do have some limitations. For example, you cannot use a macro to set up error handling or to loop through a recordset to process transactions. A macro does not return a value; therefore, it cannot be used to retrieve user input or to return a calculated value or the result of a comparison.

See Chapter 8, "Creating Macros," for more information about creating and running macros in Access.

Visual Basic for Applications (VBA)

Everything you can do with macros you can do with VBA (and a whole lot more). VBA code takes the form of a *procedure*, which is a block of code that performs a specific operation or calculates and returns a value. There are two kinds of procedures: sub procedures and functions.

Sub procedures carry out one or more operations but do not return a value; whereas *functions* not only carry out the operations but also return a value. Access provides many event procedure examples in the VBA Help topics that you can copy and paste into a control event property. Then you can make changes in the code to fit your application such as changing variable names. You can also use the Access Code Builder to create your own custom procedures that will perform any actions you want.

The following is a pair of simple sub procedures that move focus between the two pages of a form when you click the command buttons named Page1 and Page2:

```
Private Sub Page1_Click()
        Me.GoToPage1
End Sub
Private Sub Page2_Click()
        Me.GoToPage2
End Sub
```

Note: The Me expression in the procedure is a shortcut for referring to the currently active object, whether a form, subform, report, or subreport. You can leave off the form or report name completely and Access will infer that you mean the current object. However, using the Me expression eliminates any doubt or ambiguity about the object to which you are referring.

The GoToPage method moves the focus to the specified page in the current form. You learn more about methods and their syntax in Chapter 9.

Access provides many built-in functions for all types of operations: Math, Text, Error Handling, Program Flow, Database, and several other categories. You can view the list of built-in functions in the Expression Builder dialog box (see Figure 1.7). Functions return values to the program: character strings, numeric values, or true/false values. For example, the function IsNull() is often used to find out whether a field has a value. IsNull() returns True if the field is empty or False if it has a value.

Figure 1.7.
Access provides many built-in functions.

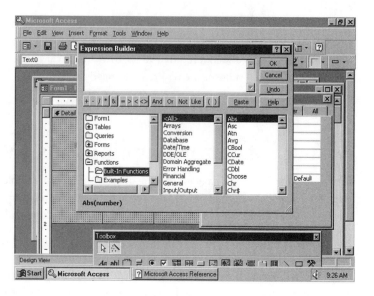

Custom functions can be created in the Expression Builder dialog box or in the Code Builder window. The following custom function displays the initials extracted from the first and last names in a form:

```
Private Function Initials() As String
' Display initials.
        Initials = Left(FirstName, 1) & Left(LastName, 1)
End Function
```

The `Initials` function uses the built-in `Left()` function to extract the first character of each name. The `&` symbol concatenates the two letters to form the returned value, `Initials`. After building and naming the function, you can use it as the control source property instead of the whole expression by entering `=Initials()` in the property sheet.

Macros can be converted into functions very easily. Select the macro in the database window and choose Tools | Macro. Then choose Convert Macros to Visual Basic. Figure 1.8 shows the macro DogMacro converted to a VBA function.

This has been a very brief introduction to VBA procedures. The remaining chapters go into much more detail about how to construct and use sub procedures and functions. Chapter 9 is devoted to programming and debugging VBA procedures.

Figure 1.8.
*DogMacro converted to a
VBA function.*

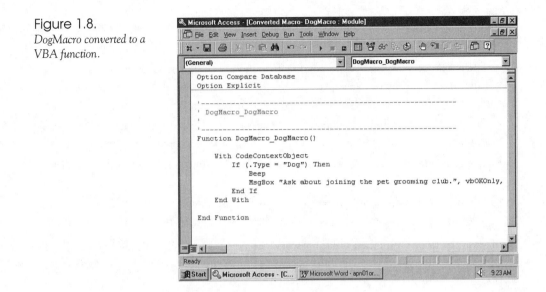

```
Option Compare Database
Option Explicit


' --------------------------------------------------------
' DogMacro_DogMacro
'
' --------------------------------------------------------

Function DogMacro_DogMacro()

    With CodeContextObject
        If (.Type = "Dog") Then
            Beep
            MsgBox "Ask about joining the pet grooming club.", vbOKOnly,
        End If
    End With

End Function
```

Deciding Which Language to Use

Each of Access's programming languages has special capabilities as well as some common functionality. For example, a query constructed in the Design View grid is coded in SQL but could just as
well be programmed as an object in VBA. As shown earlier, a macro easily can be converted to a
VBA procedure.

Queries are the primary means of viewing, changing, and analyzing data from one or more tables in
a database. The three major types of queries are select, action, and SQL. *Select* queries retrieve information, calculate totals, and build crosstabs but do not change the data in the tables. *Action* queries
affect data in tables. Both select and action queries can be used as control sources in form and report
designs. There are four types of action queries:

- The *make-table* query creates a new table from data already existing in one or more tables.
- The *delete* query deletes entire records from one or more tables based on the selection
  criteria.
- The *append* query adds complete records or only specific fields to one or more tables.
- The *update* query changes data in existing tables based on information in the Design View
  grid.

SQL queries accomplish more complex tasks and are coded using SQL statements rather than created in the query Design View grid. These include the following types:

- The *union* query combines corresponding fields from one or more tables or queries into a single field. For example, you have retail pet supply stores in several shopping centers around town and want to combine the sales data from all of them into one table.

- The *pass-through* query works directly with tables in an ODBC (Open Database Connectivity) database by dealing with the server rather than linking to the tables from Access.

- The data-definition query makes changes to a table definition such as creating and deleting tables, adding fields, and creating indexes.

- The *subquery* builds a SELECT statement within an existing select or action query. The subquery selects a subset of the records already extracted by the main query.

If you want to perform any of these tasks that work with tables, you must use the SQL language. The first three are built in the SQL view of the query window. A subquery is built by entering the SQL SELECT statement in the Criteria row of the Design View grid.

Chapter 8 covers SQL and building SQL queries in more detail.

The choice between macros and VBA code depends on what you want to do. Macros can perform simple tasks such as previewing a report or hiding a toolbar. Also, macros are easy to build. In the Macro Builder window, you are coached in the syntax and the argument definition. Some tasks can be done only with a macro (for example, performing some startup action when the database first opens or assigning an action to a keystroke or a key combination).

Programming in VBA has many advantages, and for some tasks, you must use VBA instead of a macro:

- VBA procedures are contained within the form or report definition, whereas macros are separate objects, listed in the Macros tab of the database window. If you move or copy a form or report to another database, the VBA procedures automatically move with it, but not the macros. They must be moved or copied separately.

- If none of the built-in functions do exactly what you want, you can build custom function procedures with VBA. Custom functions, once created, can also take the place of complicated expressions wherever they are used.

- Macros process an entire set of records at once by using VBA procedures. You can step through the records and process them one at a time, varying the action depending on the values encountered.

- The arguments set for a macro cannot be changed while the macro is running. While a VBA procedure is running, you can pass arguments to it or specify variables as the arguments.

- As mentioned earlier, a VBA procedure can detect an error, intercept the error message, and replace it with a more meaningful message to the user.

- VBA is extremely flexible when creating and manipulating database object definitions. You can change properties as well as add and delete controls.

In summary, the choice between building queries using the Design View grid and coding in SQL depends on the type of query you want to build. The line between the two techniques is clear. On the other hand, it is not so clear whether to use a macro or VBA to carry out actions. Macros are simple to create and easy to use, but there are many advantages to using VBA almost exclusively.

Access versions 1.*x* and 2.0 used Access Basic as the programming language. VBA is almost identical to Access Basic, and in most cases your databases will perform correctly after the conversion to Access 97. Access automatically converts the Access Basic code to VBA. Your procedures will look different, and Access might have made some changes you need to know about. There might also be some changes that you will need to make. If your application contained a lot of code, check it out carefully after conversion. Appendix B, "Converting from Earlier Versions of Access," contains more information about conversion considerations and problems.

Chapter 8 discusses macros and how to create them, and Chapter 9 takes a look at VBA procedures. Chapter 10, "Debugging VBA Procedures," discusses writing and debugging VBA sub procedures and functions.

How Do the Wizards Fit In?

The talented wizards provided by Access give you an additional step up toward creating custom databases. Access itself is an application front-end developer, and with the added expertise of the wizards, database development becomes quick and easy.

The wizards all create VBA code in the background that you can edit and augment in order to complete or add fine-tuning to the database. Chapter 4, "Creating an Application with a Wizard," shows how to create a new database beginning with one of the Database Wizard's templates. Chapter 5, "Examining and Modifying the Wizard's Code," examines the code generated by the wizard and makes some changes that modify the objects in the database.

Summary

This chapter presented an introduction to the world of programming in Access. It described the role Access plays in application development. The three Access programming languages were compared and their usage discussed.

Chapter 2 examines the Access database objects and clearly defines the terminology that Access uses. If you are already expert in using Access, you might want to skip the next chapter and go directly to Chapter 3, "Touring the World of Object-Oriented Programming," which discusses object-oriented, event-driven programming advantages, concepts, and strategies.

2

Reviewing Access Database Elements

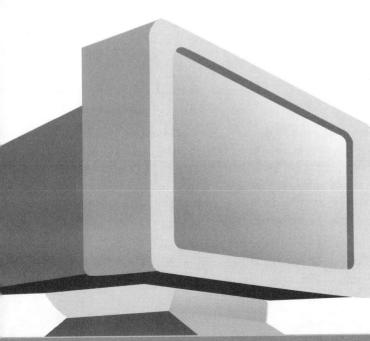

The purpose of this chapter is to review all the elements that make up the Access database environment. This chapter defines the major objects included in a database and examines the smaller components that play a part in tables, forms, and reports. In addition, you learn what makes each element look and behave the way you want.

If you are well acquainted with Access and its elements, you might want to skim over this chapter and proceed to Chapter 3, "Touring the World of Object-Oriented Programming," which addresses the characteristics of object-oriented programming and how that ties in with your Access application.

Access Objects and Collections

The catch-all term *object* refers to an element of an application. In fact, the application itself is an object that contains all the other objects. In Access, objects form a hierarchy beginning with the application in a program or library and ending with the detailed controls that make up forms and reports. Figure 2.1 illustrates the Access object hierarchy.

Figure 2.1.
The Access object hierarchy.

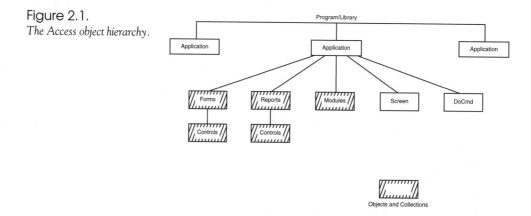

Applying property settings and methods to the top-level application object applies them to the entire application, which sets and retrieves all the options specified in the Options dialog box. For example, checking the Show Startup Dialog Box property in the View tab of the Options dialog box (shown in Figure 2.2) applies to the current application. You can also apply methods and properties to an application to change the default menu bar to a customized one, set the active object upon startup, and automatically save all files when quitting the application.

Most applications include several forms, reports, and modules. When one or more forms are open, the group is called a *forms collection*. For example, you may be looking through a Products list in a form and at the same time have the Suppliers information form open for lookup. These two forms belong to the forms collection.

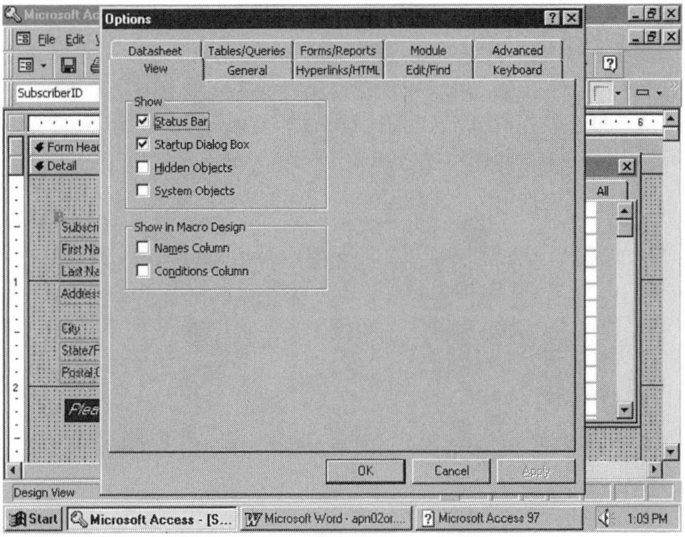

Figure 2.
You can set
properties a
Options dia

Similarly, the set of open reports or modules are members of the *reports* or *modules collection*, respectively. The objects in these collections are all the same type. That is, they are all forms, all reports, or all modules.

Tip: Collections come in handy in VBA because you can refer to a member of a collection not only by name but also by its index within the collection. Forms are indexed based on the order in which they were opened, beginning with 0. For example, the first form opened is indexed as Forms(0), where Forms is the name of the collection and (0) indicates that it was the first opened and is still open. The next forms are indexed as Forms(1), then Forms(2), and so on. If you close the first form, Forms(0), then the others move up in the index: Forms(1) now becomes Forms(0), and so on. Indexes in a reports collection behave the same way.

Access Objects

The *screen object* refers to whatever form, report, or control currently has focus. For example, while you are modifying a report design, the Report Design window becomes the screen object. You cannot open a form by referring to the screen object, but you can refer to it to find out which object is active.

The *DoCmd object* of an application lets you run most of the Access actions from a VBA procedure. For example, when you click the Save toolbar button or choose File | Save, Access carries out the

Save action. In a VBA procedure, adding the Save method to the DoCmd object creates the statement DoCmd.Save, which does the same thing as the Access Save action. Similarly, the FindNext action that executes when you click the Find Next button in the Find in Field dialog box can be converted to the VBA statement DoCmd.FindNext. A few of the Access actions, such as AddMenu and StopMacro, are not covered by DoCmd methods.

> **Note:** The terms *action* and *method* can get confusing. An action is a command in a macro or by itself that responds to a menu selection or button click. A method is a procedure that applies to an object. The Save action saves a specified Access object or the current one. The Save method carries out the Save action in VBA and applies to the DoCmd object.

An application has only one screen object and one DoCmd object, so these objects do not form collections.

> **Note:** Although you see Access tables in the database view, they are not Access objects. They are DAO (Data Access Object) objects. Earlier versions of Access included Table objects in the DAO, but they are now referred to as Recordset DAO objects. You learn more about DAO objects in Chapter 3.

Control Objects

At the lowest level, the *control objects* are contained in and subordinate to form and report objects. Controls include all the design elements you use to create forms and reports, such as text boxes, buttons, and labels. A control object can also be contained within or attached to another control.

Bound controls are linked directly to a field in a table, query, or other element of the database. *Unbound controls* are used to display information not related to any database element. *Calculated controls* are text boxes that display the results of a calculation. The control source for a calculated control is a formula or an expression using data from the underlying table or query or another control. Calculated controls can be bound or unbound.

An example of a calculated control is a text box that contains the total cost of an order by multiplying the number of items by their unit cost. The calculated control, Extended Cost, would have the following expression in its control source property box, where Qty and Unit Cost are both fields in the underlying table or query:

```
=[Qty]*[Unit Cost]
```

Table 2.1 describes the different types of Access controls you can use in form and report designs.

Table 2.1. Types of Access controls.

Control	Description
Label	Displays descriptive text such as titles and field captions. Unbound.
Text box	Displays data from a table or query, usually bound.
Option group	Displays a set of mutually exclusive alternatives, one of which must be selected. Consists of a frame containing other controls such as toggle buttons, check boxes, option buttons, and labels in its collection.
Toggle button	Displays a Yes or No value from a table or query (bound) or accepts user input (unbound).
Option button	Same as toggle button.
Check box	Same as toggle button.
Combo box	Displays a pull-down list of valid field values (bound) or stores a value for use by another control (unbound).
List box	Displays a list of valid field values (bound) or stores a value for use by another control (unbound).
Command button	Starts a set of actions stored in a macro or event procedure.
Image	Displays an object created in a different application, linked or inserted.
Unbound object frame	Contains a picture or other object that might require frequent updating.
Bound object frame	Contains a picture or other object that seldom requires updating.
Subform	A subordinate form containing data related to the data in the main or primary form.
Subreport	A subordinate report containing data related to the data in the main report.
Page break	Creates a multiple-page form.
Line	Displays a horizontal or vertical line.
Rectangle	Displays a box.
Tab	Displays information on separate form pages but as a single set.
HTML	Displays a Web page on a form. Must have Microsoft Internet Explorer installed.
ActiveX	Displays a custom control. New term for *OLE control*.

Access provides more controls than are shown on the toolbox. If you click the More Controls button on the toolbox, you will see a list of additional controls available, including ActiveX controls (see Figure 2.3). Your list might be different. This list includes all the ActiveX controls available when you have installed Microsoft Office 97 Developers Edition.

Figure 2.3.
The list of more available controls.

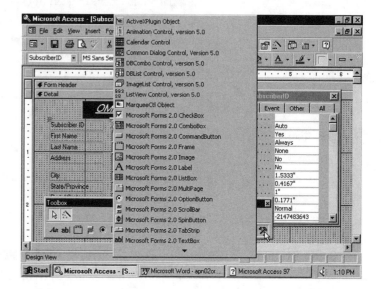

Controls Collection

Unlike a forms or reports collection, whose members are all the same type, a controls collection is composed of varying types of objects: buttons, text boxes, labels, lines, rectangles, and any other element of the design. A controls collection belongs to and is a member of the form, report, or control object that contains the controls.

> **Note:** You can use the VBA Count property to determine how many forms or reports are open or how many controls a form or report contains. Count comes in handy when setting the tab order. You can also use it to loop through the controls in a form or report and perform an operation on each one. You learn more about this and other VBA properties in Chapter 9, "Writing VBA Procedures."

A control object contained within another control becomes a member of the controls collection for that control. For example, the controls within an option group belong to the option group's controls collection. Similarly, a label control that is attached to a text box control is a member of the controls collection for that text box.

The tab control of a multiple-tab form has a special type of controls collection, called a *pages collection*, that contains the page objects that make up the tab set. Each page control, in turn, has a controls collection made up of all the controls on the page.

As with a forms or reports collection, the items in a controls collection can be referenced by name or by index number.

Using Access Control Identifiers

Being sticklers for precision, computers demand unambiguous identifiers when referring to controls. When you created formulas and other expressions using the Expression Builder, you might have noticed that each control was identified not only by name but also by the name of the object that contained it. For example, if you use the FirstName field from the Subscribers table in a formula, the Expression Builder displays the name as

```
[Subscribers]![FirstName]
```

The exclamation point operator separating the object names indicates that the item that follows, `FirstName`, is a user-assigned name.

If Access has defined the item that follows, the separator is the dot (.) operator. For example, in the statement

```
SubscriberID.DefaultValue = Forms!Subscribers!SubscriberID
```

`DefaultValue` is an Access property, so it is preceded by a dot operator. `Subscribers` is the user-assigned name of the form and `SubscriberID` is the user-assigned name for the referenced field, so they are both preceded by the `!` operator, often referred to as the "bang" operator.

The bang (`!`) operator was not available in Access versions 1.*x* and 2, so you might have to change some of the dot (.) operators in these versions to `!` in order to establish a compatible reference to an object that you have named. All subsequent versions of Access use the dot/bang convention.

> **Tip:** Instead of typing the whole explicit object reference to a control on an open form or report, you can use the `Me` keyword. The `Me` keyword implicitly refers to the current form or report controls collection and is faster than using the full reference. For example, `Me!FirstName` refers to the text box control named `FirstName` in the active form or report. If the control name contains a space, it must be enclosed in brackets: `Me![First Name]`.

Properties

Every object in Access has a specific list of attributes, called *properties*, that can be set to make the object look and behave just the way you want. The major database objects, tables, fields, queries, forms, and reports have the same set of General properties. Every control in a form or report also has a set of properties that determine the characteristics of the control as well as the appearance of any text or values it might contain.

Database Object Properties

To see the properties of one of the database objects, select the object name in the database window without opening the object, and click the Properties button. Figure 2.4 shows the property window for the DogMacro macro written in Chapter 1, "Why Program Access?"

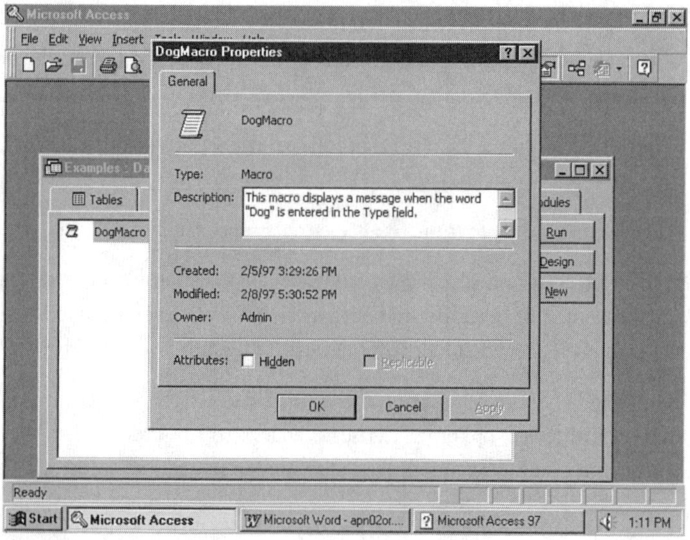

Figure 2.4.
The properties of DogMacro.

The Properties button is not usually available if the object is open in a view other than design view. Clicking the Properties button when a form or report is open in design view opens the property sheet for the currently selected object or control in the design rather than the form or report properties.

The properties of a query object are a little different. With the query open in design view, clicking the Properties button displays the General Query Properties tab if the focus is on the upper pane in the query design grid (see Figure 2.5). With the insertion point in the lower pane, clicking the Properties button opens the Field Properties sheet with two tabs: General and Lookup, as shown in Figure 2.6. If the query is open in SQL view, the General Query Properties sheet is limited to only four of the query properties: Description, Record Locks, ODBC Timeout, and Max Records.

Figure 2.5.
The properties of a query object.

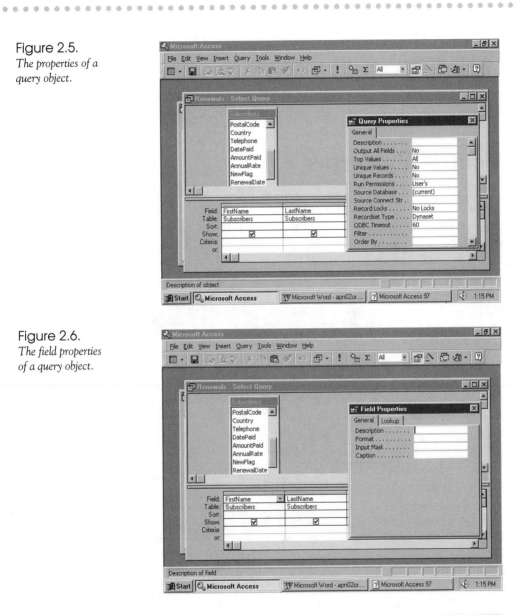

Figure 2.6.
The field properties of a query object.

Technical Note: Although it seems logical to think of a table or a query and the fields in it as Access objects, they really aren't. Any object that has anything to do with the data itself is actually a DAO (Data Access Object). These include table and query definitions, recordsets, and relationships between tables. Recordset objects are used to work with data at the record level. Field objects are contained in and subordinate to recordset objects.

> DAO objects are also grouped in collections similar to Access collections. A table definition contains a fields collection and an indexes collection; a query definition contains a fields collection and a parameters collection; a recordset contains a fields collection.

Control Properties

Each type of control has its own set of properties that can be viewed in one of the five tabs of the property sheet. Figure 2.7 shows the property sheet for a text box control. Most of the properties offer a pull-down list of valid settings for that control. Many other properties, such as the control source and the event properties, offer the assistance of the Code Builder, the Expression Builder, or the Macro Builder when you click Build (...) at the right of the property box. Still others, such as Caption, must be typed in manually.

Figure 2.7.
The property sheet for a text box control.

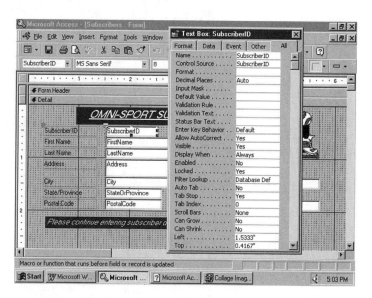

For convenience, the property sheet segregates the properties into four tabs: Format, Data, Event, and Other. To see all the properties for the selected control, open the All tab. Table 2.2 describes the four types of control properties.

Table 2.2. Types of control properties.

Type	Description	Examples
Format	Change a control's appearance	Date/Time format Number of decimal places Color and size Font style and weight
Data	Specify the source of the data and what you are allowed to do with it	Control source Input Mask Validation Rule and Text Default Value
Event	Specify how a control is to react when the event occurs	Before/After Update On Got/Lost Focus On Click On Exit
Other	Set properties that do not fit into other categories	Name Tab Stop (Yes or No) Control Tip Text Help Context ID

Tip: If you have entered a property setting that is too long to view completely in the property box, you can open a Zoom box that will show it all. Right-click the property box and choose Zoom from the shortcut menu or select the box and press Ctrl+F2.

Referencing Objects by Their Properties

There are times when you want to refer to an object by its state rather than by its name. For example, you want to work with the open form or the control that currently has focus. To do this during a procedure, you can refer to the object by the relevant property. Some properties relate to the attributes of the object itself, such as active or previous, while others refer to an object related in some way. For example, the Parent property of a control refers to the form or report that contains the control.

Referencing properties can relate to a screen object such as a control in an open report or form, to a form or report, or to a specific control. Table 2.3 describes the properties that can be used to reference Access objects.

Table 2.3. Properties used to refer to objects.

Property	Reference	Applies to
ActiveControl	Control that has focus on screen	Screen object, form, report
ActiveForm	Form that has focus or contains control with focus	Screen object
ActiveReport	Report that has focus or contains control with focus	Screen object
Form	Form itself or form corresponding to subform control	Form or subform control
Me	Form or report itself	Form or report
Module	Module associated with a form or report	Form or report module
Parent	Form or report that contains the control	Control
PreviousControl	Control that had focus just before the current one	Screen object
RecordsetClone	Clone of the recordset basis of a form	Form
Report	Report itself or report corresponding to subreport control	Report or subreport control
Section	Section of form or report that contains the control	Control

Events, Event Procedures, and Methods

An *event* is an occurrence that involves a particular object. For example, a specific key press, a mouse click, a change in data, a control getting or losing focus, a form opening, and a report closing are all events. Events usually are the result of some user action but can also be caused by a procedure or by the system itself. Access lists many events as object properties, and many more are available through VBA.

In an event-driven application such as Access, when an event occurs, some kind of action takes place. The response to the event is often to run an event procedure or a macro. An *event procedure* is a named sequence of VBA code statements that automatically executes in response to the occurrence of an event. A macro, as you learned in Chapter 1, is a list of actions written in the Access macro language that are carried out in sequence. You can also write your own custom VBA procedure as a response to an event.

Methods, on the other hand, are procedures that an object can perform. An example is the DropDown method, which executes when you click the drop-down arrow next to a combo box to display the list of values.

Events and Event Procedures

Responding to events is the way to make all the objects in the database work smoothly together. For example, when data changes, it can trigger matching changes elsewhere in the database. Or, clicking a command button can change the object on the screen or add a new record.

Events are properties of Access objects and controls. Each type of object has a specific list of event properties. Figure 2.8 shows a partial list of the events associated with a form object.

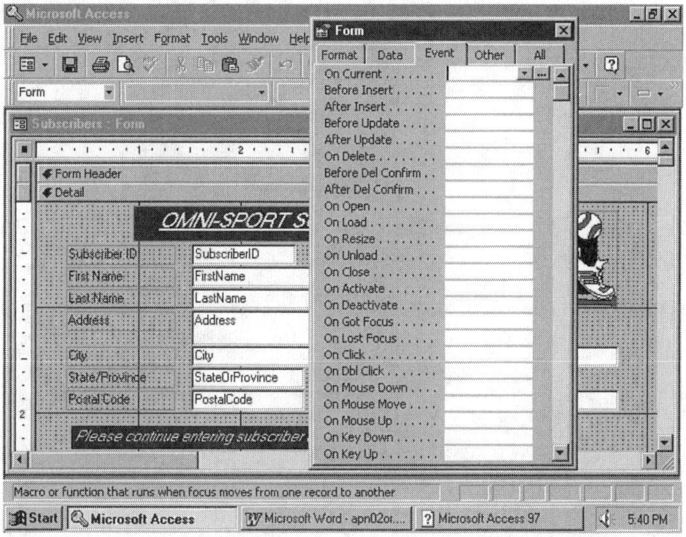

Figure 2.8.
A partial list of event properties belonging to a form object.

To define the appropriate response to an event, you can specify a macro that you have already written and stored in the database or create an event procedure. To attach a macro to an event, select the macro name from the event property pull-down menu. If you want to attach an event procedure to the event, you have two choices: call upon one of the Control Wizards when adding the control to the design, or enter the procedure statements yourself.

The Control Wizards can create event procedures for most standard form, report, and recordset operations such as close a form, add a new record, print a report, and so on. When you use a wizard to add a control to a form or report design, the wizard generates the VBA code required to execute the event procedure.

If your event procedure requires custom processes, you can use the Code Builder. To open the Code Builder, click Build (...) next to the event property and choose Code Builder from the Choose Builder dialog box. The module window opens with the first and last statements of the procedure already in place. Event procedures all begin with the `Private` (or `Public`) `Sub` statement and end with the `End Sub` statement. All the procedure statements belong between those two.

Figure 2.9 shows a form with two buttons: one added with the help of the Command Button Wizard, the other manually added and defined. The upper button, Bye Bye, closes the form when it is clicked. The first procedure in the module window is the one the wizard created to do just that. The wizard always makes allowances for errors occurring during a session, so the first statement, `On Error GoTo Err_ByeBye_Click`, branches to an error routine later in the procedure if an error occurs.

Figure 2.9.
Two button-click event procedures.

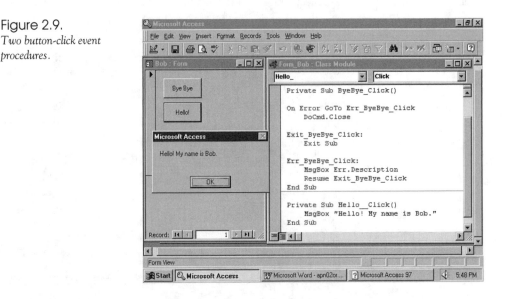

Wizards always try to consider the possibility of an error occurring so that the application won't stall out if one pops up. The next statement, `DoCmd.Close`, closes the form. The `Exit` statement simply tells Access to go from there to the end of the procedure and skip the error routine.

Chapter 10, "Debugging VBA Procedures," contains more information about writing procedures with error contingency and trapping features.

The lower button, Hello!, was added without the help of the wizard but by invoking the Code Builder to add the event procedure. The Code Builder displays a template containing the `Private Sub` and `End Sub` lines between which you enter the procedure statements. Notice the two boxes at the top of the Module window that contain Hello_ and Click. Hello, on the left, is the name of the object. If you click the pull-down arrow next to Hello_, you'll see a list of all the objects in the current form. If you want to create an event procedure for another object in the form, simply choose the object from the pull-down list.

In the top-right box you see that Click is the name of the event procedure. If you click that pull-down arrow, you'll see all the procedures that apply to the currently displayed object. Again, select a different procedure and add another event response to the object.

Methods

Each object or collection in Access has a specific set of methods it can perform. A form object has eight methods that it can perform, whereas a control has only six. Here are some form method examples:

- The `GoToPage` method moves focus to another page in the current form.
- The `Refresh` method updates all the fields in the underlying record source with the changes that were made in the form.
- The `SetFocus` method moves focus to the specified form or control.

Chapter 9 describes in more detail the use of methods in programming Access applications.

Macros and Modules

Macros and modules are both major Access database objects that determine how the application functions. In Chapter 1, you saw how to create a macro using the Macro Builder, and earlier in this chapter you were introduced to the event procedures that are stored in modules. Modules are collections of procedures that relate to the entire application or to a specific form or report.

The similarity between macros and modules lies in the fact that both types of objects determine how the application responds to events. Their principal difference is a matter of complexity and versatility. Macros are lists of actions taken one at a time. A macro can contain some conditional statements (for example, the DogMacro in Chapter 1 displayed a message box only if the Type field value was `Dog`). If you want to use complicated branching and looping, this must be done in a procedure.

Macros

Macros can accomplish many useful tasks in an application, such as the following:

- Set more powerful and flexible record or field validation rules for a control or for the field in the underlying table to which the control is bound.

- Display a customized error message for different types of data entry errors, such as a prompt to enter a Zip code if the address field is filled in.

- Synchronize records on related forms so that information from the same record appears in all the forms at the same time.

- Move between pages, records, and controls in a form by assigning specific key combinations to these actions. For example, pressing Shift+P to go back one page in a report and pressing Ctrl+P to move forward.

- Create custom menu bars and shortcut menus (new with Access 97).

- Set control, form, or report properties absolutely or conditionally. For example, if a payment is long overdue, display the value in red in the form.

- Add a conditional page break to a report that forces a new page only if a certain condition is met.

- Print a report from a form.

These are only a few of the things you can accomplish with a macro. All of these can also be done by procedures. Chapter 8, "Creating Macros," demonstrates in more detail the process of creating and running macros.

Modules

A module is a collection of statements, declarations, and procedures stored together in the database. Access includes two types of modules: class and standard. Class modules are divided into form modules and report modules. A form or report module contains all the procedures—event procedures, functions, and sub procedures—that are called from a particular form or report.

In Access 95, a class module was not available to any form or report other than the one with which it was associated. In Access 97, you can now create a special *class module* that can exist on its own without belonging on a specific form or report. It is listed in the Modules tab of the database window along with the standard module and can be used as a template to define custom objects.

Standard modules, previously called *global modules*, contain procedures not directly associated with a specific report or form. You can run a procedure in the standard module from anywhere in the database. The standard module is a convenient place to store frequently used procedures such as a function that tests to see whether a specific control is active and returns a yes or no value.

If you want to see the code that a standard or class module contains, you don't need to open the form or report. Select the object name in the database window and click the Code button on the toolbar. Figure 2.10 shows the Global Code module selected in the database window. Figure 2.11 shows the function IsLoaded(), which is the only procedure in this standard module. The IsLoaded() function tests to see whether a specified object is open, either in form or datasheet view.

Figure 2.10.
Click the Code button to see the procedures stored in a module.

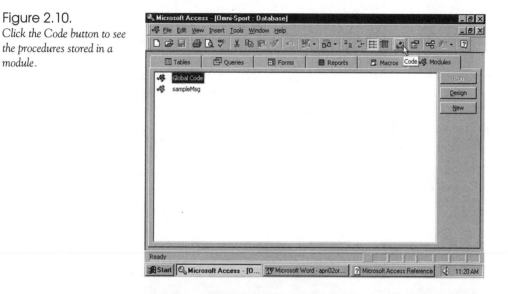

Figure 2.11.
The contents of the Global Code module.

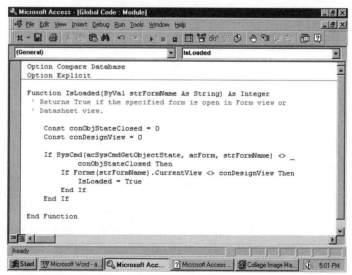

The function code might look like Greek to you now, but soon you will be reading a procedure as easily as you read the sports page.

Refer to Chapter 9 for more information about standard and class modules and how to understand, create, and use them.

Using the Object Browser

The Access 97 Object Browser is really a tool for developers of VBA code, but it is a good place to review the Access objects discussed in this chapter. The Browser is only available from the module window. To open the Object Browser, click the Object Browser toolbar button in the module window or choose View | Object Browser. The Object Browser dialog box displays information about all the objects, properties, methods, and constants in the selected project or library that can be used in VBA procedures.

Figure 2.12 shows the Object Browser displaying the classes of Access objects with the object, AcFindMatch, highlighted in the left column. In the right column, you can see the members of the AcFindMatch object. Perhaps you recognize the members of the class as the Match options in the Find in field dialog box where you tell Access what part of the field to search for the Find What text: Any Part of Field, Whole Field, and Start of Field.

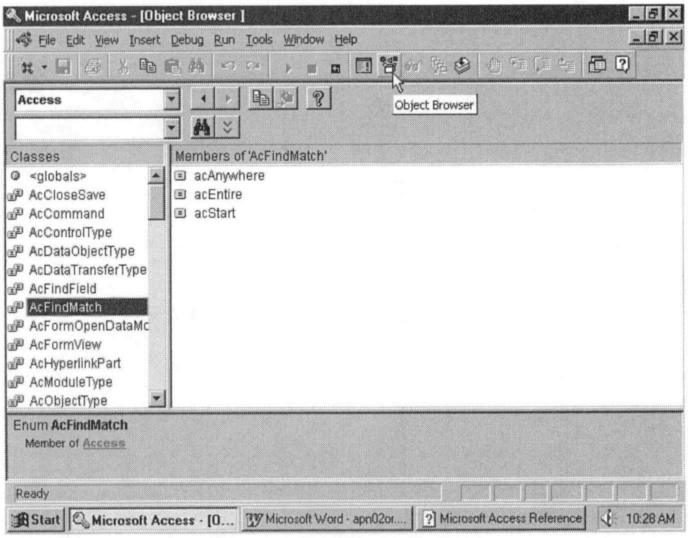

Figure 2.12.
The Object Browser displays classes of objects and their members.

> **Tip:** The Object Browser not only displays the names of the object classes and their members, but you can use it to paste code into a module by selecting the method or property and copying it to the Clipboard. Then switch to the module window and paste it in the module.

The icons preceding the class and member names indicate the type of object. For example, all the classes and members showing in Figure 2.12 are enumerated constants, values, or records. Figure 2.13 shows the Object Browser scrolled farther down the class list, which now shows object class icons and a module icon. The ComboBox class is selected, showing both property and event procedure members as you can tell from the accompanying icons.

Figure 2.13.
The Object Browser icons indicate the type of class and member.

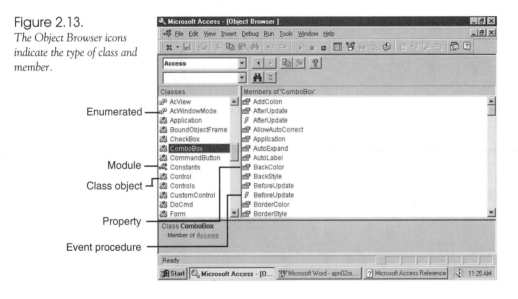

There is a lot more you can do with the Object Browser, much of which is new to Access 97. See Chapter 9 for more information about using the Object Browser to help you write VBA code.

Summary

This chapter has reviewed and examined the elements that make up an Access application and illustrated them in the object hierarchy. It has also briefly described how to build object identifiers. Object properties were also discussed. As a lead-in to the following chapters, the subject of event procedures and modules was introduced.

Chapter 3, "Touring the World of Object-Oriented Programming," follows with a more detailed picture of object-oriented, event-driven programming and how it contrasts with old-fashioned procedural programming. It also discusses the elements that make up the VBA objects and the accepted naming conventions used in VBA. In addition, it describes the DAO (Data Access Objects) used by Access.

3

Touring the World of Object-Oriented Programming

This chapter takes a closer look at the elements that are essential to object-oriented, event-driven programming. Without getting into the details of code generation, this chapter discusses properties and methods in more detail and introduces the concepts of variables and constants. It also discusses how information flows to and from functions and procedures. The elements that control the flow of database processing are also introduced.

Comparing with Procedural Languages

In procedural languages such as Fortran and COBOL, the application drives the process. The program statements determine what happens next. With event-driven languages, events control what happens next. If no events occur, nothing happens.

A program written in a procedural language begins executing at the beginning of the program and, with the bit in its teeth, runs to the end along a defined path. It might call functions and subroutines along the way or branch to a different path, but only because the program was written to behave this way.

With an event-driven program, a user action or some other system event runs the job. The user is holding the reins and the code responds. Because you don't know what the user will do next, your application must be prepared for anything. It is important to account for all possible forms of user action and make provisions for errors or exceptional events.

How Do Object-Oriented Languages Work?

In the VBA object-oriented language, there are three essential pieces: objects, events, and methods. Objects, as discussed in Chapter 2, "Reviewing Access Database Elements," are all the elements that make up an application: tables, forms and their controls, reports, queries, and so on. When something happens to an object, it is called an *event*. The object responds to the event by performing some kind of action, composed of one or more *methods*.

Not all objects are met with all events, nor can all objects perform all methods. Here are some examples of events:

- Field data changes.
- A mouse button is clicked.
- The user presses a key.
- An object gets or loses focus.
- A form opens, closes, or is resized (that is, maximized, minimized, or restored).

- A report is printed or formatted.
- A runtime error occurs.

Each type of object has a specific set of properties that determines its appearance and how it responds to a given event. The properties that rule an object's response to events are called *event properties*. When you want to specify how the object reacts, you set its event property to a macro or a procedure that contains the desired actions. Table 3.1 lists a few of the nearly 50 events that could occur. It also shows corresponding event properties and the objects to which they apply.

Table 3.1. Examples of events and event properties.

Event	Event Property	Apply to Objects
GotFocus	OnGotFocus	Forms and form controls
Activate	OnActivate	Forms and reports
Change	OnChange	Combo boxes, tabs, text boxes
NotInList	OnNotInList	Combo boxes
Print	OnPrint	Report sections
Update	OnUpdate	ActiveX, bound and unbound object frame controls

The final piece of the puzzle is the *method*. Each object has a set of methods that can be applied to it. A method is an action such as GoToRecord, ApplyFilter, and OpenForm. Such actions are specified in the object's event property settings. If you do not choose an event property for the object, it responds with a built-in behavior defined for each type of object. For example, when a text box gets focus and you have not specified its OnGetFocus event property, the built-in method changes the text box color.

If you have set the object's event property to a macro or an event procedure, Access first processes the built-in behavior and then executes your macro or procedure. For example, you click a command button that moves focus to the second page of a form. The button briefly changes to appear pressed in (the built-in behavior) and then quickly runs the macro to move to the next page in the form.

Getting Familiar with the Fundamental Elements

Objects are the fundamental building blocks in an Access application. That catch-all term includes everything from the most sophisticated form or report to the tiniest command button or check box. In Chapter 2, you examined many of the Access objects, how to refer to them, and how they behave. This chapter focuses more on the elements that directly relate to the VBA programming language, such as variables, constants, arguments used by procedures, and elements that control the program flow.

In an application, objects are tied together with macros and VBA procedures that determine the value or status of an object and pass the information along to another object.

Although this chapter discusses in detail the major elements used in database application development, the art of putting it all together in meaningful program code is examined more closely in Chapter 5, "Examining and Modifying the Wizard's Code." In that chapter, you will analyze the procedures and modules that the Database Wizard created in Chapter 4, "Creating an Application with a Wizard."

Variables

Variables are named locations in memory used to store values temporarily. Variables are used in a program to perform calculations and manipulate table data. They are similar to fields but exist only in VBA, not in a recordset. Variables must be declared before they can be used in a procedure. *Declaring* a variable can be as simple as giving it a name, or more thoroughly by also telling Access what kind of a variable you are planning on using: numeric, string, and so on.

The *scope* of a variable refers to who has access to it. This depends on where and how you declare the variable. The variable might be limited to the procedure that contains the declaration, throughout a specific module with several procedures, or to the entire application. The *lifetime* of a variable refers to how long the variable has a value. A variable gains a value when it is declared. It takes on the default value for that data type, if you don't supply a specific value. When a variable loses scope, it ceases to exist.

Variables should have unique names to avoid conflict, at least within their own scope. They are also a specified data type. The value of a variable can change over its lifetime, but the name remains the same.

Declaring Variables

You have two ways to declare variables: implicit and explicit. To implicitly declare a variable, all that is required is to use the variable name in a procedure. When you implicitly declare a variable, you are essentially throwing it out there, for better or for worse. For example, the following statements declare the variable, MyName, implicitly in a procedure:

```
MyName = "Bob"
MsgBox MyName
```

Figure 3.1 shows the results of running this short procedure.

Figure 3.1.
Declaring a variable implicitly.

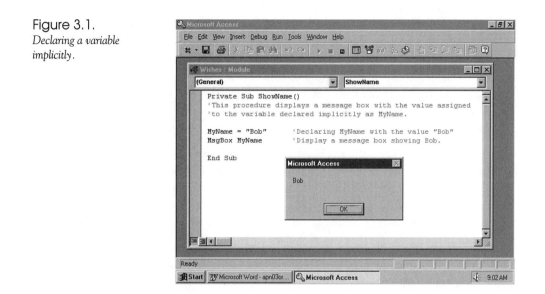

There are risks with implicitly declaring variables. For example, if you misspell an implicitly declared variable later in the procedure when referring to it, Access thinks it is just another variable and you might get some surprising results.

Peter's Principle: Be generous with comments in all the procedures you write. Even if it is crystal clear to you at the time, weeks later you will waste precious time trying to figure out what exactly the procedure is supposed to do. For example, add a comment to the line:

```
MyName = "Bob"          'Sets MyName variable to the value "Bob".
```

Comments are preceded by an apostrophe ('). Access ignores the mark and all text that follows it. You can place a comment on a line by itself or inline with a statement. In either case, precede the comment with an apostrophe.

Explicitly declaring variables means naming them and specifying their data type ahead of the first program statement. When you declare the variables explicitly, Access can spot a misspelled variable later in the procedure because it is not one of the ones you declared. You can declare variables in a procedure or a module. The location and syntax of the declaration determines the scope of the variable. The most common way to declare a variable is with the Dim statement.

Technical Note: The term Dim does not mean that the declaration appears in a subdued color. Dim is left over from earlier programming languages, where it was an abbreviated form of the Dimension statement. In those days, compilers read only the first five or six characters of a command anyway, so it was okay to abbreviate. One requirement of those early programs was to tell the computer how much memory would be needed to run the program. The Dimension statement, which appeared at the beginning of the program, specified any variables, such as vectors or arrays, that were not part of the data set but would require space.

Figure 3.2 illustrates declaring the MyName variable explicitly. Notice that Access gives you some help with the declaration. When you begin typing the data type, a list of relevant objects shows up. Automatically displaying this member list is one of the coding options available in the Module tab of the Options dialog box. If you don't want to see the member list when you begin typing, clear the option in the Options dialog box. You can choose to continue typing, press Esc to remove the list, or take one of the following actions to choose the appropriate name from the list:

- Press Tab to enter the highlighted item and remain on the same code line. Double-clicking the item also enters it into the statement.

- Press the spacebar to enter the item followed by a space so that you can continue with the declaration.

- Press Enter to enter the item and move to the next line in the procedure.

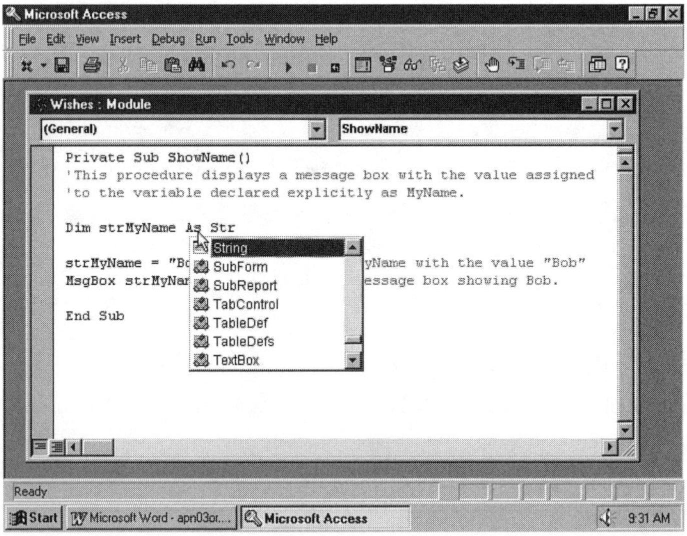

Figure 3.2.
Declaring strMyName explicitly as a string variable.

In the figure, you also see that the variable name is preceded by the `str` tag, which identifies it as a string data type. This is a good practice that improves the code readability.

A complete description of the data types that can be used in Access appears in the section, "Types of Data Variables," later in this chapter.

When you declare a variable in a procedure with `Dim`, that variable is available only within the procedure. Its scope is local and its lifetime is over when the procedure ends. You can also declare a variable in a procedure using `Static` instead of `Dim`. The scope of a `Static` variable is still within the procedure where it is declared, but the variable retains its value between calls to that procedure. The next time the same procedure is run, the value of the variable is the same as when the procedure closed. A `Static` declaration is handy for computing running totals, for example.

When a variable is declared with the `Dim` statement in the Declarations section of a module instead of in a procedure, it is available to any procedure in the module. This is useful when several procedures need access to the same information, perhaps passing values back and forth.

You can also declare a variable as `Public` in any procedure or module. A `Public` variable is available to the entire application. A `Public` variable is useful, for example, for making the company CEO's name available throughout the application.

> **Tip:** Except in special circumstances, it is best to use explicitly defined private declarations at the procedure level. This saves memory because the space the variable occupied is released as soon as the variable disappears. In addition, you don't run the risk of using the same variable name twice for two different and conflicting purposes.

When you first start a new module, Access automatically enters the first two lines (see Figure 3.3). The second statement, `Option Explicit`, requires that you explicitly declare all the variables you intend to use. If the module includes the `Option Explicit` statement, implicitly declared variables are not permitted. Figure 3.4 shows the compilation error that appears if Access encounters a variable you have not explicitly defined.

When you choose OK in the error message dialog box, Access points to the name of the procedure containing the error and highlights the variable name it doesn't recognize (see Figure 3.5), making it easy for you to find and correct the problem.

Figure 3.3.
Access includes a statement in a new module, requiring all variables be declared explicitly.

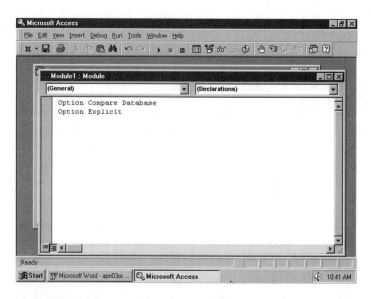

Figure 3.4.
Access displays a compile error when it doesn't recognize a variable.

Chapter 10, "Debugging VBA Procedures," contains more information about error messages and how to respond to them. It also describes many debugging techniques such as setting breakpoints and stepping through program code one statement at a time.

The alternative to declaring variables explicitly is to delete the default `Option Explicit` statement and declare variables implicitly as you refer to them. Both of these `Option` statements apply to the entire module and all the procedures and functions in it.

Figure 3.5.

Access highlights the compile error.

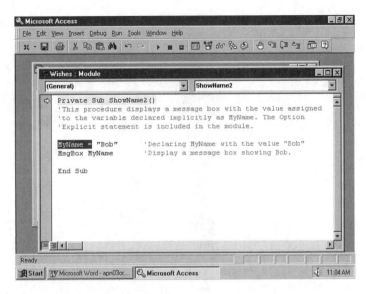

Note: The `Option Compare` statement determines how Access compares character strings in your module. Your choices are `Database`, `Binary`, and `Text`. The default option is `Database`, which uses whatever sort order you have specified for your database. `Option Compare Database` is used only in Access applications. `Option Compare Binary` uses a sort order based on the internally stored binary values in which all uppercase letters are first, followed by lowercase letters. If the `Option Compare` statement is not used at all, the default comparison method is `Binary`. The third option is `Text`, which is case-insensitive and based on your local language. Use the default `Option Compare Database` except in special cases such as in a module that uses a bookmark and must be case-sensitive. Then use the `Binary` option, which is case-sensitive. You can use different `Option Compare` statements in modules within the same database.

Using a Declared Variable

After you have declared a variable and given it a value in the procedure, you can assign that value to an object in your application. Figure 3.6 shows a procedure that runs when `MyForm` is activated. It first declares `strFavCD` as a string variable and then gives it the value `"Placido Domingo"`. The next statement changes the `MyForm` caption property from the default `"Form"` to that value. Notice that the form in the background shows Placido Domingo in the title bar.

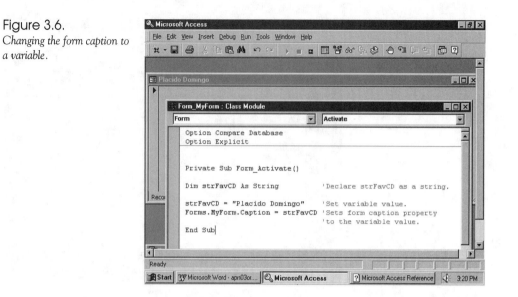

Figure 3.6.
Changing the form caption to a variable.

This procedure is included in the `Form_MyForm` class module and is available only to this form.

Naming Variables

When you declare a variable, you must give it a name. The name you assign can be very helpful when you try to maintain the program weeks after you have written it. In addition to the naming rules imposed by Access, certain naming conventions have been developed by programmers over the years to make their jobs easier. Variable base names are mixed case, using upper- and lowercase letters to help readability. For example, the name `MyFirstJob` is easier to read than `myfirstjob`. The optional tags preceding the variable base name can indicate the type of variable. `StrMyFirstJob` would indicate that it is a string variable.

The section, "Naming Conventions," later in this chapter, presents more details about the popular Leszynski Naming Conventions (LNC).

Types of Data Variables

Variables come in the same data types as fields, except they are classified as VBA data types instead of DAO data types. Table 3.2 lists the VBA variable data types and gives an example of each. Notice that each sample variable name in the table is preceded by a tag indicating its type.

Table 3.2. Variable data types.

Data Type	Description	Example
Byte	1-byte binary	`bytNewValue`
Integer	2-byte integer	`intAltitude`
Long	4-byte integer	`lngPopulation`
Single	4-byte floating-point number	`sglWeight`
Double	8-byte floating-point number	`dblNatlDebt`
Currency	8-byte number with fixed decimal	`curFebSales`
String	String of characters	`strGreeting`
Variant	Most kinds of data; 16 bytes plus one additional byte for each character in a string	`varAnyVal`
Boolean	2 bytes, True or False	`blnGiveUp`
Date	8-byte date/time value	`dtmMyBirthday`
Object	4-byte address referring to any object	`objEntryForm`
Argument	Variant by default, String or Integer	`strNewMsg`
FunctionReturn	Defined within the function	`varSqFootage`

The Variant data type can store all kinds of data: strings, numbers, dates and times, or one of its special values, `Null` or `Empty`. Variants are easy to use but require more memory space than other types of data. If you don't specify a data type when you declare your variables, Access uses Variant by default.

The Variant value `Empty` indicates the variable has not yet been assigned a value. `Empty` is replaced by a value as soon as one is assigned, even if it is `0`. `Null` indicates a database field that hasn't been initialized and the data is missing or unknown. You can use these values to test for these special values in an error-trapping procedure.

Look in Chapter 10 for information about how to detect and intercept errors.

Arrays

Arrays are groups of variables of all of the same type and with the same name. They are useful for looping through a recordset and storing a field value in the array items from a number of records. The code is simpler and has fewer statements.

Arrays are declared just like other variables, depending on the scope you want them to enjoy. If you want them to be accessible to all the procedures in the module, declare them in the declaration section of the module or declare them as Public in the procedure. For a local array, declare it with a Dim or Static statement in the procedure.

The only difference between arrays and other variables is that the arrays have an index. When you declare an ordinary (fixed size) array, you include upper and lower bounds that specify the maximum number of items you expect the array to handle. The following statements are examples of declaring arrays:

```
Dim intCountCD(25) As Integer     'Declares 25 elements, indexed 0 through 24.

Dim strSingers(15) As String      'Declares 15 elements, indexed 0 through 14.
```

To give you an idea of how arrays can be useful, suppose you run a mail-order business that specializes in CDs and you want to keep a current catalog of the most popular singers and titles.

The following statements give an example of using an array in a procedure. You have sorted the CDs by date of release with the newest ones first, and you want the names of the performers of the latest 15 recordings. The statements first declare a 15-item array for storing the singers' names. Then they loop through the recordset and copy the Singer values from the first 15 records. The DoCmd.GoToRecord.acNext is a recordset method.

```
Dim intI As Integer
Dim strSinger(1 To 15) As String
For intI = 1 To 15     'Initializes the index.
        DoCmd.GoToRecord.acNext     'Moves to next record
        strSinger(intI) = me!Singer
Next intI     'Increments the index and loops.
```

You can also declare multi-dimensional arrays with a declaration such as the following:

```
Dim int3D(5, 1 To 10, 5 To 8)
```

This declaration specifies a three-dimensional array with one dimension, indexed from 0 to 5, the second from 1 to 10, and the third from 5 to 8. Int3D(4,8,6) is an element of this array.

Warning: Be careful when you are estimating the size of your array, especially with multi-dimensional arrays. Declaring an array reserves memory for the entire array, whether you fill it up or not. Remember also that if your array contains the Variant data type variable, even more memory is used for each item.

Objects and Object Variables

Between the wizards and the design windows, you might be able to create and modify all the forms and reports you'll ever need, but it is important to know that you can do the same thing within a procedure. VBA statements can create, modify, or delete any object at runtime. An example was shown earlier in Figure 3.6, where the procedure changed the form's caption when the form was activated at runtime.

Recall that Access groups objects into collections: a forms collection, a reports collection, and so on. When you refer to an object in VBA, you use the collection identifier to help specify the object. Table 3.3 shows three ways to refer to an object in a procedure.

Table 3.3. How to refer to an object in a procedure.

Syntax	Example	Comment
identifier!objectname	Forms!MyForm	If the name contains a space or punctuation, enclose in square brackets.
identifier("objectname")	Forms("MyForm")	If the object name is a variable, do not use quotation marks.
identifier(index)	Forms(2)	Used to move through the open objects in a collection.

The first example in the table uses the ! operator, which signifies that what follows is a user-named object. If the form name were My Form, the object name would be Forms![My Form].

The second example uses quotation marks within parentheses to designate the object name. Once again, to refer to My Form, the object name would be Forms("My Form"). If the object is a declared variable, you do not use the quotation marks.

The third example in this table refers to a form by using its position in the collection as an index. Forms(2) refers to the form that was opened third. The first form opened would be Forms(0).

An object variable is used to refer to a specific object. The variable can be used later in the procedure in place of the full name of the object itself. The difference between declaring a data variable and declaring an object variable is that the data variable actually stores the value in a location in memory. The object variable stores only a pointer to the physical object in the database.

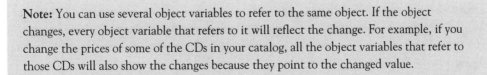

Note: You can use several object variables to refer to the same object. If the object changes, every object variable that refers to it will reflect the change. For example, if you change the prices of some of the CDs in your catalog, all the object variables that refer to those CDs will also show the changes because they point to the changed value.

To establish the connection between an object variable and the object, use the `Set` statement. For example, the following statements open the CDs table in the current database, Music:

```
Dim dbsMusic As Database
Dim rstCDs As Recordset

Set dbsMusic = CurrentDb()
Set rstCDs = dbsMusic.OpenRecordSet("CDs")
```

The two `Dim` statements declare the object variables as `Database` and `Recordset`, respectively. The first `Set` statement assigns the object variable name `dbsMusic` to the open Music database. The `dbs` tag indicates that the variable refers to a database object. The next `Set` statement defines the `rstCDs` object variable as the CDs table in the `dbsMusic` object. The `rst` tag indicates that the referenced object is a recordset.

`Set` statements can appear anywhere in a procedure or module, but the `Dim` and `Static` declaration statements must precede any action statements.

The `Set` statement comes with two keywords: `New` and `Nothing`. The `New` keyword actually creates a new instance of an existing class object, such as a form. An instance is a temporary copy of an open object. By using instances of a form, you can view several copies of the same form at once on the screen.

For example, the following statements create a new instance of the form CDs. The new instance will have all the same controls and properties as the original.

```
Dim frmNew As Form_CDs
Set frmNew = New Form_CDs
```

The new instance is hidden at first. To see both forms on-screen, add the following statement:

```
frmNew.Visible = True
```

When you are finished with an instance of an object, it is a good idea to remove it and release the memory and other system resources. To remove the instance, disassociate it from the object variable with the following statement:

```
Set frmNew = Nothing
```

Constants

Constants are named values that, once set, do not change during the execution of the module or procedure in which they are declared. Using constants makes your code much easier to read and maintain because the constant name can give you a clue as to what it represents. You set or change the value in only one place: the declaration. A constant can represent a numeric or string value, or refer to another constant. An expression containing a combination of arithmetic or logical operators can also be named as a constant.

Constants are defined by either the system or the user. After the constant is defined, you can use it anywhere within its scope, and its value remains the same. *Constant scoping* is discussed later in this section.

Access supports two kinds of constants: symbolic and intrinsic. *Symbolic constants*, also called *user-defined constants*, are defined in a module or procedure using the `Const` statement and keep their value during execution of the module or procedure. Access, VBA, and DAO provide the *intrinsic* or *system-defined constants* that can be used anywhere in all modules.

Symbolic Constants

Symbolic constants represent values that you intend to use repeatedly in a module, such as a fixed interest rate or the title of your favorite CD. After you have given the variable a meaningful name and declared the value, you can use the name in place of the value anywhere in your module. Because you declare it only once, to make a change in the value, you need to change only the declaration of the value. For example, if the interest rate (or your favorite CD) changes, you need only change the value of the constant where it is declared rather than everywhere it occurs in the code.

To declare a symbolic constant, use the `Const` statement in the declarations section at the beginning of the module or procedure. The following examples show statements declaring a numeric and string constant, respectively:

```
Const conIntRate = .075
Const conFavCD = "Placido Domingo"
```

The three-letter tag `con` in the constant names also improves the readability by clearly indicating that when the constant appears later in the code, it is indeed a symbolic constant. You need only look at the declaration section of the procedure or module to find out the value. This is just one example of the adopted naming conventions that help decipher code.

> **Tip:** You cannot change the value of the constant during the procedure—it remains the same until you change the value in the declaration. Also, be careful not to assign a name to your constant that is the same as one of the intrinsic constants. None of the intrinsic constants begin with `con`, so if you stick to that, you will be safe.

Scoping Symbolic Constants

The scope of a symbolic constant depends on where you have declared it. Similar to variables, if you declare a constant in a procedure, it is available only within that procedure. Declaring a constant in the declaration section of a module makes it available throughout the module. Constants declared in a module are considered `Private` unless specifically declared `Public`. `Public` constants are available to any module in the entire application.

Tip: Keeping all your user-defined constants `Private` is a good idea. Declaring constants `Public` might cause a conflict with other constants of the same name in another module. It is also a good idea to explicitly declare constants in a module as `Private` to avoid any doubt.

Intrinsic Constants

In addition to the constants that Access provides, you can use any of the constants from the DAO and VBA libraries available in the Object Browser dialog box. This gives you access to hundreds of constants. You also can add references to other object libraries if that is not enough. Intrinsic constants are always available.

Chapter 17, "Linking with Other Office Applications," discusses adding references to other application libraries and using their objects in VBA code.

Many intrinsic constants are directly related to a particular function, event, method, or property. For example, the `acLeftButton` constant is an Access button mask constant used in event procedures for the `MouseDown`, `MouseUp`, and `MouseMove` events to determine whether the left mouse button was involved in the event. The constant is automatically declared by Access and set to `True` or `False`, depending on whether the event occurred or not.

Tip: To find out which constants are related to a certain function, event, method, or property, open the Object Browser and scroll down the lists of constants that are available in the object libraries.

The names of the intrinsic constants have a two-letter prefix that indicates from which library they come. Access constants begin with `ac`, DAO constants with `db`, and those from the VBA library begin with `vb`. Table 3.4 describes the categories of intrinsic constants and gives some examples.

Table 3.4. Categories of intrinsic constants.

Category	Example	Description
Action	acGoTo	Used with GoToRecord method.
	acAnywhere	Used with FindRecord method.
	acFormEdit	Used with OpenForm method.
Event procedure	acLeftButton	Used with MouseDown, MouseUp, and MouseMove events.
	acApplyFilter	Used with ApplyFilter event.
	acDeleteOK	Used with AfterDelConfirm event.

Category	Example	Description
DAO	dbEditInProgress	`Edit` method has been invoked.
	dbSecNoAccess	A permissions property. User not permitted access.
	dbOpenTable	Opens a table.
Keycode	vbKey[*keyname*]	Used in event procedures for the `KeyUp` and `KeyDown` events.
Security	acSec[*permission*]	Assigns permissions to objects using VBA.
	dbSec[*permission*]	Sets permission properties of objects.
RunCommand method	acCmdInsertRows	Same as supplying `InsertRows` value for the action in a macro.
	acCmdAutoFormat	Same as supplying `AutoFormat` value for the RunCommand action in a macro.
Miscellaneous	acLBGetValue	Used with a function to fill a list box or combo box.
	acEffectChisel	Specifies the state of the `SpecialEffect` property.
VarType function	vbNull	Returns 1 if the variable is empty.
	vbCurrency	Returns 6 if the variable is of the currency data type.
	vbDate	Returns 7 if the variable is a date.

In future versions of Access, the values returned by some of the intrinsic constants might change, whereas the names will not. Therefore, it is wise to use the constant name in your code instead of the value it returns. To find the value of the constant, look it up in the Object Browser.

Arguments

Arguments are bits of information that a procedure or method uses during execution. Arguments can be required or optional. You pass them to the procedure by naming them in the procedure definition right after the name of the procedure. For example, the following statement defines the ArgProc procedure as requiring three arguments:

```
Private Sub ArgProc(strArg1 As String, intArg2 As Integer, dtmArg3 As Date)
```

The first, strArg1, is declared as a string variable, the second as an integer, and the third as a date. When you call this procedure, you can supply the actual argument values in two different ways: by position or by name.

To supply the argument by position, place the values in the same order as in the procedure definition, separated by a space and a comma:

```
ArgProc "Bob", 15, #5/5/98#
```

The string variable is enclosed in quotation marks, and the date is enclosed in date delimiter characters (#). To pass the arguments to the procedure by name, you needn't follow the order in the procedure definition because you are specifically identifying each argument. The name of the argument is followed by the colon/equal sign pair (:=), and the arguments are separated by commas. Here's an example:

```
ArgProc Arg3:=#5/5/98#, Arg1:="Bob", Arg2:=15
```

Some arguments are optional and must be labeled as such in the procedure definition:

```
OptArgProc(strArg1 As String, intArg2 As Integer, Optional dtmArg3 As Date)
```

When the procedure is called, you can omit the optional arguments. If the optional arguments are in the middle of the argument list, you must still use commas to separate the arguments even if you don't include the optional ones. For that reason, it helps to list all the optional arguments last in the list. You can set a default value for an optional argument. For example, the following sets the default value of dtmArg3 to 5/5/98:

```
OptArgProc(strArg1 As String, intArg2 As Integer, Optional dtmArg3
➥As Date = #5/5/98#)
```

When you pass arguments to a function procedure, you do not need to enclose them in parentheses unless the function returns a value. For example, the first statement in the following returns Yes or No from the MsgBox() function, and the second only displays a message and does not return a value.

```
strAnswer = MsgBox("Are you here on business?", 4, "Question 1")
```

```
MsgBox "Well done!", 0
```

Figure 3.7 shows an example of a custom procedure that uses a built-in VBA function to compute the monthly payment on a $100,000 loan with a 7.5% annual percentage rate and a 30-year duration. The complete code appears in Listing 3.1.

Listing 3.1. Calculating a payment amount.

```
Sub GetPmt()

Dim Fmt As String, varLoanVal As Variant, varFuture As Variant
Dim varAPR As Variant, varTotPmts As Variant, Payment As Variant
```

```
varLoanVal = 100000          'Loan amount $100,000
varFuture = 0                'Loan paid off at end of period.
varAPR = 0.075               'Interest rate 7.5%.
varTotPmts = 360             'Monthly payments for 30 years.
Fmt = "$###,###,##0.00"      'Define payment format.

'The arguments are passed to the Pmt() function.

Payment = Pmt(varAPR / 12, varTotPmts, -varLoanVal, varFuture)
MsgBox "Your payments will be: " & Format(Payment, Fmt) _
    & " per month."

End Sub
```

Figure 3.7.

A procedure using arguments to compute monthly payments.

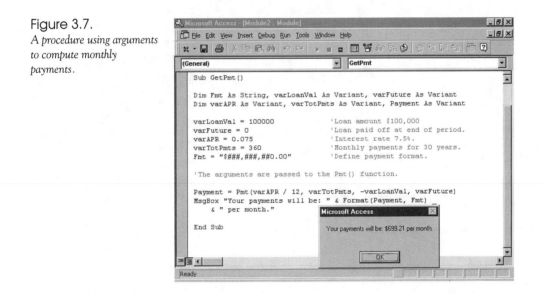

The Dim statements declare the Fmt variable as a string and all the rest as Variant because they are numbers to be used in the calculation. Numbers that are not intended for calculations, such as Zip codes, can be declared as string variables. Then four of the variables are explicitly evaluated in the next four statements.

The Fmt variable defines the format for the monthly payment amount displayed in the message box. The next statement invokes the built-in function Pmt() and passes the variable arguments to it in the proper order, separated by commas. The last statement displays a message box with the results of the calculation. This procedure would be more useful if it displayed an input box requesting the loan information from the user; however, this is a simpler example.

Arguments usually are passed by reference to a variable, but you can also pass them by value by using the ByVal keyword in the procedure declaration. In Figure 3.8, the procedure GetOct passes a value to a function named Octal to find the octal equivalent to a decimal number. The function

`Octal` is defined as receiving the argument as an integer value and uses the built-in function `Oct()` to return the octal equivalent. The procedure code appears in Listing 3.2.

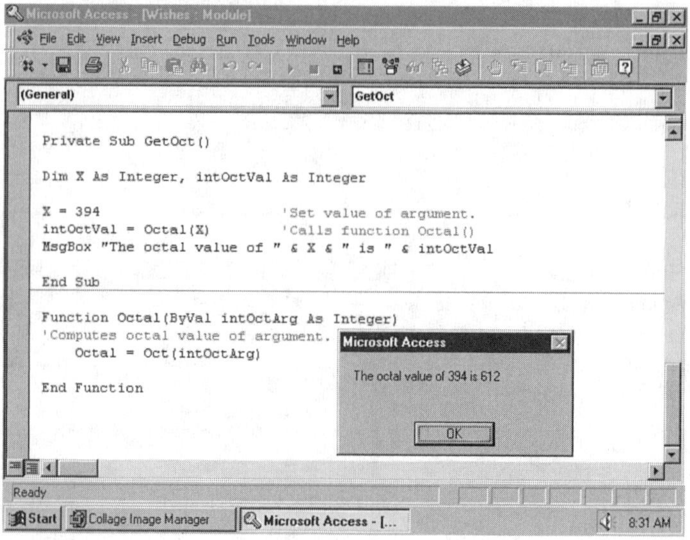

Figure 3.8.

A procedure calls a function that expects an argument by value.

```
Microsoft Access - [Wishes : Module]
File  Edit  View  Insert  Debug  Run  Tools  Window  Help

(General)                                    GetOct

Private Sub GetOct()

Dim X As Integer, intOctVal As Integer

X = 394                          'Set value of argument.
intOctVal = Octal(X)             'Calls function Octal()
MsgBox "The octal value of " & X & " is " & intOctVal

End Sub

Function Octal(ByVal intOctArg As Integer)
'Computes octal value of argument.
    Octal = Oct(intOctArg)

End Function
```

Microsoft Access

The octal value of 394 is 612

OK

Ready

Start   Collage Image Manager   Microsoft Access - [...   8:31 AM

Listing 3.2. Passing arguments by value.

```
Private Sub GetOct()

Dim X As Integer, intOctVal As Integer

X = 394                     'Set value of argument.
intOctVal = Octal(X)        'Calls function Octal()
MsgBox "The octal value of " & X & " is " & intOctVal

End Sub

Function Octal(ByVal intOctArg As Integer)

    Octal = Oct(intOctArg)    'Computes octal value of argument.

End Function
```

Note: Passing arguments by value can slow down the execution of the procedure. When you pass an argument by reference, you are really giving the procedure a pointer to the argument, which takes up only four bytes of space for any data type. Passing an argument by value copies the value, which can require up to 16 bytes and take longer to pass as well as use up more memory.

Some methods, such as the `SelectObject` method, require arguments before they can execute the corresponding action. The only argument the `SelectObject` method requires is *objecttype*, which must be one of the intrinsic constants: `acForm`, `acMacro`, `acModule`, `acQuery`, `acReport`, or `acTable`. Two optional arguments are the specific object name and whether to select the object in the database window or to select an object that is already open. For example, the statement

```
DoCmd.SelectObject acForm, "Switchboard", True
```

runs the `SelectObject` action to open a form named Switchboard in the database window. `AcForm` is the intrinsic constant for the Access form object.

In Chapter 5, you will see many examples of including arguments when calling procedures and methods. The `DoCmd.SelectObject` statement is one of them.

DAO Objects

In 1993, Microsoft Corporation introduced its Jet DBEngine and Data Access Objects (DAOs), which greatly enhanced Visual Basic 3.0 as a database application tool. The Jet became the primary means of connecting to and maintaining data in desktop databases. In contrast with Access objects such as forms and reports that are static, DAO objects are all related to the underlying data and are dynamic.

Figure 3.9 illustrates the DAO object hierarchy. All of the objects in the tree also form collections. For example, you might have more than one database in your workspace and probably more than one table definition in your database. To go even higher in the tree, there may be a workspaces collection on a network served by the same DBEngine.

Figure 3.9.
The DAO object hierarchy.

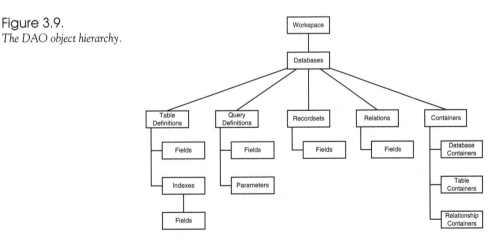

Many of the DAO objects are familiar to Access users, but a few might be new. Table 3.5 describes the DAO objects.

Table 3.5. The DAO objects.

Object	Description
Container	An object that holds information about other objects defined by Access or the Jet DBEngine, such as databases, tables, and relationships.
Database	The currently open database.
Field	A field in a table or query definition, a recordset, relation, or index.
Index	An index defined for a table.
Parameter	A parameter used in a parameter query.
QueryDef	A saved query in a database.
Recordset	A set of records in a table or a set extracted by a query.
Relation	A relationship defined between two table or query fields.
TableDef	A saved table structure in a database.

All the DAO objects in Table 3.5 can be referred to by declaring object variables. For example, the following statements declare database and query variables and then assign the current database to the variable dbs. The third statement begins to define a new query named Calif, and the last statement specifies the query name:

```
Dim dbs As Database, qry As Query

Set dbs = CurrentDB()

Set qry = dbs.CreateQueryDef()

qry.Name = "Calif"
```

Next, you would add some SQL statements in VBA code that define the query and open a form with the new query as the record source. The form would display only those records that meet the criteria in the SQL SELECT statement.

Each DAO object has a corresponding set of properties, methods, events, and functions:

- The nearly 100 DAO object properties include FieldSize, DefaultType, KeepLocal, OrdinalPosition, SourceTable, and Required.

- DAO objects can use over 50 methods including CreateField, CreateQueryDef, CreateRelation, FindPrevious, and MoveNext.

- There are 11 data events including AfterUpdate, BeforeInsert, Current, Delete, and NotInList.

- Eleven functions, all dealing with field values, can be used with DAO objects. These include `First()`, `Last()`, `Max()`, `Min()`, `Avg()`, and `Sum()`.

After you begin working in VBA code, the distinction between Access objects and DAO objects will begin to blur, and you will view them both simply as members of the Access programming family.

Several objects, methods, properties, and statements have been deleted from Visual Basic 4.0, but they are still supported in the interest of backward compatibility. For example, the terms `Dynaset` and `Snapshot` are no longer used, so all the `CreateDynaset` and `CreateSnapshot` methods have been replaced by the `OpenRecordset` method. Refer to the DAO Reference Help for more details about obsolete features.

Naming Conventions

Access imposes certain rules when naming variables and constants:

- All names must begin with a letter.
- The name can contain only letters, numbers, and the underscore symbol. No punctuation or spaces.
- The name can contain up to 255 characters.
- The name cannot contain any keywords or other words reserved by Access, such as `IF`, `LOOP`, `CLOSE`, `OR`, and `MOD`.

In addition to these rules, programmers over the years have gradually accepted a naming convention that makes their code easier to decipher months later. Such standard terminology also makes the code understandable to another programmer. You saw an example earlier when a constant was named using the `con` prefix (which is actually a tag, as you will see later). The intrinsic constants also have tags that indicate their host library. Tags are in all lowercase letters, and the names are written with mixed case.

The naming conventions outlined here are included in the Leszynski Naming Conventions (LNC) and have been in use for Visual Basic development since 1995. The following is the general structure of the LNC naming convention, where *BaseName* is the name of the object unadorned by add-ons:

`[prefix][tag]BaseName[qualifier][suffix]`

The *BaseName* is the only part of the name that can contain multiple uppercase letters. The *tag* helps to characterize the base name and identify the class of object. The *prefix* is an identifier before the tag that narrows the tag character. The prefix can indicate the scope or another characteristic of the variable.

A *qualifier* is an add-on to the base name that describes how the object appears in context. For example, `intAttendMax` is the maximum value in the `Attend` set of values. A *suffix* adds more detailed information about the object to discriminate between two members of the set that might appear identical without the qualifier. Suffixes are often separated from the base name by an underscore for better visibility.

The most useful element of the naming conventions is the tag. Table 3.6 gives some examples of tags used with VBA and Access objects.

Table 3.6. Examples of using tags with VBA and Access objects.

Object	Tag
Button	btn
Collection	col
Combo box	cbo
Control	ctl
Font	fnt
Form	frm
Image	img
Label	lbl
Menu	mnu
Menu item	mni
Submenu	msub
Toolbar	tbr

Data variables have their own set of tags, depending on the type of variable. The tags used for different data types were shown earlier in Table 3.2.

For more information about the hundreds of other examples of LNC, see *Leszynski Naming Conventions for Microsoft Access, Version 95.1 for Access 1.x, 2.x, 7.x*, published by Kwery Corporation, 1995.

Controlling the Program Flow

The last remaining major elements in event-driven programs are those that control the program flow. In addition to those statements that call a sub or function procedure, there are four major areas of flow control: exiting or pausing the program, branching to another part of the program, looping through the program code, and making decisions about what to do next.

With the End, Exit, and Stop keywords, you can quit running the program altogether, only leave the procedure and return to the previous procedure, or suspend processing while you do something else. Another keyword, DoEvents, yields the application so the operating system can attend to other events. Branching to another part of the program can be conditional, unconditional, or temporary.

The decision-making statements don't actually branch to another location in the program; instead, they choose which set of statements to execute. The If...Then...Else statement executes a series of statements if the condition is met and a second set of statements if not. When there is an expression that has several different values, you can use the Select Case statement, which executes a specific set of statements corresponding to the value of the expression.

Looping lets you repeat a series of program statements a specific number of times or until a certain condition is met. One type of loop repeats the code while or until the condition is True. Another type executes the code a specific number of times. The third type repeats the set of statements for each object in the specified collection, such as all records in the recordset or all forms in the forms collection.

Table 3.7 lists and briefly describes the keywords used to control program flow.

Table 3.7. Flow control keywords.

Keyword	Description
Actions that exit or pause	
Exit	Exits a block of code such as a Do...Loop, For...Next, a Sub, function or property procedure. Does not define the end of the code structure, only branches to the end of the block.
End	Ends a procedure or block of code. Closes files and releases variables.
Stop	Suspends execution; closes nothing.
DoEvents	A function that turns execution over to the operating system for processing other events.
Actions that branch to another set of statements	
GoTo	Branches unconditionally to the specified line number or label within the procedure.
GoSub...Return	Branches to a subroutine within the procedure and returns.
On Error	Branches to an error-processing routine if an error occurs.
On...GoSub	Branches to one of a list of destinations, depending on the value of an expression, and then returns to the next statement after On...GoSub.
On...GoTo	Same as On...GoSub, except it does not return to the next statement when finished.

continues

Table 3.7. continued

Keyword	Description
Actions that loop through code	
`Do...Loop`	Repeats the set of statements while or until the condition is `True`.
`For...Next`	Repeats the set of statements a specified number of times.
`For Each...Next`	Repeats the set of statements for each object in the specified collection.
`While...Wend`	Repeats the set of statements as long as the specified condition remains `True`.
`With`	Executes a set of statements on a single object.
Actions that make decisions	
`Choose`	A function that selects a value from a list of choices based on the index that specifies its position in the list.
`If...Then...Else`	Executes a sequence of statements if the specified condition is `True` and another set if `False`.
`Select Case`	Executes one of several alternative sets of statements, depending on the value of the specified expression.
`Switch`	A function that examines a list of expressions and returns a value or expression related to the first expression in the list that is `True`.

Each of the flow control statements has a definite syntax that must be followed. Here are some examples:

The `On...GoSub` syntax is as follows:

```
On expression GoSub destinationlist
```

where the *expression* is numeric and evaluates (or is rounded) to an integer between 0 and 255. The *destinationlist* is a list of line numbers or labels, each of which corresponds to a value resulting from the expression.

The following is the `Do...Loop` syntax:

```
Do [{While|Until} condition]      'Sets up condition for loop.
                                  'You must use While or Until.
    [statements]                  'Do while (or until) condition is met.
    [Exit Do]                     'Jumps to next statement after Loop.
    [statements]                  'Repeated while (or until) condition is met.
Loop                              'Ends loop.
```

The following is the `If...Then...Else` syntax:

```
If [conditions] Then [ifstatements] [Else elsestatements] End If
```

where at least one *condition* is required and the *ifstatements* are executed if the *conditions* evaluate to True. Otherwise, the *elsestatements* are executed. The block of code must end with an End If line.

You will see many examples of how to control program flow in the remaining chapters of this book. Refer to the Visual Basic Reference Help for specific information about each of the keywords.

Summary

This chapter has presented a lot of detail about object-oriented, event-driven programming and the elements that are behind the process. You were introduced to variables and constants, how to declare and use them, and what types are available.

One of the uses for variables is to pass them to a procedure or method as an argument to be used during execution.

DAO objects present the dynamic side of database management by addressing all the features of an Access database that are concerned with the data itself: the recordsets, queries, relations, and so on.

Finally, the elements of an event-driven program must include ways to conditionally change the flow of processing. VBA includes strategies for branching to a different course or to one of a set of different courses, or looping until a specified condition exists.

Chapter 4 shows how to create a new database, and Chapter 5 puts much of this chapter's knowledge to use.

II

Let Your Wizard Do the Coding

4

Creating an Application with a Wizard

When you were learning all about Access, you probably used many of the clever wizards Access provided. There are wizards hovering in the Access background waiting to help you create forms, reports, custom controls, links to other applications, and HTML (to name just a few). Each of these wizards creates program code behind the scenes to carry out the selections you make in the wizard dialog boxes.

In this chapter, you create a database to maintain a list of subscribers to the monthly *Omni-Sport* magazine. It is a simple database that consists of a single table, a data entry and review form, a query, and some reports and mailing labels. Chapter 5, "Examining and Modifying the Wizard's Code," explores the program code built during this development.

Welcome to the *Omni-Sport* Subscriber Database

The main purpose of the *Omni-Sport* magazine's database is to maintain current information about the magazine subscribers: their names, addresses, and payment data. It's important to know when each subscription is due for renewal so that timely notices can be sent out. Promotional material is also sent periodically to subscribers.

The first and most important effort in designing any new database is to determine what the user wants out of it. After that is specified, at least in broad terms, you can define what must go into the database in order to produce the desired output.

After specifying both the output and the input, you set about distributing the data among related tables. In this example, however, the database is limited to one table for simplicity. In real life the database would be more efficient if the data were divided among two or more tables, linked by the subscriber key field.

The completed database is contained in the `\Source\Databases` directory on the CD-ROM. However, if you choose to follow the steps in this chapter to modify the Database Wizard's creation, you can import just the table data from the CD-ROM into the new database after you define the table structure. The subscriber records are contained in the Copy of Subscribers table in the Objects to Copy database. After populating the database, proceed with modifying the form and report designs.

Peter's Principle: Creating a Database from Gathered Data

Anyone who finds a need for a database no doubt has already accumulated a lot of information. The trick in developing a database for existing data is to mold existing tools to match the requirements rather than the other way around. This and other exercises in this book will help you see what tools are available in Access and how you can use them to build a suitable database application. The cases studied in this book represent three different uses for databases—from simple data storage and retrieval to an online decision-support system. Some of the techniques presented might be of use to you during your database development.

Describing the *Omni-Sport* Output

In addition to the up-to-date list of current subscribers, *Omni-Sport* management requires a method of creating renewal notices to send to people whose subscriptions are near expiration. Other types of useful printed output include the following:

- Summaries of popular areas of subscriber interest
- Mailing labels for all or some part of the list
- Form letters announcing special offers
- Financial analyses to develop editorial strategies

Assembling *Omni-Sport* Input

In addition to the complete subscriber list with names and addresses, *Omni-Sport* might decide it needs additional information about its customers. For example, it might want to send gifts to first-time subscribers or give a discount to those who pay for more than one year. In that case, the table must include a flag for first-time subscribers and specify the amount paid. If *Omni-Sport* offers a special rate when the subscriber buys more than one year of the magazine, the database should reflect that.

If *Omni-Sport* sends personal questionnaires to new subscribers to glean information about their households (income bracket, age group, number of adults, children, or primary sports interests, for example) you need to store this information as well. Not all subscribers will respond, of course, but you still need to make room to store what information does come in. Enough readers will respond to the questionnaire to lend a measure of statistical significance to the survey.

The questionnaire responses can be used by the editorial staff in selecting articles about the most popular topics or by the peripheral sales staff (videos, tickets, memorabilia, for example) in sending promotional material to those who have expressed interest in a particular sport or activity.

Defining the Database Objects

As mentioned earlier, the *Omni-Sport* database contains a single table, Subscribers, that holds all the subscriber information. The Database Wizard creates most of the fields needed in the *Omni-Sport* database, but there still are many changes to be made.

The database must contain at least one data entry form. The form built by the wizard shows two pages. The first page contains the address information and the second contains a collection of miscellaneous data. This arrangement will work nicely for *Omni-Sport*. After removing some of the fields from the second page, there is room for the additional subscriber information submitted in response to the questionnaire.

In Chapter 5, the form is split into three linked forms for more efficient data entry and review.

The database must provide a means to print the subscriber list. A complete list is helpful for periodic error-checking and looking up information in response to reader questions.

In order to determine which subscribers need to be reminded to renew, a query should be included in the design. The query will accept the user's input about the time frame to look for—for example, any subscription that expires within 90 days from today. You might even want to send increasingly urgent letters as the expiration date approaches. Other queries can extract and summarize sales and interest data for review by management and the editorial staff.

Using the Database Wizard

When you start the Database Wizard, you have a choice of predesigned databases from which to choose. The one you want to build might not exactly match any of the Wizard's suggestions, but you can pick one that is close to meeting your requirements and modify the finished product.

No set of wizards will produce exactly the application you want, but they can give you a real head start in the process. After the wizard has finished weaving its magic, you can modify the design by changing the table structure and modifying the form and report designs to match. You can even dig into the VBA code and the macros to make changes in how the application responds to certain events.

Selecting the Application Type

When you first start Access, one of the choices in the opening screen is Create a New Database Using Database Wizard, as shown in Figure 4.1. When you click the Database Wizard option, the New dialog box opens with the Databases tab active as shown in Figure 4.2. If you are already running Access, start a new database by clicking the New button or choosing File | New. The General tab of the New dialog box appears this time, showing only a Blank Database icon. Choose the Databases tab and scroll down to see the 22 different database models. Notice that the file extension added to these templates is `.mdz`, indicating they are the property of the Database Wizard.

Figure 4.1.

The opening screen.

Figure 4.2.
The Databases tab contains more than 20 predesigned database templates.

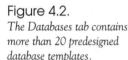

> **Tip:** If you don't see the Create a New Database dialog box when you start Access, the Startup Dialog Box option might not be checked. Choose Tools | Options, and then check Startup Dialog Box on the View tab.

The New dialog box has buttons, similar to those in the Open dialog box, that change the view of the items in the tab: Large Icons (the default), Small Icons, and Details. In addition to the filename, the Details option shows the size, type, and date of last modification. If a preview of the selected template is available, it appears in the Preview box.

After you select a template, the File New Database dialog box appears. Here, you can enter a name for the new database and tell Access where to store it. The default filename for a new database using the Address Book template is Address Book1.mdb, and the default folder is My Documents (unless you have changed that option). Keeping related files together in a folder you can find again is always a good idea. In spite of the advanced searching capability of Access, it's a lot easier if you already know where you have stored your important files.

Follow these steps to begin creating the *Omni-Sport* Subscriber database:

1. Choose the Address Book template and click OK. The File New Database dialog box appears.

2. Type the name Omni-Sport in the Filename text box.

3. Choose the folder in which you want to store the database, and click Create.

After a few moments, the Database Wizard introductory screen appears showing what information the new database will contain (see Figure 4.3). The skeleton of the empty database shows behind this window. You probably would want to store more than just the subscriber address information, but to keep it simple, the single table is used here. Click Next to move to the next dialog box for the opportunity to include additional fields in the Address table.

Figure 4.3.
The Database Wizard shows what information will be stored in the new database.

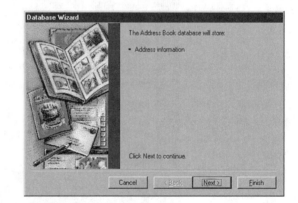

Choosing the Fields

Figure 4.4 shows the second wizard dialog box, in which you can choose the fields to add to the database. The dialog box is divided into two areas: on the left is a list of the tables that will be included in the database, and on the right is a list of the fields in the selected table. In this example, there is only one table: Address information. Other examples can have as many as five or more related tables.

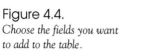

Figure 4.4.
Choose the fields you want to add to the table.

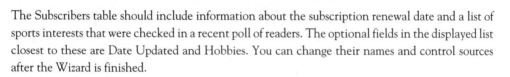

Most of the fields in the Address Book database template are required, and they appear in regular font and are checked in the list. There are, however, several optional fields that you can add to your design. These appear in italic and are not checked. The figure shows Children Names as one of the optional fields. If you try to clear any of the checked fields (not italic), Access will inform you that the field is required and cannot be removed.

Note: If you are just practicing with databases, you can ask to have sample data inserted into the database by clicking the check box labeled Yes, include sample data. When the wizard is finished, the database will contain sample records.

The Subscribers table should include information about the subscription renewal date and a list of sports interests that were checked in a recent poll of readers. The optional fields in the displayed list closest to these are Date Updated and Hobbies. You can change their names and control sources after the Wizard is finished.

To continue with the *Omni-Sport* subscribers database, follow these steps:

1. Scroll down the list of fields and check the Date Updated and Hobbies fields.
2. Click Next.

The next two dialog boxes offer 10 different screen display styles and 6 report styles. As you select different styles, a sample appears in the left pane. After the report style dialog box closes, the wizard asks for a title for the new database. Figure 4.5 shows this dialog box as it first appears. You also have the option to include a picture with all the reports that the wizard builds. This is handy for including a company logo on printed reports.

Note: If you design a report on your own later, you'll have to add the picture yourself; the Wizard will have no part in the report design.

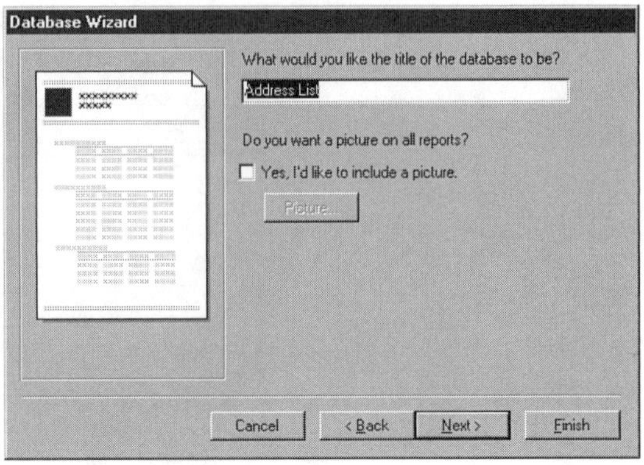

Figure 4.5.

The Database Wizard asks if you want a special title for your new database.

Follow these steps to continue with the *Omni-Sport* database design:

1. Choose Next, accepting the default style selections, until you reach the dialog box requesting a title for the database.

2. Type `Omni-Sport` in the text box.

3. Click the check box labeled Yes, I'd like to include a picture. Then, click the check box next to the Picture command button.

4. Use the Insert Picture dialog box to locate the picture you want to use. (Figure 4.6 shows a picture from the Images folder on your CD.)

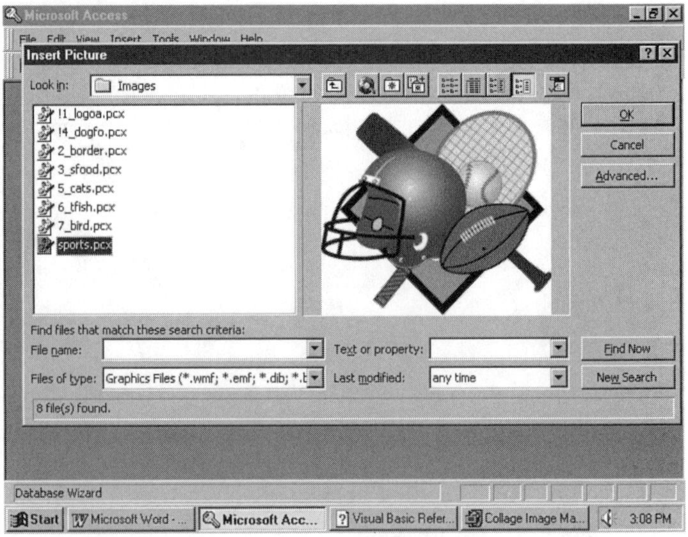

Figure 4.6.

Use the Insert Picture dialog box to locate and add a picture to all the reports in your new database.

5. Click OK to return to the Database Wizard dialog box, which now looks like Figure 4.7. The preview at the left shows the placement of the title and the picture.

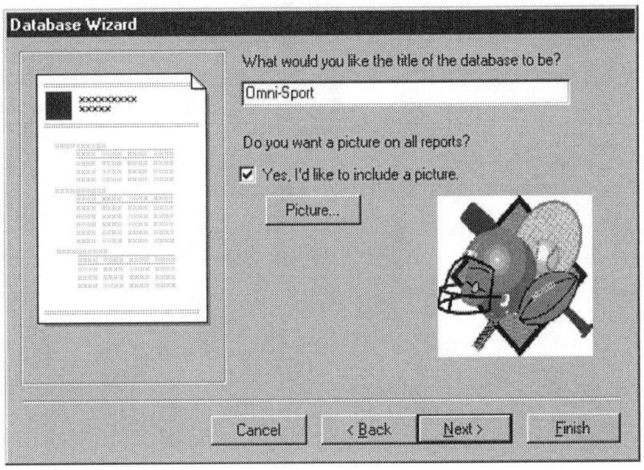

Figure 4.7.
The Database Wizard dialog box with the new database name and a picture.

6. Click Next to move to the last dialog box. Then, choose Finish to close the dialog box and start the database.

After a few moments, the Main Switchboard (see Figure 4.8) appears with a list of available actions. A *switchboard* is the user's primary point of entry into an application. It displays a list of actions you may take next to work with the information. Clicking an option triggers an event procedure or a function that opens a form, previews a report, or carries out some other action. The Database Wizard, which was new in Access 95, makes a switchboard for you, but you will see in Chapter 14, "Adding Real-Time Features," how easy it is to make one yourself.

Figure 4.8.
The first option in the Main Switchboard takes you to the Addresses data entry form.

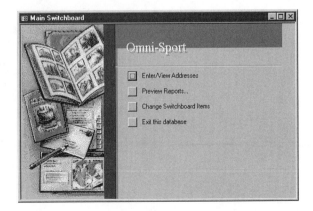

The first option in the new switchboard, Enter/View Addresses, opens the data entry form shown in Figure 4.9. Notice that this is a two-page form with additional address information on page 2. To return to the Main Switchboard, close the form window or choose Window | Main Switchboard.

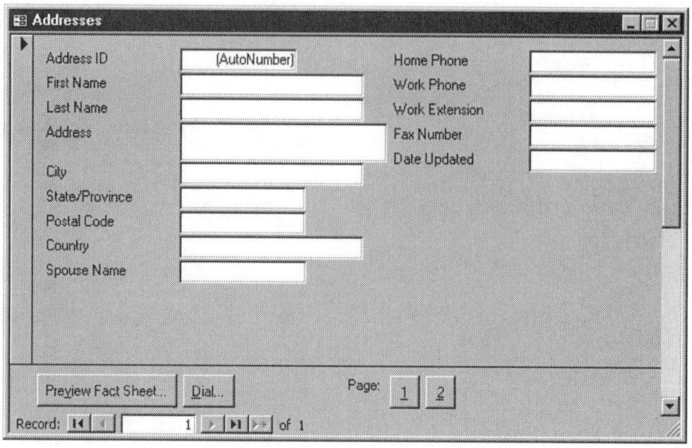

Figure 4.9.
The first page of the form shows the address fields.

This form will require some revision to make it suitable for the *Omni-Sport* database. For example, the Spouse Name and several of the phone number fields are unnecessary. Other fields would be more appropriate with different names. Several more fields need to be added to store the personal questionnaire information.

The second option on the Main Switchboard opens the Reports Switchboard (see Figure 4.10), which lists the reports the wizard has prepared. Two of these reports are irrelevant for this application and can be deleted from the database. You can create other reports that would be useful to *Omni-Sport* using the Report Wizard and add them as items to this switchboard. The final option on the Reports Switchboard returns you to the Main Switchboard.

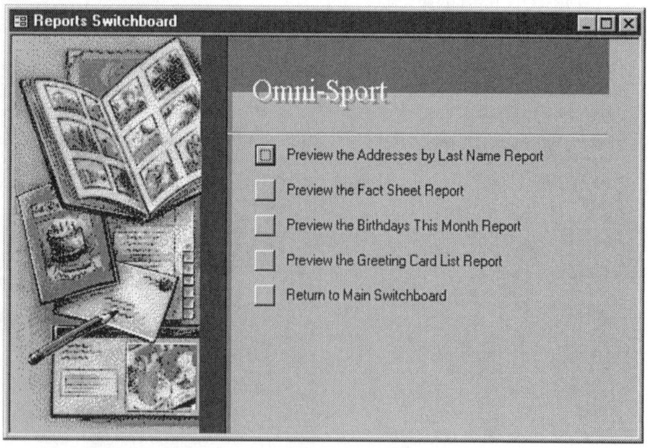

Figure 4.10.
The Reports Switchboard offers a choice of report previews.

The Change Switchboard Items option on the Main Switchboard comes in very handy for customizing both the Main and the Reports Switchboards later in this chapter. This option activates the Switchboard Manager used to change any item on any switchboard in the current database. You can edit the text of the switchboard caption that appears in its title bar or any item on the switchboard. You also can add new options and delete existing ones. When you add a new item to a switchboard, you must also specify the command Access is to execute when the item is clicked. You will learn more about this in the section, "Changing the Switchboards," later in this chapter.

Modifying the Database Design

The first step in customizing this new database is to modify the underlying table by deleting the unwanted items from the table and then adding the other fields the application needs. In addition, you need to add any default values and data validation specifications, as well as lookup tables and input masks, where appropriate. There is no data in the table yet, so Access won't object to deleting fields from the table structure.

Next, remove the unwanted items from the form and report designs. Finally, customize the switchboard captions and individual items to reflect the needs of the *Omni-Sport* application.

Restructuring the Addresses Table

Before you change the table structure, rename the table in the database view. Double-click the table name and type Subscribers in place of Addresses, and then press Enter.

Figure 4.11 shows the AutoForm-Columnar form created from the Addresses table as it was when the Database Wizard was finished. Compare this with Figure 4.12, which shows how the Addresses table must be modified for use by *Omni-Sport* for its application.

Figure 4.11.
The AutoForm showing the Addresses table fields.

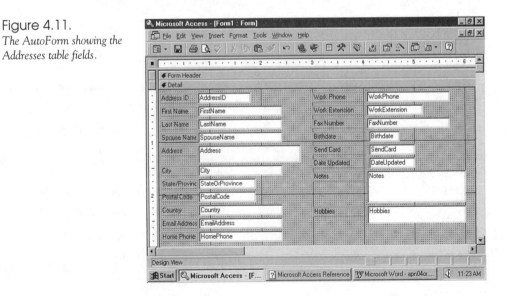

Figure 4.12.
The AutoForm showing fields changed for the Omni-Sport Subscribers table.

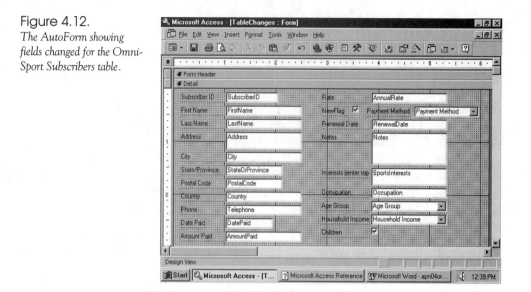

The Subscribers table structure is described in Table 4.1.

Table 4.1. Subscribers table structure.

Field	Type	Req'd	New (N)or Renamed (R)	Comments
SubscriberID	AutoNum	X	R	Key field
FirstName	Text			
LastName	Text			Indexed (Duplicates OK)
Address	Text	X		
City	Text	X		Indexed (Duplicates OK)
State/Prov	Text	X		
PostalCode	Text	X		Indexed (Duplicates OK)
Country	Text	X		Default USA
Telephone	Text		R	
DatePaid	Date/Time	X	R	Default current date
AmountPaid	Currency		N	Indexed (Duplicates OK)
AnnualRate	Currency		N	Default $29.00
NewFlag	Yes/No		N	Default No
RenewalDate	Date/Time		N	

Field	Type	Req'd	New (N)or Renamed (R)	Comments
Notes	Memo			
SportsInterests	Text		R	
Occupation	Text		N	
AgeGroup	Text		N	Lookup Table
HouseholdIncome	Text		N	Lookup Table
Children	Yes/No		N	
PaymentMethod	Text		N	Lookup Table

Five of the fields also have input masks included as field properties in the table definition that help with data entry. The first three were added by the wizard and the fourth is new.

- PostalCode input mask: 00000\-9999, which requires digits only and displays the value with a dash: 92118-2450.
- Telephone input mask: !\(999") "000\-0000, which requires digits but fills the field from left to right (that's what the ! means) and includes parentheses, a space, and a dash: (818) 555-3648.
- DatePaid input mask: 99/99/00;0, which displays a date in the short format, 10/25/97. The 0 in the second part means to store the literal characters (the slashes) with the value entered.
- RenewalDate input mask: 99/99/00;0, which is the same as the DatePaid mask.

Two new logical fields are added: NewFlag and Children. Each has a default value of No. In addition, there are three lookup fields containing lists of values that can be selected during data entry. Table 4.2 shows these fields and their respective value lists.

Table 4.2. Subscribers table lookup values.

Field	Values	
Payment Method	Cash	
	Check	
	Credit Card	
Age Group	A	<20 Years
	B	20–30 Years
	C	30–40 Years

continues

Table 4.2. continued

Field	Values	
	D	40–50 Years
	E	50–60 Years
	F	>60 Years
Household Income	1	<$15,000
	2	$15,000–$25,000
	3	$25,000–$40,000
	4	$40,000–$65,000
	5	>$65,000

To create these lookup fields, choose Lookup Wizard from the Data Type pull-down menu in the table design window. When you create a two-column list such as those for Age Group and House-hold Income, store the value in the first column in the field, using the second column only as an explanation of the codes in the first column.

Importing the Subscribers Data

Now that all the necessary changes have been made to the Subscribers table structure, you can en-ter data. You can either enter your own data or import the subscriber records from the CD that ac-companies this book. The records are contained in the Copy of Subscribers table in the Objects to Copy database. Access can import both the database definition and the data or only the definition. First, export the Copy of Subscribers table from the CD to a new table in your database, and then copy and paste the records from the new table into the empty Subscribers table.

Warning: Because your Subscribers table contains no records, you do not risk losing data by pasting. If you have already entered records, you should use an Append query to add the new records to the table without writing over the old ones.

Use the following steps to export the Copy of Subscribers table from the CD:

1. Open the Objects to Copy database in the \Source\Databases directory on the CD.
2. Right-click the Copy of Subscribers table in the Tables window and choose Save As/ Export from the shortcut menu.

3. In the Save As dialog box, choose To an External File or Database, and click OK. The Save Table "Copy of Subscribers" In dialog box appears.

4. Switch to your folder and select the *Omni-Sport* database. Then click Export. The Export Database dialog box appears.

5. Keep the Copy to Subscribers database name and the Export Definition and Data option. Click OK.

6. Open the *Omni-Sport* database. If the Main Switchboard appears, maximize the database window and open the Tables tab. The Copy of Subscribers table is now part of the database. All that remains is to copy the records from the new table to the Subscribers table.

7. Right-click Copy of Subscribers, and choose Copy from the shortcut menu.

8. Click Paste to open the Paste dialog box. Type Subscribers in the Table Name text box, and choose Append Data to Existing Table. Click OK.

9. Open the Subscribers table to view the imported records.

The record data is still in the Copy to Subscribers table in your database. You can either delete the table or keep it as a backup copy of the Subscribers table.

With the Subscribers table filled, it is time to move on and modify the rest of the database objects that the Database Wizard created.

Modifying the Data Entry Form

After you make all the desired changes to the table structure and add records to the table, the next step is to look at the data entry form design. It should contain all the fields in the table, arranged in a logical and uncluttered manner. Figures 4.13 and 4.14 show pages 1 and 2 of the original form design that the Database Wizard created for entering and reviewing the Addresses data. There are many changes to be made in the design, including adding and deleting fields, changing field names to match the changes in the table, rearranging the controls in the form, adding a title and a picture, deleting and adding command buttons, and changing several control properties. Stay in the design view to make these changes.

Tip: Don't try to run a form or report before making changes to the design that match the changes in the table structure. Access will display an Enter Parameter dialog box for each of the fields in the design that has been removed or renamed in the table structure. Instead, go directly to the design view and make the necessary changes.

Figure 4.13.
Page 1 of the Addresses form design.

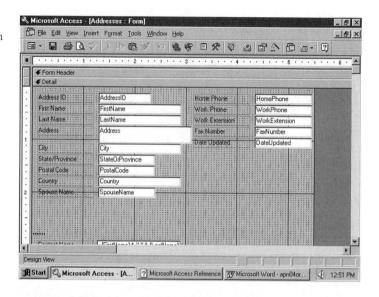

Figure 4.14.
Page 2 of the Addresses form design.

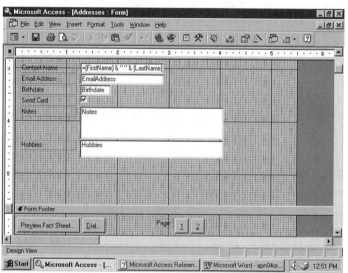

Changing Fields and Field Layout

All the fields that were renamed or removed from the table structure are now bound text box controls whose control sources Access doesn't recognize. They should be removed from the form design. To delete a control or label, select it and press the Delete button.

To change a control source, select the text box in the design and open the property sheet. Next, choose the appropriate field from the control source pull-down menu. To change a label, double-click the label, type in the new text, and then press Enter.

Tip: If you want to delete several controls at once, hold down Shift as you select the controls. This selects them as a group. Then press the Delete button to delete them all.

Table 4.3 describes the changes to make in the form's text box and label controls.

Table 4.3. Changes in text box and label controls.

Control Name	Action
AddressID	Change control source to SubscriberID
AddressID	Change label to Subscriber ID
SpouseName	Delete text box and label
HomePhone	Change control source to Telephone
HomePhone	Change label to Telephone
WorkPhone	Delete text box and label
WorkExtension	Delete text box and label
FaxNumber	Delete text box and label
ContactName	Delete text box and label
EmailAddress	Delete text box and label
Birthdate	Change control source to DatePaid
Birthdate	Change label to Date Paid
SendCard	Change control source to Children
SendCard	Change label to Children?
Hobbies	Change control source to SportsInterests
Hobbies	Change label to Sports Interests

Next, add the eight new fields that were not included in the Addresses table: AmountPaid, AnnualRate, RenewalDate, Payment Method, Occupation, AgeGroup, HouseholdIncome, and NewFlag. Refer to Table 4.1 for details of the new fields. Reposition and resize the new fields to resemble the design shown in Figures 4.15 and 4.16. Added features such as titles and other text, a rectangle, and a new button will be added later.

Figure 4.15.

Page 1 of the new Subscribers data entry and viewing form design.

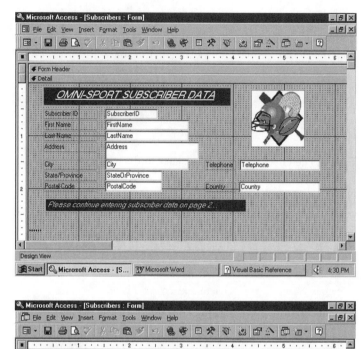

Figure 4.16.

Page 2 of the new Subscribers data entry and viewing form design.

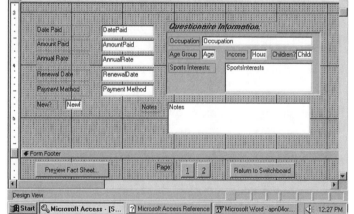

Changing the Tab Order

The *tab order* is the sequence of controls that receive focus as you press the Tab key. When you create a form, the tab order is automatically set to the order in which you placed the controls on the form design. When you enter data, the focus might not move through the fields in a logical progression. You can change the tab order to any sequence you want: logically from left to right and top to bottom or some other pattern. Also, you might want to skip some fields altogether.

You can prevent the user from being able to reach a field by removing it from the tab order, either conditionally when an event occurs or completely. For example, when RenewalDate is specified as a calculated field and filled in by an expression, the user should not be able to reach the field to change the value by pressing Tab. To keep a control from ever receiving focus, change its Tab Stop property in the text box property sheet to No.

With the form open in the design view, choose View | Tab Order. The Tab Order dialog box (see Figure 4.17) displays a list of tab stops in the currently selected section (Detail, in this case). The controls appear in the list in the same order in which they receive focus in the form when the Tab key is pressed repeatedly.

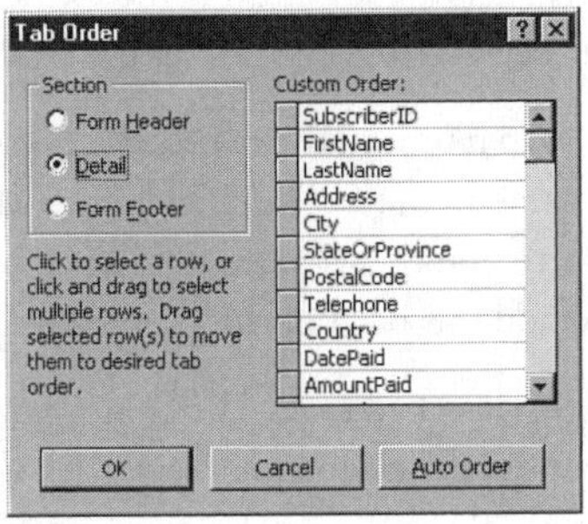

Figure 4.17.
Change the tab order on a form with the Tab Order dialog box.

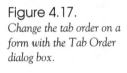

To move a tab stop to another position, select the control name and then release the mouse button. Position the mouse pointer on the small square at the left end of the selected item until the pointer appears as an up-left pointing arrow with a tiny box on its tail. You now can click and drag the line to a new position.

If you want focus to move through the form only from left to right and top to bottom, choose Auto Order in the Tab Order dialog box. The list is automatically rearranged to reflect the physical position of the controls in the form design.

Customizing the Form Appearance

Next, add a title on page 1 of the form and change its font and color properties as you want. Then, add an instruction to the user to continue entering data on page 2 of the form. If you want, locate the same picture added by the Database Wizard and place it in the upper-right corner of page 1.

On page 2, it would be convenient to group the personal questionnaire information in one place on the form. Perform the following steps to add a rectangle control that frames these fields:

1. Click the Rectangle tool on the toolbar and draw a rectangle around the group of fields. The fields seem to disappear.

2. With the rectangle selected, choose Format | Send to Back. The fields reappear.

3. Open the property sheet and change the rectangle Special Effect property to Sunken. Press Enter.

The form design now should look like the finished product (shown in Figures 4.15 and 4.16) except for the buttons in the form footer.

Changing Buttons in the Form

Because there is no need to telephone the subscribers on a regular basis, remove the Dial button from the form footer. Simply select the button and press Delete.

Leave the Preview Fact Sheet button alone for now. It opens a preview of the Fact Sheet report, which has not yet been changed to reflect the changes in the underlying table.

There are two ways to return to the main switchboard from the form view: close the form or choose the switchboard name from the Window menu (which leaves the form open). It would be convenient to have a button on the form footer that closes the form and returns to the main switchboard automatically. To add this button, call on the Command Button Wizard:

1. In the design view, make sure the Control Wizards button is activated on the toolbar, click the Command Button tool, and then click in the form where you want the button. The first Command Button Wizard dialog box shows a list of action categories and a list of actions in the selected category.

2. Choose Form Operations in the Categories list and then Close Form in the Actions list (see Figure 4.18).

Figure 4.18.
Choosing the action for the new command button.

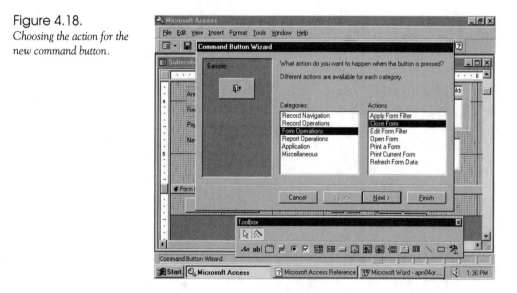

3. Choose Next. The Wizard now offers a choice between a picture or text on the button. Choose Text and type `Return to Switchboard`.

4. Choose Next and name the button `Go To Switchboard` (or something else more meaningful than the default name) and choose Finish.

> **Note:** If you have changed the Display Form Startup option from Switchboard to (none), the form will simply close without displaying the *Omni-Sport* Switchboard when you click the Return to Switchboard button.

Now is the time to test the new form by switching to form view. Figures 4.19 and 4.20 show pages 1 and 2, as well as the new form with data from the first subscriber record.

Figure 4.19.
Page 1 of the new form showing record data.

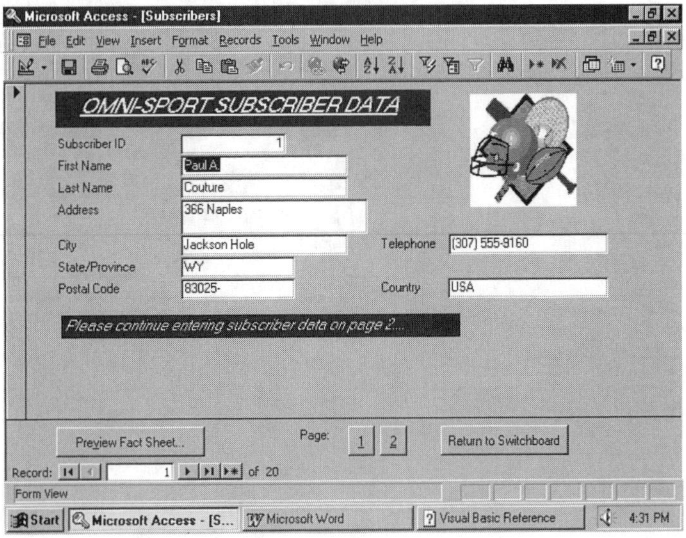

Customizing Reports

The Database Wizard provides four report designs, two of which are appropriate for the *Omni-Sport* application: Addresses by Last Name and Fact Sheet. The other two, Greeting Card List and Birthdays This Month, can be deleted and replaced by more useful reports.

The Addresses by Last Name report record source is still Addresses. Open the report in design view and change the report record source property to Subscribers. The only field that needs to be changed is the Home Phone field name, which is now Telephone. Do this by selecting the Home Phone field and changing the control source property to Telephone. Figure 4.21 shows a preview of the Addresses by Last Name report.

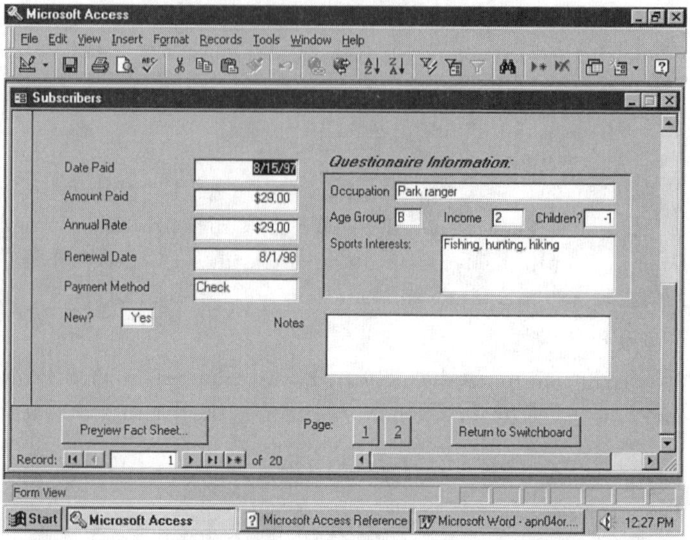

Figure 4.20.
Page 2 of the new form.

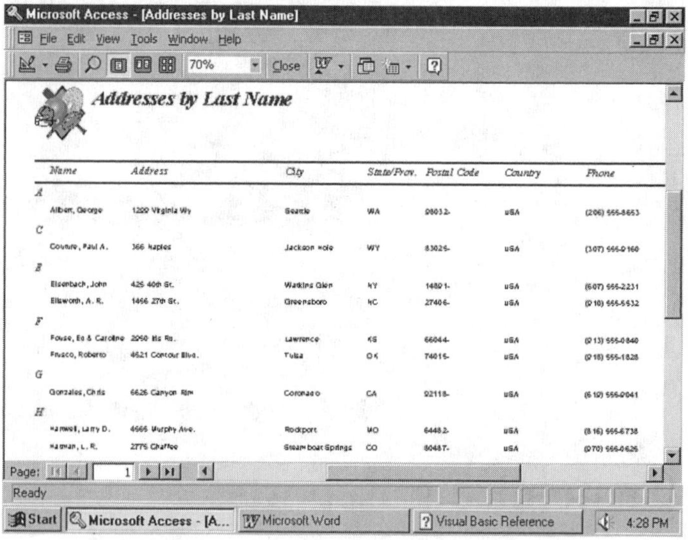

Figure 4.21.
A preview of the Addresses by Last Name report.

The Fact Sheet report, on the other hand, is a report that shows all the information for a single Addresses record on one page. Many of the fields in the Addresses table are quite different from the fields in the Subscribers table, as you saw while modifying the form design. It is easier to use the Report Wizard and start fresh to create a simple AutoReport-Columnar report based on the Subscribers table and then name it the Fact Sheet report. Figure 4.22 shows a preview of the new Fact Sheet report with an image and a dotted line added to the design.

Figure 4.22.
A preview of the new Fact Sheet report.

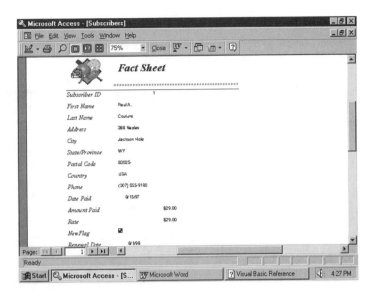

Tip: Be sure to save the new report with the same name, Fact Sheet, so that the buttons on the Report Switchboard and the Entry/Review form will open the correct report preview. Access asks for confirmation before replacing the existing report.

Note: If you viewed the Fact Sheet before changing the fields, you see that the Database Wizard included the picture that was inserted in one of the dialog boxes. When you create a new report after the wizard is finished, you must insert the picture manually.

Creating Mailing Labels

Because the *Omni-Sport* business depends heavily on mailing magazines and other information to its subscribers, a mailing label report design would be very useful. You can easily create such a report using the Label Wizard:

1. Click New in the Report window and choose Label Wizard from the New Report dialog box.

2. Choose the Subscribers table as the basis for the report and then choose OK. In the next two dialog boxes, the Wizard offers choices in label size, font, and color.

3. Choose Next until the Label Wizard displays a list of available fields and a Prototype label panel where the label will be composed.

4. Select each of the name and address fields in turn and click the right arrow. Be sure to add a space between entries and start a new line where necessary. Figure 4.23 shows the Label Wizard dialog box after the fields have been placed in the prototype label.

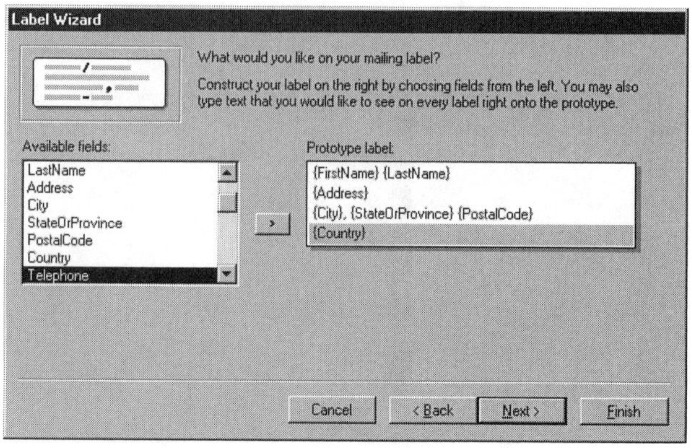

Figure 4.23.

The prototype label shows all the name and address fields.

5. In the next dialog box, the Wizard offers the option of sorting the labels by one of the fields. Choose PostalCode, and then click Next.

6. In the final dialog box, enter `Subscriber Labels - All` and the name for the report. Then click Finish. Figure 4.24 shows the preview of the new labels, sorted by Postal Code.

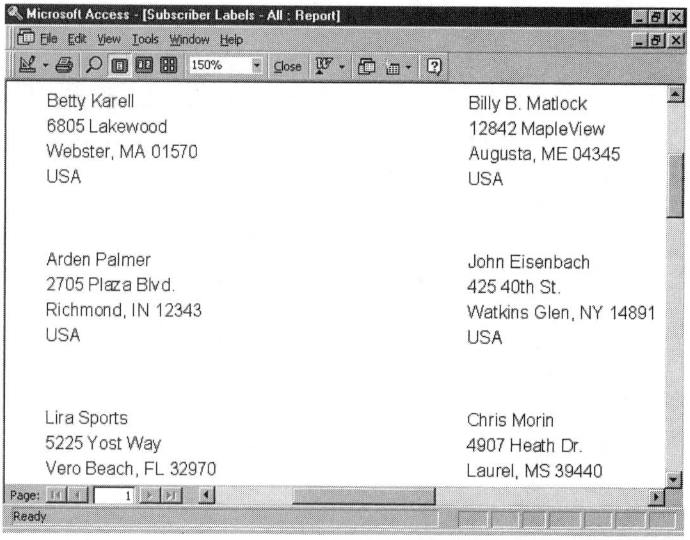

Figure 4.24.

A preview of the new mailing labels, sorted by Postal Code.

Another report that could be quite useful to the *Omni-Sport* user is a mailing label report that prints labels only for the subscribers who need to be reminded to renew their subscriptions. The easiest way to build this report is to copy the one that prints all the labels and then change the record source to a query that extracts the records in which the renewal date is close at hand.

First, create the query based on the Subscribers table, adding only the fields that comprise the address plus the RenewalDate field. Then add an expression to the query design that limits the records to those with a renewal date of less than 90 days away. Type `<Date()+90` in the criteria line below RenewalDate. Of course, the records that are extracted by the query depend on the current system date as compared with the dates entered in the table.

After the query is complete, make a copy of the Subscriber Labels - All report design and save it as Labels - Renewals.

1. Right-click Subscriber Labels - All in the Report window and choose Copy from the shortcut menu.

2. Click Paste, and then type `Labels - Renewals` in the Paste Report As dialog box and choose OK.

3. Open the new label report in design view and change its record source property to the query Renewals.

4. Close the design window.

It would help the *Omni-Sport* subscription staff keep track of the renewal correspondence by also printing a list of the subscribers who are reminded to renew. Figure 4.25 shows an example of a simple report created by the Report Wizard using the Renewals query as the record source. An unbound control was added to the report footer showing the total number of records in the list.

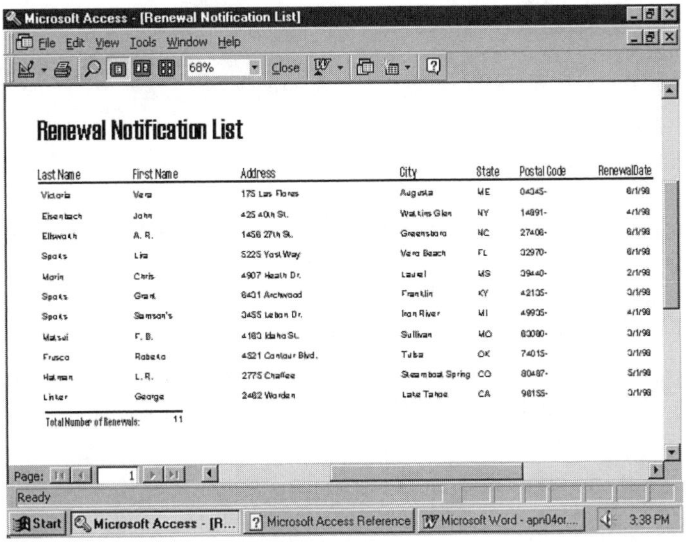

Figure 4.25.
A list of the subscribers who need to renew soon.

Changing the Switchboards

The last job you need to do to convert the Addresses database for use at *Omni-Sport* is to modify the user interface. The user deals mainly with the switchboards that the Database Wizard created. You use the Switchboard Manager to change the captions in the title bars of the switchboards as well as the items listed as actions.

To change the switchboards, return to the Main Switchboard and choose Change Switchboard Items from the list. If you are in the database window, open the Switchboard form in form view and then choose Change Switchboard Items. The Switchboard Manager dialog box shows the names of all the switchboards in the database and indicates which is the default. The default switchboard is the one that appears at startup if the startup display option is set to Switchboard.

Note: The Database Wizard has provided this convenient way to reach the Switchboard Manager. When you create your own database without the help of the wizard, you can call up the Switchboard Manager by choosing Tools | Add-ins and then clicking Switchboard Manager.

With the Switchboard Manager, you can create new switchboards, edit or delete existing ones, or change the default. Here's how to change the text in the Main Switchboard:

1. Select Main Switchboard in the list and then choose Edit. The Edit Switchboard Page dialog box appears (see Figure 4.26).

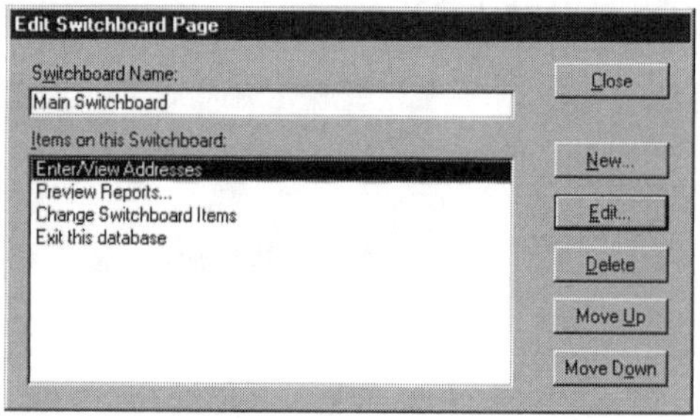

Figure 4.26.
You modify a switchboard in the Edit Switchboard Page dialog box.

> **Edit Switchboard Page**
>
> Switchboard Name:
> `Main Switchboard`
>
> Items on this Switchboard:
> Enter/View Addresses
> Preview Reports...
> Change Switchboard Items
> Exit this database
>
> Close
> New...
> Edit...
> Delete
> Move Up
> Move Down

2. Change the Switchboard Name to `Omni-Sport Switchboard`. Next, select the Enter/Review Addresses item, click Edit, and then change Addresses to `Subscribers`.

3. The command that is executed when this item is clicked is Open Form in Edit Mode. The Command pull-down menu contains several other appropriate commands from which to choose.

4. Select Subscribers from the Form pull-down menu and click OK. Then click Close.

Back in the Switchboard Manager dialog box, select the Report Switchboard to make changes in the list of report previews. Two reports were deleted and three were added. Here's how to modify the *Omni-Sport* Reports Switchboard:

1. In the Switchboard Manager dialog box, select the Reports Switchboard and then click Edit.

2. Change the name to `Omni-Sport Reports Switchboard` and then delete the birthday and greeting card reports.

3. Choose New and type `Mailing Labels - All` as the text. Select Open Report from the Command pull-down menu and select Subscriber Labels - All from the Report pull-down menu. Then click OK.

4. Repeat step 3 to add a preview of the Labels - Renewals report and the Renewal Notification List report.

Figure 4.27 shows the Edit Switchboard Page dialog box with the list of items it includes. Notice that the new items appear at the bottom of the list. It is preferable to have the exit option, Return to Main Switchboard, last in the list. To move an item in the list, select the item and click the Move Up or Move Down button until the item is in the desired position.

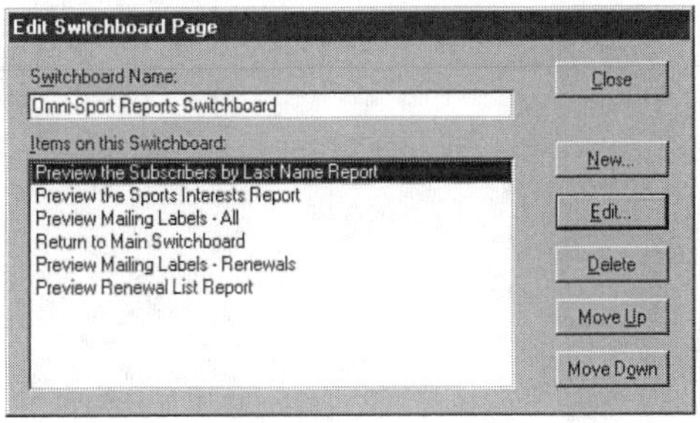

Figure 4.27.
The Edit Switchboard Page dialog box shows the new items at the bottom of the list.

In the *Omni-Sport* Reports Switchboard, select Return to Main Switchboard and click Move Down twice. Then click Close twice. When you return to the main switchboard, test the new items to see if they perform the correct operations.

When you click the Preview Fact Sheet button in the Subscribers form, Access displays an error message complaining that it can't find the field AddressID referred to in your expression. The reason is that the Fact Sheet to be previewed is synchronized with the key field of the record currently displayed in the form. The synchronization is accomplished with a VBA procedure that needs to be modified to reflect the field name change from the AddressID to SubscriberID. Chapter 5 shows how to do this.

Some applications greet the user with a special screen, called a *splash screen*, that appears for only a few seconds before launching into the main switchboard. The splash screen contains no command buttons or other input controls, it just serves as a greeting upon opening the database. Chapter 5 delves into the program code that can accomplish such a display.

Summary

This chapter has demonstrated the use of the Database Wizard to get a start on creating a new database. After selecting from the wizard's palette of choices, you modified many of the database objects to reflect the needs of the *Omni-Sport* organization.

Not only did this chapter show how to change the table structure, but it also showed how to carry the changes over into the form, report, and switchboard designs.

The next chapter continues with the *Omni-Sport* database by examining the code that resulted from the wizard's work as well as from the changes made in this chapter. Chapter 5 also shows how to make changes in the VBA code to modify object properties and to control events.

5

Examining
and
Modifying
the Wizard's
Code

This chapter examines the database objects and code generated by the Database Wizard in Chapter 4, "Creating an Application with a Wizard." Much of the VBA syntax is explained in the context of the application. After a review of the class modules, you will make some changes that add functionality and alter the behavior and appearance of some of the controls.

Inspecting the Wizard's Creation

The Database Wizard built all the necessary components for the *Omni-Sport* database. Now it is time to open up the curtains and see what the wizard has created for you.

The *Omni-Sport* Database Objects

When you open the database, the *Omni-Sport* main switchboard appears on the screen. To see the objects the wizard built into the database, click the Database Window button. Other ways to restore the database window include choosing Window | *Omni-Sport* Database or double-clicking the minimized database window at the bottom of the screen.

Tables

In the Tables tab of the database window, you'll see that there are two tables in the database: the Subscribers table, which contains all the subscriber records, and a second table named Switchboard Items. The wizard created the Switchboard Items table to hold the information about all the items on all the switchboards in the database. Figure 5.1 shows the Switchboard Items table in datasheet view.

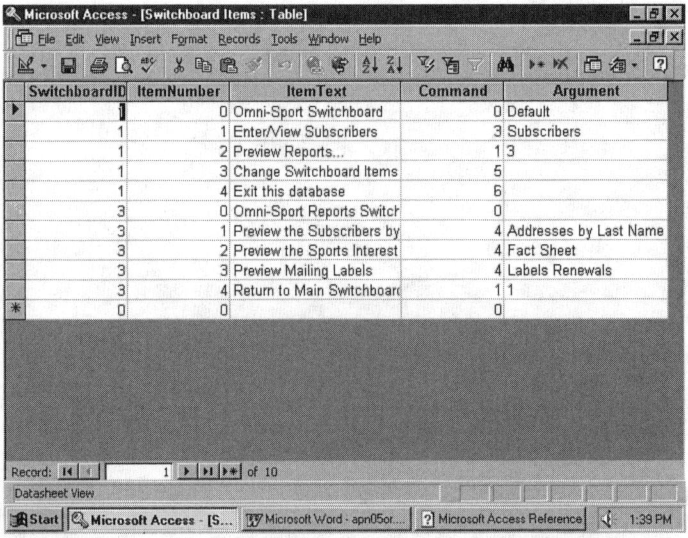

Figure 5.1.
The Switchboard Items table.

SwitchboardID	ItemNumber	ItemText	Command	Argument
1	0	Omni-Sport Switchboard	0	Default
1	1	Enter/View Subscribers	3	Subscribers
1	2	Preview Reports...	1	3
1	3	Change Switchboard Items	5	
1	4	Exit this database	6	
3	0	Omni-Sport Reports Switch	0	
3	1	Preview the Subscribers by	4	Addresses by Last Name
3	2	Preview the Sports Interest	4	Fact Sheet
3	3	Preview Mailing Labels	4	Labels Renewals
3	4	Return to Main Switchboard	1	1
*	0	0		0

The first field, SwitchboardID, identifies the individual switchboards. In this table, the main *Omni-Sport* Switchboard is named 1, and the *Omni-Sport* Report switchboard is named 3.

ItemNumber, the second field, refers to the switchboard's caption and to each of the options on the switchboard. The items are numbered sequentially within the switchboard with the caption item numbered 0. For example, the main switchboard has four options and the reports switchboard has six options. Each switchboard is limited to eight items. ItemText is just that—the text that accompanies the item button on the screen.

The last two fields, Command and Argument, are used when the corresponding option is selected. The Command value determines which of eight predefined commands to execute. The Argument specifies the name of the form or report to open, if any. In addition, the Argument for the main switchboard indicates that it is the default switchboard design (the one that appears at startup).

The Command and Argument values are passed to the event procedure, the `HandleButtonClick()` function, that is attached to the `On Click` event properties of all the switchboard items and their labels. The function is called when you choose one of the switchboard options. The values in the Command and Arguments fields are passed to the function as arguments. The function uses the passed Command value in a `Select Case` statement to execute the correct response to the button click.

For example, if you click the first item in the main switchboard, Enter/View Subscribers, the command identified as 3 (`OpenForm`) is executed with the `Subscribers` argument, telling Access to open the form named Subscriber.

If you look at ItemNumber 2 for the main switchboard, you see that the command is also 3 (`OpenForm`). But this time the argument is 3, which is the identifier for the Reports Preview switchboard. Therefore, when this item is chosen, the version of the form that represents the reports preview switchboard appears.

Forms

On the Forms tab of the database window, there are two forms: the Subscribers form that was modified in Chapter 4 from the wizard's original template and the Switchboard form. The fact that there is only one switchboard form when the application includes two switchboards might seem strange. But if you look carefully at the two switchboards, you will see that they are the same design with different items. The Switchboard Items table contains all the items from both switchboards so that when a form opens, the switchboard number (1 or 3) determines which items to display.

Reports

The Reports tab shows the two reports the wizard generated plus the three new reports used for printing labels and a list of subscribers whose subscriptions are due for renewal. These were created in Chapter 4. The Queries tab shows the query used to extract records for renewal reminders and an append query used to import records from the CD-ROM to your database (if you did so in Chapter 4).

Macros and Modules

The Macros tab is empty, but the Modules tab shows a module named Global Code that contains any procedures that the wizard wants to make available to the entire application. In the "The Global Module" section of this chapter, you'll see the code in this module as well as the code in the class modules for the forms in the database.

Changing the Startup Options

The wizard designed this database for the end user so that the main switchboard always appears when the database is opened. You might not want to see this, especially if you intend to make changes to the database elements instead of run the application. As the startup options stand, it takes extra steps to remove the switchboard and restore the database window.

One of the startup options available in the Startup dialog box (see Figure 5.2) is to display a custom form when the database opens. To open the Startup dialog box, choose Tools | Startup. In the *Omni-Sport* database, the Display Form option is set to Switchboard, which means that when you start the database, the form named Switchboard appears. To open the database and view only the database window, click the down arrow in the Display Form box and choose (None). This change affects only this database and will take effect the next time you open it.

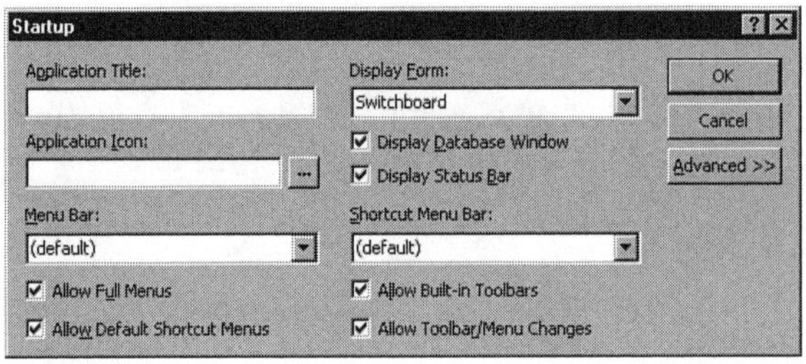

Figure 5.2.
The Startup Options dialog box.

Table 5.1 describes the options in the Startup dialog box.

Table 5.1. The Startup dialog box options.

Option	Description
Application Title	Enter a custom title to display in the title bar instead of "Microsoft Access."
Application Icon	Insert a custom icon to display in the title bar instead of the Microsoft Access key icon.
Menu Bar	Choose a custom menu bar to use as the default.
Allow Full Menus	Enables the user to have access to all menu commands.

Option	Description
Allow Default Shortcut Menus	Allows access to all default shortcut menu options.
Display Form	Specifies the form to display upon startup.
Display Database Window	Displays the database window upon startup. Can be minimized to display switchboard.
Display Status Bar	Displays the status bar upon startup.
Shortcut Menu Bar	Choose to display a custom shortcut menu as the default.
Allow Built-In Toolbars	Displays and permits use of the default toolbars.
Allow Toolbar/Menu Changes	Clear to lock toolbars and menus. Clearing this option disables the Close button on toolbars, the right mouse button, and the View	Toolbars menu option.

Note: By clicking the Advanced button, you can choose two additional startup options that deal with debugging VBA code. One enables you to view code in the module window (when an error occurs) by pressing Ctrl+Break. The other, Use Access Special Keys, lets you press special key combinations to view the database window, display the debug window, or suspend execution and display the module window.

Any changes you make in the Startup dialog box will take place the next time you open the database.

Viewing Database Code

Access offers you several ways to get to the module window to view VBA code. Without first opening the form, report, or module, you can select the name in the database window and click the Code button on the toolbar (see Figure 5.3). Access opens the object in design view and then displays the module window that contains the code. Because the module design is the code, you can also click the Design button in the Modules tab to view the code.

If a form or report is already open in design view, you can click the Code button to see the underlying code in the module window.

Figure 5.3.
Open the module window by clicking the Code button.

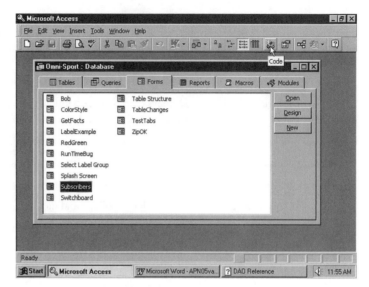

The Global Module

The Global Module contains a single function, `IsLoaded()`, created by the Database Wizard. `IsLoaded()` is a general-purpose function that sets an object's `IsLoaded` property to `True` or `False`. In this case, it checks to make sure a form is open in any view but the design view before setting the property to `True`. Excluding access to the design view is a precaution that prevents the user from making unauthorized changes in the design. The full listing of the Global Module is shown in Listing 5.1.

Listing 5.1. The Global Module.

```
Option Compare Database
Option Explicit

Function IsLoaded(ByVal strFormName As String) As Integer
  ' Returns True if the specified form is open in Form view or Datasheet view.

    Const conObjStateClosed = 0
    Const conDesignView = 0

    If SysCmd(acSysCmdGetObjectState, acForm, strFormName) <>
➥conObjStateClosed Then
        If Forms(strFormName).CurrentView <> conDesignView Then
            IsLoaded = True
        End If
    End If

End Function
```

The first Option statement sets the sort order to the same as that used in the database. The second requires that all variables be explicitly declared. Both these statements are added by default.

The Function statement names the function, IsLoaded(), and declares the return value as Integer. The ByVal keyword indicates that the argument, strFormName, will be passed by value. The strFormName is also explicitly declared as a string variable.

The comment that follows the Function statement describes the purpose of the function: to return a True value if the form named by the calling procedure is open in either form or datasheet view, but not in design view. This is done in the If...Then statements after two constants are declared and set to zero. The constants are used to compare and evaluate the results of the If...Then statements.

This procedure is a good example of nested If...Then statements. Nesting If...Then statements is a way to test for a combination of conditions. Here, the first test is to see if the form is open. If it is, then the inner If...Then condition tests the type of view. The compound condition might be worded, "If the form is open but not in form view, then...."

The first If...Then statement uses the SysCmd function to test the value of the form's object state:

```
If SysCmd(acSysCmdGetObjectState, acForm, strFormName) <>
➥conObjStateClosed Then
```

The arguments in the SysCmd() function first specify the action (GetObjectState) and then the object type (acForm) followed by the object name, which is passed by value to the argument strFormName. The object name is the one selected in the Form tab of the database window. The <> symbols mean "not equal," and the value of the constant conObjStateClosed has been declared to be 0.

The ObjectState is a property of the form and has a value of 0 if the form is closed, 1 if open, 2 if new, and 3 if changed but not saved (also called "dirty"). Therefore, with the comparison operators <>, this condition is asking if the ObjectState of the form is not equal to 0 (that is, not closed). If the form is not closed, the function goes on to the next statement, where it tests for the view. If the form is closed, the condition is not met and the function ends.

The second If...Then statement uses the CurrentView property of the form to see if it is in the design view. The values of the CurrentView property are 0 for design view, 1 for form view, and 2 for datasheet view. The condition

```
Forms.(strFormName).CurrentView <> conDesignView
```

uses the standard Forms collection identifier with the form name value that was passed to the function to compare the CurrentView property with the conDesignView constant, which was set to 0. If the CurrentView property equals 0, the form is in design view and the function ends. If the CurrentView property is any other value, the IsLoaded property is set to True. The function ends and control is returned to the calling procedure.

This is a fairly simple block of code, but you can see that even a simple function can involve many intricate details. The class modules for the Switchboard and Subscribers forms are much more complicated but still can be interpreted with patience.

The Switchboard Form Class Module

The Switchboard form class module created by the Database Wizard consists of four procedures:

- Sub procedure Form_Open minimizes the database window and opens the Switchboard form.
- Sub procedure Form_Current updates the form caption and calls the procedure that fills in the list of options.
- Sub procedure FillOptions adds the options to the switchboard. The list of options depends on which form is to be displayed. Both switchboards use the same form design with different options, as defined by the Switchboard Items table.
- Function procedure HandleButtonClick() responds to a button click that selects a switchboard option.

Each of these procedures is described in the next sections.

For more explanation about the statements in this and later modules, see Chapter 9, "Writing VBA Procedures."

Initializing the Switchboard Form

When the database first opens, the options selected in the Startup dialog box take effect. In this database, the Display Database Window option is selected so that the window opens first. The Display Form is set to the Switchboard form so that after the database window is opened and minimized, the Switchboard form appears.

The Form_Open procedure is specified in the form property sheet as the event procedure for the On Open event property (refer to Figure 5.3). When you click the build button opposite the On Open event, the module window opens showing the procedure code (see Figure 5.4). The full listing of the Form_Open procedure is shown in Listing 5.2.

Listing 5.2. The Sub Form_Open procedure.

```
Private Sub Form_Open(Cancel As Integer)
' Minimize the database window and initialize the form.

On Error GoTo Form_Open_Err

    ' Minimize the database window.
    DoCmd.SelectObject acForm, "Switchboard", True
    DoCmd.Minimize
```

```
    ' Move to the switchboard page that is marked as the default.
    Me.Filter = "[ItemNumber] = 0 AND [Argument] = 'Default' "
    Me.FilterOn = True

Form_Open_Exit:
    Exit Sub

Form_Open_Err:
    MsgBox Err.Description
    Resume Form_Open_Exit

End Sub
```

Figure 5.4.
The Form_Open *procedure is the event procedure for the* On Open *event.*

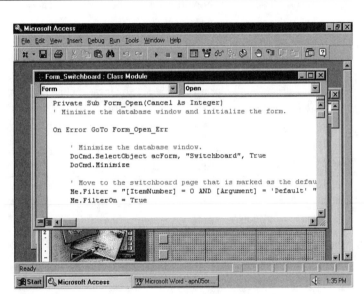

Notice that all the procedures the wizard has created include an On Error statement that branches to an error-handling routine. In this procedure, On Error sends control to the Form_Open_Err line, which displays the error message and then passes control to the Form_Open_Exit line. Form_Open_Exit: and Form_Open_Err: are line labels used as branch destinations for the GoTo and Resume commands.

Chapter 10, "Debugging VBA Procedures," contains information about adding error-handling features to your procedures.

The following DoCmd statement uses the SelectObject method to select the Switchboard form in the database window:

```
DoCmd.SelectObject acForm, "Switchboard", True
```

The arguments are acForm, which specifies the object type, "Switchboard", which names the object, and True, which indicates that the object in the database window is to be selected. If the form were already open, the last argument would be False.

This command merely highlights the form name in the database window. The next DoCmd statement minimizes the database window. The next two statements use the values in the Switchboard Items table to determine which form to open:

```
Me.Filter = "[ItemNumber] = 0 AND [Argument] = 'Default' "
    Me.FilterOn = True
```

Me.Filter sets the filter property to the Switchboard form that is specified as the default. ItemNumber and Argument are fields in the Switchboard Items table. An item with a value of 0 is a switchboard and the one with Default as the Argument value is the main switchboard. The second statement activates the filter. The switchboard is not yet displayed—the caption and options must be specified first.

Updating the Switchboard Caption

The Form_Current procedure is called when the form becomes current. It is specified as the event procedure for the form's On Current event property. If no caption has been specified in the Switchboard Items table, the title bar remains blank. The complete procedure is shown in Listing 5.3.

Listing 5.3. The Sub Form_Current procedure.

```
Private Sub Form_Current()
' Update the caption and fill in the list of options.

    Me.Caption = Nz(Me![ItemText], "")
    FillOptions

End Sub
```

Computers can behave irrationally when things are not completely defined. For example, when a computer encounters a blank where it expects a value, you should tell it how to respond.

The Nz() function is used to do just that. The first argument is the name of the field value to return, and the second is what to return if the field is blank. If the value is Null, the Nz() function can return a zero, a zero-length string, or some other value, such as N/A or Unknown.

Here, the Nz() function sets the Caption property of the current form (Me) to the ItemText value in the Switchboard Items table. If the ItemText is blank (Null), the function sets the caption to a zero-length string (""). No text will appear in the switchboard title bar.

The last statement, FillOptions, calls the FillOptions Sub procedure to add the options to the switchboard.

Filling in the Switchboard Options

Because the same form design is used for both switchboards in this database, each time you open a switchboard, the items need to be refreshed. The FillOptions procedure is called from the Form_Current procedure after the caption has been determined.

This is a rather complex procedure that uses an SQL statement to build a query that retrieves the items that go with the open switchboard. All of this happens before the switchboard finally appears on the screen. A complete listing of the FillOptions procedure is shown in Listing 5.4.

Listing 5.4. The Sub FillOptions procedure.

```
Private Sub FillOptions()
' Fill in the options for this switchboard page.

    ' The number of buttons on the form.
    Const conNumButtons = 8

    Dim dbs As Database
    Dim rst As Recordset
    Dim strSQL As String
    Dim intOption As Integer

    ' Set the focus to the first button on the form,
    ' and then hide all of the buttons on the form
    ' but the first.  You can't hide the field with the focus.
    Me![Option1].SetFocus
    For intOption = 2 To conNumButtons
        Me("Option" & intOption).Visible = False
        Me("OptionLabel" & intOption).Visible = False
    Next intOption

    ' Open the table of Switchboard Items, and find
    ' the first item for this Switchboard Page.
    Set dbs = CurrentDb()
    strSQL = "SELECT * FROM [Switchboard Items]"
    strSQL = strSQL & " WHERE [ItemNumber] > 0 AND "
    strSQL = strSQL & "[SwitchboardID]=" & Me![SwitchboardID]
    strSQL = strSQL & " ORDER BY [ItemNumber];"
    Set rst = dbs.OpenRecordset(strSQL)

    ' If there are no options for this Switchboard Page,
    ' display a message.  Otherwise, fill the page with the items.
    If (rst.EOF) Then
        Me![OptionLabel1].Caption = _
        ➥"There are no items for this switchboard page"
    Else
        While (Not (rst.EOF))
            Me("Option" & rst![ItemNumber]).Visible = True
            Me("OptionLabel" & rst![ItemNumber]).Visible = True
            Me("OptionLabel" & rst![ItemNumber]).Caption = rst![ItemText]
            rst.MoveNext
        Wend
    End If
```

continues

Listing 5.4. continued

```
' Close the recordset and the database.
rst.Close
dbs.Close

End Sub
```

The first declaration sets the constant conNumButtons, which establishes the maximum number of buttons on a switchboard equal to 8. Next, four variables are declared for later use: a database, a recordset, a string of SQL code, and an integer. The database variable, dbs, is set to the newly opened database (*Omni-Sport* in this case). The rst variable represents the records from the Switchboard Items table that belong to the form that is opening—the results of running the SQL query. The integer serves as an index for the list of switchboard items.

For more information about creating SQL statements, turn to Chapter 7, "Programming with SQL."

After the declaration section, the procedure concentrates on the switchboard options with this code fragment:

```
Me![Option1].SetFocus
    For intOption = 2 To conNumButtons
        Me("Option" & intOption).Visible = False
        Me("OptionLabel" & intOption).Visible = False
    Next intOption
```

Me![Option1].SetFocus moves focus to the first button on the form. The For...Next loop runs through the options and their labels, from number 2 to number 8, hiding them by setting their Visible properties to False, one by one.

The next block of code creates an SQL statement to extract the options and their labels from the Switchboard Items table that apply to the current form:

```
Set dbs = CurrentDb()
    strSQL = "SELECT * FROM [Switchboard Items]"
    strSQL = strSQL & " WHERE [ItemNumber] > 0 AND
    ➥[SwitchboardID]=" & Me![SwitchboardID]
    strSQL = strSQL & " ORDER BY [ItemNumber];"
    Set rst = dbs.OpenRecordset(strSQL)
```

It takes three statements to build the SQL code only because the screen is not wide enough to see the whole thing on one line. The three strings are concatenated together as they are constructed to form the complete SQL statement. The first line, SELECT * FROM [Switchboard Items] selects all the fields in the Switchboard Items table. The second line imposes the selection criterion and adds it to the first string with the & character. The criterion finds records whose ItemNumber is greater than 0 (not a switchboard, itself) and whose SwitchboardID is the same as the current form. The third line sorts the options by ItemNumber. The last line runs the SQL query and sets the rst variable to the result of the query.

The next code segment actually places the items in the Switchboard form after checking to make sure there is at least one item for it:

```
If (rst.EOF) Then
        Me![OptionLabel1].Caption = "There are no items for
        ➥this switchboard page"
    Else
        While (Not (rst.EOF))
            Me("Option" & rst![ItemNumber]).Visible = True
            Me("OptionLabel" & rst![ItemNumber]).Visible = True
            Me("OptionLabel" & rst![ItemNumber]).Caption = rst![ItemText]
            rst.MoveNext
        Wend
    End If
```

If the query has not found any records, the recordset will already be at the end of file and `rst.EOF` will have a value of `True`. The `If...Then` statement displays a message to that effect and branches to `End If`.

If there are options, the `While...Wend` loop proceeds to add each item button and label to the Switchboard form and then displays the caption in the label. The `While...Wend` loop continues until it reaches the end of the item list created by the query.

The final statements in the `FillOptions` procedure close the recordset created by the query and close the database.

Responding to Button Clicks

The `HandleButtonClick()` function is the most complex Switchboard form procedure. It is specified as the event procedure for the `On Click` event property of every button on every Switchboard form. The identity of the button that has been clicked must be passed to the function so that it can choose the appropriate action. The function uses the `Select Case` technique to recognize the button that was clicked and to select the action.

Chapter 6, "How to Get Help with Access Programming," contains information about how to get help with macros, SQL, and VBA programming.

Listing 5.5 shows the complete function.

Listing 5.5. The `HandleButtonClick()` function.

```
Private Function HandleButtonClick(intBtn As Integer)
' This function is called when a button is clicked.
' intBtn indicates which button was clicked.

    ' Constants for the commands that can be executed.
    Const conCmdGotoSwitchboard = 1
    Const conCmdOpenFormAdd = 2
```

continues

Listing 5.5. continued

```
      Const conCmdOpenFormBrowse = 3
      Const conCmdOpenReport = 4
      Const conCmdCustomizeSwitchboard = 5
      Const conCmdExitApplication = 6
      Const conCmdRunMacro = 7
      Const conCmdRunCode = 8

      ' An error that is special cased.
      Const conErrDoCmdCancelled = 2501

      Dim dbs As Database
      Dim rst As Recordset

On Error GoTo HandleButtonClick_Err

      ' Find the item in the Switchboard Items table
      ' that corresponds to the button that was clicked.
      Set dbs = CurrentDb()
      Set rst = dbs.OpenRecordset("Switchboard Items", dbOpenDynaset)
      rst.FindFirst "[SwitchboardID]=" & Me![SwitchboardID] & _
          " AND [ItemNumber]=" & intBtn

      ' If no item matches, report the error and exit the function.
      If (rst.NoMatch) Then
          MsgBox "There was an error reading the Switchboard Items table."
          rst.Close
          dbs.Close
          Exit Function
      End If

      Select Case rst![Command]

          ' Go to another switchboard.
          Case conCmdGotoSwitchboard
              Me.Filter = "[ItemNumber] = 0 AND [SwitchboardID]=" _
                  & rst![Argument]

          ' Open a form in Add mode.
          Case conCmdOpenFormAdd
              DoCmd.OpenForm rst![Argument], , , , acAdd

          ' Open a form.
          Case conCmdOpenFormBrowse
              DoCmd.OpenForm rst![Argument]

          ' Open a report.
          Case conCmdOpenReport
              DoCmd.OpenReport rst![Argument], acPreview

          ' Customize the Switchboard.
          Case conCmdCustomizeSwitchboard
              ' Handle the case where the Switchboard Manager
              ' is not installed (e.g. Minimal Install).
              On Error Resume Next
              Application.Run "WZMAIN80.sbm_Entry"
              If (Err <> 0) Then MsgBox "Command not available."
```

```
        On Error GoTo 0
        ' Update the form.
        Me.Filter = "[ItemNumber] = 0 AND [Argument] = 'Default' "
        Me.Caption = Nz(Me![ItemText], "")
        FillOptions

    ' Exit the application.
    Case conCmdExitApplication
        CloseCurrentDatabase

    ' Run a macro.
    Case conCmdRunMacro
        DoCmd.RunMacro rst![Argument]

    ' Run code.
    Case conCmdRunCode
        Application.Run rst![Argument]

    ' Any other command is unrecognized.
    Case Else
        MsgBox "Unknown option."

End Select

' Close the recordset and the database.
rst.Close
dbs.Close

HandleButtonClick_Exit:
    Exit Function

HandleButtonClick_Err:
    ' If the action was cancelled by the user for
    ' some reason, don't display an error message.
    ' Instead, resume on the next line.
    If (Err = conErrDoCmdCancelled) Then
        Resume Next
    Else
        MsgBox "There was an error executing the command.", vbCritical
        Resume HandleButtonClick_Exit
    End If

End Function
```

At the beginning of this function, eight constants are declared as numbers from 1 to 8. These are general-purpose constants that represent the set of commands that can be executed when a button is pressed. If you take a look at the Switchboard Items table, you will see three of them are not used in the *Omni-Sport* switchboards. None of the buttons in this application open a form to add new records (command 2), run a macro (command 7), or run code (command 8).

The next statement defines a message to be displayed if the user cancels the application for some reason. Then, two variables, dbs and rst, are declared as a database and recordset, respectively.

The On Error statement contains a GoTo command that branches to the HandleButtonClick_Err line to resume processing or display an error message and quit the function. The error routine appears at the end of the function.

The first block of code following the declarations section looks for the option in the Switchboard Items list that matches the button that was clicked:

```
Set dbs = CurrentDb()
Set rst = dbs.OpenRecordset("Switchboard Items", dbOpenDynaset)
rst.FindFirst "[SwitchboardID]=" & Me![SwitchboardID] & _
     " AND [ItemNumber]=" & intBtn

' If no item matches, report the error and exit the function.
If (rst.NoMatch) Then
    MsgBox "There was an error reading the Switchboard Items table."
    rst.Close
    dbs.Close
 Exit Function
End If
```

The dbs variable is set to the current database, *Omni-Sport*, and the rst variable is set using the OpenRecordSet method. The first argument in the OpenRecordSet method specifies the source of the records for the new recordset, Switchboard Items. The second argument, dbOpenDynaset, indicates the type of recordset to open. Opening a recordset as a dynaset-type stores only the primary key for each record in the recordset, not the whole record as in a table-type recordset.

Types of Recordset Objects

Recordsets are all DAO objects because they deal with actual data. Recordset objects are used to work with data at the record level. They come in five different types: table, dynaset, snapshot, forward-only, and dynamic. The table-type recordset is the one you are most familiar with. It represents the underlying table in which you can add, edit, and delete records. An index determines the order of the records, and only the current record is stored in memory.

A dynaset-type recordset represents the results of a query that can be updated. It stores only the primary key for each record rather than the actual data. Dynaset records can contain fields from more than one table or query in the database.

A snapshot-type recordset is a set of records from one or more tables that you can examine but not change. A forward-only-type recordset is similar, except that you can only scroll forward through the records.

A dynamic-type recordset contains the results of a query based on one or more tables. You and other users can add, edit, and delete records in a dynamic recordset.

The FindFirst statement sets the search criterion and searches for the item in the Switchboard Items recordset. The following search criterion looks for the item in the current switchboard that matches the passed button number argument intBtn:

```
rst.FindFirst "[SwitchboardID]=" & Me![SwitchboardID] & _
    " AND [ItemNumber]=" & intBtn
```

For example, the search criterion might read, "Find the record for switchboard #1, button #1." Looking at the Switchboard Items table, it would find that item #1 is the Enter/View Subscribers item whose Command field contains 3. Command 3 is set as the constant conCmdOpenFormBrowse in the declaration section of the function. The item also contains Subscribers in its Argument field, which is passed to the code segment that opens the form.

If there is no match between the button number passed to the function and a command constant, an error is displayed, everything closes, and the function ends.

This function presents a good example of the Select Case technique of executing alternative code segments. Cases are used when a procedure must decide among several mutually exclusive courses of action. If...Then statements are used when there are only two ways to go. Nested If...Then statements can handle one or two additional decision points, but when there are more than that, the Select Case technique is much more efficient. The following code illustrates the principle behind the Select Case structure:

```
Select Case X            'Base path on value of X
    Case 1               'If X = 1, do this:
        . . . . . . .
        . . . . . . .
        . . . . . . .
       go to end
    Case 2               'If X = 2, do this:
        . . . . . . .
        . . . . . . .
        . . . . . . .
       go to end
    Case 3               'If X = 3, do this:
        . . . . . . .
        . . . . . . .
        . . . . . . .
       go to end
    Case Else            'If X not equal to 1, 2, or, 3
        . . . . . . . 'do this:
        . . . . . . .
End Select
```

The next block of code contains the Select Case statements that execute the commands associated with the button. Most of the Case statements require the value from the Argument field in the Switchboard Items table be passed to the command. The only one that doesn't need an argument is the command to close the application.

```
Select Case rst![Command]

        ' Go to another switchboard.
        Case conCmdGotoSwitchboard
            Me.Filter = "[ItemNumber] = 0 AND [SwitchboardID]=" _
                & rst![Argument]

        ' Open a form in Add mode.
        Case conCmdOpenFormAdd
            DoCmd.OpenForm rst![Argument], , , , acAdd

        ' Open a form.
        Case conCmdOpenFormBrowse
            DoCmd.OpenForm rst![Argument]

        ' Open a report.
        Case conCmdOpenReport
            DoCmd.OpenReport rst![Argument], acPreview

        ' Customize the Switchboard.
        Case conCmdCustomizeSwitchboard
            ' Handle the case where the Switchboard Manager
            ' is not installed (e.g. Minimal Install).
            On Error Resume Next
            Application.Run "WZMAIN80.sbm_Entry"
            If (Err <> 0) Then MsgBox "Command not available."
            On Error GoTo 0
            ' Update the form.
            Me.Filter = "[ItemNumber] = 0 AND [Argument] = 'Default' "
            Me.Caption = Nz(Me![ItemText], "")
            FillOptions

        ' Exit the application.
        Case conCmdExitApplication
            CloseCurrentDatabase

        ' Run a macro.
        Case conCmdRunMacro
            DoCmd.RunMacro rst![Argument]

        ' Run code.
        Case conCmdRunCode
            Application.Run rst![Argument]

        ' Any other command is unrecognized.
        Case Else
            MsgBox "Unknown option."

    End Select
```

The first Case segment executes an option that displays another switchboard form. It sets the destination switchboard with the Filter property of the current form. The filter specifies an ItemNumber value of 0 (a switchboard), so it considers only the switchboard forms. It also sets the SwitchboardID to the value found in the item's Argument field. For example, look at the third line in the Switchboard Items table, which is item 2 on the main switchboard. The Command value is 1 (GoToSwitchboard) and the Argument value is 3, the SwitchboardID for the Reports Preview switchboard.

The second `Case` command opens a form for adding new records. The form appears with a blank record on the screen. The third opens the form for browsing and displays the first record in the recordset. The fourth command opens a report preview. The argument passed to the `OpenReport` method is the name of the report.

The fifth command takes you to the Switchboard Manager, if it is installed. If it is not installed, a runtime error occurs when the `Application.Run` command is reached. The `On Error Resume Next` statement that precedes this tells Access to skip the statement that caused the error and move to the next command after it.

If the Switchboard Manager is not installed, the `Application.Run` command will cause an error, so execution moves to the `If...Then` statement that evaluates the error number. If the error number is not `0` (that is, a runtime error did in fact occur), the error message is displayed. Then `On Error GoTo` `0` disables the error handler.

The last three statements in this `Case` block open the Switchboard form, update the caption, and call the `FillOptions` procedure to implement the changes made with the Switchboard Manager, if any.

The final code fragment, `Case Else`, is the catch-all for any alternatives that are not considered in the earlier case statements. This displays an error message saying that it doesn't recognize the option that was selected.

The last two code segments exit the function and handle any error condition. In `HandleButtonClick_Err`, an error message is displayed only if the error was a runtime error and not caused by the user canceling the execution.

> **Tip:** If you look at the property sheets for the buttons and their labels, you'll see that both controls have an event procedure attached to the `On Click` event property. This means that you don't have to click squarely on the button—you can click anywhere in the item label as well and the same event will occur. This is a standard convenience for the user.

The Subscribers Form Class Module

The Subscribers form class module is much simpler than the Switchboard module. It consists of four event procedures that correspond to the four command buttons on the form: Preview Fact Sheet, Page 1, Page 2, and Return to Switchboard (see Figure 5.5). These procedures were developed by the Button Wizard and are straightforward. The complete Subscribers form class module is shown in Listing 5.6.

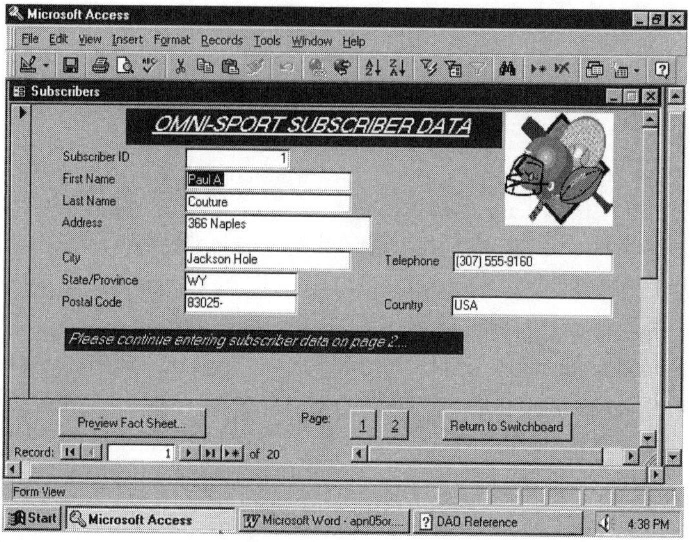

Figure 5.5.

Command buttons in the
Subscribers form footer.

Listing 5.6. The Subscribers form class module.

```
Option Compare Database
Option Explicit

Private Sub Preview_Fact_Sheet_Click()
On Error GoTo Err_Preview_Fact_Sheet_Click
    If IsNull(Me![SubscriberID]) Then
        MsgBox "Enter subscriber information before previewing fact sheet."
    Else
        DoCmd.DoMenuItem acFormBar, acRecordsMenu, acSaveRecord, , acMenuVer70
        DoCmd.OpenReport "Fact Sheet", acPreview, , "[AddressID] = " & _
            [SubscriberID]
    End If

Exit_Preview_Fact_Sheet_Click:
    Exit Sub

Err_Preview_Fact_Sheet_Click:
    MsgBox Err.Description
    Resume Exit_Preview_Fact_Sheet_Click
End Sub


Private Sub Page1_Click()
    Me.GoToPage 1
End Sub
Private Sub Page2_Click()
    Me.GoToPage 2
End Sub


Private Sub Go_To_Switchboard_Click()
On Error GoTo Err_Go_To_Switchboard_Click
```

```
    DoCmd.Close

Exit_Go_To_Switchboard_Click:
    Exit Sub

Err_Go_To_Switchboard_Click:
    MsgBox Err.Description
    Resume Exit_Go_To_Switchboard_Click

End Sub
```

The first procedure in the module is the event procedure attached to the Preview Fact Sheet command button in the form footer. In order for this button to work with the new field names in the Subscriber table, the AddressID field must be changed to SubscriberID wherever it occurs in the code. After the standard error handling statement, the `If...Then` statement tests for a value in the SubscriberID field. If the field is blank, there will be no information to display in the report preview and a message box is displayed.

```
If IsNull(Me![SubscriberID]) Then
    MsgBox "Enter subscriber information before previewing fact sheet."
Else
    DoCmd.DoMenuItem acFormBar, acRecordsMenu, acSaveRecord, , acMenuVer70
    DoCmd.OpenReport "Fact Sheet", acPreview, , "[SubscriberID] = " & _
        [SubscriberID]
End If
```

The first `DoCmd` statement executes the `DoMenuItem` action to change the intrinsic menu bar (the Form menu bar) to the Reports menu bar that you see when you are in report preview view. The two commas together with no argument between them indicate an optional argument is omitted, but the last optional argument, `version`, is included. Because the arguments are being passed by position, the commas must be included. The value `acMenuVer70` indicates code written for Microsoft Access 95 or 97 databases.

The second `DoCmd` statement executes the `OpenReport` action and defines the following:

- Which report to open: `"Fact Sheet"`
- The report view to show: `acPreview`
- Which record to display in the preview page by matching the SubscriberID value with the record in the Subscribers form

The `Err_Preview_Fact_Sheet_Click` routine displays the Access description of the runtime error and branches to the `Exit` statement.

The next two procedures, `Page1_Click` and `Page2_Click`, are the event procedures that execute when you click the 1 and 2 buttons in the form footer.

The last procedure closes the form when the Return to Switchboard button is clicked.

> **Tip:** The Return to Switchboard button returns you to the main switchboard only if you have opened the form by choosing Enter/Review Subscribers from the main switchboard. If you opened the form from the database window, you will return to the database window instead.

Maximizing the Main Switchboard

If you want the opening switchboard to fill the screen when the database opens, you can add a command to the Switchboard form class module. In the first procedure, Form_Open, add the command DoCmd.Maximize just before the Form_Open_Exit line.

Modifying the Subscribers Form

Although the Database Wizard did an admirable job creating the *Omni-Sport* database, there are still some fine touches yet to add and other things to change. For example, it would be easier to enter new subscribers records if the form had a combo box for the payment method. This way, the user could simply choose from the pull-down list instead of typing the data.

The form doesn't really need scrollbars, so they can be removed. Also, the Return to Switchboard command button lacks an accelerator key. Finally, the Preview Fact Sheet command button would be more informative with a ToolTip.

An added convenience would be to automatically calculate the new renewal date after the Amount Paid value has been entered.

In the next sections, these changes are made to the Subscribers form—some from the property sheet and others with VBA code.

Changing a Text Box to a Combo Box

To change a control type in a form, you first select the control in the design view, and then choose Format | Change To. You also can right-click the control and point to Change To in the shortcut menu. Figure 5.6 shows the Change To options for a text box control. You can change a text box to a label, a list box, or a combo box.

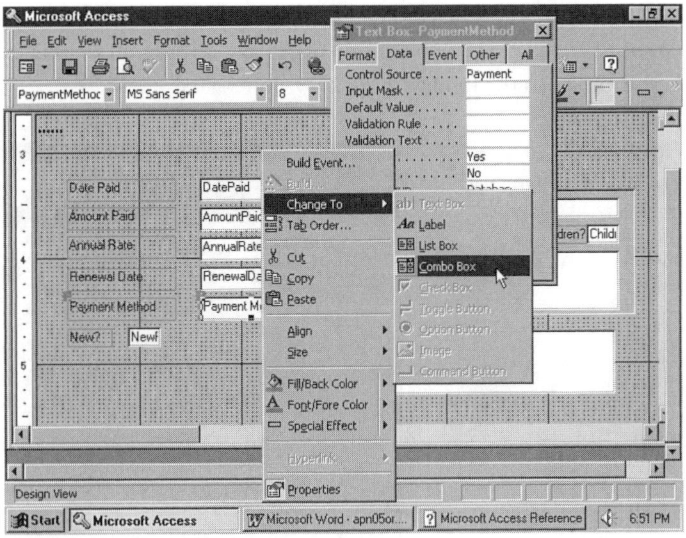

Figure 5.6.
Changing a text box control to a combo box.

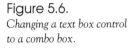

When you change a text box to either a list box or combo box, you must specify the value list from which the user can choose. After selecting Combo Box as the new control type, open the property sheet for the control and add the following property settings:

- Choose Value List as the Row Source Type.
- Type `"Check";"Cash";"Credit Card"` in the Row Source property line (see Figure 5.7).

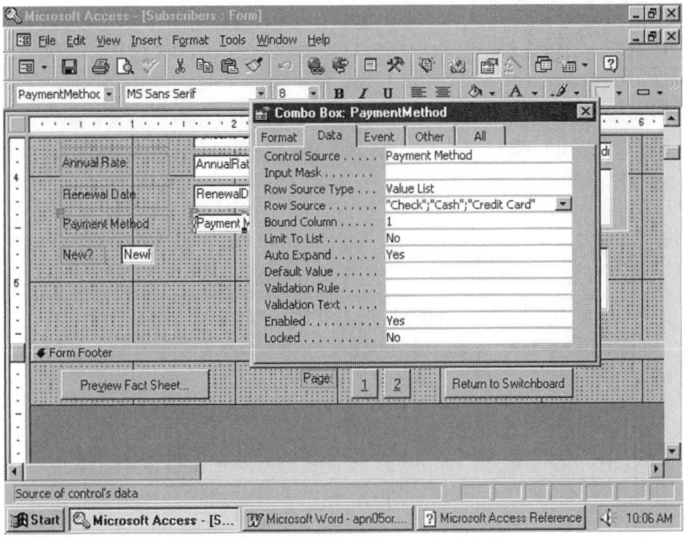

Figure 5.7.
Adding a value list as a row source.

Each of the values is enclosed in quotation marks, and they are separated by semicolons. The pull-down list in the Row Source property displays a list of all the tables and queries in the database. Figure 5.8 shows the form with the new combo box.

Figure 5.8.
The Subscribers form with the new combo box.

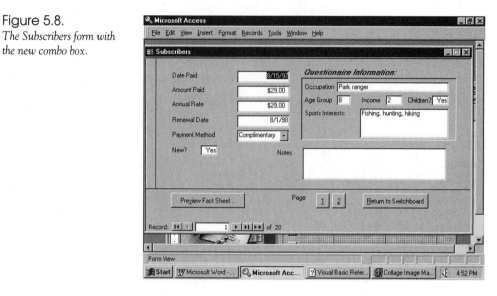

Changing Form and Control Properties with VBA

The rest of the form and control property changes are easily done with a single VBA event procedure that executes when the form is opened. To create the sub Form_Open() procedure, click the Build button next to the On Open property and choose Code Builder from the Choose Builder dialog box. The Subscribers form class module opens in the module window with the beginnings of the new procedure.

> **Tip:** While you are entering code in the module window, you can switch back and forth between the form design view and the module window by choosing from the Window menu. This is very useful for checking control names and properties.

To remove the scrollbars from the form, change the ScrollBars property to 0, which is the value for the Neither option, by typing Me.Scrollbars = 0. Me refers to the current object (which is the form), and Scrollbars is a property of the form.

Next, add a screentip to the Preview Fact Sheet command button. Type the command `Me![Preview Fact Sheet].ControlTipText = "See Fact Sheet for the Subscriber."`. The exclamation point following `Me` in this command means that what follows is not an Access-named object. The button name includes spaces, so it must be enclosed in brackets. `ControlTipText` is a property of the command button.

The last change is to change the caption of the Return to Switchboard button to identify the *R* as the accelerator key by placing an `&` symbol in front of it. Type the command `Me![Go To Switchboard].Caption = "&Return to Switchboard"`. Notice that the name of the button is not the same as the caption. If in doubt, look at the `Name` property for the button. If they don't match, you will get an error message.

The procedure looks like this after these commands are added:

```
Private Sub Form_Open(Cancel As Integer)

'Remove scrollbars and add ControlTip to Preview Fact Sheet control.

    Me.ScrollBars = 0
    Me![Preview Fact Sheet].ControlTipText = _
        "See Fact Sheet for this Subscriber"

'Add an accelerator key to the Return button caption.

    Me![Go To Switchboard].Caption = "&Return to Switchboard"

End Sub
```

Figure 5.9 shows the Subscribers form with a ControlTip and the new accelerator key.

Figure 5.9.
The modified Subscribers form.

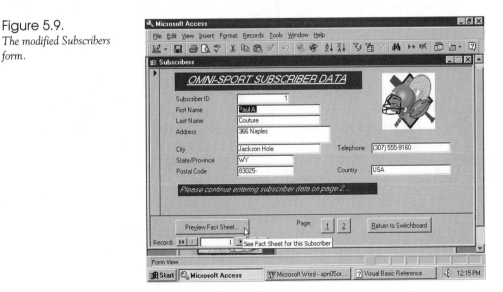

> **Tip:** When you are building VBA procedures, remember to add plenty of comments reminding you what each segment of code is intended to do. You will not be sorry.

Adding a Calculated Field

To automatically update the Renewal Date field, create a procedure that calculates the value after the Amount Paid field is updated. This requires some date arithmetic as well as computing the number of months that have been paid for. The event procedure is attached to the `AfterUpdate` event so that it changes the renewal date only if an amount has been entered in the Amount Paid field.

To create this procedure, select the Amount Paid text box and open the Code Builder from the `AfterUpdate` event property. First, declare two byte variables: `bytMonths`, which will contain the number of paid months, and `dtmResult`, which represents the value in the Renewal Date field. Type the two statements `Dim bytMonths As Byte` and `Dim dtmResult As Date`.

A problem can occur when you enter a new subscriber because the Renewal Date field is empty, which Access looks at as null. Therefore, the procedure must make provisions for a `Null` value with the `Nz()` function, which specifies a value to use if the field is null. For simplicity, set the value to today's date if Renewal Date is blank with the following statement: `dtmResult = Nz(RenewalDate, Date)`. Then, when the amount paid is entered, the renewal date is advanced by the number of months paid for.

Next, compute the number of months by dividing the amount paid by the annual rate and multiplying by 12: `bytMonths = AmountPaid / AnnualRate * 12`.

Finally, compute the renewal date by adding the number of paid months to the value already in the Renewal Date field: `RenewalDate = DateSerial(Year(bytResult), Month(bytResult) + bytMonths, 1)`.

This statement uses the `DateSerial` function to compute the new date. The arguments are year, month, and day, and the function returns a date variable. In this example, the year argument is extracted from the RenewalDate value. The month argument is also obtained from the RenewalDate field but with the `bytMonths` value added to it. The day argument is specified as 1, the first day of the month. Therefore, if a subscriber has a renewal date of February 12, 1997 and has paid for 18 months of magazines, then the new renewal date would be July 1, 1999.

If you want to see how to step through code to test it as you write it, turn to Chapter 10.

The complete procedure looks like Listing 5.7. The underline character at the end of one of the lines indicates a continuation of the statement on the next line.

Listing 5.7. Adding a calculated field.

```
Private Sub AmountPaid_AfterUpdate()
' Update the Renewal Date field after entering payment amount.

   Dim bytMonths As Byte
   Dim dtmResult As Date

'Set Renewal Date to today if new subscriber.
   Nz(RenewalDate, Date)

   bytMonths = AmountPaid / AnnualRate * 12

   RenewalDate = DateSerial(Year(dtmResult), Month(dtmResult) + _
      bytMonths, 1)

End Sub
```

Note: When a field is calculated from the value entered into another field, it can be a good idea to keep the user from having access to the calculated field. To do this, change the Tab Stop property to No. If you want the user to be able to override the automatic calculation, keep the Tab Stop as Yes.

Adding a New Report

To find out which subscribers enjoy a particular sport, you can construct a query to extract the records with baseball, for example, somewhere in the SportsInterests field. After creating a new report based on the selection query, the report can be added to the Preview Reports switchboard with the help of the Switchboard Manager.

Figure 5.10 shows a new query that retrieves all the fields in the Subscribers table but selects only those with baseball or basketball in the SportsInterests field. Figure 5.11 shows a report based on the query.

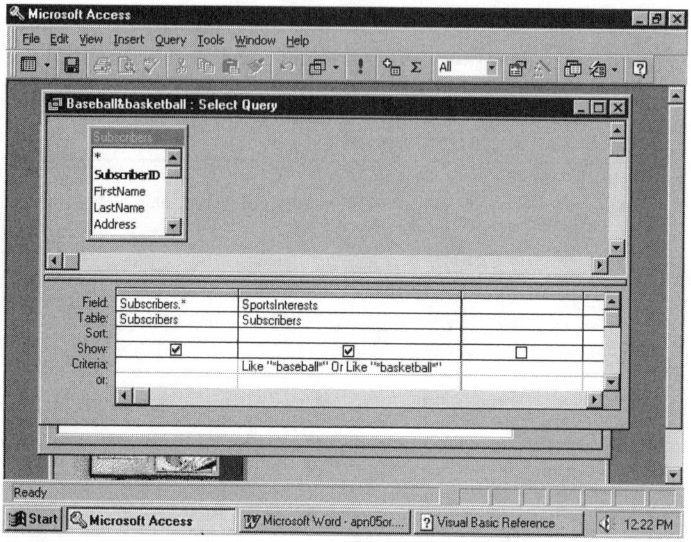

Figure 5.10.
The query that selects
baseball and basketball fans.

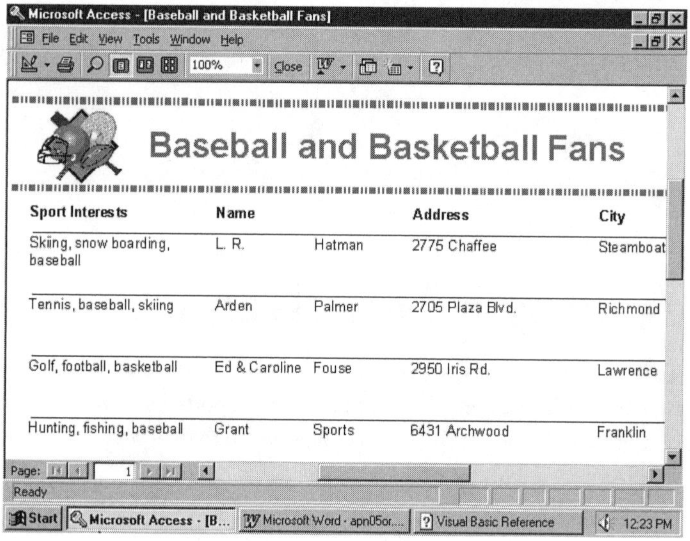

Figure 5.11.
The Baseball and Basketball
Fans report.

To add this new report to the Preview Reports switchboard, open the Switchboard Manager by choosing from the main switchboard items. Then do the following:

1. Select the *Omni-Sport* Reports Switchboard in the Switchboard Manager dialog box, and click Edit.

2. Click New in the Edit Switchboard Page dialog box.

3. In the Edit Switchboard Item dialog box, enter `Preview Baseball/Basketball Fans` as the text.

4. Select Open Report as the Command and the Baseball and Basketball Fans report, and then click OK. Click Close twice to return to the main switchboard.

Figure 5.12 shows the *Omni-Sport* Reports switchboard with the new report listed as one of the items.

Figure 5.12.
The new report item in the Omni-Sport *Reports switchboard.*

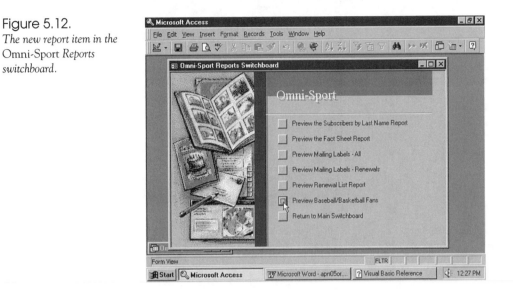

If you look at the Switchboard Items table after adding the new item, you can see the new item 6 for the *Omni-Sport* Reports switchboard that previews the new report. The last item, Return to Main Switchboard, has moved to item 7 in the list because the new item was moved up in the Edit Switchboard Item dialog box.

> **Warning:** If you try to use the ampersand (&) character in a switchboard item caption, it will turn out as a short underline character. The & symbol is a reserved character in Access.

The new report seems limited in its scope. It would be more useful if the user were able to enter the sport to look for. To do this, the command attached to the switchboard item would have to be either Run Macro (7) or Run Code (8) instead of Open Report.

The procedure would use an `InputBox()` function like this:

```
strSport = InputBox("Please enter a sport.", "Get Sport Fans")
```

This displays the input box shown in Figure 5.13. The function specifies the message to instruct the user and the title of the box. It would return the name of a sport entered by the user.

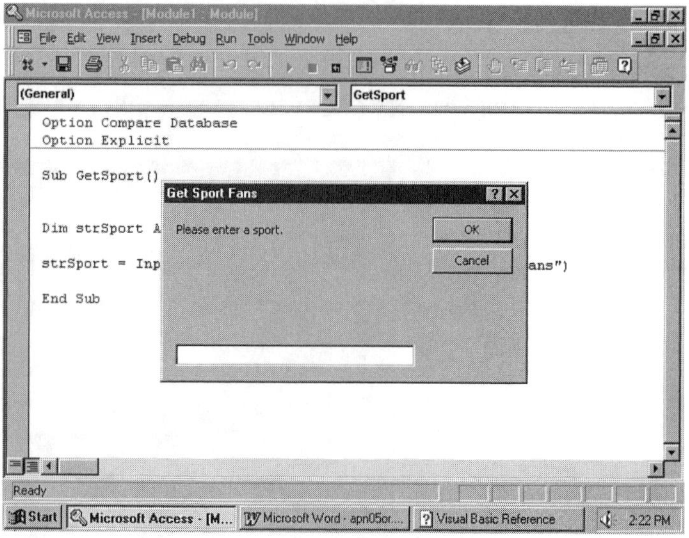

Figure 5.13.
The user enters the sport of interest.

Next, an SQL statement would use that value to create a query that selects records from the Subscribers table that contain that word somewhere in the SportsInterests field. Finally, the report based on the query is opened for preview.

You could even design the input box to accept two or three sports and then create the query to look for all of them.

Summary

This chapter has explored the tables, forms, and reports that the Database Wizard created in Chapter 4. It also closely examined the VBA modules that enable the database to function smoothly as well as how to change the database startup options.

After interpreting the code in the form class modules, changes were made to alter the form's appearance and the behavior of some of the controls. Changes were also made to the switchboards that act as the user interface.

In the next chapter, you'll see the many ways you can receive help from Access and VBA while you are building databases.

6

How to Get Help with Access Programming

Access is a very helpful mentor. It offers help, both online and as a lookup tool. If you get into trouble, you can click a button and a context-sensitive message appears with useful guidance and explanations. If you have a specific question, you can contact the omniscient Office Assistant. Help can be close at hand or as far away as the World Wide Web.

You probably have sought help while learning to use Access, but this chapter goes a little beyond the usual help features. In addition to covering how to look up special terms and access reference lists, this chapter teaches you how to get help while creating macros, SQL code, and VBA procedures. You will also get a glimpse of how to create your own customized help tools such as screentips, status bar messages, and help topics.

Asking What's This?

The What's This? button is very helpful for finding out about specific menu and shortcut menu commands, toolbar buttons, and almost any other screen item. It is available through the Help menu. To use the What's This? feature, choose Help | What's This?. The mouse pointer turns into a question mark pointer. Next, click the item you have doubts about and a screentip is displayed. To remove the tip, click anywhere on the screen or press Esc. Figure 6.1 shows the What's This? tip for the Code toolbar button. The tip not only explains the button, but it also tells you that Code is also available from the View menu.

Figure 6.1.
Viewing the What's This? tip for the Code button.

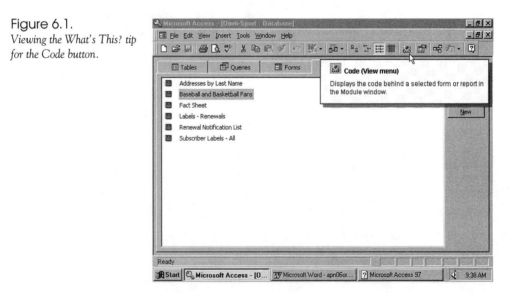

Most dialog boxes also have a What's This? button in the upper-right corner that you can use to learn about the options in the box. Click the button and then click the option. Figure 6.2 shows the tip for the Require Variable Declaration option in the Module tab of the Options dialog box. This coding option requires that all variables in the procedure be explicitly declared.

Figure 6.2.
Viewing the What's This? tip for a module coding option.

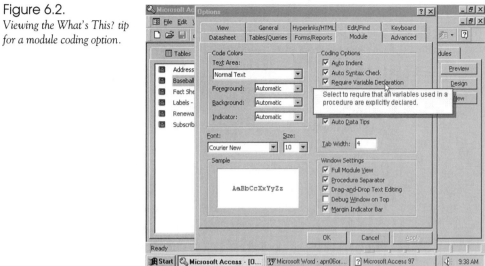

Finding and Printing Help Topics

You have three ways to reach a Help topic after you choose Help | Contents and Index. The Help dialog box has three tabs: Contents, Index, and Find. The Contents tab lists the major topic areas in the Help file. Double-clicking one of these topic books opens a list of subtopics that in turn can have additional subtopics (see Figure 6.3). Items in the list with a question mark icon are individual help topics. To close the main topic, double-click the open book icon.

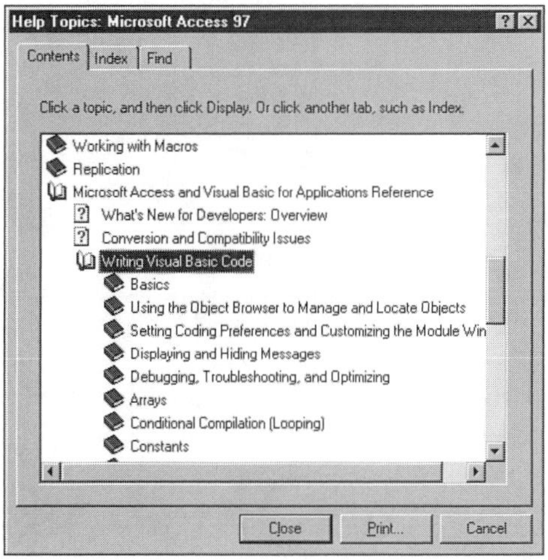

Figure 6.3.
Double-click a Help topic to see the subtopics.

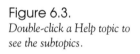

To print a topic from the Contents tab, select the topic and choose Print. Use the same technique to print all the subtopics under a main topic at the same time by selecting the main topic first, and then choosing Print. If you are already displaying a topic, choose Options | Print.

> **Tip:** If you can't see the entire title of a help topic, rest the mouse pointer on the topic and a screentip appears showing the entire name.

In the Index tab of the Help dialog box, you can type the topic you want help with. As you type, the list of topics scrolls down to the topic or as near as it can get. When you reach the topic you want to see, select it and choose Display or simply double-click the topic name. Many of the topics refer you to additional, related information with the click of a button. In addition, you can see the definition of underlined words by clicking the word. The Help buttons on all three tabs of the Help window display a message telling how to use that window to find a Help topic.

One of the useful Help topics is the Glossary, which contains definitions of all the terms used in Microsoft Office. Figure 6.4 shows the Glossary Help topic with buttons that take you to alphabetized groupings of terms.

Figure 6.4.
Look up any Access term in the Glossary Help topic.

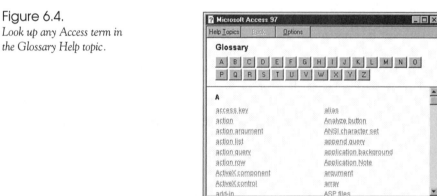

The Find tab in the Help dialog box lets you enter a subject rather than select it from the list. Access looks through the entire Help file for topics that contain the term, not necessarily in the topic title. This type of search for help takes a little longer because Access is searching through detailed abstracts of the topics rather than just the subjects and titles.

Asking the Office Assistant

The Office Assistant is a new feature in Microsoft Office 97. It has replaced the Answer Wizard from Office 95. The Office Assistant is an animated multimedia character that answers questions, offers tips for more efficient processing, and provides help with specific Access activities. You can choose to have the Assistant on screen all the time or only when summoned. It displays tips and options in a balloon when asked or when an error occurs. Figure 6.5 shows a typical Office Assistant displaying a list of help topics that you may select.

Figure 6.5.
The Office Assistant offers tips and options.

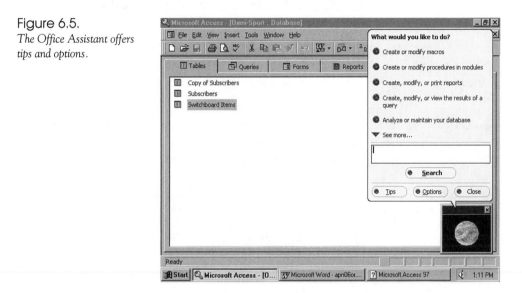

Hiding and Showing the Assistant

If the Assistant is showing, it automatically recognizes trouble and offers tips for solving or avoiding problems. If the Assistant is hidden, you can show it by doing one of the following:

- Clicking the Help button on the toolbar
- Choosing Help | Microsoft Access Help
- Pressing F1 (if that option is selected for the Office Assistant)

It is also available from many dialog boxes. To remove the Assistant from the screen, click the Close button in the Assistant window or right-click the window and choose Hide Assistant from the shortcut menu.

You can move the Assistant around on the screen by dragging the title bar just like any other window. If a balloon is showing when you move the Assistant, they move together. The Assistant window comes in two sizes. To reduce the size, drag one of the corners to the smaller size. Do the reverse to return to the larger square.

Choosing from the Assistant

As you saw in Figure 6.5, the Assistant offers a variety of Help topic options. Click an option to open the Help topic. If the option you want is not visible, there might be more options on a second page. To move to the next page, click See More. The Office Assistant disappears while a Help topic is displayed, but it returns as soon as you close the Help window.

Another way to choose an option from the Office Assistant is with the shortcut key combination Alt+*OptionNumber*: Alt+1 for the first option in the list, Alt+2 for the second, and so on. To move to the next page of options, press Alt+Down arrow; to move back to the first page, use Alt+Up arrow.

To begin a search for a specific topic not in the list of options, type the subject in the box and click Search. Figure 6.6 shows the options available after you enter Visual Basic and click Search. Next, choose one of the topics the Assistant suggests, or enter another subject.

Figure 6.6.
The Office Assistant offers
Visual Basic topics.

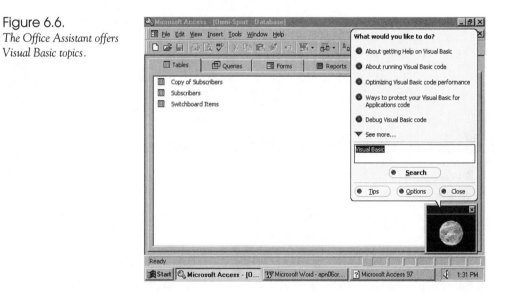

Access stores tips (see Figure 6.7) for using many Access features more efficiently and getting the most out of the application. Some tips apply to using the mouse or the shortcut keys. You can display these tips by clicking Tips in the "What would you like to do?" balloon. You can also change one of the Office Assistant startup options to have a Tip of the Day display when you start Access. The Next and Back buttons let you scroll through the tips. Each tip is displayed only once during a session, unless you specify otherwise. You can also use Alt+N and Alt+B to move to the next or previous tip, respectively.

To close the Office Assistant balloon without making a choice, choose Close or press Esc.

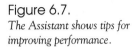

Figure 6.7.
The Assistant shows tips for improving performance.

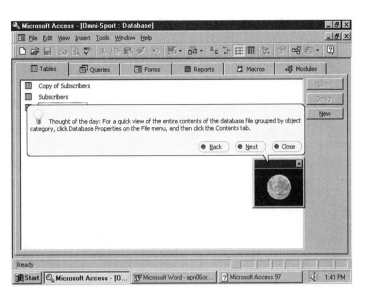

Modifying the Office Assistant

When you click Options in the Assistant balloon, the Office Assistant dialog box opens showing two tabs: Options and Gallery. The Options tab (see Figure 6.8) contains many settings related to the way the Assistant responds and the tips it displays. The figure shows the default settings. Table 6.1 describes the Office Assistant options.

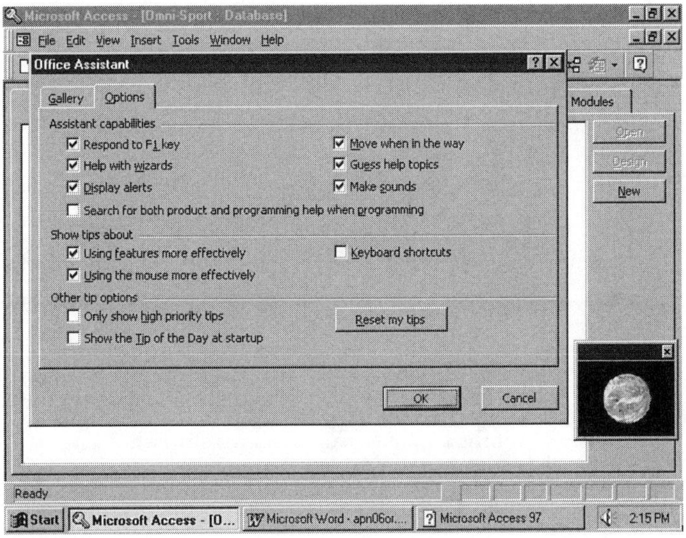

Figure 6.8.
Use the Options tab to set the Assistant options.

Warning: Be careful about making changes to the Office Assistant. The Assistant is shared with all the Office programs in your system, and any change you make will affect them as well.

Table 6.1. The Office Assistant options.

Option	Description
Assistant capabilities	
Respond to F1 key	Shows the Assistant when F1 is pressed, except in property sheets and other places where the Assistant is not used.
Help with wizards	Makes the Assistant available to wizards. Most wizards use the Assistant.
Display alerts	Shows a message when an error occurs.
Move when in the way	Moves the Assistant out of the way of dialog boxes and automatically shrinks it when it has not been used for five minutes.
Guess help topics	Shows Help topics based on what was happening when you asked for help.
Make sounds	Allows the Assistant to play sounds such as a cat meowing, a volcano erupting, or a ball bouncing.
Search for both product and programming help when programming	Adds programming Help topics to search.
Show tips about	
Using features more effectively	Suggests new features or better ways to use them.
Using the mouse more effectively	Shows tips on using the mouse.
Keyboard shortcuts	Shows tips about accelerator keys.
Other tip options	
Only show high priority tips	Shows only important tips.
Show the Tip of the Day at startup	Shows a tip when Access starts.
Reset my tips	Allows tips to be repeated.

The Respond to F1 key option always opens the Office Assistant when you press F1. If you want to go directly to the Help dialog box when you press F1 without using the Assistant, clear that option.

Note: The topics that the Office Assistant searches for depends on the window you have active. When in the module window, the Assistant looks for only programming topics plus help with actions and properties. In any other window, the Assistant searches for only product topics. To include product topics in the search while in the module window, check the Office Assistant option labeled Search for both product and programming help when programming.

When you are tired of the Office Assistant character you are using, you can change it with the Gallery tab of the Office Assistant dialog box. You have a choice of nine characters, ranging from a bouncing rubber ball to Albert Einstein. Some of their animations are fascinating. For example, a volcano erupts in the Mother Nature assistant when an error occurs. The Paper Clip assistant is an amusing cartoon character with blinking eyes and a variety of body contortions. Figure 6.9 shows the Gallery tab of the Office Assistant dialog box with a picture of each character. To change the character, you must use the installation disk.

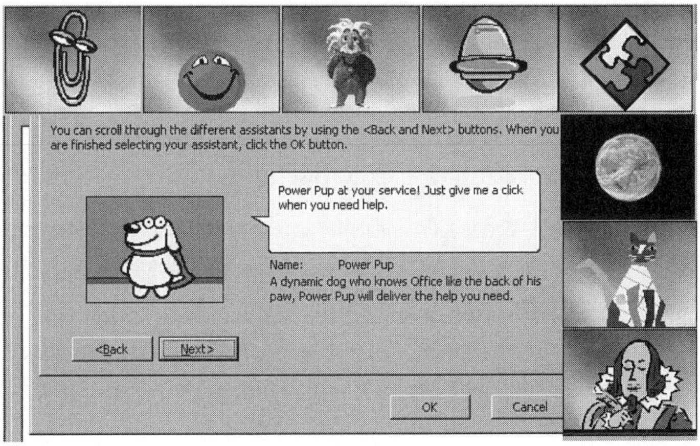

Figure 6.9.
Change the Office Assistant character in the Gallery tab.

Tip: You can customize the Office Assistant, its balloon, and all the items in the balloon by programming. The Assistant is an object itself with objects, properties, and methods of its own that can be modified using VBA.

Microsoft Office has more Office Assistants available on the Microsoft Web site. To reach them, choose Help | Microsoft on the Web, and then click Microsoft Home Page.

> **Note:** To use the Mother Nature and the Genius Office Assistants, your system must be able to support at least 256 colors. If you installed Access from 3 1/2-inch disks, those two characters are not available.

Getting Help with Macros and SQL

When you are working in the Macro Builder window, help is available directly from the Help window or through the Office Assistant. If you select an action in the Action column and press F1, the Microsoft Access Reference Help topic for that action opens automatically, whether the Assistant is set to respond to the F1 key or not.

When the Assistant is set to respond to the F1 key, if you select any other part of the macro window and press F1, the Office Assistant displays a set of three options: Run a macro, Create macros, or Debug macros. If you have cleared the Assistant's F1 key response option, pressing F1 displays either an explanation of the column that contains the insertion point or the Help Contents and Index window, where you can look for the help you need. What is displayed depends on the position of the pointer: if it is in a row that already contains an action, the column explanation is displayed; otherwise, the Help window opens.

Clicking the Office Assistant always displays the balloon with the three macro options.

Choosing Help | What's This? displays the Microsoft Access Reference Help topic for the selected action or an explanation of the column (if no action is selected).

When you are building a query either in SQL or design view, you can use the Office Assistant to look for help. Pressing F1 in either view opens the Assistant with several Help topic options (see Figure 6.10). If the Assistant is not set to respond to the F1 key, the Help window opens with no topic showing.

Asking for help with Help | What's This? while you are in the SQL view displays a definition of the SQL view regardless of the location of the insertion point. If you are in the design view, you can ask for an explanation of any of the items on the screen.

Figure 6.10.
The Office Assistant offers
help during query design.

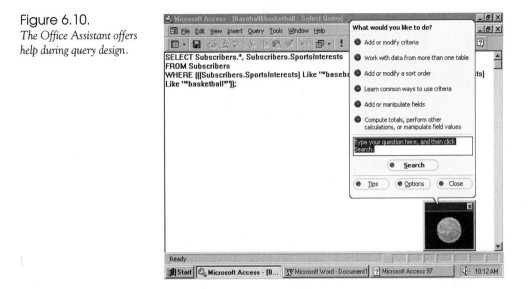

Opening the VBA Reference Help

To get help with VBA topics, use the Help Contents tab to reach the Microsoft Access and Visual Basic for Applications Reference book. From there, you can open other books to find information about VBA code, actions, constants, events, functions, and many other subjects. To print information about any of these subjects, select the book and choose Print. Topics such as events and functions have so many subtopics that they are grouped in alphabetical order (see Figure 6.11).

Figure 6.11.
Some topics are grouped
alphabetically for easier
access.

After you open a Help topic for a particular VBA term, the window offers several ways to see more information. Figure 6.12 shows the Click Event Help topic. When you click one of the jump words in the top part of the window, Access displays additional information. For example, See Also opens a dialog box with a list of related topics such as Create a command button and Event properties. To return to the Help window, choose Cancel.

Figure 6.12.
Click a jump word to see
more information.

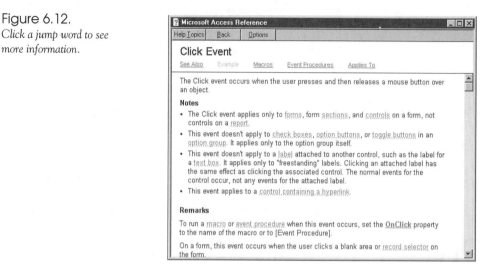

The Macros jump word opens the Click Event-Macros Help topic, which describes running a macro when the `Click` event occurs. Choose Back to return to the previous Help topic. When you click Event Procedures, the Click Event-Event Procedures Help topic appears, which describes the process of creating an event procedure. The Applies To jump word opens a dialog box that contains all the form controls to which the `Click` event applies.

Although the Example jump word is dimmed, indicating there is no example for the Click Event topic, other topics include the Example jump word, which displays sample VBA code. If the example is what you need in a procedure, you can copy it to the Clipboard and paste it into the procedure where you can make changes such as variable names, as needed.

Note: Some of the Visual Basic functions and statements might not be included in the language reference topics. The Typical Access installation does not include help for components shared with other Office programs. To install all the language reference topics, run Setup again and choose Add/Remove. Then choose Help Topics in the Custom dialog box and click Change Option. Choose Language Reference in the list of available Help options, and then end the setup.

From the Module Window

While you are writing VBA code in the module window, you can get help with a particular keyword by selecting the word and pressing F1 or by asking the Office Assistant. Pressing F1 takes you directly to the Help topic window for the selected method, property, function, statement, or object. When you click the Assistant, it displays a balloon with a list of Help topics related to the current activity. You also can type a topic and ask it to search for the information.

When an error occurs in the module window, such as a Select Case statement with no End Select statement, a message box appears describing the type of error. The box has two buttons: OK and Help. Choose Help to open the Help topic related to the error. If the Assistant is active, it displays the compile error message and also gives you the option of opening the Help topic for the error (see Figure 6.13). In the figure, the Mother Nature Assistant shows a bright red, erupting volcano complete with audio when the error occurs.

Figure 6.13.
An error message appears when a compile error occurs.

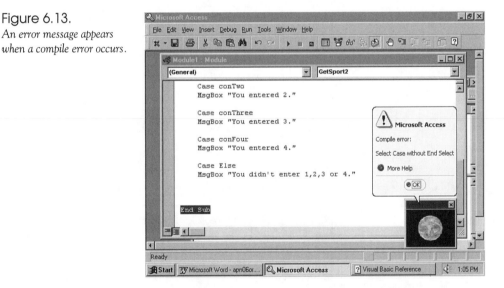

Tip: While you are writing a VBA procedure, keeping the Help window active so you can switch back and forth between Help and your application saves time. To switch between the two, press Alt+Tab or click in the Windows taskbar. If you want to copy code from the examples in the language reference Help topics, keep both windows open on-screen and move from one to the other as you copy and paste.

From the Object Browser

The Object Browser window has a Help button (a fat question mark) that you can click to get information about a selected class, method, event, or property. In Figure 6.14, the AutoExpand property of a ComboBox object is selected. Clicking the Help button displays the Help topic AutoExpand Property.

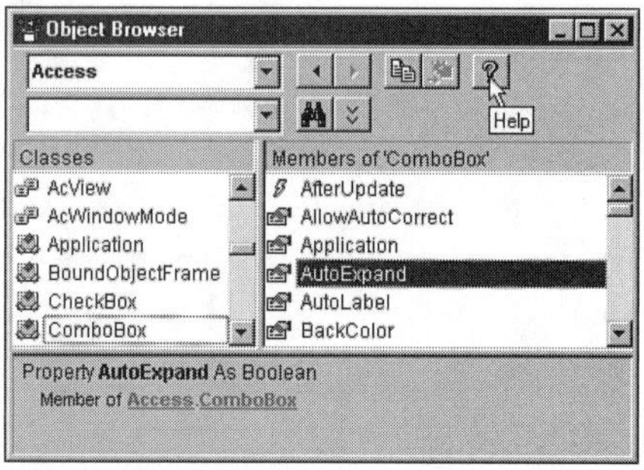

Figure 6.14.
Click Help to display the Help topic for the selected property.

You also can press F1 to see Help for the selected keyword.

See Chapter 10, "Debugging VBA Procedures," for more information about using the Object Browser.

Understanding VBA Conventions

After you have found the Help topic you want, you need to be able to interpret the information. Visual Basic uses standard typographic conventions in its documentation. Figure 6.15 shows part of the Do...Loop Statement Help topic, which includes many of the conventions.

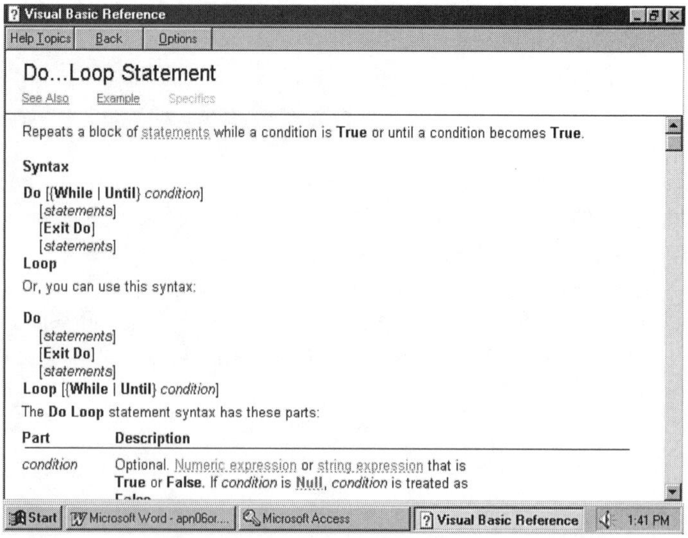

Figure 6.15.
The Do...Loop Statement Help topic uses typographic conventions.

Table 6.2 describes the conventions used in Visual Basic documentation.

Table 6.2. Visual Basic typographic conventions.

Convention	Description	Examples
Keywords	Bold with initial caps	**Do, Loop, Exit Do, True**
User entries	Bold, all lowercase	**exit, setup** (If bold, you can use positional or named-argument syntax.)
Placeholders for information you specify	Italic, all lowercase	*statements*, *condition*
Optional items	Enclosed in square brackets	**[Exit Do]**, [*statements*]
Mandatory choice	Enclosed in brackets, separated by vertical bar	**{While|Until}**
Key names	Small capitals	ESC, ENTER, TAB
Key combinations	Plus sign between key names	ALT+TAB, CTRL+P

Getting Remote Help

The Help menu also has an entry to the Internet where you can visit the Microsoft home page and browse in other forums (see Figure 6.16). You can download free software and find the answers to Frequently Asked Questions. You must have the Microsoft Internet Explorer operational in order to access the help available on the Net.

Browsing the Internet is a complex subject in itself, and entire books are devoted to the subject. This topic is covered briefly in this book. Chapter 20, "Posting Your Database to the Web," addresses the subject of converting an Access database to HTML for publishing on the Web.

Figure 6.16.
Help is also available on the Internet.

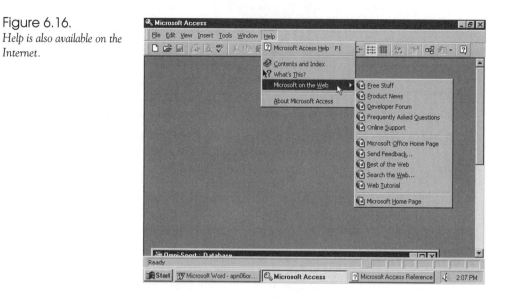

Creating Your Own Help

Although the Access help features are very comprehensive and versatile, they nevertheless are self-centered. They answer questions about using Access, creating macros, writing VBA code, and other related topics, but nothing about your application. A complete application should include customized help for its special features.

Many help tools are very easy to create while others are more complex. Screentips, the general term for those messages that appear when you rest the mouse pointer on a toolbar button, menu option or control, are easy to add and very effective. Status bar messages are also useful and easy to create, but users often do not refer to the status bar for help.

Creating your own help topics that respond to What's This or the F1 key are more complex and require access to the Windows Help Compiler.

Adding Screentips and Status Bar Messages

Screentips include ControlTips, ToolTips, and shortcut key text. All three display text when you pause the mouse pointer over the object. ToolTips and ControlTips display the custom text in a screentip. Shortcut key text displays the shortcut key combination you specify for a built-in toolbar button or menu option. If the shortcut key relates to a button, it is displayed as a ToolTip; if it relates to a menu command, it appears just to the right of the command.

ControlTip text is one of the properties of a control in a form. To add text you want to display, open the form in design view, select the control, and open the property sheet. Next, type the text in the

ControlTip Text property box. You can enter up to 255 characters. It is not necessary to enclose the text in quotation marks.

You add ToolTips and shortcut key text by customizing the command bar—either a toolbar or a menu bar. Both are toolbar properties that you reach by choosing View | Toolbars | Customize. After you select the button or menu item you want to add the help to, choose Properties. Then you can type the ToolTip text in the ToolTip property box. If you don't specify a custom ToolTip, the button's caption is displayed. For the ToolTip to appear, you must set the Show ScreenTips On Toolbars option on the Options tab of the Customize dialog box.

Enter the shortcut key combination in the Shortcut Text property box. If you want the shortcut key text to appear in the ToolTip, choose the Show Shortcut Keys In Screen Tips option in the Customize dialog box. This feature is available only for built-in toolbar buttons and menu commands, not custom ones. Entering the shortcut key text does not automatically assign the action to the keys; you still must create an AutoKeys macro.

Read Chapter 8, "Creating Macros," for more information about customizing command bars and assigning AutoKeys.

Status bar text applies to controls in a form and is also one of the control's properties. Open the form or report in design view, select the control, and type the text you want to see in the StatusBarText property box. Again, you can enter up to 255 characters but you will only see what will fit in the bar, which depends on the font and the size of the window.

Creating Custom Help Topics

Access provides context-sensitive help topics that you can bring up by pressing F1 or by choosing What's This from the Help menu. You can create your own help topics that will also respond to those user actions.

Using a word processing program or a text editor, create the help source file and save it in Rich Text Format (RTF). You can have as many topics as you want in the source file, numbered consecutively. Then, compile the Help file using the Windows Help Compiler. Save the Help file in the same folder with your application where it is readily available.

Note: The Windows Help Compiler program is included in the Microsoft Office 97 Developer's Edition, Microsoft Visual Basic for Applications, Microsoft Visual C++, and Microsoft Windows Software Development Kit (SDK).

To relate the help topics with a form or report, open the form or report property sheet and type the filename in the HelpFile property box. Next, enter the number of the topic that applies to the whole form or report in the HelpContextID property box. If you want a help topic displayed when you select a specific control and press F1, enter the same information in the control's property sheet, using the number for the topic that refers expressly to that control.

What's This tips appear when you choose What's This from the Help menu (or press Shift+F1), and then click a toolbar button or menu command. You can attach your own help topics to these command items by changing their properties. Choose Properties in the Customize dialog box (View | Toolbars | Customize) and enter the help file path and name in the HelpFile property box and the number of the topic in the HelpContextID box.

Summary

This chapter gave you several avenues to follow to get help with writing macros, SQL code, and VBA procedures. You also saw how to use the Office Assistant to help with developing an application. Access also provides a variety of ways to help you create customized help for the application end user.

In the next chapter, you'll begin programming in earnest with SQL code. Using SQL, you can create select queries as well as several types of action queries such as delete, update, append, and make-table.

III

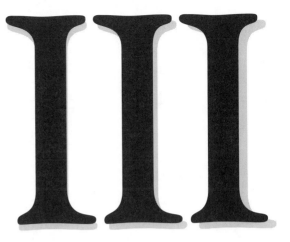

Diving into Syntax

7

Programming with SQL

Queries are the primary means of retrieving information from a database. With a query, you can select specific information and display it sorted by field values and even add summaries to the presentation. Queries are often used as a basis for forms and reports. Other queries can create new tables, append data to existing tables, delete records, and find duplicate records. Access queries are implemented in Structured Query Language (SQL) statements that you can review and edit.

This chapter reviews the types of queries and when you would use them. It also examines the SQL statements that operate behind the scenes and how to write your own SQL instructions. Other sections describe how to run SQL statements within VBA code. The examples in this and the next chapter are drawn from the Clayview City College database that is included in the Source\Databases folder on the CD-ROM that accompanies this book.

Types of Queries

When you build a query in the query design view, Access is working in the background writing equivalent SQL statements. To view the SQL code, choose View | SQL View or choose SQL View from the View pull-down menu. You can use either the SQL code or the query definition as the record source for a form or report. Using the query definition is a little faster because it is already compiled, whereas the SQL code must be compiled every time it is referenced.

Access offers several types of queries, from select queries that retrieve specific information to make-table queries that actually create new database objects.

Select Queries

The first type of query you learn about when starting with Access is the simple *select query*. The select query can retrieve information from one or more tables and often is used as the record source for a form or report. You can also run a query on a query instead of a table, thereby creating a subquery—a query within a query.

Figure 7.1 shows a query created for the Clayview City College database to serve as the record source of a report analyzing the students' grade point averages. It retrieves student information including name, class, number of units, grade, and major. The GPA Report computes the grade point average of each student based on the retrieved information. Figure 7.2 shows the query in datasheet view.

The SQL code (see Figure 7.3) demonstrates the use of statements containing keywords that define the query design. The elements of the SQL structure are discussed in the section, "Dissecting SQL Statements," later in this chapter.

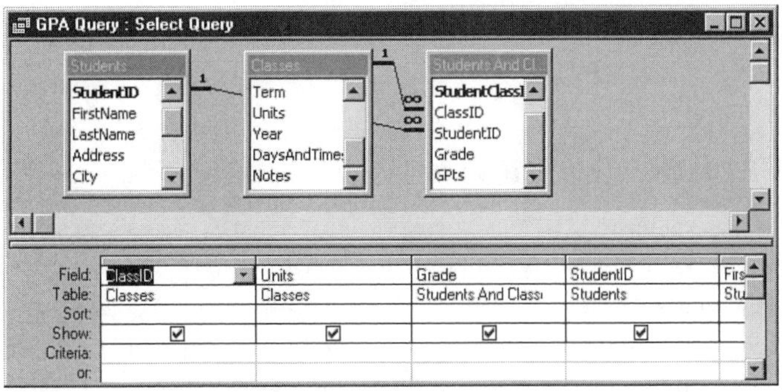

Figure 7.1.
A select query in the query design grid.

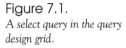

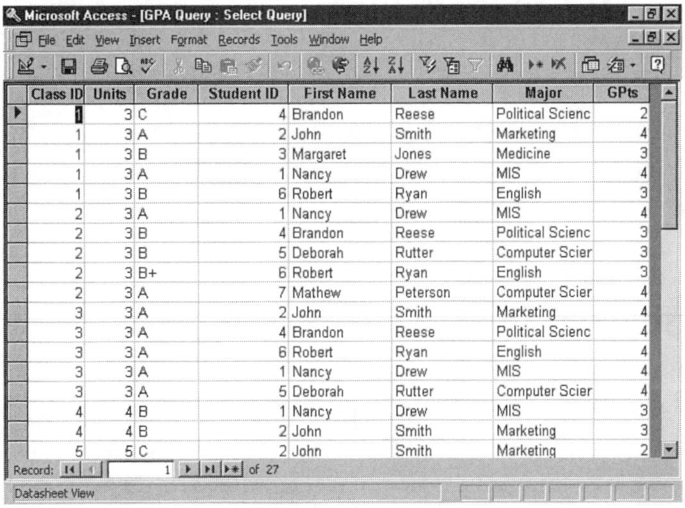

Figure 7.2.
The select query in datasheet view.

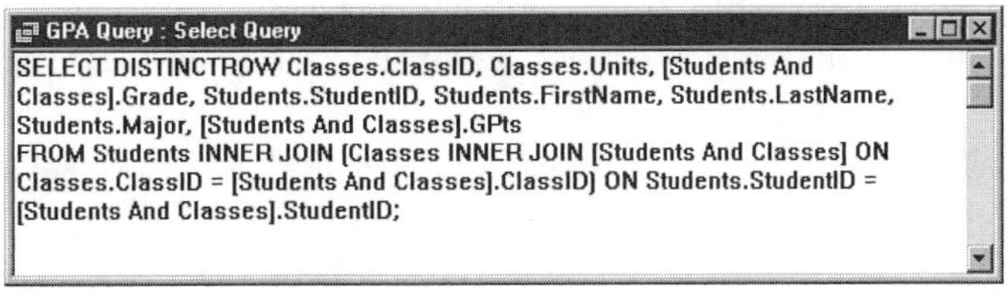

Figure 7.3.
The select query in SQL view.

```
SELECT DISTINCTROW Classes.ClassID, Classes.Units, [Students And
Classes].Grade, Students.StudentID, Students.FirstName, Students.LastName,
Students.Major, [Students And Classes].GPts
FROM Students INNER JOIN [Classes INNER JOIN [Students And Classes] ON
Classes.ClassID = [Students And Classes].ClassID] ON Students.StudentID =
[Students And Classes].StudentID;
```

Crosstab Queries

A *crosstab query* is a type of select query that helps analyze the effects of one type of information on another. It forms a two-dimensional matrix with one field as the row values and another as the column values with the information associated with the row-column pairs as the intersecting values. For example, a crosstab query could show you the grade point averages for each student for each semester. The student names would appear in the rows and the semesters in the column headings with the GPAs in the body of the matrix. The Crosstab Wizard is very helpful when you are creating a crosstab query.

Parameter Queries

A *parameter query* is a special type of select query that bases its selection of records on input from the user. A parameter query displays a dialog box prompting for information such as a student's name, a class number, or a date interval for sales transactions. You also can create a custom dialog box to receive the criteria for selecting records to include. Such queries can be used as the record source for reports and forms that can require varying criteria.

The SQL statements for a parameter query are the same as those for a select query except for a leading PARAMETERS declaration that specifies all the parameters that are requested when the query is run.

> **Note:** If you have designed a form or report based on a query and you remove or rename a field in the underlying query, Access expects you to enter the missing value. The query is treated like a parameter query, and a parameter dialog box is displayed.

Summary Queries

In some queries, it might be useful to include total or summary information such as the number of students in each class or the student's overall grade point average. Such summary queries group records and compute the requested mathematical or statistical function. To add a summary to a query, choose View | Totals. Access adds the words Group By in the total row of every field in the grid. To summarize the contents of one of the fields, click the Total down arrow and select from the list. Table 7.1 describes your choices of aggregate functions. Figure 7.4 shows a new query that counts the number of students in each class. The equivalent SQL code is shown in Figure 7.5.

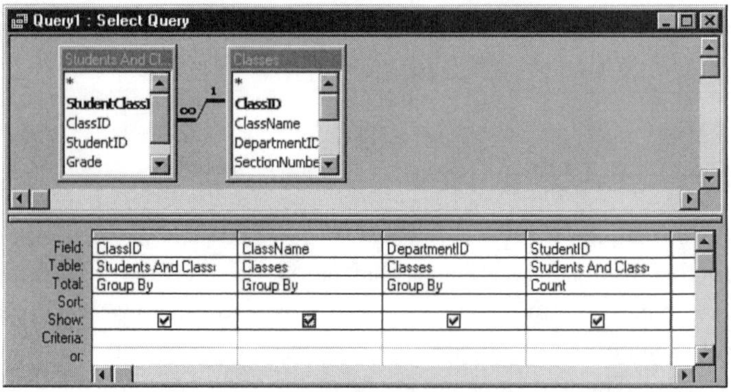

Figure 7.4.
A query that counts the number of students in each class.

Field:	ClassID	ClassName	DepartmentID	StudentID
Table:	Students And Class	Classes	Classes	Students And Class
Total:	Group By	Group By	Group By	Count
Sort:				
Show:	☑	☑	☑	☑
Criteria:				
or:				

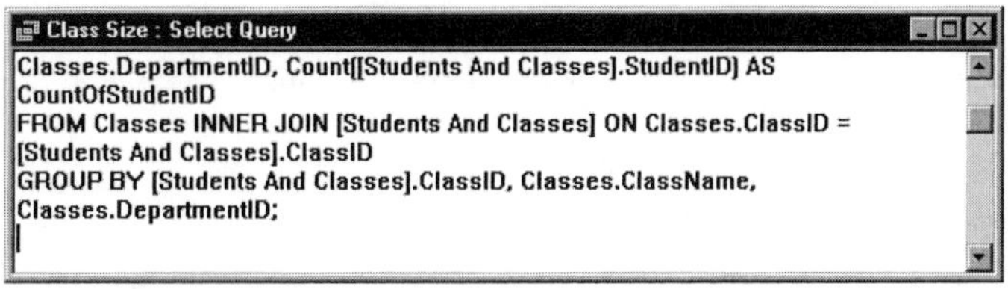

Figure 7.5.
The summary query in SQL view.

```
Class Size : Select Query                                    _ □ X
Classes.DepartmentID, Count([Students And Classes].StudentID) AS
CountOfStudentID
FROM Classes INNER JOIN [Students And Classes] ON Classes.ClassID =
[Students And Classes].ClassID
GROUP BY [Students And Classes].ClassID, Classes.ClassName,
Classes.DepartmentID;
```

Table 7.1. Summary query aggregate functions.

Function	Description
Avg	Computes the average of values in a field.
Count	Counts the number of values in a field. Does not include Null values.
First	Returns the field value from the first record in the result set.
Last	Returns the field value from the last record in the result set.
Max	Returns the highest value in a field.
Min	Returns the lowest value in a field.
StDev	Computes standard deviation of values in a field.
Sum	Computes total of values in a field.
Var	Computes variance of values in a field.

Each of these functions has an equivalent SQL aggregate function. Three additional options appear on the Totals list:

- Group By, the default option, defines the groups to perform calculations with.
- Expression creates a calculated field using one of the aggregate functions in the expression.
- Where specifies the criteria for a field that will not appear in the result set.

Note: Aggregate queries do not include records with Null values in the specified field. The Count function will not include them in the total, and they will not be included in any other calculation. To count the Null values, use the asterisk (*) wildcard with the Count function: Count(*). To make sure the records with Null values are included in other aggregate functions, you can search for the Null values and change them to 0.

Action Queries

Action queries affect the data in tables. Using Action queries, you can make changes to several records at once (such as updating a field, deleting whole records, adding new records) or make an entirely new table from fields in one or more existing tables.

You can create action queries in the query design window, and each one has an equivalent SQL statement that includes all the operators and clauses necessary to define the operation.

Update Queries

The *update query* changes the values in a field based on specific criteria. For example, you want to increase the price of certain types of items in the store by 5 percent. The query would multiply the price field value in the records for that type of merchandise by 1.05. You can change several fields at once with the same update query and also use the update query to update records in more than one table.

> **Warning:** Be careful with action queries. You cannot use Undo to reverse them. Luckily, Access displays a warning box before carrying out the action query and gives you a chance to change your mind. To be safe, always create a backup copy of the table before running an action query.

Append Queries

The *append query* adds one or more records to the end of one or more existing tables. An append query can be very useful for transferring records to an archive when the information is no longer active but worth saving. For example, at the end of each semester, student grades for each class can be appended to the existing student record archive.

Delete Queries

A *delete query* empties part or all of a table. It removes entire records rather than a single field value. If you completely empty a table, the structure, indexes, properties, and field attributes remain. You can delete records based on specified criteria such as students who have dropped a course. If you just want to delete a field value, use the update query and set the value to Null.

> **Tip:** Because the action queries are irreversible, run a select query using the criteria you would use in the delete query. This way, you can see the list of records that will be deleted and make sure you really want to remove them.

If you want to delete records on the one side of a one-to-many relationship, use the *cascade delete* option. This removes all the orphan records when the parent is deleted. For example, if you delete a specific chemistry class from the Classes table, all the records in the Students And Classes table that contain that ClassID value will also be deleted.

Make-Table Queries

The *make-table query* creates a new table from fields in one or more existing tables. This type of query is useful for creating archive tables that contain all the information for a specific period of time, such as student records for the entire school year. Make-table queries are also used to create backup tables or tables to be exported to another database.

Figure 7.6 shows a make-table query that creates a table with records for all the students with A in the Grade field. The new table includes fields from both the Students and the Students And Classes tables. In order to have a student name appear only once in the list, add the aggregate clause Count in the Total line of the ClassID field. The resulting table, Honor Roll, contains seven student records representing all the students with at least one grade of A (see Figure 7.7). The CountOfClassID field shows the number of classes in which that student earned an A.

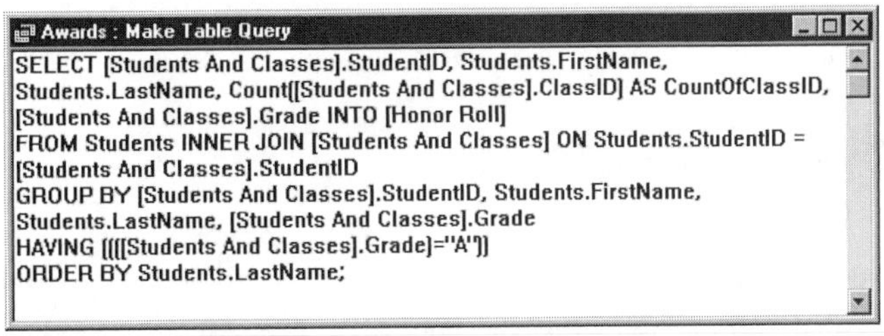

Figure 7.6.
The make-table query in SQL view.

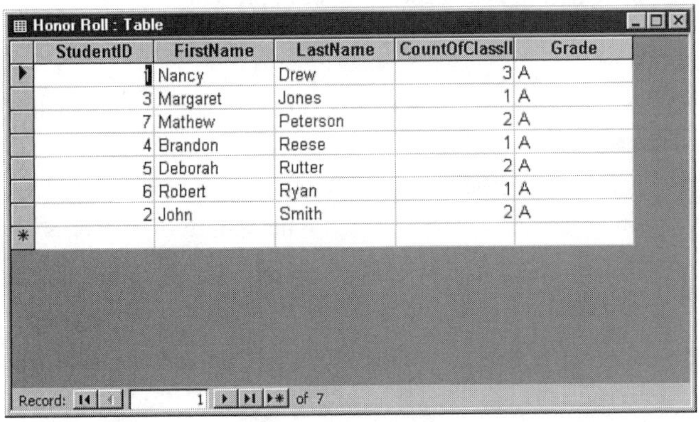

```
Awards : Make Table Query
SELECT [Students And Classes].StudentID, Students.FirstName,
Students.LastName, Count([Students And Classes].ClassID) AS CountOfClassID,
[Students And Classes].Grade INTO [Honor Roll]
FROM Students INNER JOIN [Students And Classes] ON Students.StudentID =
[Students And Classes].StudentID
GROUP BY [Students And Classes].StudentID, Students.FirstName,
Students.LastName, [Students And Classes].Grade
HAVING ((([Students And Classes].Grade)="A"))
ORDER BY Students.LastName;
```

Figure 7.7.
The Honor Roll table created by the make-table query.

StudentID	FirstName	LastName	CountOfClassI	Grade
1	Nancy	Drew	3	A
3	Margaret	Jones	1	A
7	Mathew	Peterson	2	A
4	Brandon	Reese	1	A
5	Deborah	Rutter	2	A
6	Robert	Ryan	1	A
2	John	Smith	2	A

Record: 1 of 7

As more student grades are reported to the dean's office, their records can be added to the Honor Roll using the append query. Figure 7.8 shows the append query that can be used to add the new outstanding students to the list.

Figure 7.8.

The append query that adds records of A students to the Honor Roll.

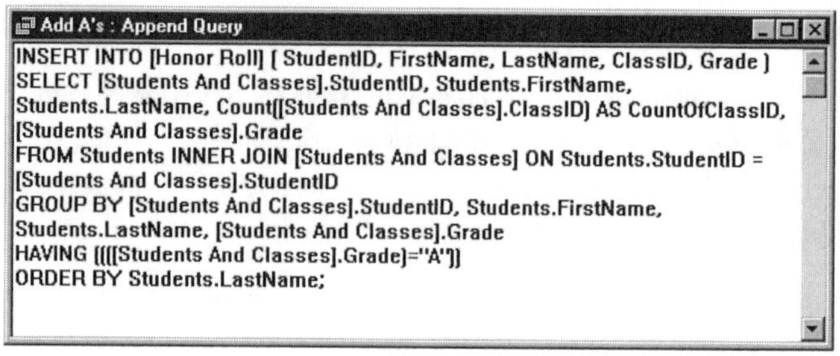

```
Add A's : Append Query                                                    _ □ ×
INSERT INTO [Honor Roll] [ StudentID, FirstName, LastName, ClassID, Grade ]
SELECT [Students And Classes].StudentID, Students.FirstName,
Students.LastName, Count([Students And Classes].ClassID) AS CountOfClassID,
[Students And Classes].Grade
FROM Students INNER JOIN [Students And Classes] ON Students.StudentID =
[Students And Classes].StudentID
GROUP BY [Students And Classes].StudentID, Students.FirstName,
Students.LastName, [Students And Classes].Grade
HAVING [[[[Students And Classes].Grade]="A"]]
ORDER BY Students.LastName;
```

Tip: If you plan to include a lot of queries in your database, creating a table with the names and descriptions of all the saved queries will help you keep track of them. It is all too easy to forget which query did what when you have a lot of them cryptically named.

SQL Queries

When you are operating in a client/server environment, you can use SQL queries to communicate with the back-end SQL server. The front end—the client—is where you sit, and the database is handled by the server at the back end. All SQL queries must be constructed in SQL code and can be run from a macro or embedded in a VBA procedure.

Here are some examples of SQL queries:

- A *union query* that combines fields from one or more tables into a single field or column in a third table.

- A *pass-through query* that works directly with the ODBC databases (for example, the Microsoft SQL Server), using commands in that server's vocabulary.

- A *data-definition query* that creates, deletes, or changes tables in the current database and also creates indexes.

- A *subquery* that places an SQL SELECT statement within another select or action query. Used in the Criteria row of the query design grid.

Union Queries

A *union query* is useful for compiling information from more than one table into a new table. For example, Clayview City College is interested in keeping track of its alumni as well as getting new graduates involved in alumni activities. A table that combines names from both the student and alumni lists with their home cities would be useful for periodic mailings.

Use the following process to create an SQL union query:

1. Click New in the Queries tab of the database window and choose Design View. Then click OK.

2. In the query design view, close the Show Table dialog box without adding any tables to the design.

3. Choose Query | SQL Specific | Union.

4. Enter the SQL SELECT statements, the first one alone and the second following the UNION operation.

   For example, the following SQL statement combines the first and last name fields from both the Alumni and Students tables and then sorts the results by City:

```
SELECT [FirstName],[LastName],[City]
FROM [Alumni]
UNION SELECT [FirstName],[LastName],[City]
FROM [Students]
ORDER BY [City];
```

Pass-Through Queries

A pass-through query works directly with the Access tables on an ODBC database server such as the Microsoft SQL Server. You can use a pass-through query to run stored procedures that update records or return specific records. A pass-through query could be used to update the grade point averages of the students at the end of the semester.

To create a pass-through query, open the query design view without adding any tables, and choose Query | SQL Specific | PassThrough. In the Query Properties sheet (see Figure 7.9) set the connection information for the database to which you want to connect. Either type in the information or click Build in the ODBC Connect Str property.

Figure 7.9.
Set the properties for a pass-through query.

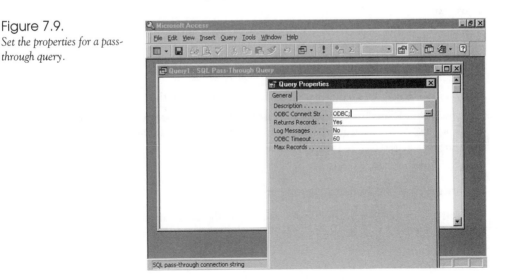

The Returns Records property allows Access to accept returned records from the query. If you don't expect records from the query, set the property to No. In addition to records, the query can return messages from the server. In that case, set the Log Messages property to Yes, and Access will create a table that contains all the returned messages.

The ODBC Timeout property sets the number of seconds to wait before triggering a Timeout error when running a query on an ODBC data source. The Max Records property sets the maximum number of records to return by a query running on an ODBC data source.

Data-Definition Queries

You can use a *data-definition query* to create a new table, change or delete an existing table in the current database, or create a new index. After choosing Query | SQL Specific | Data-Definition in the query design window, type the desired SQL statement. You have a choice of four data-definition statements to use in the query:

- CREATE TABLE creates a new table.
- ALTER TABLE adds a new field or constraint to the existing table or drops a field or constraint.
- DROP removes a table from a database or an index from a table.
- CREATE INDEX builds an index for one or more fields in an existing table.

When you use CREATE TABLE, you name the table, list the fields together with their data types, and include the primary key field. This is directly analogous to using the table design view to create a new table. You can also add indexes by using the CONSTRAINT clause. The following SQL statement is an example of a data-definition query that creates a table named Alumni:

```
CREATE TABLE Alumni
([AlumID] integer,
[LastName] text,
[FirstName] string,
      'additional fields here
CONSTRAINT [Index1] PRIMARY KEY ([AlumID]))
```

A constraint is much like an index. It places some restrictions on the table and the field values. For example, when you assign a field as the primary key, no two records can have the same value in that field. The CONSTRAINT clause above assigns the AlumID field as an index and specifies it as the primary key. You also can use the CONSTRAINT clause with two or more fields if necessary to achieve a unique value.

Here are the types of constraints you can impose on a table:

- UNIQUE—Specifies a field as a unique key. Also, the same value cannot occur in two records.

- **PRIMARY KEY**—Designates a field or a group of fields as the primary key. All primary key values must be unique and not **Null**. Only one primary key can be designated for a table.

- **FOREIGN KEY**—Designates a field from a related table as the primary key for this table.

The **ALTER TABLE** statement enables you to add a new field to a table with the **ADD COLUMN** clause or drop a field from the table with the **DROP COLUMN** clause. In addition, you can add or drop indexes with the **CONSTRAINT** clause. Some examples of using the **ALTER TABLE** are as follows:

```
ALTER TABLE Alumni ADD COLUMN Spouse TEXT(30)
```

The preceding line adds the 30-character spouse name to the Alumni table. The next line removes the Sports field from the Roster table.

```
ALTER TABLE Roster DROP COLUMN Sports
```

The following line insists that the **City** field in the Alumni table not be blank:

```
ALTER TABLE Alumni ADD CONSTRAINT City NOT NULL
```

The **DROP** statement deletes an existing table from a database or an existing index from a table. To delete a table, all you need to do is specify the table with the **TABLE** clause. To delete an index, use the **INDEX** clause and include the name of the index and its table.

The **CREATE INDEX** statement creates a new index for a table. For example, the following line creates an index named Mailing for the Alumni table using the last and first names:

```
CREATE INDEX Mailing ON Alumni ([LastName], [FirstName])
```

The statement also has several keywords, such as **UNIQUE**, **PRIMARY**, **ASC**, **DESC**, **DISALLOW NULL**, and **IGNORE NULL**, that further specify the new index.

Subqueries

You can use a subquery instead of an expression to define selection criteria for a field in the main query or define a new field to be added to the main query. Access runs the subquery first and then runs the main query on the results of the subquery. The combination returns records from the main query that meet the restrictions placed on the records that have already passed the subquery criteria. Placing a subquery in the main query design saves the trouble of storing two query definitions.

You can add the subquery **SELECT** statement to the main query in the design view or embed the statement in the SQL code. To define criteria for a field while in design view, type the **SELECT** SQL statement in the Criteria row of the field. To define a new field for the query, type the **SELECT** statement in the Field row of an empty column. The **SELECT** statement must be enclosed in parentheses. Access automatically precedes the statement with **Expr***n*, where *n* is the index of the expression, 1 if this is the only expression in the query.

In SQL, a subquery is a SELECT statement nested inside another SELECT statement or a SELECT INTO, INSERT INTO, DELETE, or UPDATE statement. The subquery SELECT statement follows the WHERE or HAVING clause of the main query.

The subquery uses the SELECT...FROM...WHERE or HAVING syntax to define the criteria. In addition, you have a choice of predicates: ANY, ALL, or SOME. ANY and SOME both retrieve records in the main query that meet the requirements of any records retrieved by the subquery. ALL is more restrictive in that is retrieves records from the main query only if they satisfy the comparison with all the records returned by the subquery.

The following SQL query uses a subquery to extract the records from the Students table who have received a grade of C as stored in the Students And Classes table.

```
SELECT * FROM Students
WHERE StudentID IN
(SELECT StudentID FROM [Students And Classes]
WHERE Grade = "C")
```

Types of Table Joins

Many of the SQL statements you've seen so far have clauses referring to joins. Now is a good time to review joins and the way related tables are linked.

You can use inner, right-, and left-outer joins in any FROM clause in an SQL statement. The type you use depends on what you want the query to select. An inner join operation is the most common type. It combines records from two tables when the values in the common fields match. Records with different values in the common field are not included. Right- and left-outer joins are used to include all the records from one table even if there are no matching records from the second table.

Inner Joins

When you add a table to a query design, Access automatically sets the join as an inner join, but you can change it to a right- or left-outer join with the Relationships feature. Choose Tools | Relationships to display all the related tables in the current database. Then, select a relationship line and choose Relationships | Edit Relationship. Click Join Type and choose the join you want from the Join Properties dialog box (see Figure 7.10).

In the figure, the first option is an inner join, the second is a left-outer join and the third is a right-outer join. The relationship between the Students and Students And Classes tables is implemented by two inner joins. If you look at the SQL view of a query linking these two tables, you will see the INNER JOIN clauses in the SQL statement:

```
INNER JOIN (Students INNER JOIN [Students And Classes] ON Students.StudentID =
[Students And Classes].StudentID) ON Classes.ClassID =
[Students And Classes].ClassID
```

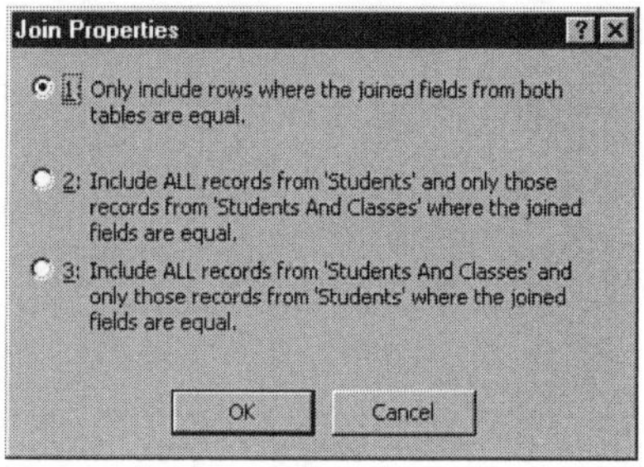

Figure 7.10.
Choose the type of join in the Join Properties dialog box.

This statement nests INNER JOIN clauses. The first links the Students table with the Students And Classes table by StudentID. The second links the Classes table with the Students And Classes table by ClassID.

You can nest all types of joins within an INNER JOIN, but you cannot nest an INNER JOIN within either a RIGHT JOIN or LEFT JOIN.

The comparison operator need not be equal. You can specify that the fields compare in other ways, such as less than (<), greater than (>), less than or equal to (<=), greater than or equal to (>=), or not equal (<>). You can also link several ON clauses within a JOIN clause, combining them with the AND or OR keywords.

Left and Right Joins

Right- and left-outer join operations refer to the sequence of listing the tables in the JOIN clause. Here's the general syntax, where *table1* is the left table and *table2* is the right:

```
FROM table1 [LEFT¦RIGHT] JOIN table2 ON table1.field = table2.field2
```

The right join operation includes all of the records from *table2* and only those from *table1* when the common fields match. The left join returns all the records from *table1* and only those of *table2* when they match. For example, the following statement would retrieve all the records from the Students And Classes table but only those from the Cumulative Class Percentiles table that have matching StudentID fields:

```
FROM [Cumulative Class Percentiles] RIGHT JOIN [Students And Classes]
ON [Cumulative Class Percentiles].StudentID = [Students And Classes].StudentID
```

Self Joins

Suppose the Students And Classes table included a field named TA (teaching assistant) that contained the StudentID value for the student assigned to the class. You could create a self join that joins two copies of the table and replace the StudentID with the student's name in one copy.

To create a self join, two copies of the same table are included in the query. The second copy is given an alias. The join combines records from the same table when the joined fields contain the same value. The SQL statement for a self join looks like any other select query with the original table and its copy. For example, creating a self join in a query using the Students table, the first instance is named Students and the second is named Students_1. Access automatically adds the_1 to form an alias.

Dissecting SQL Statements

To see the SQL statements behind a query in the design view, choose View | SQL View or click the View button and select SQL view. If you are working on a report in the design view, you can look at the SQL statements by right-clicking the report RecordSource property and choosing Zoom from the shortcut menu. Clicking Build in the RecordSource property opens the design grid. Figure 7.11 shows the SQL statement that is the RecordSource for the Class Results Summary report. Notice that the title bar indicates that the design represents an SQL statement instead of a query definition.

Figure 7.11.
The query design view for an SQL statement.

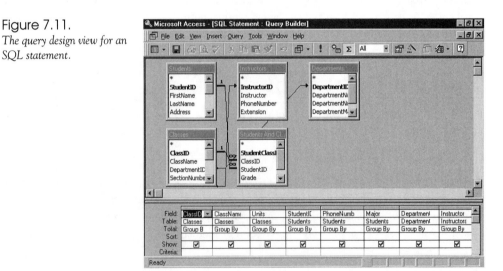

The next section looks carefully at some examples of various types of queries and the elements contained in their SQL statements. Not all features and options are examined in this chapter. For a complete description of each element of a query SQL syntax, refer to the Microsoft SQL Jet Reference in the Help Contents window.

Inspecting a Select Query Statement

The SQL code for this simple select query might look forbidding, but a close look reveals order and consistency in its construction.

Listing 7.1 shows the SQL statement used as the record source for the Class Results Summary report.

Listing 7.1. The record source for the Class Results Summary report.

```
SELECT DISTINCTROW Classes.ClassID, Classes.ClassName, Classes.Units,
Students.StudentID,
Students.PhoneNumber, Students.Major, Departments.DepartmentName,
Instructors.Instructor,
[LastName] & ", " & [FirstName] AS [Student Name], [Students And Classes].GPts,
[Students And Classes].Grade, Classes.DaysAndTimes
FROM Students INNER JOIN ((Instructors RIGHT JOIN
(Departments RIGHT JOIN Classes
ON Departments.DepartmentID = Classes.DepartmentID) ON
Instructors.InstructorID = Classes.InstructorID)
INNER JOIN [Students And Classes] ON Classes.ClassID =
[Students And Classes].ClassID)
ON Students.StudentID = [Students And Classes].StudentID
GROUP BY Classes.ClassID, Classes.ClassName, Classes.Units, Students.StudentID,
Students.PhoneNumber,
Students.Major, Departments.DepartmentName, Instructors.Instructor,
[LastName] & ", "
& [FirstName], [Students And Classes].GPts, [Students And Classes].Grade,
Classes.DaysAndTimes;
```

Several SQL keywords appear in this rather complicated statement, beginning with SELECT, which instructs the Jet DBEngine to return information as a set of records. The SELECT statement has many parts and keywords. The first word following SELECT is the predicate DISTINCTROW. The predicate restricts the number of records returned. If a predicate is not used, all the records are returned. Table 7.2 describes the alternative predicate settings.

Table 7.2. SELECT statement predicate alternatives.

Predicate	Description
ALL	Selects all the records that meet the conditions in the SQL statement. ALL is assumed if no predicate is specified.
DISTINCT	Selects only records, all of whose values in the fields listed in the SELECT statement are unique. The combination of all the selected fields must be unique. For example, if two students had the same last name, only one of the student records would be selected.

continues

Table 7.2. continued

Predicate	Description
DISTINCTROW	Omits duplicate records, all of whose fields are identical rather than just one of the selected fields. Without DISTINCTROW, the query returns any multiple rows with the same values in the selected fields.
TOP*n*[PERCENT]	Returns the specified number or percent of records from the top or bottom of an ordered list.

The next seven elements of the SQL statement define the fields to be included in the query result: `Classes.ClassID, Classes.ClassName, Classes.Units`, and so on. The next clause,

```
[LastName] & ", " & [FirstName] AS [Student Name]
```

concatenates the student's last name and first name with a comma and space between and identifies it as `Student Name`. It will appear in the report as `Student Name`. Three more fields are specified, two from the Students And Classes table and one more from the Classes table.

The FROM statement contains three nested join statements, one INNER JOIN and two RIGHT JOINs. Refer to the query design in Figure 7.11 to follow the logic. The first phrase,

```
FROM Students INNER JOIN
```

starts the linking procedure, which is completed with the last line:

```
ON Students.StudentID = [Students And Classes].StudentID
```

Together, these two lines establish an inner join between the Students table and the Students And Classes table by matching the `StudentID` field. The inner join retrieves only the records from each table that have matching values in the common field. Between these two lines, other joins are specified.

Beginning with the following line, the SQL statement begins to define the relationship lines in the query definition, first by connecting the Departments table to the Classes table with a right join by matching the `DepartmentID` fields, and then moving on to join the Classes table to the Instructors table by matching the `InstructorID` fields, again with a right join.

```
((Instructors RIGHT JOIN
```

It might look like something is missing, but Classes is implied as the table to join with the Instructors table after using it in the Departments join phrase.

Next, the Students And Classes table is joined to the Classes table by the `ClassID` field with the following statement:

```
INNER JOIN [Students And Classes] ON Classes.ClassID =
[Students And Classes].ClassID
```

The final SQL statement specifies the grouping of the records for the report. Records are grouped first by information from the Classes table and then by student information. All fields in the SELECT field list must be included in the GROUP BY list, even if it doesn't make much sense. The fields in the list appear in the same order as in the query design grid.

Inspecting a Parameter Query Statement

To create a parameter query, type a prompt in the Criteria row of the field whose value you want the user to enter. For example, to retrieve information about students in a specific class, type [Enter ClassID] in the Criteria row of the ClassID field. Listing 7.2 shows the resulting SQL code.

Listing 7.2. A parameter query.

```
SELECT DISTINCTROW Students.StudentID, Students.FirstName, Students.LastName,
[Students And Classes].ClassID, [Students And Classes].StudentID,
[Students And Classes].Grade
FROM Students INNER JOIN [Students And Classes] ON Students.StudentID =
[Students And Classes].StudentID
WHERE (([Students And Classes].ClassID)=[Enter ClassID]);
```

Notice that in the WHERE clause, the ClassID value in the Students And Classes table must equal the value entered as the parameter variable, [Enter ClassID], to be included in the query result. Figure 7.12 shows the results of running this query and entering 4 into the Enter Parameter Value dialog box.

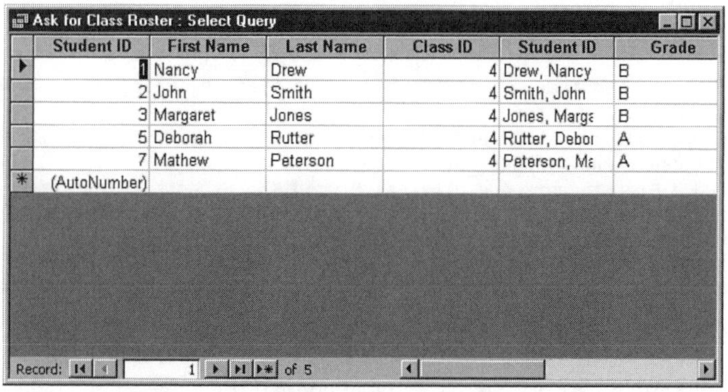

Figure 7.12.

Class roster for class number 4.

Student ID	First Name	Last Name	Class ID	Student ID	Grade
1	Nancy	Drew	4	Drew, Nancy	B
2	John	Smith	4	Smith, John	B
3	Margaret	Jones	4	Jones, Marga	B
5	Deborah	Rutter	4	Rutter, Debor	A
7	Mathew	Peterson	4	Peterson, Ma	A
(AutoNumber)					

Ask for Class Roster : Select Query

Record: 1 of 5

Inspecting Action Query Statements

Many of the same keywords and operators used in select queries are also used in action queries.

The following example of a make-table SQL query creates a new table named Alumni. The query in Listing 7.3 represents the entries you would make in the table design window, complete with defining the field names and data types and designating an index as the primary key.

Listing 7.3. A make-table SQL query.

```
CREATE TABLE Alumni
([AlumID] integer,
[LastName] text,
[FirstName] text,
[Address] text,
[City] text,
[State] text,
[Zip] text,
[Country] text,
[LastContribDate] date,
CONSTRAINT [Index1] PRIMARY KEY ([AlumID]))
```

The code in Listing 7.4 is the SQL statement that represents the append query, Add A's, which adds new student records for every student who has received an A grade in a class. The records are added to the Honor Roll table.

Listing 7.4. An append query.

```
INSERT INTO [Honor Roll] ( StudentID, FirstName, LastName, ClassID, Grade )
SELECT [Students And Classes].StudentID, Students.FirstName,

Students.LastName, Count([Students And Classes].ClassID) AS CountOfClassID,
[Students And Classes].Grade
FROM Students INNER JOIN [Students And Classes] ON Students.StudentID =
[Students And Classes].StudentID
GROUP BY [Students And Classes].StudentID, Students.FirstName,
Students.LastName, [Students And Classes].Grade
HAVING ((([Students And Classes].Grade)="A"))
ORDER BY Students.LastName;
```

The first line, INSERT INTO, establishes the action query as an append query and specifies the target table as Honor Roll. Next, the statement lists the names of the fields to include.

The FROM and GROUP BY clauses are the same as for select queries. The HAVING clause is similar to WHERE. After the records are grouped with GROUP BY, HAVING determines which records are displayed. This query displays records whose Grade value is A, ordered by the student's last name, and counts the number of students with A grades.

Inspecting an SQL Query Statement

Listing 7.5 is an example of an SQL union query that combines names and addresses from two unrelated tables into a single table.

Listing 7.5. A union query.

```
SELECT [FirstName],[LastName] AS [Alumni/LastName],[City]
FROM [Alumni]
WHERE [Country] = "USA"
UNION SELECT [FirstName],[LastName],[City]
FROM [Students]
WHERE [Country] = "USA"
ORDER BY [City];
```

The first SELECT clause in Listing 7.5 retrieves the first and last names and the city from the Alumni table. It also renames the last name as Alumni/LastName to distinguish alumni from students. The records are limited to alumni residing in the United States.

The UNION SELECT clause retrieves corresponding student information, again limiting the records to students who live in the United States. Finally, the ORDER BY sorts the records by City to make it easier for the two factions to communicate.

If you want to include duplicate records in the union, use UNION ALL instead of UNION.

Writing SQL Statements

The easiest way to write an SQL statement is to start with a query design in the Design View grid and then switch to SQL view for any necessary changes. The keywords and parentheses are already placed in their proper positions. An additional advantage is that you minimize the risk of misspelling an Access object and causing an error that must be tracked down.

When it is created, you can use the SQL code as the record source for a report or form by pasting it into the RecordSource property. To do so, select all or part of the code in the SQL view and press Ctrl+C, which copies the selection to the Clipboard. Next, place the insertion point in the RecordSource property of the form or report and press Ctrl+V. The SQL code now appears in the property sheet. To see it all, right-click the code and choose Zoom from the shortcut menu.

An alternative to pasting the SQL code in the property sheet is to save the query definition and use the query name instead of the SQL statement as the record source. This strategy has two advantages: the query definition is saved and available for use by other forms and reports, and the processing runs a little faster because the query has already been compiled. An SQL statement must be recompiled each time it is referenced.

When you use a wizard to create a report or form, it fills in the SQL statement for you and uses it as the RecordSource property. If you want to save the query for use in another form or report, click Build in the property sheet to open the query design view. Then, name and save the query definition.

If you have not already created the query to be used as the record source, click Build in the RecordSource property to open the query design view. Use the Design View grid to create the query. When you save the query, the name appears in the RecordSource property.

> **Note:** You can create most queries in the query design view. Exceptions are the SQL-specific queries that communicate with the back-end server. They must be created using SQL statements.

To see the SQL code of a query already specified in the RecordSource property, click Build to open the query design window and switch to SQL view.

Running SQL Statements

Select queries are run when you open the form or report that uses them as the record source. You can, of course, run a query from the Queries tab of the database window. You can also run action and data-definition queries by using the RunSQL action in a macro or from within a VBA procedure.

Using a Macro

Action queries that append, delete, or update records in a table and save the results in a new table can be run from a macro if the statement does not exceed 256 characters. If it does, you must use a VBA procedure, which can handle up to 32,768 characters. Figure 7.13 shows a macro that runs a short SQL statement to create a new table for listing the best text books for Clayview City College.

> **Tip:** The RunSQL action does not run a select or crosstab query. To run one of those from a macro, use the OpenQuery action and set the View argument to open the query in datasheet view. The FindA macro shown in Figure 7.14 opens the Count A select query in datasheet view, effectively running the query.

Figure 7.13.
The MakeBest macro creates a new table.

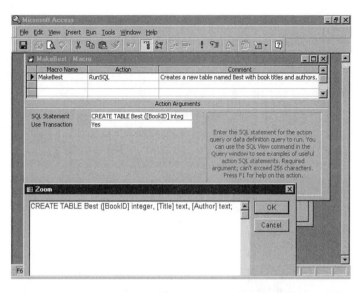

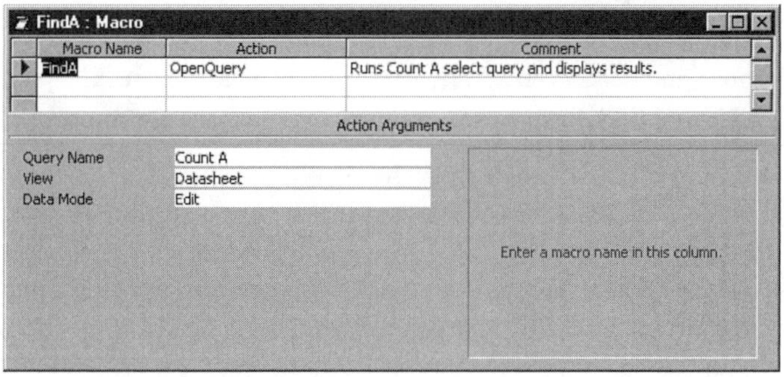

Figure 7.14.
The FindA macro opens the Count A query in datasheet view.

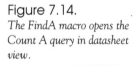

Using a VBA Procedure

To run an action or data-definition query from within a VBA procedure, use the DoCmd object with the RunSQL method. The entire SQL statement must be enclosed in quotation marks and declared as a string. The following VBA code runs the make-table query shown earlier that creates the Alumni table:

```
DoCmd.RunSQL "CREATE TABLE Alumni ([AlumID] integer, [LastName] text," & _
"[FirstName] text, [Address] text,[City] text, [State] text, [Zip] text," & _
"[Country] text, [LastContribDate] date," & _
"CONSTRAINT [Index1] PRIMARY KEY ([AlumID]));"
```

Be careful to use correct SQL structure and keywords because VBA does not check for errors in SQL syntax.

You can also create a query definition within a VBA procedure. For example, the following code fragment creates a select query that returns records from the Classes table for all classes from the fall term. The query is named Fall Semester and is saved in the current database.

```
Dim dbs As Database, qdf As QueryDef, strSQL As String
Set dbs = CurrentDb
strSQL = "SELECT * FROM Classes WHERE Term = "Fall";
Set qdf = dbs.CreateQueryDef("Fall Semester", strSQL)
```

Tip: If you are inserting an action query into a VBA procedure, the user will see a warning box asking for confirmation before running the query. To avoid this confusion for the user, turn off the Warning feature just before the query and then turn it back on in the next statement after the query.

Placing queries within VBA procedures also gives you the opportunity to control program flow and pass parameters to the query. Procedures run a little slower with embedded SQL query strings than procedures that refer to queries already constructed and saved. However, if you need the flexibility, you can sacrifice some of the processing speed.

For more information on using macros in your application, see Chapter 8, "Creating Macros." Chapter 9, "Writing VBA Procedures," contains more information on the DoCmd object and its uses.

Optimization Techniques for SQL

When databases become very large, it is important that the database management be as efficient as possible. The Microsoft Jet DBEngine automatically assesses the query specifications and determines the most efficient method of executing the query. The strategy depends on the size of the table and the index as well as a concept called the Rushmore technology.

Rushmore is used to optimize certain types of complex expressions in the criteria row of the Design View grid or in an SQL statement. Simple expressions can be optimized if they include an indexed field and one of the standard comparison operators, such as <, >, =, Between, and so on.

A small table can be queried easily by reading the table records. But, if the table contains quite a lot of information—many large records—it is more efficient to work with indexes. If the indexes are themselves large, reading the data might be just as efficient as compounding the index values.

When you create an index for a table, you are actually creating a small table with a field for each field in the index plus a pointer to the record it represents. An index table has as many records as the base table but each record is much smaller. The Rushmore technology works only with the indexes without reading the table records directly. The concept uses indexes to process the WHERE and JOIN clauses in an SQL statement. It looks at all the indexes and applies the criteria to the specified index and tags the index entries that meet the criteria. After scanning all the indexes, it compares tags and combines the results with AND or OR operators, depending on the criteria.

Rushmore can optimize a complex expression combining two simple, optimizable expressions with the OR or AND operators. If one or both of the simple expressions is not optimizable, Rushmore is not used. Rushmore queries also work with Microsoft FoxPro and dBASE tables.

Even more time is saved when the query returns a count based on a field contained in the index. Rushmore doesn't bother with the records—it just counts the items in the indexes.

Another technique used by the Jet DBEngine is a process that displays the first few records retrieved by the query while completing the query process in the background.

Jet also uses multithreading to process queries involving searching multiple indexes. It reads through one index on the first thread and retrieves entries that match the criteria. These retrievals are simultaneously passed to another thread for further matching and retrieval. This process is called "read ahead and write behind" and is a form of parallel processing.

Summary

This chapter examined the types of queries that you can use to retrieve information from Access tables. It has also demonstrated how to use SQL to define queries that feed report and form designs. The processes of running an SQL statement with a macro and from a VBA procedure were also discussed.

8

Creating Macros

Macros are easy-to-build, easy-to-use collections of actions that can make your application run smoothly. A simple macro can consist of a single action that causes the system to beep when you click a button. A more complex macro can contain multiple actions that open a form and automatically update fields in the form.

Chapter 1, "Why Program Access?," briefly discusses macros as one of the Access programming languages. This chapter looks into programming with macros in more detail and shows you how to use them in an application. It also describes when it is better to use a VBA procedure instead of macros and how to convert macros to VBA event procedures.

What Can Macros Do?

Each macro action performs a specific operation, such as setting a value, opening a form, or closing a dialog box. Any task you perform repeatedly is a candidate for a macro. The macro runs in response to an event, such as a button click or a field update. Each action in the macro is carried out in sequence. To run a macro, you refer to it by name, often attaching it to the appropriate event property of a form, control, or report.

Macros are easy to create and can be used to perform quite a variety of operations, including the following:

- To open a report to preview or print
- To synchronize data in two or more forms
- To navigate between controls, records, and form pages
- To set object properties, often based on another value
- To validate newly entered data
- To perform alternative actions depending on conditions
- To perform actions at startup
- And almost anything else you can think of

Macros work like robots. They perform a series of actions one at a time until they run out of actions. The exception is when you have added a macro condition such as `IsNull()` that tests for a blank value. If the condition returns `True`, the action is carried out; if not, the macro skips to the next action. By skillfully arranging the macro actions, you can create an `If...Then...Else` program flow.

After the macro is completed and checked out, you can attach it by name to an event property.

Individual related macros can be grouped into a macro group for easier handling. For example, you could group all the macros that are attached to the command buttons in a form.

When an event occurs, Access automatically responds with a built-in behavior that varies by object. For example, when you click a button, it appears pressed in, and newly entered data is automatically checked for correct data type. When you attach a macro or event procedure to an object's event property, the built-in response occurs first and then the macro or event procedure is executed.

The most important thing a macro cannot do is trap errors. For that, you must use a VBA event procedure and attach it to the object's OnError event property.

Touring the Macro Design Window

To start a new macro, click New in the Macros tab of the database window or choose Insert | Macro. The macro design window (see Figure 8.1) has two parts: the upper pane, which contains the action and comment columns, and the lower pane, in which you specify any action arguments. The number and type of arguments depend on the action you have added. The lower pane also displays a box with instructions about the currently selected part of the macro window. In Figure 8.1, the insertion point is in the Action column, so the instruction is "Enter an action in this column."

Figure 8.1.
An empty macro design window.

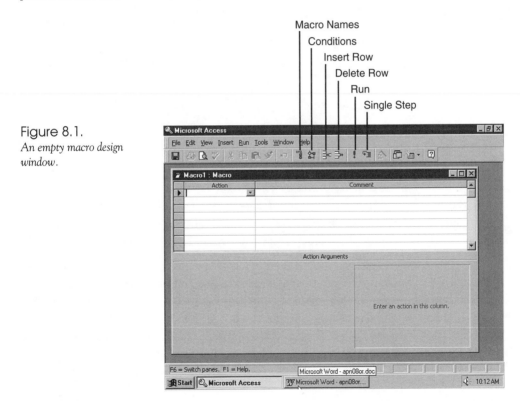

The macro design window has four new buttons on the toolbar and four corresponding menu items. The Macro Names and Columns buttons show or hide the corresponding columns in the macro design. The View menu also has those options. The Run button (with the large exclamation point) runs the macro, and the Single Step button runs the macro one action at a time. These two options are found on the Run menu. The Insert Row button inserts a blank row above the selected row. The Delete Row button deletes one or more selected macro rows. You can also choose Insert | Row to add a blank row and Edit | Delete Rows to delete selected rows.

When you begin to add actions to the macro, the lower pane displays the action argument list. Figure 8.2 shows a new macro named GoStudents with a single action, OpenForm. The design window now has four columns, with the addition of the Macro Name and Condition columns. These two columns are optional, and you can view or hide them by choosing View | Macro Names or View | Conditions or by clicking the Macro Names or Conditions toolbar buttons.

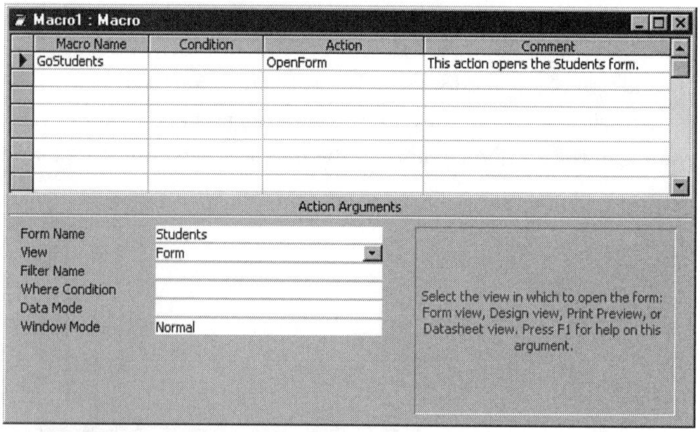

Figure 8.2.

Adding an OpenForm *action to the macro.*

After you add the OpenForm action to the macro, the arguments for the action appear in the Action Arguments pane. They include the name of the form, the view you want to see, any Filter Name or Where Condition you want to impose, the data mode, and the window mode. To select these arguments, you often select from a pull-down menu. For example, with the OpenForm action, the Form Name argument displays a list of all the forms in the current database. From the View argument list, you can choose Form, Design, Print Preview, or Datasheet, as the instruction box describes.

Enter an expression or the name of a saved query in the Filter Name argument. In the Where Condition line, you can click Build to get help from the Expression Builder to create the correct expression. The Data Mode argument lets you decide whether to allow the user to edit or enter data or to keep the form read-only. The last argument for this action, Window Mode, lets you select from Normal, Hidden, Icon, and Dialog. The Normal setting displays the form the way it is specified in the form properties. Hidden hides the form, and Icon displays the form minimized. The Dialog setting sets the form's Modal and Pop-up properties both to Yes, which makes the form act like a dialog box.

Other actions have a different group of arguments, and some have none.

Looking at Macro Structure

The only required elements in a macro are the actions and corresponding action arguments. Many of the arguments are optional, such as the Filter Name and Where Condition arguments for the OpenForm action.

Access provides over 50 actions that you can use in macros. Table 8.1 in the section, "Setting Actions and Arguments," lists the macro actions. They fall into several categories such as working with data in forms and reports, executing other commands and applications, transferring objects and data among applications, manipulating Access objects, and other miscellaneous tasks such as beeping and displaying information on the screen.

You use the Condition column to set conditions under which the macro action is to run. For example, if the student's grade is A, then display a message box with a congratulatory message. This condition is not to be confused with the Where Condition in the Action Arguments pane, which is used to limit the records that are to appear in the form or report.

Action arguments provide more specific information about how you want Access to carry out the action. For example, the form name, record number, or filter condition.

Creating and Debugging Macros

To begin creating a new macro, choose New in the Macros tab of the database window. The macro design window opens where you can add the actions and arguments that will accomplish the objective of the macro. The ample use of comments in building a macro will help in later interpretation of what it is supposed to do and when.

Preceding the macro names with the characters "mac" helps to differentiate macros from other objects in the database.

Setting Actions and Arguments

The Action column contains a pull-down menu from which you can select the action you want the macro to execute (see Figure 8.3). Another way to enter the action is to type the first few characters of the action. Access completes that action name as you type; when it reaches the action you want, press Enter. The Action Arguments pane then shows the arguments for that action.

Enter the action argument for each action, or select from the pull-down menu. If the action requires the name of a form or other database object, the pull-down menu displays the names of all the objects of that type in the current database. Be sure to begin at the top of the argument list in the Action Arguments list because a setting in one of the arguments might change the choices in a later argument.

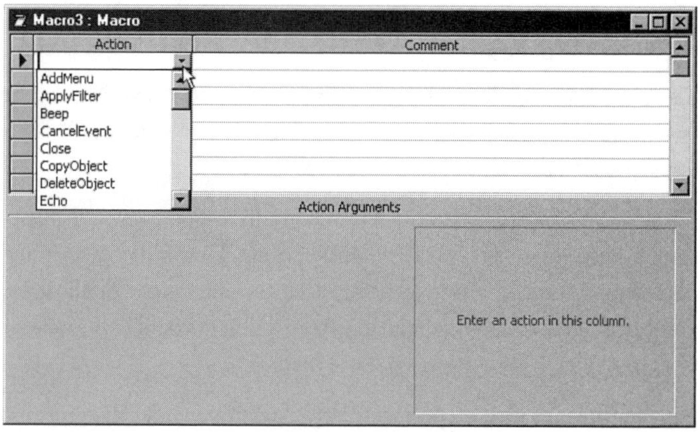

Figure 8.3.
*Choose an action from the
pull-down menu.*

Adding a Where Condition limits the records that appear in a form or report. You can use the Expression Builder to help with the condition expression or type it directly in the argument line. Figure 8.4 shows an OpenForm action that includes a Where Condition argument that will show only records whose ClassID value matches that in the active Students form. The complete Where Condition in the macro is

```
[ClassID]=[Forms]![Students]![ClassID]
```

The form is opened as read-only, and the user will not be able to add or edit any of the records.

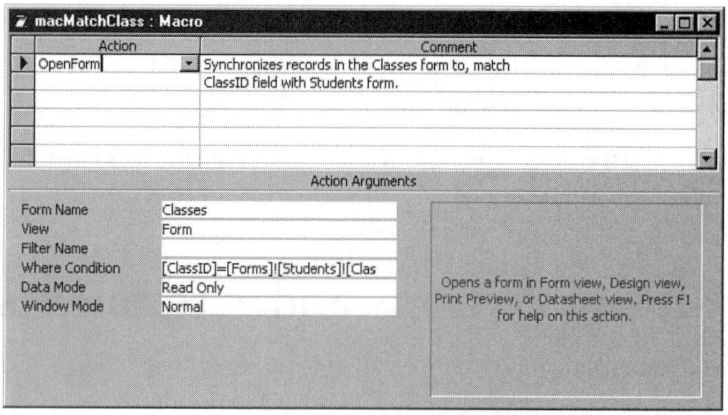

Figure 8.4.
*Adding a Where Condition
to the macro.*

You can use this type of macro to synchronize records between two forms that are open.

Table 8.1 lists the actions that you can add to a macro and the reasons for using each one.

Table 8.1. Macro actions.

Purpose	Actions
Limit data in form or report	ApplyFilter
Navigate through data	FindNext, FindRecord, GoToControl, GoToPage, GoToRecord
Execute a command	RunCommand (replaces DoMenuItem in Access 95)
Exit Access	Quit
Run a query, a procedure, another macro, SQL code, or another application	OpenQuery, RunCode, RunMacro, RunSQL, RunApp
Stop execution without exiting Access	CancelEvent, Quit, StopAllMacros, StopMacro
Export Access object to other applications	OutputTo, SendObject
Exchange data with other data formats	TransferDatabase, TransferSpreadsheet, TransferText
Manipulate Access objects	CopyObject, Rename, Save, DeleteObject, Close, OpenForm, OpenModule, OpenQuery, OpenReport, OpenTable
Print an Access object	OpenForm, OpenQuery, OpenReport (setting the view to Print Preview)
Resize or move a window	Maximize, Minimize, MoveSize, Restore
Specify the value of a field, control, or object property	SetValue
Update data or the screen	RepaintObject, Requery, ShowAll Records
Create a custom or global menu bar or shortcut menu	AddMenu
Specify the state of an item on a custom or global menu bar	SetMenuItem
Show item or information on the screen	Echo, HourGlass, MsgBox, SetWarnings
Generate keystrokes	SendKeys
Show or hide a command bar	ShowToolbar
Sound a beep	Beep

Creating a Macro Group

When you have several macros that are used with the same form or related in some other way, keeping track of them is easier if they are in a macro group. In earlier versions of Access, such groups were called macro libraries. To create a macro group, choose New in the Macros tab of the database window and open the Macro Names column in the design window. As you create the macros for the group, give each one a name and add the desired actions. Leaving a blank line between the individual macros in the group makes it easier to read the list.

One of the easiest ways to add a macro action that involves a database object is to drag the object from the database window to the Action column of the macro design. Access automatically adds the appropriate arguments, which you can change or add to, as you want.

With this method, you can create several macros at once by having both the database window and the macro design window open at the same time. Figure 8.5 shows a switchboard for the Clayview City College that gives the user a list of forms he or she can open. The switchboard shows five items: four to enter or view data and one to return to the main switchboard.

Figure 8.5.
A switchboard for opening forms.

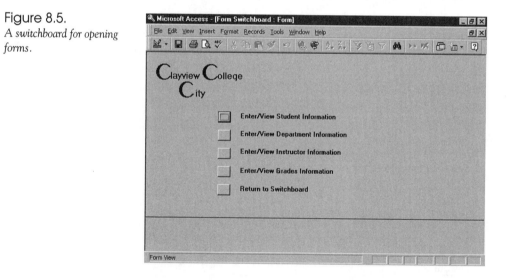

To create the macros that open the forms listed in the Clayview City College switchboard, follow these steps:

1. With the database window open, click the Macros tab and choose New to open the macro design window.

2. Choose Window | Tile Vertically to show both windows on the screen.

3. Click the Forms tab, and then click and drag the Students form name to the Action column of the first row. The form name is automatically entered into the Action Arguments pane.

4. Repeat step 3 for the other forms named in the switchboard items: Classes, Departments, Instructors, and Grades, leaving a blank line between each one.

5. Enter a name for each macro, using the `mac` tag preceding each macro to identify the object as a macro.

6. Finally, add the last macro, the `Close` action, which responds to the Return to Switchboard item.

Figure 8.6 shows the results with the action `OpenForm` automatically entered and the last form name, Grades, in the argument list.

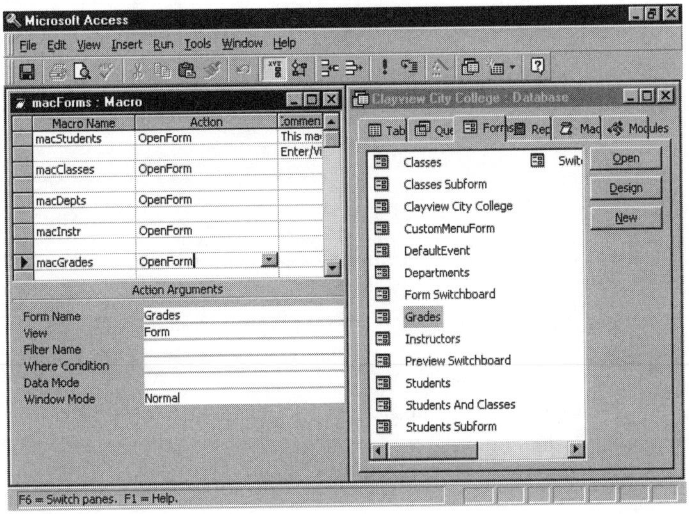

Figure 8.6.
Dragging an object from the database window builds a macro.

Notice that the macro group has a different name than any of the macros in the group. When you refer to a macro in the group, use the group name as well as the macro name. For example, to attach the `macClasses` macro to the `OnClick` event property of a button, use `macForms.macClasses`.

The same technique can be used to create the macro group for the Preview Switchboard items that preview various reports.

Assigning AutoKeys

Instead of assigning an action or set of actions to a macro name, you can use a specific key combination, such as Ctrl+F3, by creating macros in an AutoKeys macro group. Each key combination can trigger a list of actions or simply execute the `RunMacro` action with the name of an existing macro.

To assign a key combination to a macro action, use the key combination as the macro name, using the key name syntax. For example, the caret symbol (^) represents the Ctrl key and the plus sign (+) represents the Shift key. Key names are enclosed in curly brackets ({}).

Figure 8.7 shows an example of an AutoKeys macro group with a macro that runs when you press Ctrl+L. The resulting message box is also shown.

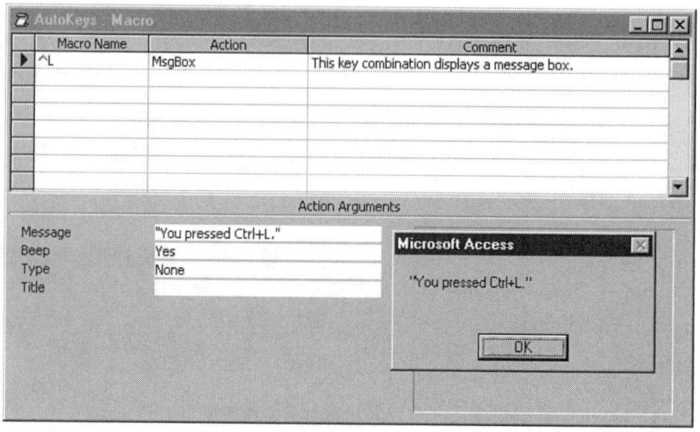

Figure 8.7.
An AutoKeys key combination that displays a message box.

Macro Name	Action	Comment
^L	MsgBox	This key combination displays a message box.

Action Arguments

Message   "You pressed Ctrl+L."
Beep   Yes
Type   None
Title

Microsoft Access

"You pressed Ctrl+L."

OK

Warning: Access uses certain key combinations for special operations such as Ctrl+C and Ctrl+V for Copy and Paste. If you assign different actions to any of these key combinations, your actions will replace the ones Access specified. You might get some surprising results.

Table 8.2 lists the key combinations that are available as AutoKeys key combinations and shows examples of the syntax.

Table 8.2. Available AutoKeys key combinations.

Key Combination	Examples
Ctrl+*any letter or number*	^F or ^9
Any function key by itself	{F7}
Ctrl+*any function key*	^{F3}
Shift+*any function key*	+{F6}
Insert	{INSERT}
Ctrl+Insert	^{INSERT}
Shift+Insert	+{INSERT}
Delete	{DELETE} or {DEL}
Ctrl+Delete	^{DELETE} or ^{DEL}
Shift+Delete	+{DELETE} or +{DEL}

You can run a macro named as a key combination by selecting it in the Macros tab of the database window and choosing Run. To run the macro by pressing the keys, it must be saved in the AutoKeys macro group.

The macro AutoKeys feature is analogous to the SendKeys statement in VBA.

Debugging a Macro

If an error occurs while you are running a macro as a whole rather than step-by-step, an error message appears and it is up to you to find which action caused the error. The easiest way to debug the macro is to change to Single Step and run the macro one action at a time. With Single Step, the macro executes the actions, one at a time. That way you can pinpoint the action that is causing the trouble.

To start Single Step, in the macro design window, choose Run | Single Step (or click the Single Step button) and then choose Run. The Macro Single Step dialog box appears displaying the specifics of the first action (see Figure 8.8). The dialog box displays the macro name, the condition, and the action name and its arguments.

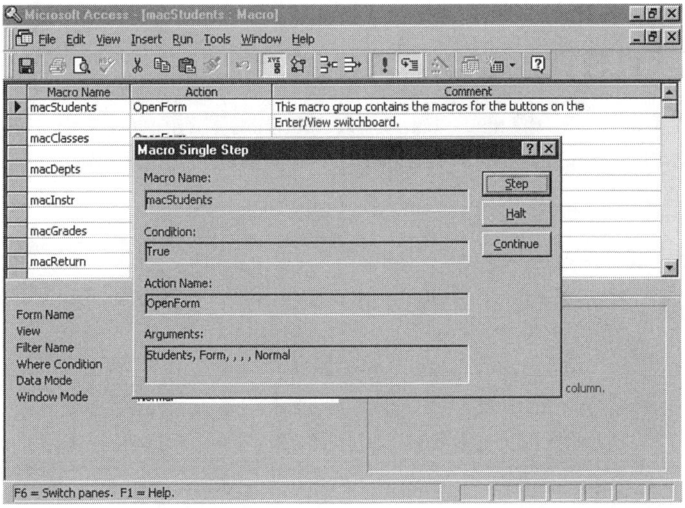

Figure 8.8.
The Macro Single Step dialog box gives information about the current action.

The Macro Single Step dialog box has three options:

- Step—Executes this action and displays the next action in the macro.
- Halt—Stops the macro and closes the dialog box.
- Continue—Turns off the single step mode and runs the rest of the macro in normal mode.

If an error occurs in one step, the appropriate Access error message appears. Choosing OK to close the error message opens the Action Failed dialog box, which displays the action that caused the error together with its arguments. This dialog box is similar to the Macro Single Step dialog box, but it has only one option: Halt. You must close the dialog box and correct the error in the action before you can run the macro again.

Note: You can stop the execution of a macro and change to single step at any time by pressing Ctrl+Break.

The single step mode remains in effect until you cancel it. To discontinue Single Step execution, click the Single Step button again or choose Run | Single Step to clear the option.

Warning: You can copy, move, or delete a macro just like any other object. However, when you rename a macro, Access does not update the macro name in the property sheet. You must remember to change all references to the macro to the new name.

Running a Macro

You must save the macro before you can run it. There are several ways to run a macro: directly from the macro design window or the database window, from another macro or procedure, or in response to an event.

Here are the ways you can run a macro:

- From the macro design window, click Run on the toolbar or choose Run | Run. If the macro refers to a field or other object in a form that is not open, it will not run from the macro design window or the database window.
- From the database window, select the macro name and choose Run or right-click the macro name and choose Run Macro from the shortcut menu.
- From another macro, use the `RunMacro` action and enter the macro name in the Action Argument list.
- From a VBA procedure, use the `DoCmd` object and the `RunMacro` method, for example, `DoCmd.RunMacro "macForms.macClasses"`.
- In response to an event, attach the macro to the object's corresponding event property.

Note: If you try to run a group macro from the macro design window or the database window, only the first macro in the group executes.

Attaching a Macro to an Event Property

After you have created the macro that contains the desired response for a specific event, such as a button click or a text box update, you can attach the macro to the event property of the object. To do this, open the property sheet for the object and click the Events tab. Then, choose the macro name from the pull-down menu in the desired property.

If you haven't created the macro yet, click the Build button in the event property and choose Macro Builder from the Choose Builder dialog box. Then, name and create the macro. The new macro is automatically attached to that event and is also stored in the database where it is available for use with other events.

To attach a macro to the same property of more than one object, select all the objects and then select the macro name from the pull-down menu in the event property sheet. Figure 8.9 illustrates attaching the `macForms.macGrades` macro to the `OnClick` property of both a button and its label in the Forms switchboard. When you view the switchboard, clicking either the button or the label opens the Grades form. Notice that the property sheet indicates a multiple selection, and only the events common to all selected objects are listed.

Figure 8.9.
Attaching a macro to two objects.

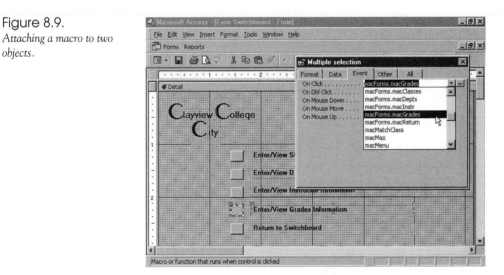

Forms, form controls, reports, and report sections all have events associated with their object types. For example, a toggle button can respond to a click event while a report section can respond to a format event. Table 8.3 lists the events, describes when they occur in relation to other events for the same objects, and shows the types of objects to which they apply.

Table 8.3. Event properties and their objects.

Event	Occurs When...	Applies To
Activate	Object becomes the active window.	User form objects
AfterDelConfirm	After user confirms deletions and when records are deleted or deletion is canceled.	Forms
AfterInsert	After new record is created.	Forms
AfterUpdate	After changed data in a record or form control is updated.	Forms and form controls
ApplyFilter	User applies or removes a filter.	Forms
BeforeDelConfirm	Between the user performing a delete action and Access asking for confirmation of deletion.	Forms
BeforeInsert	User types the first character of the record but before the record is created.	Forms
BeforeUpdate	Before changed data in a record or form control is updated.	Forms and form controls
Change	Contents of a text box or combo box are changed. Also when moving from one form page to another.	Combo box, text box, and tab controls
Click	User presses and releases the left mouse button.	Forms and form controls
Close	Form or report is closed and removed from the screen.	Forms and reports
Current	Focus moves to a record, or form is refreshed or required.	Forms
DblClick	User presses and releases the left mouse button twice.	Forms and form controls
Deactivate	An object is no longer the active window.	User form object
Delete	User performs delete action but before record is deleted.	Forms
Enter	Before control receives focus from a control on the same form.	Form controls
Error	A runtime error occurs. Includes Jet DBEngine but not VBA errors.	Forms and reports

Event	Occurs When...	Applies To
Exit	Before control loses focus to another control on the same form.	Form controls
Filter	User chooses Filter By Form or Advanced Filter/Sort.	Forms
Format	Access assigns data to a report section before formatting the section for preview or print.	Report sections
GotFocus	Form or control receives focus.	Forms and form controls
KeyDown	User presses a key while a form or control has focus.	Forms and form controls
KeyPress	User presses and releases a key or key combination that matches an ANSI code. Only while form or control has focus.	Forms and most form controls, except the text box control
KeyUp	User releases a key while form or control has focus.	Forms and most form controls
Load	Form is opened and records are displayed.	Forms
LostFocus	Form or control loses focus.	Forms and form controls
MouseDown	User presses a mouse button while pointer is on form or control.	Forms and form controls
MouseMove	User moves the mouse pointer over a form, form section, or control.	Forms and form controls
MouseUp	User releases a pressed mouse button over a form or control.	Forms and form controls
NoData	After empty report is formatted for printing, before printing.	Reports
NotInList	Value entered in combo box is not in the combo box list.	Combo box controls
Open (form)	When form is opened but before first record is displayed.	Forms
Open (report)	When report is opened but before previewing or printing.	Reports
Page	After report page is formatted for printing, before printing.	Reports

continues

Table 8.3. continued

Event	Occurs When...	Applies To
Print	After report section is formatted for printing, before printing.	Report sections
Resize	When a form is opened and when its size changes.	Forms
Retreat	On return to previous report section.	Report sections
Timer	At regular intervals set by form's TimeInterval property.	Forms
Unload	After form is closed but before it is removed from the screen.	Forms
Updated	When data has been modified.	OLE object controls on a form

Sequence of Events

In order for your macro or event procedure to perform the operations you want when you want them to, it is important to understand the sequence of events. You need to know which of the control event properties to attach a macro to in order to accomplish the desired outcome. Many events occur when you are moving from one record to another entering and editing data in a form. Even moving the mouse pointer around on the screen triggers events.

The following sections show some sequences of events that occur under specific circumstances. There are many more scenarios that can play out as you work in an application, but these can give you an idea of the way events trigger.

Events for Forms and Controls

When a *form is first opened* the following events occur:

```
Open↓
 Load↓
  Resize↓
   Activate↓
    Current
```

If the form has no active control when it opens, the GotFocus event for the form triggers after the Activate event but before Current. If there is an active control, it gets focus.

The Current event can be used to set a property such as the caption or the size of the form or report when it first opens. For example, the SetValue macro in Figure 8.10 sets the caption of the Classes form to the value found in the Class field. The Item argument identifies the form property, Caption, and the Expression argument determines the new value as the same as the Class Name field. You can use the Expression Builder to create the expression or enter it yourself. The important thing to remember is not to use an equal sign in the Expression argument.

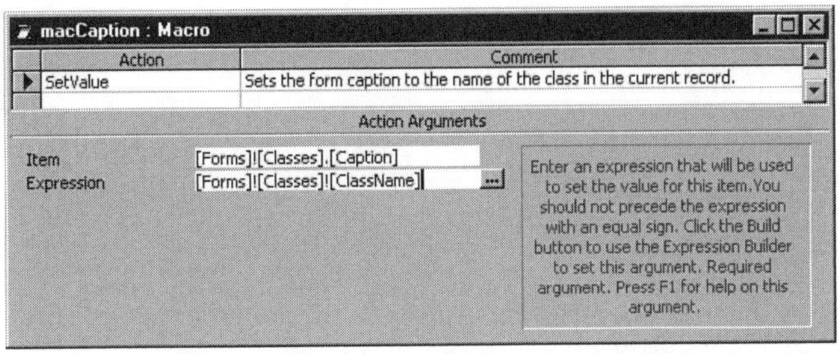

Figure 8.10.
A macro that changes the Classes form caption to the value of the Class field.

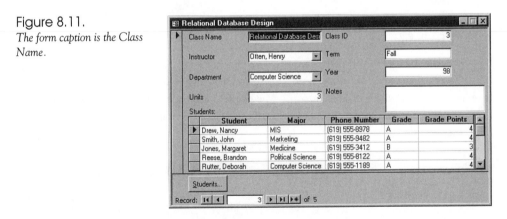

Attaching the macCaption macro to the OnCurrent property of the form causes the caption to change as you move through the records. Figure 8.11 shows the form with the new event property setting.

Figure 8.11.
The form caption is the Class Name.

You can also use the Current event to show or hide custom menus and toolbars. More about creating such menus and toolbars with macros in the section, "Creating Menus and Toolbars from Macros," later in this chapter.

When the *form closes*, the following events occur:

    Unload↓
    Deactivate↓
    Close

If the form has no active control when it closes, the LostFocus event for the form is triggered between Unload and Deactivate. If there was an active control, it would lose focus when the form closes, after the Close event.

When you *open a form and move between controls* on that form, the first series of events opens the form and moves to the first control (C1).

> Open↓
> Load↓
> Resize↓
> Activate↓
> Current↓
> Enter(C1)↓
> GotFocus(C1)

As you move from control to control on the form, the Exit and LostFocus events occur for the control you are leaving (C1) and Enter and GotFocus events occur for the control that you are moving to (C2). You can attach a macro to any of the control properties associated with these events.

> Exit(C1)↓
> LostFocus(C1)↓
> Enter(C2)↓
> GotFocus(C2)

The OnGotFocus and OnEnter properties are often used to execute an action when you move to a field or other control. Figure 8.12 shows the results of a macro that triggers when the insertion point enters an empty Grade field in the Classes subform. The macro is attached to the OnGotFocus property of the Grade field and to the OnLostFocus property of the Telephone field, which precedes the Grade field in the tab order.

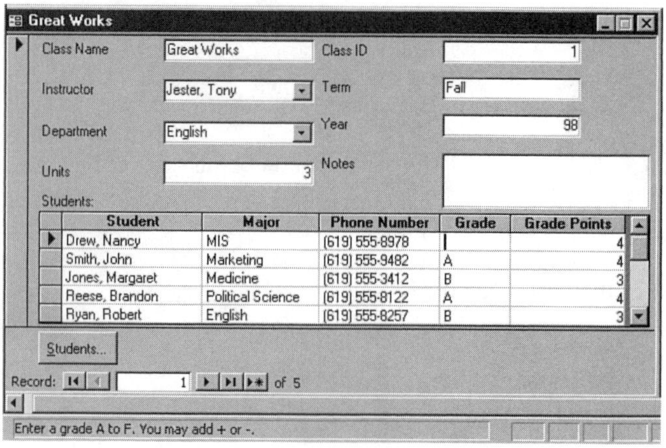

Figure 8.12.

The OnGotFocus event property displays a message in the status bar.

The macro tests for a blank Grade field and, if blank (Null), carries out the SetValue action, which displays the message in the status bar. The Expression Builder was used to designate the status bar text property as the Item argument (see Figure 8.13). The Expression argument is the text to be displayed, enclosed in quotation marks. Figure 8.14 shows the completed macCaption macro.

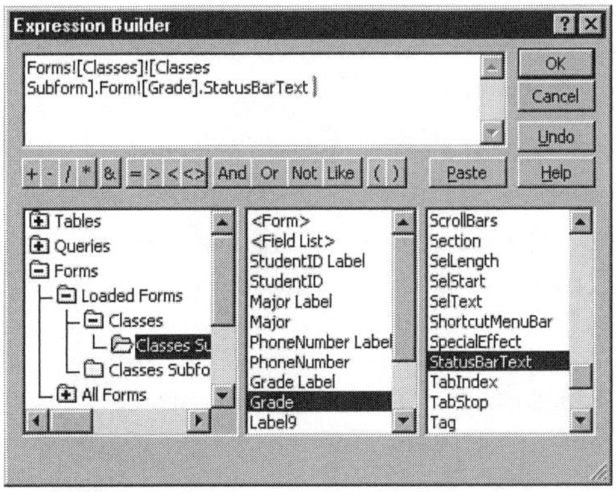

Figure 8.13.
The Expression Builder helps
with complex expressions.

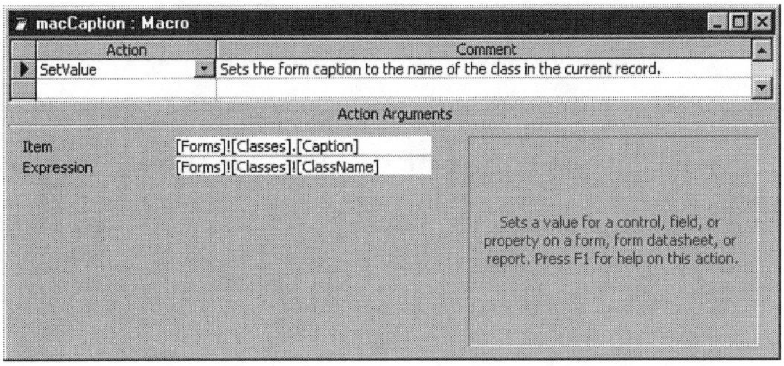

Figure 8.14.
The completed macCaption
macro.

Another macro is developed in the section, "Controlling the Flow with Macro Conditions," later in this chapter that updates the GdPts field with the value corresponding to the grade that is entered. This requires a more complex action condition that is equivalent to a SELECT CASE statement. This macro is attached to the AfterUpdate event for the Grade field.

If you switch to another form, the last active control remains active on the first form. When you return to the first form, you are right back where you left off.

When you *save a new record* by choosing Records | SaveRecord, the following events occur:

```
BeforeUpdate(C2)↓
 AfterUpdate(C2)↓
  BeforeUpdate(form)↓
   AfterUpdate(form)↓
    AfterInsert(form)
```

When you *delete a record*, Access displays a dialog box asking for confirmation of the deletion with the following events:

```
Delete↓
Current↓
 BeforeDelConfirm↓
 (display deletion confirmation dialog box)↓
  AfterDelConfirm
```

The `BeforeDelConfirm` places the record in a buffer, and then Access displays the confirmation dialog box. If you cancel the `BeforeDelConfirm`, the dialog box is not displayed and the `AfterDelConfirm` does not occur. The `AfterDelConfirm` occurs after the Deletion Confirm dialog box is displayed and returns the response to the confirmation.

You can attach a macro or procedure to the `OnDelete` event property of a control that will prevent a record from being deleted or deleted only under special circumstances.

> **Note:** If you select multiple records and choose Delete, the `Delete` event occurs for every one of the records first and then triggers the `Current` event.

Events for Keystrokes and Mouse Clicks

A keyboard event occurs when you press a key or send keystrokes while a form or control has focus. A mouse event occurs when you use the mouse buttons while the pointer is on a form, section, or control. A mouse event can also occur when you move the mouse pointer over part of the form, section, or control.

Pressing and releasing a key causes the following events to occur:

```
KeyDown↓
 KeyPress↓
 KeyUp
```

If the keystroke changes the value in a text box, the `Change` event occurs once for every key you press before reaching `KeyUp`.

> **Note:** A change in the value of a calculated control or the selection of a value from a combo box does not trigger a `Change` event.

Updating data in one text box and then *clicking a second text box* triggers the update and exit events before passing focus to the second control. The sequence looks like this (the `KeyDown`, `KeyPress`, and `KeyUp` loop repeats for each key pressed):

```
KeyDown↓
 KeyPress↓
  KeyUp↓
   BeforeUpdate(C1)↓
    AfterUpdate(C1)↓
     Exit(C1)↓
      LostFocus(C1)↓
       Enter(C2)↓
        GotFocus(C2)↓
         KeyDown(C2)↓
          KeyPress(C2)↓
           KeyUp(C2)
```

If the keystroke you press while in the first control moves focus to another control instead of entering a character, the KeyDown event applies to the first control and the KeyPress and KeyUp events apply to the second.

> **Note:** If you enter a value in a combo box that is not in the list of values and you have set the LimitToList property for the control to Yes, you will get an error message. Actually, the NotInList event occurs, which triggers an error event to which you can attach a macro or event procedure to the OnError property to display a custom message.
>
> ```
> KeyDown↓
>  KeyPress↓
>   Change↓
>    KeyUp↓
>     NotInList↓
>      Error
> ```

To *add a new record*, move to the blank record and begin by entering a single character in the first control in the record. The following sequence of events occurs:

```
Current(new record)↓
 Enter(C1)↓
  GotFocus(C1)↓
   KeyDown(C1)↓
    KeyPress(C1)↓
     BeforeInsert(new record)↓
      Change(C1)↓
       KeyUp(C1)
```

Then, *click another text box* in the same record (no longer new) and enter text.

```
BeforeUpdate(C1)↓
 AfterUpdate(C1)↓
  Exit(C1)↓
   LostFocus(C1)↓
    Enter(C2)↓
     GotFocus(C2)↓
      MouseDown(C2)↓
       MouseUp(C2)↓
        Click(C2)↓
         KeyDown(C2)↓
          KeyPress(C2)↓
           Change(C2)↓
            KeyUp(C2)
```

In the preceding sequence, you can see that clicking a mouse button also triggers the MouseDown/ MouseUp/Click sequence of events. You have already seen how to attach macros to the OnClick property of command buttons.

Using the mouse to move from one control to another causes the following sequence of events:

```
Exit(C1)↓
 LostFocus(C1)↓
  Enter(C2)↓
   GotFocus(C2)↓
    MouseDown(C2)↓
     MouseUp(C2)↓
      Click(C2)
```

Double-clicking the mouse button causes both Click and DoubleClick to occur. The MouseMove event, which is independent of the other mouse events, occurs whenever you move the mouse pointer over a control, form, or section. This event can be used to display screentips when the pointer pauses on a button on a form.

Events for Reports and Report Sections

Reports and report sections have fewer event properties than forms and controls. When you *open a report to preview or print it* and then close it or make another window the active window, the following events occur:

```
Open↓
 Activate↓
  Close↓
   Deactivate
```

The Format and Print events happen to report sections after the report is activated.

Open(report)↓
Activate(report)↓
Format(section)↓
Print(section)↓
Close(report)↓
Deactivate(report)

Default Events

More than three quarters of the macros used in an application are attached to objects' default events. Default events are not triggered automatically; they simply are the events that are most often associated with a particular object. For example, the Click event is the most common event associated with toggle and command buttons, and Open is the most common event for reports. Not all objects have default events.

Table 8.4 lists the default events and their associated objects.

Table 8.4. Default events for Access objects.

Default Event	Objects
Click	Form detail section, image control, check box, command button, label, option button, rectangle, toggle button
BeforeUpdate	List box, option group, text box, combo box
Updated	Bound and unbound object frames, chart
Enter	Subform
Load	Form
Open	Report
Format	Section

Access provides a shortcut for creating a macro or event procedure that responds to the default event. Choosing Build Event from the shortcut menu and then choosing Macro Builder opens the macro design window. The macro you create here will automatically be attached to the default event property of the object. This saves you the step of attaching it yourself.

To see how this works, follow these steps:

1. Create a new blank form based on the Classes table and add two of the text box controls, such as Class Name and InstructorID, to the form.

2. Right-click the Class Name text box control and choose Build Event from the shortcut menu.

3. Choose Macro Builder from the Choose Builder dialog box and name the macro DefaultEvent.

4. In the blank macro design window, choose MsgBox in the Action column and enter a message such as "This is a default event for a text box" (see Figure 8.15) and close the macro window. Be sure to enclose the message text in quotation marks.

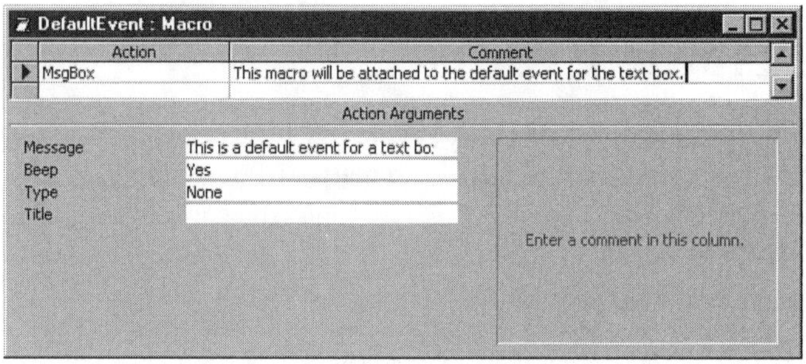

Figure 8.15.
Building a macro to be attached to the default event property.

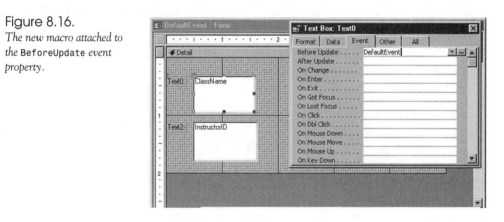

5. Open the property sheet for the text box control and look at the event properties. The new macro, DefaultEvent, is attached to the BeforeUpdate event property for the text box (see Figure 8.16).

Figure 8.16.
The new macro attached to the BeforeUpdate event property.

When you open the DefaultEvent form, enter a value in the Class Name field, and then tab to the InstructorID field, the BeforeUpdate event occurs, which displays the message from the macro definition.

Controlling the Flow with Macro Conditions

By listing macro actions with conditions, you can control the flow of operations in an application. In some cases, you might want to carry out the action only if the condition returns True. If the condition is not True, the macro stops or moves on to the next action, if there is one. You can even construct actions and conditions to mimic If...Then...Else and SELECT CASE situations.

Figure 8.17 shows a straightforward macro that uses the MsgBox() function to request confirmation before deleting an Instructor record from the table. The DeleteConfirm macro that cancels the event is attached to the OnDelete form event property and is triggered when you choose Edit | Delete Record. The figure also shows the Instructors form and the message box that asks for confirmation.

Figure 8.17.
The DeleteConfirm macro asks for confirmation before deleting an Instructor's record.

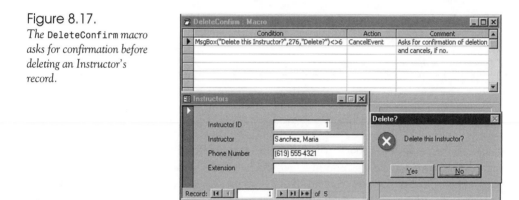

The complex action condition uses the MsgBox() function to display a special message box. The first argument in the function is the actual message, the second specifies the box type, and the third is the box caption. The number, 276, determines what you will see in the box and is the total of the values that represent the display elements: button type Yes/No (4 points); icon style Stop sign (16 points); and the second button (No) as the default (256 points). The condition returns the value of the button selected: Yes = 6, No = 7. Therefore, the condition allows the action (CancelEvent) to take place if the value of the selected button is not 6. If it returns 6, the Delete event takes place. Table 8.5 lists the MsgBox() box type elements and their values.

Table 8.5. MsgBox() function arguments.

Box Type Element	Value
OK button	0
OK, Cancel buttons	1

continues

Table 8.5. continued

Box Type Element	Value
Abort, Retry, Ignore buttons	2
Yes, No, Cancel buttons	3
Yes, No buttons	4
Retry, Cancel buttons	5
No icon	0
Stop sign icon	16
? Question mark icon	32
! Exclamation mark icon	48
I Information icon	64
First button default	0
Second button default	256
Third button default	512

The MsgBox() function returns a value depending on which button was selected: OK = 1, Cancel = 2, Abort = 3, Retry = 4, Ignore = 5, Yes = 6, and No = 7.

You can also use macros to validate data beyond what is specified in the table definition. For example, the Grades macro group shown in Figure 8.18 contains a macro with two conditions. One makes sure the Grade field is not blank by displaying a message box with a prompt to enter a grade if the user leaves it empty. The other appears if the user enters a letter grade other than a letter between A and F. You put both conditions in the same macro because they apply to the same event, BeforeUpdate.

The figure shows the macro, the Grades form with an invalid entry, and the message box with the error message.

> **Tip:** If you want to be even more precise, you could add another criterion to the macro Condition precluding a grade of E. The Condition expression would read [Grade]>"F" OR [Grade]<"A" OR [Grade]="E". Then you would want to change the message to "You have entered an invalid grade."

The AddGrade macro demonstrates the use of an ellipsis to extend the condition beyond one action. The IsNull([Grade]) condition applies to both the MsgBox action on the first line and the CancelEvent action on the second line. If the first condition returns False, Access skips to the next action that does not have an ellipsis in the Condition column.

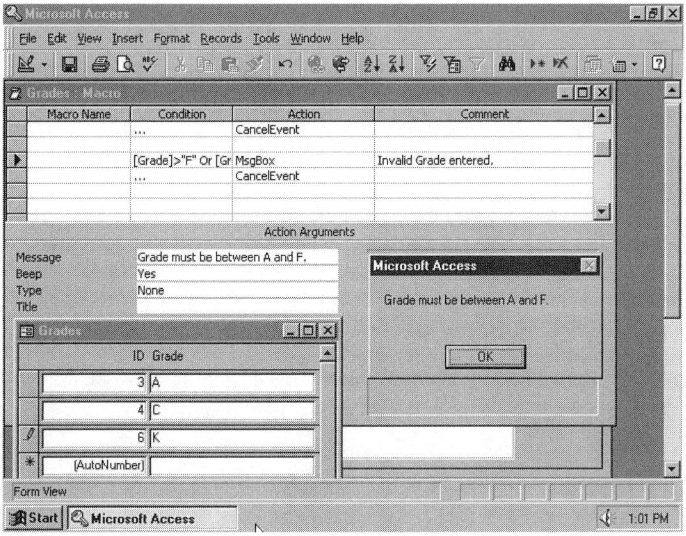

Figure 8.18.
The Grades *macro group validates entered grade values.*

The second condition that tests for a valid grade also extends to the CancelEvent action on the next line. CancelEvent stops the BeforeUpdate event and leaves the insertion point in the Grade text box.

The SetGdPts macro in Figure 8.19 is an example of using a macro to perform a SELECT CASE statement. It includes a series of conditions that, one by one, determine what value to place in the GdPts field. If the grade entered is A, 4 is entered automatically in the GdPts field when the Grade text box control loses focus. The comparison LIKE "A*" uses the * wildcard to allow for A+ and A– grades. The default value of the GdPts field is set to 0 in the table definition so if none of the conditions in the macro are met, the field reverts to 0, the implied CASE ELSE clause.

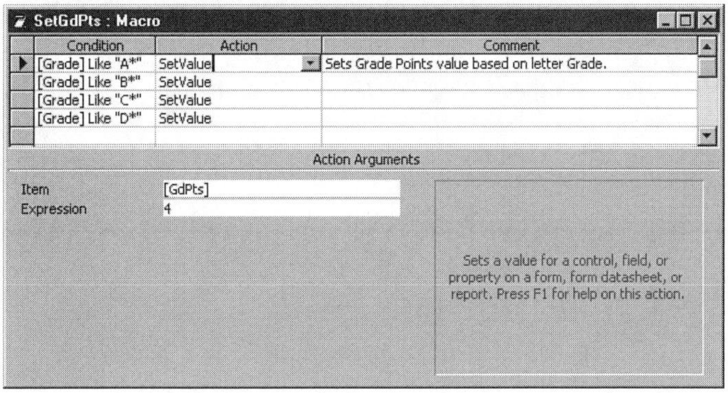

Figure 8.19.
The SetGdPts fills in the GdPts value depending on the grade entered.

The SetGdPts macro is attached to the Grade OnLostFocus event property. After the grade is entered and the focus moves to another field, the GdPts field value is set.

Creating an **AutoExec** Macro

If there is one particular action or series of actions that you want to execute whenever you open the database, you can create a special macro named AutoExec. You can use it to do such things as open a switchboard form, request a password, or ask the user to enter his or her name.

A database can contain only one AutoExec macro. When Access starts a database, it looks for a macro named AutoExec and, if it finds one, executes it. You can set many of the same options in the macro that appear in the Startup dialog box.

Warning: The AutoExec runs after the startup options are applied, so if you include a conflicting action in the AutoExec macro, it will override the startup options. For example, suppose you have set the Display Form setting in the Startup dialog box to Main Switchboard and then you include an OpenForm action in the AutoExec macro that opens the Students form. When you start the database, the Main Switchboard opens briefly and then gives way to the Students form.

To bypass the AutoExec macro, press Shift when you open the database. This also bypasses the other options set in the Startup dialog box.

Note: The database object has an AllowByPassKey property that you can create and set to keep the user from pressing Shift to bypass the startup settings and the AutoExec macro. This property is useful when you deliver the application to an end user who should not be allowed to change the way the application starts. When set to True (-1), the property enables the user to use Shift to bypass both. When set to False (0), the Shift key doesn't bypass anything.

Be sure to set this property to True until all the bugs are out of your application.

Creating Menus and Toolbars from Macros

Using the AddMenu macro action, you can create custom menus and shortcut menus for a database object. The AddMenu action has three arguments: the Menu Name, the Menu Macro Name, and optional Status Bar Text. The Menu Name is the text that appears in the main menu bar at the top of the window. The Menu Macro is the macro that contains the actions you want to see in the menu when you click the menu name. Figure 8.20 shows a form with a custom menu bar containing two menus: Reports and Forms. The items in the menus are taken from macro groups that contain the responses to buttons on the Forms and Preview Switchboards. Notice that the custom menu has replaced the default Access menu because it was attached to the MenuBar property of the form. The figure also shows the CCC Main Menu macro that produced the menu.

Figure 8.20.
A custom menu bar with two menus.

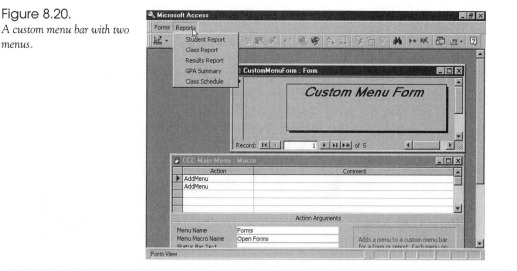

To create a line between two menu items in the custom menu, enter a hyphen in the macro name column between the two macros you want to separate. To add an accelerator key to a menu item, type & just before the letter in the macro name. To create a submenu for any of the menu items, add an AddMenu action to the macro and name another menu macro.

After you create the menu macro, attach it to the MenuBar or ShortcutMenuBar property of a form, form control, or report. A customized shortcut menu replaces the built-in shortcut menu for form, form control, and report objects.

Although you can still create custom menus with AddMenu macros, Microsoft recommends that you use the new Access 97 Customize dialog box. To open it, choose View | Toolbars | Customize or choose Customize from the toolbar shortcut menu. See Chapter 11, "Creating an Application from an Existing Database," for more information about creating your own customized menus and toolbars without using macros. With Customize, you can even add icons to a custom menu or toolbar item.

Custom toolbars created with earlier versions of Access are automatically converted to the new Access 97 style. Custom menu bars and shortcut menus created with the Access 95 Menu Builder are interpreted as the new style when you open a converted database, but they are not actually converted. Until they are converted, you cannot use the Customize dialog box to make changes in them.

A quick way to convert a menu or shortcut menu is to use the Tools menu. Select the menu macro in the database window and choose Tools | Create Menu From Macro (or Toolbar or Shortcut Menu).

The new menu appears immediately at the top of the window above the built-in main menu. A new toolbar appears in the lower-right corner of the window. You can drag both around on the screen wherever you want them to appear and even dock the new toolbar. A new shortcut menu does not appear until you open the Customize dialog box.

Figure 8.21 shows the database window after creating a menu from the CCC Main Menu macro and a toolbar from the Preview Reports macro. Both have been repositioned for better viewing. Right-clicking on the toolbar displays the toolbar shortcut menu with the list of active toolbars.

Figure 8.21.
A new menu bar and toolbar created from macros.

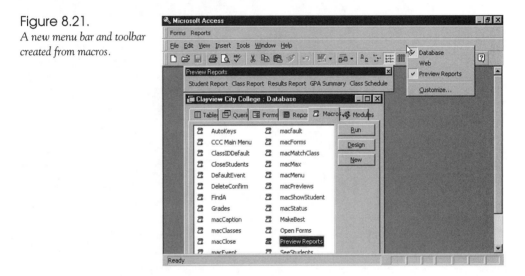

To remove the toolbar from the screen, right-click any toolbar and clear the check mark next to the name, or simply click the Close button. To remove the menu, you must use the Customize dialog box available from the View | Toolbars menu or from the toolbar shortcut menu. On the Toolbars tab of the Customize dialog box, clear the check mark next to CCC Main Menu. To delete a menu bar or toolbar altogether, select it and choose Delete.

When you create a shortcut menu from a macro, it does not display immediately like the menu bar and toolbar. To see the new shortcut menus, you must open the Customize dialog box and check Shortcut Menus in the Toolbars list. Then, click the Custom pull-down menu. Figure 8.22 shows three new shortcut menus in the shortcut menu bar. When you close the Customize dialog box, the shortcut menus are removed from the screen.

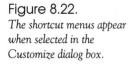

Figure 8.22.

The shortcut menus appear when selected in the Customize dialog box.

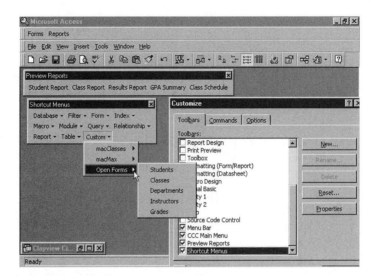

Looking Up Macros

If you want to see the names of all the macros in the current database, choose File | Properties and then click the Contents tab. All the database objects are listed in the Contents box, beginning with the tables. Scroll down the list until you come to the Macros section of the list. Figure 8.23 shows some of the macros in the Clayview City College database.

Figure 8.23.

The Contents tab shows a list of all the application database objects.

To keep a record of the specifications of a macro, you can print the description. The Print button is dimmed on the toolbar but you can open the Print dialog box using File | Print. This opens the Print Macro Definition dialog box, which gives you the option of including any of three features of the macro: the macro Properties, the Actions and Arguments, and the Permissions by User and Group. After making your selections, choose OK and the macro definition is printed. Figure 8.24 shows the first page of the macForms macro group.

Figure 8.24.

The printed macForms *macro group definition.*

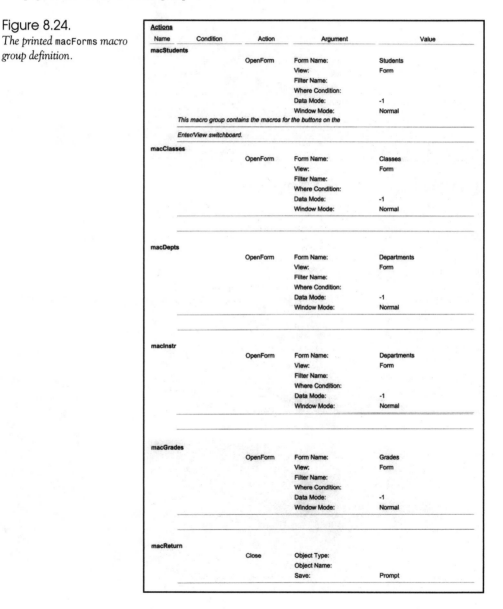

Actions

Name	Condition	Action	Argument	Value
macStudents				
		OpenForm	Form Name:	Students
			View:	Form
			Filter Name:	
			Where Condition:	
			Data Mode:	-1
			Window Mode:	Normal
	This macro group contains the macros for the buttons on the			
	Enter/View switchboard.			
macClasses				
		OpenForm	Form Name:	Classes
			View:	Form
			Filter Name:	
			Where Condition:	
			Data Mode:	-1
			Window Mode:	Normal
macDepts				
		OpenForm	Form Name:	Departments
			View:	Form
			Filter Name:	
			Where Condition:	
			Data Mode:	-1
			Window Mode:	Normal
macInstr				
		OpenForm	Form Name:	Departments
			View:	Form
			Filter Name:	
			Where Condition:	
			Data Mode:	-1
			Window Mode:	Normal
macGrades				
		OpenForm	Form Name:	Grades
			View:	Form
			Filter Name:	
			Where Condition:	
			Data Mode:	-1
			Window Mode:	Normal
macReturn				
		Close	Object Type:	
			Object Name:	
			Save:	Prompt

Converting Macros to VBA Code

Many activities in an application can easily be carried out using macros. Others, such as error trapping, transaction processing, and passing arguments to a procedure while it is running require VBA procedures. You can convert any macro or all macros for a form or report to VBA procedures. Some programmers feel more comfortable with all operations done with procedures.

To convert a single macro to a procedure, select the macro name in the database window and choose Tools | Macro | Convert Macros to Visual Basic. You cannot convert a macro that is open in the design window. A Convert Macro dialog box opens with two options, both selected by default:

- Add error handling to generated functions
- Include macro comments

The first option includes OnError statements that branch to error-handling routines in the procedure. The second option adds all the comments you placed in the macro design as comments in the VBA code. Choose Convert to complete the conversion. Figure 8.25 shows the macShowStudent macro both in the macro design window and as a VBA function procedure.

Figure 8.25.
The macShowStudent *macro converted to VBA.*

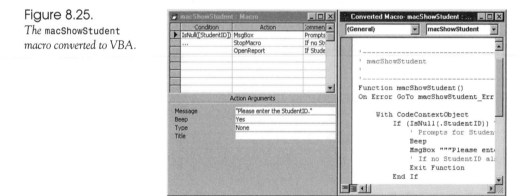

Another method of converting macros to VBA is to select the macro name in the database window and choose File | Save To/Export to open the Save As dialog box. Then, choose Save as Visual Basic Module. The same Convert Macro dialog box offers the options of adding error-handling and including the comments. The conversion produces the same procedure as using the Tools menu.

You can also convert all the macros that are associated with a form in one operation. First, open the form in design view and then choose Tools | Macro | Convert Form Macros to Visual Basic. The Convert Macros dialog box opens as before. Choose Convert, and Access converts all the macros for that form into functions and procedures in the class module for the form. You can do the same with all macros associated with a report.

Summary

In this chapter, you have seen some of the operations that you can do with macros. Macros are easy to create and attach to events that affect the database objects. There are more than 50 actions that you can execute under the control of a macro. The chapter also introduced the importance of the sequence of events so that you attach the macro to the correct event property.

Macros can also be used to carry out conditional branching and even act as SELECT CASE constructs. You have also seen how to build custom menus and toolbars from special macros. In the final section, you learned how to convert macros to VBA procedures. The next chapter discusses VBA procedures and how to use the Module Builder.

9

Writing VBA Procedures

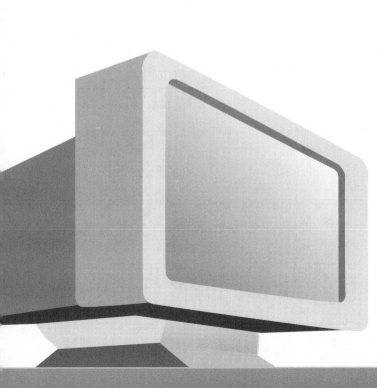

In Chapter 5, "Examining and Modifying the Wizard's Code," you had a chance to examine the code that the Database Wizard created while building the *Omni-Sport* database. In this chapter, you create your own VBA code to further customize the database forms, reports, and switchboards.

In addition to using the Module window to enter and modify VBA code, this chapter demonstrates the flexibility of VBA procedures. It also discusses the convenient Object Browser, which Access provides to assist in creating code.

Planning Ahead

> **Peter's Principle:** As with any endeavor, especially in the computer realm, it is best to plan ahead and try to anticipate how the user will interact with the system and how the system should respond. In planning a VBA program, divide the process into small increments, each with a specific purpose. Then, create a procedure or function for each one separately. Splitting the program into short, single-purpose tasks makes debugging and maintenance much easier. Adding frequent comments also helps to interpret the code later on.

Another good practice is to use consistent names for variables and objects, such as *rst* for recordsets and *dbs* for databases. Following a standard naming convention also makes it easier for another programmer to be able to maintain the code.

Generalizing where possible saves time and space. You can write a procedure that can be used in more than one instance or by more than one object. For example, the IsLoaded() function in the module window of the *Omni-Sport* database is a global function and is accessible to any form in the database. The code needn't be repeated in each form in the database that uses the function.

Another good policy is to create object-specific class modules with code for a certain form or report. These modules are stored with the form or report and are accessible only to the host object. Keeping procedures in class modules also helps to prevent conflicts among procedures that use the same variable names.

After you have determined what your application should contain and how it should respond to all the expected events, you can start to build the application using the Access wizards. They give you a good starting point to begin customizing the database.

Which Language Should You Use?

Although macros and SQL statements are easy to create and use in an application, there are certain times when you should or must use VBA. For example, to make an application more comfortable for the user, you can intercept the cryptic error messages so popular with database management systems and replace them with diagnostic messages that are more informative. You can even add some advice about getting out of the problem. You can do this only with VBA programming.

Macros can run with arguments you have supplied, but if you want to be able to change their values during execution, you must write a VBA procedure.

Access provides many built-in, intrinsic functions such as Date() and Pmt() that return values when you supply the arguments. Intrinsic functions are available to both macros and VBA procedures. If you want to create your own custom functions, you must do so with a VBA function procedure. VBA procedures can also create and modify objects just like a wizard. You can change the appearance and behavior of form controls and other objects with procedures.

Procedures are also easier to keep track of because they are stored in groups as modules. Macros are stored individually in the Macro tab of the database window.

How Does VBA Work?

Visual Basic for Applications is an event-driven programming language, which means it responds to events as they happen. *Events* are actions recognized by a form, a form control, or a report. Using VBA code, you can make the object respond to the event any way you want.

You've already seen many examples of procedures and functions that respond to events, such as the form that opens when you click a command button or the calculated field that is updated when you enter data in another field. Events are not always user initiated—the system can generate events as well.

Before continuing, a review of VBA terms is in order. Table 9.1 defines a few of the more commonly used programming terms.

Table 9.1. Event-driven programming terms.

Term	Definition
Module	Container for procedures and functions.
Class module	Collection of procedures and functions belonging to a form or report.
Standard module	Module whose general procedures are available to the application as a whole.
Procedure	Self-contained series of statements that executes as a whole to perform a single task.
Sub procedure	Type of procedure that performs a specific purpose.

continues

Table 9.1. continued

Term	Definition
Function	Procedure that returns a specific value.
Event procedure	Procedure that causes an object to respond to a specific event.
Method	Procedure that operates on a specific type of object. Similar to a statement or function.
Statement	Combination of instructions with keywords, symbols, constants, and variables. A single line or a line continued with a line continuation pair (space and underline).
Keyword	Word that has a special meaning to the VBA compiler.
Argument	Additional information passed to a function or sub procedure. Also called a parameter.

Touring the Module Window

VBA code is written, edited, and displayed in the module window. Figure 9.1 shows the module window with a function that creates a full name from the first and last names in the Subscribers table. You can open the module window for a class module associated with a form or report whether the object is open or not. To see the code for a class module, do one of the following:

- Select the form or report name in the database window and click the Code toolbar button or choose View | Code.
- In the form or report design view, click Code on the toolbar or choose View | Code.
- Click Build in an event property for an object in the report or form design.
- Select the module name in the database window, choose Design, click Code on the toolbar, or choose View | Design.

Note: If you open the class module for a form or report from the database window, the design view opens first. When you close the module window, the design view remains open.

If no procedures exist for the object you have selected, Access starts one for you. Only the two Option statements appear in the module window, Option Compare Database and Option Explicit, ready for you to create the new procedure.

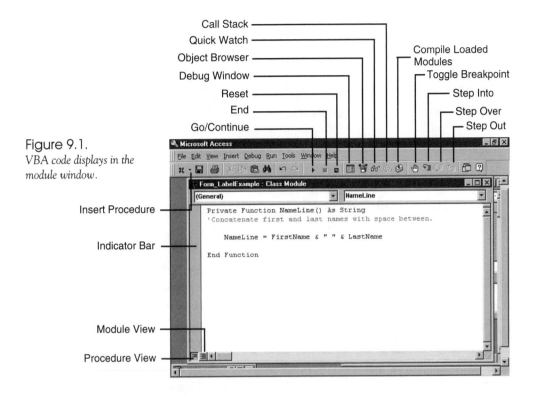

Figure 9.1.

VBA code displays in the module window.

The module window has several new toolbar buttons and menu items specifically related to writing and debugging VBA code. The left-most toolbar button is Insert Module, from whose pull-down menu you can choose what you want to create: Module, Class Module, or Procedure. If you choose Procedure, a dialog box opens in which you can specify the procedure name, type, and scope. These options are also available from the Insert menu. The other new toolbar buttons are explained in Table 9.2.

Table 9.2. The module window toolbar buttons.

Button	Description
Go/Continue	Runs the procedure containing the insertion point. If the procedure is in a class module, the form or report must be open in design view.
End	Ends code execution following a runtime error. Module-level variables retain their values.
Reset	Stops all code running and resets all variables.

continues

Table 9.2. continued

Button	Description
Debug Window	Opens the Debug window in front of the module window.
Object Browser	Opens the Object Browser window.
Quick Watch	Opens the Quick Watch dialog box, in which you can see a selected expression and, if in context, its current value.
Call Stack	Displays a list of procedures that have begun but have not finished. The most recently started procedure is at the top of the list.
Compile Loaded Modules	Compiles the loaded modules and displays any syntax or other compilation errors.
Toggle Breakpoint	Sets and removes breakpoints in the code.
Step Into	Steps through the code, one statement at a time.
Step Over	Runs a called procedure without stepping through it and then executes the next statement after the procedure call.
Step Out	Runs the rest of the current procedure and returns to the next statement in the previous procedure.

These actions are also available through the Run, View, and Debug menus.

Note: To view a single procedure instead of all the procedures in a module, use the two small buttons in the bottom-left corner of the window. The left one changes to Procedure View and the right one changes to Module View.

To navigate among procedures in a module, press Ctrl+PgUp to move to the previous procedure and Ctrl+PgDn to move to the next. You can also use the Object and Procedure boxes in the module window to move to a specific procedure. Click the Object box arrow and select the object whose procedure you want to see in the Object box. Then click the Procedure arrow to select from the list of events that apply to the selected object. Any event that has a related event procedure appears in bold in the list. Figure 9.2 shows the module window listing all the events for the Go To Switchboard button. The Click event is bold, indicating that an event procedure exists for this button.

Select the event from the list to see the event procedure or select an event that is not bold to start a new event procedure for that event.

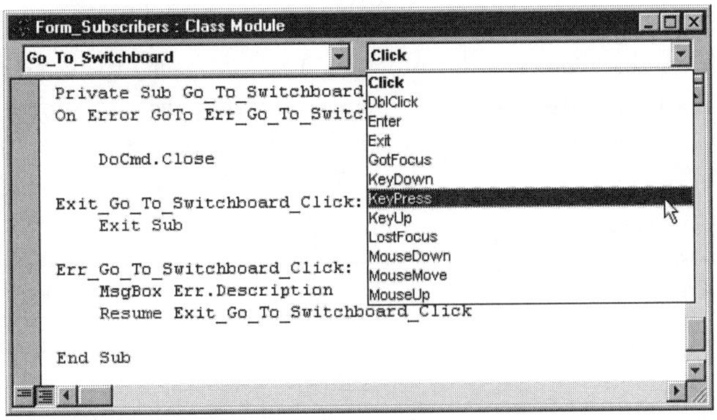

Figure 9.2.
Choose from the procedure
box to move to a specific
procedure.

Setting Module Window Options

To change some of the features of the module window, choose Tools | Options and open the Module tab (see Figure 9.3).

Figure 9.3.
Setting module window
options.

The options are divided into four categories:

- Code Colors establishes the colors for various types of text in the module.
- Font and Size determine the appearance of the text.
- Coding Options provides many useful aids while writing procedures.
- Window Settings determines how the module window looks and behaves.

The Code Colors options can be applied to normal, selection, syntax error, comment, keyword, iden-tifier, and several other types of text. You can specify the foreground, background, and indicator colors. Each of those pull-down menus displays a palette of colors from which to choose. The coding options and window settings are described in Table 9.3.

Table 9.3. Module window coding options.

Option	Description
Auto Indent	Automatically indents a line of code to match the previous line.
Auto Syntax Check	Checks for syntax errors as you type.
Require Variable Declaration	Automatically includes `Option Explicit` in the declaration section of every new module in the database, including class modules.
Compile on Demand	Compiles a complete module when you compile a procedure in the module. If cleared, it compiles all other procedures that may be called by this one as well.
Auto List Members	Displays a list of valid choices as you type a statement.
Auto Quick Info	Displays syntax information when you type a procedure or method name. The current element you are entering appears in bold in the syntax statement.
Auto Data Tips	Shows the current value of a variable when you pause the mouse pointer on the variable name. Must be in break mode to see it.

Tip: If Auto List Members is checked, Access helps you complete statements as you type by displaying a list of relevant objects, properties, and methods that are appropriate to the statement you are typing. If you don't want this assistance, clear the option in the Modules Options dialog box.

Changing the Window Settings

The module window settings available in the Tools | Options dialog box give you some help during debugging. The Window Settings options include the following:

- Full Module View—Shows all the procedures in the module as the default view. Clear this option to change the default view to show a single procedure. It has the same effect as using the buttons at the bottom of the window.

- Procedure Separator—Draws a line across the screen between procedures.

- Drag-and-Drop Text Editing—When selected, this option lets you drag and drop text as an alternative to cutting and pasting. Use this technique to drag selected text to another location in the same module or to the Debug window.

- Debug Window on Top—Keeps the Debug window on top when it is inactive. This helps you to see what is happening as you step through code.

- Margin Indicator Bar—Appears down the left side of the window and displays symbols that show the current statement and the location of breakpoints and bookmarks.

There are additional debugging options on the Advanced tab of the Options dialog box, which are discussed in Chapter 10, "Debugging VBA Procedures."

Types of VBA Modules

Modules are containers for code segments and can contain declarations, event procedures, sub procedures, and functions. VBA includes three types of modules, one of which is new to Access 97. *Standard modules* are separate objects in the database that store code you want to use anywhere in the application. Standard module names appear on the Modules tab of the database window.

When you create a new form or report, Access creates a *class module* for it and includes it in the design. When you add an event procedure to the form or report, Access adds it to the class module. If you copy the form or report to another database, the class module is copied along with it. Deleting a form or report also deletes its module.

In Access 97, you can now create class modules independent of any form or report that appear with the standard modules on the Modules tab of the database window. An independent class module can be used to build a custom object on the same level as forms and reports.

The Modules collection contains all open modules in the application, class, or standard, compiled or not.

Types of Procedures and Their Elements

There are two kinds of procedures in VBA: sub procedures and functions. A *sub procedure* performs an operation but does not return a value to the application and, because it does not return a value, it cannot be used in an expression. Functions, on the other hand, return a value and thus can be used in an expression. Access provides many built-in functions, and you can also create your own custom functions.

Procedures contain declarations, statements, and expressions. *Declarations* explicitly establish the data type of variables and constants that appear in the procedure or module. The declaration section must appear at the beginning of the procedure. A *statement* expresses a specific operation, declaration, or definition. Statements are usually placed singly on one line of the procedure. You can combine two or more statements on a single line by separating them with a colon (:). For example, the following statement puts three statements on one line:

```
intA = 1: intB = 2: intC = 3
```

Note: The disadvantage of placing more than one command on a line comes during debugging when you try to set a breakpoint. Although you can step through the code, one statement at a time, a breakpoint is attached to the whole line rather than to one of the statements on the line.

If a statement is long, it can be continued on the next line by using the line continuation pair, a space followed by an underscore. For example, the statement that evaluates an expression and sets the `LabelAddress` to that value runs to three lines.

```
'The first two lines end with a space and an underscore.
LabelAddress = NameLine & strLineFeed & _
    Address & strLineFeed & City & ", " _
    StateOrProvince & " " & PostalCode
```

Expressions such as the preceding one set the value of the object on the left of the equal sign to the value derived from the terms on the right.

Use the standard Access naming rules when you name procedures, constants, variables, and arguments in VBA:

- The first character must be a letter.
- The name can contain letters, numbers, and the underscore character but no other punctuation.
- The name can contain no more than 255 characters.
- Do not use the same name as any VBA function, method, or statement and do not use the same name twice in the same procedure.

Sub Procedures

A sub procedure is a set of one or more distinct operations. You use a sub procedure to automate tasks that you perform repeatedly. You can even assign one to a menu item so that you can run it from the menu.

Sub procedures are also useful for operations you might want to run under different circumstances, such as by clicking a button on a form or when a certain control gets focus. Both the event properties of the two controls would call the same procedure. The procedure code need not be repeated in each event procedure.

Event procedures are by far the most common sub procedures that you will find in an application. They are actually sub procedures that have been assigned as the responses to events that happen to an object. A sub procedure that is not used as a response to an event is referred to as a *general procedure*.

Warning: Be sure you have settled on the names of the controls you are going to attach event procedures to before you create the procedures. However, if you do change the control's name after writing the procedure, remember to change the name of the procedure, as well. If Access does not associate the procedure with the event property of a control, the procedure becomes a general procedure.

The sub procedure statement specifies the procedure name, arguments, and code statements and has the following syntax:

```
[Private¦Public][Static]Sub name [(arglist)]
    [statements]
    [Exit Sub]
    [statements]
End Sub
```

In this standard syntactic definition, the words in bold are keywords and must be typed exactly as shown. The words in italic are user-provided names. Any element in square brackets ([ ]) is optional. Keywords separated by a vertical line (¦) indicate a mutually exclusive option. For example, you can use Public or Private, but not both. If an argument list is included, the list must be enclosed in parentheses and the arguments are separated by commas. All of these elements are described in the next section, "Functions," because they are shared by functions.

Note: Two or more keywords separated by vertical lines but enclosed in braces ({}) indicate a mandatory entry. You must choose one of the keywords or the default option will automatically be used. An example is the Option Compare statement, which includes {Binary ¦ Text ¦ Database} in its syntax. One of them must be used with Option Compare. Database is the default keyword.

The Sub keyword declares the procedure by name. Everything between the Sub and End Sub lines are executed when you run the procedure.

Functions

A *function procedure* derives a value and returns it to the application. The returned value has the same name as the function and can be used in an expression elsewhere, such as in a calculated field in a form, or in a `Select Case` branching operation. You can even assign the function as a control property setting. For example, the `NameLine` function builds a full name from the `FirstName` and `LastName` field values. The value returned by the function is named `NameLine` and can be used by another procedure in the module:

```
Private Function NameLine() As String
'Concatenate first and last names with space between.
    NameLine = FirstName & " " & LastName
End Function
```

The `Function` statement has the following syntax:

```
[Private|Public][Static]Function name [(arglist)][As type]
    [statements]
    [name = expression]
    [Exit Function]
    [statements]
    [name = expression]
End Function
```

The value the function returns is the value assigned by the expression to the name of the function. If the function does not assign a value to its name, the function returns a default value: `0` if a numeric function, zero-length string (`""`) if a string function, or `Empty` if a variant function.

To use the value returned by the function, place the function name on the right side of an expression in another procedure.

Procedure Elements

Both types of procedures share most of the same syntactic elements. Table 9.4 describes their use and limitations.

Table 9.4. Procedure elements.

Element	Description
Public	Makes the procedure available to all other procedures in all other modules in application. (Optional.)
Private	Limits procedure to other procedures in this module. (Optional.)
Static	Preserves the value of local variables between procedure calls. Has no effect on variables used by this procedure but created in another procedure. (Optional.)

Element	Description
name	Name of sub or function. (Required.)
arglist	List of variables passed to the procedure when it is called. Names in list are separated with commas. (Optional.)
As type	Indicates the data type of the value returned by function: Boolean, Byte, Currency, Date, Double, Integer, Long, Object, Single, String, Variant. If you don't specify a data type, Access uses Variant. (Optional.)
statements	Group of statements to be carried out in procedure. (Optional.)
Exit Sub(Function)	Exits from the procedure before the normal End statement. Processing resumes at the statement following the statement that called the procedure. Procedure may contain more than one Exit statement.
expression	Return value from a function. (Optional.)

The argument list also has a required structure and syntax that applies to both types of procedures:

[Optional][ByVal][ByRef][ParamArray]varname[()][As type] [=defaultvalue]

Table 9.5 describes the argument list elements.

Table 9.5. Argument list elements.

Element	Description
Optional	Argument not required. (Optional.)
ByVal	Value of the argument is passed. (Optional.)
ByRef	Argument is passed by referring to another variable. (Optional.)
ParamArray	Indicates that the argument in the list is an array of variant elements. Enables you to pass a varying number of variant arguments. Must be the final argument in the list. (Optional.)
varname	Name representing the argument used in the procedure. (Required.)
type	Same as in procedure statement. (Optional.)
=defaultvalue	Any constant or constant expression to be used as the default value for an optional argument. (Optional.)

Declaring Variables and Constants

You use declaration statements, usually the Dim statement, to define variables for the procedure or module. To declare constants, use the Const statement. Where and how you declare them defines their scope and lifetime. Declarations are placed at the top of a procedure to define procedure-level variables and constants. To have them available to all procedures in the module, place the declarations at the top of the module, right after the two Option statements.

If you don't specify a data type in the declaration, the Variant type is assumed. Refer to Chapter 3, "Touring the World of Object-Oriented Programming," for a complete discussion of VBA data types and declarations as well as how to reference objects in code.

You can use the Public, Private, and Static keywords in declaration statements to set the scope of the variables and constants the same way as in Sub and Function statements.

What Can You Do with a Procedure?

The principal use for procedures in Access is to define a response to an event and accomplish the purpose of the application. If the application is designed properly, each procedure performs a separate operation such as validating newly entered data, opening a form, displaying a report for preview, or evaluating an expression and branching to the next procedure.

This section contains a sampling of some of the things you can do with procedures.

Enter Data

Listing 9.1 is an example of a function that responds to data input. If the user has entered a value between 00000 and 99999 in the PostalCode field, "USA" is automatically entered into the Country field and the cursor moves to the first field on the second page. The event is AfterUpdate, and it occurs when the cursor leaves the PostalCode field. If you look at the event property sheet for the PostalCode text box control, you will see [Event Procedure], indicating a sub procedure is attached to this event.

Listing 9.1. A function that responds to data input.

```
Private Sub PostalCode_AfterUpdate()
'Fill in the Country field if the PostalCode is between 00000 and 99999.
    If PostalCode > "00000" And PostalCode < "99999" Then
        Country = "USA"
        GoToPage 2                      'Moves focus to the second page.
        DatePaid.GetFocus               'First control on second page.
    End If
End Sub
```

The GoToPage action moves focus to the first control on the second page of the form. Without this action, the form moves up on the screen to expose the DatePaid field without displaying the complete second page. The DatePaid.GetFocus statement is not really necessary because the GoToPage moves the cursor to the first control on the page automatically. No declaration statements are necessary for this procedure because it contains only field names from the database and no variables.

Asking the User a Question

Using the MsgBox() function is a good way to impart information to the user. You can also use the function to get quick input from the user, especially if there are only two or three options from which to choose. The button responses are coded so that you can interpret the response and perform other operations depending on the response.

Figure 9.4 shows a message box that asks the user a question to which the response is Yes or No. The 36 argument in the function statement is the sum of 4, which specifies the Yes and No buttons, and 32, which means to display the question mark icon. If the user clicks Yes, the function returns 6, whereas No returns 7. The message box caption, Reader Poll, is also specified by the MsgBox() function.

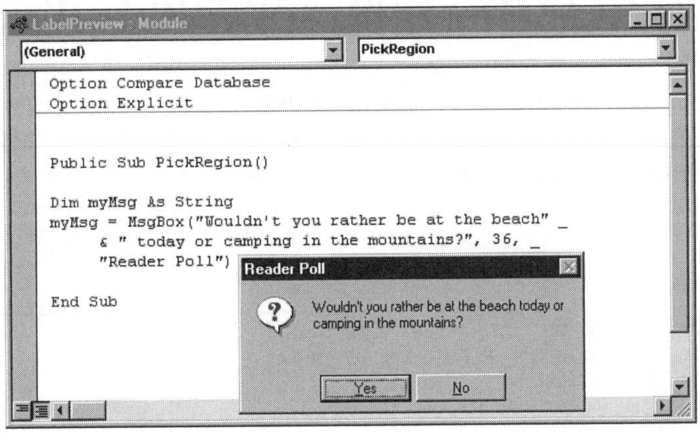

Figure 9.4.
The MsgBox() function can ask simple questions.

Set Startup Properties

Listing 9.2 is an example of a way to set custom startup properties instead of using the Tools | Startup dialog box.

Listing 9.2. Setting custom startup properties.

```
Sub Getgoing()
'Change startup properties for a database.
Dim dbs As Database
    Set dbs = CurrentDB
    dbs.StartupForm = "Subscribers"
```

continues

Listing 9.2. continued

```
    dbs.StartupShowDBWindow = False
    dbs.StartupShowStatusBar = True
    dbs.StartupPosition = 2
    dbs.StartupMenuBar = "MyOwnMenu"
    dbs.AllowBreakIntoCode = False
    dbs.AllowByPassKey = True
End Sub
```

In this procedure, the database is set to the current database, and the Subscribers form is set as the startup form rather than the database window. The status bar is displayed and the `StartupPosition` value 2 places the startup form in the center on the whole screen. Other properties display a custom menu bar named MyOwnMenu, prevent the user from viewing VBA code following a runtime error, and allow the user to skip the startup options by pressing the Shift bypass key as the database opens.

Trap Errors and Validate Data

When a wizard creates an event procedure for a control, it always adds an error contingency plan. Usually, it just branches to the end of the procedure and lets Access display whatever message it feels is appropriate. However, you can insert your own messages in place of the default messages. For example, Listing 9.3 was generated by the Button Wizard for the Go To Switchboard button in the Subscribers form.

Listing 9.3. An `On Click` event procedure.

```
Private Sub Go_To_Switchboard_Click()
On Error GoTo Err_Go_To_Switchboard_Click
    DoCmd.Close
Exit_Go_To_Switchboard_Click:
    Exit Sub
Err_Go_To_Switchboard_Click:
    MsgBox Err.Description
    Resume Exit_Go_To_Switchboard_Click
End Sub
```

The `On Error` statement branches to the statement labeled `Err_Go_To_Switchboard_Click`, which displays the `Err.Description` in a message box and then branches back to the `Exit_Go_To_Switchboard` line. Any line that ends with a colon (`:`) is a line label rather than a statement. It marks the destination for the `GoTo` statement. This structure is standard for error handling. If you wanted to show a different message based on the type of error, you could change the `MsgBox` statement—perhaps after testing for the code number of the error that occurred.

If you want to make sure that the user has entered a Postal Code after entering an address, you could use an If...Then...Else structure in a procedure attached to the form's BeforeUpdate event to test for the missing values.

Filter Records for a Report

It is not as easy for the user to filter information in a report preview as it is in a form. To filter records for a report, you usually base the report on a query. If you want the user to be able to decide how to filter the report in real time just before previewing it, you can use an InputBox() function to acquire the criteria from the user.

For example, suppose you want to be able to preview the fact sheets for subscribers from a certain state. An InputBox() function can ask for the state value and add the response to a filter argument for the OpenReport method. The only real trick is to include quotation marks around the two-character state abbreviation that the user enters. This requires embedding the quotation marks within the criteria string so that the criterion becomes [StateOrProvince] = "CA".

You can use either single or double quotation marks to embed a string within a string. In this example, double quotation marks are used to concatenate the string variable, strFilter. Listing 9.4 shows an event procedure that is attached to the On Click property of the Preview Fact Sheets for State button on the GetFacts form. The form is based on the Subscribers recordset. Figure 9.5 shows the GetFacts form with a single command button and the GetState event procedure.

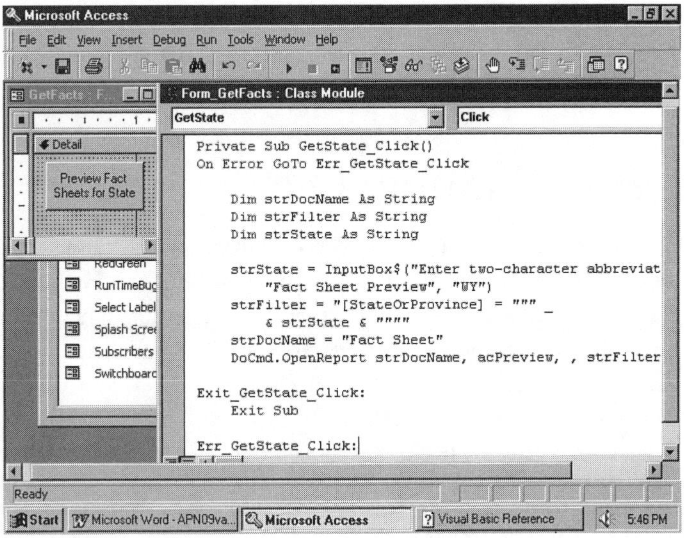

Figure 9.5.
The user can filter records for a report preview.

Listing 9.4. Creating a filter from user input.

```
Private Sub GetState_Click()
On Error GoTo Err_GetState_Click
    Dim strDocName As String
    Dim strFilter As String
    Dim strState As String

    strState = InputBox$("Enter two-character abbreviation for state.", _
        "Fact Sheet Preview", "WY")
    strFilter = "[StateOrProvince] = """ _
        & strState & """"
    strDocName = "Fact Sheet"
    DoCmd.OpenReport strDocName, acPreview, , strFilter
Exit_GetState_Click:
    Exit Sub
Err_GetState_Click:
    MsgBox Err.Description
    Resume Exit_GetState_Click
End Sub
```

In this example, WY is specified as the default value in the InputBox() function. The default value argument is optional.

> **Tip:** Using double quotation marks instead of single lets you include apostrophes in the string, which would not be allowed if you used single quotation marks.

Another way to embed quotation marks in the filter is to assign a variable to the ASCII character 34: Chr$(34). The dollar sign ($) in the Chr$() function specifies that the value returned by the function be the string equivalent of the ANSII code.

Create Mailing Labels

The two functions shown in Listing 9.5 build a label report from the database field values. If either the LastName or the Address field is blank, no label is created in the report. The first function creates the name line for the label. Writing this as a separate function enables you to use the function for other purposes within the form class module. The second function uses the results of the NameLine function in an expression that builds the rest of the label. The two characters, Chr(13) and Chr(10), are the ASCII character codes for carriage return and line feed. Used together, they place the next characters on the next line just as though the user had pressed Enter.

Listing 9.5. Creating mailing labels.

```
Private Function NameLine() As String
'Concatenate first and last names with space between.
    NameLine = FirstName & " " & LastName
End Function
```

```
Private Function LabelAddress() As String
'Build mailing label address from Subscribers fields.
Dim strLineFeed As String
'Set strLineFeed to the carriage return and line feed ASCII code.
strLineFeed = Chr(13) & Chr(10)
'Check for blank LastName or Address.
If IsNull(LastName) Or IsNull(Address) Then
    LabelAddress = ""
Else
    LabelAddress = NameLine & strLineFeed & _
        Address & strLineFeed & City & ", " & _
        StateOrProvince & " " & PostalCode
End If
End Function
```

Figure 9.6 shows a split screen with the function code in the module window with the LabelExample form in form view. The `NameLine` is an unbound text box whose Control Source property is set to =NameLine() on the property sheet. `LabelAddress` is another unbound text box with =LabelAddress() as the Control Source property.

Figure 9.6.
Results of NameLine *and* LabelAddress *functions.*

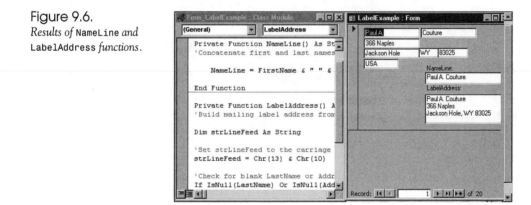

Change Form Control Properties

The ColorStyle form contains two label controls that have procedures attached to their `Click` events (see Figure 9.7). Both of the procedures use the `InputBox()` function to display a box requesting user input. The message asks the user to enter a number between 1 and 4. Each number causes a change in back color for one of the labels and font style for the other. Figure 9.8 shows the color label changed to green and the style label changed to italic.

Listing 9.6 shows the two procedures that change the properties of the label controls based on user entry in the input box.

Figure 9.7.
The ColorStyle form can change label control properties.

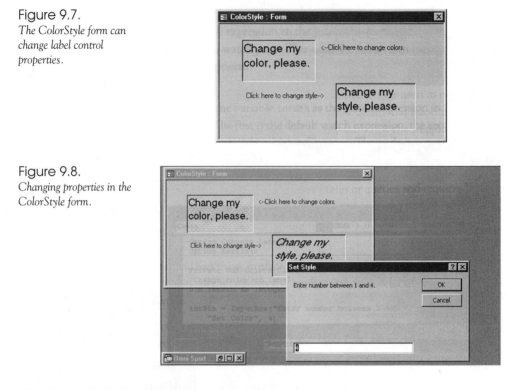

Figure 9.8.
Changing properties in the ColorStyle form.

Listing 9.6. Changing label color and style properties.

```
Private Sub Colors_Click()
'Change color of label.
Dim intBtn As Integer
intBtn = InputBox("Enter number between 1 and 4.", _
    "Set Color", 4)

Select Case intBtn
    Case 1              'Sets to red.
        Colors.BackColor = 255
    Case 2              'Sets to blue.
        Colors.BackColor = 16711680
    Case 3              'Sets to green.
        Colors.BackColor = 845388
    Case 4              'Returns to gray.
        Colors.BackColor = 12632256
End Select
End Sub

Private Sub Styles_Click()
'Change font size, italic or bold.
Dim intBtn As Integer
intBtn = InputBox("Enter number between 1 and 4.", _
    "Set Style", 4)

Select Case intBtn
```

```
    Case 1                'Sets font size to 8 pts.
        Styles.FontSize = 8
    Case 2                'Sets to italic.
        Styles.FontItalic = True
    Case 3                'Sets to bold.
        Styles.FontBold = True
    Case 4                'Resets original style.
        Styles.FontSize = 14
        Styles.FontItalic = False
        Styles.FontBold = False
End Select
End Sub
```

These procedures are good examples of how to refer to Access objects in VBA code. After the label controls were added, they were named Colors and Styles, respectively. The default names, Text1 or whatever, could have been used as reference but it is easier to see what the procedures do if the controls have more relevant names. For example, `Styles.FontSize` refers to the Styles label control, and `FontSize` is the property to set. Both `InputBox()` functions specify 4 as the default value.

Add an Item to a Combo Box

The `NotInList` property of a combo box control lets you create an event procedure that will allow the user to add a new item to the list. There is a combo box in the Subscribers form that lists three types of payment methods: Cash, Check, or Credit Card. You might want to include advertisers in your subscription list and send free copies to them. Entering a payment method that implies money changing hands could confuse the bookkeeping department, so you need to be able to add another value to the list.

The first time you enter an advertiser and specify that the subscription is complimentary, you will trigger the event `NotInList` for which you can create the event procedure shown in Listing 9.7 that adds Complimentary to the combo box list (see Figure 9.9).

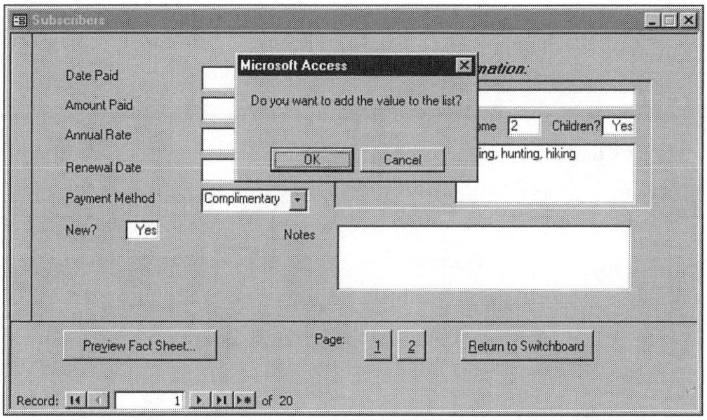

Figure 9.9.
The NotInList *event displays a message box.*

Listing 9.7. Adding to a combo box list.

```
Private Sub PaymentMethod_NotInList(NewData As String, Response As Integer)
'Allows user to add a new item to the list.
    Dim ctl As Control
    'Set the control object to the combo box.
    Set ctl = Me!PaymentMethod
    'Ask user to confirm they want to add the vew value.

    If MsgBox("Do you want to add the value to the list?", vbOKCancel) _
          = vbOK Then
        'Set Response argument to show a value is to be added.
        Response = acDataErrAdded
        'Add string to value list in row source.
        ctl.RowSource = ctl.RowSource & ";" & NewData
    Else
        'If user chose Cancel, undo change and suppress error msg.
        Response = acDataErrContinue
        ctl.Undo
    End If
End Sub
```

This procedure does not explicitly add the new item to the value list in the Row Source property; however, the next time you click the combo box list you will see that value (see Figure 9.10). The Complimentary value does appear in the Subscribers record after the record is saved.

Note: The Response argument indicates how the event is to be handled. The argument is set to one of three intrinsic values, depending on the user's response to the MsgBox(). In the preceding procedure, if the user responds OK, the Response is set to the constant, acDataErrAdded, which adds the entry and updates the combo box list. If the user chooses Cancel, the Response is set to acDataErrContinue and the combo box is not changed. The third constant for Response is the default acDataErrDisplay, which displays the default error message, and the user is not allowed to add a new value to the combo box list.

Tip: The *Omni-Sport* Subscribers table in this chapter uses the Lookup property in the table structure to specify the items in the combo box list. The NotInList() function cannot add to this list. Any value you add in the Subscribers form is temporarily approved and added to the displayed list but not to the list of values stored in the Lookup property. When you open the form again, the new value is no longer displayed in the combo box. You must add values to the table definition or to the Row Source property in the property sheet. The Row Source property shows the values from the Lookup table.

If, however, the combo box references a separate table as the source of the list of values, the Row Source property shows the name of the lookup table. The NotInList event procedure can be used to add new values to this table.

Figure 9.10.

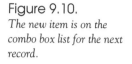

*The new item is on the
combo box list for the next
record.*

Use **DoCmd** to Run a Macro

Many applications greet the user with a welcoming screen that displays for a short time, then gives way to the main switchboard for the application. Figure 9.11 shows a splash screen for the *Omni-Sport* application. The form includes only the magazine logo and a brief message. It is unrelated to any table data.

Figure 9.11.

*The Omni-Sport splash
screen.*

The macro group, SplashScreen, has two macros: Splash, which opens and maximizes the splash screen, and GoSwitchboard, which closes the temporary screen and opens the main switchboard. A new independent procedure, ShowSplash, uses the DoCmd object to run the Splash macro (see Figure 9.12).

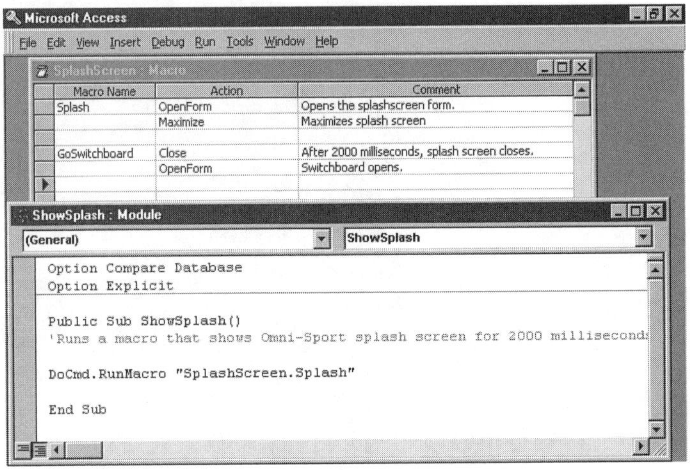

Figure 9.12.
The DoCmd runs the
SplashScreen.Splash
macro.

To make the screen temporary, set the form's Timer Interval property to the number of milliseconds you want the screen to remain on the screen. If you want the screen to appear for only two seconds, set the property to 2000. Then you must tell Access what you want it to do when the time runs out. In this case, the macro SplashScreen.GoSwitchboard runs when the time is up (see Figure 9.13).

Figure 9.13.
Changing the Splash Screen
form timing properties.

To run the procedure, select ShowSplash in the module window and choose Run.

Note: To include this welcoming screen in the application, change the startup options to show it at startup instead of the Switchboard form. The timer properties will still be in effect. You could even add a check box in the temporary screen that gives the user the choice of preventing the screen from appearing again at startup. When checked, the check box's Click event procedure will change the startup option to go directly to the main switchboard.

Creating a Procedure

Creating a new procedure involves a series of steps. First, if the procedure responds to an event such as a button click, use the appropriate wizard to get started. Then, declare all the necessary variables and constants. The body of the procedure contains the response to the event or other operations. The last section cleans up afterward by closing objects, restoring values, and adding error-handling statements, if necessary.

After planning the procedure, open the Access module window and type the VBA code. The module window contains many helpful tools and menu items to enable you to create bug-free code. In an earlier tour of the module window, you saw the toolbar buttons and the object and procedure boxes. You also learned how to set the module options by choosing Tools | Options. You will now see how some of these options can help when you are entering code.

Design the Form

The procedure created in this section is an event procedure to be attached to a command button. The form shown in Figure 9.14 is designed to be opened when the user selects Preview Mailing Labels - All from the Preview Switchboard. The form offers the choice of previewing labels for one of three geographic regions or labels for all the subscribers. The procedure uses the value returned by the option group to set the filter for the report. Figure 9.15 shows the form in design view.

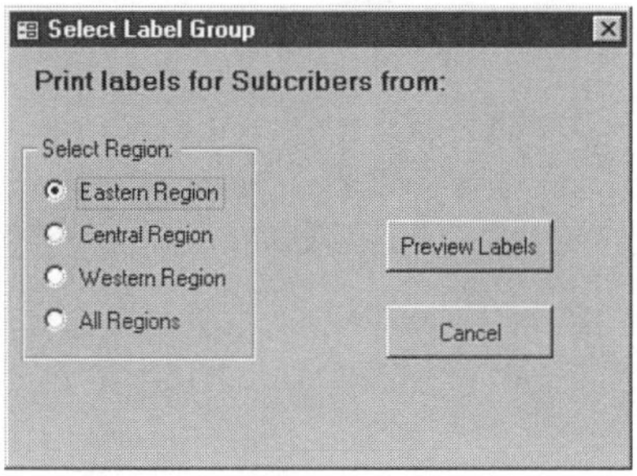

Figure 9.14.
The Select Label Group form
offers four choices.

Figure 9.15.
The Select Label Group form design.

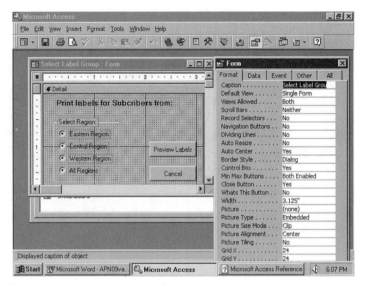

In order for the form to act like a pop-up window, some of the form properties need to be changed. In the form property sheet, change the following properties:

- Type `Select Label Group` in the `Caption` property.
- Set `Scrollbars` to `Neither`.
- Set `RecordSelectors` to `No`.
- Set `Navigation Buttons` to `No`.
- Set `AutoCenter` to `Yes`.
- Set `Border Style` to `Dialog`.

Declare Variables and Set Values

It is always easier to start an event procedure for a command button control with the help of the Button Wizard. Figure 9.16 shows the module window with the procedure created by the wizard. The procedure specifies which report to open and in what view. It also includes the default error-handling statements. Now comes the job of completing the procedure by adding a filter based on the value returned by the Region option group.

Declare the string variable `strFilter` in the declaration section. As you type `Dim strFilter As Str`, the Auto List displays an alphabetical list of valid choices to fill out the declaration (see Figure 9.17). To choose from the list, do one of the following:

- Press Tab to accept the highlighted name and remain on the same line with no space after.

- Press the spacebar to accept the highlighted name, add a space, and remain on the same line.

- Press Enter to accept the highlighted name and move to the next line in the procedure.

Figure 9.16.

The Click *procedure created by the Button Wizard.*

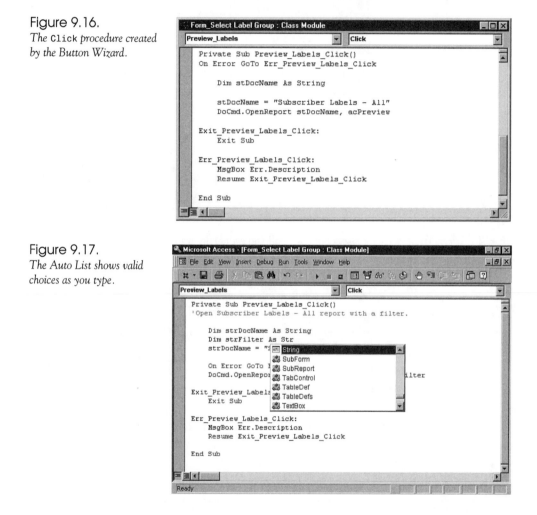

```
Private Sub Preview_Labels_Click()
On Error GoTo Err_Preview_Labels_Click

    Dim stDocName As String

    stDocName = "Subscriber Labels - All"
    DoCmd.OpenReport stDocName, acPreview

Exit_Preview_Labels_Click:
    Exit Sub

Err_Preview_Labels_Click:
    MsgBox Err.Description
    Resume Exit_Preview_Labels_Click

End Sub
```

Figure 9.17.

The Auto List shows valid choices as you type.

```
Private Sub Preview_Labels_Click()
'Open Subscriber Labels - All report with a filter.

    Dim strDocName As String
    Dim strFilter As Str
    strDocName = "S [String]
                    SubForm
    On Error GoTo I SubReport
    DoCmd.OpenRepo TabControl        ilter
                    TableDef
Exit_Preview_Labels TableDefs
    Exit Sub        TextBox

Err_Preview_Labels_Click:
    MsgBox Err.Description
    Resume Exit_Preview_Labels_Click

End Sub
```

One of the options in the option group is All Regions, which previews all the labels, regardless of region. When this option is chosen, there will be no filter; therefore, set the strFilter variable to a zero-length string before running the case. Add a line below the line that sets the strDocName to the report name: strFilter = "".

Many of the options from the Module Options dialog box are also available from the module short-cut menu. If you have turned any of the coding options off, use the shortcut menu for temporary help. Figure 9.18 shows the module window shortcut menu.

Figure 9.18.

The module window shortcut menu.

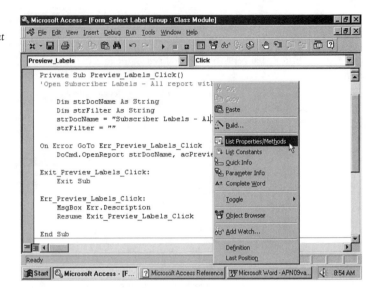

- List Properties/Methods displays a list of all the properties and methods in the current database beginning with the property or method closest to the selected word in the procedure (see Figure 9.19). You can tell that strDocName is a property by the icon next to it.

- List Constants is available only if the insertion point is in an enumerated constant. For example, with the insertion point in the word acPreview, the list shows three other view constants: acViewDesign, acViewNormal, and acViewPreview.

- Quick Info displays information about the current object such as name, type, scope, and value. For example, with the insertion point in Region in the Select Case line, Quick Info displays Region As OptionGroup.

- Parameter Info displays syntax information for the statement that contains the insertion point. The current argument appears in bold in the syntax (see Figure 9.20).

- Complete Word finishes the word you have begun if it is unambiguous; otherwise, it displays a list of words beginning with the characters you entered.

Tip: The Module tab of the Options dialog box shows an Auto Quick Info coding option which, when selected, displays syntax information as you type. This is analogous to the Parameter Info selection in the shortcut menu rather than the Quick Info option. Maybe that will be changed to be more consistent in later versions of Access, but for now don't let it confuse you.

Figure 9.19.
The List Properties/Methods option displays a list of all properties and methods in the current database.

Figure 9.20.
The Parameter Info option displays syntax information for the current statement.

All of these shortcut menu items are also available from the Edit menu.

You use the other options in the shortcut menu when you are debugging a procedure. See Chapter 10, "Debugging VBA Procedures," for more information about these items.

Add the Case Structure to Create the Filter String

A case structure based on Region as the test expression can use the value returned by the Region option group as the differentiating value. Option buttons in a group return default or specified values, depending on how you define the controls. In this case, the default sequential integers are accepted so that the buttons return the values 1 through 4. The regions are roughly divided by postal code, so the filter specifies a range of postal code values as follows:

- Between 00000 and 39999—Eastern region.
- Between 40000 and 69999—Central region.
- Between 70000 and 99999—Western region.

The final option, All Regions, leaves the filter as the zero-length string. Type the following statements immediately below the On Error GoTo statement, omitting the final quotation mark, and then press Enter:

```
Select Case Region            'User's choice of region
    Case 1                    'Eastern Region selected.
        strFilter = "[PostalCode] > '00000' And [PostalCode] < '39999'
```

You will see that the closing quotation mark was automatically added when you pressed Enter. Continue with the next statements, which set the other filters for the Central and Western regions. Listing 9.8 shows the complete listing for the Select Label Group form class module. The listing includes a procedure the Command Button Wizard created for the OnClick event for the Cancel button on the form. Be sure to add plenty of comments as you enter the code statements.

Listing 9.8. The Select Label Group class module.

```
Private Sub Preview_Labels_Click()
'Open Subscriber Labels - All report with a filter.
    Dim strDocName As String
    Dim strFilter As String

    strDocName = "Subscriber Labels - All"
    strFilter = ""

On Error GoTo Err_Preview_Labels_Click
    Select Case Region    'User's choice of region.

    Case 1      'Eastern Region selected.
        strFilter = "[PostalCode] > '00000' And [PostalCode] < '39999'"

    Case 2      'Central Region selected.
        strFilter = "PostalCode > '39999' And PostalCode < '69999'"
```

```
    Case 3      'Western Region selected.
        strFilter = "PostalCode > '69999' And PostalCode < '99999'"

End Select

    DoCmd.OpenReport strDocName, acPreview, , strFilter
    DoCmd.Close acForm, "Select Label Group"

Exit_Preview_Labels_Click:
    Exit Sub
Err_Preview_Labels_Click:
    MsgBox Err.Description
    Resume Exit_Preview_Labels_Click

End Sub

Private Sub Cancel_Preview_Click()
On Error GoTo Err_Cancel_Preview_Click
    DoCmd.Close
Exit_Cancel_Preview_Click:
    Exit Sub
Err_Cancel_Preview_Click:
    MsgBox Err.Description
    Resume Exit_Cancel_Preview_Click

End Sub
```

Note: If you want to create a new procedure for one of the objects in the form without relying on a wizard, you can use the object pull-down menu at the top left of the module window to see a list of all the objects in the current form or report. To start a new event procedure for one of these controls, select the control from the object pull-down. Then use the pull-down menu on the right, which lists all the procedures that apply to that object. Select the procedure you want to create, and type the code statements.

Change the Switchboard

Now that you have a form that offers a selection of label previews and a procedure that responds to the Preview Labels button, you need to insert it into the application. Because it applies to reports, it would make sense to place the access to the report on the Preview Switchboard. You can either add a new option or change an existing option.

To divert the Preview Switchboard item to a different object (a form in this case instead of a report), all you need to do is change the Switchboard table. The table also determines the switchboard item text and caption.

Open the Switchboard table in datasheet view and make the following changes:

- Change the ItemText for item 3 on switchboard 3 to Preview Labels By Region.
- Change the Command on the same line to 3 (OpenForm).
- Change the Argument to Select Label Group.

Close the table and try out the new option. Figure 9.21 shows the new dialog box in which you se-lect the labels you want to preview.

Figure 9.21.
Choosing from the Preview Switchboard opens the new form.

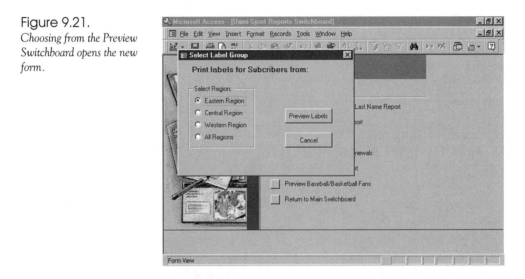

The Object Browser

The Object Browser is a useful tool for looking up objects available to Access and to see which methods and properties can be used with each object. The information includes definitions of objects and their properties, methods, events, and constants as well as their related functions and statements. When you find the item you want, you can copy and paste it into the procedure. As procedures become more complicated, the Object Browser can ensure correct spelling and pairing up of objects with their methods and properties.

You must be in the module window to use the Object Browser. To open the Object Browser, click the Object Browser button or choose View | Object Browser. The Definition option in the module shortcut menu also opens the Object Browser window and displays the definition of the current term.

When you open the Object Browser window, you have a choice of projects and libraries, including the current database, *Omni-Sport* (see Figure 9.22). Each library has a slightly different collection of objects and associated members. The left half of the window shows the list of all the object classes in the current library, while the right side shows a list of members of the selected object class. The lower pane displays the definition of the currently selected class and member.

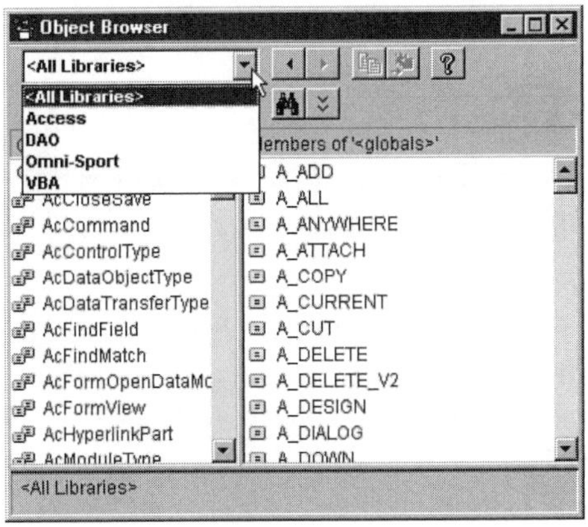

Figure 9.22.
The Object Browser offers a choice of libraries.

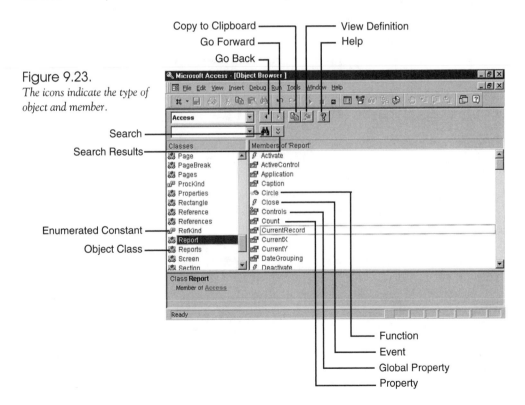

Members of a class of objects refers to all the functions, properties, events, and constants that belong to that class and also includes related functions and statements. The icons preceding the names in the lists indicate the type of class and member. Figure 9.23 shows the class Report as a member of the Access library and some of the members of the Report class.

Figure 9.23.
The icons indicate the type of object and member.

The Access 97 Object Browser has many new features in addition to the Copy to Clipboard button. Here are some other new features:

- The <globals> item that appears at the top of the class list displays a list of all the members in the selected library that can be accessed globally.

- The Go Back and Go Forward buttons navigate through the items you have previously selected.

- View Definition opens the module window and displays the user-defined sub or function procedure. For example, choose *Omni-Sport* from the Project/Library list, select the `Form_Select Label Group` from the `Class` list and `Preview_Labels_Click` from the `Members` list, and then click Show Definition. The procedure code will appear in the module window.

- To find a class or member in the current library, type the name in the Search Text box, and then click Search. After the search is completed, click the Show Search Results button to open the results pane.

- If you need help with a specific object, method, property, or event, select it and click the Help button or press F1. The Help topic for that item opens. When you close the Help window, you return to the Object Browser.

The Object Browser window can remain open while you are writing a procedure, and you can continue to reference it by switching back and forth between windows.

Run a VBA Procedure

To check out a new procedure, you must be able to run it. You can run an event procedure by causing the event to occur. Any procedure that does not take arguments can be run from the module window by choosing Run | Go/Continue (or click Go/Continue on the toolbar) with the cursor anywhere in the procedure. If the procedure does take arguments, the underlying object must be open in design view. General procedures stored in the Modules tab of the database window can be run from the module window.

> **Tip:** If your procedure stopped before execution was completed and the Run | Go/Continue option is dimmed, you might need to switch the underlying form to design view. The procedure will not run from the module window if the form is in form view.

You can also call a procedure from another procedure or run it from a macro by using the `RunCode` action.

Functions cannot be run like sub and general procedures from the module window. To check out a function procedure, use it in an expression in another procedure and run the procedure to see if the function gives the right return value. You can also test a function from the Debug window.

Summary

In this chapter, you became acquainted with the module window and saw how to change some of the coding and window options. Many of the options offer automatic help during code generation. The chapter also discussed the types of modules and procedures and their syntax.

Many procedures were developed demonstrating the wide variety of operations that can be accomplished with VBA procedures. Examples included displaying a message to the user, filtering records for a report, and creating a temporary welcoming screen.

Finally, the chapter briefly approached the subject of running VBA procedures, which is resumed in Chapter 10 when you explore the debugging process for VBA procedures.

10

Debugging VBA Procedures

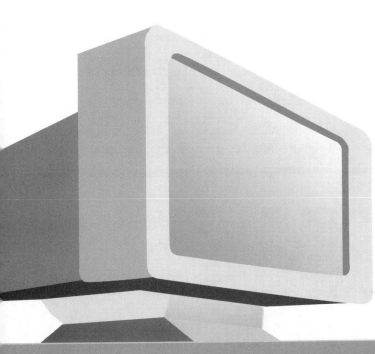

In Visual Basic for Applications, sub procedures are supposed to perform some operation, and functions are supposed to return a value. When the operation is not what you intended or the returned value is not what you expected, the debugging process begins. This chapter discusses the many tools Access provides to help you track down and correct the errors in VBA code.

With these tools, you can monitor variables and properties while code is running, move slowly through code execution, and suspend execution at specified locations in the procedure.

Types of Bugs and How to Avoid Them

According to the *Academic Press Dictionary of Science and Technology*, a bug is "an error in either the mechanics or the logic of a computer program." In an Access application, you can encounter three major types of bugs. First, *compile errors* are the result of an incorrect statement. For example, a variable might be misspelled, the End If might be missing from an If...Then...Else structure, or some required punctuation might be missing. Access automatically displays an error message when a compile error occurs unless you have cleared the Auto Syntax Check option in the Module Options dialog box.

Runtime errors occur when the program tries to execute an impossible operation such as dividing by zero, passing an invalid argument, or writing to a floppy disk that is not in place. You can expect runtime errors when you are developing new procedures, especially if they are complex. They are one more reason to keep procedures short and limited to a single operation.

Errors in *logic* cause a procedure to produce the wrong answer or not do what is expected. Procedures containing logic errors might compile and run correctly but still give incorrect results. For example, you based a case structure on the value returned from a message box and used the wrong button code. You can spot logic errors by stepping through the code one statement at a time and analyzing the results of each step.

VBA provides the tools you need to find all three types. With these debugging aids, you can execute your code one line at a time, watch the results of each step, and trace through a list of nested procedure calls.

Peter's Principle: Prevention Is Still the Best Medicine

Instead of chasing bugs after you write the procedures, it is better to avoid them, if possible. You've heard this before, but it is still good advice. Break up the program into single-purpose sub and function procedures and be generous with comments. Explicitly declare all variables to help prevent misspelled variable names that can cause compile errors. Using a naming convention that gives information about variables such as data type and what it stands for can help prevent errors caused by misunderstanding the purpose of the variable. For example, the variable strFilter cannot be mistaken for anything but a string expression to be used as a filter for a recordset.

The trick to successful debugging is to zero in on the statement where the error occurs by processing the code a piece at a time in the debug window. When you find where the program goes astray, you can work backward and locate the cause of the problem. Using the debug window, you can also insert different values in variables and properties to see the effects on the outcome.

Dealing with Compile Errors

If the Auto Syntax Check option is in force, many errors are caught as you type. Syntax errors such as failing to end a statement with the proper characters or placing two operators together with no expression between them are noticed when you press Enter to move to the next line. Access automatically corrects some simple omissions such as leaving out the closing quotation mark. If you don't want to be interrupted with syntax error alerts as you type, clear the Auto Syntax Option in the Module tab of the Options dialog box. Syntax will be checked later during compilation.

When a syntax error occurs, Access displays an error message explaining the type of error. Figure 10.1 shows the result of leaving a trailing quotation mark at the end of the statement. The offending statement is shown in red in the module window.

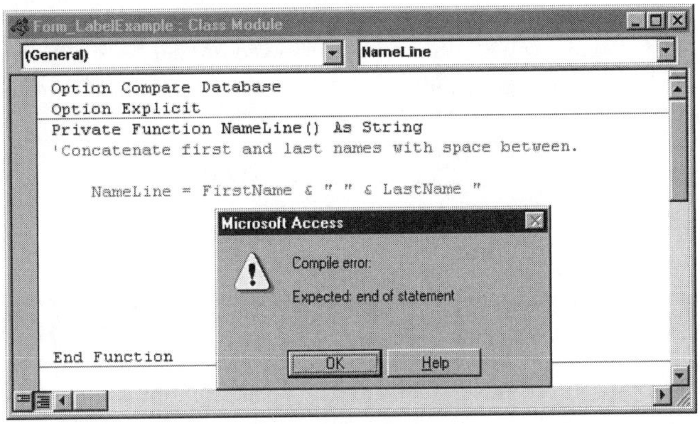

Figure 10.1.
The message box explains the compile error.

The box also contains a Help button that displays the relevant Help topic. When you click OK, you return to the module window where the mistake is highlighted in dark blue (see Figure 10.2). If the Auto Syntax Check option is cleared in the Module Option dialog box, this type of error will not be sensed while you type. It will be picked up when the procedure is compiled.

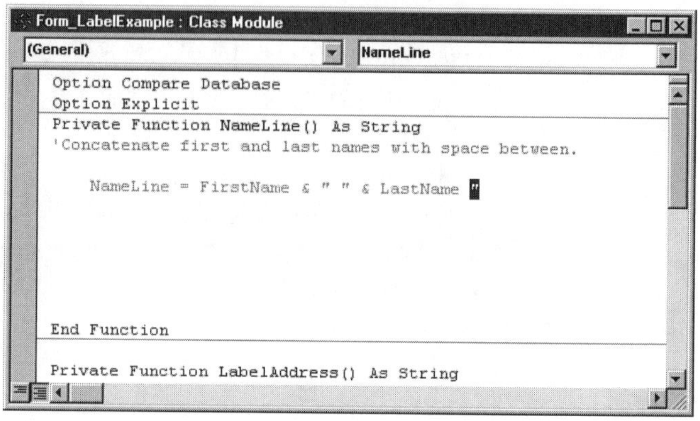

Figure 10.2.
The error is highlighted in dark blue.

```
Form_LabelExample : Class Module                        _ □ X
(General)                              NameLine
Option Compare Database
Option Explicit
Private Function NameLine() As String
'Concatenate first and last names with space between.

    NameLine = FirstName & " " & LastName ▮

End Function

Private Function LabelAddress() As String
```

During the compilation process, Access reads the entire procedure and tries to reconcile all the pieces. Does every If...Then...Else structure have an End If to match? Does every Select Case have an End Select? Is every variable declared? To compile the procedures in a module, click the Compile Loaded Modules toolbar button or choose Debug | Compile Loaded Modules. When these types of errors occur, Access displays error messages, and you can correct the code in the module window.

Note: Two additional compilation options are available on the Debug menu. The Compile All Modules option includes modules that are not currently loaded in the compilation process. Compile And Save All Modules is a new option that saves all modules in compiled form. This can save time the next time you want to run the procedures because Access does not have to compile the code before running it. Large modules can take some time to compile. Another time-saving feature is the Compile On Demand option in the Module Options dialog box. When this is checked, modules are not compiled until they are called to run by another module.

More complex errors require the assistance of the debug window, in which you find all the tools necessary to track down elusive bugs.

Touring the Debug Window

A lot of information is available in the debug window while you are running VBA code. When a module is open in the module window, click the Debug Window toolbar button or choose View | Debug Window to open the debug window. The status bar at the top of the window displays the name of the current database, the module that contains the procedure that is running, and the procedure name. If nothing is running, the status bar shows <Ready>. The window consists of three panes, only two of which are visible at a time (see Figure 10.3):

- The *immediate pane*, which is always visible, is the lower part of the window. You can run any sub or function procedure from the immediate pane and also test stand-alone expressions.

- The *locals pane* in the upper pane shows the parent object with a list of variables with their underlying expression, current value, and type. The information is updated whenever there is a break in execution.

- The *watch pane* alternates with the locals pane and lets you see the value of an expression or variable while code is running. You specify which expressions or variables you want to monitor in the watch pane.

Figure 10.3.
The debug window showing the locals and immediate panes.

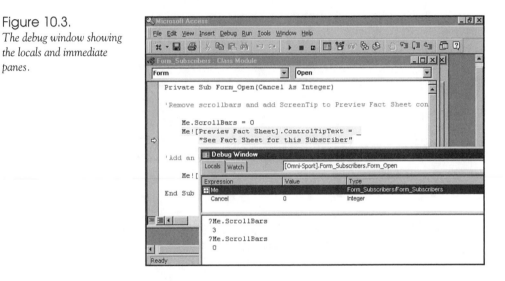

The debug window in Figure 10.3 shows the name of the active procedure in the top line: [Omni-Sport].Form_Subscribers.Form_Open. The Form_Open sub procedure from the Subscribers form class module is executing one step at a time.

One of the exercises in Chapter 5, "Examining and Modifying the Wizard's Code," added VBA statements to the Subscribers form's Form_Open procedure to include a controltip and an accelerator key in the Subscribers form design. In the module window, the current line, which sets the ControlTipText property, is highlighted in yellow and the arrow in the indicator margin also points to the current line. The highlighted line is the statement to be run next.

The locals pane shows the list of variables encountered in the procedure. The first in the list is the system-defined variable Me, which is an object reference to the current object, the Subscribers form. The plus sign to the left of the Me reference indicates that it can be expanded to show all the data members and properties in the form. If the current module is a standard module rather than a class module, the list begins with the name of the current module instead of Me.

The second variable in the list is the VBA-defined variable, `Cancel`, which is passed as an argument to the `Form_Open` sub procedure. The locals pane shows `Cancel` has a value of `0` and is an integer data type.

Typing a question mark means "`Print`" to the immediate pane. When you type an expression preceded by `?` and then press Enter, the value of the expression is displayed in the immediate pane. Also in Figure 10.3, the `?Me.ScrollBars` line was typed in when the previous line in the procedure was current and the `ScrollBars` property was still set to `3`, the value for displaying both scrollbars. After the next line was executed, the value changed to `0`, which removed the scrollbars from the form design.

You use the watch pane to keep an eye on the value of specific variables and expressions during code execution. Figure 10.4 shows the debug window with the `Me.ScrollBars = 0` line highlighted, indicating that it is the next statement to be executed. The watch pane shows that the value of the `ScrollBars` variable is still `3`. You will have a chance to try out both of these panes in the sections "Working in the Immediate Pane" and "Working in the Locals Pane" later in this chapter.

Figure 10.4.
The watch pane shows the `ScrollBars` *property is* `3`.

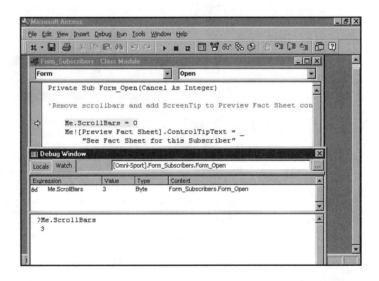

The principle difference between the locals and watch panes is that all the variables and expressions are listed in the locals pane, but only those you select are displayed in the watch pane. Also, values in the locals pane are updated when code is suspended, whereas values in the watch pane change while code is running. Limiting the elements to keep track of can speed up the code execution. You can use either pane to change the value of a variable or expression in place during a break. The locals pane empties when the procedure ends. The watch pane retains the watches you have added until you delete them.

The debug window is quite flexible. You can drag the pane separator to change the height of the immediate pane or drag the column dividers to resize the column headers in the watch and locals panes. To switch between the watch and locals pane, click the tab at the top of the debug window.

Tip: You can open the debug window any time without opening the module window first by pressing Ctrl+G.

If you have checked the module option, Debug Window On Top, you can always see what is going on during code execution. With the debug window moved to the lower right of the screen, you can easily see the important parts of the module window as well as the debug window. The debug window remains visible after the module window closes, until you close it.

Note: After a procedure has ended and the module window closes, you can still use the debug window to run another procedure in a class module. For example, type `Form_Subscribers.Form_Open` in the immediate pane and press Enter. Because the module window toolbar and menu are not visible, you cannot step through the code or set breakpoints. The procedure runs through from beginning to end.

Working in the Immediate Pane

You can do a lot in the debug window's immediate pane. The immediate pane can display the results of a single line of code, including values of controls, fields, and properties or the result of an expression. You can use the immediate pane to assign new values to variables, fields, or properties and run the procedure with the new values.

You saw earlier that typing `?`, which is the shorthand for `Print`, followed by a property displayed the property's value in the debug window. Another way to show the value in the immediate pane is to add the statement `Debug.Print Me.ScrollBars` to the code. When the code stops running, you can view the value in the immediate pane by pressing Ctrl+G.

What you ask for in the immediate pane need not be part of the form or report associated with the current module—it can be any type of expression as long as it does not refer to an object it doesn't have access to.

For example, you can use the `WeekDay()` function to find out what day of the week your birthday falls on in 1999. Open any procedure in the module window and choose View | Debug to open the debug window. Next, type the following, using the # delimiters for the date value:

```
MyDate = #January 15, 1999#
?WeekDay(MyDate)
```

Now press Enter. The immediate pane in Figure 10.5 shows that the date falls on a Friday (day number 6).

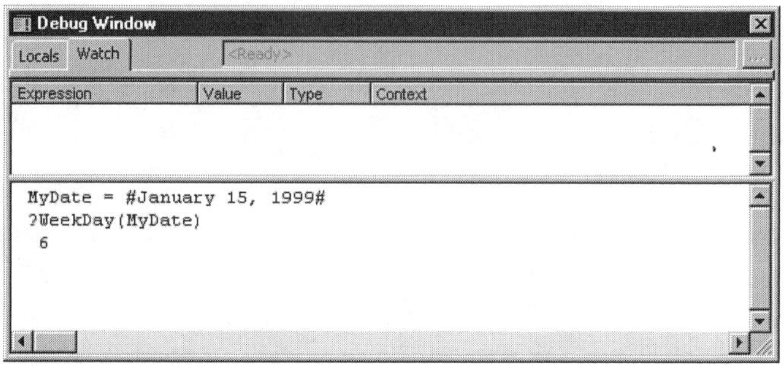

Figure 10.5.
Showing the day of the week.

The immediate pane also lets you evaluate more complicated expressions such as calculating the number of days between two dates or the price to charge for a product given the cost and the markup percentage. Figure 10.6 shows the immediate pane with the results of two such expressions.

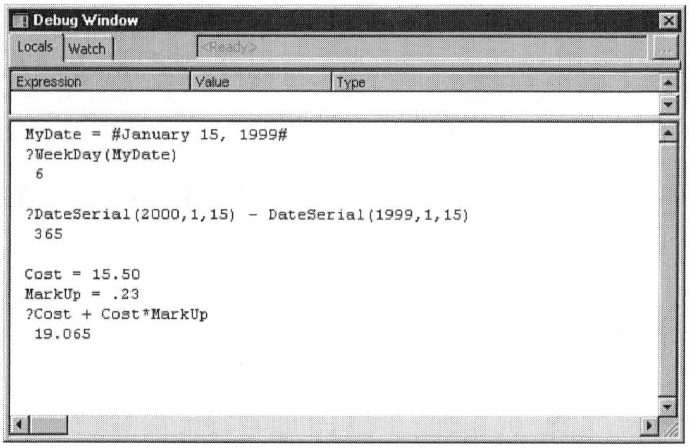

Figure 10.6.
Evaluating other expressions in the immediate pane.

To run a sub procedure from the immediate pane, type the name and the arguments, and then press Enter. For example, typing `MySub arg1, arg2, arg3` would run the sub procedure `MySub`.

When you run a sub, you do not use `?` or `Print` because subs do not return values. The procedure simply runs and then you need to examine the objects it worked on to see if it executed properly.

To execute or test a function, you use `?` or `Print` to display the returned value. For example, you can test the `IsLoaded()` function in the Global Module of the *Omni-Sport* database using the following steps:

1. Open the Subscribers form in form view, and then press Ctrl+G to open the debug window.

2. In the immediate pane of the debug window, type strFormName = "Subscribers" and press Enter.

3. On the second line, type ?IsLoaded(strFormName) and press Enter. The pane shows -1 (True), indicating that the form is loaded.

4. Type strFormName = "Get Facts" and press Enter. Then repeat the line from step 3 and press Enter. The returned value is 0 (False) this time because the Get Facts form is not loaded. Figure 10.7 shows the immediate pane with the results of the IsLoaded() function.

Figure 10.7.
Testing a function in the immediate pane.

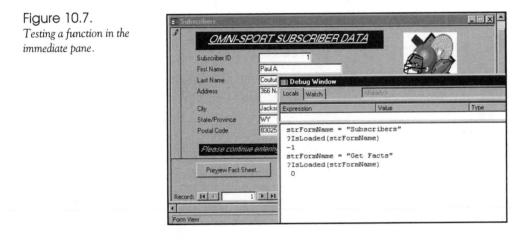

Tip: When you want to repeat a line in the immediate pane, you don't need to retype it. Simply place the insertion point anywhere in the line and press Enter. The line will execute with the latest values.

When a procedure has suspended execution, you can assign or change the values of variables and properties in the immediate pane and then continue execution. More about this in the section, "Controlling Execution."

The immediate pane keeps all the entries as you work in the debug window; the list can become quite lengthy. You can delete lines as you go along by selecting them and pressing Delete. If you keep them, you can navigate through the entire list using the standard mouse, arrow keys, Home, End, and PgUp/PgDn keys. Ctrl+PgUp moves the insertion point to the top of the list and Ctrl+PgDn moves it to the bottom.

Working in the Locals Pane

The locals pane displays a list of the variables used by the procedure. The list shows the variable expression, value, and type. The first item in the list indicates the current module: the module name for a standard module or the variable, Me, for a class module.

The values in the list are updated every time execution is suspended. The execution mode changes from run to break when you are stepping through code or when a breakpoint is encountered. In break mode, you can change the value of a variable in the list and continue execution.

Working in the Watch Pane

The watch pane list is similar to the locals list except that it includes only the variable and expressions you specify, and they are updated while code is running. The watch list also includes the context of the expression, usually the name of the procedure in which it originates. The watch pane can be more efficient during debugging because it updates only the expressions and variables you are interested in. When the watch pane is visible, the locals pane no longer updates all the expressions.

Items added to the watch pane remain there until you remove them.

As in the locals pane, you can click the plus sign next to the module reference to expand the hierarchical information and see all the variables in the module. You can also change the value of an expression or variable in place in the watch pane.

When you add a watch to the list, you can set the expression to any variable, property, function call, or other expression in the module. You can also ask Access to stop execution when the expression changes value, reaches a certain value, or when a loop has iterated a specific number of times. You learn more about specifying and adding watches in the next section.

Controlling Execution

Because errors are often embedded deep in the code, you can't always locate them after the procedure ends, whether it ends prematurely or normally. It is very helpful to be able to step through code and execute only the parts that are still causing errors. Access gives you several ways to control code execution while the code is displayed in the module window:

- Stepping through code one statement at a time
- Setting breakpoints where you want the code to stop after running part of the procedure
- Skipping over called procedures
- Skipping to the statement that contains the cursor
- Exiting the code and resetting the variables and expressions to their original values
- Moving to a specified statement when code stops

Stepping Through Code

To enter the step mode of code execution, click the Step Into toolbar button or choose Debug | Step Into, and then click Go/Continue or choose Run | Go/Continue. The first line of the current procedure is highlighted in yellow and an arrow in the left indicator margin points to the line as the next one to be executed.

When you click Go/Continue again, that statement is executed and the indicator moves to the next line. As you step through the code, the local pane displays the value of the expressions and variables that are encountered.

Figure 10.8 shows the ColorStyle form's `Colors_Click` event procedure in the module window running in step mode. When the `intBtn` input box was displayed, the value 2 was entered. The locals pane shows the `intBtn` expression with the entered value. The `Debug.Print intBtn` statement in the procedure code displays the same value in the immediate pane.

Figure 10.8.
Stepping through the
`Colors_Click` *event*
procedure.

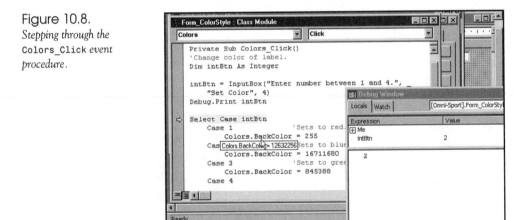

When the mouse pointer rests on the `Colors.BackColor` property, the AutoData Tip option displays the current value of the property. It still has the default color because the case statements have not yet evaluated the `intBtn` expression.

At this point, you can change the value of the `intBtn` expression by typing `intBtn = 3` in the immediate pane and pressing Enter. Figure 10.9 shows the results: the locals pane value has changed to 3 and the mouse pointer displays `intBtn = 3` when paused over the expression in the `Select Case` statement.

You could also change the `intBtn` value by selecting the value in the locals pane and typing a new value.

Stepping through the rest of the procedure moves to `Case 1` and then to `Case 2`. When `Case 3` is executed, it finds a match with `intBtn` and executes the statement that follows, which changes the background color of the Colors box in the form to green. Go/Continue then skips directly to the End Select line and then to End Sub.

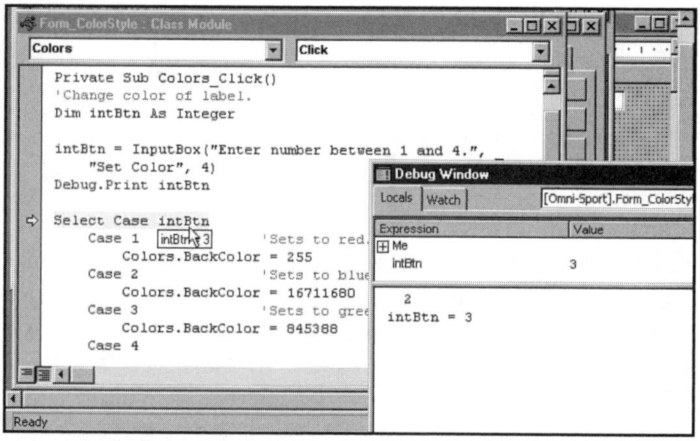

Figure 10.9.
Changing the value of an expression during step through.

Figure 10.10 shows the Debug menu with the step-through options as well as options for setting breakpoints and adding expressions to the watch pane.

Figure 10.10.
The Debug menu with options for stepping through code and adding watch expressions.

When a procedure calls another procedure, Step Into moves into the called procedure and steps through it line by line as well. If you know that the called procedure is already bug free, use Step Over to run the whole procedure as a unit and return to the next statement in the calling procedure.

For example, you are stepping through Proc A and reach a statement that calls Proc B. You don't want to step through Proc B, so you click Step Over. Proc B runs and when finished, the next statement in Proc A is highlighted and ready to execute.

If you want to run the rest of the current procedure and return quickly to the next line in the procedure that called this one, use Step Back. If this procedure was not called by another, it runs to the end. If the current procedure calls others, they too are run before returning to the calling procedure.

When you want to skip over part of a procedure that is already checked out, you can use the Run To Cursor option. Place the cursor in the statement where you want processing to stop, and then choose Debug | Run To Cursor or click the right mouse button and choose Run To Cursor from the shortcut menu.

Two other options are available on the Debug menu that let you skip over parts of the code or even back up and run a segment again: Set Next Statement and Show Next Statement. Place the insertion point in the statement you want to run next, and choose Debug | Set Next Statement. The yellow highlight and indicator move to the line containing the cursor. The Show Next Statement option moves to the statement that will be executed after the current one. These two options are not available unless the execution was stopped by a breakpoint or a Stop statement. These two options are also available in the module window shortcut menu.

> **Tip:** If fixing a bug requires moving a block of code from one place to another in a procedure, select the statements and press Ctrl+X, which places the code on the Clipboard. Then, move to where you want the code and press Ctrl+V to paste it in place.

Setting Breakpoints

A breakpoint suspends execution and leaves the procedure still running, but just in idle state. Everything stands still; the variables and properties keep the same values. When execution is suspended, the debug window becomes active.

To pause execution, do one of the following:

- Set a breakpoint at a line
- Add a Stop statement to the code
- Press Ctrl+Break

A *breakpoint* is a statement that you have marked as a stopping place for VBA. Setting a breakpoint couldn't be easier. Simply click in the indicator margin next to the line you want to mark as the breakpoint—the next statement to be executed. The line changes color to bold white text on a dark-red background and a dark-red dot appears in the margin (see Figure 10.11). If you have set another color combination in the Module Options dialog box, this will show instead.

Clicking the Toggle Breakpoint toolbar button and choosing Debug | Toggle Breakpoint also set and clear breakpoints at the line that contains the insertion point. You can have as many breakpoints in a procedure as you want.

Figure 10.11.
*Two lines are set as
breakpoints.*

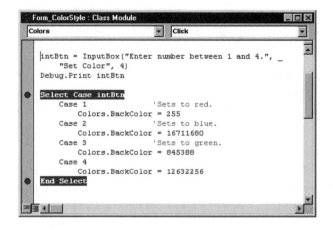

When the breakpoint line is reached, execution is suspended and you can take a look in the debug window to see the current expression values. If the error has not yet occurred, it might be caused by the breakpoint line, which is the next one to be executed. When you reach a breakpoint, you can continue stepping through the code with Step Into until you find the problem.

Breakpoints are automatically removed when you close the module; however, to remove them while the module is still open, choose Toggle Breakpoint or Debug | Remove All Breakpoints.

Another way to suspend code execution is to insert a Stop statement in the procedure just before the line where you want to stop. A Stop statement works like a breakpoint except that it stays in the code until you remove it. Breakpoints need to be reset when you start the procedures again, but Stop keeps the stopping point throughout a long debug process. The only problem is remembering to remove all the Stop statements when debugging is over.

Warning: Be careful about setting breakpoints in event procedures, especially mouse and key event procedures. For example, if you stop execution in a Mouse Down procedure and then resume, Access thinks the mouse button is still down. You must press the mouse button down before the Mouse Up event occurs, but pressing the mouse button down executes the mouse down event procedure again. Mouse_Up might never occur. It is safer to use Debug.Print to test for the values in such event procedures.

When you decide to stop running the procedure, you can use End or Reset. Clicking End on the toolbar or in an error dialog box stops code execution and leaves the module-level variables with their current values. End is also available on the Run menu. If you want to restore the module-level variables to their original values, click Reset on the toolbar or choose Run | Reset.

Watching Results

Instead of showing the changing values of all the variables and expressions in the locals pane, the watch pane is a more efficient tool for monitoring just the expressions of interest. By specifying one or more expressions to watch, their values are continuously displayed in the watch pane. Another alternative is Quick Watch, which gives you a snapshot of the current value of a single selected expression.

Setting a watch on an expression involves three specifications: what expression to monitor, when to monitor it, and how Access is to respond to the expression. All of these are set in the Add Watch dialog box.

To add an expression to the watch pane of the debug window, choose Debug | Add Watch to open the Add Watch dialog box (see Figure 10.12). If the insertion point is already in an expression in the module window, the expression appears in the dialog box; otherwise, type the expression in the Add Watch dialog box. You can watch a variable, property, function call, or any other valid expression. Add Watch is also available on the debug window shortcut menu and on the module window shortcut menu when code is suspended.

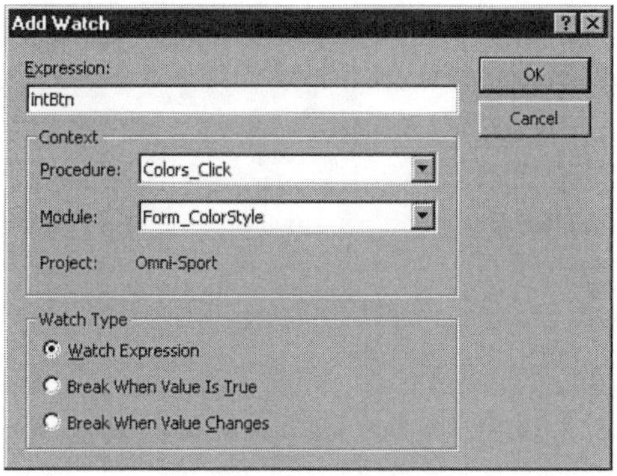

Figure 10.12.
Add an expression to the watch pane.

The Context entries in the Add Watch dialog box define the range over which to monitor the expression. By default, the context is the procedure and module in which the expression occurs. Setting the scope as narrow as possible is more efficient than setting the context to all modules in the current project. The Procedure pull-down menu lists all the procedures in the current module, and the Module pull-down menu lists all the modules in the current database.

The Watch Type option group gives you a choice of what to do with the expression. The first option, Watch Expression, is the default, which displays the value in the watch pane continuously while code is running. If you want to stop execution when the watch expression evaluates to True, choose Break When Value Is True. The third option, Break When Value Changes, suspends execution when the watch expression value changes.

Tip: If you want to add another watch expression to the list in the watch pane, select it in the module window and drag it to the watch pane. This adds the watch expression using the default context and watch type options.

Figure 10.13 shows the watch pane with the variable intBtn as the watch expression in three watch types, each indicated by a different icon. The first is the default watch expression, the second is Break When Value Is True, and the third is Break When Value Changes. The code has executed to the point where 2 was entered in the input box that requested the variable to be used in the Select Case structure.

Figure 10.13.
Watching the intBtn *variable.*

```
Form_ColorStyle : Class Module                          _ □ ×

Colors                        ▼    Click                       ▼

    Option Compare Database
    Option Explicit

    Private Sub Colors_Click()
    'Change color of label.
    Dim intBtn As Integer

    intBtn = InputBox("Enter number between 1 and 4.", _
        "Set Color", 4)
```

```
Debug Window                                                  ×

Locals  Watch          [Omni-Sport].Form_ColorStyle.Colors_Click   ...

Expression          Value      Type      Context
66  intBtn          2          Integer   Form_ColorStyle.Colors_Click
    intBtn          2          Integer   Form_ColorStyle.Colors_Click
    intBtn          2          Integer   Form_ColorStyle.Colors_Click


    2
```

To edit a watch expression, select the expression in the watch pane list and choose Debug | Edit Watch or choose Edit Watch from the shortcut menu. The Edit Watch dialog box is the same as the Add Watch dialog box, except that it also has a Delete button. Change the watch type of context and then choose OK. To delete the watch expression, choose Delete in the Edit Watch dialog box or choose Delete Watch from the shortcut menu.

If you just want a temporary look at an expression, use the Quick Watch feature. After selecting the variable or expression in the module window, choose Debug | Quick Watch or click the Quick Watch toolbar button. The Quick Watch dialog box opens, showing the context and value of the watch expression (see Figure 10.14). If you want to add the expression to the watch pane now, choose Add in the Quick Watch dialog box.

If the procedure that contains the expression is not running, the context and expression boxes show the proper entries, but the value shows <Out of context>.

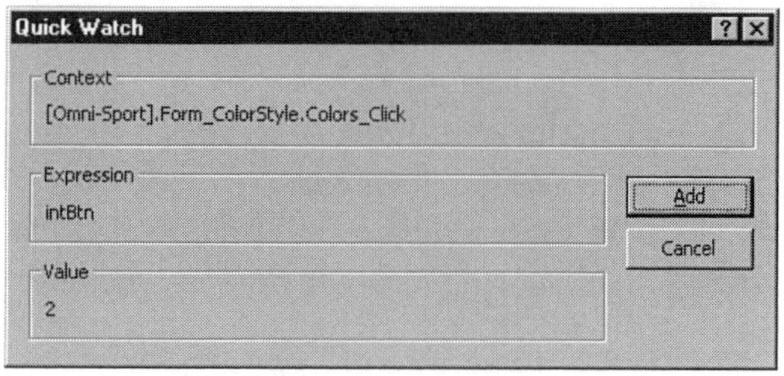

Figure 10.14.
Quick Watch gives you a
snapshot of the expression.

Access provides many shortcut keys to maneuver around the module and debug windows to accomplish debugging tasks. Table 10.1 describes some of them.

Table 10.1. Shortcut keys used during testing and debugging.

Press This:	To Do This:
F2	Display the Object Browser
Ctrl+Down arrow	Display the next procedure in the module
Ctrl+Up arrow	Display the previous procedure
F1	Display context-sensitive help about a keyword
Ctrl+J	List properties and methods
Ctrl+Shift+J	List constants
Ctrl+I	Display Quick Info
Ctrl+Shift+I	Display Parameter Info
Ctrl+Spacebar	Complete the VBA keyword
Ctrl+G	Open the debug window
F8	Step into a procedure (single step)
Shift+F8	Step over a procedure
Ctrl+Shift+F8	Step out of a procedure
Ctrl+F8	Run code to the cursor
Shift+F9	Show Quick Watch for selected expression
F9	Toggle breakpoint at selected line
Ctrl+Shift+F9	Clear all breakpoints
Ctrl+Break	Suspend code execution
F5	Continue code execution
Shift+F5	Reset execution

Warning: If you have assigned a set of actions to one of these key combinations, they will replace the actions shown in Table 10.1, and you might get some unexpected results when you try to use them during debugging. Try always to use key combinations that Access hasn't reserved for a special purpose.

Tracing Procedure Calls

When the module contains several procedures, some of which call upon others to perform operations, the calling procedure and all those it has called are active at the same time. To see the currently active nested procedures, use the Call Stack feature. *Stack* is a term used in programming to indicate a first-in-first-out list in which the top item in the list is the most recently added item and the first to be removed from the list.

The Call Stack dialog box helps to trace how an application runs through a series of procedures. To see the list of procedure calls, suspend code execution and do one of the following:

- Click the Call Stack toolbar button
- Choose View | Call Stack
- Click Build in the debug window status bar at the top of the window

Figure 10.15 shows the Call Stack dialog box after the Omni-Sport Switchboard form class module was suspended with Ctrl+Break. It shows the names of the database, module, and procedures. The first procedure to execute was the `Form_Switchboard.Form_Open` event procedure, followed by some non-BASIC code and the `Form_Current` event procedure. The procedure that was interrupted is the `Switchboard.FillOptions` sub procedure. The non-BASIC code contains the instructions that set the filter during the `Form_Open` procedure.

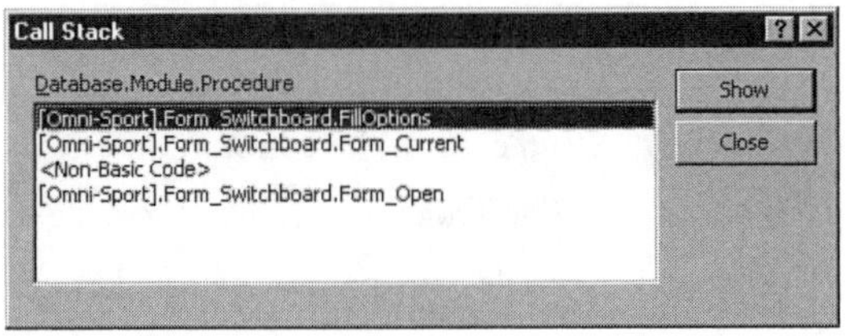

Figure 10.15.
Use Call Stack to see nested procedure calls.

Call Stack	? ✕
Database.Module.Procedure	
[Omni-Sport].Form_Switchboard.FillOptions	Show
[Omni-Sport].Form_Switchboard.Form_Current	Close
<Non-Basic Code>	
[Omni-Sport].Form_Switchboard.Form_Open	

If you want to see the statement that called one of the procedures in the list, select the procedure below it in the list and choose Show. The module window shows the calling procedure with an indicator pointing to the calling statement, `FillOptions` (see Figure 10.16).

Figure 10.16.
Choose Show to see the calling statement.

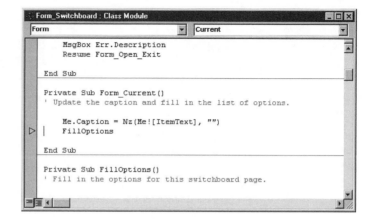

If you choose Show with the current procedure selected in the Call Stack dialog box, the statement that was current when the code was suspended is highlighted in the module window.

Getting Help

In addition to the help offered by the Help menu and the Office Assistant, the error message dialog boxes include a button that opens a Help topic that explains the error that has occurred. While in the module window, you can get help with a specific method, function, property, object, or statement by clicking the keyword and pressing F1.

If you are having trouble with a specific VBA object, method, property, or constant, the Object Browser might be able to help. Click the keyword and choose View | Definition or choose Definition from the shortcut menu. The Object Browser opens, showing the definition of the selected keyword. Figure 10.17 shows the Object Browser with the definition of the acForm constant, which was selected in the module window.

To open the Object Browser for general use, click the Object Browser toolbar button, choose View | Object Browser, or choose Object Browser from the shortcut menu.

Sometimes it is necessary to backtrack through the sequence of breakpoints and other stopping places in the database modules. The Last Position option on the module window shortcut menu moves to the last statement where the cursor stopped in any module and procedure in the current database. If the module was closed, it is reopened and the cursor appears at the line that stopped the code execution. Repeatedly choosing Last Position retraces your steps through the entire session in the module window.

Figure 10.17.
The Object Browser displays the definition of the selected keyword.

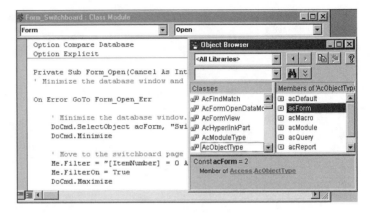

Handling Runtime Errors

Runtime errors are errors that Access can detect only when running the application. They can happen during the debug phase of development or after the application has reached the hands of the end user. Runtime errors occur in macros as well, but you can't trap errors in macros because macro errors do not have key code numbers like VBA runtime errors. This is another good reason to use VBA procedures in an application.

Error handling is a process of anticipating errors and adding code that will execute when an error occurs. This may be no more than displaying the default VBA message and branching to an Exit or End statement, or it might identify specific errors by code number and display custom messages. The Access wizards always include error handling in their event procedures.

During Debugging

Runtime errors that occur during debugging are not as much a concern as those that appear after the application has been completed. The error message is usually clear enough for a developer to understand. Such errors happen when you have misspelled a field name or referenced a nonexisting property. If you have misspelled a variable, the error is caught during compilation. Figure 10.18 shows an example of a runtime error occurring as a result of misspelling the TryMe command button name in the Form_Load event procedure for the RunTimeBug form.

The error message box offers the choices of Debug, End, and Help. Choosing Debug returns to the module window with the faulty statement highlighted in yellow. Choosing End stops code execution and the module window remains active (if that's where you ran the procedure). If you choose End and close the form, the runtime error message reoccurs the next time you try to load the same form.

After you correct the error, you might have to reset the code before you run it again.

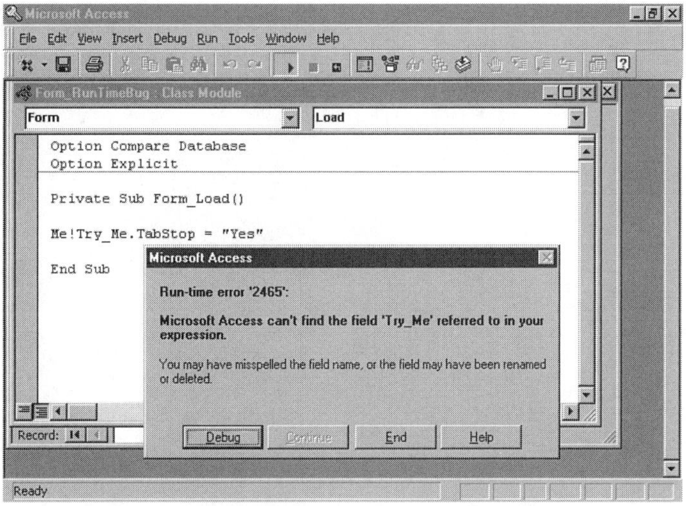

Figure 10.18.
*A runtime error occurs
during debugging.*

> **Note:** While you are in the debug phase, make sure you have checked the Allow Viewing
> Code After Error option in the Startup dialog box. This enables you to press Ctrl+Break to
> stop execution and to look at the VBA code after a runtime error has occurred. If the
> option is cleared, you can still view the code by pressing Ctrl+Break if the Allow Special
> Keys option is selected. Both of these options are in the Advanced expansion of the
> Startup dialog box.

Access 97 has some new error-trapping options for handling runtime errors in your VBA code. They
let you decide how to enter the break mode when an error occurs in the procedure. The Error Trapping options have moved from the Module tab to the Advanced tab of the Options dialog box. You
have three choices (see Figure 10.19):

- Break on All Errors does just what it says—it breaks on all handled and unhandled errors in
  all modules: class or standard. The module that contains the error appears in the debug
  window with the offending line highlighted.

- Break in Class Module is useful for debugging class modules. This option breaks on all
  unhandled errors in both class and standard modules. If the error is in a class module, the
  module becomes active in the debug window and the line with the error is highlighted.

- Break on Unhandled Errors breaks on unhandled errors in a standard module. If the error is
  in a class module, VBA breaks on the line that called the class module containing the error
  rather than on the line in the class module that contains the error.

Figure 10.19.
*Set error trapping options in
the advanced Options dialog
box.*

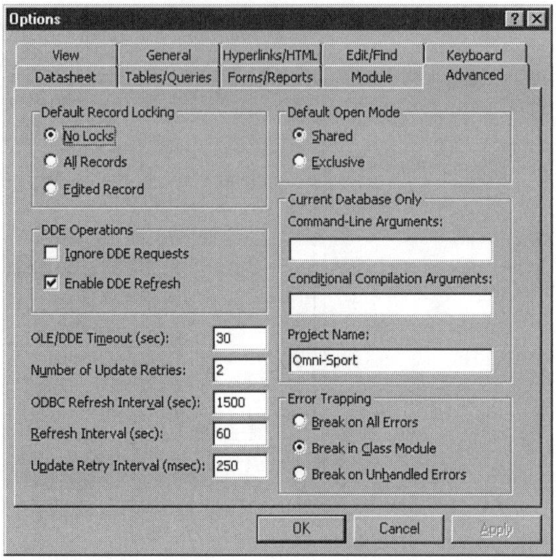

Sometimes it is necessary to simulate a runtime error to check out the error-handling code. The `Raise` method can simulate any VBA or user-defined error. For example, the following line of code would generate the error caused by a type mismatch:

```
Err.Raise Number:=13    'Simulates "Type mismatch" runtime error.
```

The method also takes optional named arguments that specify the object or application that generated the error, an expression describing the error, a path to where help for the error can be found, and the Help topic related to the reason for the error rather than the error message.

For the User

The messages that appear when runtime errors occur might be clear to the developer, but the user might be confused by some of the messages. Replacing them with more meaningful messages and appropriate courses of action often helps the application run more smoothly in its intended environment. You obviously cannot foresee all possible errors, but you can anticipate a few likely ones and provide for them. Unexpected errors can also route to general-purpose error-handling code.

Errors in VBA and DAO are objects in themselves and have properties just like any other object. The VBA `Err` object holds information about one error at a time. Two of the properties of interest to error handlers are the error number and description. You can use these properties to determine what kind of error has occurred.

An error involving a data access operation (DAO) results in the creation of an `Error` object and an `Errors` collection. `Error` objects also have number and description properties. The number and description properties of the first `Error` object in the `Errors` collection should match the number and description of the VBA `Err` object.

Error handling is a four-step process:

1. When an error occurs, route processing to the error handler.
2. Find out what kind of error occurred.
3. Branch to the appropriate error-handling operation.
4. Resume or exit the procedure.

Routing After an Error

The `On Error` statement enables error-handling code and specifies the location of the routine. You can also use `On Error` to disable error handling during debugging. You can place the `On Error` statement anywhere in the procedure, but you should insert it before any statement that could cause an error. The statement syntax is as follows:

```
On Error GoTo label
```

> **Note:** The error-handling code marked by a line label or number is not a separate function or sub procedure. It is a block of code within a procedure.

The label argument is required and can be a line label such as `ErrHandler:` or a line number. The line must be in the current procedure or you will get a compile error. When an error occurs, execution branches to the line that marks the beginning of the error handler. For example, the following statements branch to the line labeled `ErrHandler:`.

```
Sub Procedure PossibleError()
'Enable error handler.
On Error GoTo ErrHandler
'Code that may cause a runtime error.
.
.
ErrHandler:
'Code to handle errors.
.
.
End Sub
```

Two other versions of the `On Error` statement disable error handling or ignore the error entirely:

- `On Error GoTo 0` disables error handling, which is helpful during development because code execution suspends at the statement that caused the error instead of branching to the error handler. `On Error GoTo 0` also clears the number and description properties of the `Err` object.

- `On Error Resume Next` ignores the error and executes the statement following the one that caused the error. This can be helpful if you want to check the properties of the error object and respond to the error right in the code.

At the end of the error-handling routine, the optional `Resume` statement sends execution back to the main part of the procedure. Use `Resume` if you want to specify where to continue execution. You have three choices with the `Resume` statement:

- `Resume` or `Resume 0`—Branches back to the statement that caused the error.
- `Resume Next`—Branches back to the statement following the line that caused the error.
- `Resume label`—Branches to a specific line in the procedure.

`Resume` and `Resume 0` are handy when the user responds incorrectly to a request for information, such as entering a table or query name. The error handler can display instructions to reenter the value and then branch back to the statement that requested the entry in the first place.

`Resume Next` is used when the error handler can correct the error and continue with the procedure instead of repeating the statement that caused the error.

`Resume label` is used when you want to branch to another location in the procedure (often an `Exit Sub` or `Exit Function` routine).

Identifying and Dealing with the Error

It is the job of the error-handling code to find out what error occurred and to execute the code specified for that error. Several language elements are used in error identification, including the `Err` VBA object, the DAO `Error` object and `Errors` collection, and the `Error` event. The elements you use depend on what kind of errors you expect to occur in the procedure. You might need to use different elements in different parts of an application.

After a VBA error occurs, the `Err` object contains the error code number, which you can examine to find out which error occurred. Only a few of the hundreds of VBA errors can be expected to occur as a result of user interaction or a system situation. Determine which are most likely to occur and include code to intercept them. The rest can be treated as a group in the error-handler code and can fall back on the default error messages.

The following code demonstrates how to use the `Err` object to respond to a `Disk Not Ready` error (VBA error number 71). First, declare a constant and set it to the anticipated error number; then test for that number in the error-handling code. If that is the error that occurred, a custom message is displayed in a message box. Then, execution is returned with `Resume` to the line that caused the error where the user again has the opportunity to save the file to disk. If a different error occurred, the `Else` statement displays a message with the error number and description. Then, `Resume Next` branches to the statement that follows the one that caused the error. Here's the code:

```
Sub Procedure PossibleError()
'Declare constant as an anticipated error.
Const conDiskUnready As Integer = 71
'Enable error handler.
On Error GoTo ErrHandler
'Code that may cause a runtime error.
.
.
.
ErrHandler:
'Check Err object property.
    If Err = conDiskUnready Then
        MsgBox "Be sure a disk is in the drive and the door closed."
        Resume
    Else
'Display error number and description.
        MsgBox "Error number " & Err.Number & ": " & Err.Description
        Resume Next
    End If
End Sub
```

You can also use a Select Case structure to branch to different error-handling code by first declaring a series of constants as specific error numbers. Then, use the constant names as case expressions.

DAO errors that happen while dealing with data access objects, such as table and query definitions, often occur in a group forming a collection. When a DAO error occurs, the VBA Err object contains the number and description of the first DAO error. The same error recognition and trapping routine that relies on the Err properties can be used here.

You can also use the Error event to trap errors that occur in form or report class modules by attaching an event procedure to the object's On Error property. The Error event procedure requires the DataErr argument, which is the integer number of the error that occurred. The VBA Err object does not contain the error number after the Error event occurs. The Error event is maintained for backward compatibility with earlier versions of Access.

Exiting the Procedure

Any procedure that contains an error-handling routine should also have an Exit routine that exits the procedure before reaching the error handler. Placing the Exit routine before the error-handling routine does not upset the procedure flow and guarantees that the error-handling routine will not be executed unless an error occurs. If an error occurs, the error handler can branch to the Exit routine upon completion to end execution.

The structure of a typical procedure that includes error handling looks like this:

```
Sub Procedure PossibleError()
'Enable error handler.
On Error GoTo ErrHandler
.       'Code that may cause a runtime error.
.
.
Exit_PossibleError:
```

```
    Exit Sub
ErrHandler:
'Code to handle errors.
.
.
.
Resume Exit_PossibleError
End Sub
```

Runtime Errors in Nested Procedures

In an application that includes nested procedures, an error can occur in any one of them. If the procedure containing the error has no error-handling routine, VBA looks back up the chain for the nearest error handler. When it finds one, the error is passed to that error handler for processing. If no handler exists in any of the procedures, execution stops and the default error message is displayed.

When the procedure can't handle the error that occurred, you can use the `Raise` method to regenerate the error and look back through the calls list for a procedure that can. First, save the error number as an integer variable, such as `intErr`, and clear the `Err` number property with `Err.Clear`. Then, regenerate the runtime error with the following statement:

```
Err.Raise Number:=intErr.
```

Conditional Compilation

Conditional compilation is a method of including or excluding blocks of code in the final product. For example, suppose an application contains debugging procedures that you don't want to remove and yet don't want to include in the delivered application. A conditional compilation could skip the debugging code and compile the rest. Perhaps you are preparing an application for delivery to another country that uses different date and currency formats. You could write two separate procedures for each operation that displays these values and compile one or the other, selectively.

First, declare the conditional compiler constant, `#Const`, in the module that contains the blocks of code; then embed the code segments in the conditional compilation directive. The directive looks much like the normal `If...Then...Else` structure, except that each statement is preceded by a pound sign (`#`). A sub procedure that contains debugging routines can be conditionally compiled with the following directive:

```
Sub condComp()
#Const conDebug = True
#If conDebug Then
.           'debug statements
.
.
.
#Else
```

```
.           'other statements
.
.
.
#End If
```

The first expression must evaluate to `True` or `False`. Additional `If` statements can be nested within the first when there are more than two conditions to consider. The compiler compiles the blocks of code based on the value of the declared `#Const` constant. The code excluded by the conditional compilation is omitted from the executable file.

> **Note:** Unlike the usual `If...Then...Else` structure, which you can combine on one line of code separated by colons, conditional compilation directives must all appear on separate lines.

Another way to specify the conditional compilation constant is with the Advanced Options dialog box. In the Current Data Base Only group, enter the arguments in the Conditional Compilation Arguments box. If you have more than one, separate them with colons as follows:

```
conDebug = True: conMgmt = False.
```

Here, the `#Const` directive is implied. Conditional compilation can also be used to compile an application for different platforms. For example, suppose the application is developed on a 32-bit platform but must run on a 16-bit platform, or vice versa.

Summary

This chapter has been devoted to finding and trapping errors during code generation, compilation, debugging, and running. It examined the three panes that make up the debug window and the ways each one can help create error-free VBA code. The features include monitoring and changing the values of variables and expressions in the locals or watch pane. In addition, you can control execution during debugging by stepping through code and setting breakpoints to suspend execution at critical points.

A later section in this chapter addressed the problem of trapping runtime errors in an application so that error messages can be more informative to the user. Finally, the chapter discussed the process of conditional compiling code to exclude segments from the final product.

The next chapter introduces you to a retail pet store application of Access, which includes all the data and processes required for day-to-day operation of the store, inventory management, and long-range strategic planning for expansion and improvement of customer services.

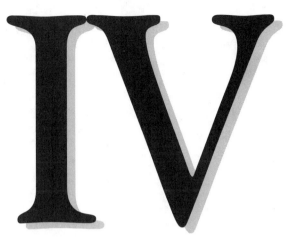

IV

Developing a Multiple- Table Application

11

Creating an Application from an Existing Database

This chapter examines the current information management system in place at Pat's Pets, a suburban retail pet supply store, and preparing it for upgrading to a more sophisticated and automatic system. Their current system is predominantly manual with only a single table maintained in a small computer. The importance of involving the user in design decisions is emphasized in this chapter.

The first part of this chapter focuses on the development aspects of database applications. Even if development is not your responsibility, it is essential that you have a clear picture of how development and programming work together to optimize the usefulness of the application. This is especially true when you are converting from a manual database management system to an advanced technology such as Access.

Analyzing the Existing System

The first thing to consider when you are designing a new database system is to think of all the ways the user wants to use the information and to describe all the products of the system. Determine what kinds of reports can be used and how the information should be filtered, grouped, and summarized. The user interface, usually a data entry and viewing form, must be carefully thought out with the end user in mind. A beginning user needs more help in the form of screentips, help messages, and error trapping. A more advanced user might not need a very sophisticated environment but still requires a smoothly running data management system.

Rarely does a developer get the opportunity to start from scratch to design an information management system. The organization usually has a semi-automated system in place and wants to upgrade. Human nature puts limits on the amount of change a user will tolerate. They are reluctant to accept drastic changes in their method of operating. It is essential to take the existing procedures into consideration when you are designing a new system so that it can evolve smoothly. Unless the current operation is completely at odds with a more automated system, it is best to try to absorb at least the general procedures into the new system.

This chapter, together with the next three chapters, focuses on Pat's Pets, a suburban retail store in Southern California that deals in supplies as well as food and services for dogs, cats, fish, birds, and small animals. The customer base is growing rapidly, and the product lines are also expanding to the point where the current data-handling system is inadequate.

The manager-owner of Pat's Pets feels that her business would improve if the store's information management system were more automated. Fewer mistakes in product ordering and pricing would be made, better customer relations could be maintained, and less time would be spent digging through files in search of a specific piece of information. In addition, if historical sales data were organized and stored, she could examine trends in seasonal sales and product popularity. Expansion possibilities into the surrounding growing community could also be tested against the historical data.

Current Operations

In the current system at Pat's Pets, the only table that is maintained is the inventory list of products. This is updated weekly from the sales receipts, at which time the list is examined for products whose stock level has reached a point where they should be reordered. All sales figures are accumulated at the cash register.

The Products table includes the following information (see Figure 11.1):

Note: Although Figure 11.1 shows the product information as an Access table, the store data is not yet computerized.

- Product ID—The store's unique number for this product.
- Description—A text field that describes the product.
- Main Supplier Name—A text field that shows the name of the principal supplier of the product.
- Supplier2 Name—A text field that shows the name of the backup supplier of the product.
- Unit Cost—A currency field showing the cost of the item, not including shipping and handling. It is updated only when the supplier changes prices.
- Sell Price—A currency field containing the current selling price of the product. It is updated when the cost is changed or when a promotional sale is planned.
- In Stock—A number field that shows the actual count of items in stock. It must be updated regularly.
- Re-order—A number field that shows the level at which the product should be reordered. This amount can change depending on demand.

On a daily or weekly basis, store clerks update the Products inventory list by subtracting items that were sold or damaged in the store during the period. At the same time, shipping invoices showing items received are used to add quantities to the In Stock field. Any new products are added to the list, and products that have been dropped are removed. The inventory list provides a relatively current status of the store but keeps no records of past performance of individual products or product categories.

Quarterly, or more often if necessary, the inventory list is compared with the actual quantity of each item in the store, either on display or in the storage area.

Figure 11.1.

The Pat's Pets Products list.

Product ID	Description	Main Supplier Name	Supplier2 Name	Unit Cost	Sell Price	In Stock	Re-order
1000	Cage cover, bird	T. M. Cages	Kal Pets, Inc.	$6.30	$9.95	6	4
1001	16 oz dog dish	Pet Supply Whse.	J&J Breeders	$2.60	$7.00	12	5
1002	Hamster vitamins	West Coast Whse.	Kal Pets, Inc	$2.00	$3.00	8	5
1003	Mealworms (50)	West Coast Whse.	Kal Pets, Inc	$1.00	$5.00	10	8
1004	6 oz scratch-card	T. M. Cages	Kal Pets, Inc	$1.75	$2.50	8	8
1005	Goldfish	Gull Wing Ranch	Aquatic Foods	$0.30	$0.75	79	60
1006	Flea comb	Kal Pets, Inc	West Coast Whse.	$2.59	$7.69	7	5
1007	Lovebirds	T. M. Cages	Kal Pets, Inc	$15.00	$45.00	2	6
1008	Nail clippers	Kal Pets, Inc	West Coast Whse.	$3.75	$7.00	10	5
1009	Kitty tease	Kal Pets, Inc	West Coast Whse.	$2.50	$6.00	3	10
1010	Flea and tick dip	Pet Supply Whse.	J&J Breeders	$6.16	$15.49	12	4
1011	Mouse house	T. M. Cages	Kal Pets, Inc	$2.00	$4.50	1	2
1012	Spiral stake, 16"	Pet Supply Whse.	J&J Breeders	$4.50	$10.00	1	2

Record: 1 of 31

Unique product identifier. Primary key and link to Transaction table.

Periodically, the store manager scans the products list and notes products that have fallen below the desired restocking level and makes a note to place an order for the products. If several orders are to be placed with the same supplier, she might look for other products whose in-stock level is close to the reorder level. Ordering these at the same time might save shipping costs. Orders are prepared manually either on the supplier's or the Pat's Pets order form. The addresses and telephone numbers of the suppliers are kept in a card file.

All data entry is now done in the single Products table while displayed in datasheet view. Currently, there are no data validation criteria to help prevent errors from entering the database, other than not allowing duplicate Product ID values.

Investigating Improvements

To provide complete sales and inventory management, additional tables must be defined and related to one another. For example, a transaction table that keeps track of all the transactions as they occur should be added. This table will become the focal point of the new system and will be related to the products table by the unique product identifier. If the new system included automated point-of-sale registers linked to the inventory control system, the transaction data would not need to be manually entered. In the Pat's Pets example, this is not the case.

In addition to the transactions table, a supplier table could contain the name, address, telephone numbers, and a personal contact name for each of the suppliers. The supplier table would relate to the product table with a unique supplier ID. A separate table containing the definition of the product category would eliminate the need to repeat the full category term in every product and transaction record.

A new table containing customer information would be nearly stand-alone except for the category of products they are interested in. Additional tables could be included to manage employee information, but such data will not be included in this case study.

The heart of any application is the user interface, which must be easy to use and as nearly foolproof as possible. Many of the users are employees who have little or no experience with computer systems. The system must be so simple to use that the training period will be brief. The data entry form that is central to this inventory control application is the transaction log, which is updated every day. The form must be armed with data validation features in the background and clearly marked interactive tools, informative messages, and custom Help in the foreground.

Figure 11.2 shows a typical data entry form. The five fields within the rectangle at the top of the form are entered by the user. Much of the information below that is acquired from related tables. The form can be used for sales, purchases, and shrinkage.

Figure 11.2.
The Transaction data entry form.

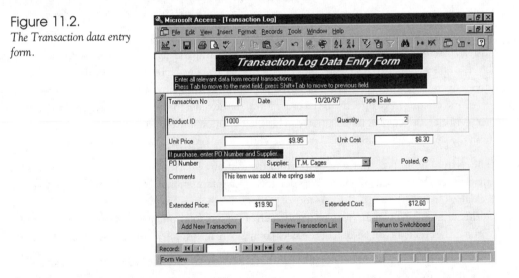

Lookup forms are also essential to a good application. What good is it to store data if you can't get it back as useful information? Some helpful lookup forms could display all the products from a particular supplier, all customers who have dogs or raise tropical fish, or all the stocked items in a specific product category. Figure 11.3 shows a lookup form that lists all the products currently acquired from one supplier. This form is actually a form with a subform.

The physical inventory process would go much faster if the product list included the item's display location in the store and in storage. The list could then be sorted by location, printed, and carried around the store to verify the current inventory level.

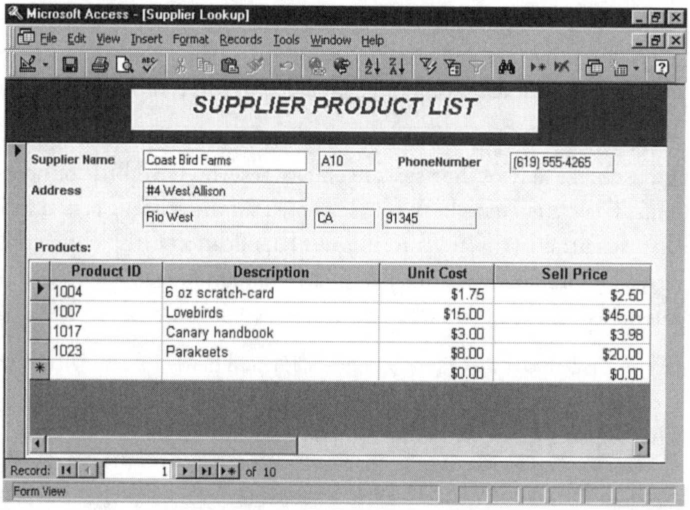

Figure 11.3.
*A lookup form showing
products from one supplier.*

Instead of scrolling through the products table and comparing the quantity in stock with the reorder level, a query could extract the records for items that need to be reordered. If this is vital to the store's operation, a prompt can be displayed at startup showing how many items need to be reordered and offering to go directly to the order form. In the order form, after the user enters the product identifier, the supplier information can be filled in automatically and a list of the other products from the same supplier can be displayed for adding to the order list, as desired.

The variety of reports that can be printed from an application is limited only by the user's imagination. Many useful reports can be designed with information from one or more tables, such as a catalog report with each major category of products beginning on a new page. The products can be further arranged in columns by subcategory such as pet, pet food, and pet supplies. A catalog listing without the cost data can be kept at the sales counter where customers can look up items of interest.

Another useful report would be a supplier list that relates products to their suppliers (see Figure 11.4). This information would also be online in a form, but the printed report is also helpful. A report listing the products that need to be ordered complete with the supplier name and telephone number could also be printed for reference when placing orders.

Figure 11.4.
A report listing suppliers and their products.

SUPPLIER PRODUCT LIST

Supplier Name   Coast Bird Farms   A10   **PhoneNumber**   (619) 555-4265

Address   #4 West Allison

                    Rio West   CA   91345

Products:

	Description	Unit Cost
1004	6 oz scratch-card	$1.75
1007	Lovebirds	$15.00
1017	Canary handbook	$3.00
1023	Parakeets	$8.00

Supplier Name   Gull Wing Ranch   A12   **PhoneNumber**   (619) 555-8356

Address   615 De Hesa Rd

                    Corona Mar   CA   91228

Products:

	Description	Unit Cost
1005	Goldfish	$0.30
1026	Feeder guppies	$0.20

Supplier Name   T.M. Cages   B15   **PhoneNumber**   (619) 555-1178

Address   1400 Lemon Ave

                    Del Mesa   CA   91228

Products:

	Description	Unit Cost
1000	Cage cover, bird	$6.30
1011	Mouse house	$2.00
1022	Wild bird feeder	$3.00
1024	Rabbit cage	$10.00

A helpful historical report could summarize the purchasing activities over a period of time, organized by supplier. The report could summarize the purchases from each supplier, keep a subtotal, and provide a grand total at the end of the report. Figure 11.5 shows the first page of a Transactions by Supplier report.

Figure 11.5.

A report summarizing purchases from each supplier.

Transactions by Supplier

Supplier Name	Date	Description	Quantity	Unit Cost	Extended Cost
Aquatic Foods					
	10/27/97	Live ghost shrimp	10	$7.00	$70.00
	10/27/97	Brine shrimp	10	$2.00	$20.00
		Total This Supplier:			**$20.00**
		SubTotal So Far:			**$90.00**
Bill's Kennel					
	10/20/97	Small dog biscuit (50#)	1	$10.20	$10.20
	10/20/97	Rawhide bone	3	$0.86	$2.58
	10/21/97	Rawhide bone	4	$0.86	$3.44
	10/21/97	Small dog biscuit (50#)	1	$1.30	$1.30
	10/23/97	Rawhide bone	3	$0.86	$2.58
	10/26/97	Rawhide bone	2	$0.86	$1.72
	10/27/97	Rawhide bone	3	$0.86	$2.58
		Total This Supplier:			**$22.58**
		SubTotal So Far:			**$114.40**
Coast Bird Farms					
	10/20/97	Lovebirds	2	$15.00	$30.00
	10/21/97	Parakeets	1	$8.00	$8.00
	10/22/97	Lovebirds	2	$15.00	$30.00
	10/24/97	Lovebirds	2	$15.00	$30.00
		Total This Supplier:			**$52.58**
		SubTotal So Far:			**$212.40**
Gull Wing Ranch					
	10/23/97	Goldfish	20	$0.30	$6.00
		Total This Supplier:			**$58.58**
		SubTotal So Far:			**$218.40**
Kal Pets, Inc					
	10/20/97	Flea comb	3	$15.00	$45.00
	10/20/97	Nail clippers	3	$3.75	$11.25
	10/22/97	Cat harness	2	$1.95	$3.90

Sunday, March 23, 1997   Page 1 of 3

Similar summarizing reports can be designed to monitor sales activity. A report that includes charts and graphs can be very helpful in analyzing the store's performance. Figure 11.6 shows a chart that can be created from Access data using the Microsoft Chart applet from within Access.

Other reports that would be useful to Pat's Pets are the following:

- Current price list in alphabetical order or grouped by category or by main supplier
- List of products grouped by major category such as birds, cats, and dogs
- List of customers grouped by pets of interest
- Summary of transactions, including calculated profits
- Form letters reminding customers of dog grooming services due
- Form letters and mailing labels for sales promotions

Figure 11.6.
Sales performance for Pat's Pets, summarized in a bar chart.

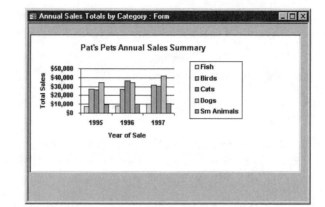

Enhancements to be considered for later implementations include tracking cost fluctuations over time that might prompt price changes. Adding a second vendor for some of the products would allow you to compare their performance and cost strategies. Seasonal product performance is also a valid analysis to add to the design. As the application design matures, additional ideas for improvement can come forward. It is important to freeze the design at some point and proceed with development, saving the new ideas for the next phase.

The Application Development Process

The application development process consists of seven distinct phases that begin after you determine the informational and operational needs of the user. It is important to realize that although these steps appear to be sequential, the design process is actually iterative. You often return to a previous step and make changes as the goals of the application become more distinct. Users invariably expand their expectations when they begin to realize the power and flexibility that is available to them with an Access application.

The first step is an analysis of the data requirements and how the elements relate to one another. In this step, data is grouped by subject and frequency of use into separate tables, and the links among the tables are defined.

The second step involves actually creating the table definitions, defining indexes, key fields, required fields, and data validation rules. If any of the fields can be linked to a lookup table, these are also defined. After completing the table definitions, you add enough data to be able to test the application thoroughly. These two steps are covered in this chapter.

The principal user interface in a database management system is a form used for entering and viewing the data that is the basis for the application. In Pat's Pets, the basic data is the product inventory and sales activity. Of secondary interest is supplier and customer information. The third step in application development is the design of the main data entry form. The fields in the form must be carefully arranged in a logical order and with meaningful labels to help prevent entry errors.

In the fourth step, macros, event procedures, and functions are added to the form design so that it will perform appropriately to user actions.

Chapter 12, "Customizing Data Entry," demonstrates steps 3 and 4 with the development of the Pat's Pets application.

Additional forms and reports are added to the application in the fifth stage of development. These can include lookup forms to retrieve selected information, filtered and sorted in useful ways. You can design reports to filter, sort, group, and summarize information in any number of ways.

Chapter 13, "Customizing Reports," teaches you how to create additional forms and a variety of reports for Pat's Pets, including sales summaries with charts and graphs.

The sixth step adds features that connect all the pieces together into a smoothly functioning operation, such as command buttons, customized menus and toolbars, and pop-up forms for user input.

The seventh and final step creates a starting place such as a main switchboard that gives the user the opportunity to decide what to do next. Subordinate switchboards are also added as necessary (for example, to choose one from a list of reports to open for preview).

In Chapter 14, "Adding Real-Time Features," you finish the Pat's Pets application by adding switchboards, error trapping, and some management-decision features.

Designing the Pat's Pets Database

In most cases, the bulk of the necessary data is available in the current system, and the main task is to rearrange it into related tables to reduce the redundancy of data and improve processing efficiency. If the current system is inadequate—really inadequate, not just unable to keep up with the volume— then you must give some extra thought to procedures for collecting the necessary data. For example, if you want to build a mailing list for sending out promotional material, you can offer free dog or cat treats to customers as an incentive to sign up.

The Pat's Pets current system does not accumulate transaction data. It concentrates on the more static physical inventory that is affected by the flow of products in and out of the store. What is really needed here is a way to measure this flow to be able to track progress and extract information that can be used in making business decisions.

Defining and Relating Tables

"The data that is used together stays together" should be the motto of the database developer. Items of data used for the same purpose should be stored in the same table unless there will be a lot of repetition. If that is the case, you should separate the repeated data into another, related table and add a field that links the two tables. The frequency of use is also a factor in data distribution. Store little-used data out of the way in a separate table.

In the new Pat's Pets database design, the transaction data is in one table, the product data in another, and the supplier data in a third. Customer data is stored in a fourth table.

Access requires a key field in every table to ensure that each record is unique. In the Pat's Pets database, you can assign a unique product code to each product in the store and a unique identifier to each supplier and each customer.

The transaction table poses a slightly different problem. Neither the product code nor the date can guarantee a unique record. You might sell more than one of a given item in one day, and you certainly hope to make more than one sale per day. You might also receive a shipment of a product the same day you sell some of the same items. Even combining the values in both the date and product code fields fails to create a unique value. Unless you want to maintain your own transaction record numbers, you can use Access to create a special field that will always contain a unique value. The transaction record number field has no other use than to create a unique record.

Because the tables in a relational database are related by common fields, you must define these fields. They must contain the same kind of data (number, text, date, and so on), and they must be the same length. They need not have the same name because part of the database design is specifying which fields you want to use to join the two tables.

For Pat's Pets, the product and supplier tables are related by the supplier's name. This can cause problems with long names that are easily misspelled. Computers are perfectionists and often disregard what you mean in favor of what you actually enter. Using a short code for each supplier is not only easier to remember, but it also saves space. The Supplier table can correlate the code with the supplier's full name and other information.

If the Transaction table is to be used to update the current inventory in the Products table, these two tables must be related as well. Once again, you could use the full name of the product, but a code would be more efficient both in time and space. The product code serves a dual purpose by also having a unique value that can make sure there are no duplicate records in the database. The Category table, which is used for looking up category codes, stores the category names and code numbers. Figure 11.7 shows how the four tables are related by common fields.

The Relationships window in Figure 11.7 shows the types of relationships that exist between the four tables. The Category table is related to the Products table by the Cat Code field with a one-to-one relationship. A one-to-one relationship is typical of lookup tables.

The Products table is related to the Transactions table by Product ID in a one-to-many relationship, indicating that a single product could be involved in many transactions. The Suppliers table is related to the Products table by the Supplier ID field with a one-to-many relationship, indicating that a supplier can offer more than one product for sale.

Figure 11.7.
The Pat's Pets database includes four related tables.

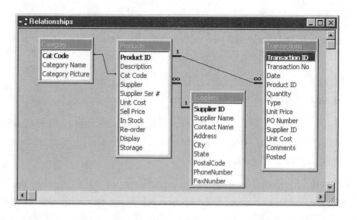

Peter's Principle: Creating a Many-to-Many Relationship

In a many-to-many relationship, a record in one table (call it Table A) can have several matching records in another table (Table B), and vice versa. Neither table is considered the parent because the linking field is not the primary key in either table. The only way you can create such a relationship is by creating a third table, called a *junction table*. This new table has a primary key that is actually a combination of at least the primary keys from Tables A and B. The junction table then acts as the bridge between Tables A and B when you build two one-to-many relationships among them. You can add other fields to the junction table like any other table.

Figure 11.8 shows a junction table linking two tables. Because several products could be included in a single order and several orders could include the same product, this represents a many-to-many relationship. To solve the relationship problem, the junction table, Order Details, was created with a primary key that combines the foreign keys from the Products table (ProductID) and from the Orders table (OrderID). Two one-to-many relationships then link the Products and Orders tables to the Order Details table.

Figure 11.8.
Creating a junction table for a many-to-many relationship.

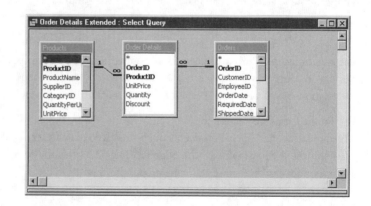

Tables 11.1, 11.2, and 11.3 describe the definitions of each of the three principal tables in the Pat's Pets database.

Table 11.1. Transactions table definition.

Field Name	Data Type	Description
Transaction ID	AutoNumber	Primary key field, provided by Access
Transaction No	Number	User-entered transaction number
Date	Date/Time	Date of the transaction
Product ID	Text	Linking field to Products table
Quantity	Number	Number of items sold or purchased
Type	Text	Three valid values: Sale, Purchase, or Shrinkage
Unit Price	Currency	Selling price
PO Number	Number	Purchase Order number
Supplier ID	Text	Lookup table of suppliers
Unit Cost	Currency	Purchase cost
Comments	Memo	Additional information about the transaction
Posted	Yes/No	A check box, automatically checked when the Products table is updated with the transaction

Field properties, validation rules, default values, and secondary indexes for the Transactions table are discussed in the next section of this chapter.

Table 11.2. Products table definition.

Field Name	Data Type	Description
Product ID	Text	Unique product identifier. Primary key and link to Transaction table.
Description	Text	Item description.
Cat Code	Text	Product category, one of a list of valid values.
Supplier	Text	Short field containing a supplier code. Used to relate to Supplier table.
Supplier Ser #	Text	Supplier item number for product.
Unit Cost	Currency	Cost of item, not including shipping and handling.
Sell Price	Currency	Normal retail price.

continues

Table 11.2. continued

Field Name	Data Type	Description
In Stock	Number	Quantity in stock. May be negative if back ordered.
Re-order	Number	Lower limit of stock level below which the item should be reordered.
Display	Text	Code for display location in store.
Storage	Text	Code for storage location.

Additional information about the Products table appears in the next section of this chapter.

Table 11.3. Suppliers table definition.

Field Name	Data Type	Description
Supplier ID	Text	Unique supplier identifier. Primary key field and link to Products and Transactions tables.
Supplier Name	Text	Supplier company name.
Contact Name	Text	Person to contact at supplier.
Address	Text	Supplier street address.
City	Text	Supplier city.
State	Text	Supplier state.
PostalCode	Text	Supplier postal code.
PhoneNumber	Text	Supplier voice phone number.
FaxNumber	Text	Supplier Fax phone number.
Comments	Memo	Information about delivery schedule and lead times.

One additional table is part of the Pat's Pets application: the Customer table, which contains customer names, addresses, and a memo field with comments about the types of purchases made and services used at the store. The Customer table is unrelated to the other tables in the application. The purpose of the Customer table is to maintain a mailing list of clients and their interest in pets.

Defining Field Properties

Each table already has a unique key field that ensures no two records will be identical. Other field properties can be anticipated at this stage of application development. For example, considering how the data can be filtered and sorted will lead to adding indexes. Filtering and sorting records works much faster if the records are indexed on the fields of interest.

It is also not too early to define data validation rules for fields and records. Field validation rules ensure that the field contains proper values, whereas record validation tests for conflicts between field values in the same record.

Indexes and Sort Orders

To summarize the coverage Pat's Pets provides in all types of pet supplies, sort the products by category code. To isolate the products for a specific type of pet, filter the records by category code. To analyze sales, sort the transactions first by type—sales as opposed to purchases or shrinkage—and then by product or product category. To make mailing quicker, sort both the suppliers and customers by postal code. To target dog owners for a special mailing, filter the customer records by the major category code for dog-related items.

Many other possibilities can be imagined and indexes can be added at any time, even after the tables are populated. For the Pat's Pets application, the following indexes seem appropriate at this time:

- Products table by Cat Code and an index combining values from the Supplier field with the Category field.
- Suppliers and Customer tables by Postal Code.
- Transactions table by Product ID and Supplier ID.

All the added indexes allow duplicate values in the indexed fields. Figure 11.9 shows the indexes that have been defined for the Products table, and Figure 11.10 shows the indexes for the Transactions table.

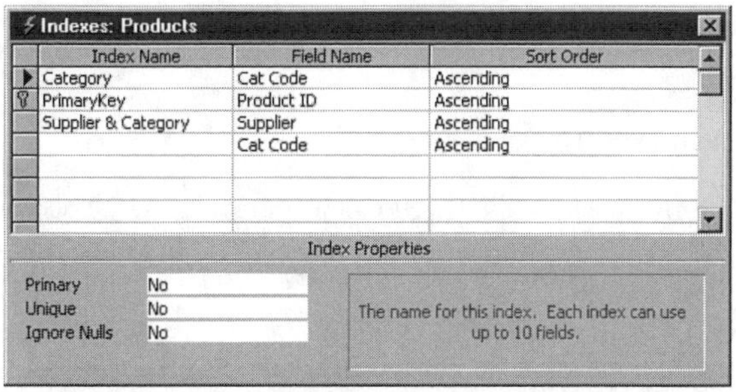

Figure 11.9.
The Products table indexes.

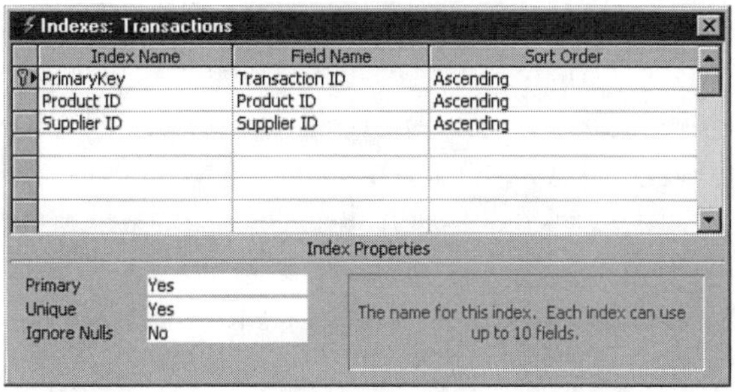

Figure 11.10.
The Transactions table indexes.

The indexes appear in alphabetical order in the Indexes dialog box, and the primary key field shows the key icon. The primary key index also has the `Primary` and `Unique` properties set to `Yes`. None of the indexes will ignore null values unless you so specify.

Default Values and Data Validation Rules

One of the most crucial aspects of maintaining a database is to prevent errors from creeping in. It is easier to prevent errors than to find them and correct them after they are hidden in the forest of data. Access provides several ways to make sure the data you enter is valid and error free.

One way is to specify the field as required. Access will not let you save a record without an entry in a required field. Other validation rules insist a value fall within a given range of values or may never be negative.

The following rules are appropriate for the Pat's Pets application:

- The Product ID in the Transactions table must match a value in the Products table.
- The Re-order quantity in the Products table must be between 1 and 100, with a default value of 0.
- The Date field in the Transaction table has a default value of the current date.
- The Supplier field in the Transaction table has a blank default value because the Supplier name should appear only when the transaction is a purchase.
- The Sell Price in the Products table must be greater than the Unit Cost (a record validation rule) and cannot be zero (a field validation rule).

More requirements will no doubt turn up as the application develops.

Data Formats

Display formats can make the user's job much easier. You can impart additional information by customizing the appearance of field values. The following field format properties are suggested for the Pat's Pets database:

- Using the format `@;"Unk"` for the suppliers FaxNumber field displays the number, if any; otherwise, it displays Unk, for unknown.
- Using `>` as the format for the Suppliers ID field in both the Suppliers and Products tables converts all letters to uppercase to conform to the customary ID code.
- Using the format `0;!0![Red];"Out";"N/A"` for the In Stock field in the Products table will display at least one digit if the value is greater than zero. If the value is negative, the product is back ordered and the value is displayed in red and enclosed in exclamation marks. If it is zero, the word Out is displayed, and if blank, N/A is displayed.
- The Posted Yes/No field is displayed as a check box rather than a text field containing the words Yes or No.

Adding Lookup Tables

Access provides three ways to link a field to a list of valid values: by entering the values in the field definition, by listing the values as the row source in the property sheet of the text box control, or by naming a separate table or query as the row source for the field values.

The advantage of using a separate table or query for the list of values is that the user can add values to the list by responding to the NotInList() function. Because you want the user to be able to add new product categories as the store expands, use the Category table as the lookup row source for the Cat Code field.

You might not want the user to be able to add to the list of valid transaction types, however, in which case enter the values in the field property pane of the table definition or in the property sheet in the form design.

Populating the Database

If the existing Products table was stored in an earlier version of Access, it can easily be converted to Access 97. The other tables must be filled in manually. At this stage of application development, add only enough data to be able to test the system thoroughly. For example, include enough data to produce a report with two pages. This way you check out headers and other elements on a page other than the first page. Also, be sure to have enough items to test filters and sort routines as well as summaries and calculated fields. Filling up the database at this time is unnecessary and wastes processing time.

If the table has few fields, the easiest way to enter data is in datasheet view. A table with too many fields to fit on the screen can be viewed in form view by creating an AutoForm object that will show all the fields for one record at once on the screen. You needn't save the form, just create it again the next time you need to enter more data.

User Interaction

At this point, development slips quietly into programming. After you have defined all the pieces of the application (development), it is time to decide how they will work together in response to user actions (programming). It is important to step through all possible scenarios and try to anticipate the user's actions. The user has one entry point into the application, which is usually a main switchboard showing a list of major activities from which to choose. Each of these items leads to further defined subactivities until the user reaches a specific operation or goal.

The most common activities in a database application are data entry/edit and data retrieval. Data entry and editing is usually done in forms that can be helpful if properly designed to take into account the user's actions. Command buttons can give the user options for further action, and validity checks can help prevent entry errors.

Screentips, help options, and status bar messages can provide guidance to new users as necessary. In addition, pop-up forms can be displayed on demand that will show additional information about items in the current form. For example, the user could place the cursor in the Supplier field and press a key combination that would run a macro that displays a pop-up dialog box with the supplier's name and other information.

Data retrieval usually involves a report based on one or more tables or queries and requires little or no user interaction, once selected. Some reports can ask for user input to set a specific filter or other parameter. If the application includes sensitive information, security measures can be added that limit access to certain data.

You can create customized command bars to use in place of the default menu bar, toolbar, and shortcut menus. The items would be specifically related to the application with selected general-purpose options, such as Print and Save.

The next paragraphs step through scenarios in which the user enters new data, edits existing data, and previews a report. The processes of posting and archiving transactions are also described.

The Transactions Data Entry/Edit Scenario

Most of the data activity occurs with the Transactions table. The transactions are intended to be entered daily. Changes to the Products table other than in-stock quantities are not as frequent, although new products are added and prices are changed now and then. New suppliers are also added to the suppliers list, and changes in telephone numbers or contact personnel also occur.

In this scenario, the user has some recent transactions to enter into the Transactions table. When the Pat's Pets application starts up, a main switchboard appears and one of the options is Enter/Edit Transactions. Other options on the main switchboard can include the following:

- Enter/Edit Other Data—Opens up a second switchboard with options for the other tables in the database.
- Preview Reports—Opens up another switchboard with a list of the available reports, including customer mailing labels and supplier order forms.
- Post and Archive Transactions—Enables the user to update the Products table with recent transactions and remove completed transactions from the table.
- Exit the Database—Closes the database and returns to the Access window.

If the user selects Enter/Edit Transaction Data, the Transaction Log form opens showing the first record in the table (refer to Figure 11.2 for a sample form). In the form, the following actions are taken:

1. To add new records, click Add New Transaction or click the New Record button in the navigation bar. To edit an existing record, use the navigation buttons to locate the record. The records are ordered by the Transaction ID value that Access assigns, which is not displayed in the form. It is not ordered by the Transaction No field. If this creates a problem, the table can be sorted by transaction number before the form opens.

2. Enter the transaction number. The Transaction No does not contain a unique value. Together, the Transaction No and Product ID fields form a unique combination.

3. Press Tab to move to the next field, Date, which is by default the current system date. Change it if necessary, and press Tab to move to the Type field.

4. Enter the transaction type here. It must be one of three values: Sale, Purchase, or Shrinkage. A combo box is appropriate for this text box control (with no added items allowed).

5. Move to the Product ID and enter the value. When this text box control loses focus, the Unit Price and Unit Cost fields are filled in with values from the Products table for that item. If the transaction is Shrinkage, the Unit Price should be set to $0 because no revenue was received from the transaction. The price and cost fields should not be in the tab order in the form because they are automatically filled in.

6. Next, if the transaction is a purchase, focus moves to the PO Number field and then to the Supplier field.

7. The Posted field is not available to the user. It is for information only and is automatically checked when the transaction is posted to the Products table in a separate operation. The Posted field is also tested when the user wants to archive transactions to the history file. Records that contain this field unchecked are not ready for archiving no matter what the date of the transaction may be.

8. Enter any comments in the Comments field, such as the reason for the shrinkage—shoplifting, rain damage, or chewed by mice.

9. The Extended Price and Extended Cost fields are automatically calculated with the values from the Products table after the Product ID number is entered. They are not in the tab order for the user.

10. The buttons in the form footer let the user choose what to do next: Add another transaction, print the list, or return to the switchboard.

The only trouble the user could get into with this form is entering an invalid Product ID number. When this happens, Access displays a message that the value must match the join key. You can trap the error and replace the message with something more helpful to the user. Even though the cost and price fields are not in the tab order, the user can click in the fields and change the data, if they want. Any changes made in a record in this form are also made to the Products table.

The user should not be allowed to delete any records from the Transactions table because they represent past events. However, errors might have been made that need correcting, in which case, allowing deletion only with a password may be an alternative.

Entering or Editing Product Data

To reach the Products form for data entry and editing, the user selects Enter/Edit Other Data from the main switchboard. A second switchboard gives the user the option of opening a form for each of the other tables in the database: Products, Suppliers, or Customers. Choosing Products opens a form, such as the one shown in Figure 11.11, and the following actions can be taken:

- To add a new product, click the Add New Product command button or click the new record navigation button. To edit an existing record, use the navigation buttons to locate the record.

- Enter a unique Product ID value followed by the product description. Because the categories are stored in a lookup table, click the combo box arrow and choose from the list. The list shows the name of the category as well as the code. The code is the value that is stored in the record.

- Enter the Supplier ID code and the supplier's serial number for the new product. If the Supplier ID value is not in the Suppliers table, Access will display an error message that you should intercept and replace with a more understandable message.

- The rest of the form should not present any problems for the user. The command buttons in the form footer give the user a choice of the next operation—print the list of products or close the form and return to the main switchboard.

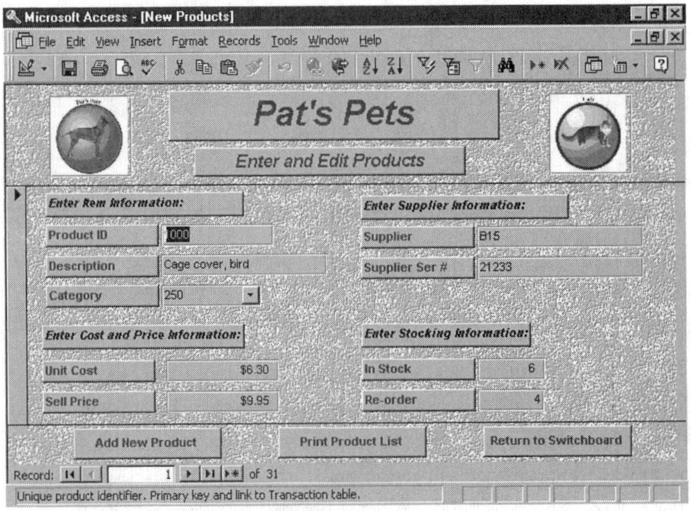

Figure 11.11.
A Products data entry form.

The Suppliers table is quite straightforward, with little or no error checking required except for the unique ID value. The Customers table requires no error checking or data validation.

Previewing Reports

A preview switchboard lists the reports that have been designed for the Pat's Pets application. Many of the reports can accept a user-specified filter. For example, for a report that lists all the products related to small animals, the user would enter the major category code. Other reports require a specified time period, such as quarter or year.

One of the reports will print mailing labels for customers. This report can be filtered to include only those customers with specific pet interests.

If no records meet the criteria set by the user, a message is displayed indicating there is no information for this selection rather than displaying a blank page.

From the preview window, the user can print the report or close the window. When printing is completed, the main switchboard returns to the screen.

Posting Transactions

The Pat's Pets manager posts the day's transactions to the Products table at the close of business or at some other regular interval. Transaction posting is an item on the main switchboard. Little user interaction is required once the transaction posting operation begins. You might want to give the user the choice of posting all unposted transactions or only those that occurred on a certain date or during a particular time period. If no date is chosen, all transactions are posted.

If you want, you can place a command button on the Transactions Log form that will post transactions after data entry is complete.

The posting module performs the following tasks:

1. Filters out the transaction records that show the Posted field as unchecked.
2. Creates an update query that updates the In Stock field in the Products table, subtracting the quantities listed as sales and shrinkage transactions and adding quantities listed as purchase transactions.
3. After updating each In Stock quantity, the Transaction record Posted field is checked.
4. When all the transactions have been posted, a message is displayed to the user indicating the number of records updated.

After the operation is complete, the main switchboard returns to the screen.

This set of procedures must be carefully tested to ensure that each transaction is posted only once. The user should have no trouble with this operation.

Archiving Transactions

Posting and archiving transactions are separate activities. Keeping recent transactions in a current table is a handy reference, but the Transactions table could become infinitely large if it is not purged from time to time. Saving historic transaction information can be quite useful in analyzing marketing and sales trends. Archiving can be done periodically, monthly or quarterly, depending on the level of activity.

When the user chooses to archive transactions, an input box is displayed asking for the time period of the transactions to remove from the active table. This can be expressed as a range of dates or a single cutoff date; for example, "Archive all transactions that occurred before November 1, 1997." Only those records with the Posted field checked will be transferred to the archive table, even if the date falls within the selected range.

The archiving module performs the following tasks:

1. Extracts the transactions whose date meets the criterion and whose Posted field is checked.
2. Creates an append query that adds the records to the transaction history table.
3. Displays a warning showing the number of records that are about to be added to the archive and deleted from the current table. The user can cancel the operation at this point.
4. Deletes the records from the current Transactions table.
5. Displays a message box showing the number of records moved from the current table to the archive table.

After the user closes the message box, the main switchboard returns to the screen.

These procedures must also be checked out thoroughly in development to make sure no information is lost in the transfer.

Summary

Although you were not exposed to much programming in this chapter, you did get a view of what must go into the design of an application before the programming begins. Much time is wasted by beginning the implementation of an application before the design is carefully thought out. The design process begins with an analysis of the existing system and interviews with the users to determine how the new application should perform.

This chapter discussed the distribution of data among related tables and how to minimize the possibility of errors in the database by the use of data validation rules. Finally, user interaction with the system was discussed, and several scenarios stepped through the most common operations.

In the next chapter, the data entry forms for the Transactions and Products tables are designed with the underlying class modules that contain event procedures and error-trapping code.

12 Customizing Data Entry

The data entry form is the primary interaction tool that links the user with a database. It is essential that there be a high level of understanding between human and machine if the application is to succeed. In many situations, difficulties can occur at points where two different mediums connect. For example, in a building the line where the wall material meets the flooring can present interface problems or where one type of plumbing material joins with another.

Computer-based applications are no different. The point at which data moves from mind to machine can present interpretation difficulties. A properly designed and implemented data entry system can minimize the possibility of data errors. This chapter discusses several of the data entry vehicles in the Pat's Pets application.

Create Simple Data Entry Forms

When you need to create a relatively simple data entry tool, you can save some work by using the Form Wizard to build the basic structure and then add your own custom features. The Products and Suppliers tables lend themselves well to simple forms because there is not a lot of interaction with other tables, and neither insists on elaborate data validation. However, both have unique key fields that can cause an error if two records contain the same values. You can add a procedure to trap this error.

After the Form Wizard is finished, you can rearrange and resize the controls as well as add a title and pictures, if desired. After arranging the fields, recheck the tab order and make any necessary changes in the control properties.

Next, add command buttons to the form footer with the help of the Button Wizard, which also writes the Click event procedure code for the buttons. At this point, you can modify these procedures and add some new ones of your own. New procedures can change the form appearance upon opening, trap data errors, and calculate field values.

The forms designed in this chapter are all quite different for a reason: You can see how simpler forms may be easier to use than ones that are more cluttered. One form has explicit instructions for the user; both use the labels on the command buttons to convey their purpose.

The New Products Data Entry Form

The Pat's Pets New Products form was started by the wizard; then the controls were rearranged and resized (see Figure 12.1). A title, subtitle, and instructions for each area of data were added. Next, three command buttons were added:

- Add New Products, which moves to an empty record at the end of the table.
- Preview Product List, which opens the Product List report for preview. The Button Wizard needs a name for the target report. This report can be a simple AutoReport now, named Product List. A more useful report can be designed later and substituted for it.

- Return to Switchboard, which closes the form and brings up the switchboard (if the New Products form was opened via the switchboard). This button should appear on every form to give the user an escape route other than clicking the Close button.

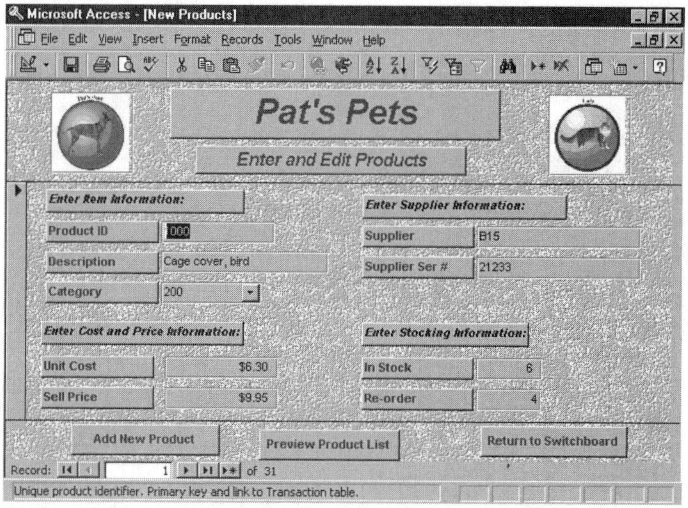

Figure 12.1.
A data entry form for the Products table.

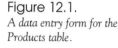

After the Button Wizard has helped to add the three command buttons, the New Products class module contains the three Click event procedures shown in Listing 12.1.

Listing 12.1. The New Products form class module.

```
Private Sub Return_to_Switchboard_Click()
On Error GoTo Err_Return_to_Switchboard_Click

    DoCmd.Close

Exit_Return_to_Switchboard_Click:
    Exit Sub

Err_Return_to_Switchboard_Click:
    MsgBox Err.Description
    Resume Exit_Return_to_Switchboard_Click

End Sub

Private Sub Add_Record_Click()
On Error GoTo Err_Add_Record_Click

    DoCmd.GoToRecord , , acNewRec

Exit_Add_Record_Click:
    Exit Sub
```

continues

Listing 12.1. continued

```
Err_Add_Record_Click:
    MsgBox Err.Description
    Resume Exit_Add_Record_Click

End Sub

Private Sub ProdList_Click()
On Error GoTo Err_ProdList_Click

    Dim stDocName As String

    stDocName = "Product List"
    DoCmd.OpenReport stDocName, acPreview

Exit_ProdList_Click:
    Exit Sub

Err_ProdList_Click:
    MsgBox Err.Description
    Resume Exit_ProdList_Click

End Sub
```

The wizards are notoriously closemouthed about comments in their procedures. It is up to you to add sufficient comments for later reference.

Add a Form Startup Procedure

When a form opens, it might not be maximized, depending on the window that was open before it. Many forms are large and need to be maximized in the window in order for all the controls to be seen. An event procedure that executes when the form opens can use the Maximize method.

To add this procedure, open the module window for the New Products form and choose Form from the Object list and Load from the Procedure list. Figure 12.2 shows the beginnings of the new procedure. Although this procedure is simple enough not to require explanation, get into the habit of commenting all procedures. Just below the Private Sub line, enter the following code:

```
'Maximize the form window at startup.
DoCmd.Maximize
```

Change a Control Type

Changing a text box to a combo box, thus giving the user access to the value list, can save time entering data as well as ensure valid values. One of the tables discussed in the previous chapter is the Category table, which can be used as a lookup table wherever the Cat Code field appears. The New Products form includes the Category field, which stores the category code. To change the text box to a combo box, carry out the following steps:

Figure 12.2.
Starting a `Form_Load` *event procedure.*

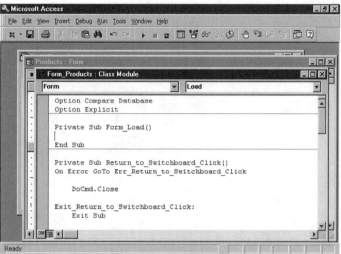

1. Open the New Products form in design view.

2. Right-click the Cat Code text box and point to Change To in the shortcut menu and then choose Combo Box. A down arrow appears in the Cat Code control indicating it is now a combo box.

3. The category codes are not yet in the combo box list. Open the property sheet for the Cat Code control and make the following changes to the Data properties:

   Change `Row Source Type` to `Table/query`.

   Change `Row Source` to `Category`, the table with the Cat Code values.

   Change `Bound Column` to `1`, the column in the Category table that contains the value you want stored in the Cat Code field.

   Change `Limit to List` to `No` so the user can add new categories if necessary.

4. Click the Format property sheet tab and make these changes:

   Set `Column Count` to `2` so you will see both the Cat Code and the Category Name.

   Change `Column Heads` to `No`.

   Type `0.4";1.25"` in the `Column Widths` property to specify the width of both columns when the list is displayed.

   Type `1.65"` in the `List Width` property to increase the width of the pull-down list to wider than the control in the form.

5. Switch to form view and click the Category combo box (see Figure 12.3).

Figure 12.3.
The new Category combo box.

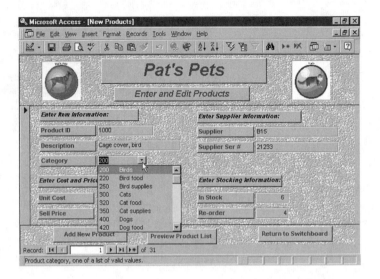

Set the Tab Order

The progress of focus through the controls in the form by pressing Tab is called the *tab order*. By default, the tab order is the sequence in which the controls were added to the form design. If you move controls around after the wizard has started the form design, the tab order does not automatically change to match the new positions without help. You can set the order any way you like or use the Auto Order option, which moves the cursor from left to right and top to bottom.

You have two ways to set the tab order within a form section: by changing the tab index property of the control or using the Tab Order dialog box. To use the tab index property, change the number in the property sheet. You can enter any number between 0 and one less than the number of controls in the section. When you enter a number already used by a control, the others are adjusted accordingly.

To use the Tab Order dialog box, choose View | Tab Order (see Figure 12.4). The dialog box shows a list of all the controls that can receive focus in each of the form sections. To move a control within the order, select it and drag it to a new position in the list. To revert to the automatic sequence, click Auto Order. To change the order of controls in another section, click the appropriate section. The New Products form has two controls in the header (the two images), and three in the footer (the command buttons).

In the New Products form, the order is set in the dialog box to move the cursor down through the item information, to the supplier fields, to the cost and price fields, and finally to the stocking data. Notice that pressing Tab after filling out the Re-order field, instead of moving focus to the command buttons, causes Access to display the next record with the cursor in the first text box. If you want the user to be able to reach the buttons with the Tab key, you must place the buttons in the detail section with the text boxes and other data-related controls.

Figure 12.4.

Change the tab sequence in the Tab Order dialog box.

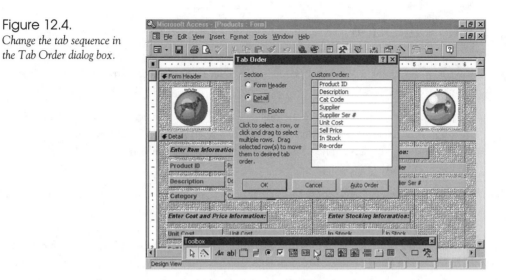

By setting the `Tab Stop` property to `No`, you can keep the user from reaching the control by pressing Tab. He or she can still reach it by clicking the mouse, but it does not automatically receive focus. For example, the section that discusses the Transaction Log form later in this chapter shows how to reach or skip a tab stop based on the value selected for the transaction type.

By combining the settings for the `Enabled` and `Locked` properties, you can regulate the amount of access the user has to a control. You can use the two properties together with the following effects:

- Set both to `Yes`. The control is accessible and the data is displayed normally and can be copied but not changed.

- Set `Enabled` to `Yes` and `Locked` to `No`. The control is accessible and the data is displayed normally and can be copied or changed.

- Set `Enabled` to `No` and `Locked` to `Yes`. The control is inaccessible and the data is displayed normally but cannot be copied or changed.

- Set both to `No`. The control and data both appear dimmed.

Tip: Setting the `Enabled` property in an `AfterUpdate` event procedure lets you have conditional control over the accessibility of command buttons and other controls. For example, suppose a form has a Preview Report button that opens one of a set of product reports based on a product category. Until the user chooses the category to use in the report's filter, the button should not be available. Set the `Enabled` property to `No`, and when the user selects a category from an option box or a combo box, the `AfterUpdate` event procedure runs and sets the `Enabled` property to `Yes`. Be sure to reset the property to `No` after previewing the report. When you set `Yes` and `No` property values in VBA, you use `True` and `False`.

Data Validation

The only data validation the Products table requires is that the Product ID field have a unique value. If you try to save a new record with a duplicate Product ID field, Access will display the following error message:

"The changes you requested to the table were not successful because they would create duplicate values in the index, primary index, or relationship. Change the data in the field or fields that contain duplicate data, remove the index, or redefine the index to permit duplicate entries and try again."

While this message may make sense to some, it is not specific about which field is in question. It would help the user if you trapped this error and displayed a more definitive message. You can write a procedure to attach to the form's `Error` event. In order to trap the error, you need to find out the error code number that Access stores in a system variable named `DataErr`. Look in the Help index for Trappable Microsoft Jet and DAO Errors to see a complete list of trappable data-related errors. Access also has an extensive list of error codes that relate to Access objects. The `Error` event applies to both forms and reports.

The `Form_Error` procedure statement has the following syntax:

```
Private Sub Form_Error(DataErr As Integer, Response As Integer)
```

Note: The words appearing in bold in a syntax statement are keywords that must be typed exactly as shown.

The `DataErr` argument is the error code that is returned by the `Err` object when an error occurs. It is passed automatically to the procedure. The `Response` argument determines whether to display an error message.

If you set the `Response` argument to the intrinsic constant `acDataErrContinue`, the default error message is not displayed and the error is ignored. Then, it is up to you to deal with the error, such as by displaying your own error message and focusing back on the key field. The other `Response` setting, `acDataErrDisplay` (the default), displays the Access error message.

Add the `Form_Error` event procedure to the New Products form by choosing Form from the Object list in the module window and Error from the Procedure list. Then, type the following code between the `Private Sub` and `End Sub` lines, once again starting with a comment:

```
'Trap duplicate Product ID value and display message.

Dim strMsg As String
Const conDupKey = 3022

    If DataErr = conDupKey Then
        strMsg = "You have entered a duplicate Product ID. "
        strMsg = strMsg & "Please enter a unique value."
        MsgBox strMsg
```

```
      Product_ID.SetFocus
      Response = acDataErrContinue
End If
```

The `Dim` statement declares a string variable to represent your error message. Next, a constant is declared with the value 3022, which is the code number for the duplicate key field error. The `If...Then` statement tests the `DataErr` value and, if it is 3022, displays the message you stored in `strMsg`. The next line, `Product_ID.SetFocus`, returns focus to the Product ID field where you can correct the error. The last line before `End If` sets the response to skip displaying the default message and continues processing. That is, it gives control back to the user to enter a unique value in the Product ID field.

Figure 12.5 shows the message caused by trying to save a record with a duplicate Product ID value.

Figure 12.5.
The new error handling message.

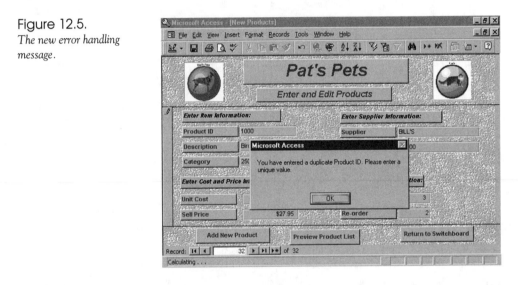

Tip: This procedure is general in nature and can be copied to other form class modules with minor changes to the field name.

The Supplier Data Entry Form

The second form, Supplier Form, is similar to the New Products form. The form itself is at risk of overdoing the user instructions (see Figure 12.6). How much guidance you give in the form depends on the skill level of the prospective user. When in doubt, keep it simple. Elaborate forms also take longer to load.

Once again, the Button Wizard has helped to create the event procedures for the command buttons in the form footer. Supplier ID is the key field for the table and must not contain any duplicates, so an Error event procedure is also appropriate for this form. Listing 12.2 shows the finished class module for the Supplier form with added comments.

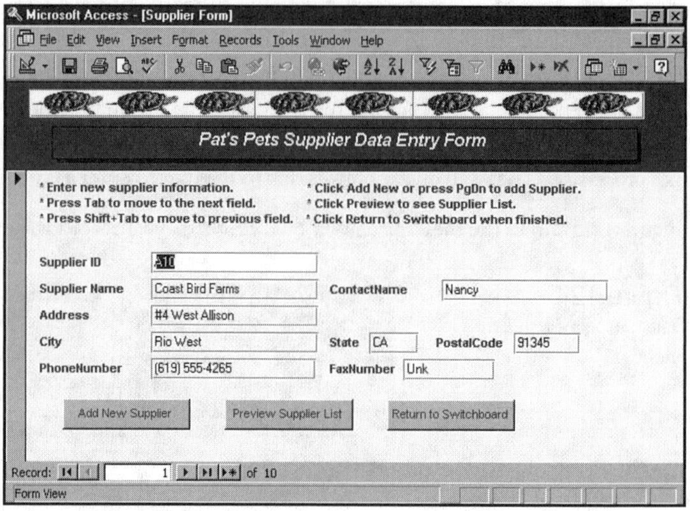

Figure 12.6.
The completed Supplier form.

Listing 12.2. The Supplier Form class module.

```
Option Compare Database
Option Explicit

Sub Close_Form_Click()
'Close form and return to switchboard.
On Error GoTo Err_Close_Form_Click

    DoCmd.Close

Exit_Close_Form_Click:
    Exit Sub

Err_Close_Form_Click:
    MsgBox Err.Description
    Resume Exit_Close_Form_Click

End Sub

Private Sub AddSuppl_Click()
'Add new Supplier record.
On Error GoTo Err_AddSuppl_Click

    DoCmd.GoToRecord , , acNewRec

Exit_AddSuppl_Click:
    Exit Sub

Err_AddSuppl_Click:
    MsgBox Err.Description
    Resume Exit_AddSuppl_Click
```

```
End Sub

Private Sub Form_Error(DataErr As Integer, Response As Integer)
'Trap duplicate Supplier ID value and display message.

Dim strMsg As String
Const conDupKey = 3022

    If DataErr = conDupKey Then
        strMsg = "You have entered a duplicate Supplier ID. "
        strMsg = strMsg & "Please enter a unique value."
        MsgBox strMsg
        Supplier_ID.SetFocus
        Response = acDataErrContinue
    End If

End Sub

Private Sub Form_Load()
'Maximize the form window on startup.

DoCmd.Maximize

End Sub

Private Sub PrevSuppl_Click()
'Preview the Supplier List report.
On Error GoTo Err_PrevSuppl_Click

    Dim stDocName As String

    stDocName = "Suppliers"
    DoCmd.OpenReport stDocName, acPreview

Exit_PrevSuppl_Click:
    Exit Sub

Err_PrevSuppl_Click:
    MsgBox Err.Description
    Resume Exit_PrevSuppl_Click

End Sub
```

Note: The only trick to adding command buttons to a form is to understand the difference between the button caption and the button name. When you use the Button Wizard, you have a chance to give the button a meaningful name, which helps you to remember which button does what. This name identifies the control the event procedure belongs to and, if you inadvertently use the button caption instead, nothing happens when you click the button. On the other end, no error occurs when a procedure in the class module refers to a control not in the form.

Create the Transaction Log Data Entry Form

The purpose of the Transaction Log data entry form is to acquire and store the information about transactions that have occurred during the business day. Granted, it is a bit unreasonable to expect a store manager or clerk to sit at the computer and log in every box of birdseed and every goldfish that has moved through the store during the day. This type of information would be automatically entered by a point-of-sale system at the register. However, this example can give you some useful ideas about the interactivity among related tables in an inventory control environment.

The Transaction Log form is by far the most active of the Pat's Pets database forms and requires the most attention to the details of events and responses (see Figure 12.7). Some of the data in the form comes from the Products table and is included so that it will present a complete picture at a later date. For example, the transaction shows the actual cost and price, and the Products table furnishes the cost and price that were current at the time of the transaction. After the transaction data has been accumulated over a period of time, this comprehensive information can be used in summaries and analyses.

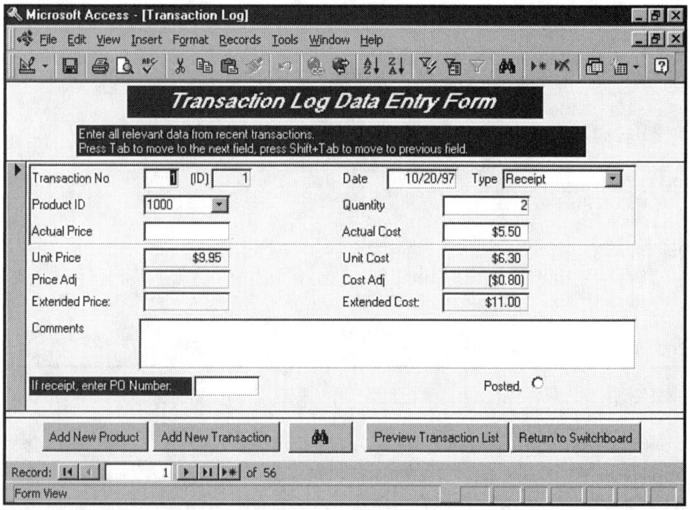

Figure 12.7.

The completed Transaction Log form.

Modify the Wizard's Form

The form shown in Figure 12.8 is the result of using the Form Wizard to create a columnar form with all the fields from the Transactions table and the Unit Cost and Sell Price fields from the Products table. The style is Colorful 2. The tables are already related so that the price and cost data will correspond to the Product ID.

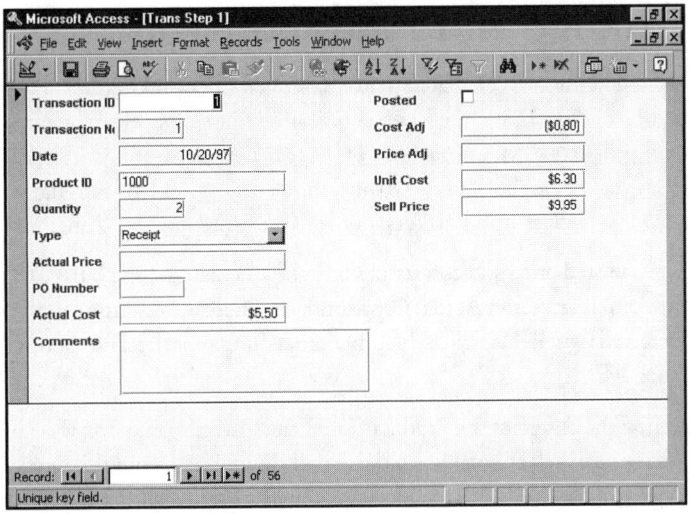

Figure 12.8.
The form finished by the Form Wizard.

Microsoft Access - [Trans Step 1]

File Edit View Insert Format Records Tools Window Help

Transaction ID	1		Posted	☐
Transaction N(	1		Cost Adj	($0.80)
Date	10/20/97		Price Adj	
Product ID	1000		Unit Cost	$6.30
Quantity	2		Sell Price	$9.95
Type	Receipt			
Actual Price				
PO Number				
Actual Cost	$5.50			
Comments				

Record: 14 | ◄ | 1 | ► | ►I | ►* | of 56

Unique key field.

The next step is to move the controls to a more logical sequence on the form. For example, gather the text boxes (into which the user will enter data) and place them in a rectangle at the top of the form. Then, arrange the Products fields and the calculated fields beneath the box. The adjusted price and cost figures are bound to fields in the Transaction table, but the extended price and cost figures are calculated fields and are not stored. They can easily be calculated later from information that is stored.

The unique key field, Transaction ID, is included and placed next to the Transaction No field for reference only. This is the AutoNumber field generated automatically by Access for each new record and is not available to the user. It corresponds to the line item in the transaction rather than the complete transaction.

The PO Number field is used only when the transaction is a receipt; therefore, it is placed at the bottom of the form. In the section, "Change Text Box Appearance and Tab Order," you will see a procedure that sets and resets the tab stop property of the PO Number field so that it receives focus only when the user selects Receipt as the Type value. An error is also generated if the user tries to save a record for a receipt transaction without entering a PO number. A procedure is added in the section, "Add Error-Handling Procedures," to handle this error.

The Posted check box is also placed out of the way because the user never checks this box. It is automatically checked when the Transactions table is used to post recent transactions to the Products table.

In Chapter 14, "Adding Real-Time Features," procedures are written that post the transaction data and archive posted records to a transaction history file.

Most of the controls are much larger than they need to be. Resizing the controls as you rearrange them gives the form a more open look.

Change and Add Controls

Next, add the two calculated fields: Extended Price and Extended Cost. After adding the unbound text box controls, use the Expression Builder or simply type the expression in the `Control Source` data property. Type `=[Quantity]*[Actual Price]` as the expression for Extended Price and `=[Quantity]*[Actual Cost]` for the Extended Cost field. Recall that if a field name includes a space, you must enclose it in brackets, but to be consistent, Access encloses them all in brackets.

The adjusted price and cost values must be calculated using VBA's `Lost Focus` event procedures for the Actual Price and Actual Cost controls. These are discussed in the section, "Calculate Adjusted Price and Cost fields," with the other procedures that the Transaction Log form requires to function properly.

During the design of the Products form, the Category text box was changed to a combo box so that the user can select a value from the pull-down list. Doing the same thing in the Transaction Log form with the Product ID field would help the user select (or at least verify) the proper code. Follow the same steps as before:

1. Right-click the Product ID text box and point to Change To and choose Combo Box.

2. Open the Data property sheet for the text box and make the same changes as before to set the `Row Source Type` to `Table/Query`, the `Row Source` to `Products`, and the `Bound Column` to 1. You might not want the user to be able to add to the Product ID list, so leave the `Add To List` property `No`.

3. Change the Format properties to set the `Column Count` to 2, remove the `Column Heads`, and then widen the columns and the list width to be able to see the full name of the products.

The Type field was already specified in the table definition as a lookup field, and the values were entered into the field property pane in the table design window.

Change Text Box Appearance and Tab Order

To distinguish quickly between text boxes that require data entry and those that just offer information, change the back colors. The Wizard shows only the text box with focus in white and the others in the same color as the form background. Change the back color of all the data entry text boxes in the rectangle to white and the others to the light yellow of the form. Figure 12.9 shows the modified form so far.

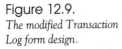

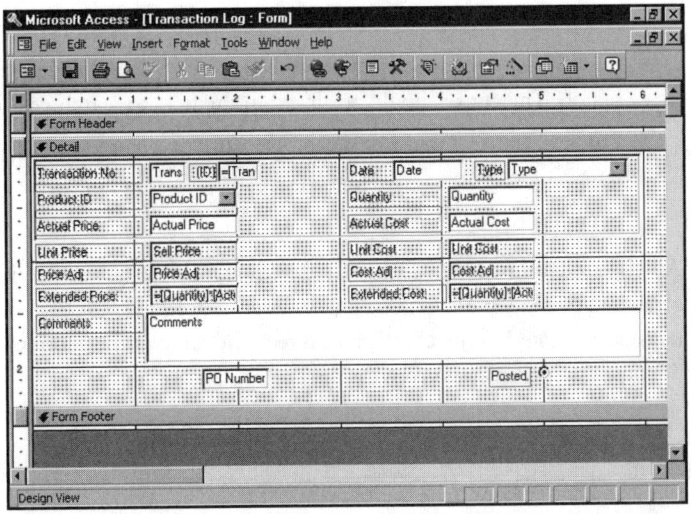

Figure 12.9.
The modified Transaction Log form design.

Tip: When you look at the format property sheet for the selected text box and click the Back Color build button to open the color palette, you will see that the selected color is already white. This is because the control gets focus when you select it in the design, and white is the default color for text boxes with focus. Clicking the white square in the color palette will keep the text box background white even after it loses focus.

Next, add a title and some explanatory text, as necessary, to the form header as well as an instruction about the PO Number text box.

The final step in working with the controls in the design is to modify the tab order and set the Tab Stop property of all the passive text boxes to No. The Enabled property of the Posted check box should be set to No and the Locked property to Yes to keep the check box bright but unavailable. Later, when the transactions are posted to the Products table, the Posted properties are changed so that the field can be checked after updating the product inventory.

Add Command Buttons

The completed Transaction Log form shows five command buttons in the form footer that carry out the following operations when clicked:

- Add New Product, which moves to an empty record at the end of the table and copies the transaction number, date, and type to the new record.

- Add New Transaction, which moves to an empty record at the end of the table.
- Find, which opens the Find dialog box where the user can enter the value for which to search. The cursor should be placed in the field to search before clicking the button.
- Preview Transaction List, which opens the Transaction List report for preview.
- Return to Switchboard, which closes the form and returns to the switchboard (if it was open before this form opened).

All of these buttons can easily be added to the form design with the Button Wizard. The procedures generated by the wizard, with added comments, are shown in Listing 12.3 (notice that the button name as indicated in the Click procedure is the same as the caption on the button because that is the name the wizard was given for the button).

Listing 12.3. The command button's OnClick event procedures.

```
Sub Preview_Transaction_List_Click()
'Opens Transactions report for preview.
On Error GoTo Err_Preview_Transaction_List_Click

    DoCmd.OpenReport "Transactions", acViewPreview

Exit_Preview_Transaction_List_Click:
    Exit Sub

Err_Preview_Transaction_List_Click:
    MsgBox Err.Description
    Resume Exit_Preview_Transaction_List_Click

End Sub

Sub Add_New_Record_Click()
'Adds new transaction record and disables PO Number tab stop.

On Error GoTo Err_Add_New_Record_Click
    DoCmd.GoToRecord , , acNewRec
    Me.PO_Number.TabStop = False
    Me.Transaction_No.SetFocus

Exit_Add_New_Record_Click:
    Exit Sub

Err_Add_New_Record_Click:
    MsgBox Err.Description
    Resume Exit_Add_New_Record_Click

End Sub

Private Sub Return_to_Switchboard_Click()
'Closes form and returns to switchboard.
On Error GoTo Err_Return_to_Switchboard_Click

    DoCmd.Close
```

```
Exit_Return_to_Switchboard_Click:
    Exit Sub

Err_Return_to_Switchboard_Click:
    MsgBox Err.Description
    Resume Exit_Return_to_Switchboard_Click

End Sub

Private Sub Add_New_Product_Click()
'Adds new product to current transaction.

On Error GoTo Err_Add_New_Product_Click

DoCmd.GoToRecord , , acNewRecord

Exit_Add_New_Product_Click:
    Exit Sub

Err_Add_New_Product_Click:
    MsgBox Err.Description
    Resume Exit_Add_New_Product_Click

End Sub

Private Sub Find_Record_Click()
'Opens Find dialog box.
On Error GoTo Err_Find_Record_Click

    Screen.PreviousControl.SetFocus
    DoCmd.DoMenuItem acFormBar, acEditMenu, 10, , acMenuVer70

Exit_Find_Record_Click:
    Exit Sub

Err_Find_Record_Click:
    MsgBox Err.Description
    Resume Exit_Find_Record_Click

End Sub
```

All of these procedures will do what is intended except for Add New Product. All the wizard knew
was that it was to go to a new record in the form. The current transaction data must be copied from
the previous record so that the user need enter only the product information. To do this, add the
following code to the Add_New_Product_Click procedure right after the On Error statement:

```
    Dim strTransNo As String
    Dim strType As String
    Dim dtmDate As Date

'Store previous transaction data.
    strTransNo = Me.Transaction_No
    strType = Me.Type
    dtmDate = Me.Date
```

```
'Copy transaction data to new record.
    DoCmd.GoToRecord , , acNewRec
    Me.Transaction_No = strTransNo
    Me.Type = strType
    Me.Date = dtmDate
    Me.Product_ID.SetFocus
```

The first three statements declare variables in which to store the transaction data temporarily. The next three copy the data to the variables. Then comes the DoCmd statement the wizard included that goes to a new record in the form. The next three statements copy the transaction data to the new record. The last statement moves focus to the Product ID field because the transaction data is already filled in.

After entering the new code, compile the entire module to catch any errors in spelling or syntax.

Add Data Validation and Other Procedures

The Transaction Log form needs at least six more procedures to complete a smooth-running user interface. One procedure maximizes the form and turns off the tab stop for the PO Number text box. Another sets the PO Number tab stop on if the transaction is a receipt. Two procedures calculate the adjusted cost and price values and two others handle potential errors.

The first procedure in Listing 12.4, Form_Load, is similar to those for the other two forms except for the TabStop setting. The second procedure examines the value in the Type field and sets the PO Number tab stop accordingly.

Listing 12.4. Added Transaction Log event procedures.

```
Private Sub Form_Load()
'Maximize the form window at startup.
'Reset PO Number tab stop to false.
On Error GoTo Err_Form_Load

    DoCmd.Maximize
    Me.PO_Number.TabStop = False

Exit_Form_Load:
    Exit Sub

Err_Form_Load:
    MsgBox Err.Description
    Resume Exit_Form_Load

End Sub

Private Sub Type_AfterUpdate()
'Allow tab to PO Number field, if transaction is a receipt.
On Error GoTo Err_Type_AfterUpdate

    If Me.Type = "Receipt" Then
        Me.PO_Number.TabStop = True
    Else
```

```
        Me.PO_Number.TabStop = False
    End If

Exit_Type_AfterUpdate:
    Exit Sub

Err_Type_AfterUpdate:
    MsgBox Err.Description
    Resume Exit_Type_AfterUpdate

End Sub
```

Calculate Adjusted Price and Cost Fields

After entering the Actual Price and Actual Cost values, Access can calculate the values to place in the Adjusted Price and Cost fields. These are bound text box controls that store the values in the Products table, so you cannot use an expression as the control source. The two procedures in Listing 12.5 calculate the values when the ActPrice and ActCost text boxes lose focus. They also refresh the form to add the adjusted values right away and then move to the next control.

Listing 12.5. Calculating fields from entered costs and prices.

```
Private Sub ActPrice_LostFocus()
'Calculates and updates Price Adjustment then moves to ActCost.
On Error GoTo Err_ActPrice_Lostfocus
    [Price Adj] = [Actual Price] - [Sell Price]
    Me.Refresh
    ActCost.SetFocus

Exit_ActPrice_LostFocus:
    Exit Sub

Err_ActPrice_Lostfocus:
    MsgBox Err.Description
    Resume Exit_ActPrice_LostFocus
End Sub

Private Sub ActCost_LostFocus()
'Computes and updates Cost Adjustment then moves to Comments.
On Error GoTo Err_ActCost_Lostfocus

    [Cost Adj] = [Actual Cost] - [Unit Cost]
    Me.Refresh
    Comments.SetFocus

Exit_ActCost_LostFocus:
    Exit Sub

Err_ActCost_Lostfocus:
    MsgBox Err.Description
    Resume Exit_ActCost_LostFocus

End Sub
```

There is a potential problem in these procedures. If the Product ID field is blank, the connection to the Sell Price and Unit Cost fields cannot be made and Jet engine error #3101 occurs: "The Microsoft Jet database engine can't find a record in the table Products with key matching field Product ID."

This is a form error that could be trapped by the Form_Error event. The problem is that this happens before you try to save the form, so any error-trapping procedure you attach to Form_Error will not be reached. You must handle the error before trying to calculate the adjusted values.

Add Error-Handling Procedures

To intercept the Jet engine error before it happens, add a procedure that runs when the Quantity text box gets focus before any value is entered. The following procedure checks for a Null value in the Product ID field and then composes an error message to display in place of the default message. After the message is displayed and the user has clicked OK, focus is returned to the Product ID field for a value to be entered. Listing 12.6 shows this error-handling procedure.

Listing 12.6. Ensuring a receipt has a PO Number value.

```
Private Sub Quantity_GotFocus()
'Checks to make sure Product ID has value.
On Error GoTo Err_Quantity_Gotfocus
Dim strMsg As String

'Display error message if Product ID field is blank.
    If IsNull(Product_ID) Then
        strMsg = "The Product ID field must have a value. Select a "
        strMsg = strMsg & "value from the combo box. If you want to "
        strMsg = strMsg & "delete this record, select any value for "
        strMsg = strMsg & "the Product ID then choose Edit¦Delete Record."
        MsgBox strMsg
        Product_ID.SetFocus
        GoTo Exit_Quantity_GotFocus
    End If

Exit_Quantity_GotFocus:
    Exit Sub

Err_Quantity_Gotfocus:
    MsgBox Err.Description
    Resume Exit_Quantity_GotFocus

End Sub
```

Figure 12.10 shows the message displayed when the Product ID field is blank and focus reaches the Quantity field. If you wait until focus reaches the Actual Price field, you will get the Jet engine error message after clicking OK in the custom message.

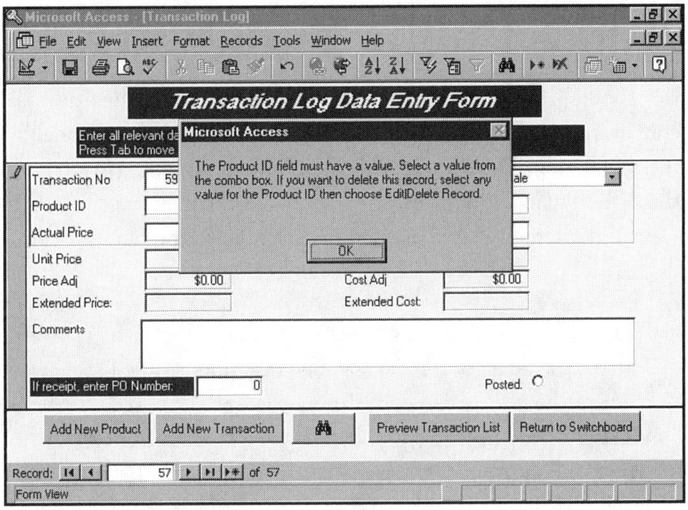

Figure 12.10.

The adjusted price cannot be calculated without a Product ID value.

The last error handler checks for the record validation rule that says if the transaction is a receipt, there must be a PO number. A slight complication is that PO Number field is the last tab stop on the form, so when you leave that field, focus moves to the next record. The error procedure must include a statement that returns to the previous record. The following event procedure runs when the PO Number field loses focus:

```
Private Sub PO_Number_LostFocus()
'Display error message if Receipt transaction has no PO Number.
On Error GoTo Err_PO_Number_LostFocus

Dim strMsg As String
strMsg = "You must enter a PO Number for a Receipt transaction."

'Check for Receipt type and no PO Number.
If [Type] = "Receipt" And PO_Number = 0 Then
    MsgBox strMsg
    DoCmd.GoToRecord , , acPrevious      'Returns to previous record.
    [PO_Number].SetFocus
End If

Exit_PO_Number_LostFocus:
    Exit Sub

Err_PO_Number_LostFocus:
    MsgBox Err.Description
    Resume Exit_PO_Number_LostFocus

End Sub
```

Add a Public Function

In Chapter 4, "Creating an Application with a Wizard," the Database Wizard built a Global module containing a single function, `IsLoaded()`. This function is available to all the other procedures in the application. The purpose of the function, as explained in Chapter 5, "Examining and Modifying the Wizard's Code," is to test the state of a form object and return `True` if the form is open in form view. If the form is closed or open in design view, the function returns `False`.

Tip: Such a function will be necessary for the Pat's Pets application when you add a pop-up form in the next section. This public function is called `IsOpen()`, but it contains exactly the same code. You can copy it from the Omni-Sport database or enter the code yourself. Click the Modules tab of the database window, and click New to open the module window. The two default `Option` statements are already in the window, so just enter the following code:

```
Public Function IsOpen(ByVal strFormName As String) As Boolean

Const conDesignView = 0
Const conObjStateClosed = 0

IsOpen = False
If SysCmd(acSysCmdGetObjectState, acForm, strFormName) <> conObjStateClosed
➥Then
    If Forms(strFormName).CurrentView <> conDesignView Then
        IsOpen = True
    End If
End If

End Function
```

Refer to Chapter 5 for an explanation of the `SysCmd()` function.

This is an important function because errors can occur if you try to carry out an operation that requires an open form, such as to change the records it displays, and the form is closed. You will call upon this function when you add a pop-up form to the Transaction Log form.

Create a Pop-Up Form

There may be times while you are entering transactions in the Transaction Log form that you would like to know what other transactions have taken place lately with the same product. A pop-up form can display all these transactions without closing the Transaction Log form.

Use the Form Wizard to create a new form based on the Transactions table. Select only the Product ID, Transaction No, Date, Quantity, and Type fields. Then, on the Other tab of the Property sheet, set Pop Up to Yes, which keeps the form on the screen while you are working with the other form. Switch to the Data tab and set Allow Edits, Allow Deletions, and Allow Additions all to No. Leave the Modal property as No so that you can work in other areas of the screen without having to close the form. Save the form with the name ThisProduct.

The new form is maximized in the window. Click and drag the window borders to resize the window so you will be able to see all the record data without obscuring the Transaction Log form.

Next, use the Command Button Wizard to add a command button to the Transactions Log form that will display the new form as a pop-up form. Follow these steps with the Wizard dialog boxes:

1. In the first dialog box, choose Form Operations and Open Form.

2. In the second, choose ThisProduct as the form to open.

3. Next, choose the option labeled Open the form and find specific data to display.

4. In the next dialog box, choose Product ID from both the Transaction Log and the ThisProduct field lists (see Figure 12.11).

5. In the last two dialog boxes, enter Transactions This Product as the button caption and ThisProduct as the button name.

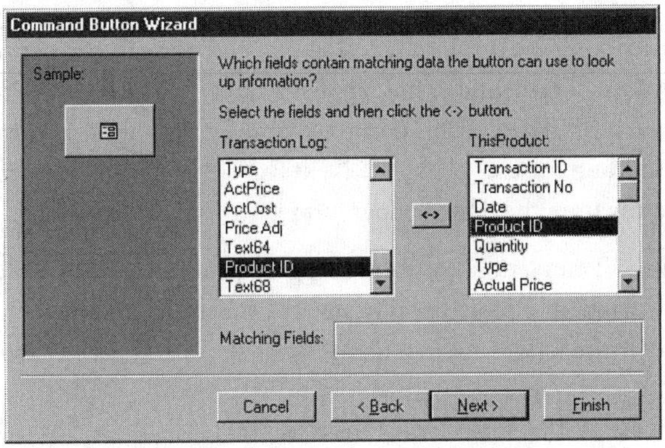

Figure 12.11.
Select the linking fields in the Command Button Wizard dialog box.

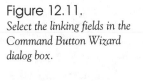

The following code is generated by the Command Button Wizard after you have made the previous selections:

```
Private Sub ThisProduct_Click()
On Error GoTo Err_ThisProduct_Click

    Dim stDocName As String
    Dim stLinkCriteria As String

    stDocName = "ThisProduct"

    stLinkCriteria = "[Product ID]=" & "'" & Me![Product ID] & "'"
    DoCmd.OpenForm stDocName, , , stLinkCriteria
```

```
Exit_ThisProduct_Click:
    Exit Sub

Err_ThisProduct_Click:
    MsgBox Err.Description
    Resume Exit_ThisProduct_Click

End Sub
```

The two declared variables, stDocName and stLinkCriteria, store the name of the pop-up form and the linking fields that connect the two forms. Then, the DoCmd statement opens the ThisProduct form with the Product ID filter. The wizard uses the "st" tag instead of "str" to declare string variables.

The pop-up form stays open until the user closes it by clicking the Close button. When you move to a different record in the Transaction Log form, the records in the ThisProduct form still show the first products, unless you click the new button again. It would be helpful if the forms were synchronized so that the pop-up form always showed the same product as the current record in the Transaction Log form.

Synchronize the Forms

To synchronize the two forms, add a procedure to the Transaction Log form that checks to see if the pop-up form is open and, if it is, applies a filter that changes the records in the pop-up form to match the main form. The event procedure is attached to the GotFocus event for the Transaction Log form because when the user clicks the Next Record or another record navigation button, the form takes focus away from the ThisProduct form.

Select the Transaction Log form in the database window and click the Code toolbar button. In the module window, choose Form from the Objects list and then choose GotFocus from the Procedures list. Enter the following statements:

```
Private Sub Form_GotFocus()
'Synchronize the ThisProduct form if it is open.

Dim strProduct As String

strProduct = Product_ID
    If IsOpen("ThisProduct") Then
        Forms!ThisProduct.Filter = strProduct
        Forms!ThisProduct.FilterOn = True
    End If

End Sub
```

The procedure first stores the current Product ID value in the string variable, strProduct. It then uses the new IsOpen() function to determine if the ThisProduct form is open. If so, it sets the ThisProduct filter to the value in strProduct and sets the FilterOn property to True. If the ThisProduct form is not open, the procedure ends.

Figure 12.12 shows the ThisProduct form displaying the transaction records that involve product #1013. Notice the record navigator in the ThisProduct form shows that there are five records and that a filter is applied to the recordset.

Figure 12.12.
The pop-up form shows the transactions for product #1013.

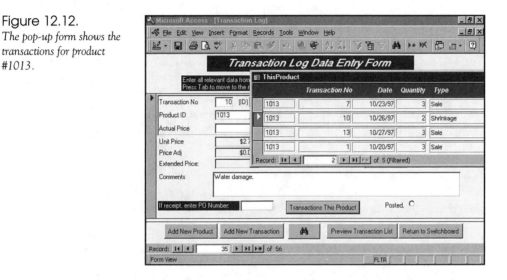

Note: Although the record selector shows that the current record in the ThisProduct form is the same as the current record in the Transaction Log form, this does not happen automatically. The record selector was moved prior to capturing the figure.

Close the Pop-Up with the Transaction Log

When you close the Transaction Log form, the pop-up form does not automatically close as well, so you need a procedure that closes it when the main form closes. If it is not open, then it doesn't need to be closed, so the IsOpen() function is used again in this procedure to check the current state of the form object.

Return to the module window and choose Close from the Procedures list with Form still showing in the Objects list. Then enter the following statements:

```
Private Sub Form_Close()
'Close ThisProduct popup form if still open.

    If IsOpen("ThisProduct") Then
        DoCmd.Close acForm, "ThisProduct"
    End If

End Sub
```

This simple procedure checks to see if the ThisProduct form is open and, if so, closes it.

Switch to the Transactions Log form view and test the new synchronized pop-up form.

Create a Tabbed Form

Access 97 has a new tool in the toolbox: the Tab control. With this tool, you can make multitabbed forms like many of Access's own dialog boxes that have related controls grouped on each tab. The Transaction Log form would be much less cluttered if you used a tabbed form with the sales data on one tab, the receipt data on another, and the shrinkage data on a third. It would be easier to enter all the data for one type of transaction at once and then move on to the next type.

The Tab control tool is simple to use. The first tab control you add to a new form creates two tabs. To add another tab, right-click on the last tab and choose Insert Tab from the shortcut menu. You can add any type of control to a tab control except another tab control. After creating the multitabbed form, change the tab captions to indicate the contents of the tab and other properties, as desired.

Start a new form for the transaction data, which will have three tabs, each with one type of transaction data. To create the form, follow these steps:

1. In the Forms tab of the datasheet window, click New and then choose Design View and select Transactions as the record source. An empty form appears in the design window.

2. Open the toolbox if it's not already visible and click the Tab Control button and draw the control to the entire size of the new form. Figure 12.13 shows the form with two tabs, labeled Page 1 and Page 2.

3. Add a third page by right-clicking anywhere in the form and choosing Insert Tab from the shortcut menu. Access adds Page 3 to the form.

4. Next, change the tab captions to **Sales**, **Receipts**, and **Shrinkage** by entering the new values in their respective Name properties on the Other tab of the property sheet.

Figure 12.13.
Creating a tabbed form.

Tab control

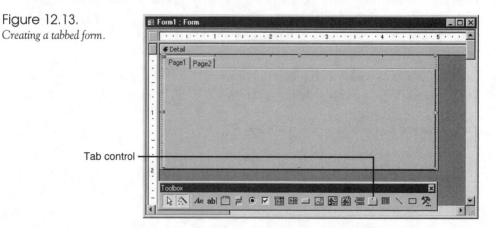

You are now ready to add the Transaction fields to the form pages. To display the field list, click the Field List toolbar button. The list of all the fields in the TransQuery appear in a window to the right of the new tabbed form (see Figure 12.14). One by one, click and drag the field names to the tab and then resize and reposition them for appearance.

Figure 12.14.
Drag the field names from Field List to the tabbed form.

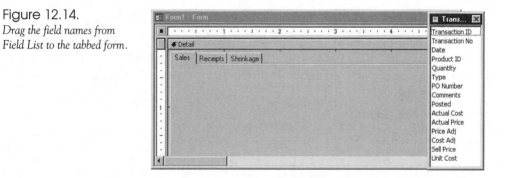

Add the common transaction fields and the price-related fields to the Sales tab and then add a command button that closes the form. Each tab should have an escape hatch so that the user can exit from any one of them. Next, add the common fields and the cost-related fields to the Receipts tab and only the common fields to the Shrinkage tab. The cost data is available in the Products table when you post the shrinkage transactions. Figure 12.15 shows the design of the Sales tab of the TabTransForm form.

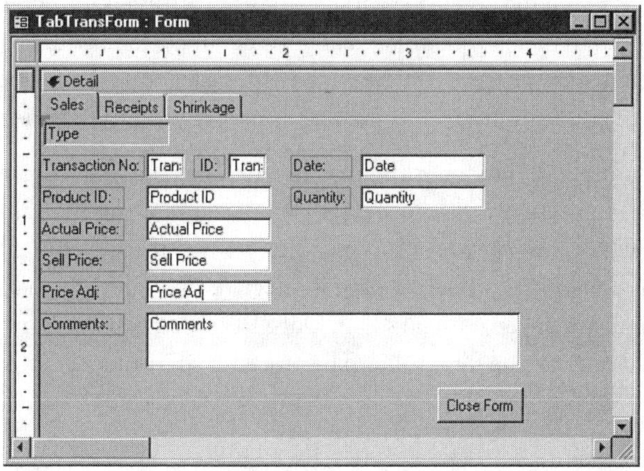

Figure 12.15.
The finished Sales tab design.

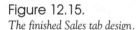

Note: When you drag the same fields to the second page of the tabbed form, the label is not the field name. You must change the label of these text boxes to the field names.

The Type control at the top of the design is no longer a combo box, and the properties are deliberately set to make it unavailable for data entry. A default value is specified so that when the user adds a new record to this tab, the value is automatically set to Sale. The control is there only for confirmation when the records are viewed. Similar changes are made to the Type field on the other two tabs.

After laying out the form design, some procedures are required to filter the records so that only sales transactions appear in the first tab, receipts in the second, and shrinkage in the third. When the form first opens, the first tab is always the active page, so an event procedure can be attached to the form OnLoad property that filters the records to those with "Sale" in the Type field. The following code accomplishes this:

```
Private Sub Form_Load()
'Filter records to show transactions for first page.

Dim tbc As Control
Dim strFilter As String

Set tbc = Me!TabCtl0
strFilter = "Sale"

Me.Filter = "Type = " & "'" & strFilter & "'"
Me.FilterOn = True

End Sub
```

The first statement declares the variable tbc as a control and then sets the reference to the Tab control in the current form, TabCtl0. In the Me.Filter statement, be sure to include the single quotation marks around the strFilter variable so that the filter is interpreted literally as Type = "Sale". When you need to include quotation marks in the filter, embed single quotation marks within double quotation marks. The two "'" groups on either side of and concatenated with the strFilter variable pass the quotation marks to the Filter property with the variable value.

The procedure that filters the records when the active tab changes is a little more complicated because it must set the filter depending on the current page. For this, use a Select Case structure based on the tab control Value property. The Value is the index number of the page in the tab control's Pages collection. If the first page is selected, the index number is 0. If the second page is selected, the index number is 1, and so on. Once the index number is determined, you can use it in the Case structure to set the filter value. The procedure in listing 12.7 is attached to the tab control OnChange property.

Listing 12.7. Segregating transactions by type on the tabbed form.

```
Private Sub TabCtl0_Change()
'Filter records to show transactions for specific page.

Dim tbc As Control
Dim intPge As Integer
Dim strFilter As String
```

```
Set tbc = Me!TabCtl0
strFilter = ""

intPge = tbc.Value + 1
Select Case intPge
    Case 1
        strFilter = "Sale"
    Case 2
        strFilter = "Receipt"
    Case 3
        strFilter = "Shrinkage"
End Select
Me.Filter = "Type = " & "'" & strFilter & "'"
Me.FilterOn = True

End Sub
```

The `intPge` declared integer is calculated by adding 1 to the tab control `Value`; it is then used in the `Select Case` statement to add the transaction type to the filter. You cannot use 0 as a `Case` value. Figure 12.16 and 12.17 show the Receipts and Shrinkage pages of the new tabbed form. Notice that the record navigation bar shows the number of transactions of that type on the page.

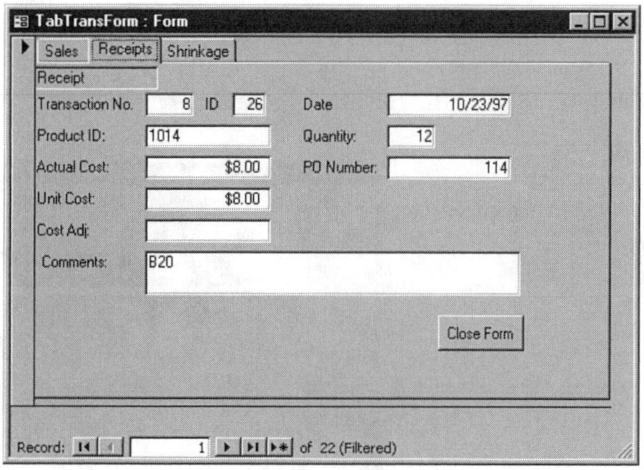

Figure 12.16.
The Receipts page of the tabbed form.

Note: If you want to delete a page from the tabbed form, right-click anywhere in the page you want to remove and then choose Delete Page from the shortcut menu. To change the page order in the tab control, choose Page Order from the shortcut menu. Choosing Tab Order from the shortcut menu lets you change the tab order for the controls on the current page.

Three additional procedures are in the TabTransForm form class module that were created by the Command Button Wizard. These close the form when the Close Form button on any of the pages is clicked.

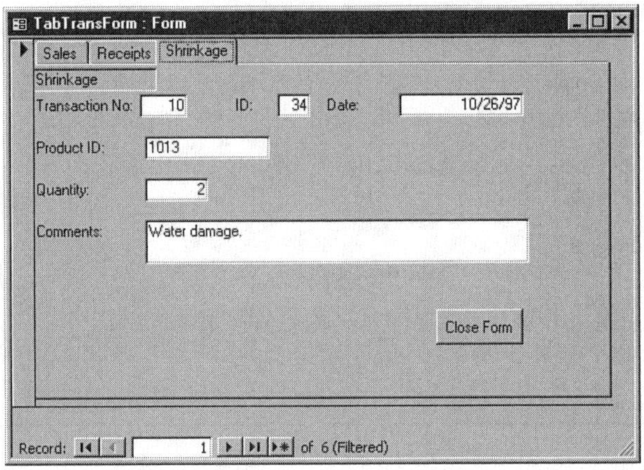

Figure 12.17.
The Shrinkage page of the tabbed form.

Add Controltips and Other User Help

Until the user becomes accustomed to the data entry forms in the application, tips and reminders can be helpful. *Controltips* are short messages that pop up when the mouse pointer rests on a control in the form. To specify a controltip, enter the text in the `ControlTipText` property box. You can enter up to 255 characters in the tip, but shorter is better. Figure 12.18 shows a controltip that advises the user to place the cursor in the field to search before clicking the Find button.

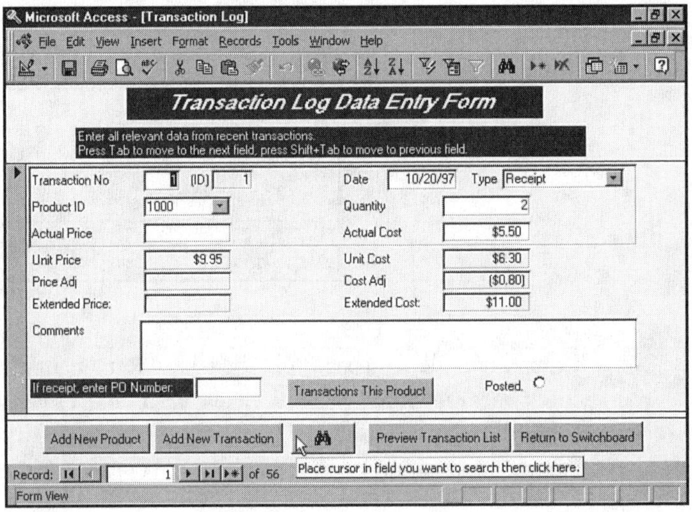

Figure 12.18.
A controltip for the Find button.

Status bar messages are also helpful and can be attached to a control or the form itself. Again, you can enter up to 255 characters in the StatusBarText property box, but Access displays only as many as will fit in the status bar line. Figure 12.19 shows a message in the status bar when the Shrinkage page is active that reminds the user to enter a reason for the loss.

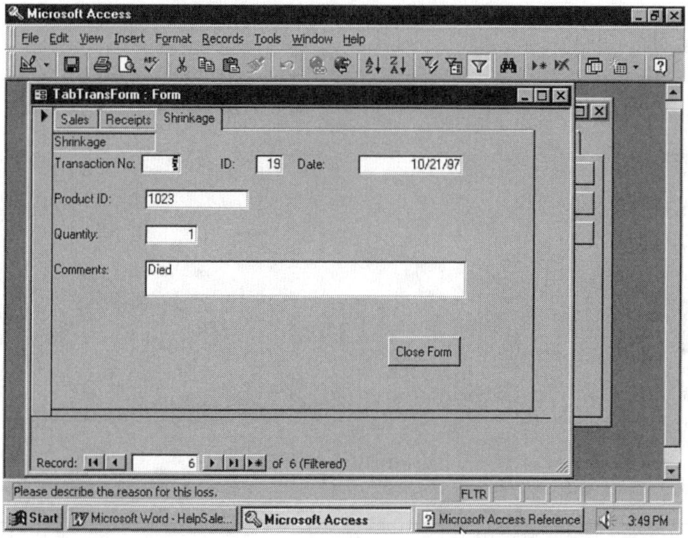

Figure 12.19.
The status bar reminds the user to enter a reason for the loss.

As discussed briefly in Chapter 6, "How to Get Help with Access Programming," you can also create compiled Help topics that display when the user presses F1 or clicks the What's This? button.

Summary

This has been a rather intensive chapter dealing with the important issue of data entry and how to prevent errors during the process. Carefully designing forms can enhance the user's understanding of the requirements of the application and can reduce the likelihood of mistakes.

Four different types of forms were designed in the chapter: two were rather simple, one contained fields from two tables, and the last contained multiple pages. VBA code was created to add new records, preview reports, validate data, filter records, and trap errors. Where multiple forms were displayed, a procedure was written to synchronize the records in the forms.

In the next chapter, reports are discussed for the Pat's Pets application—reports that sort, group, and summarize the information stored in the application.

13

Customizing Reports

Preparing and printing Access reports requires far less user interaction than forms. However, you still have the opportunity to make some changes in the format and other properties of a report at runtime. This chapter gives some examples of manipulating the Pat's Pets reports with custom features.

The Report Wizard

The Access 97 Report Wizard can do just about anything you could want for a report. It can group records and provide totals, counts, and other summaries; it can sort the records based on the value in one or more fields; it can automatically shrink or grow a section based on the contents; and it can even provide a custom report style.

For most applications, the Report Wizard can create the reports you need; however, there might be some things you need that it can't do. All the report properties are set before the report opens. After that, the wizard has no jurisdiction. Any changes you want to make based on the value of the data to be included in the report are up to you. For example, if you want products whose stock levels have fallen below the restocking level to appear in bold font in the report, you must add VBA code to accomplish this.

Another example is adding a filter to the report that is specified by the user at runtime. If you have already created queries that include the filters from which you want the user to select, your code will set the report record source property to the appropriate query at runtime.

Report Events

In order to be able to attach the code to the correct event, it is important to review what events apply to reports and report sections. There are far fewer events for reports than for forms. They fall into two main categories: *general events*, which apply to the report as a whole, and *section events*, which apply to the report sections—the page, group headers and footers, and the detail section.

The general events are as follows:

- The `Open` event occurs before the report is previewed or printed. `Open` is the default event for report objects.
- The `Close` event occurs when the report is closed and removed from the screen.
- The `Activate` event occurs when the report receives focus and becomes the active window.
- The `Deactivate` event occurs when the report loses focus to another window.
- The `NoData` event occurs when a report is being formatted for printing when the report is bound to an empty recordset.

- The Page event occurs after a report page has been formatted for printing, but before printing occurs.
- The Error event occurs when a runtime error occurs in a report that has focus.

The events that apply to report sections include the following:

- The Format event occurs when Access selects the data for the section but before Access actually formats it. Format is the default event for report sections.
- The Print event occurs after formatting but before printing.
- The Retreat event occurs when Access has to back up to do additional formatting operations with the section. Retreat applies to all sections except page headers and footers.

The Sequence of Report Events

As with forms, it is important to understand the sequence of events so that you can attach the event procedure to the right event. Generally speaking, report and report section events occur when you open a report for previewing or printing, or when you close the report.

When you open a report to print or preview it and then close it or switch to a different window, the following sequence of events occurs:

```
Open↓
 Activate↓
 Close↓
  Deactivate
```

If you have more than one report open and you switch between them, the Deactivate event occurs for the first report followed by the Activate event for the second report. This also occurs when you switch to another Access window. The report remains active, and the Deactivate event does not occur if you switch to a dialog box or a pop-up form or to a window in another application. The Activate event can be used to hide or display custom toolbars and other window-related features.

If the report is based on a query, the query is run after the Open event has occurred for the report. This is very useful for setting the query criteria with a macro or event procedure after the report opens but before the query is run. A macro or event procedure can also open a dialog box so the user can specify the desired filter criteria.

The NoData event occurs after all the Format events have occurred for all the report sections and before the first Page report event occurs. NoData is used to cancel printing of a blank report. This event does not occur for a subreport if there are no records in it. You must use a different strategy to hide empty subreports. One way is to use the HasData property in a procedure to test for the empty control. Then attach the procedure to the subreport section's Format or Print event.

The Sequence of Report Section Events

The report section events begin to occur after the Open and Activate report events and before the Deactivate and Close events. The sequence of events is as follows:

> Open (report)↓
> Activate (report)↓
> Format (section)↓
> Print (section)↓
> Page (report)↓
> Close (report)↓
> Deactivate (report)

The Format event occurs with every section in the report; you can use it as a trigger for procedures that run calculations and make other runtime adjustments. In a detail section, the Format event occurs for each record in the section. In group headers, the Format event occurs for each new group and can change data in the header as well as in the first record of the detail section. In group footers, the Format event applies to the data in the footer and in the last record of the detail section. With a Format event procedure, you can use the data in the current record to change properties or hide or display special text.

If you want to make changes that don't affect the page layout or format, use the Print event. The Print event occurs after all the formatting is done for the section and before it is actually printed. In the detail section, Print occurs for each record just before Access prints it; thus, a Print event procedure can be used to examine the data in the record before printing. In a group header, the Print event occurs for each new group, and the event has access not only to the data in the header but also the first record to the data in the detail section. Similarly, the Print event in the group footer has access to the data in the footer as well as the data in the last record of the detail section.

You can use the Print event to work with the data Access has ready to print. For example, you can use a macro or event procedure to calculate running totals to be printed in the page or group header or footer. If you want to change the page layout, you must use the Format event instead of Print because the page is already prepared by the time you reach the Print event. You would also use the Format event to access data in sections that you are not going to print. For example, you don't plan to print all the pages of a report but you still want to calculate a running total of sales or receipts.

The Page event occurs after all the Format events have occurred for all the report sections and after the Print event has occurred for the current report page, but before the page is printed. If you want to change the appearance of the printed report, you can attach a macro or event procedure to the Page event. For example, using the Line or Circle methods in a procedure can add graphics to the page. You can also add pictures or other images at report printing time rather than have them embedded in the report design where they take up disk space.

Under some circumstances, Access must return to a previous section to carry out the placement of controls and sections in the report. For example, a group might not fit in the space left on a page if the KeepTogether property is set to Yes for either the Whole Group or With First Detail in the Sorting and Grouping dialog box. Subforms and subreports whose CanGrow or CanShrink property is set to Yes can also affect the formatting of a previous report section. The sections on the last page of the report can also trigger the Retreat event.

After the Format event has occurred for every section on the page to determine how the controls are to be placed, the Retreat event will occur if the sections can't be printed. Access backs up to a previous section and moves it to the following page. The Retreat event occurs for every section passed over. After the Retreat events have occurred, Format occurs again to get ready to actually print the report.

> **Tip:** An event procedure that runs in response to a Retreat event can undo any changes made during the previous Format event such as summarizing values by page or deciding whether to print a page header.

Change Format and Properties at Runtime

The Transactions by Number report described in this section is an example of changing report and section properties at runtime. The report is designed to list the Pat's Pets transaction data grouped by transaction number.

All the transaction records in the current Transactions table are included with no filtering. The Report Wizard was used to create the basic report; then the text boxes containing information relating to the transaction number rather than the line item were moved to the group header section. A group footer was also added so that a light line could be drawn across the page to separate the groups. After some resizing and font changes, the design looks like what is shown in Figure 13.1.

The Comments field does not have text in many of the records and it appears as the sole control on the second line in the Detail section. An event procedure can be run when the Format event occurs for the Detail section that can test for a value in the field and, if none, omit the Comments label and close up the Detail section.

By default, Access leaves space for the text box value even if it is blank. The next step is to change the Detail section and the Comments control so that they will vertically close up if the text box control has no data. Setting the Can Shrink property of the text box control does not automatically set the equivalent property of the Detail section, so you must set them both.

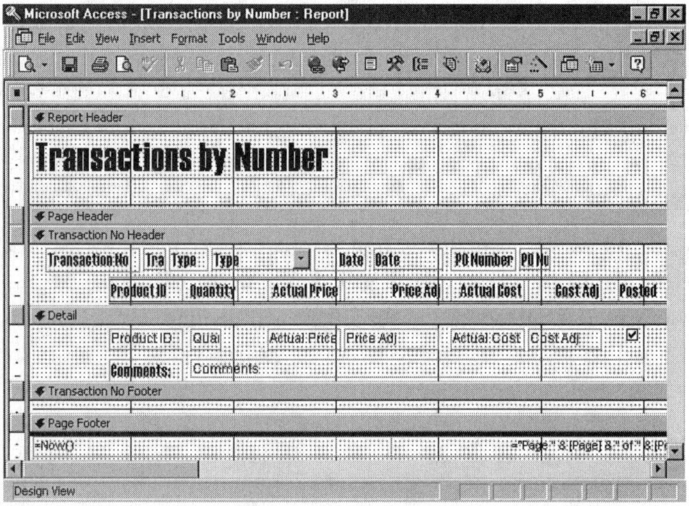

Figure 13.1.
The Transactions by Number report design.

The Can Shrink property when set to Yes (True in VBA) shrinks the section or control vertically so that no blank lines are printed. The Can Shrink property and its counterpart, Can Grow, can be set only in the control's property sheet. They do not apply to page header and footer sections.

The Can Shrink property takes care of blank Comments fields, but the label will still be printed unless you specify that it can disappear if there is no value associated with it. You can do this by attaching the code in Listing 13.1 to the Format event for the detail section.

Listing 13.1. The Detail_Format event procedure.

```
Private Sub Detail_Format(Cancel As Integer, FormatCount As Integer)
'If the Comments field is blank do not print the label.

Dim blnComments As Boolean

'Test for blank Comments field.
blnComments = Not IsNull(Comments)

'Set the visible property for the Comments label.
CommentsLabel.Visible = blnComments

End Sub
```

In this procedure, the statement

```
blnComments = Not IsNull(Comments)
```

sets the value of the Boolean variable blnComments to False if the Comments field is blank or to True if the field contains text. IsNull() returns True if the argument is blank, and then the Not keyword converts it to False. If there is text in the Comments field, IsNull() returns False and the Not keyword converts this to `True`. The last statement before `End Sub` sets the `Visible` property of the `CommentsLabel` control to the value of the Boolean variable.

> **Note:** You must know the name of the label control for the Comments text box in order to set its visible property. Look at the Name property in the Other tab of the property sheet.

Another improvement to this report is that if the transaction type is not Receipt, there is no PO number, so omit the PO Number label from the group header section. You don't need to set the `Can Shrink` property for the group header section to `Yes` because not printing the PO number does not change the group header height.

This event procedure is also run in response to the `Format` event, but this time when the event occurs for the group header. The code (see Listing 13.2) for this runtime property adjustment is similar to the code for the Comments field.

Listing 13.2. The `Format` event procedure for the group header.

```
Private Sub GroupHeader0_Format(Cancel As Integer, FormatCount As Integer)
'If the transaction is not a receipt, do not print the PO Number label.

Dim blnPONum As Boolean

'Test for blank PO Number.
blnPONum = Not IsNull(PO_Number)
PO_Number_Label.Visible = blnPONum

End Sub
```

The `Not IsNull()` test is run for the value in the PO Number text box and if it is blank, the `Visible` property of the PO Number Label control is set accordingly.

Images, pictures, and other graphics take up disk space if they are embedded in a report or form design. To reduce the amount of space the report requires and also to speed up loading the report, you can link the object at runtime. You can even display a pop-up box asking the user if he or she wants to include the object.

For the Transactions by Number report, the user might like to classify the printed report with the Confidential classification watermark. This can be added as a background image centered on the page and can be printed on every page of the report. The procedure in Listing 13.3 runs when the report's `Open` event occurs. The picture used in this example is one of the bitmaps in the Office subfolder in the Microsoft Office folder. Your path may be different.

Listing 13.3. The Open event procedure for the Transactions by Number report.

```
Private Sub Report_Open(Cancel As Integer)
'Add "Confidential" watermark before printing.

Me.Picture = "C:\Program Files\Microsoft Office\Office\Bitmaps\" & _
    "Styles\Confidential.bmp"
'Set picture properties to Clip, Linked and Center.

Me.PictureSizeMode = 0
Me.PictureType = 1
Me.PictureAlignment = 2

End Sub
```

The last three statements before End Sub set the report properties as follows:

- PictureSizeMode to Clip (0 in VBA).
- PictureType to Linked (1 in VBA).
- PictureAlignment to Center (2 in VBA).

Figure 13.2 shows a preview of the new Transactions by Number report. Notice that in the records that have no Comment text, the line is closed up and the group headers for sales transactions do not include a PO Number label. The Confidential watermark appears centered on the page both horizontally and vertically.

Figure 13.2.
The Transactions by Number report preview.

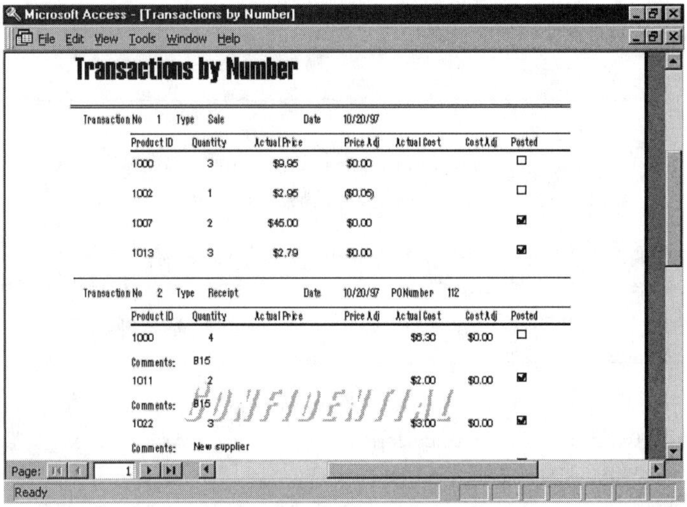

Preparing for User Input

If you have several reports that present the same basic information in different ways, you may consider using a dialog box to ask the user which report he or she would like to see. For example, three reports show transaction data in three different ways: grouped by transaction number, grouped by supplier with group totals and a running total, and grouped by transaction type. The previous section discussed the first report. This section discusses the other two as well as a form for user input to select which report to preview.

First, let's create the two new reports and then tie all three together with a dialog box form.

The Transactions by Type Report

Once again, let the Report Wizard start the report design by making the following choices in the Wizard dialog boxes:

1. Choose the query TransQuery as the basis for the report. This query combines data from the Transactions table and the Products table so that the unit cost and sell price are available for calculations in the report.

2. Include all the fields in the query except the Transaction ID, the AutoNumber Access uses as the primary key for the Transactions table.

3. Group the records by Type and sort by Transaction No.

4. Choose the Align Left 1 layout and the Soft Gray style, and then name the report Transactions by Type.

After the wizard is finished, the report layout is 21 inches wide. You need to resize and reposition many fields to fit on a page even in landscape orientation. Also, add three unbound text box controls to hold the calculated fields: extended price, extended cost, and the net difference between the two. Use the Expression Builder or type the following expressions in the Control Source properties for the new text boxes:

- ExtPrice = [Quantity]*[Sell Price]
- ExtCost = [Quantity]*[Unit Cost]
- Net = [ExtPrice]-[ExtCost]

Be sure to name the first two calculated fields so you can use the names in the third expression.

The Type field would look better in the group header if the font size and style were the same as the label: Arial, 9 point, and heavy weight. The completed report design looks like the one shown in Figure 13.3.

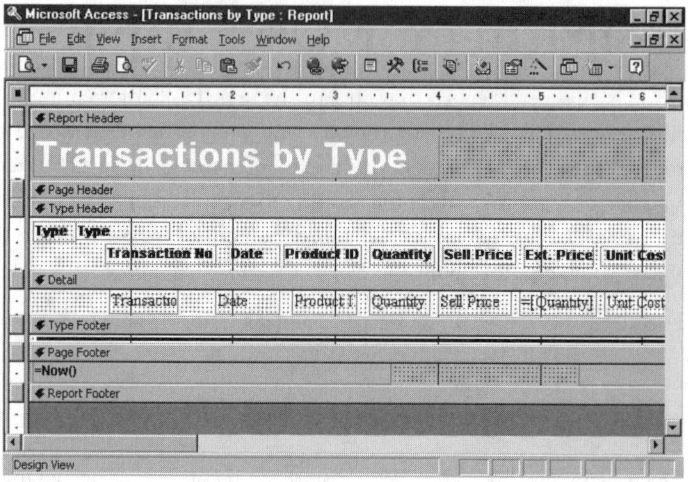

Figure 13.3.
The Transactions by Type
report design.

In the Transactions by Number report, some of the text box controls and label controls were not printed, depending on the type of transaction. With this report, the Unit Cost and Sell Price values always appear regardless of the transaction type because they are from the Products table. Some VBA code attached to the Detail section Format event can keep these fields from being printed when they do not apply to the transaction type. For example, the Sell Price does not relate to a receipt or a shrinkage transaction.

This report needs two event procedures: one to set the Visible property of several of the text box controls and their labels, and a second one to restore the Visible properties to Yes after the report is printed. If not reset to Yes, the property remains No, which could affect later use of the controls.

The procedure in Listing 13.4 runs when the Format event occurs for each Detail section. It first resets all the Visible properties to Yes. This is necessary because the previous Detail section might have set some of the Visible properties to No. Then, the procedure tests the value in the Type field with a nested If...Then block.

Listing 13.4. Formatting the report Detail sections.

```
Private Sub Detail_Format(Cancel As Integer, FormatCount As Integer)
'Select the fields to display depending on the type of transaction.
'If sale, display all fields but PO Number.
'If receipt, remove cost data.
'If shrinkage, display only cost data.
'Reset all the visible properties to True then
'change detail section display depending on type of transaction.
```

```
        Me.Unit_Cost.Visible = True
        Me.ExtCost.Visible = True
        Me.Net.Visible = True
        Me.Unit_Cost.Visible = True
        Me.ExtCost.Visible = True
        Me.Net.Visible = True
        Me.Sell_Price.Visible = True
        Me.PO_Number.Visible = True
        Me.ExtPrice.Visible = True

If Me.Type = "Receipt" Then
        Me.Unit_Cost.Visible = False
        Me.ExtCost.Visible = False
        Me.Net.Visible = False
    ElseIf [Type] = "Shrinkage" Then    .
        Me.Sell_Price.Visible = False
        Me.ExtPrice.Visible = False
        Me.Net.Visible = False
End If

End Sub
```

The `If...Then` structure tests only for Receipt and Shrinkage because if the transaction is a Sale, all the fields apply except for PO Number, which is blank anyway for a sale. The corresponding labels could also have been set to invisible, but that creates a report page with large gaps. It is easier to read with the column headings left in the report.

The `Report_Close` procedure resets all the affected `Visible` properties to `Yes`:

```
Private Sub Report_Close()
'Reset all the visible properties to True.

    Me.Unit_Cost.Visible = True
    Me.ExtCost.Visible = True
    Me.Net.Visible = True
    Me.Unit_Cost.Visible = True
    Me.ExtCost.Visible = True
    Me.Net.Visible = True
    Me.Sell_Price.Visible = True
    Me.PO_Number.Visible = True
    Me.ExtPrice.Visible = True

End Sub
```

Figures 13.4, 13.5, and 13.6 show the three pages of the Transactions by Type report with all three types of transactions.

Figure 13.4.
Receipt transactions.

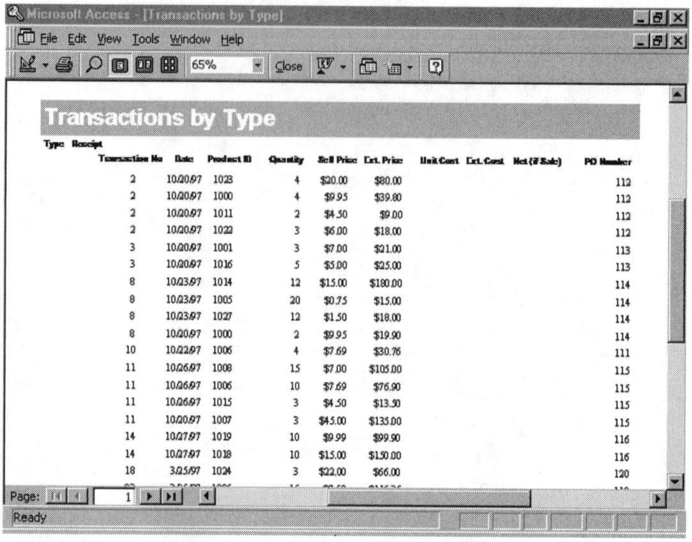

Microsoft Access - [Transactions by Type]

Transactions by Type

Type: Receipt

Transaction No	Date	Product ID	Quantity	Sell Price	Ext. Price	Unit Cost	Ext. Cost	Net (If Sale)	PO Number
2	10/20/97	1023	4	$20.00	$80.00				112
2	10/20/97	1000	4	$9.95	$39.80				112
2	10/20/97	1011	2	$4.50	$9.00				112
2	10/20/97	1022	3	$6.00	$18.00				112
3	10/20/97	1001	3	$7.00	$21.00				113
3	10/20/97	1016	5	$5.00	$25.00				113
8	10/23/97	1014	12	$15.00	$180.00				114
8	10/23/97	1005	20	$0.75	$15.00				114
8	10/23/97	1027	12	$1.50	$18.00				114
8	10/20/97	1000	2	$9.95	$19.90				114
10	10/22/97	1006	4	$7.69	$30.76				111
11	10/26/97	1008	15	$7.00	$105.00				115
11	10/26/97	1006	10	$7.69	$76.90				115
11	10/26/97	1015	3	$4.50	$13.50				115
11	10/20/97	1007	3	$45.00	$135.00				115
14	10/27/97	1019	10	$9.99	$99.90				116
14	10/27/97	1018	10	$15.00	$150.00				116
18	3/25/97	1024	3	$22.00	$66.00				120

Page: 1

Figure 13.5.
Sale transactions.

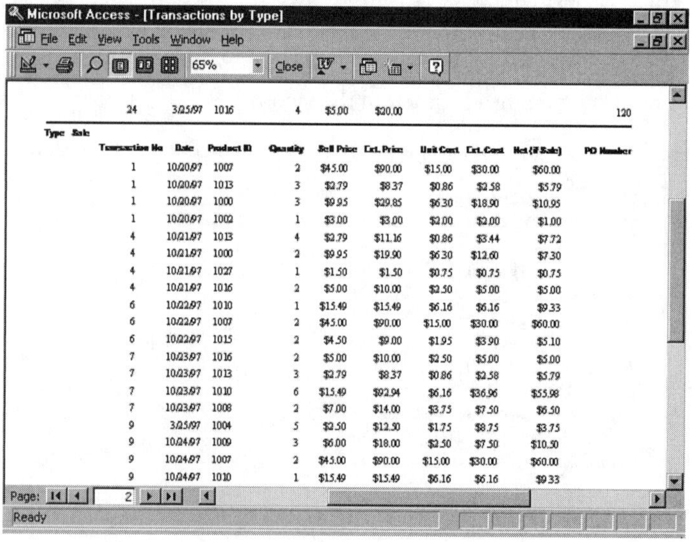

Microsoft Access - [Transactions by Type]

Transaction No	Date	Product ID	Quantity	Sell Price	Ext. Price	Unit Cost	Ext. Cost	Net (If Sale)	PO Number
24	3/25/97	1016	4	$5.00	$20.00				120

Type: Sale

Transaction No	Date	Product ID	Quantity	Sell Price	Ext. Price	Unit Cost	Ext. Cost	Net (If Sale)	PO Number
1	10/20/97	1007	2	$45.00	$90.00	$15.00	$30.00	$60.00	
1	10/20/97	1013	3	$2.79	$8.37	$0.86	$2.58	$5.79	
1	10/20/97	1000	3	$9.95	$29.85	$6.30	$18.90	$10.95	
1	10/20/97	1002	1	$3.00	$3.00	$2.00	$2.00	$1.00	
4	10/21/97	1013	4	$2.79	$11.16	$0.86	$3.44	$7.72	
4	10/21/97	1000	2	$9.95	$19.90	$6.30	$12.60	$7.30	
4	10/21/97	1027	1	$1.50	$1.50	$0.75	$0.75	$0.75	
4	10/21/97	1016	2	$5.00	$10.00	$2.50	$5.00	$5.00	
6	10/22/97	1010	1	$15.49	$15.49	$6.16	$6.16	$9.33	
6	10/22/97	1007	2	$45.00	$90.00	$15.00	$30.00	$60.00	
6	10/22/97	1015	2	$4.50	$9.00	$1.95	$3.90	$5.10	
7	10/23/97	1016	2	$5.00	$10.00	$2.50	$5.00	$5.00	
7	10/23/97	1013	3	$2.79	$8.37	$0.86	$2.58	$5.79	
7	10/23/97	1010	6	$15.49	$92.94	$6.16	$36.96	$55.98	
7	10/23/97	1008	2	$7.00	$14.00	$3.75	$7.50	$6.50	
9	3/25/97	1004	5	$2.50	$12.50	$1.75	$8.75	$3.75	
9	10/24/97	1009	3	$6.00	$18.00	$2.50	$7.50	$10.50	
9	10/24/97	1007	2	$45.00	$90.00	$15.00	$30.00	$60.00	
9	10/24/97	1010	1	$15.49	$15.49	$6.16	$6.16	$9.33	

Page: 2

Figure 13.6.
Shrinkages.

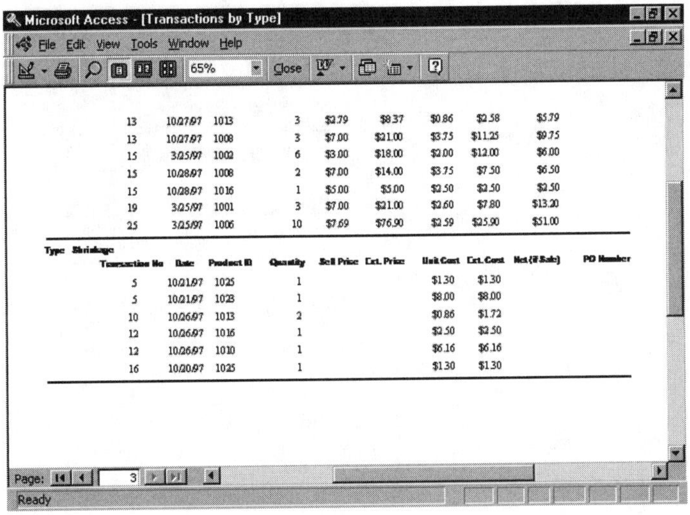

The Transactions by Supplier Report

The third transaction report groups the receipt transactions by supplier. The extended cost is calculated for each supplier, and a running total is also added to the group. Figure 13.7 shows a preview of the completed report, and Figure 13.8 shows the report design after modifying the Report Wizard's product.

Figure 13.7.
The Transactions by Supplier report preview.

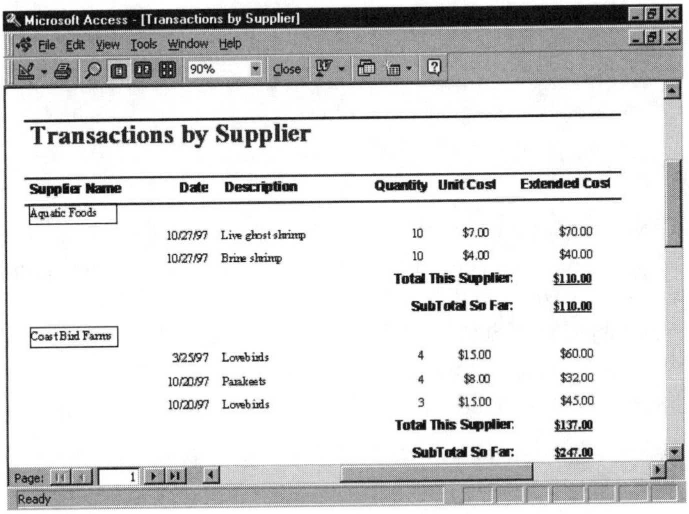

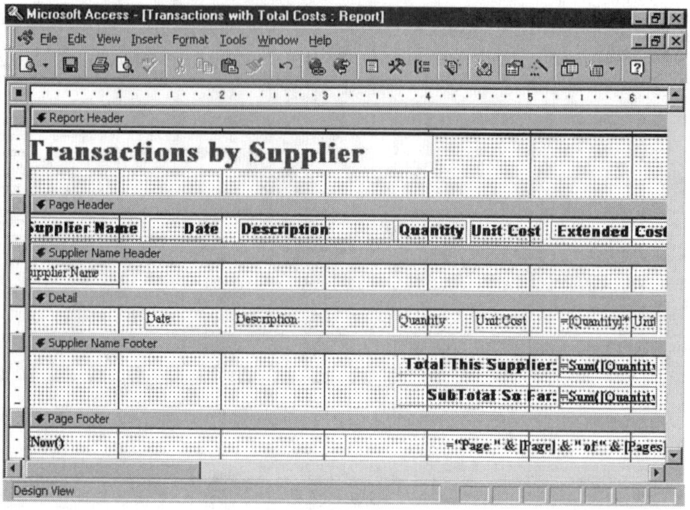

Figure 13.8.

The Transactions by Supplier report design.

![Screenshot of Microsoft Access report design view showing "Transactions by Supplier" report with Report Header, Page Header, Supplier Name Header, Detail, Supplier Name Footer, and Page Footer sections. Columns include Supplier Name, Date, Description, Quantity, Unit Cost, and Extended Cost.]

An expression is used to define both of the unbound text box controls, Total This Supplier and SubTotal So Far, that are placed in the group footer. The expression =Sum([Quantity]*[Unit Cost]) can be used for both the controls. Placing the Total This Supplier in the group footer automatically totals the value for the group. The Subtotal So Far value is a running total that can be specified in the control's property sheet by setting the Running Sum property to Over All.

Note: You could show a running total within the group as each line item is added to the transaction by placing the control in the detail section. Then, you could remove the Sum operator and change the Running Sum property to Over Group. If you use this setting for the control in the group footer, it shows only the value of the last item in the group. In the footer, you must use the Sum() function.

The Transactions by Supplier report is based on an SQL statement that includes fields from three tables: Transactions, Suppliers, and Products (see Figure 13.9). An inner join is formed linking the Transactions table to the Products table by the Product ID field. Another join links the Transactions table to the Suppliers table with the Supplier ID field. A WHERE clause limits the records to those with Receipt in the type field. To see the report's SQL statement, right-click the Record Source property and choose Zoom from the shortcut menu.

This report has no procedures in the class module. All the design work was done in the property sheet and with the SQL statement.

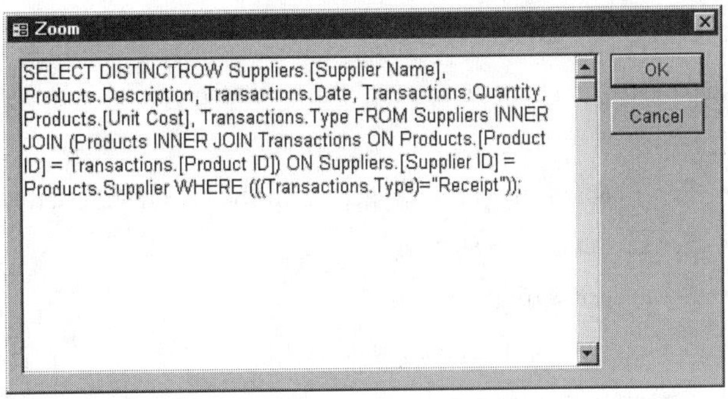

Figure 13.9.
*An SQL statement is the
record source for the
Transactions by Supplier
report.*

Zoom

SELECT DISTINCTROW Suppliers.[Supplier Name],
Products.Description, Transactions.Date, Transactions.Quantity,
Products.[Unit Cost], Transactions.Type FROM Suppliers INNER
JOIN (Products INNER JOIN Transactions ON Products.[Product
ID] = Transactions.[Product ID]) ON Suppliers.[Supplier ID] =
Products.Supplier WHERE (((Transactions.Type)="Receipt"));

OK

Cancel

The User Input Form

The final piece of the scenario is the form that lets the user decide which report to preview. The form design contains an option group with the three reports as choices (see Figure 13.10). It has two buttons, one to preview the selected report and the other to close the form without making a selection.

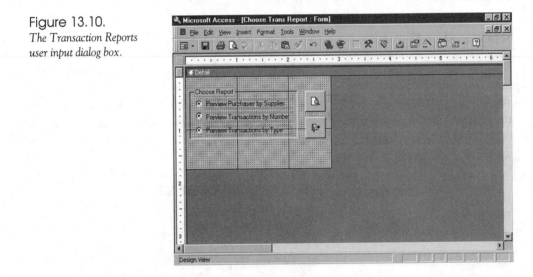

Figure 13.10.
*The Transaction Reports
user input dialog box.*

Create the form without the help of the Form Wizard, and add an option group with the three options. Then, add two command buttons with the help of the Command Button Wizard: one that opens a report for preview and the other to close the form. When you tell the wizard you want to use the button to open a report, it wants to know which report. Select one of the transaction reports—you will change that with code later.

Setting Properties

To make the form behave and look like a dialog box, change some of the form's properties as follows:

- Enter Choose Transaction Report in the Caption property.
- Set Scrollbars to Neither.
- Set Record Selectors to No.
- Set Navigation Buttons to No.
- Set AutoCenter to Yes.
- Set Border Style to Dialog.
- Switch to the Other property tab and set Popup to Yes.
- Set Modal to Yes.

Setting the form as modal means that the user will not be able to click anywhere outside the form while it is open. Most of the dialog boxes in Access are modal and require a response from the user before moving on, even if it is only a click of the Cancel button.

Sizing the Form

To make the form the right size when it opens in the Access window, click the Resize button if the form design window is maximized. Then, drag the borders of the window to match the form itself and save the form design. Figure 13.11 shows the completed form with controltips added to explain the options. These are added with code in the Form_Load event procedure in later paragraphs. You create them by typing the text in the ControlTip text box on the control and the label property sheets.

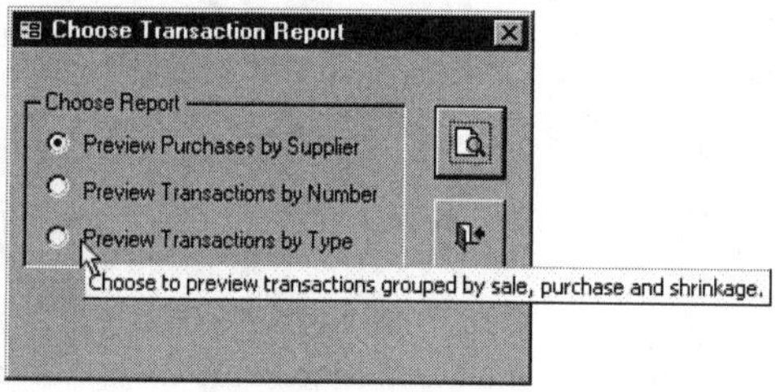

Figure 13.11.
The completed Choose Transaction Report form.

Next, you need to write an event procedure for the Preview command button that will select the report for preview. The Command Button Wizard has already taken care of the Cancel button Click event procedure with the code shown in Listing 13.5.

Listing 13.5. The Cancel_Click event procedure.

```
Private Sub Cancel_Click()
On Error GoTo Err_Cancel_Click

    DoCmd.Close

Exit_Cancel_Click:
    Exit Sub

Err_Cancel_Click:
    MsgBox Err.Description
    Resume Exit_Cancel_Click

End Sub
```

When the Preview command button is clicked, the OnClick procedure tests for the value returned by the option group, and then opens the specified report for preview. By default, the options in a group return integer numbers beginning with 1, the value from the first selection. So, if the value is 1, the Transactions by Supplier report should open for preview; if 2, the Transactions by Number, and so on. The form also must be removed from the screen after a selection is made.

The event procedure in Listing 13.6 runs when the Preview button is clicked in the Choose Transaction Report form.

Listing 13.6. The Preview button OnClick event procedure.

```
Private Sub PrevSuppTrans_Click()
'Open a report for preview depending on returned value from
'option group.
On Error GoTo Err_PrevSuppTrans_Click

Dim strDocName As String
'Use ChooseReport option group in Case structure
    Select Case ChooseReport
        Case 1
            strDocName = "Transactions by Supplier"
        Case 2
            strDocName = "Transactions by Number"
        Case 3
            strDocName = "Transactions by Type"
    End Select
'Remove dialog box from the screen and open report.
    Me.Visible = False
    DoCmd.OpenReport strDocName, acPreview

Exit_PrevSuppTrans_Click:
    Exit Sub

Err_PrevSuppTrans_Click:
    MsgBox Err.Description
    Resume Exit_PrevSuppTrans_Click

End Sub
```

This procedure uses a `Select Case` block based on the value returned by the option group named ChooseReport to set the name of the report to preview. Just before the `DoCmd.OpenReport` statement, the form's `Visible` property is set to `False`, removing it from the screen.

Adding Controltips

An added touch to the form is the display of explanatory controltips when the mouse pointer hovers over a control or a label (refer to Figure 13.11). You can add these by typing text in the `ControlTip` property of the control or in code in the `Form_Load` event procedure. Listing 13.7 adds controltips to both the option button controls and their labels.

Listing 13.7. Adding controltips when the form loads.

```
Private Sub Form_Load()
'Set the text of controltips for the options in the option group.
    Me.Option9.ControlTipText = "Choose to preview transactions " & _
        "grouped by Supplier with totals."
    Me.OptionLabel1.ControlTipText = "Choose to preview " & _
        "transactions grouped by Supplier with totals."
    Me.Option11.ControlTipText = "Choose to preview report of " & _
        "transactions by number."
    Me.OptionLabel2.ControlTipText = "Choose to preview " & _
        "report of transactions by number."
    Me.Option13.ControlTipText = "Choose to preview transactions " & _
        "grouped by sale, purchase and shrinkage."
    Me.OptionLabel1.ControlTipText = "Choose to preview " & _
        "transactions grouped by sale, purchase and shrinkage."

End Sub
```

Forms such as this one can be used as mini-switchboards that branch out from a selection made on the main switchboard. For example, a main selection could be to enter or edit records, which opens a form from which the user selects the table to work with.

In Chapter 14, "Adding Real-Time Features," the Pat's Pets application will be integrated with a main switchboard, the branching form created in this chapter, and other forms and dialog boxes that complete the project.

Add Conditional Totals

In the next report design, which is a summary of the product inventory in Pat's Pets, the products are grouped by major product category, and products that must be reordered are emphasized by printing them in heavy font weight. In addition, a count of the number of items that need to be ordered is added to the group footer.

Use the Report Wizard to build the beginnings of the Summary of Product Inventory report, choosing the Products Query as the record source. The Products Query joins the Category table with the Products table so that you have access to the name of the category that corresponds to the code. Group the records by Cat Code and sort them within the group by Product ID.

Next, add two text box controls and labels to the group footer to hold the total number of products in the group and the number of products that need to be ordered. Enter names for the new unbound text boxes that resemble the field names so that you can use them in the code to set their properties. The Name property is on the Other tab of the property sheet.

Type the expression =Count([Product ID]) in the control source box for the unbound text box that will show the total number of products in the category. The control source for the number of products that need to be ordered will be defined by code at runtime.

> **Tip:** If you preview the report now, you see that the supplier codes contain lowercase letters. The Suppliers table included a formatting provision that converted them to uppercase, which is not carried over to a report design. To add this feature to the report, change the control source from Supplier to the expression =UCase([Supplier]). You must include the equal sign or you will get a prompt to enter the parameter value. Figure 13.12 shows the report design after these changes have been made.

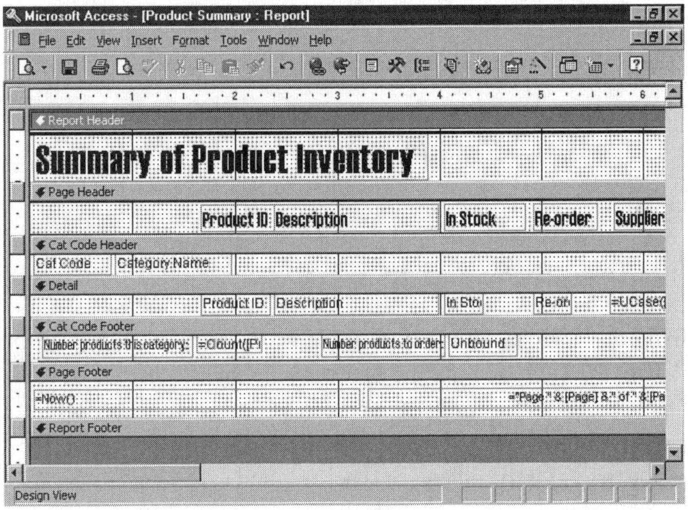

Figure 13.12.
The Summary of Product Inventory report design.

When you add a conditional count to a group, you need to initialize it to 0 every time the report opens a new group. A procedure to do this should run when the group header is formatted and ready to print so that you can use the group header OnPrint event as the trigger.

The code that changes the appearance of the In Stock and Re-order values depending on their relative values belongs in the `Detail_Print` event procedure. The calculation of the conditional count of products to reorder is also in that procedure. Listing 13.8 shows the Products Inventory report class module with both procedures.

Listing 13.8. The Products Inventory report class module.

```
Private Sub GroupHeader0_Print(Cancel As Integer, PrintCount As Integer)
'Reset number of products to order to 0.
ReOrdNum = 0

End Sub


Private Sub Detail_Print(Cancel As Integer, PrintCount As Integer)
'If the In-stock value is less than or equal to the Re-Order level,
'print both values in bold style.
'Define constants with normal and bold font weight values.
Const conNormal = 400
Const conBold = 800
Dim lngDiff As Long

lngDiff = [In Stock] - [Re-order]

If lngDiff < 0 Or lngDiff = 0 Then
    [In Stock].FontWeight = conBold
    [Re-order].FontWeight = conBold
Else
    [In Stock].FontWeight = conNormal
    [Re-order].FontWeight = conNormal
End If

'Add 1 to number of products to order to the group total.

If PrintCount = 1 Then
    If lngDiff < 0 Or lngDiff = 0 Then
        ReOrdNum = ReOrdNum + 1
    End If
End If

End Sub
```

In the declaration section of the `Detail_Print` procedure, three variables are declared: two constants that set the VBA value for the `Font Weight` properties `Normal` and `Bold`, and a numeric variable that represents the difference between the In Stock value and the Re-order value. Next, the difference is calculated and the `If...Then...Else` segment sets the Font Weight properties of both text box controls to `Normal` if the difference is positive and `Bold` is zero or negative.

Next, the ReOrdNum value is incremented if the difference between the product levels is equal to or less than 0. You would think that you could just add a statement to the `If...Then` block used to set the font property, which tests the same expression. However, it is not that easy because of the `PrintCount` property that appears as an argument in the `Detail_Print` procedure. `PrintCount` identifies the number of times the OnPrint property for the section is evaluated. It is incremented if the section runs over to a second page, for example. Because you don't want to count any product twice, increment the total only if PrintCount equals 1 (that is, the first time any part of the section is printed).

Figure 13.13 shows a preview of the beginning of the Summary of Product Inventory report. You might be able to see that the Live ghost shrimp and Feeder guppies products need to be reordered. Their In Stock and Re-Order values appear in bold and the Number products to order shows 2. There is one product to order in the Fish supplies category.

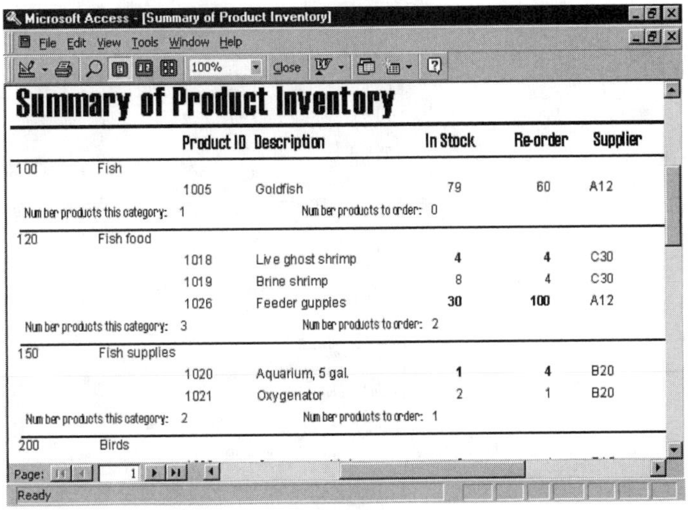

Figure 13.13.
A preview of the Summary of Product Inventory report.

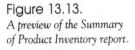

Microsoft Access - [Summary of Product Inventory]

Summary of Product Inventory

	Product ID	Description	In Stock	Re-order	Supplier
100 Fish					
	1005	Goldfish	79	60	A12
Number products this category: 1		Number products to order: 0			
120 Fish food					
	1018	Live ghost shrimp	**4**	**4**	C30
	1019	Brine shrimp	8	4	C30
	1026	Feeder guppies	**30**	**100**	A12
Number products this category: 3		Number products to order: 2			
150 Fish supplies					
	1020	Aquarium, 5 gal.	1	4	B20
	1021	Oxygenator	2	1	B20
Number products this category: 2		Number products to order: 1			
200 Birds					

Using Subforms to Print Purchase Orders

When the inventory of a product falls below the recommended stocking level, the store manager issues purchase orders to the suppliers. Access can be of help in identifying the products that should be ordered and printing selected purchase orders. To display the products with low levels together with information about their suppliers, you can create a form with a subform control.

The form is based on the Suppliers table, and the subform is based on the Products table. The linking field is the Supplier ID from the Suppliers table and Supplier from the Products table. In order to show only those products whose levels are low, base the subform on a query with the criterion that the In Stock quantity is less than or equal to the Re-Order level ([In Stock] < [Re-Order] + 1). The subform's Default View property is set to Datasheet.

After placing the text box controls and the subform control on the form, add three command buttons with the Command Button Wizard. One prints the current purchase order, the second prints all the orders, and the third closes the form.

Figure 13.14 shows the Reorder List form design with the Reorder subform, and Figure 13.15 shows the same form in form view.

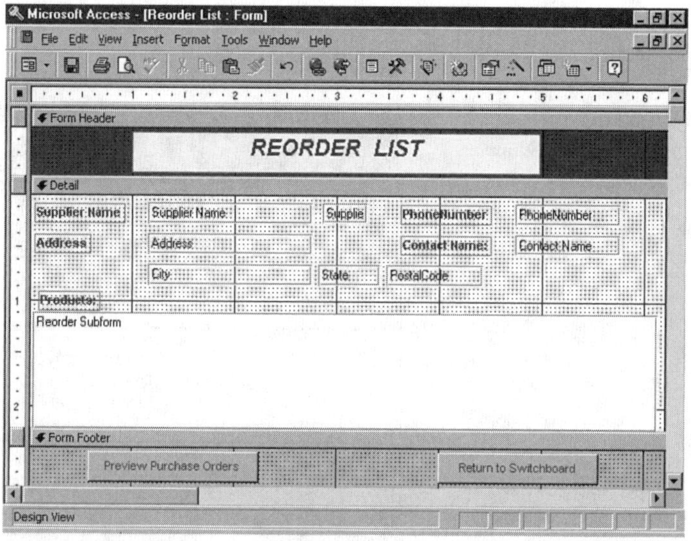

Figure 13.14.
The Reorder List form design.

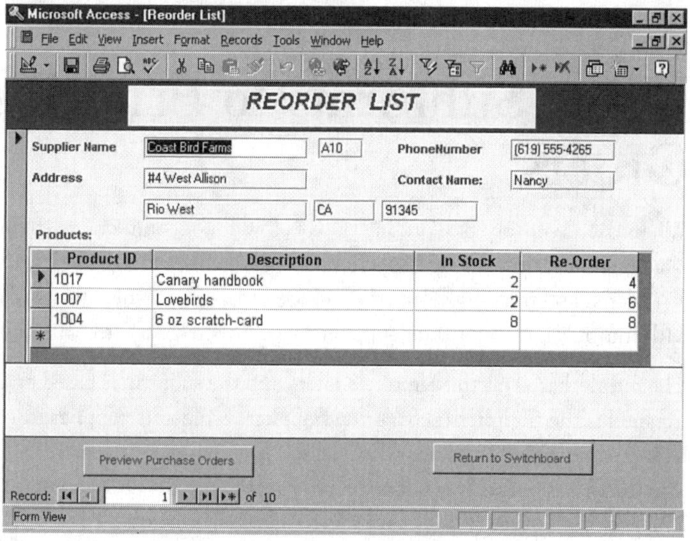

Figure 13.15.
The completed Reorder List form.

As you navigate through the supplier records, notice that some suppliers have no products in the subform. This form is meant to be used to add other products to the order lists as necessary, and not rely on the query to decide what and how much to order.

The event procedure that the Command Button Wizard creates prints all the records in the Order Products report by default. If you want to restrict the report to the current record, you must add a filter condition based on Supplier Name to the DoCmd.OpenReport statement. With the filter, the event procedure contains the code in Listing 13.9.

Listing 13.9. Filtering records before printing purchase orders.

```
Private Sub Print_PO_Click()
On Error GoTo Err_Print_PO_Click

    Dim strDocName As String, strFilter As String
    Dim strName As String

    strName = [Supplier Name]
    strFilter = "[Supplier Name] = " & "'" & strName & "'"
    strDocName = "Order Products"

    DoCmd.OpenReport strDocName, acViewNormal, , strFilter

Exit_Print_PO_Click:
    Exit Sub

Err_Print_PO_Click:
    MsgBox Err.Description
    Resume Exit_Print_PO_Click

End Sub
```

The declaration statements create variables for the report name, the field to filter on, and the filter itself. The next three statements set the variable values before the DoCmd statement that prints the purchase order for the supplier currently displayed in the form view. Figure 13.16 shows the printed report for the Coast Bird Farms.

The Print All Orders Click procedure requires no additional code statements.

The Order Products report design has some special features. To have each order print on a separate page, change the Force New Page property of the group footer to After Section. This moves to the next page after printing the data in the group footer.

> **Tip:** If you have any data in the page header and choose to print only the current record, the page header information will print again on a second page. To prevent this problem, place all the page header text and controls in the group header. Figure 13.17 shows the Order Products report design with all the header information in the group header.

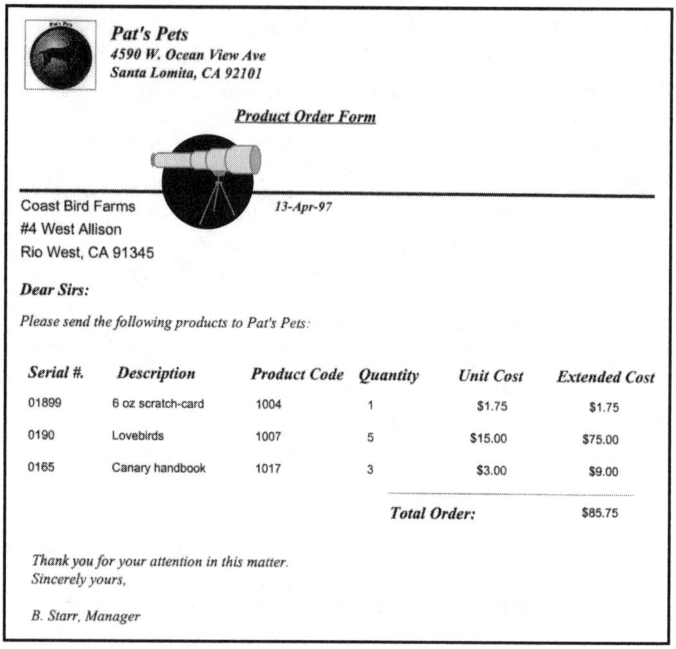

Pat's Pets
4590 W. Ocean View Ave
Santa Lomita, CA 92101

Product Order Form

Coast Bird Farms
#4 West Allison
Rio West, CA 91345

13-Apr-97

Dear Sirs:

Please send the following products to Pat's Pets:

Serial #.	Description	Product Code	Quantity	Unit Cost	Extended Cost
01899	6 oz scratch-card	1004	1	$1.75	$1.75
0190	Lovebirds	1007	5	$15.00	$75.00
0165	Canary handbook	1017	3	$3.00	$9.00
				Total Order:	$85.75

Thank you for your attention in this matter.
Sincerely yours,

B. Starr, Manager

Figure 13.16.
A printed purchase order.

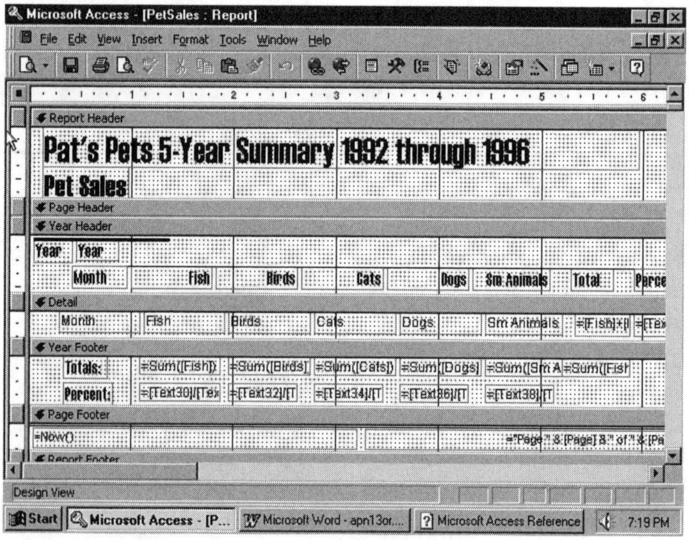

Figure 13.17.
The Order Products report design.

Summarize Archived Data

Storing information from the past helps plan for the future if the information is stored carefully and in an organized manner. The Pat's Pets store has been keeping track of sales data for several years by totaling monthly sales for each of the five major product categories.

The granularity of the data is sufficient to be able to arrange and analyze it in several ways. For example, you can detect quarterly trends by grouping the monthly data in groups of three. In addition, one can analyze the growing or waning interest in a particular type of pet over the years. One hardly sees pot-bellied pigs anymore.

Sharp changes in the data in short periods of time can be traced to extraordinary events such as earthquakes, the invasion of a large competitor in the neighborhood, a new residential community developing nearby, or a change in management personnel.

More important for business decisions are the subtle changes that occur over time. The Access Chart Wizard is a good tool to use for graphically illustrating and comparing these trends.

Another way to illustrate trends is to send the data to Excel for analysis and then import the results back to your report. Chapter 17, "Linking with Other Office Applications," includes several examples of exchanging data.

The report generated in this section is a dual-purpose report. It will print the details of the monthly sales figures for a five-year period or print only the yearly summaries. The same report design is used for both, and the required formatting changes are done at runtime by VBA procedures. A pop-up form is also designed that will open either version of the report.

Create the Dual-Purpose Report

The Report Wizard is always a good place to start with a new object. The modified report design shows the records grouped by year with both a group header and footer (see Figure 13.18). Each Detail line has two calculated fields at the right end of the section: the total amount of sales for that month and the percentage of the year's sales represented by that month. The Year group footer also contains calculated fields that total the sales for the whole year and compute the percentage of the year's sales that came from each product category.

Figure 13.18.
The PetSales report design.

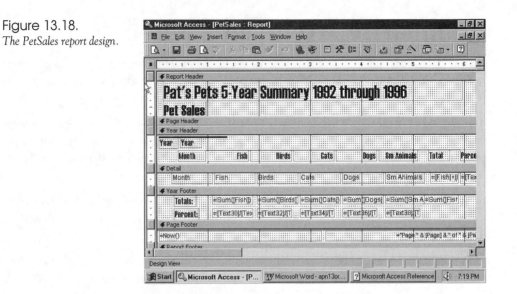

Figure 13.19 shows the first page of a three-page preview of the Monthly Sales Summary report. This one has all the details for every month of the five-year period. To be able to use the same design for a report that summarizes the data and doesn't show the details, some changes need to be made to the report properties.

Determine the Differences

The first step is to make a list of how the two reports differ. The most obvious difference is that the detail section does not appear in the Annual Summary, only the subtotals for each year and the grand totals in the report footer. Also, it would look more professional if the column headings that refer to fields only in the detail section were removed from the report when it is the Annual Summary version. Finally, it is convenient to have a custom caption in the title bar when previewing reports that can appear to be similar.

Each section, control, and label in the report design has a name even if it is only `Label56`. You use this name when you want to make changes. The sections are numbered, and when you want to change a section property, you refer to it by its index number, such as `Section(3)`, which is the page header section. Table 13.1 shows the index numbers for the report sections.

Table 13.1. Report sections and their index numbers.

Index	Section
0	Detail section
1	Report header
2	Report footer
3	Page header
4	Page footer
5	Group 1 header
6	Group 1 footer
7	Group 2 header
8	Group 2 footer

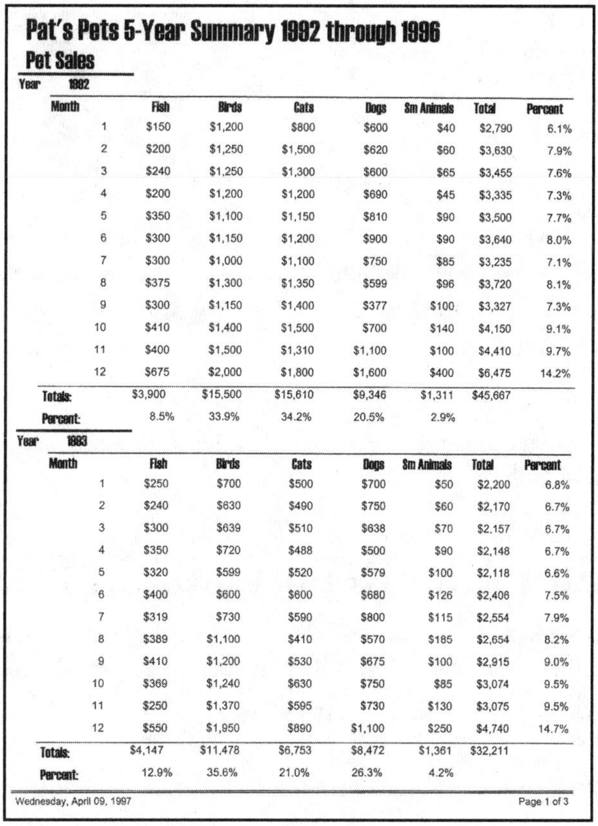

Figure 13.19.
The first page of a preview of the Monthly Sales Summary report.

Pat's Pets 5-Year Summary 1992 through 1996
Pet Sales

Year 1992

Month	Fish	Birds	Cats	Dogs	Sm Animals	Total	Percent
1	$150	$1,200	$800	$600	$40	$2,790	6.1%
2	$200	$1,250	$1,500	$620	$60	$3,630	7.9%
3	$240	$1,250	$1,300	$600	$65	$3,455	7.6%
4	$200	$1,200	$1,200	$690	$45	$3,335	7.3%
5	$350	$1,100	$1,150	$810	$90	$3,500	7.7%
6	$300	$1,150	$1,200	$900	$90	$3,640	8.0%
7	$300	$1,000	$1,100	$750	$85	$3,235	7.1%
8	$375	$1,300	$1,350	$599	$96	$3,720	8.1%
9	$300	$1,150	$1,400	$377	$100	$3,327	7.3%
10	$410	$1,400	$1,500	$700	$140	$4,150	9.1%
11	$400	$1,500	$1,310	$1,100	$100	$4,410	9.7%
12	$675	$2,000	$1,800	$1,600	$400	$6,475	14.2%
Totals:	$3,900	$15,500	$15,610	$9,346	$1,311	$45,667	
Percent:	8.5%	33.9%	34.2%	20.5%	2.9%		

Year 1993

Month	Fish	Birds	Cats	Dogs	Sm Animals	Total	Percent
1	$250	$700	$500	$700	$50	$2,200	6.8%
2	$240	$630	$490	$750	$60	$2,170	6.7%
3	$300	$639	$510	$638	$70	$2,157	6.7%
4	$350	$720	$488	$500	$90	$2,148	6.7%
5	$320	$599	$520	$579	$100	$2,118	6.6%
6	$400	$600	$600	$680	$126	$2,406	7.5%
7	$319	$730	$590	$800	$115	$2,554	7.9%
8	$389	$1,100	$410	$570	$185	$2,654	8.2%
9	$410	$1,200	$530	$675	$100	$2,915	9.0%
10	$369	$1,240	$630	$750	$85	$3,074	9.5%
11	$250	$1,370	$595	$730	$130	$3,075	9.5%
12	$550	$1,950	$890	$1,100	$250	$4,740	14.7%
Totals:	$4,147	$11,478	$6,753	$8,472	$1,361	$32,211	
Percent:	12.9%	35.6%	21.0%	26.3%	4.2%		

Wednesday, April 09, 1997 — Page 1 of 3

If you have more than two groups, their index numbers continue with 9 for the index for the Group 3 header, 10 for the Group 3 footer, and so on. To refer to the detail section of the current report in VBA code, use the following syntax:

```
Me.Section(0)
```

Create the Pop-Up Form

Before you start writing the code that will make the changes you need, create the form that will invoke the print previews. You must use the response from the pop-up form to determine which version of the report to display. The form is quite similar to the one used to choose which transaction report to preview, except that it has only two options: monthly sales or annual sales (see Figure 13.20). The Preview button opens the report, and the value of the option selected in the option group is available to the Report_Open procedure.

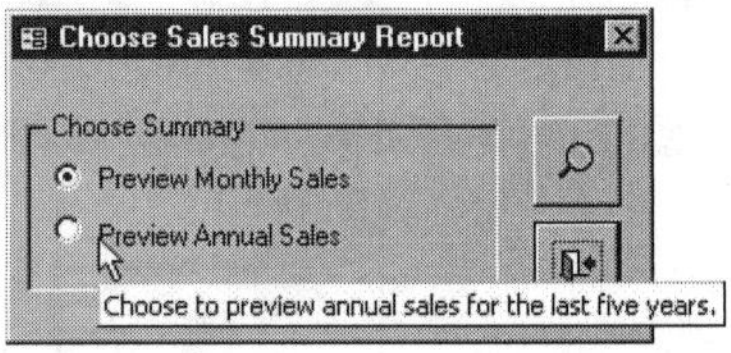

Figure 13.20.
Choose the report to preview
from the pop-up form.

The only change you need to make in the code generated by the Form Wizard is for the Preview button's OnClick event. Because the form is a pop-up, you must close it before opening the report or else it will stay on the screen in front of the report. Add the following statement to the event procedure:

```
Me.Visible = False
```

You make the rest of the changes after the report opens so that you make them in the report's Open event procedure.

Add to the Report's **Open** Event Procedure

With the report in design view, click the Code toolbar button. In the report class module, choose Report from the Objects box and Open from the Procedures box, then enter the following code:

```
Private Sub Report_Open(Cancel As Integer)
'Declare a variable for the option group value.
Dim intOpt As Integer
On Error GoTo Report_Open_Error

intOpt = Forms![Choose Summary]!ChooseSummary
    Select Case intOpt
    Case 1       'Preview Monthly Sales, the first option.
```

```
        Me.Caption = "Monthly Sales Summary"
        Me.Section(0).Visible = True      'Detail section.
        Me.Label98.Visible = True         'Month column label.
        Me.Label97.Visible = True         'Percent column label.

    Case 2       'Preview Annual Sales, the second option.
        Me.Caption = "Annual Sales Summary"
        Me.Section(0).Visible = False     'Detail section.
        Me.Label98.Visible = False        'Month column label.
        Me.Label97.Visible = False        'Percent column label.
    End Select

Exit Sub

Report_Open_Error:
    MsgBox Err.Description
    Exit Sub

End Sub
```

The statement `intOpt = Forms![Choose Summary]!ChooseSummary` sets the value of the integer variable to the value of the selected option in the ChooseSummary option group in the Choose Summary form. This value is used in the `Select Case` block.

The first `Select Case` block sets the report preview caption to Monthly Sales Summary. Then, it sets the detail section and the Month and Percent column labels' `Visible` properties to `True`. The second `Case` statement changes the caption and reverses the other settings so that the detail section and the two column labels do not appear. If you wanted to get into precise report design, you could change the length and weight of some of the lines or change any other control properties.

After adding the procedure to the report class module, close the report design and open the form in form view. Make a choice from the option group and see the report preview. Figure 13.21 shows a preview of the Annual Sales Summary opened by choosing Preview Annual Sales in the Choose Transaction Report form. Notice the caption text that was set by the event procedure code.

Note: Unless you need to change report properties at runtime, use the control and report property sheets. It is faster to set them in the property sheets because they don't need to be compiled.

These reports can be greatly enhanced with charts and graphs that visually represent trends and fluctuations. In Chapter 14, some charts are added to this and other reports.

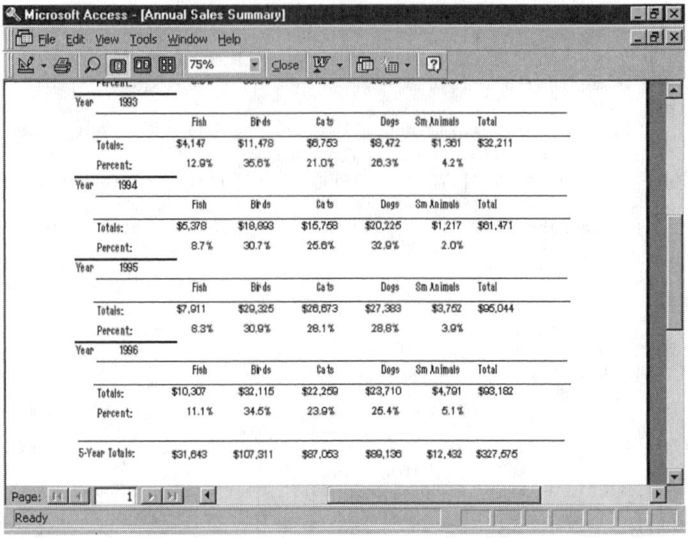

Figure 13.21.
Previewing the Annual Sales Summary report.

Combining Report Run-Time Properties

Access reports have three other runtime properties that you can combine to create a template for printing the report. They change the report's layout when it is previewed, printed, or copied to a file for printing later. The MoveLayout property indicates whether to move to the next printing location on the page. The NextRecord property indicates whether to move to the next record. The PrintSection indicates whether to print the section.

All three of these properties are set to True by default and are reset to True before the Format event of each section. To change one of these settings, attach a macro or event procedure to the OnFormat of the section.

These properties are used in combination with varying results, as shown in Table 13.2.

The True/False/True combination can be used when the data in a section exceeds the space allowed in the layout. This permits the data to be printed in the space that would normally be occupied by the next section. Because the NextRecord property is set to False, no record is omitted, just postponed.

Table 13.2. The effects of combining the runtime property settings.

MoveLayout	NextRecord	PrintSection	Result
True	True	True	Moves to the next print location; gets next record and prints it.
True	True	False	Skips a record and leaves the space blank.
True	False	True	Moves to the next print location but doesn't advance to next record. Prints the data.
True	False	False	Leaves a blank space without skipping a record.
False	True	True	Prints the data in the current record as an overlay on top of the previous record.
False	True	False	Skips a record without leaving a blank space.
False	False	True	Not permitted.
False	False	False	Not permitted.

Summary

Even though there's not a lot of interaction between the user and reports, there are many things that can be done behind the scenes in a report's design that can change the way it looks and behaves. This chapter has touched on a few of the ways you can program Access to customize reports.

14

Adding Real-Time Features

The last three chapters have provided nearly all the pieces of the Pat's Pets puzzle. All that remains is to tie everything together with a single point of user entry to the database and add some additional VBA code to handle the transaction-processing feature. This chapter completes the application by creating a switchboard which has options that branch to all the capabilities required of the database.

Top-Down Versus Bottom-Up Implementation

Systems analysts are split into two schools of thought about implementing a database application: the top-down approach and the bottom-up approach.

With the top-down implementation process, the first piece that is developed is the user interface, a switchboard, or other tool from which the user can select what to do next. This switchboard has all the options but they are not linked to any form, report, or procedure at this stage. Next, the branching elements are created that give the user additional options such as which form to open or which report to preview. Finally, the forms and reports are created that are in turn linked to the choices made in the branching tools.

A top-down analysis of the Pat's Pets inventory control system yields the information management structure described in Table 14.1.

Table 14.1. A top-down analysis of the Pat's Pets application.

Top Layer	Second Layer	Third Layer
Enter/edit data	Transaction data	(none)
	Product data	
	Supplier data	
	Customer data	
Preview data	Transaction data	Summarized by supplier
		Summarized by number
		Summarized by type
	List of suppliers	
	Summary of current inventory	By product code
		By category
		By value
	Sales summaries	Monthly
		Quarterly
		Annually

Top Layer	Second Layer	Third Layer
Look up specific information	Product categories Suppliers	(none)
	List of shortages	Print purchase orders
Update inventory with recent transactions	(none)	(none)

Although the top-down approach is valid for analysis, it is difficult to put into practice with Access because of the wizards. When you add an option group to the switchboard, the wizard wants to know to what object the selection applies: which report to open for preview or which form to open for data entry. If you have not created these objects yet, it is difficult to use the wizards.

Starting at the Bottom

With the bottom-up approach, the implementation starts at the lowest level and works its way up, grouping the elements into option groups. This method is more convenient with Access because the wizards are a big help with the option groups, command buttons, and other controls you need to make the application operate smoothly.

After defining all (or nearly all) of the input and output requirements of the application, begin by designing the forms and reports, grouped together by data or activity. Much of this has been accomplished in the previous three chapters.

Accumulating the Form and Report Objects

There is usually a separate data entry form for each table in the database, but you might be able to combine two tables into one entry form. For example, to add a new category, you can add it to the combo box list while entering new products in the Products form. The Transaction Log, Supplier Form, and Products data entry forms were created in Chapter 12, "Customizing Data Entry." To round out the data entry for the retail store application, the Customers data entry form is added to the database. This can be used later for mailing promotional material or for reminding customers of upcoming events (see Figure 14.1).

Some additional forms would be useful for looking up specific data such as the product list grouped by category, the suppliers together with the products they provide to the store, and a list of the products that are in low supply. The Category Lookup form is composed of a form based on the Category table and a subform with data from the Products table. Records in the form and subform are linked by Cat Code in both the parent and child recordsets (see Figure 14.2).

Figure 14.1.
The new Customers data entry form.

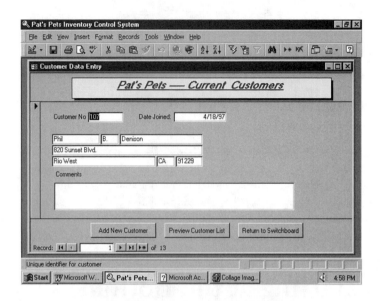

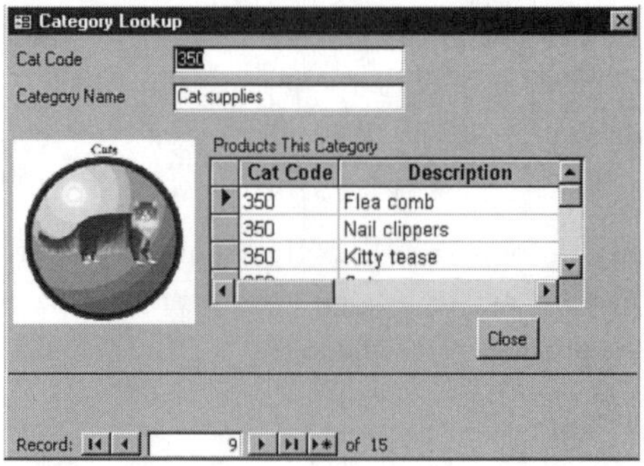

Figure 14.2.
The Category Lookup form.

The Supplier Product List form was introduced in Chapter 11, "Creating an Application from an Existing Database," and shows information about each supplier in the form with a subform that contains details of their products. The Re-order List form was created in Chapter 13, "Customizing Reports," using a similar layout as the Supplier Product List form, but using the results of a query as the record source for the subform. The query selects products whose In Stock value is less than or equal to the Re-Order quantity. The product fields are also slightly different: the Supplier Product List shows the Product ID, Description, Unit Cost, and Sell Price; the Reorder List shows In Stock and Re-Order quantities instead of cost and price. It also has buttons to print one or more purchase orders using the Order Products report.

Several of the necessary reports were developed in Chapter 13, such as the following:

- Transactions by Supplier, which groups all purchases by supplier and shows totals both for the individual suppliers as well as a running total over all.

- Transactions by Number, which lists all transactions in the table and shows a Confidential watermark on each page. The Comment label is not printed if there is no text in the Comment field. The detail section is allowed to shrink to close up the space.

- Transaction by Type, which separates sales from receipts and shrinkage and lists all the details of the transaction.

- Product Summary, which summarizes products within their category, prints some quantities in bold if their stock level is low, and counts the number of products in the category and the number that needs to be ordered.

- Product List by Category, which is a simple report grouped by product category with no added calculated fields.

- Order Products, which is the report used to print purchase orders from the Re-order List form. It is not called by itself, but only through the Re-order List form.

- Inventory Summary, which totals the value of the products in stock in each category and provides a grand total.

- PetSales, which is the report design used for both monthly and annual sales summaries.

The only report that is missing is the Quarterly Sales Summary. A table containing sales summarized by quarter was prepared separately for this report from the same sales data as the other reports. The Quarterly Sales report design resembles the monthly sales report (see Figure 14.3). A preview of the report is shown in Figure 14.4.

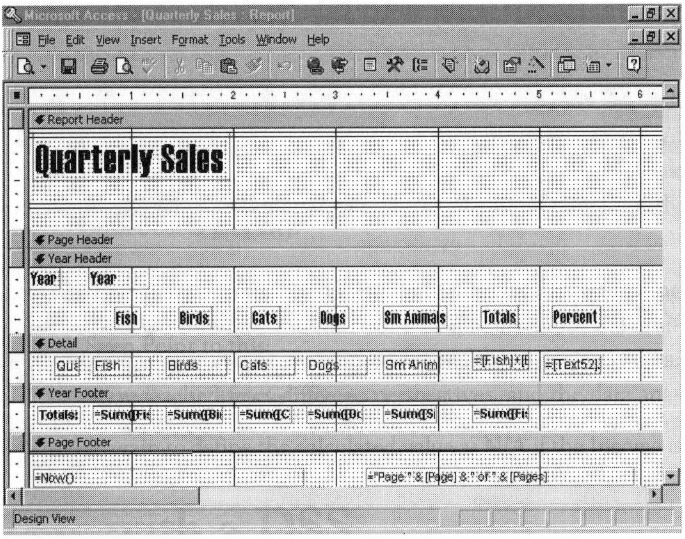

Figure 14.3.
The Quarterly Sales Summary report design.

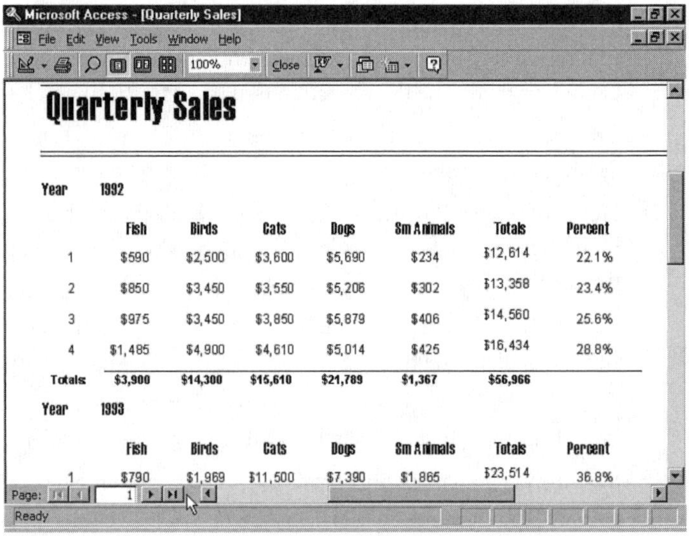

Figure 14.4.
Preview of the Quarterly Sales Summary report.

Building Option Pop-Up Forms

With all the lowest-level objects built, it is time to arrange them into logical groups and link them to a pop-up form showing a list of options for the user to choose. Two of these pop-up forms were developed in Chapter 13 for choosing which transaction or which sales summary report to preview.

Entering new transactions is likely the most frequently performed task, so it will stand alone in the main switchboard and not require the user to take time choosing from a secondary option box. Entering data in the other database tables can be lumped together into one pop-up form. Reviewing miscellaneous reports and looking up specific information can also be conveniently grouped into separate pop-up forms.

The pop-up form used to choose which table to enter data into contains three choices: Enter/Edit Products, Enter/Edit Suppliers, and Enter/Edit Customers (see Figure 14.5).

If the user requires more help in using the form, you could add, "and click Open" to the Choose Data label. Use the name of the option group in the OnClick event procedure for the Open Form command button. When you add the command button with the help of the Command Button Wizard, you can choose only one form to open. Then you must change the code to include the options in the option group. Listing 14.1 shows the OnClick event procedure for the OtherData button.

Figure 14.5.
The Choose Other Data pop-up form.

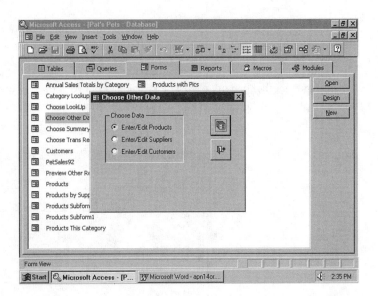

Listing 14.1. The OtherData button `OnClick` event procedure.

```
Private Sub OtherData_Click()
On Error GoTo Err_OtherData_Click

    Dim strDocName As String
    Dim intChoice As Integer

    intChoice = Me!ChooseData
    Select Case intChoice
    Case 1
        strDocName = "Products"
    Case 2
        strDocName = "Supplier Form"
    Case 3
        strDocName = "Customers"
    End Select

    Me.Visible = False
    DoCmd.OpenForm strDocName, acNormal

Exit_OtherData_Click:
    Exit Sub

Err_OtherData_Click:
    MsgBox Err.Description
    Resume Exit_OtherData_Click

End Sub
```

The procedure uses two variables in the `Select Case` structure. The `intChoice` variable is set to the value of the option selected in the option group, and the `strDocName` is the name of the form to be opened. The pop-up form is a modal form and remains visible in front of the newly opened form unless you set its visible property to `False` before opening the data entry form.

Miscellaneous reports that may be of interest but that are accessed less frequently can be grouped together into another pop-up form. The Preview Other Reports pop-up form includes four reports listing suppliers, current stock levels, categorized products, and the current inventory value (see Figure 14.6).

Figure 14.6.
The Preview Other Reports pop-up form.

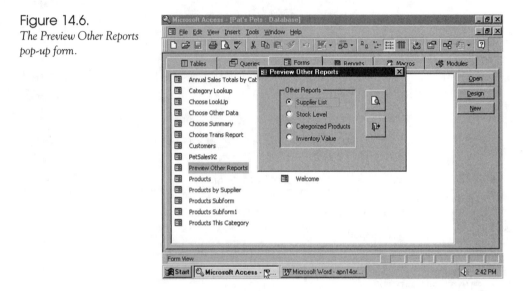

The event procedure for the Preview button's `OnClick` event (see Listing 14.2) is similar to that for the OtherData button. They both use a `Select Case` structure to define the string variable `strDocName` with the integer variable `intChoice` set to the value of the selected option in the option group. Once again, the form's `Visible` property is set to `False` before opening the report preview.

Listing 14.2. The Preview button's `OnClick` event procedure.

```
Private Sub Preview_Click()
On Error GoTo Err_Preview_Click

    Dim strDocName As String, intChoice As Integer
    intChoice = ChooseReport
    Select Case intChoice
        Case 1
            strDocName = "Supplier Lookup"

        Case 2
            strDocName = "Product Summary"

        Case 3
            strDocName = "Product List by Category"
```

```
        Case 4
            strDocName = "Inventory Summary"

    End Select
    Me.Visible = False
    DoCmd.OpenReport strDocName, acPreview

Exit_Preview_Click:
    Exit Sub

Err_Preview_Click:
    MsgBox Err.Description
    Resume Exit_Preview_Click

End Sub
```

Three additional forms that can be used for looking up specific information are grouped together in a pop-up form (see Figure 14.7). Information such as the product categories with their specific items (refer to Figure 14.1), suppliers and all their products, and suppliers with products that are in short supply. This last form (the Re-order form) is used to print the purchase orders with the Order Products report.

Figure 14.7.
The Choose LookUp pop-up form.

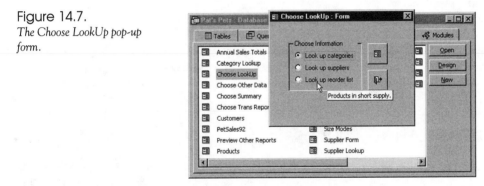

The event procedure for the Open Form button is the same as that for the Choose Other Data pop-up form except for the names of the forms to open. All of these pop-up forms also have a Close or Cancel button with the following OnClick event procedure that closes the form and maximizes the switchboard or other window on-screen:

```
Private Sub Cancel_Click()
On Error GoTo Err_Cancel_Click

    DoCmd.Close
    DoCmd.Maximize

Exit_Cancel_Click:
    Exit Sub
```

```
Err_Cancel_Click:
    MsgBox Err.Description
    Resume Exit_Cancel_Click

End Sub
```

Transaction Posting and Archiving Procedure

Posting transactions involves adding or subtracting the quantity of the product in the transaction to or from the In Stock quantity in the Products table. The easiest way to do this is to build a query that relates the Transactions and Products tables and filters the resulting recordset to those records whose Posted field is `False`. Then, working with the query results, the posting procedure can update the values and set Posted to `True`. Here is the Post Query SQL statement:

```
SELECT DISTINCTROW Products.[Product ID], Products.[In Stock],
Transactions.[Product ID], Transactions.Quantity, Transactions.Type,
Transactions.Posted, Transactions.[Transaction No]
FROM Products INNER JOIN Transactions ON Products.[Product ID] =
Transactions.[Product ID]
WHERE (((Transactions.Posted)=False))
ORDER BY Products.[Product ID];
```

One way to begin to write and test the code for this procedure is to make copies of the Transactions and Products tables with different names, or make copies in another database and work there. The trigger for the procedure can be a command button on an otherwise blank form.

Transaction Processing

This event procedure uses the trilogy of transaction methods: `BeginTrans`, `CommitTrans`, and `Rollback`. These methods are used to manage transaction processing during a session defined by a workspace object. Recall that a workspace object is a member of the `Workspaces` collection of the DBEngine. A workspace contains open databases, connections, groups, and users. You refer to the workspace by its name or index number: `DBEngine.Workspaces("MyWork")` or `DBEngine.Workspaces(0)`.

Technical Note: The transactions referred to by `BeginTrans` and `CommitTrans` are the changes made to the recordset, not to be confused with the sales and receipt transactions in the pet store.

Using the transaction methods helps to maintain the integrity of the database by ensuring that all the changes have been completed (committed) for all of the affected tables. If an error occurs during the transaction processing, the changes are undone (rolled back). After you have committed the transactions, they cannot be rolled back. If you close the workspace object while some transactions are still pending, all the changes will be rolled back.

BeginTrans starts a new transaction, and CommitTrans ends the current transaction and saves all the changes to the table. Rollback ends the current transaction and restores the table to its original condition before the transaction began. Using these methods treats many data updates as a single process, which saves time and space.

Archiving Records

A table such as the Transactions table will reach infinite proportions if it is not purged now and then. If you are not interested in the historical information, you can simply delete the old records. In this case, however, the management at Pat's Pets wants to maintain historical sales records in an effort to improve store performance. A procedure can extract transaction records that have been posted and no longer are of immediate interest, and then copy them to an archive table. After safely archiving the information, the procedure can delete the same records from the Transactions table.

The archiving procedure is combined in this application with the posting procedure as a subroutine. They would normally be carried out at the same time in the store. After the transaction posting is completed, the user is asked if he or she wants to go ahead and archive older records. If the response is Yes, the user is asked to enter a cutoff date. Two action queries are then run: the first is an Archive query that uses the INSERT INTO clause to copy the records to the archive; the second uses the DELETE clause to remove the same records from the Transactions table.

> **Note:** When constructing the Archive query, you can use Transactions* in the SQL statement to include all the fields in the table, even the AutoNumber primary key field. Access takes care of it when you archive records and makes sure that no two records have the same Transaction ID value.

The user can run the archiving procedure even if there are no records to post. After displaying a message that there are no records to post, the procedure branches to the question about archiving.

The **Sub Post** Procedure VBA Code

The full procedure is included in Listing 14.3, and the paragraphs that follow explain some of the segments of code in it.

Listing 14.3. The Post button's OnClick event procedure.

```
Private Sub Post_Click()
'Automatically posts transactions and updates Products InStock value.
'Then offers to archive records before specified date.

Dim wsp As Workspace, dbsCurrent As Database
Dim rstPost As Recordset
Dim intCount As Integer, blnInTrans As Boolean
Dim varReturn As Variant, strMsg As String
Dim strSQLArchive As String, strSQLDelete As String
Dim dtmCutOff As Date, intChoice As Integer
Dim strParm As String

On Error GoTo Err_Post_Click

blnInTrans = False
Set wsp = DBEngine.Workspaces(0)
Set dbsCurrent = CurrentDb()
Set rstPost = dbsCurrent.OpenRecordset("Post Query")

'Check for empty recordset and if so, display a message,
'close the recordset and exit the procedure.

If rstPost.RecordCount = 0 Then
    MsgBox ("No transactions to post.")
    GoTo ArchiveTrans
End If

'Start of transaction and set blnInTrans to True.
wsp.BeginTrans
blnInTrans = True
'Move to the first record.
rstPost.MoveFirst

'Set the counter to 0 and start the Do While loop.
'Display message in status line.
strMsg = "Posting transactions, please wait..."
varReturn = SysCmd(acSysCmdSetStatus, strMsg)
intCount = 0

Do Until rstPost.EOF
    If rstPost![Type] = "Receipt" Then
        rstPost.Edit
        rstPost![In Stock] = rstPost![In Stock] _
            + rstPost![Quantity]
    Else                    'The transaction is either sale or shrinkage.
        rstPost.Edit
        rstPost![In Stock] = rstPost![In Stock] _
            - rstPost![Quantity]
    End If
    rstPost![Posted] = True
    rstPost.Update
    intCount = intCount + 1
    rstPost.MoveNext
Loop
'Remove message from the status line.
varReturn = SysCmd(acSysCmdClearStatus)
```

```
If MsgBox("Save all changes?", vbQuestion + vbYesNo, _
    " Save changes") = vbYes Then
    wsp.CommitTrans                'Commit the updates.
Else
    wsp.Rollback                   'Undo the updates.
End If
'Display the number of transactions posted and close form.
MsgBox (intCount & " transactions posted.")

'Subroutine to archive transactions and delete them from the
'Transactions table.
```

The archiving subroutine begins here:

```
ArchiveTrans:
intChoice = MsgBox("Do you want to archive transactions now?", _
    vbYesNo + vbQuestion, "Archive?")
If intChoice = 7 Then
    GoTo Exit_Post_Click
Else
    dtmCutOff = InputBox("Please enter cutoff date.", "Cutoff Date")

'Turn off the Access warning message.
DoCmd.SetWarnings False

    strSQLArchive = "INSERT INTO [Transaction Archive] " & _
        "SELECT Transactions.* FROM Transactions " & _
        "WHERE (Transactions.Date)<= #" & dtmCutOff & "# " & _
        "AND ((Transactions.Posted)=True);"
    DoCmd.RunSQL (strSQLArchive)

    strSQLDelete = "DELETE Transactions.* " & _
        "WHERE (Transactions.Date)<= #" & dtmCutOff & "# " & _
        "AND ((Transactions.Posted)=True);"
    DoCmd.RunSQL (strSQLDelete)
'Reset the warning message.
DoCmd.SetWarnings True
End If

Exit_Post_Click:
    rstPost.Close
    Exit Sub

Err_Post_Click:
    MsgBox Err.Description
    If blnInTrans Then
        wsp.Rollback
    End If
    Resume Exit_Post_Click

End Sub
```

First, the declaration section declares the following variables, which are set in subsequent statements:

- wsp as the current workspace, set to DBEngine.Workspaces(0), the first workspace in the collection.

- dbsCurrent as the active database, set to CurrentDB().

- **rstPost** as the recordset that results from the **Post** query.

- **intCount** as an integer that is used to count the number of transactions posted.

- **blnInTrans** as a Boolean value representing the status of the transaction processing.

- **varReturn** as the Variant value used with the **SysCmd()** function to display text in the status bar while the transactions are being processed.

- **strMsg** as the message to display in the status bar.

- **strSQLArchive** as the SQL statement to use for the archive action query.

- **strSQLDelete** as the SQL statement to use for the delete action query.

- **dtmCutOff** as the date entered by the user to be used as the criterion for both queries.

- **blnChoice** as the Yes/No response to whether to archive records now.

Next, the **If...Then** segment checks for an empty recordset. If there are no records that meet the query criteria (**Posted = False**), a message is displayed and control is sent to the **ArchiveTrans** subroutine, which is described later. If the recordset is not empty, transaction begins, the transaction status is set to **True**, and the cursor moves to the first record in the recordset:

```
wsp.BeginTrans
blnInTrans = True
rstPost.Movefirst
```

The following two lines use the **SysCmd()** function to set the status bar text:

```
strMsg = "Posting transactions, please wait..."
varReturn = SysCmd(asSysCmdSetStatus, strMsg)
```

It can also be used to display a progress meter in the status bar instead of text. There are many other intrinsic constants that you can use with the **SysCmd()** function to return the state of Access or one of the Access objects.

After initializing the counter to zero, the **Do Until** loop begins and will continue to process the statements between **Do Until** and **Loop** until the end of the **rstPost** file is reached:

```
Do Until rstPost.EOF
    rstPost.Edit
    If rstPost![Type] = "Receipt" Then
        rstPost![In Stock] = rstPost![In Stock] _
            + rstPost![Quantity]
    Else                    'The transaction is either sale or shrinkage.
        rstPost![In Stock] = rstPost![In Stock] _
            - rstPost![Quantity]
    End If
    rstPost![Posted] = True
    rstPost.Update
    intCount = intCount + 1
    rstPost.MoveNext
Loop
```

The **Edit** method is used to copy the record to a buffer for editing. Then, the **If...Then** structure first asks if the Type field contains "Receipt." If so, the Quantity value from the Transactions record is added to the In Stock value from the Products table.

If the transaction is not a receipt, then it is either a sale or a shrinkage, both of which will decrease the In Stock quantity. Therefore, the `Else` clause subtracts the Quantity from the In Stock value.

The next three statements change the Posted value to `True`, use the `Update` method to put the updated record back in the recordset, and increment the counter. Then, the `MoveNext` method moves to the next record. If `MoveNext` moves past the last record, the `EOF` property changes to `True` and the loop stops.

The `varReturn` statement removes the text from the status bar and a message box asks if you want to save all the changes made during the transaction processing. If you respond Yes, then the transactions are committed; if No, they are rolled back. Next, another message box displays the number of transactions that were posted (see Figure 14.8).

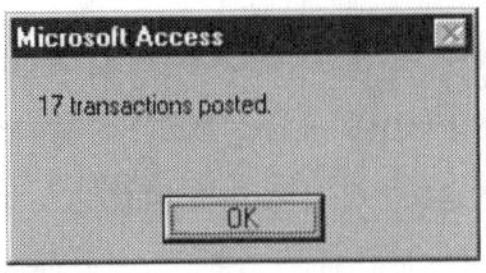

Figure 14.8.
A message box shows the number of transactions posted.

After completing the posting, the procedure enters the `Archive` subroutine and asks if you want to archive records now. If the response is No, the procedures ends. If Yes, you are asked to enter the cutoff date for the action queries. The first SQL statement performs an archive query that extracts transaction records whose Date field value is earlier than the date entered in the input box and appends them to a table named Transaction Archive. The second SQL statement deletes the same records from the Transactions table.

> **Warning:** Both of these queries prompt a warning message to the user. It is important to turn them off before the queries begin. If you do not turn them off, the user might accept one of the operations and not the other, resulting in inconsistent tables. Use `DoCmd.SetWarnings False` to turn them off, but be sure to turn them back on right after the queries are run with `DoCmd.SetWarnings True`.

After the two action queries are completed, the procedure exits.

Creating the Main Switchboard

After building all the necessary option pop-up forms and procedures, the next step is to create a main switchboard that serves as the single point of entry into the application. The user chooses from the list of options to accomplish an inventory task. When the task is completed, control always returns to the main switchboard.

You saw what the Switchboard Manager was able to do with the Omni-Sport switchboard in Chapter 4, "Creating an Application with a Wizard." You can use the same tool to create a switchboard for the Pat's Pets inventory control system now that you have all the pieces completed.

> **Tip:** If you know you are going to have to make a lot of changes to the switchboard the Manager builds, you are better off creating the switchboard yourself from a blank form. You'll see how to do that in Chapter 16, "Customizing Input and Output."

Using the Switchboard Manager

You used the Switchboard Manager in Chapter 5, "Examining and Modifying the Wizard's Code," to make changes in the Database Wizard's switchboards by choosing the Change Switchboard Items option on the switchboard, itself. Creating a new switchboard is not much different.

Most of the switchboard items you need for Pat's Pets will open one of the forms you created in Chapter 13, such as the form to choose which sales summary you want to preview. Two of the options involve running procedures: post transactions and return to Access.

To start the Switchboard Manager, choose Tools | Add-Ins | Switchboard Manager. The Switchboard Manager dialog box shows a single entry, Main Switchboard (Default). After you create the switchboard, you can copy the `Post_Click` event procedure into the switchboard form class module and change the name to simply `Post` because it will not be an event procedure but a called procedure by the `HandlebuttonClick()` function the Manager wrote. For the Return to Access procedure, you can write a simple procedure that closes the switchboard form and maximizes the database window.

To add items to the empty switchboard page, follow these steps:

1. Choose Edit to open the Edit Switchboard Page dialog box (see Figure 14.9).

Figure 14.9.
*The Edit Switchboard Page
dialog box.*

```
┌─ Edit Switchboard Page ──────────────────────────────┐
│                                                       │
│  Switchboard Name:                          ┌───────┐ │
│  ┌─────────────────────────────────────┐    │ Close │ │
│  │ Main Switchboard                    │    └───────┘ │
│  └─────────────────────────────────────┘              │
│  Items on this Switchboard:                 ┌───────┐ │
│  ┌─────────────────────────────────────┐    │ New...│ │
│  │                                     │    └───────┘ │
│  │                                     │    ┌───────┐ │
│  │                                     │    │ Edit  │ │
│  │                                     │    └───────┘ │
│  │                                     │    ┌───────┐ │
│  │                                     │    │ Delete│ │
│  │                                     │    └───────┘ │
│  │                                     │    ┌───────┐ │
│  │                                     │    │Move Up│ │
│  │                                     │    └───────┘ │
│  │                                     │    ┌─────────┐│
│  └─────────────────────────────────────┘    │Move Down││
│                                              └─────────┘│
└───────────────────────────────────────────────────────┘
```

2. Click New to open the New Switchboard item dialog box, in which you enter the text and the commands for each of the switchboard items.

3. Type Enter or edit transaction data as the text for the first item, and then choose Open Form in Edit Mode from the list of eight standard commands.

4. Select Transaction Log from the list of form names in your database (see Figure 14.10). If you had chosen a command to preview or print a report, the list would have contained the names of all the reports in the database.

Figure 14.10.
Entering an item in the Edit Switchboard Item dialog box.

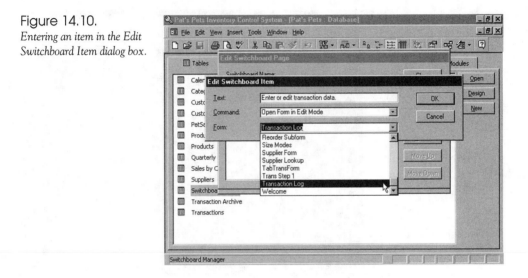

5. Repeat steps 2 through 5 to specify the items shown in Table 14.2.

6. After entering all the items, choose Close twice to return to the database window.

Table 14.2. Switchboard item specifications.

Text	Command	Form or Other
Enter or edit transaction data	Open Form in Edit Mode	Transaction Log
Enter or edit other data	Open Form in Edit Mode	Choose Other Data
Preview transactions	Open Form in Edit Mode	Choose Trans Report
Preview other reports	Open Form in Edit Mode	Preview Other Reports
Look up information	Open Form in Edit Mode	Choose Lookup
Sales analysis	Open Form in Edit Mode	Choose Summary
Post transactions	Run Code	Post
Return to Access database	Run Code	Return To Access window

If you look now in the Tables tab of the Pat's Pets database window, you will see the new table named Switchboard Items that the Manager has created based on your input to the Switchboard Manager dialog boxes. Now move to the Forms tab and open the new Switchboard form in form view (see Figure 14.11). You probably will want to make a few changes to the appearance of the form, such as adding the store logo and adding a button that quits Access altogether.

Figure 14.11.
The new switchboard after the Manager is finished.

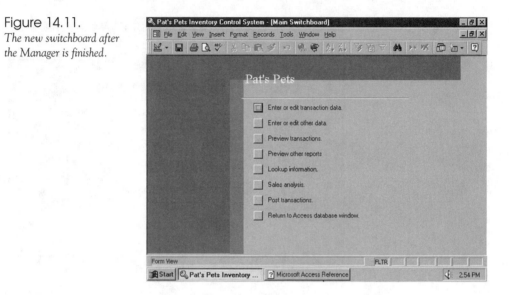

Making Changes to the Switchboard

First, increase the length of the title, which now shows only Pat's Pets, the name of the database. When you resize it to move into the wide, colored left margin, the text disappears. Select the colored box and choose Format | Send to Back. This places it in back of the text.

Next, add the company picture logo to the upper-left corner. Choose Insert | Picture and locate the !1_logoa.pcx file in the Images folder on the CD-ROM included with this book and choose Insert. Resize the picture to fit the space and change its Size Mode property to Stretch.

Now add a command button that quits Access by using the Command Button Wizard. Choose Application from the Categories list and Quit Application from the Actions list. Following the style set so far in this application, use text "Quit Access" on the button. Figure 14.12 shows the completed switchboard form.

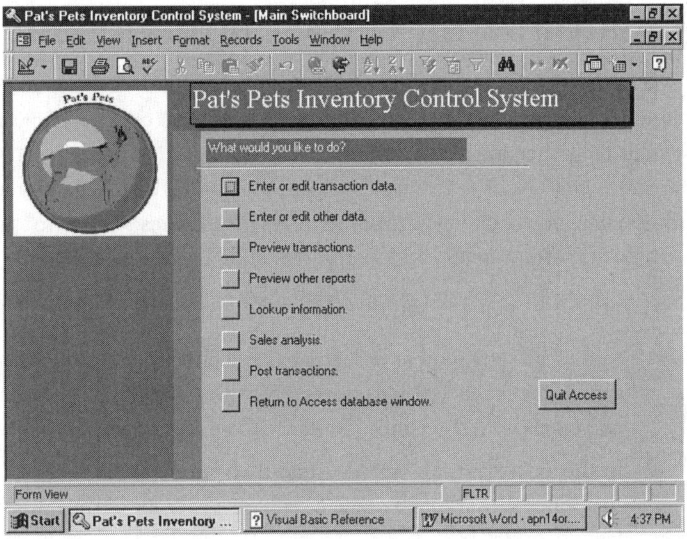

Figure 14.12.
The Pat's Pets switchboard.

Finishing the Form Class Module

The `Post_Click` procedure was developed as an event procedure for a button on a blank form. Copy this procedure to the switchboard module and change its name to `Post`. Remember to change the `On Error GoTo` and `Exit` lines as well.

Next, create a new procedure to close the form and return to the Access database window with the following code:

```
Private Sub Return_To_Access()
'Close the switchboard and return
'to the Access database window.

DoCmd.Close
DoCmd.Maximize

End Sub
```

Return to the form view and check out each item on the switchboard. Make any necessary changes.

Troubleshooting Tip: If you have trouble getting the two items that call procedures to work, you can always create `OnClick` event procedures using the code you have and attach them to both the button and the label.

Customizing the Command Bar

The options represented by the buttons on the switchboard can also be made available through a custom command bar. Access 97 has new tools for creating custom menu bars and toolbars, now grouped together and called *command bars*. When you have started a custom menu bar, you can add your own commands to it as well as any of the hundreds of Access built-in menu commands. Access also enables you to change the properties of menu items, such as to show only icons, icons and text, or only text. You can also add tooltip text and Help text associated with a What's This? button.

To create a custom menu bar for the Pat's Pets application, perform the following steps:

1. Right-click any toolbar or menu bar and choose Customize from the shortcut menu. You can also point to Toolbars in the View menu and click Customize. The Customize dialog box opens with three tabs: Toolbars, Commands, and Options.

2. In the Toolbars tab, click New and then enter `Pat's Pets` for the name of the menu bar; then click OK. A small menu bar appears in front of the Customize dialog box, as shown in Figure 14.13.

Figure 14.13.
Starting the Pat's Pets custom menu bar.

3. Click Properties and choose Menu Bar from the Type box in the Toolbar Properties dialog box, and then choose Close. Your other options for command bar type are Toolbar and Popup.

4. Reposition the newborn menu bar and the Customize dialog box so you can see both at once; then open the Commands tab. Scroll down the Categories list, and select New Menu.

5. Drag New Menu from the Commands list (not the Categories list) to the new menu bar and drop it in the bar. Right-click the new menu item and type the name you want in the shortcut menu (see Figure 14.14). The first menu item is Enter Data, so type `&Enter Data` in the shortcut menu. The ampersand (&) designates the next character as the access key for the menu command.

Figure 14.14.
Adding and naming a new menu item.

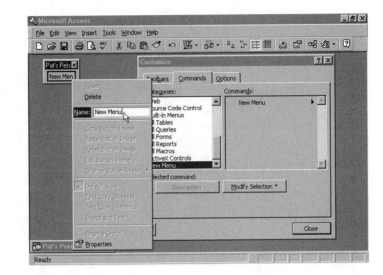

6. Repeat step 5 to add the other menu items. Then, scroll up in the Categories list and select Built-in Menus. Drag Tools from the Commands list to the end of the new menu bar.

7. Now it's time to add commands to the menu so that something happens when you click an item. Click the Enter Data menu item and a small empty box appears just below it. This is where the menu commands will be placed.

8. The Enter Data menu item opens a variety of data entry forms, so select All Forms in the Categories list. The Commands list now shows the names of all the forms in the Pat's Pets database. Drag and drop Transaction Log from the Commands list to the submenu box. Right-click the new item and remove the word Log from the name and add an ampersand (&) before the T to assign an access key.

9. Repeat step 8 to place the other form commands in the submenu box. Change their text from the form name to something consistent and understandable, if necessary. Figure 14.15 shows the completed Enter Data menu item.

10. The Preview Reports menu presents a special case: the Transactions report has three different layouts. This calls for another New Menu item with lower-level submenu commands. Drag a New Menu item to the box below Preview Reports and name it &Transactions. Next, click the right-pointing arrow to add a small box to the right of the Transactions item.

11. Select the All Reports category and drag and drop the three transaction report names from the Commands list to the new box. Right-click Suppliers in the menu list, and choose Begin a Group from the shortcut menu. This places a line above Suppliers separating the rest of the reports from Transactions. Figure 14.16 shows the completed Preview Reports menu.

Figure 14.15.

Adding commands to a custom menu.

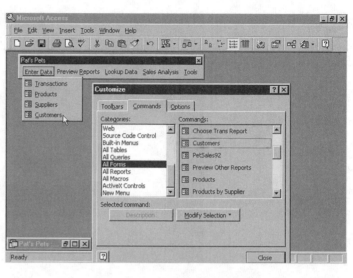

Figure 14.16.

Creating a submenu.

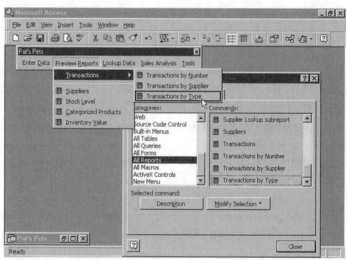

12. Finish adding the remaining menu commands, and then drag the menu to the top of the screen to dock it.

Command bar items have many properties that you can change to create the appearance and behavior you want. The shortcut menu contains properties that can change the appearance of the menu item (see Figure 14.17). Choose Properties from the shortcut menu to open the Pat's Pets Control Properties dialog box (see Figure 14.18) where you can add Help text, specify a macro or function procedure that will run when the item is selected, or specify other runtime properties. Table 14.3 describes these properties.

Figure 14.17.

Select from the shortcut menu to change the menu item appearance.

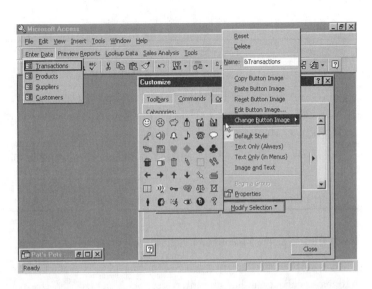

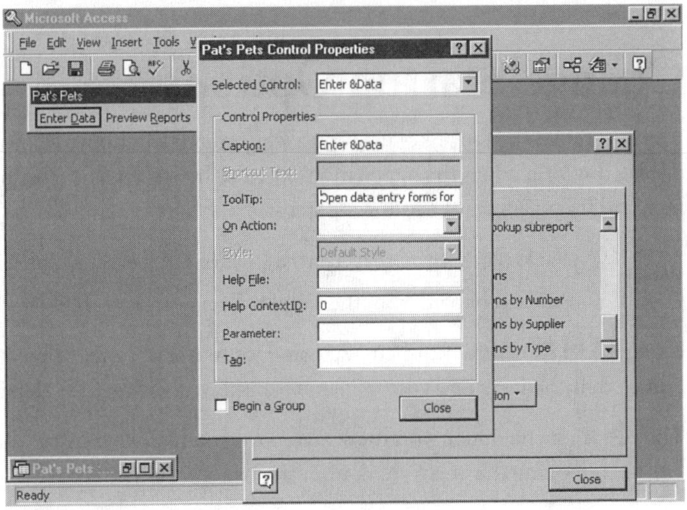

Figure 14.18.

Use the Properties dialog box to change other menu control properties.

Table 14.3. Pat's Pets menu bar control properties.

Property	Description
Caption	Text that appears in the menu bar.
Shortcut Text	The shortcut key or key combination that activates the menu item, such as ^K or ^F3. Create an AutoKey macro to carry out the menu option.
ToolTip	Text to display when the mouse pointer rests on the menu item.
On Action	Name of macro or VBA function to run.

continues

Table 14.3. continued

Property	Description
Style	Default Style, Text Only (Always), Text Only (in Menus), or Image and text.
Help File	Path to Help file that contains the answer to the What's This? button.
Help ContextID	Identifier for the topic in the Help file.
Parameter	Parameter passed to the function named in On Action.
Tag	String that can be used later in a VBA event procedure.
Begin a Group	Places a line in the menu list above the selected menu item.

If you want to delete a menu item, right-click it and choose Delete from the shortcut menu.

There is much more to creating and customizing menu bars and toolbars. Chapter 16 contains more information about building user interfaces.

Change Startup Options

The last step in the process of creating a welcoming switchboard is to change the startup options to display the form when the application opens. Choose Tools | Startup to open the Startup dialog box, and then perform the following steps:

- Type Pat's Pets Inventory Control System in the Application Title box.

- Choose Switchboard from the Display Form list, and then choose Close.

Figure 14.19 shows the finished Welcome form as it appears when the Pat's Pets database opens. Notice that the Pat's Pets custom menu is displayed without the default toolbar.

The custom menu remains on the screen until you remove it by right-clicking any toolbar or menu bar and removing the check mark from the list of command bars.

Tip: You can also toggle between the global menu bar and the custom menu bar by pressing Ctrl+F11. This works only when you are not in the switchboard form view. To leave the switchboard form view, choose the Return to Access database window from the switchboard to close the form. Then you can toggle to the global menu.

Figure 14.19.
The finished Welcome switchboard.

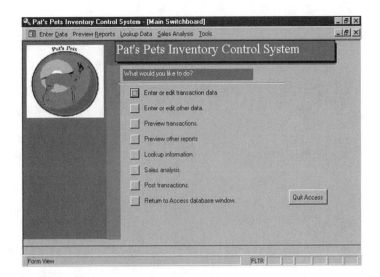

Adding Charts for Visual Trend Analysis

Charts are used for two basic purposes: to track the changes that occur in one or more series of data over time and to compare relative proportions to the whole. Line charts are the most common example of the time-trend type of chart, although bar charts, column charts, and area charts can also convey the same information. Pie charts are the most common type of chart used to illustrate proportions.

The time spent planning how you want information visually represented more than pays off by resulting in the intended interpretation of the underlying data. In the Pat's Pets application, it is important to track the popularity of types of pets by comparing the sales of each category over a period of time. A simple line chart with a line for each category tracking the total sales for each year can show a major trend.

Another chart that would be useful is a bar chart showing quarterly sales in each category, one chart for each year. A pie chart can be used to illustrate the relative sales among the five categories. Pie charts have no time line, so the sales would be totaled for a single year in each chart.

Creating a Line Chart

The first chart to create in this application is the line chart tracking the sales of each category over the five-year period. Each category is represented by a separate line. To create a chart, start a new form or report, choose Chart Wizard and the table or query that has the information you want to illustrate (in this case, the PetSales table).

The Chart Wizard builds a query based on the choices you make in its dialog boxes. Make the following choices in the Chart Wizard dialog boxes:

- In the first dialog box, choose the fields you want in the chart (maximum of six). Select Year and all five categories.
- Choose the line chart style in the second box (see Figure 14.20).

Figure 14.20.
Choose the chart type from the Chart Wizard.

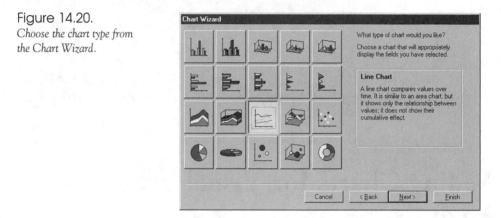

- The third dialog box (see Figure 14.21) helps you arrange the data in a series on the chart. First, drag and drop Year down to the X-axis at the bottom of the chart. Then, one by one drag and drop the category sales totals to the chart. Click the Preview Chart button in the upper-left corner of the window to see how the chart will look as you go along.

Figure 14.21.
Move Year and drag the sales data to the chart.

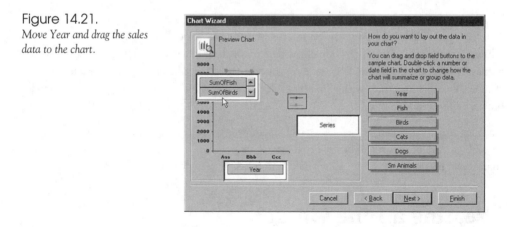

- In the last dialog box, enter Annual Sales Line Chart as the name for the new chart, and choose Finish. Don't forget to save the new form containing the chart.

Figure 14.22 shows how the chart looks when the Wizard is finished with it. Obviously, it needs a little adjusting to make the legend fit in the chart, and the dollar values should be formatted as currency. A title on the vertical axis would also help. If you want to make changes in the data, you do that in Access, but for changes in appearance you must open the Microsoft Graph applet.

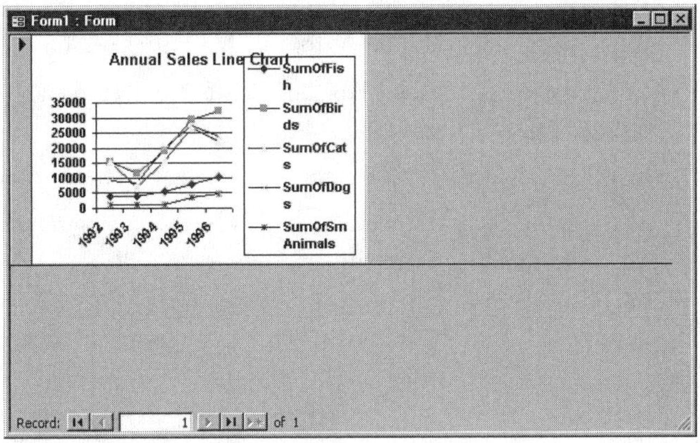

Figure 14.22.
The Chart Wizard's product.

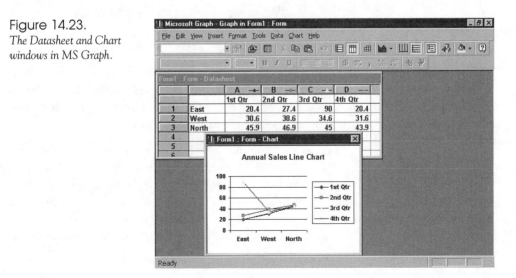

First, switch to form design view and increase the width of the chart in the form design. Then, double-click in the chart to open MS Graph. The Graph window has two child windows: the Datasheet window (where you can add, change, or delete data and change column headers used in the legend), and the Chart window (see Figure 14.23). The Graph toolbar and menu bar contain all the operations you need to modify the chart. The shortcut menu also has many of the commonly used operations.

Figure 14.23.
The Datasheet and Chart windows in MS Graph.

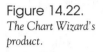

Don't worry about the data in the Graph window, it is just an example, not the real thing. To improve the chart's appearance, perform the following steps:

1. Widen the chart so there will be enough room for the legend. Then, click and drag the legend box to the right.

2. Select the chart and resize it as necessary, and then right-click the Y-axis (the dollar values) and choose Format Axis from the shortcut menu.

3. In the Format Axis dialog box, choose the Number tab, and choose Currency with no decimal places. Choose OK.

4. Select the chart title and change it to read `Pat's Pets - Annual Sales`.

5. Move to the Datasheet window and change the column headers to the names of the categories and the row identifiers to the years 1992, 1993, and so on.

6. Choose File | Exit & Return to Form1:Form, and then switch to form view (see Figure 14.24).

Figure 14.24.
The finished line chart.

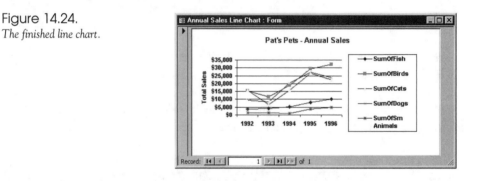

You might need to return to Graph several times before the chart looks just the way you want it.

The line chart clearly shows a significant decline in sales of dog and cat products and a steady increase in the sales of the other three product categories. Store management may be able to speculate on why this is so—the neighborhood has become more crowded and less conducive to walking dogs or more apartments are restricting the types of pets their occupants may have.

When the chart design is finished, save the form with the same name so that you will know where to find it when you want to insert it into a report. To insert the chart into a report, open the report in design view and use the Subform toolbar button to draw a frame for the subform. Select the name of the form that contains the chart from the Reports and Forms list displayed by the Subform/Subreport Wizard. After adding the subform, you can move it and resize it to meet your needs. Figure 14.25 shows a preview of the PetSales Annual Report with the chart added to the report footer.

Figure 14.25.
The line chart is added to the PetSales Annual Report.

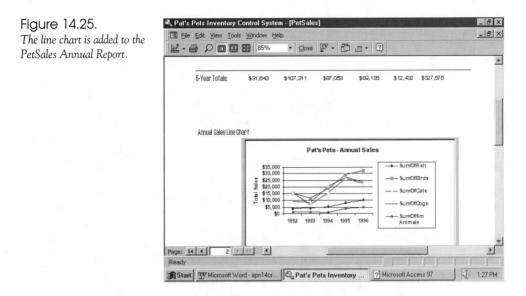

Creating a Bar Chart for One Year

Seasonal trends might be even more important for inventory management than annual sales totals. Using the Chart Wizard again, you can create a bar chart based on the Quarterly Sales table and include all the product categories. Then, in Access you can limit the data to one year, such as 1996.

During the preparation of the chart, the Chart Wizard builds a query based on the information you have provided in the dialog boxes. It has no way of filtering the data, so you have to do that in Access by changing the SQL statement that represents the Row Source property of the chart. Figure 14.26 shows the SQL statement with the HAVING filter clause added.

Figure 14.26.
Change the SQL statement to limit the data to 1996.

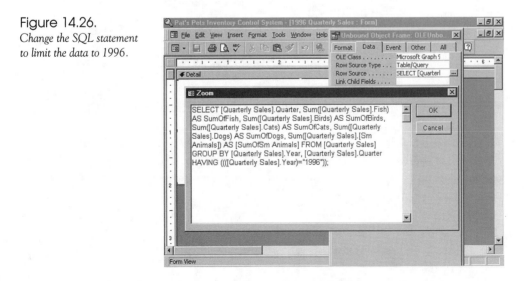

To make some changes in the appearance of the chart, double-click it in design view to open Graph. After changing the chart title, you can add a subtitle by typing in the chart. The text appears in the center of the chart, but you can drag it to a location below the title (see Figure 14.27).

Figure 14.27.
Adding a subtitle.

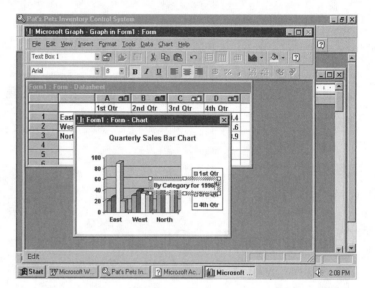

Figure 14.28 shows the finished chart in the form named Quarterly Sales Bar Chart. To create similar charts for the other years, all you need to do is change the HAVING clause of the SQL Row Source property to a different year.

Figure 14.28.
The 1996 Quarterly Sales Bar Chart form.

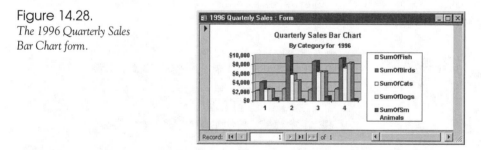

This bar chart (actually called a "column" chart in Access) shows a definite 2nd- and 4th-quarter rise in sales of bird-related products. Small animal products seem to become popular during the 3rd quarter—perhaps as caged pets for classrooms at the beginning of the school year.

Creating a Pie Chart of Product Categories

Pie charts showing proportion of sales for each category by year can be useful in allocating storage for the different products. Figure 14.29 shows a pie chart that illustrates the proportion of total sales in 1996, attributable to each product category. Cat and dog products together accounted for approximately half the total sales. Pie charts contain only a single series, so they cannot represent trends over time.

Figure 14.29.
The 1996 Product Sales pie chart.

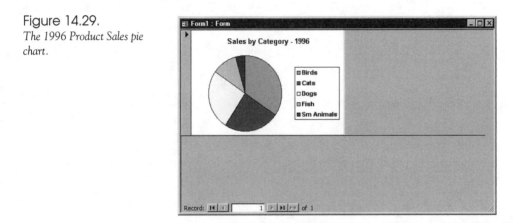

There are many more things you can do with charts—more than can be covered in this chapter. In Chapter 17, "Linking with Other Office Applications," you will see how to import spreadsheet data from Excel to use in charts.

Summary

This chapter covered a lot of material related to implementing the complete application. Links in the form of pop-up option groups were created to tie together forms and reports that related to the same subject matter. A complete procedure for posting and archiving transaction records was also developed. All of these operations were then attached as event procedures to a main switchboard.

A custom menu bar was designed and set to display whenever the switchboard was in form view. Then, the startup options were changed to display the switchboard with a new application title when the Pat's Pets database opened.

The final section of this chapter briefly addressed the visual objects you can create with Access and the Microsoft Graph applet. Such charts and graphs can help users interpret the underlying database information.

V

Programming Access for Decision Making

15

Introducing a Database Decision Support System

The goal of this chapter is to show you how easily you can use an Access database application as a tool for decision making. You have already seen how Access accomplishes simple and complex data management tasks as well as how the flexible input and output capabilities can be customized to fit nearly any purpose. The decision-making environment presents new challenges to the database developer, but the Access event-driven database management system is the perfect tool for designing a valuable decision support system.

What Is a Decision Support System?

A Decision Support System (DSS) is a computerized system that supports the process of making a decision. A DSS focuses on the process of making a decision rather than on the outcome of the decision or the content of the problem. For example, setting marketing budgets is a process, whereas placing specific offers on the Internet is the outcome. A DSS is more of a service than a product.

Basically, a DSS is a number cruncher and a data manipulator that processes information and presents results to the decision maker for intuitive evaluation. It is not designed around a static model—one that produces the same answer every time. Each user represents a unique problem-solving situation. One might be interested mainly in cash flow, and the next more interested in long-term appreciation.

Decisions come in roughly three major types: *structured*, *unstructured*, and *semi-structured*. Structured decisions such as inventory ordering, determining the most profitable product mix, and choosing the most economical plant location, are well supported by traditional computer models and data management systems. The majority of the information used in a structured decision is quantitative, and the decision model is static. Given the same input, a structured problem has the same solution every time it is solved.

Unstructured decisions are called unstructured either because they cannot be explicitly modeled or because there is insufficient information. These decisions must be made using human intuition rather than computer support. There is little data for a computer to work with. Examples of unstructured decisions are selecting the perfect photo for a magazine cover, hiring the appropriate upper-management personnel, and planning a research and development investment portfolio.

It is with the remaining type, the semi-structured decision, that a DSS can become a hero. Semi-structured decision making cannot rely solely on managerial judgment because there is too much information for humans to process accurately in the limited time the decision demands. Yet, you can't rely completely on the computer because there are human values to be considered as well. Here are some examples of semi-structured problems:

- Tracking the municipal bond market, where the many facts involved with yield, maturity, and the state of the market must be combined with judgment and subjective opinions. You would use the computer to search the database and make computations and then analyze the resulting alternatives.

- Setting market budgets for consumer products, where the DSS first computes and projects anticipated trends; then human judgment takes over and superimposes external values and influences unknown to the computer.

- Analyzing the effects of different financial strategies and assumptions when planning to acquire capital for a new business.

Each of these examples combines the high-speed information processing capabilities of the computer with the human intuitive powers of the decision maker to provide a complete DSS.

Note: It is interesting to note that over the years, the lines between types of problems have shifted toward structure as knowledge and technology advance. Problems such as inventory management, which were once considered so complicated as to require an experienced manager with a large staff, are now routinely handled by a computer as a simple, structured problem.

In another example of how knowledge redefines a problem is the five-year-old who plays tic-tac-toe and considers it an unstructured problem—one that is uncertain and exciting, not knowing who will win. When she gains knowledge and experience with the problem, it becomes more structured and predictable.

Compare DSS with Transaction Processing

A DSS design differs greatly from a transaction processing system such as the inventory control system featured in the previous chapters. A DSS must be flexible, whereas transaction processing is bound by rules and procedures. If you deviate from the rules, the system fails and the data becomes corrupted. Rigid protocol and prescribed interfaces with the outside world preclude flexibility. Think of a banking system and imagine what would happen if the rules and procedures were not explicitly followed.

A DSS, on the other hand, must be flexible if it is to be useful. Like an event-oriented programming language, you never know what action the user will want to take next or how he will want to arrange his priorities; the DSS must be prepared for any sequence of events and arrangement of data. Most semi-structured problems can be approached from different perspectives, and the data analyzed in different logical patterns.

Solving Problems with a DSS

Getting back to decisions and the problems that demand the decisions, take a look at the decision makers. In an organization, there are usually three levels of management with corresponding decision-making responsibilities: operational control, management control, and strategic planning (see Figure 15.1).

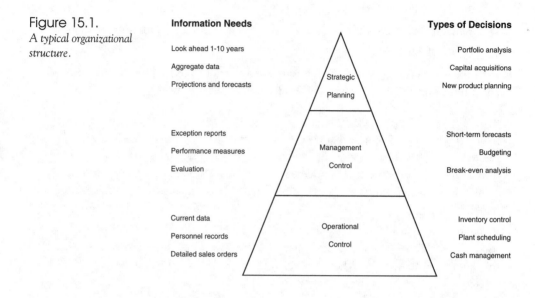

Figure 15.1.
A typical organizational structure.

Information Needs

Look ahead 1-10 years

Aggregate data

Projections and forecasts

Exception reports

Performance measures

Evaluation

Current data

Personnel records

Detailed sales orders

Strategic Planning

Management Control

Operational Control

Types of Decisions

Portfolio analysis

Capital acquisitions

New product planning

Short-term forecasts

Budgeting

Break-even analysis

Inventory control

Plant scheduling

Cash management

At the operational control level, decisions are made daily that concern supervision of personnel and operations within a limited scope such as a single department or region. At the middle level, decisions are based on information that is summarized over a period of time and across two or more departments or regions. Top-level management decisions depend on aggregated information in the form of charts and graphs that can be almost instantly assimilated for speedy decisions.

Table 15.1 describes the characteristics required of information used for decision making and how they differ between high-level strategic planning and daily operational control. The information requirements of management control level falls in between.

Table 15.1. Information characteristics by decision area.

Characteristic	Strategic Control	Operational Control
Accuracy	Low	High
Level of detail	Aggregate	Detailed
Time horizon	Future	Present
Frequency of use	Infrequent	Frequent
Major source	External	Internal
Scope	Wide	Narrow

Characteristic	Strategic Control	Operational Control
Type of info	Qualitative	Quantitative
Currency	Older	Current
Access time	Quick	Slower

In Table 15.1, there might seem to be an inconsistency between the currency and the access speed requirements. Currency relates to the age of the information. Operational managers need up-to-the-minute information in order to respond quickly to problems, whereas strategic planners prefer to look back at information after it has seasoned. They do insist, however, on immediate response to questions they might have regarding information they need to access for their decisions.

A commercial property investment search sponsored by Elgin Enterprises is used in this and the remaining chapters as an example of a DSS that can be of use to a single investor or shared with many investors, even over the Internet (see Figure 15.2). The problem can be simply stated as finding the most appropriate property in view of the client's financial status and personal preferences. The alternative decisions are the available properties listed in the database.

Figure 15.2.
Introducing the Elgin Enterprises Investment Property Search Facility.

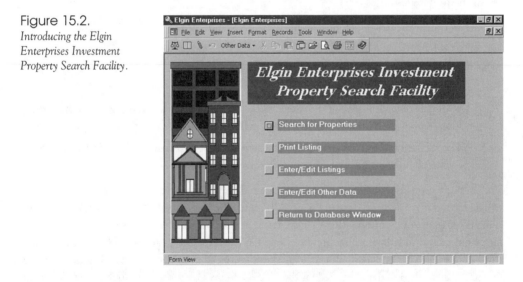

The Players in DSS Development

A DSS is viewed differently by the three major players in its development: the user, the developer, and the programmer. From the user's point of view, a DSS must fulfill most of the following objectives:

- Support decision making for hard or under-specified problems.
- Support decision making at all levels, providing each level with the desired degree of detail.

- Support all phases of decision making: collecting and processing raw data; devising, developing, and analyzing courses of action; and recommending the course of action that best fits the user's specifications.

- Support a variety of decision-making processes that fit the decision maker's cognitive style such as primarily factual or more intuitive.

- Above all, the DSS must be understandable and easy to use.

The user of the Elgin Enterprise Property Search Facility wants to be able to express his preferences in a comfortable manner and to be able to adjust them easily. The information presented by the DSS must be clear and organized in a logical manner, perhaps layered in accordance with the level of detail and interest. For example, if a property seems interesting, the client can explore additional information about it and even run some financial analyses.

The developer has other concerns that also fall into three categories: the dialog, data, and model subsystems. The developer is the "great explainer" who must translate the imprecise needs of the decision maker into extremely precise terms for the programmer to implement. In many cases, the developer and the programmer are the same person, especially when using an advanced database management system such as Access.

Of the three areas the developer must address, the *dialog subsystem* is the most visible and the most important. It consists of three major parts:

- The action language—What the user does to communicate with the DSS (click buttons, choose from menu lists, enter data, and so on).

- The display language—What the user sees as a result of actions taken (forms on the screen, printed reports, graphics and audio output, and so on).

- A knowledge base—What the user must know in order to use the DSS. This can include on-screen help and tips or a printed user's manual.

The *data subsystem* contains the information required for the decision process, often a wide variety of data from both inside and outside the organization. The higher up in the organization the decision maker is, the more information that comes from external sources. For example, the CEO of a large computer firm will be more interested in what his competitors are doing (external information) than in how his salesmen in Seattle are doing (internal information). In addition, the higher up the decision, the less detail needed for the process. Many DSSs must also include personal judgment data related to the decision process and reflecting the inclination of the decision maker.

The Elgin data subsystem holds all the available information about the available properties, including a description, present value, expenses and income, and a photograph, if available.

The *models subsystem* defines the structure of the decision process. It includes equations, formulas, logical comparisons, and other building blocks for processing the information appropriately. The developer can often become mesmerized by the structure of the decision model at the expense of a simple, modular approach of taking the process one step at a time.

The Elgin model subsystem consists of a scoring algorithm that credits each property with points in proportion to the emphasis the client places on the attributes of the property, such as price, location, or cash flow. For example, if the property is in the desired price range and the client has specified the price attribute as essential, 100 points are added to the property's total score.

From the programmer's point of view, the DSS also consists of three subsystems similar to the developer's, but dealing more with the computer software. The *dialog management subsystem* focuses on the display technology and implementation of required user interaction. Figure 15.3 shows a typical dialog object that Access uses to acquire user input. The form is from the Clayview City College database described in Chapter 7, "Programming with SQL."

Figure 15.3.
A typical Access dialog object.

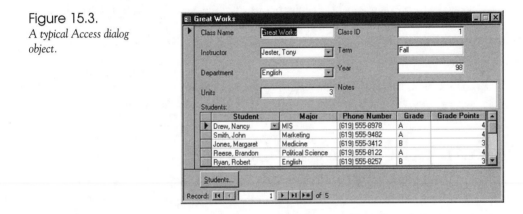

The *data management subsystem* handles the storage, retrieval, and validation of the information needed for the decision. The programmer creates the relational database system, extracting information from other sources as needed.

The *model management subsystem* explicitly defines the interrelationships among the variables in the decision and acts out the "What if?" scenarios. In the Elgin DSS, the model is the comparison of the values in the property database with the values selected by the client. The model consists of a series of event procedures that respond to the client's actions.

Access provides all three subsystems for the Elgin DSS. With Access, you can store all the necessary data as well as retrieve, filter, and sort it any way you want. Using VBA procedures, you can generate mathematical models to manipulate the data. The input and output design capabilities provide the ideal dialog with the client.

Designing a DSS

The DSS design process is evolutionary, with the design and implementation phases nearly inseparable. There is no clear break between the two, no precise end to design because new ideas keep cropping up as users learn more about what the DSS can do for them. The decision environment might also be shifting as the problem becomes more clear. For example, the Elgin DSS might start out to be a tool for searching for residential housing and then be expanded to include all types of commercial real estate. Later, it might shift again to include real estate investment trust (REIT) funds.

The Elgin system accepts input from the potential investor in the form of a list of requirements based on property attributes such as price, cash flow, location, type of property, and gross receipt multiplier (GRM). Each attribute is ranked on a scale from "essential" to "nice to have" and "don't care," depending on the user's preferences.

The DSS model then examines all the properties listed in the database and scores them based on how well they meet the user's requirements. The results are displayed for the investor to examine the details of the listings more closely. Further economic analyses are available if desired, or the client can return to the original form and change some of the selections.

This is an example of the multi-attribute utility model in which several features of the property are considered, each one weighted according to its relative importance in the view of the decision maker.

Identify the Right Problem

The most important facet of designing a DSS is to choose the right problem to work on. It is possible that each person involved in the DSS development has a different concept of the problem. For example, in a portfolio management system, the investment research folks want to solve the problem by hiring more high-quality analysts. They are treating the problem as an unstructured problem, solvable only with human intuition.

The computer branch of the company treats it as a structured problem to be solved by improving their automated trust accounting system. In actuality, this is a semi-structured problem that can be solved by a combination of mathematical models that optimize the portfolio and the intuition of an experienced manager.

It is also important to concentrate on the problem rather than on a symptom of the problem. Sometimes it is hard to distinguish between the two. For example, the client is earning a low rate of return on a money market account, which is a symptom, not the basic problem. The problem is how to invest funds to get the best return (or the safest, if that is more important) on the capital.

The solution to the problem can also be confused with the problem itself. For example, suppose your 10-year-old car is giving you trouble, so you decide to buy a new one. You state your problem as, "How do I find the right car?" when the problem is really how to ensure you have reliable transportation. One of the potential solutions is to buy a new car. Other solutions might be to lease a car, ride your bike to work, or take the Metro. After you decide that buying a new car is the appropriate solution to the first problem, the next problem becomes how to decide which car to buy.

At Elgin Enterprises, the major problem is matching the investor with the property that best meets his requirements and preferences. To do this, you must be able to express these factors quantitatively and find a way to match them to the stored information about the properties.

What Is the Main Objective?

When defining the main objective of a new DSS, the focus is on what the DSS is supposed to do rather than on how it will look. The dialog and results displays are designed later in the process. For example, what is the DSS intended to accomplish: optimize a portfolio strategy, pick out the best location for a new store, or identify potentially profitable investment opportunities? Keep in mind that the computer is not allowed to make the decision, only to come up with possible solutions to the problem as you have defined it.

The main objective of the Elgin Enterprises DSS is to help the client find suitable commercial real estate properties for investment. Clients can specify the factors that play a part in their particular decision styles and reflect their requirements.

What Are the Decision Factors?

After determining what the major objective of the DSS is, you must examine the factors that affect the decision. What would cause you to choose one solution over another?

The Elgin DSS will ask questions such as, "How important is location to you? Is location more important than cash flow?" Clients will be able to state their requirements both quantitatively and qualitatively. For example, one client might specify a price range between $200,000 and $300,000 and an annual cash flow of at least $15,000. At the same time, they will tell Access that the type of property is more important than the cash flow.

After entering all the criteria and their relative importance, Access searches the database and accumulates a numeric score for each property based on how well it fits the client's requirements and preferences. Information about the listings that meet the selection criteria is then displayed. If the client desires, additional analyses can be run on a specified property to compute future values, return on investment, and other statistical predictions.

If none of the properties meet the client's requirements, he has the option of relaxing the requirements and rerunning the operation. This is part of the flexible feature of DSSs: the capability to trade off one factor against another. With a carefully designed dialog subsystem, the client can play "What if?" games with the information to see the outcome of different choices.

For example, the client could ask the question, "If I do this, what will it look like 10 years from now?" Using the information in the database, a projection can be run based on estimated inflation rates, property value fluctuations, or other trends.

There certainly will be subjective as well as objective decision criteria. For example, clients might prefer one location because it is close to their place of business and it will be more convenient to oversee. Or, one might prefer to invest in an apartment building because the mother-in-law could move into it as the manager.

The decision factors must be quantifiable in some way. If they are not actually numeric values, you can assign relative values to the factors. For example, assign a value of 100 to an attribute that is essential and a value of 50 to one that is only half as important.

How Can Access Help?

Access can provide all the data manipulation that is required by a DSS, including interactive dialog and flexible mathematical models. The Chart Wizard can supply visual interpretations of many of the analyses for Elgin's clients.

An added strength of Access is that it can call upon its fellow Office applications for their specific help. The financial data can be stored in Excel, where many types of charts and graphs are available. Figure 15.4 shows a 3-D column chart from the Excel array of sample charts. A column chart is useful for illustrating trends over a period of time, such as comparing the cash flow of two or three properties over a 10-year period. Figure 15.5 shows a sample exploding pie chart that can be used to show proportions of a whole, such as the relative number of properties in each region.

Figure 15.4.
A sample 3-D column chart from Excel.

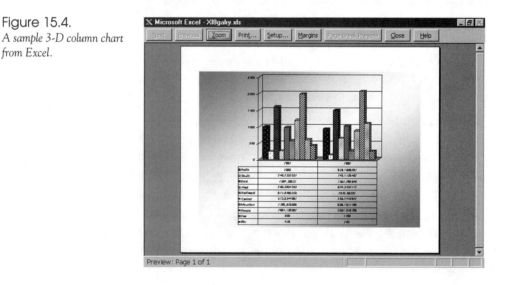

Figure 15.5.
A sample pie chart from Excel.

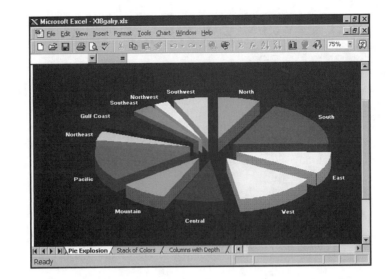

Using the Access Web Wizard, you can create a home page and post your database to the Web. Figure 15.6 shows a sample of a Web page advertising the Elgin Enterprises Investment Property Search Facility.

Figure 15.6.
Use the Access Web Wizard to create a home page on the Web.

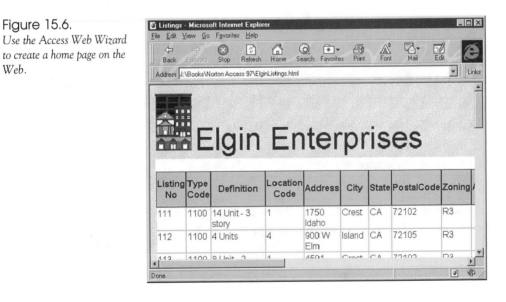

An Overview of the Elgin Enterprises Database

You already have a good idea of what the Elgin DSS is all about and what kind of decision it is intended to support. As the system develops in this and the next chapter, keep in mind that although the database is limited, it is as close to reality as possible. If loan information such as current interest rates and amount financed were included, other analyses could follow the property search. Another more qualitative factor would be the future use of such property as buildable land.

> **Note:** The data in the Elgin database is totally fictitious, although you will see photographs of actual properties. The pictures were taken of local buildings to serve as sample properties only and should not be construed to be actually for sale.

The Elgin Enterprises database consists of four related tables, as follows:

- The Listings table contains all the relevant information about the listed properties.
- Location is a lookup table that contains descriptions of the Location Code field in the Listings table. This table has a one-to-one relationship with Listings. It includes information such as the population, average income, size in square miles, and a short description of the environment.
- Type is also a lookup table that defines the Type Code field values in the Listings table.
- The Agent table contains the names and telephone numbers for the agents referenced in the Listings table. Agents is related to Listings with a one-to-many relationship.

Table 15.2 lists the data contained in the Listings table.

Table 15.2. The Listings table data.

Field	Data
Listing No	Unique key field entered by Elgin Enterprises
Type Code	Four-digit code indicating the type of property
Definition	Short description of the property
Location Code	Code representing approximate location of property
Address	Address of property
City	City
PostalCode	Postal code
Zoning	Specific zoning category

Field	Data
Age	Approximate age of the structure (if any)
Size	Approximate size of the structure
List Date	Date of most recent listing
Agent Code	Code referring to the listing agent
List Price	Currently listed price
GRM	Gross Revenue Multiplier (the ratio of list price to income)
Previous List	Previous list price (if listed before)
Taxes	Annual property tax
Expenses	Total annual expenses
Income	Total annual income
Cash Flow	Net annual income after expenses and taxes
Total Score	Computed score based on user's stated requirements and rankings (to be computed by the search program)
Picture	Photograph of the property (if available)

Figure 15.7 shows the data entry form for the Elgin Enterprises Listings table.

Figure 15.7.
The Listings data entry form.

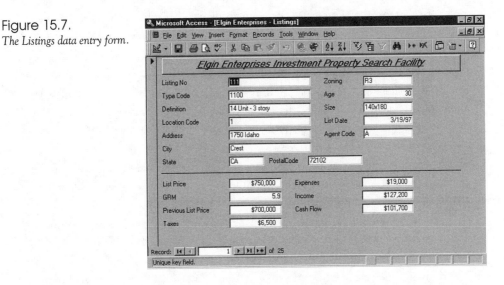

The Elgin Enterprises assistants maintain the information in the database behind the scenes. The data is not volatile, so no exotic data entry operations are required.

Chapter 16, "Customizing Input and Output," continues with the development of the Elgin DSS. Chapter 17, "Linking with Other Office Applications," describes how to interface and share data with the Excel and Word applications in Office 97 to add more functionality to the DSS.

Pioneers in Decision Support Systems

Professors William A. Wallace and Frank De Balogh published a paper titled, "Decision Support for Disaster Management" in the *Public Administration Review, Volume 45, Special Issue* in January 1985. In this paper, Drs. Wallace and De Balogh described several DSS models dealing with preparing for and reacting to disasters such as nuclear power plant incidents, ocean accidents that required Coast Guard search and rescue, and earthquake mitigation.

The Federal Emergency Preparedness Agency has broken down disaster management into four stages: preparedness, mitigation, emergency response, and recovery. Each stage has specific information requirements, and specific decisions are required from different levels of management at each stage.

The earthquake disaster mitigation DSS was designed at the University of Southern California Decision Support System Laboratory to help planners and other public officials make appropriate decisions to prepare for an earthquake and when an earthquake occurs.

The database contains several tables detailing building characteristics, population distribution, quake intensity, and projected costs of upgrading and retrofitting to meet the new safety standards. The information used in this prototype DSS was obtained from the City of Los Angeles Planning Department.

The system uses mathematical models to predict damage assessments by local region.

After the decision maker enters an intensity factor for the quake, the DSS computes the percentage of square footage and dollar value lost for each type and age of building. These estimates are then used to assess the potential damage an earthquake can do to existing and proposed buildings.

The model then couples the damage assessment with the estimated costs to improve buildings to new standards to compute the estimated savings that would be realized by making the improvements.

The DSS also provides summary statistics that estimate the total damage caused by an earthquake of a specific intensity, indicating the area that would be hardest hit, and which types of buildings would suffer the most.

The decision maker can use this DSS to play "What if?" games by varying upgrade costs and earthquake intensity.

Summary

Although somewhat pedantic, this chapter has expanded the use of Access to the realm of decision support. Access has all the objects that a DSS requires: a dialog subsystem, a database subsystem, and a model subsystem. All it takes to implement a DSS with Access is a little imagination and some programming skill. The next chapter completes the development of the Elgin Enterprises DSS by creating an interactive user interface and a series of procedures that operate the decision model.

16

Customizing Input and Output

In Chapter 15, "Introducing a Database Decision Support System," you were introduced to the Elgin Enterprises database. This chapter turns it into a decision support system by adding the user dialog feature, the decision model, and a means to display the results of the search for potential investment properties. You also will design some analytical computations and summaries as additional decision-making tools.

Note: Keep in mind that the properties featured in the Elgin Enterprises database are for example only and not actual investment opportunities.

Creating the User Input Form

Clients who come to Elgin Enterprises have some idea of what kind of investment property they are looking for. They definitely have a price range in mind and might also have a preference for apartment buildings or shopping centers. There are five major categories of property attributes that can be of interest to a potential investor:

- Location. The area is divided into six major regions.

- Type of property, including apartments, industrial, offices, commercial, and miscellaneous.

- Price range.

- Cash flow.

- Gross Revenue Multiplier (GRM), which is the ratio of the listed price to the annual income.

The last three can be broken down into intervals from which to choose. For example, prices less than $100,000, between $100,000 and $200,000, and so on. All of these attributes must be displayed to the client together with a tool for ranking the perceived importance of each attribute.

This structure is an example of the multi-attribute utility model mentioned in Chapter 15. The decision maker considers multiple attributes (price, location, GRM, and so on, in this case) and weights them according to their individual importance in the decision process.

The Choice Form Design

Five lists of attributes is a lot of information to display in a single form on-screen, so the Elgin Enterprises developer has divided the data into a two-page tabbed form. Figure 16.1 shows the first page of the form, which includes the Location and Type selections. Beneath each option group is a list box containing the five ranking selections. After the clients choose one of the values in an attribute box, they can choose the ranking from the drop-down list. All attributes need not be selected. If an attribute is selected but no ranking is specified, it is ignored in the evaluation of the properties in the Listings table.

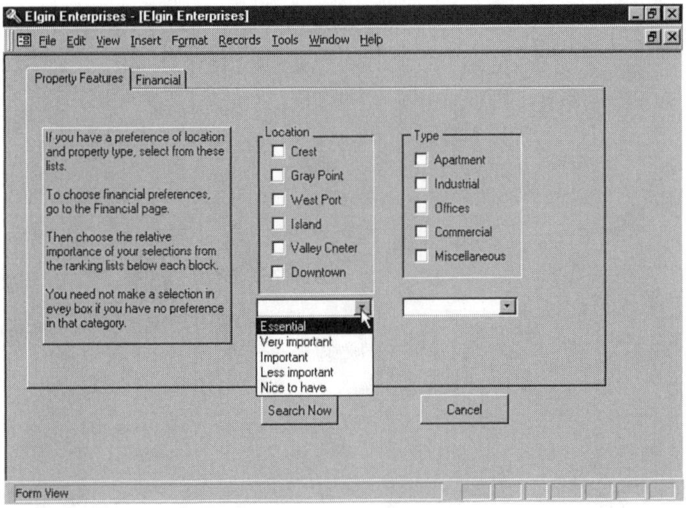

Figure 16.1.
The Property Features tab of the Choice input form.

> **Note:** The Type and Location attribute lists are shown as check boxes in option groups in this example. This precludes adding more types or locations to the lists without adding to the option groups. If you need to be able to add to these lists, change the option groups to combo boxes. There would also be some minor changes to the VBA code that interprets the choices.

The ranking list is an unbound combo box whose row source is a two-column value list entered directly in the control property sheet. The value list equates each level of importance to a number value:

- Essential = 100
- Very important = 50
- Important = 35
- Less important = 20
- Nice to have = 10

Figure 16.2 shows the form design with one of the value lists expanded in the Zoom window. These scores are accumulated as Access evaluates each property in the Listings table with respect to the client's preferences.

Figure 16.2.

The ranking controls are based on a value list.

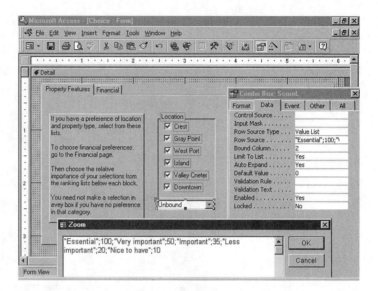

Warning: If you have set the Choice form's Allow Update property to No, you will not be able to make choices in the attribute lists or the value lists. Set the Allow Update property to Yes and set the Allow Deletions, Allow Additions, and Allow Filters all to No.

The second page of the Choice form gives the client choices in price, cash flow, and GRM ranges (see Figure 16.3). Each of these also has a ranking drop-down list for rating the relative importance of the attribute. Two buttons are placed in the form footer so that they are available from both pages of the form. One starts the search for properties that meet the entered criteria, and the other closes the form.

The Choice form class module contains only four event procedures. The first two (OnLoad and OnGotFocus) maximize the form. Attaching the Maximize method to both events guarantees that the form will be maximized no matter what has gone on in the meantime. The event procedure that runs when the Cancel button is clicked simply closes the form. The Search Now button triggers a much more complicated procedure, which is described in the next section.

Figure 16.3.

The Financial tab of the Choice input form.

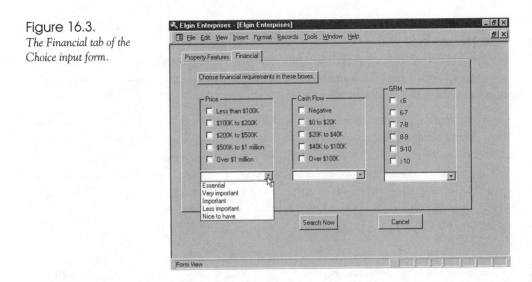

The Search Process

The search process moves through all the listings in the Listings recordset and compares each property, attribute by attribute, with the stated preferences from the Choice form. When a property is found to meet the desired condition, the value from the corresponding ranking list is added to the property's Total Score field. At the end of the process, the properties that have a Total Score above 0 are displayed in a results form.

If the client has specified an attribute as essential, only properties with a Total Score over 100 are displayed in the result. It is, of course, possible for a property to accumulate more that 100 points and still not have the specified "essential" attribute, but scoring high without it might actually place the property within the realm of consideration.

The Search Procedure

The Search Now button `OnClick` event procedure contains four major routines as well as a rather extensive declarations section. In addition to the usual database and recordsets, integer variables are declared for each of the option group choices—`intOptLoc`, `intOptType`, and so on. Then, variables are declared for the selected value in each attribute group. The `strType` and `strLoc` attribute variables are String type. For the other three attributes that specify value ranges, you need variables for both the upper and lower values in the selected option. Finally, variables are assigned to the score value chosen for each attribute group.

The first section after the declaration section checks to make sure at least one attribute has been selected before proceeding. An If...Then block tests the values returned by the options groups. If they are all zero, nothing has been selected and a message box displays, "You must select at least one category before searching." If at least one attribute has been selected, five integer variables are set to the values returned by the option groups.

The second routine uses Select Case structures to assign the option numbers of the selected attribute values to variables for later comparison with the values in the recordset. The preferred location attribute can use the selected value directly without the Select Case logic because the Location Code field in the Location table very conveniently has integer values from 1 to 6, which is the same set of integers returned by the option group selection. Of course, you can have the Option Group Wizard set any integers as the returned value for each option. Ascending integer values beginning with 1 are the default.

Note: The lowest range of the cash flow attribute is <0, a range with only one limit. In the Select Case, the lower limit is set artificially to a large negative number, one that would never be exceeded. Similarly, the upper limit of the highest range is set to a very large number, $1,000,000. This magnitude of annual cash flow is not likely from the types of properties Elgin lists in the database. The highest range limit of the Price attribute is defined as $1 to $10 million.

The third routine moves through all the records in the recordset, adding points to the property's Total Score field whenever a field value meets the stated attribute value. The number of points to add to the score is determined by the choice made in the corresponding ranking list.

The fourth and final routine displays the results of the search, displaying only those whose total score is over 100, if one of the attributes was deemed essential.

The complete listing for the Search Now command button, interspersed with comments, is shown in Listing 16.1.

Listing 16.1. The Search Now button's OnClick event procedure.

```
Private Sub Search_Click()
On Error GoTo Err_Search_Click
'Declare variables for all the attributes and scores.

Dim dbsCurrent As Database, rstList As Recordset
Dim rstResults As Recordset
Dim intOptLoc As Integer, intOptType As Integer
Dim intOptPrice As Integer, intOptGRM As Integer
Dim intOptCash As Integer
Dim strType As String, strLoc As String
Dim curHiPrice As Currency, curLoPrice As Currency
Dim intHiGRM As Integer, intLoGRM As Integer
```

```
Dim curHiCash As Currency, curLoCash As Currency
Dim intScore As Integer, intScoreL As Integer
Dim intScoreT As Integer, intScoreC As Integer
Dim intScoreP As Integer, intScoreG As Integer

Set dbsCurrent = CurrentDb
Set rstList = dbsCurrent.OpenRecordset("Listings")
'Check for at least one option selection.
If LocBox = 0 And TypeBox = 0 And PriceBox = 0 And GRMBox = 0 _
        And CashBox = 0 Then
    MsgBox ("You must select at least one category before searching.")
    Me.[Property Features].SetFocus
    Me.Visible = True
End If

'Define the variables from the option group selections
intOptLoc = LocBox
intOptType = TypeBox
intOptPrice = PriceBox
intOptGRM = GRMBox
intOptCash = CashBox
```

The next code clears the strType variable and then uses the Select Case to equate the returned option group value to the property type code in the Listings table.

```
'Set the selected property type.
strType = ""
Select Case intOptType
    Case 1
        strType = "1100"
    Case 2
        strType = "1200"
    Case 3
        strType = "1300"
    Case 4
        strType = "1400"
    Case 5
        strType = "1500"
End Select
```

The next statement uses the CStr() function to set the Location attribute value to the string equivalent of the integer returned by the Location option group. Then, the next three Select Case structures set the upper and lower values for the selected Price, Cash Flow, and GRM ranges attributes:

```
'Set the selected location.
strLoc = CStr(intOptLoc)

'Set the selected price range.
Select Case intOptPrice
    Case 1
        curHiPrice = 100000
        curLoPrice = 0
    Case 2
        curHiPrice = 200000
        curLoPrice = 100000
```

```
        Case 3
            curHiPrice = 500000
            curLoPrice = 200000
        Case 4
            curHiPrice = 1000000
            curLoPrice = 500000
        Case 5
            curHiPrice = 10000000
            curLoPrice = 1000000
End Select

'Set the selected cash flow range
Select Case intOptCash
        Case 1
            curHiCash = 0
            curLoCash = -100000
        Case 2
            curHiCash = 20000
            curLoCash = 0
        Case 3
            curHiCash = 40000
            curLoCash = 20000
        Case 4
            curHiCash = 60000
            curLoCash = 40000
        Case 5
            curHiCash = 100000
            curLoCash = 60000
        Case 6
            curHiCash = 1000000
            curLoCash = 100000
End Select

'Set the selected GRM range.
Select Case intOptGRM
        Case 1
            intHiGRM = 6
            intLoGRM = 0
        Case 2
            intHiGRM = 7
            intLoGRM = 6
        Case 3
            intHiGRM = 8
            intLoGRM = 7
        Case 4
            intHiGRM = 9
            intLoGRM = 8
        Case 5
            intHiGRM = 10
            intLoGRM = 9
        Case 6
            intHiGRM = 100
            intLoGRM = 10
End Select
```

 Before beginning to process the recordset, integer variables set the individual attribute scores to the selections made in the corresponding ranking drop-down lists. Then, the procedure moves to the first record in the recordset to begin comparing field values with the selected attribute values. A Do Until EOF loop is used to move through the recordset, and If...Then statements determine whether to add the score to the Total Score of the property. When the attribute is a range of values, the And operator is used to combine the upper and lower criteria.

You must include the rstList.Edit statement in order to be able to write the Total Score to the current record. Just before the end of the loop, the rstList.Update statement writes the score to the record:

```
'Set the weight values from the Ranking lists.
intScoreT = ScoreT
intScoreL = ScoreL
intScoreP = ScoreP
intScoreG = ScoreG
intScoreC = ScoreC

'Move to the first record in the Listings table.
rstList.MoveFirst

'Compute the total score for each property in the Listings table.
Do Until rstList.EOF
    intScore = 0
    rstList.Edit
'Get score for Location.
    If rstList![Location Code] = strLoc Then
        intScore = intScore + intScoreL
    End If

'Add score for Type.
    If rstList![Type Code] = strType Then
        intScore = intScore + intScoreT
    End If

'Add score for Price.
    If rstList![List Price] >= curLoPrice And _
        rstList![List Price] < curHiPrice Then
        intScore = intScore + intScoreP
    End If

'Add score for GRM.
    If rstList!GRM >= intLoGRM And _
        rstList!GRM < intHiGRM Then
        intScore = intScore + intScoreG
    End If

'Add score for Cash Flow.
    If rstList![Cash Flow] >= curLoCash And _
        rstList![Cash Flow] < curHiCash Then
        intScore = intScore + intScoreC
    End If

    rstList![Total Score] = intScore
rstList.Update
rstList.MoveNext
Loop
```

Warning: The `Do While` loop does not automatically advance to the next record in the recordset. You must be sure to include the `rstList.MoveNext` statement just before the `Loop` line or else your procedure will run forever. (Or at least until you press Ctrl+Alt+Del.)

The last routine in the procedure prepares the results for display in the Results form. Actually, two versions of the display form are involved. One is based on a query that limits the records to those with a total score greater than or equal to 100. This version, `Results100`, is used if any of the attributes were deemed "essential." The other report displays all the properties that have a score over 0:

```
If intScoreL = 100 Or intScoreT = 100 Or intScoreP = 100 _
    Or intScoreG = 100 Or intScoreC = 100 Then
    Set rstResults = dbsCurrent.OpenRecordset("Results100")
    DoCmd.OpenForm "Results100", acNormal
Else
    Set rstResults = dbsCurrent.OpenRecordset("Results")
    DoCmd.OpenForm "Results", acNormal
    End If

Exit_Search_Click:
    Exit Sub

Err_Search_Click:
    MsgBox Err.Description
    Resume Exit_Search_Click

End Sub
```

Displaying the Results of the Search

Once again, the new Access 97 feature of tabbed forms is used—this time to display the results of the property search. The property attributes are divided into three categories: information about the location and type of property, financial and environmental features, and listing information. The arrangement is based on the relative importance of the information to the client. Price, type, and location were considered to be of primary interest and were placed on the first page (see Figure 16.4). The Listing Number, Price, and Definition information appear on all three pages so that the client can easily correlate the information.

The four buttons in the form footer are used to do the following:

- Print the complete information in report format for the current listing
- Print a report including all the listings
- Open the window for further analysis of the current listing
- Close the form and return to the switchboard

Figure 16.4.
The first page of the results form.

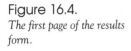

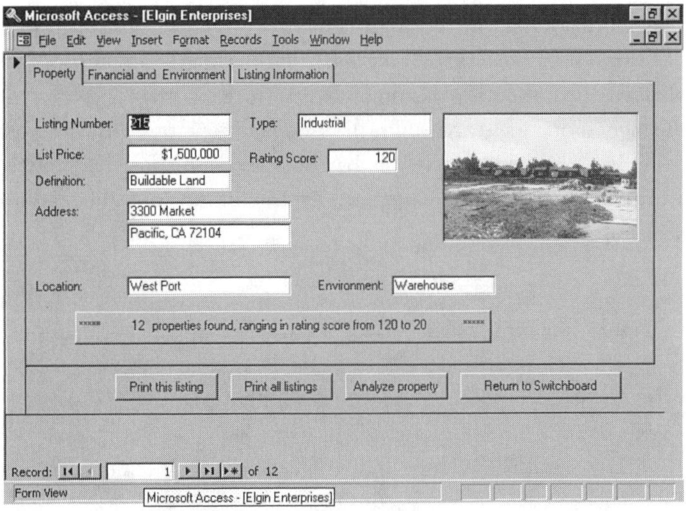

There are several special features in this form design. The first page shows a summary of the results of the search. The rectangle at the bottom of the form tells how many properties were found and the range of scores among them. Figure 16.5 shows the first page of the form in design view.

Note: Just a reminder that the data in the Elgin Enterprises database is fictitious, although the properties pictured in the database are real. They serve only as sample properties and should not be construed to be actually for sale.

Figure 16.5.
The design of the first page.

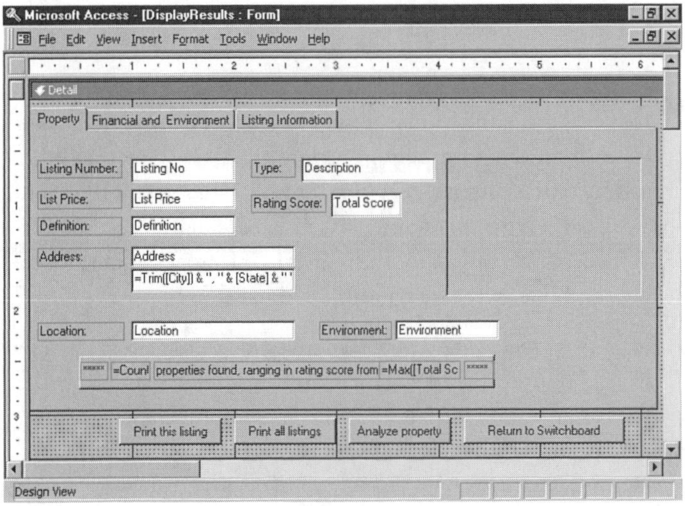

The information in the rectangle combines two expressions with some label text in between. The first expression, `=Count([Listing No])`, returns the total number of properties found. After the explanatory text, the second expression, `=Max([Total Score]) &" to "& Min([Total Score])`, returns the highest and lowest scores in the group of properties with the word "to" in between. This summary gives the clients an idea of how restrictive or liberal their preferences are. If too few properties are found, perhaps the requirements are too limiting and the search should be rerun with relaxed demands.

Tip: In the form design, you can see the address line containing an expression concatenating the city, state, and postal code field values. If you see nothing in the text box but `#Error` when you switch to form view, there might not be anything wrong with the expression. Check for errors in the expression and if you don't find any, delete the message and reenter it. The Expression Builder might be of some help, but it occasionally creates an expression that also evokes the `#Error` message.

The picture of the property appears on this page and again on the third page of the form. They are embedded bound objects that display the bound OLE object that is stored in the Picture field of the Listings table. Not all pictures are going to be the same size because they are cropped to show the property at its best. It is important to set the OLE object properties so that there is not an unattractive gap between the picture and the frame. You also must preserve the ratio of picture height to width. Set the following OLE object properties:

- Size Mode to Zoom
- Special Effect to Sunken
- Border to Transparent
- Back Style to Transparent

The second page of the Display Results form (see Figure 16.6) shows the financial and environmental information about the current listing. The only thing that needs attention on this page is the formatting of the currency text box controls. These fields were formatted in the table design and appear in datasheet view as currency with no decimal places, but that formatting does not carry over to a form design. You must set the format in the property sheet for these controls. Select them all as a group, and change the format of all of them at once.

If the property seems like a potential investment, the client can move to the other pages for more details, ending up on the Listing Information page where she can find the name and telephone number for the listing agent (see Figure 16.7). The form includes a command button that automatically dials the agent's phone number.

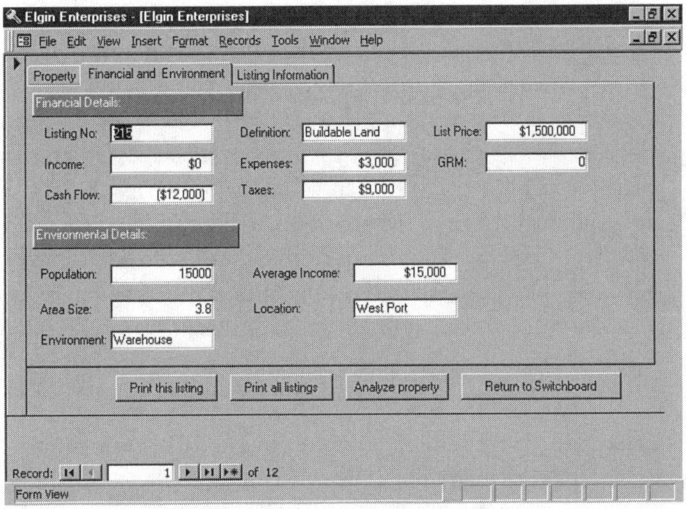

Figure 16.6.
The Financial and Environment page of the Results form.

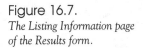

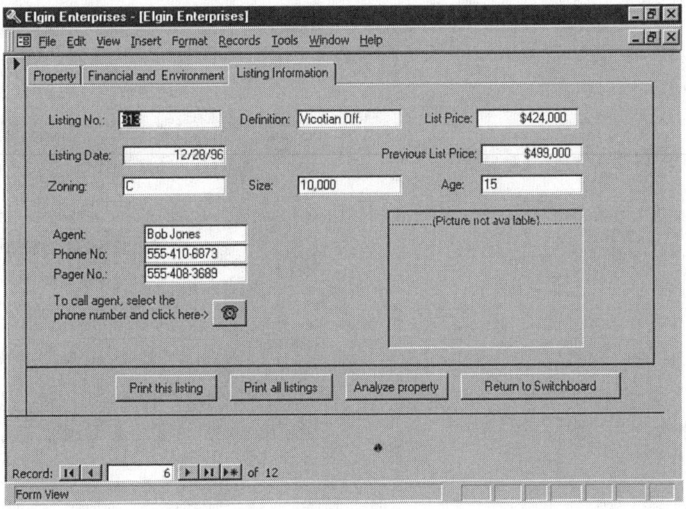

Figure 16.7.
The Listing Information page of the Results form.

To use the AutoDialer, you need a Hayes or Hayes-compatible modem installed in your computer. To add the command button to the form, use the Command Button Wizard and choose Miscellaneous in the Categories box. Then choose AutoDialer from the Actions box. The button you see in the Display Results form uses the smaller of the two telephone icons. To use the AutoDialer button, first select the telephone or pager number, and click the button.

Another feature you can see on this page is the text that appears in the empty OLE control frame when there is no picture for the property. The text is actually a bit of text art created with Microsoft WordArt 3.0. You insert this object instead of a photo file into the Picture field of each record that does not have a picture. If you acquire a picture later, simply write over the text art.

Note: The photographs in the Elgin database were scanned in black and white with a rather coarse resolution to save disk space. Adding images to a database can dramatically increase its size, especially if the images are in 256 colors. If you are really short of disk space, you can display an icon representing the image instead of the whole image. To change a bound image to an icon, select the object in form view or in the datasheet and choose the appropriate object command—Photo Editor Photo Object for an Elgin photo—and then choose Convert. In the Convert dialog box, check Display as Icon. If the object is unbound, you can convert it from the form or report design window. When you want to view the image itself, double-click the icon; the OLE server is launched, and the image is displayed.

To create and add the text art, open the table in datasheet view, place the cursor in an empty Picture field, and then follow these steps:

1. Choose Insert | Object to open the Insert Object dialog box.

2. Choose Create New, scroll down the Object Type list, and select Microsoft WordArt 3.0 (see Figure 16.8).

Figure 16.8.
Inserting a WordArt object.

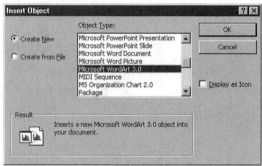

3. Type ....(Picture not available)............. in the Enter Your Text Here box and make any changes you want to the font style, size, and color; then choose OK (see Figure 16.9).

Tip: Without the preceding and trailing dots, the text is expanded to the width of the bound object frame because of the Zoom Size Mode property. This creates a large obtrusive message. With the dots, the line is wide enough without expanding. If you had set the Size Mode for the bound object control to Stretch, the text would be expanded both horizontally and vertically to fill the frame. That gives the message a very distorted appearance.

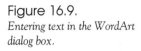

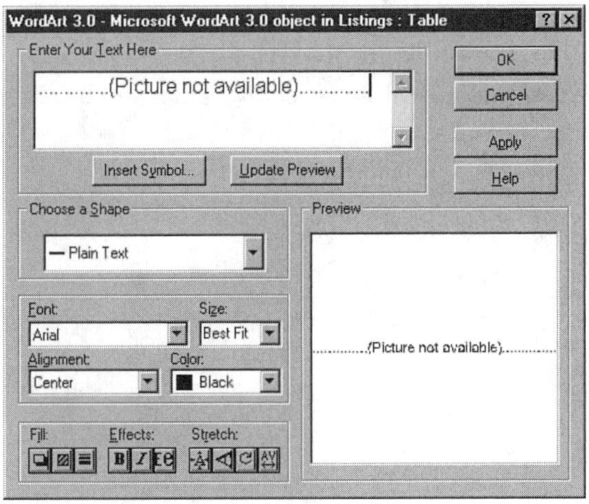

Figure 16.9.
Entering text in the WordArt dialog box.

4. Back in the datasheet view, select the new object and click Copy; then paste it in each of the other empty Picture fields.

The Display Results Form Code

The VBA code in the Display Results form class module is relatively straightforward. It includes the usual Maximize method when the form opens and the Close method when the Close button is clicked.

The first procedure was created by the Command Button Wizard when the AutoDialer button was added. It finds the telephone number you have selected. The nested If...Then statements test for the type and contents of the control that had focus just before the button was clicked. An IIf() function then tests the contents of the previous control and, if it is not blank, returns the value in the control, presumably the phone number. If it is blank, an empty string is returned.

> **Note:** The IIf() function (immediate If) provides a quick way to return one value if the value of an expression is true and another if it evaluates to false. The function takes three arguments: the expression to be evaluated, the true value and the false value. The If...Then statement offers more versatile branching options, and the Select Case is the most sophisticated of the three structures.

If the previous control was not one of the three types of boxes—text, list, or combo—the phone number is set to an empty string because those are the only controls that could contain a phone number. Then the following statement calls the AutoDial application and passes the phone number variable, stDialStr:

```
Application.Run "utility.wlib_AutoDial", stDialStr
```

The wizard sets two constants in the procedure to trap specific errors and resume processing without exiting. The message for the Jet 3.0 Error 91 is "Object variable or With block variable not set." Error 2467 displays a similar message saying that the object variable does not exist. If any other error occurs, the procedure exits.

Listing 16.2 shows the complete listing of the Display Results form class module.

Listing 16.2. The Display Results form class module.

```
Private Sub Form_Load()
DoCmd.Maximize
End Sub

Private Sub Dial_Click()
On Error GoTo Err_Dial_Click

    Dim stDialStr As String
    Dim PrevCtl As Control
    Const ERR_OBJNOTEXIST = 2467
    Const ERR_OBJNOTSET = 91

    Set PrevCtl = Screen.PreviousControl

    If TypeOf PrevCtl Is TextBox Then
      stDialStr = IIf(VarType(PrevCtl) > V_NULL, PrevCtl, "")
    ElseIf TypeOf PrevCtl Is ListBox Then
      stDialStr = IIf(VarType(PrevCtl) > V_NULL, PrevCtl, "")
    ElseIf TypeOf PrevCtl Is ComboBox Then
      stDialStr = IIf(VarType(PrevCtl) > V_NULL, PrevCtl, "")
    Else
      stDialStr = ""
    End If

    Application.Run "utility.wlib_AutoDial", stDialStr

Exit_Dial_Click:
    Exit Sub

Err_Dial_Click:
    If (Err = ERR_OBJNOTEXIST) Or (Err = ERR_OBJNOTSET) Then
      Resume Next
    End If
    MsgBox Err.Description
    Resume Exit_Dial_Click

End Sub

Private Sub PrintAll_Click()
'Opens report of all listings in results of search.

DoCmd.OpenReport "All Results", acViewPreview

End Sub
```

```
Private Sub PrintThis_Click()
'Opens Print Property report for preview.
'Asks for Listing No for the property to print.

DoCmd.OpenReport "Property Listing", acViewPreview

End Sub

Private Sub Analysis_Click()
'Opens form for selecting type of financial analysis.
On Error GoTo Err_Analysis_Click

    DoCmd.OpenReport "Analysis", acViewPreview

Exit_Analysis_Click:
    Exit Sub

Err_Analysis_Click:
    MsgBox Err.Description
    Resume Exit_Analysis_Click

End Sub

Private Sub Close_Click()
'Closes form and returns to switchboard.
DoCmd.Close

End Sub
```

The code for the Results100 form that displays the result of a search containing an "essential" attribute is the same except for the reports that open for preview when you click to print or analyze the results. The Print All Listings button on the Results100 form opens the Results100 report, which uses the same Results100 query that the form used as the record source. Similarly, the Analysis Results100 report is the report the opens for preview when you click the Analyze property button in the Results100 form. You could compose the SQL statements in the class modules for these forms each time they run, but processing is quicker if the queries are already constructed.

Previewing Reports

Two reports are available from the Display Results form: One includes the information for a single listing and the other for all the listings that were found in the search. The single listing report is based on a parameter query, and the client must enter the Listing Number of the desired property. This enables the report to be accessed from other points in the application rather than only from the Display Results form. Figure 16.10 shows a preview of the single listing report, and Figure 16.11 shows a two-page preview of the All Results report. If the search was limited to properties scoring 100 points or more, the Results100 report opens for preview instead of the All Results report.

Figure 16.10.
Previewing a single listing.

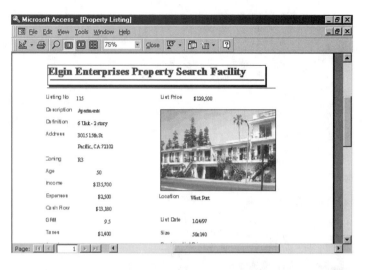

Figure 16.11.
Previewing two pages of the All Results report.

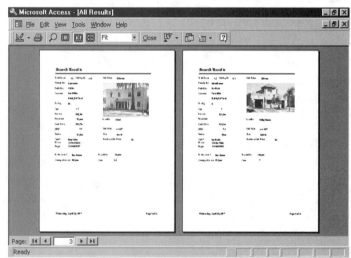

Including Computations and Trade-Offs

When clients find properties that look promising as investments, they might like to see some financial analyses of the properties. If the number of properties found during the search is small enough—less than six—comparative analyses can be performed. The results show how the properties compare with respect to such things as long-term appreciation, the annual rate of return, a 10-year projection of cash flow, or the break-even point at which the income has offset the price paid.

The Analysis command button opens a report that includes the percent annual return on the investment and the estimated break-even point. The report that is based on the same query as the form is opened for preview. Figure 16.12 shows an analysis report containing information for five properties.

Elgin Enterprises - [Analysis 100]
File Edit View Tools Window Help
100%
Close
Analysis of Results
Listing No List Price GRM Taxes Expenses Income Cash Flow Total Score
215 $1,500,000 0 $9,000 $3,000 $0 ($12,000) 100
Break Even Pt. (yrs): N/A Percent Return: 0.0%
214 $119,500 9.3 $1,350 $2,500 $12,800 $16,650 100
Break Even Pt. (yrs): 9.3 Percent Return: 10.7%
213 $75,000 9 $1,000 $1,500 $8,300 $5,800 100
Break Even Pt. (yrs): 9.0 Percent Return: 11.1%
115 $129,500 9.5 $1,400 $2,500 $35,700 $31,800 100
Break Even Pt. (yrs): 3.6 Percent Return: 27.6%
413 $350,000 6.5 $4,500 $8,000 $53,100 $39,600 100
Break Even Pt. (yrs): 6.6 Percent Return: 15.2%
Page: 1
Ready

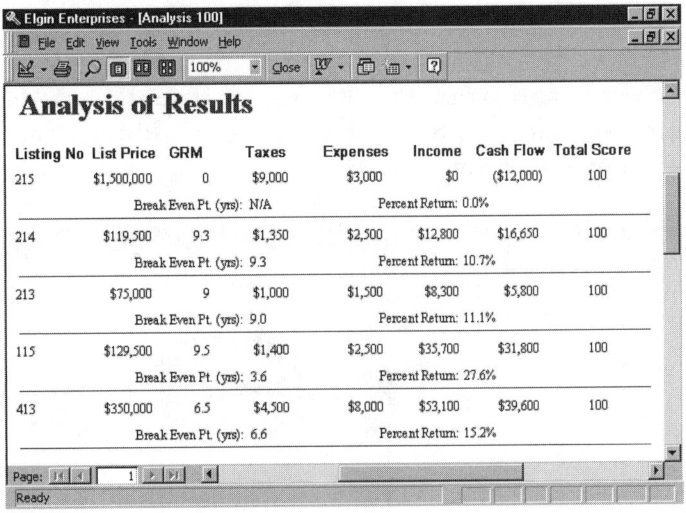

Figure 16.12.
Analyzing selected properties.

Here are the two calculated fields shown in the analysis report:

- Break Even Point, which is the result of the list price (considered the present value divided by the net annual income). Enter the following expression in the Control Source property of the calculated field:

```
=[List Price]/[Listings.Income]
```

- Percent Return, which is the result of dividing the income by the list price. Enter the following expression in the Control Source property:

```
=[Listings.Income]/[List Price]
```

The only problem occurs when the Income is 0. You get an error if you try to try to divide by 0. Change the expression for the Break Even Point to this:

```
IIf([Listings.Income]=0, "N/A",[List Price]/[Listings.Income])
```

This expression uses the `IIf()` function again to define the calculated value as N/A if the Income is 0 and the result of the division, if not.

Tip: If you let the Expression Builder help you with this expression, it automatically changes [Listings.Income] to [Listings].[Income], which will cause an error message, possibly because when the Expression Builder spots a period, even within brackets, it recognizes it as the dot operator and moves the brackets. Then, because Income is a user-named element rather than an Access object, an error occurs.

Other analyses can compare the density of listed properties in the different locations or by property type (see Figure 16.13). Such analyses can be of use to the Elgin Enterprise management in an effort to balance their inventory or concentrate on the more promising areas or types of properties.

Figure 16.13.

The relative number of properties in each location.

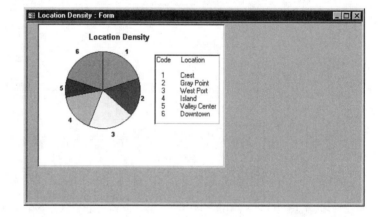

Although Access has many features you can use for numerical and statistical analysis, Excel is the Office application that specializes in these types of studies. In Chapter 17, "Linking with Other Office Applications," you will have a chance to let Excel do the work and ship the results back to the Access reports.

Putting It All Together in an Application

Once again, the final task is to wrap up all the pieces that make up the application into a single package with one point of entry for the user. Most of the end products—the forms and reports—have been created, now build the model that links them all together. Figure 16.14 shows how the objects are related and how to get from one to another.

Figure 16.14.
Model of the Elgin Enterprises decision support system.

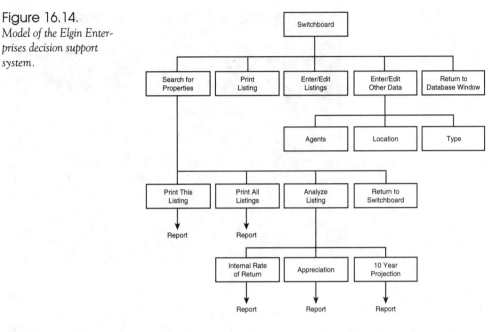

Adding a Switchboard

The main switchboard is the customary tool for branching to the desired operation. The order of items in the switchboard should be by priority and frequency of use. Because the Elgin Enterprise application is intended for the decision maker, the option to search for properties is placed at the top of the list (see Figure 16.15).

The options in the switchboard carry out the following actions:

- Search for Properties opens the Search form for the client to begin scouting for suitable investments from the available listings.

- Print Listing is a utility operation that prints a specified listing.

- Enter/Edit Listings opens the Listings data entry form, shown in Chapter 15.

- Enter/Edit Other Data opens other data entry forms. Although the Location and Type tables have data entry forms, adding records to those lists would require adding to the attribute lists in the Search form.

- Return to Database Window closes the switchboard and returns to a maximized Access database window with the Elgin Enterprises database still current.

Figure 16.15.
The Elgin Enterprises main switchboard.

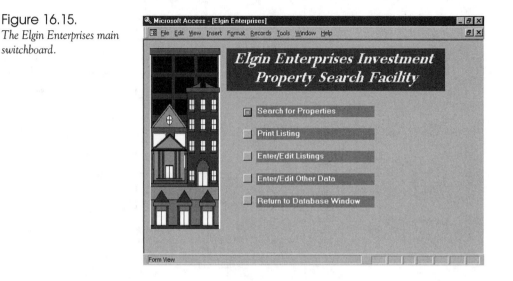

Unlike the switchboards you have seen in earlier chapters, the options in this one are command buttons. Command buttons do not have attached labels, so you must attach the event procedure to the label as well as the button if you want to be able to trigger the operation by clicking on either the button or the label. You can select both controls and click Build to create a macro or an expression that will run when you click either the button or the label. You cannot, however, create an event procedure for a multiple selection. The code for the switchboard form contains pairs of identical event procedures, one for the button and one for the corresponding label. This may seem a little redundant, but it works very well.

Listing 16.3 shows all the event procedures associated with the Elgin Enterprises Switchboard form.

Listing 16.3. The Switchboard form class module.

```
Private Sub Form_GotFocus()
DoCmd.Maximize
End Sub

Private Sub Form_Load()
DoCmd.Maximize
End Sub

Private Sub Find_Props_Click()
'Event procedure for Search for Properties label.
On Error GoTo Err_Find_Props_Click

    Dim strDocName As String
    Dim strLinkCriteria As String

    strDocName = "Choice"
    DoCmd.OpenForm strDocName, , , strLinkCriteria
```

```
Exit_Find_Props_Click:
    Exit Sub

Err_Find_Props_Click:
    MsgBox Err.Description
    Resume Exit_Find_Props_Click

End Sub

Private Sub Search_Click()
'Event procedure for Search button.
On Error GoTo Err_Search_Click

    Dim strDocName As String
    Dim strLinkCriteria As String

    strDocName = "Choice"
    DoCmd.OpenForm strDocName, , , strLinkCriteria

Exit_Search_Click:
    Exit Sub

Err_Search_Click:
    MsgBox Err.Description
    Resume Exit_Search_Click

End Sub

Private Sub Print_Click()
'Event procedure for Print Listing label.
On Error GoTo Err_Print_Click

    Dim strDocName As String

    strDocName = "Property Listing"
    DoCmd.OpenReport strDocName, acPreview

Exit_Print_Click:
    Exit Sub

Err_Print_Click:
    MsgBox Err.Description
    Resume Exit_Print_Click

End Sub

Private Sub Prop_Listing_Click()
'Event procedure for Print Listing button.
On Error GoTo Err_Prop_Listing_Click

    Dim strDocName As String

    strDocName = "Property Listing"
    DoCmd.OpenReport strDocName, acPreview

Exit_Prop_Listing_Click:
    Exit Sub
```

continues

Listing 16.3. continued

```
Err_Prop_Listing_Click:
    MsgBox Err.Description
    Resume Exit_Prop_Listing_Click

End Sub

Private Sub Enter_Listings_Click()
'Event procedure for Enter/Edit Listings button.
On Error GoTo Err_Enter_Listings_Click

    Dim strDocName As String
    Dim strLinkCriteria As String

    strDocName = "Listings"
    DoCmd.OpenForm strDocName, , , strLinkCriteria

Exit_Enter_Listings_Click:
    Exit Sub

Err_Enter_Listings_Click:
    MsgBox Err.Description
    Resume Exit_Enter_Listings_Click

End Sub

Private Sub Update_Listings_Click()
'Event procedure for Enter/Edit Listings label.
On Error GoTo Err_Update_Listings_Click

    Dim strDocName As String
    Dim strLinkCriteria As String

    strDocName = "Listings"
    DoCmd.OpenForm strDocName, , , strLinkCriteria

Exit_Update_Listings_Click:
    Exit Sub

Err_Update_Listings_Click:
    MsgBox Err.Description
    Resume Exit_Update_Listings_Click

End Sub

Private Sub Edit_Other_Click()
'Event procedure for Enter/Edit Other Data button.
On Error GoTo Err_Edit_Other_Click

    Dim strDocName As String
    Dim strLinkCriteria As String

    strDocName = "Choose Data to Edit"
    DoCmd.OpenForm strDocName, , , strLinkCriteria

Exit_Edit_Other_Click:
    Exit Sub
```

```
Err_Edit_Other_Click:
    MsgBox Err.Description
    Resume Exit_Edit_Other_Click

End Sub

Private Sub Enter_Other_Click()
'Event procedure for Enter/Edit Other Data label.
On Error GoTo Err_Enter_Other_Click

    Dim strDocName As String
    Dim strLinkCriteria As String

    strDocName = "Choose Data to Edit"
    DoCmd.OpenForm strDocName, , , strLinkCriteria

Exit_Enter_Other_Click:
    Exit Sub

Err_Enter_Other_Click:
    MsgBox Err.Description
    Resume Exit_Enter_Other_Click

End Sub

Private Sub Return_Click()
'Event procedure for Return to Database Window label.
On Error GoTo Err_Return_Click

    DoCmd.Close
    DoCmd.Maximize
Exit_Return_Click:
    Exit Sub

Err_Return_Click:
    MsgBox Err.Description
    Resume Exit_Return_Click

End Sub

Private Sub Close_Click()
'Event procedure for Return to Database Window button.
On Error GoTo Err_Close_Click

    DoCmd.Close
    DoCmd.Maximize
Exit_Close_Click:
    Exit Sub

Err_Close_Click:
    MsgBox Err.Description
    Resume Exit_Close_Click

End Sub
```

If you want the switchboard form to appear when you start the application, change the startup option. Choose Tools | Startup and select Elgin Enterprises Switchboard from the Display Form list.

Customizing the Command Bar

Instead of a custom menu bar, this application will have a custom toolbar with buttons. To create a custom command bar, as shown in Figure 16.16, choose View | Toolbars | Customize, and then perform the following steps:

1. In the Toolbars tab, choose New. A new command bar appears in the dialog box.

2. Choose Properties, and select Toolbar as the type of command bar. Move the Customize dialog box and the new command bar on the screen so that you can see both.

3. In the Commands tab, choose All Forms in the Categories list and Choice from the list of forms in the database. Then drag the form name from the Customize dialog box to the new command bar.

4. Choose All Reports in the Categories list and drag the Property Listing report from the Commands list to the bar. Repeat to drag the All Listings report to the bar.

5. To add the Enter/Edit Other Data option to the bar, you must add a New Menu item and attach the three data entry forms as submenu items.

6. Right-click each of the new buttons and select Properties from the shortcut menu. Add tooltip text for each new button.

7. To change the button icon, right-click the button and point to Change Button Image in the shortcut menu. Then select from the palette of icons. If you are artistic, you can choose Edit Button Image instead and draw your own.

8. Select other categories such as File, Edit, and View and drag some of the built-in command buttons to the command bar. Figure 16.16 shows the switchboard with the custom command bar containing both custom and built-in commands.

Figure 16.16.
The Elgin switchboard with the custom toolbar.

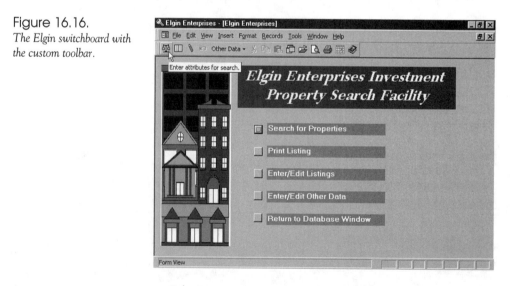

After you add the desired buttons to the toolbar and create tooltips for the custom buttons, the DSS development is fully functional. "Complete" is not the correct term for a DSS because you can always see where you can make improvements and changes.

Summary

The display forms and reports created in this chapter complete the development of the Elgin Enterprises DSS. Perhaps you have acquired a feel for the extensive capabilities Access has to offer to a DSS developer. Access can literally do whatever you need in support of quantitative and qualitative decision analysis. You will visit the Elgin database briefly in the next chapter, where it asks for assistance from Excel.

17

Linking with Other Office Applications

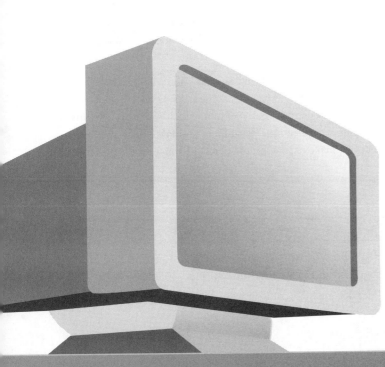

Like its human counterpart, the diverse and talented office staff, each of the Microsoft Office 97 applications has a special area of expertise. In addition to being able to import and export data between programs, you can create live links to make the objects available for cooperative efforts.

The Automation feature of Office 97 is the medium that makes these talents so easily available to all the other Office applications. Whenever necessary, Access can call upon one of its Office team to help out with a special task. This chapter explores Automation and sharing information among the Office applications.

Copying Access Objects

The easiest way to exchange objects among Office applications is to copy them. You can copy Access objects from one Access database to another or to a different application.

To copy an object to another Access database, select the object name in the database window and click Copy on the toolbar to copy it to the Clipboard. Next, close the current database and open the one in which you want to place the copy and click the Paste toolbar button. Then, enter a name for the newly pasted object. If you are copying a table, in the Paste As dialog box, you have a choice of pasting the table structure only, both the structure and the data, or appending the data to an existing table. Pasting an Access object copies all the object's properties, as well.

> **Note:** When you cut or copy data from an Access form or datasheet to an Excel spreadsheet, the font, alignment, and number formatting settings you have specified for the column headings and the data are preserved when you paste the data into the spreadsheet.

After you have copied the object you want to the Clipboard, you can also choose Edit | Paste Special instead of Paste. The type of information you want to paste from the Clipboard varies with the source and destination applications. Table 17.1 describes the types from which you may choose in the Paste Special dialog box with each pair of applications. Both Paste and Paste Special let you access the source application from Access to make changes in the object. If you want the object to keep up-to-date with the original information as it changes, you need to create a link.

Table 17.1. Paste Special choices.

Source	Destination	Paste As Types
Access	Excel	Biff5, text, or CSV
Access	Word	Formatted text (RTF) or unformatted text
Word	Access	MS Word document, picture, or text

Source	Destination	Paste As Types
Word	Excel	MS Word document object, picture (enhanced metafile), Unicode text, or text
Excel	Access	MS Excel worksheet, picture, bitmap, or text
Excel	Word	MS Excel worksheet object, formatted text (RTF), unformatted text, picture, bitmap, or picture (enhanced metafile)

In the Paste Special dialog box, you also have a choice of Paste Link, which creates a link to the source application. Then any changes made to the source object are reflected in the pasted object. A final option is to display the object as an icon. This is handy when you are working on a report and need to see it without the pasted object's getting in the way.

Using the drag-and-drop method is another way to copy Access objects to other databases or other applications. You can drag a table or other object to another database if it is open in another instance of Access. To drag objects between applications, you can either have both applications visible at once and drag the object between them (see Figure 17.1) or drag the object first to the Windows desktop where it becomes a shortcut and then open the destination application and drag the shortcut into that window. You can drag a table, query, or report from the database window to another application to make a copy of it.

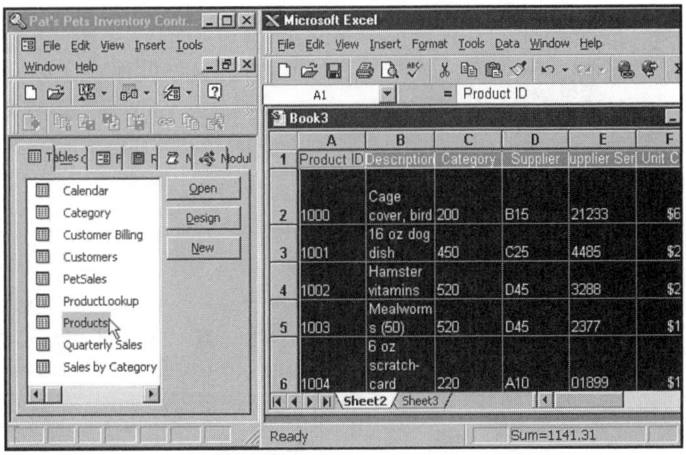

Figure 17.1.
Dragging an Access table to an Excel spreadsheet.

If you want a range of cells from an Excel worksheet, you can drag them to the Tables tab of a database window. You can also drag standard modules between Access and Excel.

Importing, Linking, and Exporting Data

Importing data into Access creates a copy of the information in a new table in a database. Importing data has no effect on the source of the data. You can make changes to your new copy, which also have no effect on the original information. Imported data is not updated when the source data is changed. For that, you must link the data to the source.

When you create a link to external data, you can read and usually update the data without making a copy of it in your database. This saves space in the database, but you must keep track of the location of the external data. If the original information is moved to a different folder, your database might not be able to locate it. You can use either the application that created the data or Access to add, delete, or edit its data.

Before importing or linking data to Access, you must open an existing database or create a new one to use as the destination.

Importing from Another Access Database

To import or link data from another Access database to your database, open your database and then follow these steps:

1. Click New in the Tables tab of the database window.

2. In the New Table dialog box, choose Import Table or Link Table and then choose OK. You can also choose File | Get External Data | Import (or Link Tables) to select the database objects for importing.

3. In the resulting Import or Link dialog box, locate the database from which you want to get information and click Import or Link.

4. If you chose Import Table, the Import Objects dialog box opens, closely resembling the database window itself. You can select any of the database objects to import. If you chose Link Table, you can select only table objects. Click the object name to include it in the operation. If you change your mind, click it again to deselect it. You can also select or deselect all the objects in the list.

5. Click Options in the Import Objects dialog box to specify additional options for the import (see Figure 17.2):

   • The Import check boxes let you also import the relationships that exist between the tables and queries you select, import the custom menus and toolbars, and include all the import/export specifications in the imported database. If a custom menu or toolbar is named the same as one in the destination database, it will not be imported.

- Import only the table definition or both the definition and the data.

- Import queries as queries or as tables.

6. After completing the selections, choose Import (or Link) and you are returned to the database window where you can see the new Access objects (see Figure 17.3).

Figure 17.2.
Selecting objects to import.

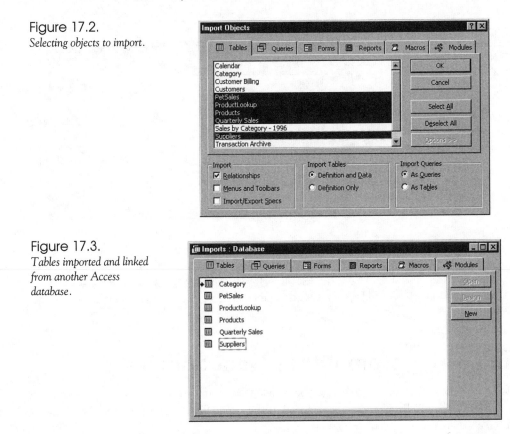

Figure 17.3.
Tables imported and linked from another Access database.

Importing objects from one Access database to another is effectively the same as copying and pasting the objects.

> **Note:** To import all the objects from one database to another, choose File | Get External Data | Import. Then choose Microsoft Access (.mdb) in the Files of Type box. After you locate the database you want to import, choose Select All on each of the object tabs. With the Tables tab, you can import only the table definition, if you want. With queries, you can import them as tables or queries.

Tip: The linked tables are identified in the database window with an arrow and an icon representing the origin of the data, if it is other than Access (see Figure 17.4). If you delete a table name with an icon, you remove the link in Access to the external database or other application, but you do not remove the table itself from the external source.

Figure 17.4.
Tables linked from other sources show an icon.

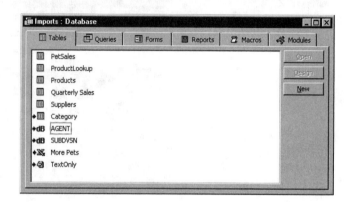

Note: You cannot append most imported data to an existing table in your database. The exceptions are spreadsheet data and text files. However, after you import the data, you can run an append query to add it to the existing tables.

Importing from Other Data Sources

Table 17.2 shows the other data sources from which you can import or link data. Drivers for Lotus 1-2-3 and Borland's Paradox are not included in the Office 97 Setup. If you have the Office 97 ValuPak, you can install them from there.

Table 17.2. Other data sources supported by Access.

Data Source	Format or Version
dBASE databases	III, III+, IV and 5
Excel spreadsheets	3.0, 4.0, 5.0, 7.0/95, and 8.0/97
FoxPro	2.x and 3.0 for importing only
Lotus 1-2-3 spreadsheets	.wks, .wk1, .wk3, and .wk4 (when linked, data is read-only)
Paradox databases	3.x, 4.x, and 5.0

Data Source	Format or Version
Delimited text files	MS-DOS or Windows ANSI text format files with values separated by commas, tabs, or other specified characters
Fixed-width text files	MS-DOS or Windows ANSI text format files with values arranged in fields all the same width
HTML	1.0 (list), 2.0, 3.x (table or list)

You also can import from or link to SQL tables and data from databases and programs that support the Open Database Connectivity (ODBC) protocol.

When you import data from Excel, you invoke the Import Spreadsheet Wizard, which gives you a choice of worksheets (if there are more than one in the selected workbook) or named ranges. The wizard then asks you to specify whether the first row in the sheet contains the names you want for the fields in the new table (see Figure 17.5). Then, you can choose to store the information in a new table or in an existing table.

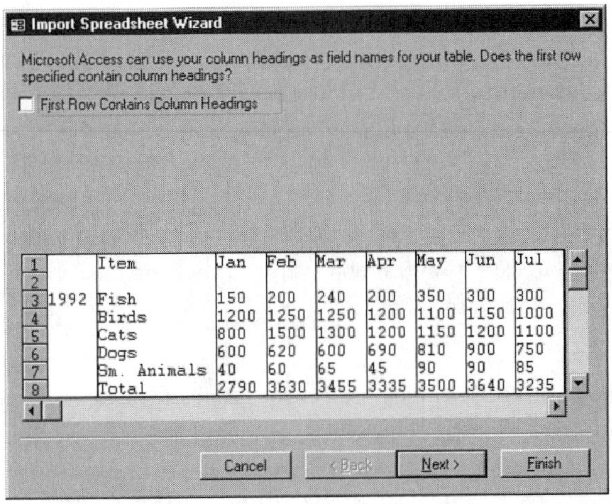

Figure 17.5.
Selecting field names from a spreadsheet.

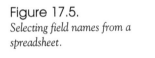

The next Import Spreadsheet Wizard dialog box lets you specify information about the fields, such as renaming the fields and identifying a field as an index field, or even leaving a field out of the import (see Figure 17.6). Select each field and make changes in its options, as necessary. The last steps with the wizard deal with setting a primary key field and naming the new table that will contain the spreadsheet data.

When you import a table from dBASE or some other database program, the table goes right into the open database. If you link a table from dBASE, you are asked to select associated index files as well and then select a unique record identifier. This arranges the data in the source program the way you want to see it in Access.

Figure 17.6.
Specify information about each field.

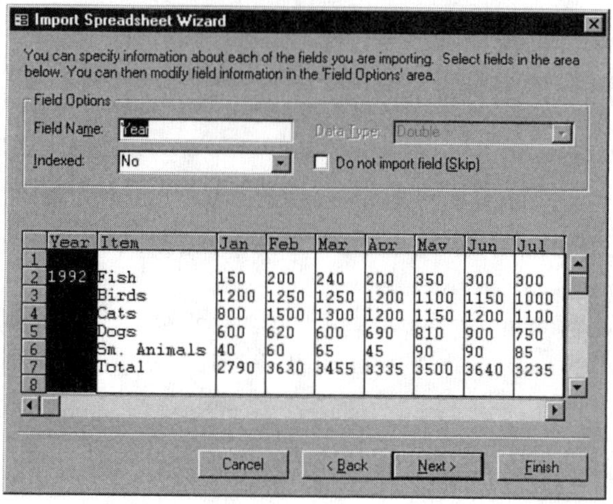

Exporting from Access
=====================

Exporting from one Access database to another is just another way of looking at importing Access objects, but exporting to other programs is a little different. A special case is exporting an Access table containing names and addresses to Word for use in a mail merge operation. More about mail merge in the section, "Mail Merge," later in this chapter.

> **Tip:** Because you can export only one object at a time, you might want to turn things around to export several objects to another database. Open the destination database and import the objects all at once.

To export an Access object, select the name of the table or query you want to export and choose File | Save As/Export or choose the same option from the shortcut menu. The Save As dialog box gives you the choice of saving to an external file or database or within the current database with a new name. Choose the external file option and click OK.

In the Save Table *"tablename"* In dialog box, choose the destination for the table or query; then choose the file type from the Save As Type list and enter a name for the exported file. When you are finished, click Export.

> **Note:** Although you can export tables, queries, and macros from Access 97 to Access 95, you can export only tables to previous versions of Access.

New in Office 97 are two ways to use Excel data in Access. To create an Access report with Excel spreadsheet data, choose Data | Access Report in the Excel spreadsheet window to start the Access

Report Wizard. Using the wizard, you can format the report just as any other Access report. Another option in the Excel Data menu is Convert to Access, which permanently converts an obsolete Excel spreadsheet to an Access database.

If you are exporting to Excel or to another database application, Access creates the new file using the field names as column headings. To export to Word, you must choose either a rich text format (.rtf) file type or export to the mail merge data source file. Table 17.3 shows the data formats that Access can export.

Table 17.3. Access export data formats.

Destination	Format or Version
dBASE databases	III, III+, IV and 5
Excel spreadsheets	3.0, 4.0, 5.0, 7.0/95, and 8.0/97
FoxPro	2.x and 3.0
Lotus 1-2-3 spreadsheets	.wk1 and .wk3
Paradox databases	3.x, 4.x, and 5.0
Delimited text files	MS-DOS (PC-8) or Windows ANSI
Fixed-width text files	MS-DOS (PC-8) or Windows ANSI
HTML and IDC/HTX	1.1 (list), 2.0, 3.x (table or list)

Creating Live Office Links

Before getting into programming live links to other Office applications through Automation, take a look at other ways you can use wizards and menu choices.

Access is useful as a repository for names and addresses that can be used for form letters and mailing labels. Excel, in turn, is very helpful to Access for analyzing numeric data and creating charts and graphs to illustrate trends and comparisons.

The new Office Links option in the Tools menu contains three choices: Merge It with MS Word, Publish It with MS Word, and Analyze It with MS Excel.

Interchanges with Word

There are three ways to exchange data with Word: send an Access table to Word via the Mail Merge Wizard; export an Access table as an external file and specify the file type as Mail Merge; or save the datasheet, form, or report as a rich text format file. When you save the object as an .rtf file, you can also automatically open it with Word and be ready to work on it. In addition, from Word, you can specify an Access table or query as the data source for a mail merge operation.

Mail Merge

The cooperation between Access and Word is an example of letting the member who can best do the job do it. Although both applications can accomplish a mail merge operation alone, the most efficient way is to let the database manager handle the list of addressees and the word processor handle the main document—the form letter or other text.

This collaboration can work from either end: Word can create the main document and then call upon Access for the file to use as the Data Source in a Mail Merge operation; or Access can merge the table into a Word Mail Merge setup with the main document.

As an example, the Pat's Pets store has a form letter to send to customers who have recently registered with the store. The basic letter, called the Main Document, has been written in Word without any of the merge fields added. The letter is contained in the New Letter.doc file in the Imports folder on the CD. When you open the table that contains the names and addresses of the customers, you can export it to Word and connect it with the mail merge Main Document as follows:

1. Select the Customers table name in the Pat's Pets database window and choose Tools | Office Links | Merge It with MS Word. The Mail Merge Wizard dialog box opens (see Figure 17.7).

Figure 17.7.
The Mail Merge Wizard dialog box.

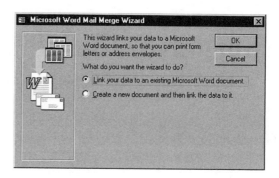

2. Choose the first option, Link your data to an existing Microsoft Word document, and then choose OK.

3. Choose New Letter.doc in the Select Microsoft Word Document dialog box. You might need to change to the folder to which you copied the files from the CD. Then choose Open.

4. This launches Word and another instance of Access to use as the live link. The Insert Merge Field drop-down list in the Mail Merge toolbar displays the fields in the Customer

table of the Pat's Pets database. Select the customers' first names, middle initials, and last names from the Access table and place them in the form letter (see Figure 17.8).

Figure 17.8.
Selecting fields from the Access Customer table.

5. After placing the remaining merge fields in the letter, the Word document looks like Figure 17.9. The Field Shading option (Tools | Options | View) has been set to Always for the figure.

Figure 17.9.
The form letter with all the merged fields.

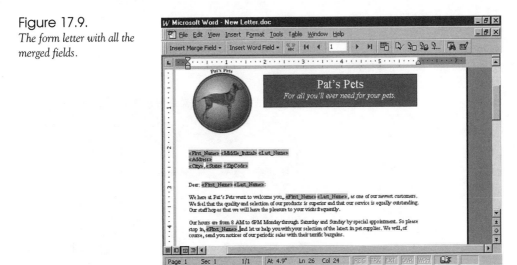

6. Click the Merge to New Document on the Word Mail Merge toolbar and print the first page of the form letter (see Figure 17.10).

Figure 17.10.

The finished printed form letter.

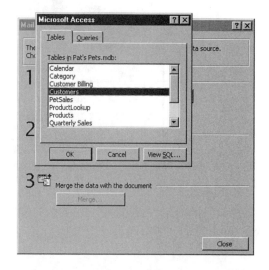

If you have worked in Word to create the form letter and want to select an Access table as the data source, choose Get Data in the Mail Merge Helper dialog box, and select Open Data Source. Then choose .mdb in the Files of Type box, and select the database file that contains the table or query with the names and addresses you want for the dialog box (see Figure 17.11). If you want to use a query as the data source, you can look at the SQL statement that defines the query by clicking the Query tab and choosing View SQL.

Figure 17.11.

Selecting an Access table as the data source.

Note: When you use an Access table or query as the data source for a Word mail merge operation, the field names are used as the merge fields. If you have already completed a main document with the merge fields and the field names of the Access table or query don't match, edit the field names in the data source or in the main document so that they do match. Word formatting rules also state that the field names can be no longer that 20 characters (additional characters are truncated). Characters other than letters, numbers, and underscores are all changed to underscores.

Publishing in Word

If you simply want to add some of the information from Access to a Word document, use the Publish option. You can save a table, query, form, or report by loading it in Word as an .rtf file. To do this, select the object you want to save, and choose Tools | Office Links | Publish It with MS Word. The output is automatically saved to the same folder as the Access application, and then Word automatically starts and opens the file. Figure 17.12 shows the Elgin Enterprises Property Listing report as published with Word.

Figure 17.12.
An Access report published with Word.

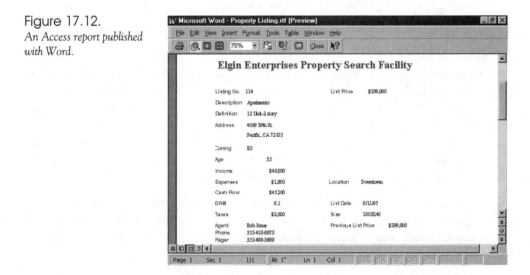

You can see in the figure that the picture of the property that was included with the Access report does not appear in the Word file. When you save a file as .rtf format, only the text is saved. If you want to include other objects, they must be inserted after the file is exported to Word.

If there is a version of Word open, the file is saved to that version. If not, the file is saved to the latest version that is installed in the system. Watch the status bar for messages as the file is saved. It can take a few minutes.

If you want to save only part of an Access datasheet, select that part before choosing from the Tools menu.

Exporting to Word

To export an Access table or query to a Word document, save the object as a rich text format (.rtf) file, and then open it from Word. Then, within Word, save the file as a document file. This creates a copy of the Access table or query and retains no connection with the original Access object.

Interchanges with Excel

You can export a table, query, form, or report to an Excel worksheet where you can call upon Excel's analytical capabilities to process the data. If you want to create a copy in an Excel spreadsheet that will always contain current information, create a link instead. Choosing Tools | Office Links | Analyze It with Excel stores the selected Access object as an .xls file and automatically starts Excel and loads the new file.

If you just want to save a copy of the Access information in an Excel worksheet, save the Access table or query by choosing File | Save As/Export and specifying where and how you want it saved.

Using Office Link

The financial information in the Elgin Enterprises database offers an excellent example of linking Access with Excel. Excel can perform many more types of analysis of numeric information because that's its job. To link the Listings table from Access to a new worksheet in Excel, select Listings in the database window and choose Tools | Office Links | Analyze It with MS Excel. The status bar displays the message "Outputting object" during the process. Then, Excel launches with the new worksheet containing the Listings data (see Figure 17.13). The field names from your Access table or query become the values in the first row of the Excel spreadsheet.

In Excel, you can create a range of cells containing summary information such as the average percentage of return by property category or the average break-even point by category. Figure 17.14 shows the Excel summaries on a separate sheet. Using the Excel Chart Wizard, you can create column charts depicting these summaries, as shown in Figure 17.15.

Now all that remains is to copy the charts to an Access report that will include text information about Elgin Enterprises and its investment opportunities. The easiest way is to start a new report or open an existing report and copy the charts into it one at a time.

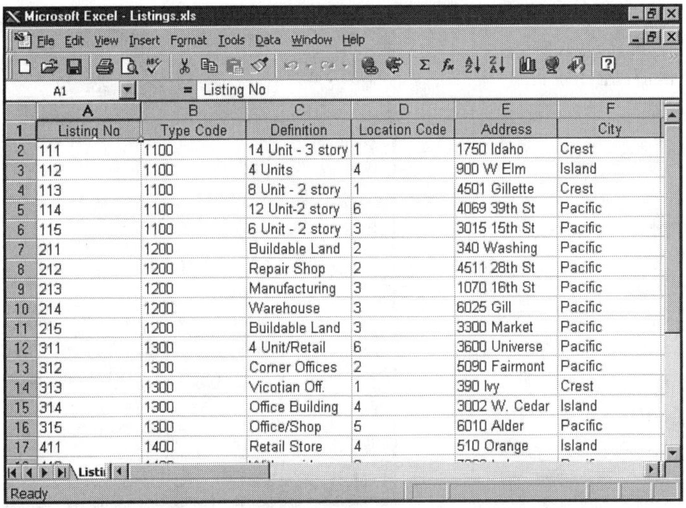

Figure 17.13.
The Listings table data exported to Excel.

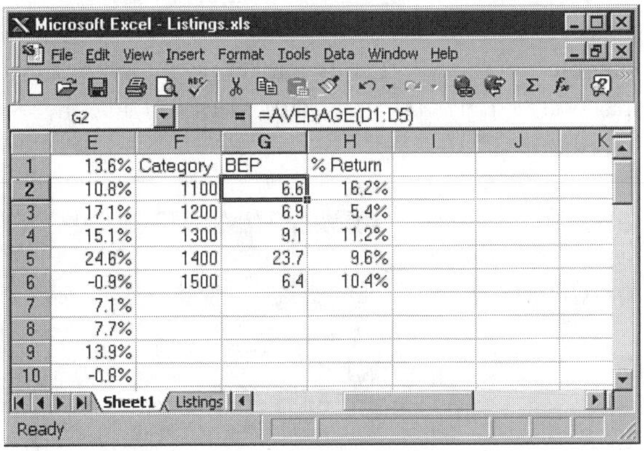

	Listing No	Type Code	Definition	Location Code	Address	City
1	Listing No	Type Code	Definition	Location Code	Address	City
2	111	1100	14 Unit - 3 story	1	1750 Idaho	Crest
3	112	1100	4 Units	4	900 W Elm	Island
4	113	1100	8 Unit - 2 story	1	4501 Gillette	Crest
5	114	1100	12 Unit-2 story	6	4069 39th St	Pacific
6	115	1100	6 Unit - 2 story	3	3015 15th St	Pacific
7	211	1200	Buildable Land	2	340 Washing	Pacific
8	212	1200	Repair Shop	2	4511 28th St	Pacific
9	213	1200	Manufacturing	3	1070 16th St	Pacific
10	214	1200	Warehouse	3	6025 Gill	Pacific
11	215	1200	Buildable Land	3	3300 Market	Pacific
12	311	1300	4 Unit/Retail	6	3600 Universe	Pacific
13	312	1300	Corner Offices	2	5090 Fairmont	Pacific
14	313	1300	Vicotian Off.	1	390 Ivy	Crest
15	314	1300	Office Building	4	3002 W. Cedar	Island
16	315	1300	Office/Shop	5	6010 Alder	Pacific
17	411	1400	Retail Store	4	510 Orange	Island

Figure 17.14.
Summarizing Access data in Excel.

G2 = =AVERAGE(D1:D5)

	E	F	G	H
1	13.6%	Category	BEP	% Return
2	10.8%	1100	6.6	16.2%
3	17.1%	1200	6.9	5.4%
4	15.1%	1300	9.1	11.2%
5	24.6%	1400	23.7	9.6%
6	-0.9%	1500	6.4	10.4%
7	7.1%			
8	7.7%			
9	13.9%			
10	-0.8%			

Note: Copy the charts one at a time if you want to create a link with the Excel worksheet. You can select both charts in Excel by holding down Shift while you select them and then clicking Copy. When you paste them in the report, they are considered unbound OLE images instead of linked charts.

To place the charts in an Access report, follow these steps:

1. Select one of the charts in the Excel worksheet, and click Copy.

2. Switch to the Access database window, and click New in the Reports tab. Then, choose Design View to open a blank report design window.

3. Click Paste. The chart appears in the report design detail section.

4. Return to the Excel window, select the other chart, and then click Copy again.

Figure 17.15.
Adding charts to the summarized data.

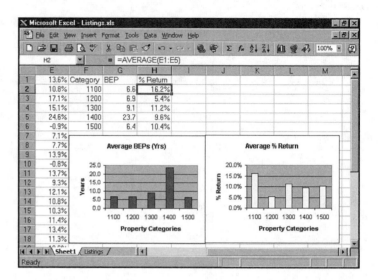

5. Return to the Access window and click Paste. This gets confusing because when you paste an object in the report design, it always appears at the upper-left corner of the design. This places it on top of the first chart. Click and drag the second chart away from the first one (see Figure 17.16).

Figure 17.16.
The new Access report with two Excel charts.

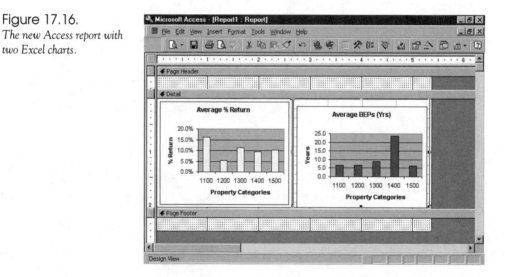

The link between Access and Excel is now complete. If you want to make a change in one of the charts, double-click the chart in the report design and then Excel, the source application, opens with the chart selected on the Listings sheet in the window. Right-click the chart, and choose Chart Options from the shortcut menu to change any of the formatting options (see Figure 17.17). The chart was moved in the figure so you can see it with the Chart Options dialog box open. Notice that the data used in the chart is outlined in the sheet. You also can change the data in the sheet, and the changes will be reflected in the chart.

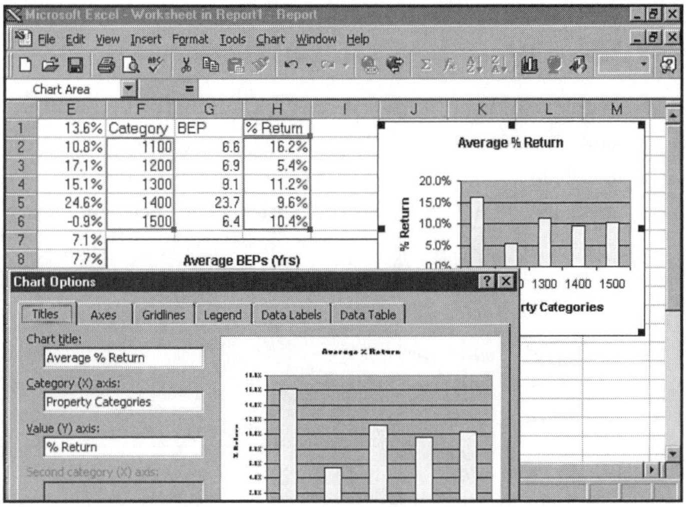

Figure 17.17.
Activating the link with Excel to change chart options.

To return to Access, choose File | Close and Return to Report1.

Exporting to Excel

To export a table or query to an Excel spreadsheet, select the object name in the database window, and then choose File | Save As/Export. In the Save As dialog box, choose to save the file to an external file or database. Next, choose a spreadsheet format and the spreadsheet where you want to save it in the Save In dialog box; then click Export. You also can create a new spreadsheet to save it in.

> **Warning:** If you attempt to export an Access table or query to an existing Excel spreadsheet file from an early version of Excel, you might delete and replace the contents of the worksheet. Exporting to an Excel version 5.0, 7.0/95, or 8.0/97 copies the data to the next available worksheet instead. Be careful to add an empty worksheet if you are exporting to one of the earlier versions.

The only objects you can save to an Excel spreadsheet are tables and queries. You can, however, save the output of any object in an Excel spreadsheet using the same File | Save As/Export process. In the Save In dialog box, choose one of the newer Excel formats (Excel 5–7 or Excel 97) or RTF. Then, the Save Formatted option in the Save In dialog box preserves the data in the Lookup fields as well as the fonts and the field widths as they were in Access. It also saves any group levels in a report as Excel outline levels. This option slows down the saving but will conserve time in the long run if you need consistency.

Creating a PivotTable

A PivotTable is similar to a crosstab query except that it is interactive. It performs calculations such as sums and counts on the underlying data, depending on how you have arranged the rows and columns. Excel can use data in an Access table to create a PivotTable in an Access form. Figure 17.18 shows an example of a PivotTable summarizing Pat's Pets' annual sales over the last five years.

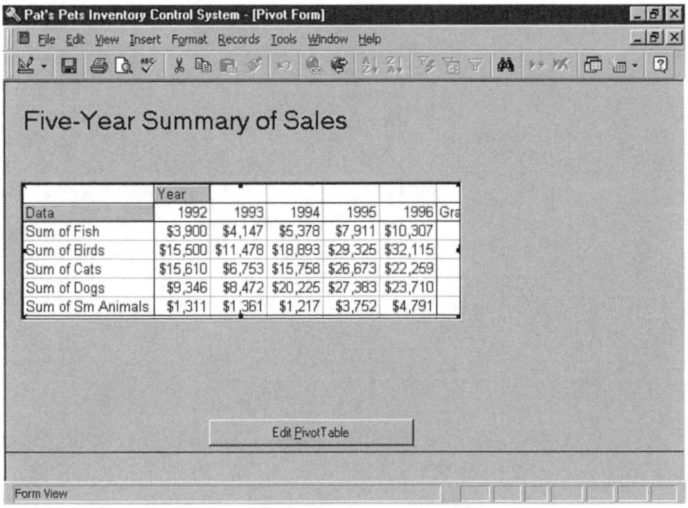

Figure 17.18.
A PivotTable in an Access form.

The table was created by calling up the PivotTable Wizard from Access, as follows:

1. Start a new form, choosing the PivotTable Wizard and the PetSales table. The Wizard shows an explanatory dialog box followed by a dialog box in which you can choose which fields to include in the table.

2. Select Year and the five pet category fields; then choose Next. The next PivotTable Wizard dialog box displays a diagram into which you drag the fields (see Figure 17.19).

3. Drag the Year field to the Column heading position in the diagram and the product category field to the Sum block. Then choose Next. The finished form appears in Access form view.

The Edit PivotTable button takes you back to Excel, where you can make changes to the table formatting such as formatting the sales figures as currency with no decimal points. The form shown in Figure 17.18 has also been resized and a title added.

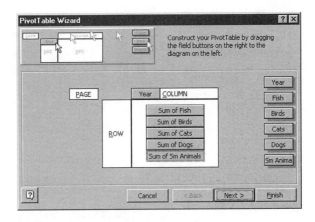

Figure 17.19.
Using the PivotTable Wizard.

Because the data is not stored in the PivotTable, each time you use the form with the table, you must refresh the data if there have been any changes.

Introducing Automation

If you recall OLE Automation in Office 95, this version of Automation will not be a stranger. Automation is a feature of the industry-standard technology known as Component Object Model (COM), which its members use to expose their objects to other members of the model. For example, a database application can expose a report, form, or table as a separate, identifiable object for use by Word, Excel, or any other application that supports Automation.

If an application supports Automation, you can access its objects through VBA and then manipulate the objects with methods or by setting the object's properties. Access is an ActiveX component that supports Automation. An ActiveX component is defined as an application that can use objects supplied by another application or expose its own objects for use by another. Such applications were formerly known as OLE Automation servers and controllers.

Create a New Automation Object

If you want to use an object from another Automation component, you first must set a reference to that application's type library. After you set the reference, you have access to all the objects in the library, together with their properties and methods. After setting a reference to a VBA project in another Access database, you can also call any of the public procedures in that project. Setting a reference to an ActiveX control enables you to add the control to an Access form.

To set a reference to another Automation component's applications, choose Tools | References. The References option is available only when the module window is open. You can, however, set a reference from a VBA procedure. Figure 17.20 shows the References dialog box displaying a list of more than 35 different available references. Scroll down the list and check the object libraries for Excel 8.0, Graph 8.0, and Word 8.0 to add them to your list of available libraries.

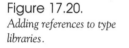

Figure 17.20.

Adding references to type libraries.

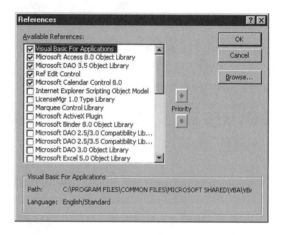

In Chapter 9, "Writing VBA Procedures," you were introduced to the Object Browser, where you can select the desired type library from a list. After you have set new references with the References dialog box, their libraries appear in the Object Browser list (see Figure 17.21). When you select one of the new libraries, you can see all the objects in the Object Browser together with their methods and properties. This makes it much easier to know what is available to each object in another application with which you are not all that familiar.

Through Automation, you can manipulate the objects in the other applications by referring to them by class. For example, a Word 8.0 document is referred to as `Word.Document` and an Excel worksheet as `Excel.Worksheet`.

From Access, you can now create a new Excel object (or other component application object) and change its properties and call its methods just as you would with an Access object. There are two ways to create a new application object: by using the `New` keyword in the declaration statement or by calling the `CreateObject()` function after declaring the application object variable as follows:

```
Dim appExcel As New Excel.Application
```

or

```
Dim appExcel As Excel.Application
Set appExcel = CreateObject("Excel.Application")
```

Figure 17.21.
The new libraries appear in the Object Browser.

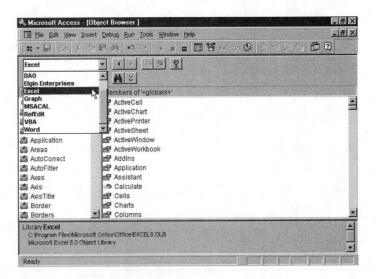

After the object is created, you can manipulate it in VBA code by using the object variable name you assigned to it.

You can also use `CreateObject()` to create one of the other application objects, such as a Word document or an Excel worksheet. For example, the code in Listing 17.1 creates a new Excel application that automatically starts Excel. After setting the other variables to a new workbook and worksheet, the code adds text to cell A1. Then, the worksheet is saved in the specified directory and Excel closes. Here's the code.

Listing 17.1. Creating a new Excel application.

```
Sub GetWorkSheet()
'Create a new Excel workbook with one worksheet.
Dim xlApp As Excel.Application
Dim xlBook As Excel.Workbook
Dim xlSheet As Excel.Worksheet

Set xlApp = CreateObject("Excel.Application")
Set xlBook = xlApp.Workbooks.Add
Set xlSheet = xlBook.Worksheets(1)

'Make the worksheet visible.
xlSheet.Application.Visible = True
```

continues

Listing 17.1. continued

```
'Add text to cell A1 and change the font properties.
With xlSheet.Cells(1, 1)
    .Value = "This is Cell A1"
    .Font.Size = 14
    .Font.Name = "Arial"
    .Font.Italic = True
End With

'Save the new worksheet, close Excel and clear the object variable.
xlSheet.SaveAs "C:\Test.xls"
xlSheet.Application.Quit
Set xlSheet = Nothing

End Sub
```

The preceding `With...End With` block of code keeps `xlSheet.Cells(1, 1)` active for changing several properties at once. The index for `Cells` must be numeric, so `Cells(1, 1)` refers to cell A1.

Figure 17.22 shows the new Excel worksheet with the formatted text in cell A1.

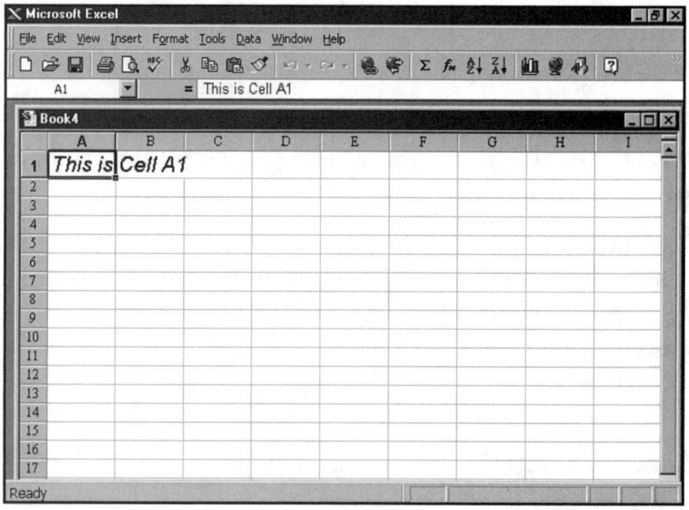

Figure 17.22.
The new worksheet created from an Access procedure.

Note: In this example, declaring and setting the application, workbook, and worksheet variables bind the new object when the module is compiled. If you set only the worksheet object, the binding does not occur until the code is run. You will get an error message if you try to run the code from the module window without first setting the application and workbook objects.

The GetObject() function accesses an ActiveX object from a file and assigns the object to an object variable you have declared. The GetObject() syntax is GetObject([*pathname*][,[*class*], where both arguments are optional. However, if you omit the *pathname* argument, you must include the *class* argument. The *class* argument uses the syntax *appname.objecttype*, where *appname* is the name of the application providing the object and *objecttype* is the type or class of the object you want to access. For example, the following line of code will create a reference to an existing Word document:

```
Set objDoc = GetObject("C:\Winword\Letters\Sams.doc")
```

If you already have the application running, you can also use the Get Object() function as an alternative to creating a new object by specifying the path name as a zero-length string (""). If you omit the *pathname* argument, GetObject returns the currently active object that matches the type you declared for the object variable, if any. If none is active, an error occurs.

You can also use VBA procedures to work with Word documents from Access. Word has its own set of objects, properties, and methods that you can scan through with the help of the Object Browser by choosing the Word type library. The following fragment of VBA code uses the GetObject() function to open the Word document named New Letter, which is in the Imports folder on the CD.

```
Sub OpenLetter()
Dim wrd As Object

Set wrd = GetObject(, "Word.Application")
wrd.Visible = True
Documents.Open "C:\My Documents\Sams\New Letter"
End Sub
```

Change the Documents.Open statement to refer to the path to the file on your hard drive.

Working with ActiveX Controls

An ActiveX control is another object you can insert into a form, like the built-in controls on the toolbox—text boxes, list boxes, combo boxes, images, and so on. In previous versions of Access, they were called OLE controls or custom controls. To see a list of the ActiveX controls you have available, click the More Tools button on the toolbox. The list shows the built-in controls as well as ActiveX controls such as the ImageList control and the popular Calendar control (see Figure 17.23).

The subject of ActiveX controls is far too extensive to cover adequately here. A useful example is the Calendar control, which can be bound to a table that contains a list of events with their dates and other related information. To use this control, start a blank form based on the table named Calendar in the Elgin Enterprises database that contains the event information; then do the following:

1. Choose More Controls on the toolbox, and choose Calendar Control 8.0 from the list. You can also choose Insert | ActiveX Control to open the same list in a dialog box.

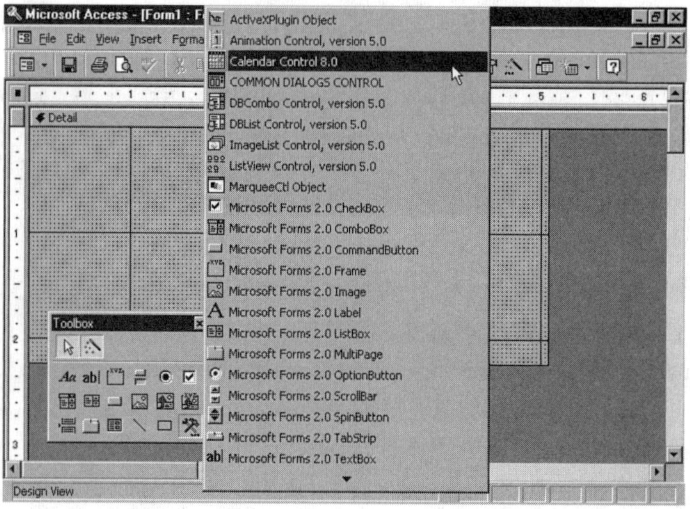

Figure 17.23.
*The More Controls list
shows available ActiveX
controls.*

2. Click the plus sign with the little hammer icon where you want the upper-left corner of the calendar.

3. In the Calendar Control property sheet, set the Control Source property to Date, the name of the date field in the table.

4. Resize and move the calendar control as necessary.

5. Add two text boxes to display the name of the event and the list of attendees. Then add a title.

Figure 17.24 shows the completed Schedule form. The navigation buttons at the bottom of the form move you through the records in the Calendar table, highlighting the corresponding date on the control as you go.

The calendar control has many properties that you can change with the property sheet, but it also has a custom property dialog box in which you can set more appearance properties. To see this dialog box, click the Build button next to the Custom property in the property sheet. The dialog box has three tabs: General, Font, and Color (see Figure 17.25). Choosing Calendar Object | Properties also opens the Calendar Properties dialog box.

The General tab sets the length of the day and month name text, the first day of the week, and what items to show in the calendar. The Font tab lets you choose different font settings for each section of the calendar, and the Color tab does the same with standard and custom colors.

Figure 17.24.
The completed Schedule form.

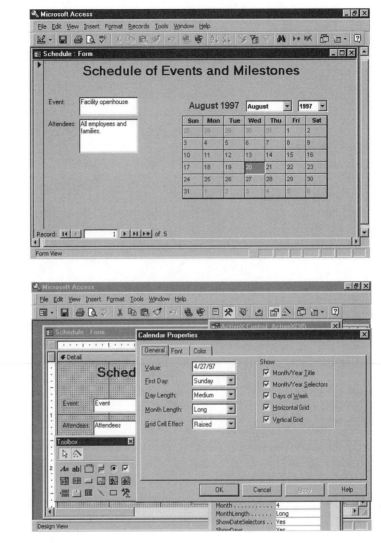

Figure 17.25.
The Calendar Properties dialog box.

Summary

Office 97 offers many ways for its members to interact with one another. This chapter has investigated some of them, beginning with simple copy-and-paste operations from one to another and then moving into creating live links through Office Links. Word becomes an important tool for Access as a publishing arm, and Access returns the favor by providing the data source for mail merge operations. Excel has many analytic capabilities to offer to Access, including the PivotTable Wizard.

The Automation environment makes it easy for all the members to share their objects for use in VBA code. Properly written procedures can use the type libraries of other components of the Automation model to work with objects from other applications. The final topic in this chapter briefly addressed the subject of ActiveX controls.

VI

Advanced
Access
Programming

18

Working in a Multiuser Environment

So far in these chapters, the Elgin Enterprises database has been described as if it's a straightforward, single-user database that exists on only one computer in the Elgin Enterprises offices. Nothing could be further from the truth. Consider for a moment the wide variety of data stored in this database: real-estate descriptions, income and expenses data, agents' names and phone numbers, and so on. This information is intended to be used by several different people at Elgin Enterprises as well as the company's customers and clients.

The Need for Multiuser Data Access

Back when personal computers were first becoming popular in business environments, there was no easy way to share information among several users. Sharing data often meant having to copy files onto floppy disks and physically carry the disks from computer to computer. Each user then copied the files onto his or her own computer before beginning to work. Keeping the data coordinated under these conditions was a nightmare. Often, only one user could make updates to the data at a time. If more than one user added new records, deleted old records, or changed the data in existing records, someone had to be responsible for ensuring that the changes were collected and coordinated to keep the data synchronized on all computers in the office.

The situation is actually worse when the shared information resides in an Access .MDB file. Most .MDB files are quite large and would never fit on a single floppy disk, making it impossible to share data using this type of disk medium. Also, because all of the database objects, including tables, forms, and reports, reside in the same file, any time changes are made to these objects, they must be imported or exported into the working database—a tedious, time-consuming process at best.

Over the last 10 years or so, computer networks have become a standard part of most offices. Now, more than 80 percent of the business computers in the United States are connected to a network of some kind. The network usually is a *local area network* (LAN) serving all of the computers in an office or building. Often, a company's network extends beyond a single building to multiple buildings or even across the country as a *wide area network* (WAN).

When computers are connected via a network, making information available to multiple users is greatly simplified. The data can reside on a single place on the network and be made accessible to all users. Data files do not have to be copied onto floppy disks and carried from computer to computer. Other operations such as backing up the data to protect it from catastrophic loss are made much easier by keeping the data files in a single location in the business.

However, as soon as more than one user is working with the data at the same time, several new problems arise. For example, a method must be devised to make sure that only one user can make changes to a record at a time. If more than one user is able to edit the same record, important changes might accidentally be overwritten. Also, because data is so important, very often the data must be protected by limiting access to it with passwords and other protective mechanisms.

This chapter answers two very important questions about multiuser databases: how to set up Access databases so the data can be shared by all users and how to protect the data from being changed by more than one user at a time. This chapter does not discuss networking or network architecture. Instead, it concentrates on the steps a developer must take to ensure that the data in an Access database is efficiently shared among several users. Chapter 19, "Adding Security to the Application," discusses how to secure a database by adding password protection to the tables and other database objects.

The good news is that Microsoft Access was created with multiuser capabilities in mind. As you'll soon see, you have all of the options and capabilities you could ever ask for at your disposal as you begin sharing your databases with other users. In fact, as you'll see near the end of this chapter, sharing more than just the data in Access databases is quite easy. Access 97 makes it easy to share new forms and reports with other users regardless of the multiuser architecture you choose for your environment.

Where to Put the Data

Obviously, the data in a multiuser environment must be put someplace on the network that is accessible to all users who need the information. Even though all of the database objects such as tables, forms, and reports in an Access database live in a single .MDB file, you'll soon see that you are not limited to this arrangement. As a developer, you have several options when it comes to determining your database's architecture. In this context, *architecture* simple means where on the network you put all of the tables, forms, reports, and code in your application. Often, the best solution involves breaking the .MDB file into several pieces and distributing the pieces where they'll do the most good.

The Simple Approach

An easy solution is to simply put the Access .MDB file on a *server* computer on the network. Depending on the network configuration, the server might be the network's file server (most often in a Novell-type LAN) or a computer that is designated as the database server (in the case of a Windows 95 or Windows NT network). Figure 18.1 illustrates this type of network arrangement.

The arrangement you see in Figure 18.1 is easy to implement. In the case of the Elgin database, the single .MDB file is moved or copied to the computer on the network that is working as the database file server. As mentioned earlier in this chapter, this computer might be the actual file server in a Novell LAN or a designated server on a Microsoft Windows Networking network. Each of the desktop computers in this figure has its own copy of Microsoft Access installed.

Figure 18.1.
One option for multiuser database access.

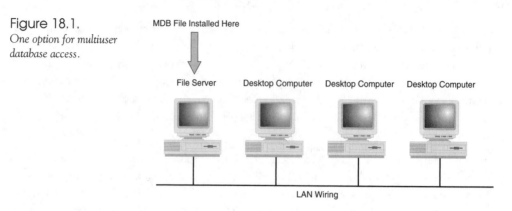

Unfortunately, there are several problems with this approach. Every time a user opens a form or report in the centrally located .MDB file, a large amount of information must flow across the network from the .MDB file to the local copy of Access. This information includes a lot more than the data behind the form or report. All of the information necessary to display the form or report must also travel across the network. This information includes the form's or report's design details such as the size, position, and color of the controls, the text that appears in the labels on the form or report, and other details such as the size and position of the form or report on the screen.

If very few users are working with the database at one time, or if the network is otherwise very lightly loaded, the network traffic generated by the arrangement you see in Figure 18.1 probably is not much of an issue. In these cases, a user might notice a very slight delay as the form or report is opened on his or her computer. If, however, there is a large number of users trying to use the same database or if the network is being used for printing, Internet access, or file sharing with other applications, the delay can be quite long.

Many other factors enter into the network performance equation, including the speed of the database server, the type of LAN wiring used in the network, how many other applications are moving data across the network at the same time, and so on. It is hard to generalize the performance you can expect from this simple approach to sharing Access databases, but performance is bound to become an issue in this arrangement sooner or later.

A Better Solution

Figure 18.2 illustrates an alternative approach to sharing Access databases. In this arrangement a *back-end* database is installed on the server, and *front-end* databases exist on each desktop computer. The back-end database contains the data tables, and each front-end .MDB contains the forms, reports, code, and other user-interface components of the database. The tables in the back-end database are linked to each front-end .MDB on the users' desktops.

Figure 18.2.
Splitting a database for multiuser access.

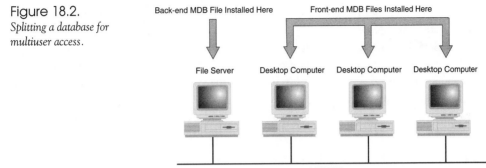

There are several big advantages to this arrangement. Because the forms, reports, and other user interface components are kept in the local copy of the front-end database, they load very quickly. No information moves across the network as a form opens unless that form contains data. Therefore, loading unbound forms such as switchboards and dialog boxes takes very little time.

Second, because the user interface components are kept separate from the tables, updating a form or report is as easy as replacing the front-end .MDB on a user's desktop computer. In fact, the easiest way to keep users updated is to put a copy of the front-end database on the file server and instruct each user how to copy that .MDB file to his or her own desktop computer.

A third big advantage of the database architecture you see in Figure 18.2 is that different users can have "custom" front-end databases. For example, the needs of the order entry people in a company are quite different than the folks in the Sales department. Figure 18.3 shows how you might set up your database system so that each department has its own customized user interface, including the switchboards, data and dialog forms, and reports that make the most sense for the department. All of these departments are sharing the same data reservoir in the back-end .MDB file.

Figure 18.3.
A custom front-end database for each department.

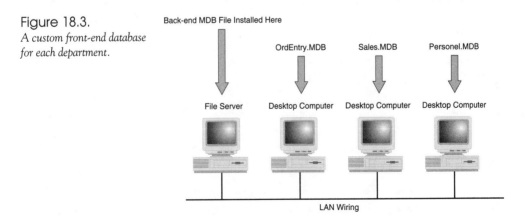

The arrangement you see in Figure 18.3 is incredibly powerful. Using this architecture, you can treat each department as a separate client or customer. With different front-end databases, it's easy to provide an individual department with a customized form or report or to update an existing form or report. Because each department has its own user interface, the people in the Sales department don't even need to know about the Human Resources department's information stored in the back-end database. A high level of security is provided by simply "hiding" sensitive tables in the back-end database by making the tables unavailable to departments that have no need for the information stored there.

Obviously, there is more work involved in setting up the scheme illustrated in Figure 18.3. You must create a separate database for each department, doubling or tripling the work involved in creating the database system. One way to minimize the work involved is to create a "master" database that contains all of the forms, reports, code, and other objects needed by all of the departments. You (the developer) keep the master database on your computer, making it easy for you to make changes to any of the objects used by the users. The master "development" database makes it easy for you to apply the same appearance attributes to all of the forms and reports used by everyone.

After you have a reasonably complete master database, copy it once for each department, assigning an appropriate name to each copy. Then, make the final adjustments to each copy to suit the intended audience. As you complete each departmental database, copy it as a "department master" onto the server computer to make it available to its intended users. Later, as you update each individual departmental database, export the updated component to the department master and let your users make copies from the master.

Figure 18.4 illustrates the principle of maintaining a development master on one computer and the department masters and the department back-end databases on the server. It shouldn't be too hard to train users how to copy the department master.

You're probably wondering just how you're going to produce the separate front-end and back-end databases. Later in this chapter (in the section titled "Using the Database Splitter"), you'll learn all about a utility built into Access 97 that makes splitting databases a fast and easy process.

Fine-Tuning for Performance

So far, the process of splitting a database into separate front-end and back-end pieces seems relatively straightforward. All of the tables go into the back end, and all of the user interface and code goes into the front end to minimize network traffic and improve performance. There's one final step to take to optimize this arrangement.

Most databases contain a number of tables that contain largely static data. For example, a table of Zip codes and cities isn't likely to change very much. The table is there simply to make it easy to find the city corresponding to a particular Zip code. Such a table is often referred to as a *lookup table*.

Figure 18.4.
Keep the master database on the developer's computer.

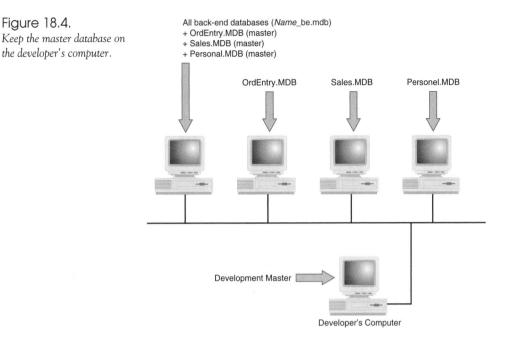

All back-end databases (*Name*_be.mdb)
+ OrdEntry.MDB (master)
+ Sales.MDB (master)
+ Personal.MDB (master)

OrdEntry.MDB   Sales.MDB   Personel.MDB

Development Master

Developer's Computer

In contrast, the data stored in an orders or employees table is likely to be quite dynamic, constantly changing and being updated. There is no reason to keep static data in the back-end database on the server computer.

As you set up your databases as distinct front-end and back-end components, look for opportunities to keep lookup tables on the user's desktop computer in the front-end database. Each time an inquiry is made against a lookup table stored in the front-end database, you save a considerable amount of network traffic. In the rare event that a lookup table needs to be updated, you can put the updated table in the master front-end database on the server and let users copy the master to their own computers.

As a final consideration, if your application creates any temporary tables, the temporary tables should always be stored on the local computer. Not only will this arrangement help minimize network traffic, it will prevent the inevitable conflicts that arise if more than one user tries to create the same temporary table on the back-end copy of the database.

Using the Database Splitter

The "split database" design has become so common in many environments that Microsoft built a splitter utility into Access 97. The Database Splitter add-on simplifies the process of creating a back-end database, exporting files to the back end, and linking the tables between the two halves. In fact, the Database Splitter does not actually "split" an existing database. Instead, it creates an entirely new back-end database and exports all of the tables to that database. After verifying that the tables have been exported without error, the Database Splitter then deletes the tables in the current database and creates links to each of the tables in the back-end portion. In this way, the Database Splitter preserves the original database architecture so that you can use it as a development master.

> **Warning:** Because the Database Splitter's actions are not easily reversed, you should make a backup of the database if possible before commencing.

To start the splitter utility, select the Database Splitter command from the Add-Ins fly-out menu (you'll find Add-Ins under the Tools menu). The opening dialog box of the Database Splitter opens in response (see Figure 18.5).

Figure 18.5.
The Database Splitter is a powerful tool for multiuser databases.

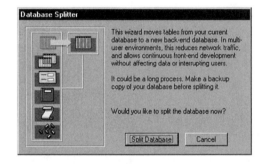

Be prepared for the Database Splitter to require a lot of time when it is splitting large databases. Creating the back-end database takes only a few seconds. What can take a long time is exporting the tables to the back-end database. Exporting the tables will also generate a tremendous amount of network traffic, assuming you're posting the back-end database on a server computer on the network. Click the Split Database button in the dialog box you see in Figure 18.5 to continue.

The next dialog box of the Database Splitter lets you specify where to drop the back-end part of the split database (see Figure 18.6). Notice that the Database Splitter suggests appending _be to the end of the database name. This convention makes it easy to recognize when a database is serving as the back-end to another database.

The Save In drop-down box at the top of the Create Back-end Database dialog box in Figure 18.6 is network-aware. There is a Network Neighborhood entry on the drop-down list that lets you locate any computer on the LAN to use as the database server. As soon as you click the Split button in the Create Back-end Database dialog box, Access begins the splitting process. You should not interrupt the splitting process unless it is absolutely necessary. Keep in mind that Access is actually deleting the tables in the current database, which could lead to a problem if Access is not allowed to complete the task.

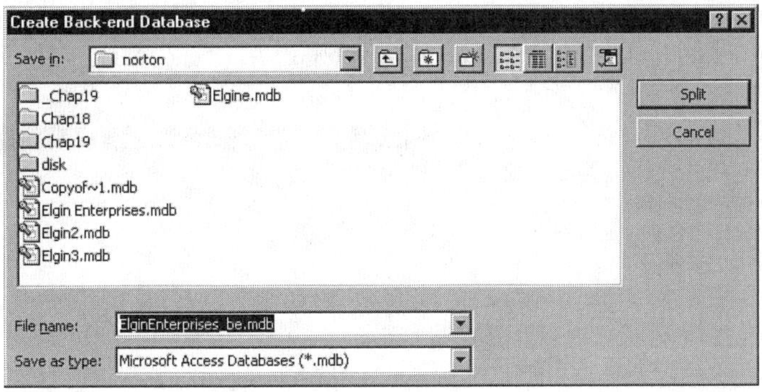

Figure 18.6.
Put the back-end database on the database server.

Figure 18.7 shows the Tables tab of the Database window after the splitting process is complete. Notice that all of the tables are actually links to another database. Figure 18.8 shows the Linked Table Manager dialog box (accessed through the Linked Table Manager command in the Add-Ins menu) showing that the tables in the Elgin Enterprises database are linked to Elgin Enterprises.MDB on the computer named Gandalf on the LAN.

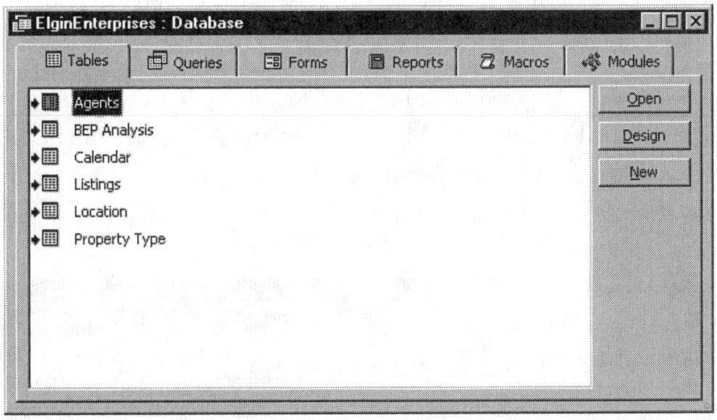

Figure 18.7.
The tables after the splitting process.

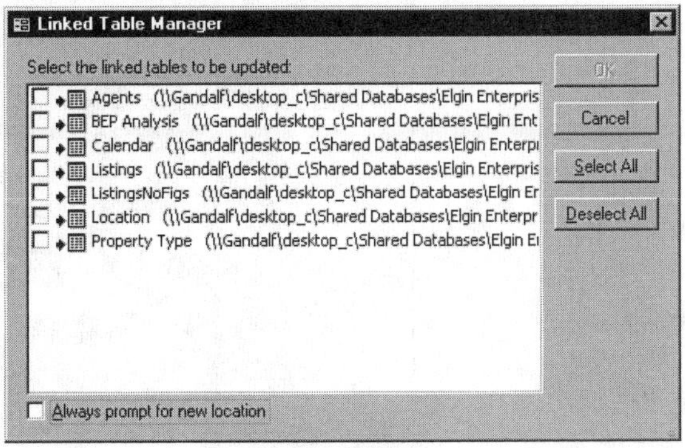

Figure 18.8.
All tables are now links to the back-end database.

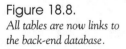

Figure 18.9 shows the Tables tab in `ElginEnterprises_be.MDB`. This database actually contains all of the data tables for the split database system. Any data changes will actually occur in this database.

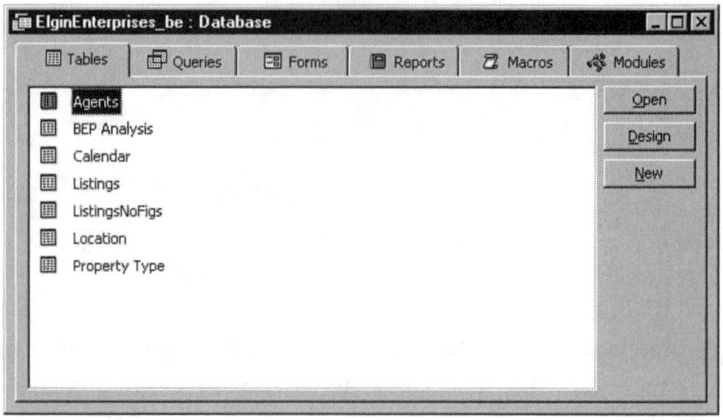

Figure 18.9.
`Elgin-`
`Enterprises_be.MDB`
contains the tables for the
split database.

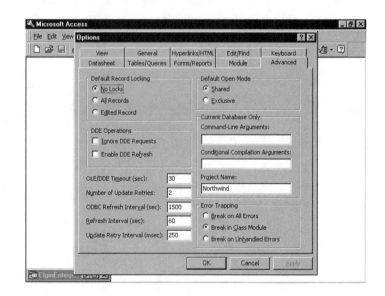

The next step in the splitting process is to import any lookup tables from the back-end database back to the front-end component. Notice that the Database Splitter moved every table to the back-end `.MDB` file. This might or might not be what you prefer in your final application. Be sure to move the lookup tables before distributing to users.

As a last check of your new multiuser database system, make sure that the Shared option button is selected in the Default Open Mode area on the Advanced tab of the Options dialog box (see Figure 18.10). (Open this dialog box with the Options command on the Tools menu.) The Shared option means that Access will enable more than one person to use the data in a database at a time.

Figure 18.10.
The Shared option button
enables multiple users to
open the same database at
the same time.

Record Locking: Controlling Access to Records

Now that you've installed the back-end database on the file server, the users each have their own copy of a front-end database, and databases are being opened in shared mode, look at how Access helps you protect the data in the tables.

One of the most serious problems that can occur in shared databases happens when more than one user makes changes to the same record at the same time. Consider the situation in which no control is maintained over multiple access to the records in database tables. Suppose two users (Shirley and Bob) are updating some records in the Elgin Enterprises database. Even though they each have a copy of the front-end database installed on their desktop PC, the data with which they are both working is stored on the same back-end database on the server. Therefore, if they both are working on a particular listing, they both actually are working on the same record in the Listings table.

Imagine the confusion that would occur if Bob gets a call from a client as he's working on the listings in the Elgin Enterprises database. The call is from a client who has decided that the new list price he arranged with Shirley the day before isn't quite what he thinks will best sell his property. During the phone call Bob opens the listing in question and continues his dialog with the client. Meanwhile, Shirley is in her office inputting the "old" list price she discussed with the client the day before. Bob completes his phone call, saves the record with the new list price, and moves on to another record in the database. Coincidentally, the second after Bob saves the record he's been working on, Shirley completes her changes and moves on to another record.

In this particular scenario, even though Shirley's data was incorrect, she "won" the changes in the database because she saved her changes after Bob completed his. Keep in mind that one of the preconditions of this scenario was that no control over access to database records is in place. This means that neither Bob nor Shirley was aware that the other was making changes to the client's record at the same time. When Shirley saved the record, she was not informed that she was overwriting changes made by another user while she had the record open.

The situation described in the preceding paragraphs would be disastrous in many environments. In the case of the Elgin Enterprises database, the worst that could happen is that a sale would be lost if the incorrect list price was too high to sell the property. Or, the client might be forced into an awkward situation if the incorrect list price was lower than the correct price and a buyer insisted that the client honor the too-low price. In either case, Elgin Enterprises is exposed to possible legal action as a result of mishandling the client's listing.

The very least that would happen is that the incorrect list price would show up on forms and reports for a few days until someone noticed the error. Eventually, someone would realize the incorrect price had been stored in the database and would correct the error.

Fortunately, the Access *locking* mechanism reduces the chance that errors such as this will damage the data in the tables. As soon as a user begins editing the data in a record (this includes adding new records to the database), Access notices the edit activity and imposes a *lock* on the record, preventing other users from making changes to the same record. Access provides several levels of record locking that you can fine-tune to suit how your users work with their data.

Pessimistic Locking

In many cases, simultaneous changes to the same record is an undesirable situation. In environments where it is important that the data in a record be completely updated before another user can begin making changes to the same record, *pessimistic locking* is required. Under this scheme, as soon as a user begins making changes to a record, Access clamps down on the edited record, preventing other users from making changes to it. The other users can view the record in a form or report, but they cannot make changes to it. Figure 18.11 illustrates pessimistic locking at work.

Figure 18.11.
Pessimistic locking is needed in many situations.

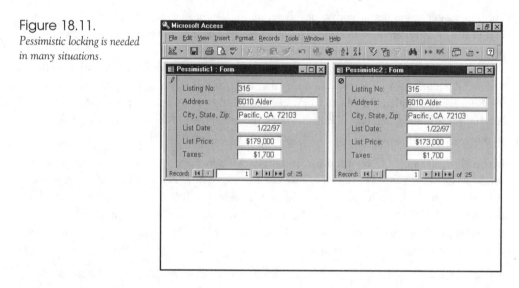

In Figure 18.11, the List Price text box on the form on the left is being changed from $173,000 to $179,000. Notice that the icon in the form's record selector (the vertical gray bar along the left edge of the form) is a pencil, indicating the current record is being edited. The record selector on the form on the right (Pessimistic2) displays the international "Not" symbol, indicating that the record in Pessimistic2 is unavailable for editing.

The Not symbol tells you that Access has locked the recordset behind the Pessimistic2 form. This means that only the person using the Pessimistic1 form is able to make changes to the record at this time. The Pessimistic2 user will have to wait until the Pessimistic1 user is finished with his edits before proceeding.

The Not symbol does not appear instantly. In an effort to reduce processing overhead, Access checks the lock state of a form's recordset at intervals specified by the Refresh Interval setting in the Advanced tab of the Options dialog box. (The refresh interval appears in the lower-left corner of Figure 18.10.) If, at the end of the refresh interval, Access determines the records in the form's recordset are locked, the Not symbol will appear in the form's record selector area. By default, the refresh interval is set to 60 seconds, which might be too long in dynamic environments. Set it to a lower value if users complain that they can't tell when another user has locked records they are trying to use.

Access also checks the lock state as soon as a user tries to edit a record. Even if the refresh interval has not expired, Access will instantly display the Not symbol as the user begins changing data in a locked form.

Pessimistic locking must be specified; it is not the default setting for Access 97 forms. You set pessimistic locking by specifying Edited Record as the value for a form's Record Locks property (see Figure 18.12). The next section describes *optimistic locking*, an alternative locking scheme that is the default for all new forms in Access databases.

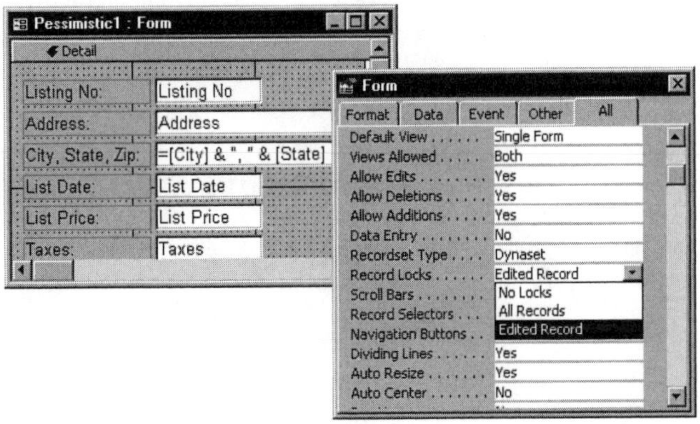

Figure 18.12.
You establish pessimistic locking by setting Record Locks to Edited Record.

Optimistic Locking

The default lock setting in Access is *optimistic locking*. Optimistic locking assumes that record conflicts will be a rare event. The assumption is that in most cases, a user will complete an edit on a record before another user tries to edit the same record. Therefore, there is minimal need to handle edit conflicts.

You set optimistic locking in your application by setting a bound form's Record Locks property to No Locks (see Figure 18.13). The edited records are locked only at the instant they are actually being saved in the database. Using optimistic locking, a true lock conflict is a rare event. A *write conflict*, however, occurs if two users try to save a record at the same time (more on write conflicts later in this section).

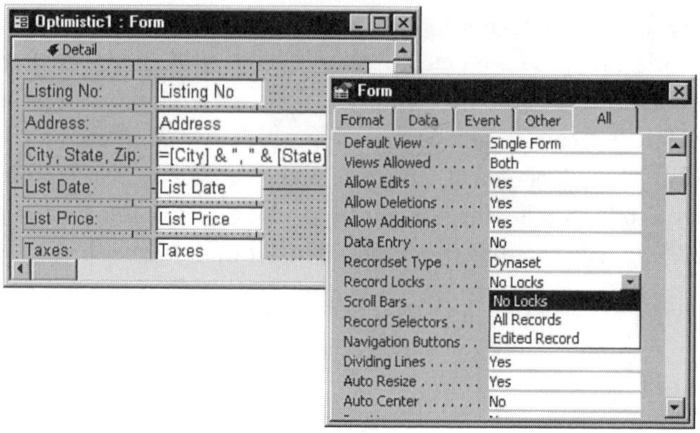

Figure 18.13.
Optimistic locking is appropriate in many situations.

Figure 18.14 illustrates optimistic locking in action. In this figure, two forms are displaying the same data from a single record in the Elgin Enterprises database. Optimistic1 (the form on the left) is in the middle of an edit (the list price is being changed from $179,000 to $170,000). Notice that the icon in the form's record selector (the vertical gray bar along the left edge of the form) is a pencil, indicating that the current record is being edited. The record selector on the Optimistic2 form on the right is also displaying the pencil icon, indicating the same record is being edited in the Pessimistic2 form (the Taxes field is being changed to $1,750).

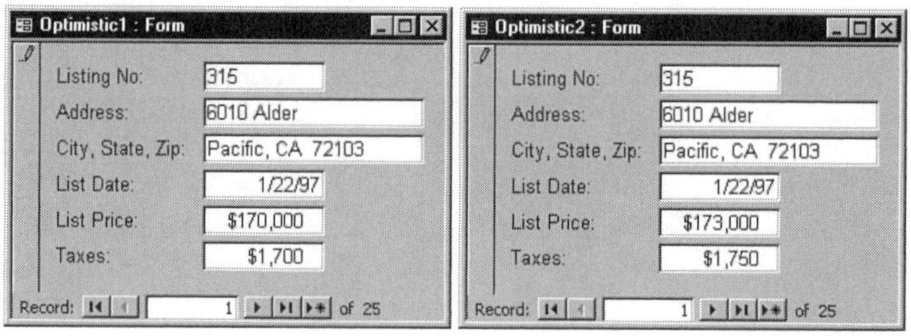

Figure 18.14.
More than one user can be editing the same record under Optimistic locking.

The Optimistic2 form remains available and editable forever. No matter how long the user on the left holds the edit state on the current record, the record selector in form Optimistic2 does not change to the Not symbol. The only time the Optimistic2 user will be aware that a problem exists is when he tries to commit his changes. If Optimistic1 completes her edits and commits the changes by moving on to another record, when Optimistic2 tries to save his changes, the dialog box shown in Figure 18.15 appears.

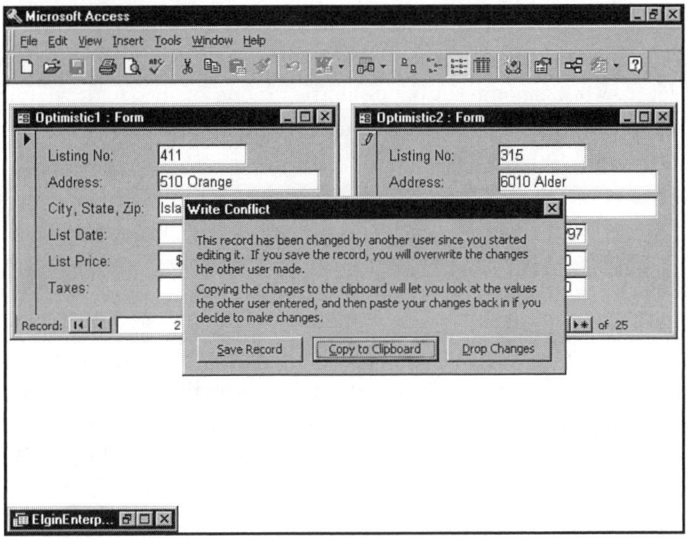

Figure 18.15.
A write conflict occurs when two users make changes to the same record.

The Write Conflict dialog box informs the user that someone else on the network has made changes to the record while he was making his edits. Here are the options available to him at this point:

- Go ahead and save the record, overwriting the changes made by the user on form Optimistic1. This means the change made to the list price by the Optimistic1 user will disappear from the database.

- Copy the new data to the Windows 95 Clipboard so that the changes made by the other user can be viewed on the form.

- Discard edits and allow the other user's edits to be displayed on the form. In this case, the Optimistic2 user will have to re-enter his changes to the data.

If you choose to use optimistic locking, you'll have to train your users how to deal with the Write Conflict dialog box. Experiment with the three write conflict options to see which one is best suited for your users' data.

Locking Entire Tables

The last locking scheme you'll learn is obtained by setting a form's Record Locks property to All Records. In this case, Access locks all of the records in the tables providing information to a form. While the All Records lock is in place, of course, no other users can make changes to the data. In most environments this is an unacceptable situation, but there are times when the All Records setting is needed. For example, if the form runs an update or delete query that is going to modify the data in several different records, you'll want the query to lock all records so that it is able to complete its work. If optimistic or pessimistic locking are used in these situations, some records might be held open by other users, and the update or delete query would either fail or incompletely modify the data in the table.

The .LDB File

You might have noticed a file with the same name as an open database but with an .LDB filename extension in the Windows Explorer. This file contains the information that Access needs to manage locks on the open database. Do not delete this file while a database is open. In fact, there should almost never be a reason for you to manually delete this file. Under normal conditions, Access will automatically remove this file when the last user working with the data has closed the database.

Choosing a Locking Scheme

There are several factors you should consider when you select a locking scheme for your database:

- You should use pessimistic locking whenever it's important to prevent a user's changes from being overwritten by another user. Pessimistic locking allows only a single user to access a record at a time.

- Pessimistic locking almost always locks more than one record at a time.

- Generally speaking, you'll get fewer complaints from users with optimistic locking because more users can get to more records without encountering locks.

- You'll have to train your users how to deal with the Write Conflict dialog box if you choose optimistic locking.

The preceding discussions have described the Access locking schemes as if they affect individual records at a time. Unlike many other database systems, however, Access does not actually lock a single record at a time. Access uses a *page locking* mechanism that actually locks a 2KB (2048 bytes) buffer in the .MDB file. The page locking used by Access means that more than one record will be affected by a lock imposed by a user as he or she edits data. The effect of page locking becomes especially important when working with very small records in tables. It's possible that 20 or 30 records will be locked if each record contains 100 or fewer bytes of data. If you've selected pessimistic locking and your users frequently complain that they can't edit records because some other user is making changes, you should consider changing to optimistic locking.

Setting the Default Locking Scheme

Refer to Figure 18.10. The Advanced tab of the Options dialog box contains several settings that affect the locking implemented in your applications. You've already learned about the Default Open Mode setting in the upper-right corner of this dialog box and the Refresh Interval in the lower-left corner. Notice the Default Record Locking setting in the upper-left corner. When Access is first installed, the Default Record Locking is set to No Locks (optimistic locking), as you see in Figure 18.10. If you decide that pessimistic locking is more appropriate for your environment, select the Edited Record setting. This means that all new forms in the database will automatically be set to pessimistic locking at the time they are created.

The locking settings in the Options dialog box affect all databases created from this point on.

Implementing Locking in VBA Code

So far, this chapter has dealt with locking as if the only way locking is implemented in Access databases is by setting a form's Record Locks property. In Chapter 16, "Customizing Input and Output," and Chapter 17, " Linking with Other Office Applications," you saw code such as the following:

```
Dim dbsCurrent As Database
Dim rstList As Recordset
Set dbsCurrent = CurrentDb
Set rstList = dbsCurrent.OpenRecordset("Listings", dbOpenDynaset)
```

These statements, of course, set up and build a dynaset-type recordset object that contains data from the Listings table. By default, all Access recordsets implement pessimistic locking.

There are times, however, when the default setting is not appropriate for the recordset you've created. You might want to use optimistic locking in situations in which performance is critical and users complain that they can't get their work done.

All dynaset and table-type recordsets have a LockEdits property that enables you to specify optimistic or pessimistic locking. The following statements create a recordset named rstList and set its locking to optimistic:

```
Dim dbsCurrent As Database
Dim rstList As Recordset
Set dbsCurrent = CurrentDb
Set rstList = dbsCurrent.OpenRecordset("Listings", dbOpenDynaset)
rstList.LockEdits = False
```

Setting LockEdits to False is the same as setting a form's RecordLocks property to No Locks. LockEdits is set to True by default (pessimistic locking).

Snapshot-type dynasets have no LockEdits property. Because a snapshot cannot be updated, there is no need to provide a locking mechanism for these objects.

Keeping Data Views Up-To-Date

Consider for a moment a form that is designed mostly for data review. Perhaps the form is intended as part of an online orders support application. Customers call in to check on the status of their orders, and the clerk uses the form to confirm the items and quantities ordered, as well as to see if the order has been packed or shipped. In this kind of application, it is critical to make sure that the data view the clerk sees is completely up-to-date. In dynamic environments such as large mail-order companies like LL Bean, Sears & Roebuck, and JC Whitney, the data in the order entry database changes by the second. Giving a customer incorrect information about an order could be very damaging.

Access provides several options that control the "timeliness" of the data displayed on forms. The most important of these are the refresh interval and the Refresh and Requery methods. A *refresh* updates the data displayed on the screen, whereas a *requery* completely rebuilds the recordset underlying the form. Either a refresh or requery will be called for, depending on the needs of your users.

In either case, the view the user sees will change before his eyes as the refresh or requery cycle is completed. As long as the data displayed on the screen is from a dynaset or table-type recordset, Access maintains live connections back to the tables underlying the form. As soon as the data changes and the refresh or requery cycle ends, the data displayed on the form will be updated to reflect the changes.

Refresh

You've already visited the Refresh Interval setting in the Options dialog box. By default, this value is set to 60 seconds, much too long in truly dynamic environments. If it is critical that users see an up-to-date view of the data, set the refresh interval to something smaller, perhaps as low as 10 or 15 seconds. Be careful not to set it too low, of course, because each refresh cycle generates network traffic and consumes CPU cycles on the computer. The increased overhead is a small price to pay when accurate views are essential. Keep in mind, however, that the Refresh Interval setting in the Options dialog box affects all recordsets in all forms in the application.

A user can also force a refresh by selecting the Refresh command from the Records menu. If you'd prefer that the user clicks a button on a form to refresh the data, use the following code in the `Click` event procedure for the button:

```
Me.Refresh
```

All forms have a `Refresh` method that can be triggered at any time. Alternatively, you can use the form's timer interval (measured in milliseconds) to trigger the `Timer` event. Use the same `Refresh` method in the `Timer` event procedure and set the timer interval to the desired number of milliseconds between refresh intervals. Using the `Timer` event lets you set the refresh interval on a form-by-form basis, rather than affecting the overall application with the Refresh Interval setting in the Options dialog box.

A refresh does not guarantee 100 percent accuracy in its view of the underlying data. For example, records that have been added to the database since the recordset was constructed for the form are not displayed. Or, if the sort order has changed for some reason, the records underlying the form are not resorted. Finally, deleted records are marked with #Delete in all fields.

Requery

A requery is a more drastic view update than the refresh. When the form's Requery method is invoked, Access completely rebuilds the recordset underlying the form. A requery guarantees that the data view is completely accurate: new records are displayed, the data is sorted in the proper order, and deleted records are removed from the recordset. The only problem from the user's perspective is that the data in the form returns to the first record in the recordset. Therefore, if the user is working on a particular customer's order before the requery, she'll have to return to that customer's record before continuing.

You trigger a requery by pressing the Shift+F9 key combination or by running the form's Requery method:

```
Me.Requery
```

Choosing **Refresh** or **Requery**

You should consider using either the Refresh or Requery methods when it's important that your users see an up-to-date view of the data. A refresh provides a fast update to the form's data and is easily triggered in code with a button or Timer event, but it might not show a completely accurate view of the data. A requery provides a 100 percent accurate view of the data, but it takes more time, consumes more resources, and generates more network traffic than a refresh. A requery is also easily triggered in code but has the disconcerting effect of returning the user to the first record in the underlying recordset.

Summary

This chapter has explored the challenges of preparing Access databases for multiuser use. Turning a database into a multiuser environment involves much more than copying the .MDB file to the file server. You must consider how the users will be working with their data, the importance of maintaining data integrity while providing adequate performance, and keeping data views in forms up-to-date.

Microsoft has done an outstanding job in providing the developer with a wide variety of options when setting up databases for multiuser access. Your choices will be driven by the business requirements of the users and their data.

19

Adding Security to the Application

Chapter 18, "Working in a Multiuser Environment," described all of the issues to consider when you are moving an Access application from the individual desktop to a multiuser environment. However, simply splitting a database, setting locking options, and training users how to work in a shared environment is only part of the story. After you move a database from a controlled local environment to a public server on the network, you must consider the security implications of the database's increased exposure.

The Need for Security

Usually, when we think of database security, our major concern is unauthorized access to the information stored in a database's tables. The primary job of security in a database is to protect the data from being viewed or edited by unauthorized people. In this way, security ensures that the data can't be corrupted or stolen by a competitor or a disgruntled employee.

Everyone has heard horror stories about the employee who steals a company's secrets just before quitting or being fired. With the proliferation and widespread use of laptop computers, a large portion of many company's assets are vulnerable to theft or accidental loss. Access 97 security can guarantee that unauthorized people are unable to view or use the data stored in its tables.

A second, equally important job is to protect the database design from modification by unqualified individuals. Let's face it—application development is time-consuming and costly. It's a mistake to expose your carefully designed and painfully implemented application to modification by summer interns or temporary help with a hankering to explore.

Access 97 applications are particularly vulnerable to modification by unqualified people. Microsoft has distributed millions of copies of Access as part of the Microsoft Office package and as a stand-alone product. This means that there are millions of copies of Access available to do-it-yourself database engineers who'd like nothing more than to change the design of a form or report in your databases.

Although the majority of do-it-yourselfers are well-intentioned, unless they fully understand and appreciate the rationale behind a particular design element of an application, they can unknowingly damage the application's integrity or performance. Sometimes, seemingly trivial details such as a validation rule on a field or the name of a text box can have profound impact on the operation of the database. Even seemingly benign changes such as moving or changing the size of a control on a report can cause unexpected results.

For all of these reasons, you will more than likely want to establish a reasonable and rational level of security in your Access 97 applications. This is particularly true of the back-end database residing on the server. This is where the majority of the valuable information is stored and vulnerable to intentional or accidental loss or corruption. (In this context, "corruption" means inaccurate or incorrect data entry as well as data loss due to scrambled or unusable entry.)

The Database Password: The First Level of Security

You can quickly and easily protect your Access 97 databases by using the database password feature. Using this security feature, you assign a single password that all users utilize when they begin work with the database. You open the Set Database Password dialog box with the Tools | Security | Set Database Password command (see Figure 19.1).

Figure 19.1.
The database password provides blanket protection for your databases.

The database must be opened in exclusive mode when setting the database password. You select the exclusive open option by marking the Exclusive check box under the buttons in the upper-right corner of the Open dialog box (you open this dialog with the File | Open command as shown in Figure 19.2). You will not be able to open the database in exclusive mode if another user is working with the database.

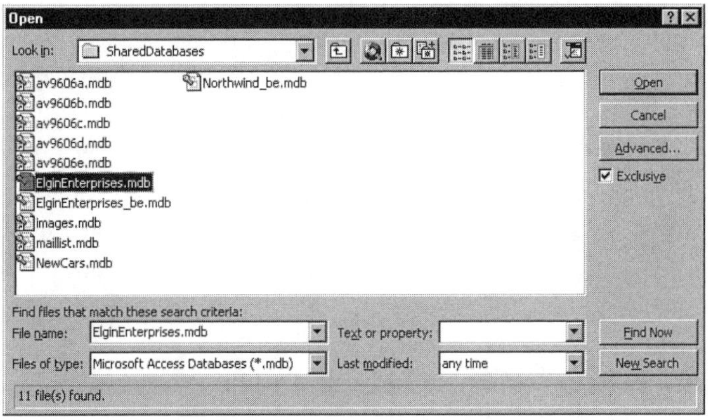

Figure 19.2.
Open the database in exclusive mode before setting the Database Password.

After you set a database password, all users are challenged by the Password Required dialog box you see in Figure 19.3. Notice that nothing but the password is required for entry to the database. When a user is admitted to the application, every object is available to him or her.

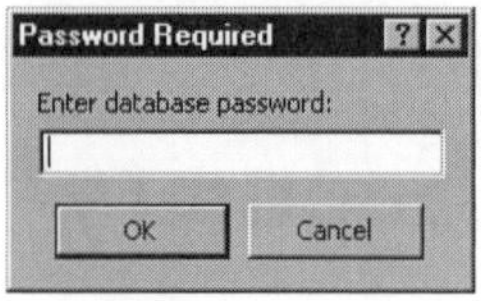

Figure 19.3.
*A single password services
all users.*

Password Required   ? X
Enter database password:
[   ]
OK   Cancel

The database password provides a mediocre level of security to an Access database. Because a single password must be shared by all of the database users, it is impossible to control exactly who knows the password. It would be very easy for an unauthorized user to learn the password in most cases.

The database password provides no way to identify an individual. All users are logged into the database as Admin, a powerful and dangerous user (as you'll read later in this chapter). When using the database password there is no way for Access to differentiate between one user and another. All users are the same "person" to Access.

Also, because the database password provides no object-level protection, there is no way to secure individual components of the database. As you'll see later in this chapter, Access security is based on user and group accounts. The owner of a database object such as a table or form is the ultimate authority over the object. Only the owner is able to grant access permission to other users and groups in the database. When using database password security, every user is a database administrator and has complete authority over all objects in the database. In other words, a database password provides virtually no security at all.

Finally, the database password represents a distinct danger to a database. Anyone who knows the database password can invoke the Tools | Security | Unset Database Password command (this command is seen only when a password is imposed on the database) to remove the current password. When the password has been disabled, this person can then maliciously assign a bogus password to the database, effectively locking every other person out of the database.

All things considered, the database password does not provide a significant level of security. In most environments where security is an issue, a stronger and more capable form of security is called for. Fortunately, Access has one of the best security features of any desktop database.

Understanding the Access Security Model

The Access security model is designed around the notion of *workgroups*. A workgroup can contain several other groups within it. Consider a large company with sales, marketing, and production departments. Each department might be considered a workgroup because they share certain responsibilities within the company. Within the sales workgroup, you might have regional, international, and government sales groups, each having specific sales objectives.

Elgin l...   ee has a different title even though
all em...   ore, we'll have a single workgroup
with se...   me business function, such as sales
or mar...   more groups and will have certain
securit...   ong to.

One in...   " You don't need to explicitly enable se...   Access security measures until you
assign a...   istrator (more on this later in the
chapter...   .

Un...   p File

As you...   . You can use the Access installation on...   tabases. Needing to assign users,
groups,...   nightmare. Consider the amount
of redun...   group, a marketing group, and a
manager...   helps you set up security, you'd
have to...   used in the company.

Fortunat...   soft Access. You must set up the
group an...   ation you enter is stored in a special datal...   es that this file stores workgroup
informati...   e is System.mdw. Figure 19.4 illustrates thi...

Figure 1...
Group and...
is stored in...
information...
System.md...

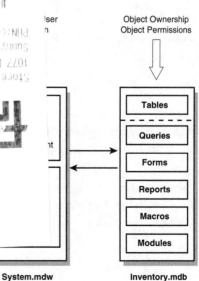

| | Object Ownership Object Permissions |

| Tables |
| Queries |
| Forms |
| Reports |
| Macros |
| Modules |

Orders.mdb   System.mdw   Inventory.mdb

This arrangement enables the same group and user information to be shared among several different databases. Figure 19.4 shows how two databases (Orders and Inventory) at the Elgin Enterprises company both use the same System.mdw file. In this illustration, System.mdw contains information about three groups (Sales, Marketing, and Management) and five users (Jones, Bond, Gibbs, Bache, and Johns). Each of the five users belongs to one or more of the groups in the System.mdw file.

Tip: The workgroup file does not have to be named System.mdw. In fact, in most cases it is a good idea not to use the default System.mdw file. Instead, you should create a custom workgroup file that is associated with the workgroup that will be using Access on its network.

Creating a Workgroup

Access 97 includes a "hidden" utility called the Workgroup Administrator that establishes a new workgroup file. Wrkgadm.exe resides in the Windows System folder (usually C:\Windows\System). This utility, which is not installed into the Office 97 or Access 97 folders during installation, creates a completely new workgroup information file for your Access installation. In a secured environment, you usually do not want to use the default System.mdw in order to avoid "contamination" from users or groups that might have been installed in the past. A nice, new clean system file is the best start to a new security scheme.

Use the Run command on the Start menu to run Wrkgadm.exe. Use the Browse button on the Run dialog box to locate Wrkgadm.exe (see Figure 19.5).

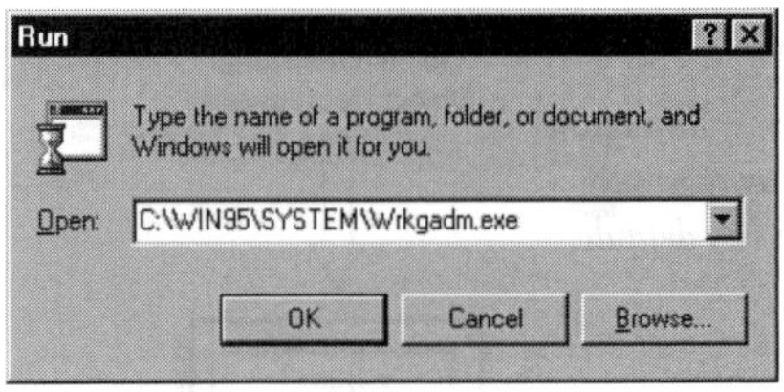

Figure 19.5.
Use the Run dialog box to
run Wrkgadm.exe.

The Workgroup Administrator is quite simple. The first dialog box (not shown here) explains that the Workgroup Administrator is intended to be used to create the workgroup information file for an Access installation. The first dialog box contains three buttons that let you create a new workgroup information file, join an existing workgroup, or exit the Workgroup Administrator. Because you're installing security for the first time on the computer, use the Create button to build an entirely new workgroup information file.

The second dialog box ("Workgroup Owner Information," shown in Figure 19.6) actually asks for the information needed to identify the owner and other information needed by the workgroup information file. Of these bits of information, the most interesting is the Workgroup ID (WID). The WID is a case-sensitive string of 4–20 characters. Be sure to record the WID you use and keep it in a safe place. Think of the WID as a "password" you need to reconstruct the workgroup information file in the unlikely event it is ever lost though accidental erasure or hardware failure.

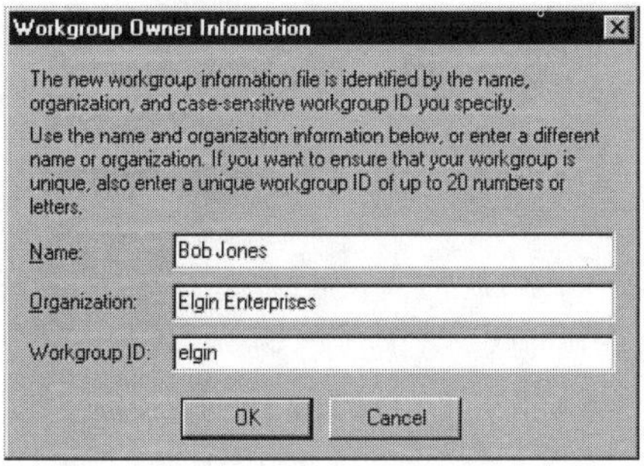

Figure 19.6.
This information is important when you are reconstructing a workgroup information file.

If you try to create a new workgroup information file and use the wrong owner information (including the WID), you will not be able to open any databases using the workgroup information file. Storing this information in a safe location is imperative. If you use an obvious, easily guessed owner, organization, and WID, an unauthorized user will be able to construct his own workgroup information file and use the built-in administrator account in the new workgroup information file to gain access to your databases. This is the primary reason you don't want to use the default workgroup information file (System.mdw) with a secured application.

When you click OK on this dialog box, you are asked where you want Access to create the new workgroup information file. Normally, you'll want the file placed in a shared folder on a file server on the network. In Figure 19.7, Elgin Enterprises is using the networking built into Microsoft Windows 95, and the developer's computer is the designated file server for the company. Therefore, the workgroup information file is being placed in the Shared Databases folder on the developer's computer.

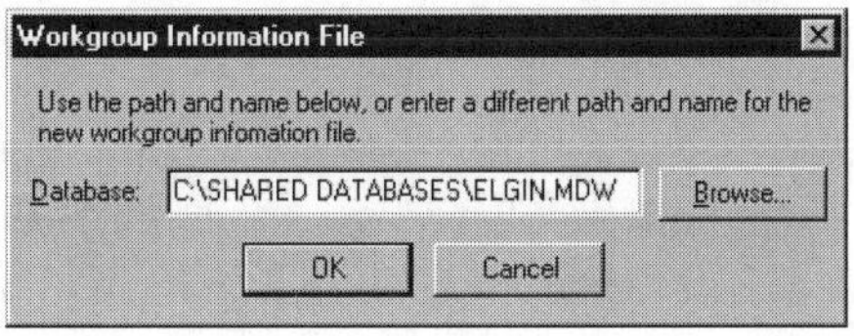

Figure 19.7.
Put the workgroup information file in a shared folder on an accessible computer.

The last dialog box of the Workgroup Administrator asks you to confirm the information you've provided to create the workgroup information file (see Figure 19.8). This is your last chance to verify and record this data for safe-keeping. After you press OK, the Workgroup Administrator builds the workgroup information file and changes the computer's system Registry to point Access to the new file. Only one workgroup information file can be used on a computer at a time.

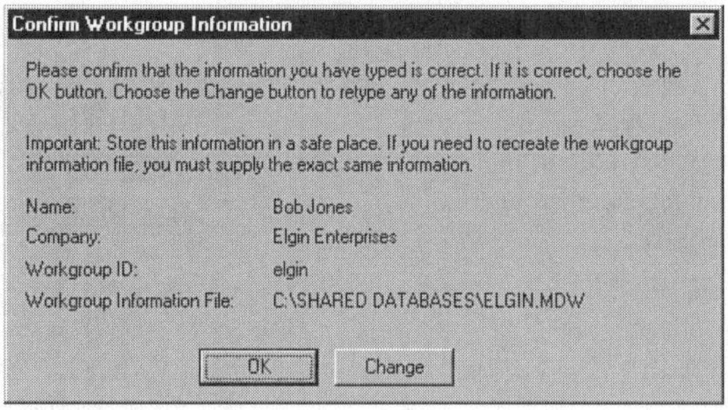

Figure 19.8.

Confirm and record this information before proceeding!

Confirm Workgroup Information	

Please confirm that the information you have typed is correct. If it is correct, choose the OK button. Choose the Change button to retype any of the information.

Important: Store this information in a safe place. If you need to recreate the workgroup information file, you must supply the exact same information.

Name:	Bob Jones
Company:	Elgin Enterprises
Workgroup ID:	elgin
Workgroup Information File:	C:\SHARED DATABASES\ELGIN.MDW

OK   Change

You can, however, use a different workgroup by specifying its location with the /wrkgrp command-line switch. Look for the "command line" topic in the Access 97 online Help for instructions on setting command-line arguments under Windows 95.

Working with Groups and Users

The security within an Access database is built around the groups, users, and objects in the database. There are several groups in most Access database security schemes, each with many users. In most cases, the security groups parallel functional groups within the company using the database. A user can belong to more than one group, particularly when a person's responsibilities overlap more than one functional group.

Later in this chapter, you'll see how to assign permissions to the objects in a database. Permissions protect the data and objects in the database. A group or user might or might not have permission to look at the data in a table, run a query, or modify the design of a table, query, form, or some other database object. In this way, you can grant relatively comprehensive permissions to skilled and responsible users while keeping things locked up and out of the reach of less privileged individuals.

Back in Figure 19.4 you saw how the security information in an Access database is divided between the workgroup information file (System.mdw, by default) and individual databases. This design permits multiple databases to share the group and user information stored in the workgroup information file while maintaining object permissions with the .MDB database file.

When you start Access 97 in a secured environment, you are asked for your user name and password (see Figure 19.9). Access checks this information against the group and user data stored in the workgroup information file to verify that you are a valid Access user on the system. If Access cannot match your user name with any of the entries in System.mdw, or if the password you provide does not match your password in the workgroup information file, the logon fails and you are not permitted entry into Access.

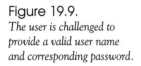

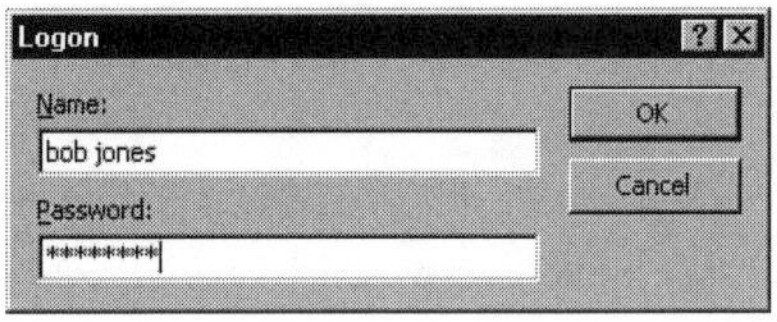

Figure 19.9.
The user is challenged to
provide a valid user name
and corresponding password.

This first barrier to unauthorized access is more than adequate to stop casual unauthorized browsers from trying to open any databases in Access 97. Later in this chapter, in the section titled "Adding New Users," you'll see how a user is assigned a password.

Built-In Groups

Every copy of Access has many built-in groups and users. These groups and users become important when you are considering the implications of improperly setting up security in an Access database. As you'll see, one of the steps of securing an Access database is to disable a dangerous default user:

- Admins—All members of the Admins group are administrators of the Access database. An administrator is able to add new groups and users, change ownership of database objects, and change permissions on any database objects. Administrators, therefore, are powerful individuals in the database.

- Users—Every user is a member of the Users group. Normally, the Users group has no real authority in the database and is provided for "guests" who might not be part of a database's security scheme.

Neither the Admins nor the Users group can be deleted or renamed. They are permanent and immutable parts of the Access 97 security scheme.

Built-In Users

There is one built-in user account. The Admin user, a member of the Admins group, is in every copy of System.mdw that is created when Access 97 is installed. This means that millions of copies of System.mdw exist, each with a default user who is able to open, view, and modify all of the data and database objects in every Access database ever created. Later, you'll see how to change the Admin user's group and permissions in your databases.

Understanding Object Ownership

All objects (tables, queries, forms, and so on) in an Access database must be owned by some user. By default, all objects are owned by the owner of the database, itself. By default, the owner of all databases and all objects within all databases is Admin. When security is implemented in an Access installation, each user is able to create new databases and objects (with appropriate permissions, of course).

Groups can own objects just as users do. In fact, in many cases it makes more sense to have group ownership than individual user ownership of most objects. As an administrator, your job is complicated whenever you have to change the ownership of database objects each time a person's job responsibilities change or a person leaves the company. Later in this chapter, in the section titled "Assigning Object Ownership," you'll see how to set an object's ownership.

The owner of an object is the ultimate authority of that object. This means that an object's owner can modify the design of the object, view any data the object holds, and export or import the object to other Access databases. There are other permissions; for example, printing the object's design or outputting the object to various formats such as HTML (hypertext markup language) or RTF (rich text format). An object's owner is also able to grant permissions to other groups and users.

Activating Security in Access 97

Earlier in this chapter you read that you don't have to explicitly install security or turn it on. Security is always in place in your databases and becomes visible only when you assign a password to the Admin user.

Because the default user is Admin, each time you open an Access database in an unsecured environment, you log on as Admin. This means that you are the database owner and administrator and own all of the objects in the database.

Open the User and Group Accounts dialog box (see Figure 19.10) by selecting Tools | Security | User and Group Accounts. This dialog box contains three tabs when you log on as Admin. The first two tabs, Users and Groups, let you create new users and groups, and the third tab, Change Logon Password, has the text boxes required for you to assign a password to Admin.

Because there is no password for the Admin user to start with, leave the Old Password box blank and tab to the New Password box. Enter the new password for Admin; then, tab to the Verify box and retype the password. When you've completed this simple operation, security is enabled, and anyone trying to use the database will encounter the dialog box shown in Figure 19.9. Nothing more is required to make security visible in an Access 97 database.

You should shut down Access and restart it to test the new Admin password. Notice that you must provide the password before you open any databases. When you're in Access as the Admin user, you can open any database and set up the security within that database.

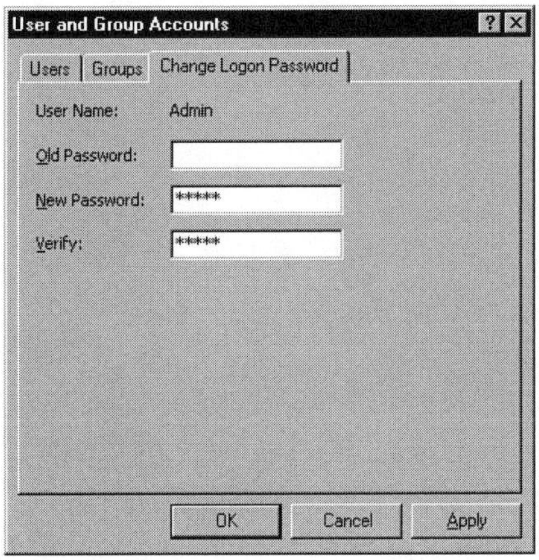

Figure 19.10.
Set the Admin user's password in the User and Group Accounts dialog box.

Designing an Access Security System

The first step in designing a security system for an Access database is to decide which users should belong to which group. Generally, this process is quite straightforward. Table 19.1 shows a reasonable security setup for the Elgin Enterprises database.

Table 19.1. User and Group information for Elgin Enterprises.

User Name	Job Title	Group
Bob Jones	Owner	Management
Jane Bond	Vice President	Management, Marketing, Sales
Shirley Gibbs	Marketing Assistant	Marketing
Joe Bache	Sales Associate	Sales
Betty Johns	Office Manager	Management, Sales

Notice that Jane Bond and Betty Johns belong to more than one group. Jane Bond (the sales and marketing manager) often works as a salesperson in addition to her marketing tasks, whereas Betty Johns (the office manager) sometimes participates in sales activities.

The Elgin Enterprises database, therefore, requires three security groups (Management, Sales, and Marketing) and five user accounts (Bob Jones, Jane Bond, Shirley Gibbs, Joe Bache, and Betty Johns).

Adding New Groups

While you are logged on as Admin, open the Tools | Security | User and Group Accounts dialog box. Click the Groups tab to begin adding groups (see Figure 19.11).

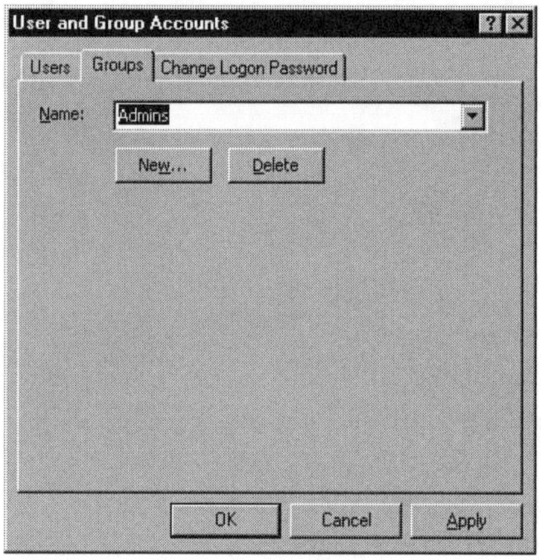

Figure 19.11.
Adding groups to an Access
database is straightforward.

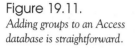

The drop-down list at the top of the User and Group Accounts dialog box contains the names of all of the groups in the current workgroup information file (you'll recall that user and group information is stored in the workgroup information file and not in the database).

Click the New button to open the New User/Group dialog box (see Figure 19.12). Enter the name of the group and a *personal identifier* (PID) for the group. Be sure to record the PID you assign. It is a case-sensitive string between 4 and 20 alphanumeric characters in length, and you'll need it if you ever have to reconstruct the workgroup information file. The PID you see in Figure 19.12 is formed using a "one off" code. For each character in the alphabet, the next character in the alphabet is chosen for encoding purposes. Using this scheme, an "a" becomes "b," a "q" becomes "r," and so on. Given Management as the group name, the encoded group name is nbobnfnfou (all characters are coded in lowercase for simplicity).

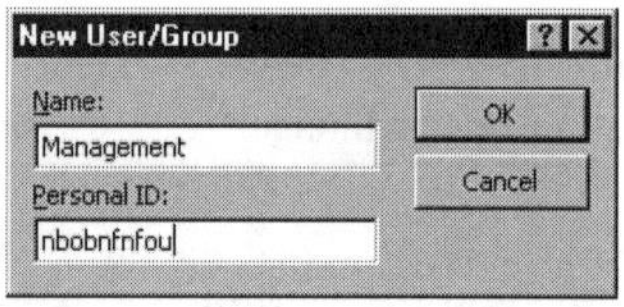

Figure 19.12.
Be sure to record the PID
you assign to the new group.

The group name and PID you assign are combined by Access to create a *SID* (security ID). Access actually uses the SID to verify a group's identification. The SID is "tagged" onto all objects owned by the group and is used to look up a group's permission on objects in the database.

In this way, the database administrator actually controls security. Because a group (or user) is not able to assign their own PID, there is no chance that an unauthorized user is able to create a group or user account and gain access to the database and its objects. Unless you make the PID something obvious and easily guessed, you needn't worry about unauthorized groups in your security environment.

Adding New Users

After the three Elgin Enterprises groups have been added, it is time to add the five users. Select the Users tab in the User and Group Accounts dialog box to enter the information needed to create group accounts (see Figure 19.13). The drop-down list at the top of the dialog box contains the names of all users in the workgroup information file.

Figure 19.13.

You assign a user to the available groups as you create the user account.

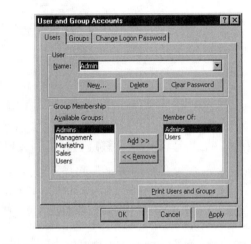

Clicking the New button in the top half of the Users tab opens the New User/Group dialog box you saw in Figure 19.12. Again, you are required to assign a case-sensitive PID to the new user. As with the other IDs in the Access security scheme, be sure to record the PID and store it in a safe location. Click OK in the New User/Group dialog box after you've provided the required information.

Notice the selection lists at the bottom of the Users tab. The left list contains the names of all the groups in the workgroup information file, and the right list contains the names of the groups to which the current user has been assigned. In Figure 19.14, notice that Jane Bond has been assigned to the Management, Marketing, and Sales groups as well as the Users group. The Users group membership happens by default and cannot be removed from the membership list. The other groups are completely configurable and can be deleted or renamed.

As the database administrator, it is a good idea to close Access and log on as each of the users you create. Once you have logged on to Access, use the Change Logon Password tab of the User and Group Accounts dialog box to assign the initial password to each user. It is a bad idea to leave this important step up to the individual users. Many people won't bother setting a password for themselves, creating a serious security breach. If nothing else, their account will be protected by the initial password you assign to them. Your users are able to establish new passwords at any time.

Figure 19.14.
Jane Bond belongs to more than one group.

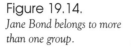

Assign a New Administrator

Before moving on to permissions, you should create a new administrative user. This is an essential step in securing your database. As long as you leave an Admin user in your database who is a member of the Admins group, your database is vulnerable to unauthorized snooping. Every workgroup information file contains an Admin user who is a member of the Admins group. Therefore, as long as this user exists in your databases, an unauthorized user is able to use *any* workgroup information file to open and access your database. Unfortunately, because Admin is a default user in all Access databases, you cannot actually remove this person. You can, however, reassign the group to take Admin out of the Admins group and remove permissions from the Admin user account.

Here are the steps required to disable the Admin user in your database:

1. Create a new user account and assign the user a password.
2. Add the new user to the Admins group.
3. Log off and log back on as the new administrator to test the new account.
4. Assign a completely bogus password to the (old) Admin user.
5. Remove the Admins group from the membership list for the Admin user.

Later, in the section titled "Assigning Object Permissions" you will learn how to revoke permissions to all objects from the Admin user. This multistep process effectively disables the Admin user by establishing an alternative administrator, removing the Admin account from the Admins group, and assigning an unguessable password to the Admin account. When this process is complete, even if an unauthorized user is able to finagle a bogus workgroup information file to try to open the secured database, he'll discover the Admin user is no longer an administrator in the secured database. As a member of the Users group, the Admin user has no special privileges or power over the data and objects in the database.

Assigning Object Ownership

By default, the owner of the database owns all of the objects in the database. This means that, until security is activated, all objects are owned by the Admin user. In most situations, it is appropriate to assign ownership to other users or groups in the database.

The owner of an object is the ultimate authority over the object. An owner has all permissions on the object and is able to change its design, the data it contains, and to grant permissions to other users or groups. In many cases, you might want an administrator to retain ownership of the database objects because there is no one within a group who is qualified to make changes to the objects. In other cases, however, it makes sense to let a group write its own queries and make changes to forms and reports (within reason, of course!).

Access lets you assign ownership of an object to a user or group, but not to multiple users or groups. To begin assigning ownership, open the User and Group Permissions dialog box (see Figure 19.15) by selecting Tools | Security | User and Group Permissions. Click the Change Owner tab to see the object ownership options.

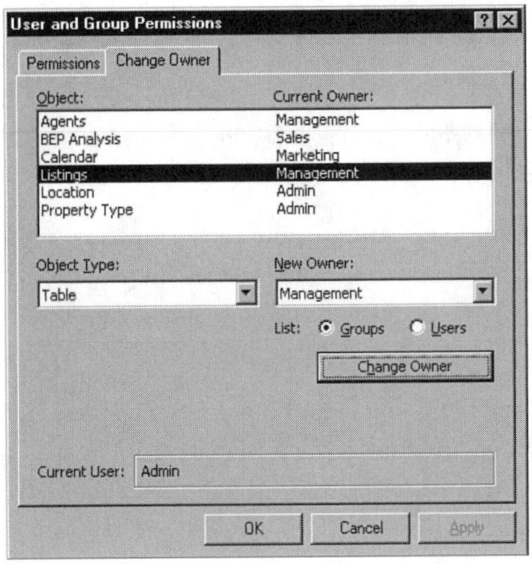

Figure 19.15.
Assign object ownership where appropriate.

The list at the top center of the Change Owner tab contains all of the objects specified in the Object Type drop-down list in the lower-left side of the dialog box. The New Owner drop-down list to the right contains the names of all the users or groups in the workgroup information file, depending on which option button (Groups or Users) is selected. By default, the Users option button is selected, letting you assign ownership to individual users of the database.

Changing ownership is easy. Select the object type from the Object Type drop-down list, and tell Access whether you want to assign ownership to a user or group. Then use the New Owner drop-down list to select the new owner. You must explicitly click the Change Owner button for the ownership assignment to take effect.

> **Tip:** You are generally better off assigning ownership to groups than you are assigning ownership to individuals. Groups such as Sales and Marketing are unlikely to disappear entirely from a company even if the individual people in each of those groups change. If you assign ownership to individual users, you must go back into the security setup and change ownership as the people in the organization change jobs within the company or leave the company. There is no reason for Shirley Gibbs, a marketing assistant, to retain ownership of any of the marketing objects if she takes a job with the Sales department.

Keep in mind that all members of a group share permissions and privileges equally. That means anyone from the marketing group will have complete access to any object owned by the marketing group unless specific permissions are revoked. For this reason, you might find it necessary to create distinct MarketingManagement and Marketing groups. Only true managers would then have access to objects owned by the MarketingManagement group, even though the functions of the two groups are similar.

Understanding Access Permissions

At this point, you have many groups and users in the database. The Admin user has been assigned to a harmless account, and a new administrator is in place. It is now time to assign permissions to the objects in the secured database.

Permissions give users access to the data, forms, and reports in the database. Both individual users and groups can have permissions assigned. In fact, the permissions granted to an individual user are the sum of all the permissions given to any groups the user belongs to, plus the individual permissions assigned to the user.

Consider Jane Bond, the Elgin Enterprises vice president. Jane is a member of both the Marketing and Sales groups in addition to the Management group. Therefore, Jane's permissions will be all those permissions granted to the Management, Sales, and Marketing groups, as well as any permissions assigned to her as a user.

Generally, you will find it much less work to assign permissions to groups and let users have the permissions they enjoy by virtue of their membership in the various groups. Trying to set all the permissions on all the objects in several databases for the dozens of users in most environments is a daunting task, indeed!

All objects in an Access database have several permissions associated with them. For the most part, these permissions reflect how the objects are used in the database. For example, a table has Read Design, Modify Design, Read Data, and other permissions related to its role as a repository of data. A module, on the other hand, has only Read Design, Modify Design, and Administer permissions. Table 19.2 lists all of the permissions possible for Access database objects.

Table 19.2. Object permissions in Access 97.

Object	Open/ Run	Read Design	Modify Design	Read Data	Update Data	Insert Data	Delete Data
Tables		X	X	X	X	X	X
Queries		X	X	X	X	X	X
Forms	X	X	X	X			
Reports	X	X	X	X			
Macros	X	X	X	X			
Modules		X	X	X			

Here is a brief description of each of these types of permissions:

- Open/Run—Open a database, form, report, or macro. This permission is required for a user or group to be able to work with a form or report. If this permission is denied, the user or group cannot view the form or report and cannot run any macros associated with the form or report.
- Read Design—Open an object in Design view. This permission is required by any users or groups who are responsible for changing the design of a table, query, form, report, macro, or module.
- Modify Design—View and change the design of a database object. This permission is required before changing the design of any database object.
- Read Data—View the data in tables or queries.
- Update Data—View or modify the data in a table or query, but don't add new records or delete existing records.
- Insert Data—Insert new data, but don't modify existing data.
- Delete Data—Delete existing data, but don't insert new data.

You can assign virtually any or all of these permissions to users and groups in the workgroup information file. Certain permissions, such as Read Design, are required by other permissions (Modify Design). Therefore, you will not be able to assign Modify Design to a user or group without also assigning Read Design. When you select the Modify Design permission you'll notice that Access automatically selects Read Design. If you notice this behavior, do not try to remove the Read Design permission because Access will then remove the Modify Design permission. Don't worry if you notice Access removing or adding permissions as you change a group or user's permissions. Rest assured that Access will only change the permissions required to satisfy the permissions you specify in the User and Group Permissions dialog box.

Planning Object Permissions

As a database administrator, you have a tremendous amount of flexibility in designing the security scheme for your database. At the same time, this flexibility means that assigning security is a complex process. You must plan which permissions to assign to which users and groups. Table 19.3 shows the permissions that might be given to the tables in the Elgin Enterprises database.

Table 19.3. The table security scheme for Elgin Enterprises.

Table	Management	Sales	Marketing
Agents	Yes	No	No
BEP Analysis	Yes	Yes	No
Calendar	Yes	Yes	Yes
Listings	Yes	Yes	No
Location	Yes	Yes	No
Property Type	Yes	Yes	No

It's easy to see how complicated designing database security can be. In this case, there are only three groups and six tables. In addition to these tables, there are queries, forms, and reports to consider, as well as the macros and modules needed to support the forms and reports. All in all, it's quite a complex task.

Imagine how difficult security would be if you had to individually assign permissions to every user. The Elgin Enterprises database contains just five users, more than enough to keep the database administrator busy for an hour or more setting up security.

Assigning Object Permissions

Finally, you are ready to actually assign object permissions to the users or groups in the organization. Open the User and Group Permissions dialog box once again (select Tools | Security | User and Group Permissions). This time, click the Permissions tab to reveal the permissions assignments in the database (see Figure 19.16).

The Permissions dialog box operates much like the other security dialog boxes you've seen. The large User/Group Name list in the upper-left corner of the dialog box contains the names of all the users or groups in the category selected by the option buttons below the list. In Figure 19.16, the Groups option button has been selected, so you see all of the groups in the Elgin Enterprises database in this list.

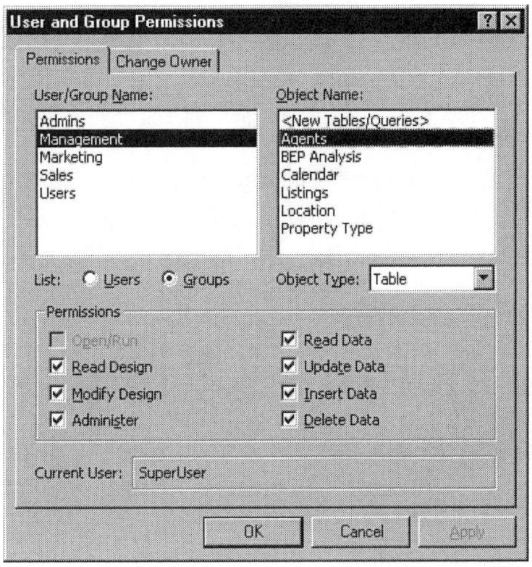

Figure 19.16.
Assigning permissions to the Elgin Enterprises database.

The large Object Name list in the upper-right corner of this dialog box contains the names of all the objects of the type selected in the Object Type drop-down list just below the Object Name list. In this case, the list shows you the names of the tables in the database.

At the bottom of the Permissions tab is a text box displaying the name of the current user. In this case, the current user is SuperUser, the system administrator who has replaced the Admin user in this database.

The Permissions area contains all of the permissions that are possible for the objects in the database. Check or uncheck permissions as needed to give the groups (or users) in the database the appropriate permissions.

Keep in mind that an individual user's actual permissions are the sum of the permissions granted by group membership plus any individual ownership you assign to him or her. Carefully planning the security scheme goes a long way to making the assignment process a painless task.

Disabling the Users Account

Make sure you remove all permissions to all objects in the database from the default Users group. You can select multiple items in the Object Name list (hold down the Ctrl key and click objects, or hold down the Shift key and scroll though the Object Names list). Use this feature to remove all permissions from the Users group. This will prevent unauthorized users from logging in to Access with a dummy name and viewing or changing the objects in the database.

Testing the Security Scheme

As administrator, it is your responsibility to properly assign permissions to groups and users and to verify the operation of the security scheme you've implemented. The only way to fully test security is to log on to Access as some user and try opening a table or form the user is not supposed to be able to view. It's often surprising how many gaps exist in an otherwise well-designed security scheme because of some simple oversight during the setup process.

Implementing Other Security Measures

In addition to the rather rigorous security measures built into Access, there are several other measures you can take to truly ensure the protection of your databases and the data they contain.

Encryption

Although the .MDB file is stored on the hard disk in a binary format, there is nothing to prevent an experienced computer user from using a sector editing tool such as the Norton Utilities to view the raw data on the disk. The text and numeric data in a database is there in the bits and bytes stored on the computer's disk, exposed to prying eyes.

Normally, this is not a problem. There is no way to use a sector editor to view the relationships between tables or to decipher OLE or the other binary data in the .MDB file. However, if absolute security is important, Access provides an encryption tool for scrambling and descrambling data as it is written to or read from disk.

To encrypt an Access database, select Tools | Security | Encrypt/Decrypt. This command—which requires the database to be open in Exclusive mode—uses a secret algorithm to quickly convert the database contents to a totally random sequence of bits on the computer's disk. No password is required for encryption or decryption. Access simply encrypts the database contents and stores the encrypted format on the computer's disk. Encryption can take a few minutes or more, depending on the size of the database.

Reading an encrypted database requires no special steps. Simply open the database and Access performs the decryption as the database is opened. You might notice a slight delay as the decryption process occurs, but the user is not challenged for an encryption password.

The biggest noticeable difference between an encrypted and unencrypted database is that an encrypted database cannot be compressed by utilities such as PKZip. Because the byte sequence on the disk is totally random, there are no repeating patterns for a compression utility to exploit. An encrypted database may take longer to transmit electronically for the same reason. Even modems that use efficient real-time compression routines to shorten transmission times will have trouble applying those routines to an encrypted Access database.

Disguising Database Objects

One popular security technique is to simply assign a misleading name to an object that must be kept secret. This can be as simple as naming a table that contains salary information something like HireDates or another misleading name. In a large database, even the most diligent snooper is discouraged from going to the trouble of poking through dozens of tables looking for something interesting.

Along similar lines, if keeping certain data secret is important, set up a dummy table with a very attractive name such as RegionalSales1997 and fill it with completely erroneous information. Then, if there is a security leak, you can be assured the correct information did not leak out of the company, and you have the chance to locate the source of the leak.

Hiding Database Objects

A simple technique that is easy to implement in Access databases is to prefix sensitive objects with USys (USysSalaries, for example). Anything with a USys (or MSys, for that matter) prefix is invisible in the Database window. You must use the System Objects check box in the View tab of the Options dialog box to see objects hidden with the USys prefix trick (see Figure 19.17).

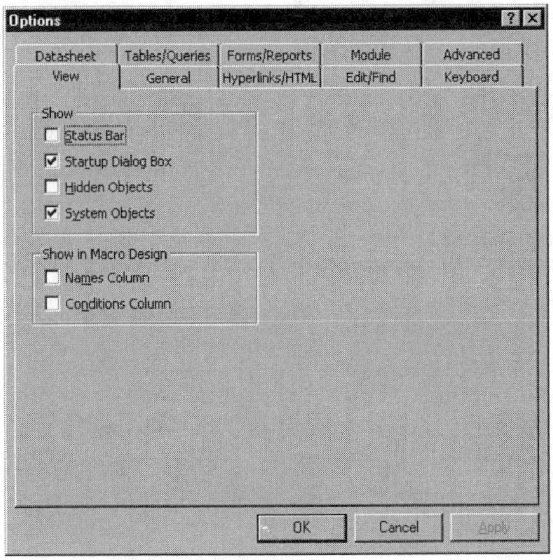

Figure 19.17.
The System Objects option is helpful when you are hiding objects.

All but the most diligent and motivated snoopers will be unable to find objects hidden with the USys prefix. In fact, many experienced Access developers are unaware of this feature.

Utilizing Network and Operating System Security

Most network operating systems provide some level of security. For example, the networking built into Windows 95 and Windows NT provides a password verification mechanism that prevents unauthorized users from simply turning on a computer and having full access to the files on that system. In addition, each folder on a Windows 95 or Windows NT computer can have certain sharing privileges imposed that restrict admission to certain individuals.

Although the network security in Windows 95 is fairly easy to circumvent (by booting the computer from a floppy disk) the security in Windows NT is much more stringent. If the simple password security in Windows 95 is inadequate for your users, you should investigate the more rigorous user registry system built into Windows NT. Access 97 runs equally well under both of these operating systems.

Summary

Implementing database security in an Access database can be a daunting exercise. You first must understand the Access security model, which includes user and group information stored in the System.mdw file. Next, you must master the hierarchy of object ownership and the permissions granted to groups and users within a database. Good planning is essential to implementing an effective security system in an Access database.

Security does not end with the password-based system in an Access database. There are other measures such as hiding or disguising sensitive tables, forms, and queries that go a long way toward keeping out all but the most experienced Access developers. Finally, encrypting a secured database will ensure total protection from unauthorized access to the data.

20

Posting Your Database to the Web

Now that you have created a database full of valuable information and written an application to maintain and use the data, wouldn't it be great to share it with the world? Or even your company or close friends? Microsoft Access 97 introduced some revolutionary features that make it almost trivial to convert database tables, queries, forms, and reports to formats usable by Web browsers such as Internet Explorer and Netscape Navigator. As with any kind of automated code generation, there are some limitations, but you have reasonable flexibility in publishing data.

This chapter assumes that you are familiar with the Internet and know a little bit about HTML and how Web pages work. This doesn't mean that you have to know enough to create Web pages from scratch, but that you've surfed the Web a bit. If you want to learn more, there are gazillions of books available at your local bookstore.

Two terms are used repeatedly in this chapter, and you should be familiar with them:

- HTML (HyperText Markup Language)—This is the set of codes and tags that a Web browser uses to display a Web page. Sometimes, a scripting language, such as VBScript or JavaScript, is embedded within the page as well.

- URL (Universal Resource Locator)—A URL is the address of the document you want to open in a Web browser. Typically, it is the address of a Web page out on the Internet, but it can also be a Word document on your local machine, or almost any type of file located anywhere.

This chapter continues to use the Elgin real-estate listing database, introduced and used in earlier chapters, to create the HTML pages.

Static Versus Dynamic Web Pages

In the prehistoric days of the Web, until early 1996 or so, Web pages were static, unchanging entities. Web developers laid out a Web page like a page in a book; when they saved the .HTML file, it was set in stone. When users fired up browsers and connected to Web servers, they got the page exactly as designed by the developer, except that the users could elect to not download graphics. Every user got the exact same page, possibly with minor variations depending on the browser he or she used. These are called *static* Web pages.

Web pages have become far more responsive these days, which means you can log onto a site and get something completely different from the last user who logged on, depending on the time of day, the type of browser you are using, and almost any other condition that the Web page developer chooses. With these Web pages, the Web server is creating pages on the fly in response to specific requests the user makes. These *dynamic* Web pages function much like a custom application, responding to choices the user makes, the type of data requested, whether the user has logged on to this site before, and so on.

An example of a dynamic Web page is the result of a Web search using engines such as AltaVista or Excite. When you first log onto the search site, you receive a static Web page, the same as any other user sees (except that the ad banner changes, but let's not quibble). After you set your search parameters, the search engine responds by sending you a dynamic Web page with hot links to the sites that meet your search criteria. It creates this page by receiving your search definition, searching its database for the sites that meet your requirements, and creating an HTML page listing those sites.

Using Access and the other tools in Microsoft Office, you can create either static or dynamic Web pages that display your data, or both. The type of page you decide to use to publish your data on the Internet or an intranet depends on how frequently the data changes, the need to allow users to perform custom searches, the amount of data you want to publish, and other factors specific to particular types of data.

For example, the sample Elgin Enterprises real-estate database contains information about property for sale. Depending on the size of Elgin Enterprises and the volume of real estate it sells or leases, the data is unlikely to change daily. However, it could change weekly, so you'll want to build a Web page that uses the latest information. A user-friendly Web page would let a user customize a search instead of slogging through the entire list of properties.

One other important difference between static and dynamic Web pages is the method you use to actually expose the page to the network. You can copy static pages via FTP to your Web server; then users open them in their browsers in the same way that you open a text file in Notepad. Dynamic pages, however, require a more sophisticated server that can receive requests from users, retrieve the recordset, and then create Web pages on the fly to send back to the users. The end result, from the user's perspective, is the exact same: an HTML page displayed in the browser showing your data. Microsoft's Internet Information Server, shipped with Windows NT, performs such functions and is easiest to use with Access databases. However, Netscape and many other companies have servers that can perform the same functions.

Unfortunately, the tools available in Access aren't quite advanced enough to enable you to create pages that let users perform custom queries on your data. But these kinds of tools are available as part of programs dedicated to creating Web pages, such as Microsoft's Visual InterDev (for more information, check out http://www.microsoft.com/vinterdev/ or http://www.microsoft.com/vstudio/). With Access, you at least have some basic tools for publishing your data.

Converting an Access Database to HTML

In general, Microsoft Access has four ways to save data from your database as HTML documents and publish it on the Internet:

- *Save data as static HTML documents.* You can create static HTML documents from tables, queries, form datasheets, and reports. When you save data as static HTML documents, the resulting pages reflect the state of the data at the time it was saved, like a snapshot. If your data changes, you must save the pages again to publish the new data.

- *Save data as IDC/HTX files.* You can save your tables, queries, and form datasheets as Internet Database Connector/HTML extension (IDC/HTX) files that generate HTML documents by querying a copy of your database located on a Web server.

- *Save data as Active Server pages.* You can save tables, queries, form datasheets, and forms as Active Server pages (ASPs). Saving forms this way acts like the forms in Access and displays data from a database located on a Web server.

- *Automate the publishing of dynamic and static HTML documents.* You can use the Publish to the Web Wizard to automate the process of saving multiple objects to any combination of all three of the preceding file types.

Which method you use primarily depends on the timeliness of the data and the server that you have available for making the HTML pages available.

There are a couple of limitations in using the built-in Access tools for publishing data this way. One is that there is no way to save OLE Object fields to the HTML page, so you can't include any images stored in the database and automatically include them in the HTML page. You can always edit the HTML page by hand to include them, but that kind of defeats the purpose of automating the page generation.

You also can't control which fields are included in the HTML page when you create a page from an Access table. If you want to include only certain fields, sort the data, or otherwise massage it, you need to create a query and then create the HTML page from the query. With Dynamic HTML pages, you can also manually edit the SQL statement in the resulting pages.

Saving Data As Static HTML Documents

The simplest way to create static HTML pages with Microsoft Access 97 is to save tables, queries, form datasheets, and reports using File | Save As from the Access main menu:

1. In the Database window, select the table, query, form, or report you want to save.
2. On the File menu, select Save As/Export.

3. In the Save As dialog box, click the To An External File Or Database radio button, and then click OK.

4. In the Save As Type combo box, select HTML Documents (*.htm;*.html). The file extension will change to .html.

5. If you want to preserve formatting, select the Save Formatted check box. To automatically open the resulting HTML document in your Web browser, select the Autostart check box (this isn't required, but the new page will immediately load into your browser, as shown in Figure 20.1).

6. Enter the filename and directory location where you want to save the file, and then click Export.

7. In the HTML Output Options dialog box, if you want Microsoft Access to merge an HTML template with the resulting HTML document, specify that as well, and then click OK. (See the "Using an HTML Template for Customization" section for more information about this option.) If you don't want to use a template, just click OK without entering the name of a template file.

You can't save a regular Access form as an HTML document because a form, by nature, is not a static document. A typical form has navigation buttons, which require an underlying mechanism for navigating a recordset and refreshing the data in the bound controls on the form. This is outside the realm of capabilities of a static HTML page. Therefore, Access saves a form as the underlying datasheet.

The end result of saving the Listings table from the Elgin database is shown in Figure 20.1. This will load into your browser automatically if you selected the Autostart option when you created the page. Otherwise, you must open the page yourself.

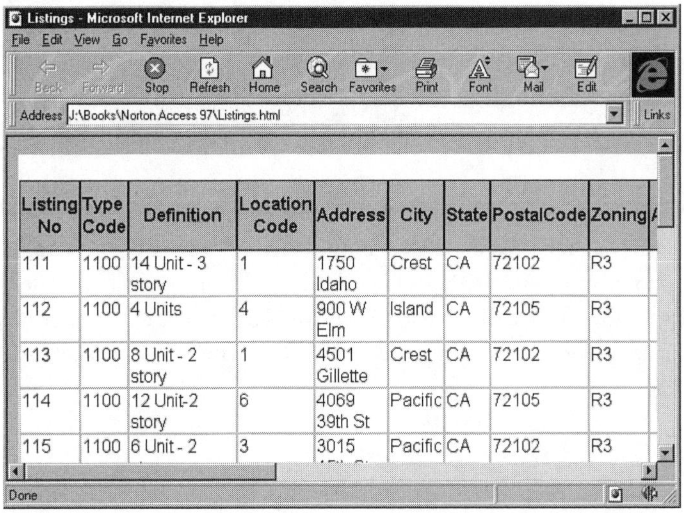

Figure 20.1.
Elgin's Listings table as a static HTML page.

Publishing Tables, Queries, and Form Datasheets

When you save a table, query, or form datasheet as an HTML document, the resulting HTML document is based on the table or query associated with the datasheet, including the current setting of the `OrderBy` or `Filter` property of the table or query.

If you select the Save Formatted check box, the HTML document contains an HTML table that reflects as closely as possible the appearance of the datasheet by using the appropriate HTML tags to specify color, font, and alignment. The HTML document follows as closely as possible the page orientation and margins of the datasheet. Whenever you want to use settings that are different from the default orientation and margins for a datasheet, you must first open the datasheet, and then select File | Page Setup to change settings before you save the datasheet as an HTML document. The HTML document will then reflect these new settings, more or less. Access does its best to maintain consistent formatting, but HTML has far less flexible formatting options. Figure 20.2 shows the HTML page generated from the same table as in Figure 20.1, but with Save Formatted left unchecked.

Listings - Microsoft Internet Explorer
File Edit View Go Favorites Help
Back Forward Stop Refresh Home Search Favorites Print Font Mail Edit
Address J:\Books\Norton Access 97\Listings.html
Links
315 1300 Office/Shop 5 6010 Alder Pacific CA 72103 C 45 3,450 1/22/
411 1400 Retail Store 4 510 Orange Island CA 72105 CR 35 50x140 4/4/
412 1400 With residence 2 7229 Lake Pacific CA 72102 C 40 100x140 5/15/
413 1400 2 Blds/2 Lots 3 300 Polke Pacific CA 72104 C 30 10,000 11/25/
414 1400 Retail Corner 1 3601 C St Crest CA 72102 C 25 7,000 11/11/
415 1400 Medical 6 7000 Pacific CA 72105 C 10 .5 3/20/
Done

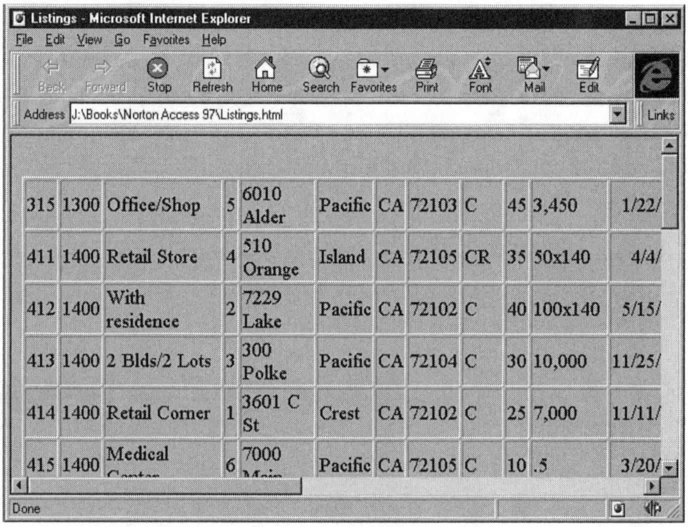

Figure 20.2.
Elgin's Listings table as a static HTML page without formatting.

With the Save Formatted check box, when a field has a `Format` or `InputMask` property setting, those settings are reflected in the data in the HTML document. For example, if a field's `Format` property is set to `Currency` and you have English (United States) selected in the Windows Regional settings in the Control Panel, the data in the HTML document is formatted with a dollar sign, a comma as the thousand separator, and two decimal places. The HTML page will reflect the regional settings in Windows.

Note: If you are using a particular international version of Windows, Access doesn't always pick up all of the applicable regional settings. For example, in the United States version of Windows NT 4.0, setting the Regional Settings to German (Standard) causes currency to be displayed in the HTML page with a dollar sign ($) but with a decimal as the thousands separator. Be sure to test for all combinations of Windows versions and regional settings where your application will be used.

Publishing Access Reports

When saving table, query, and form datasheets, Microsoft Access saves each datasheet to a single HTML file, but it saves reports as multiple HTML documents, with one HTML file per printed page. To name each page, Microsoft Access uses the name of the object and appends `_PageXX` to the end of each page's filename after the first page. Therefore, if you save the Listing report from the Elgin real-estate database, the first page is `Listing.htm`, followed by `Listing_Page2.htm`, `Listing_Page3.htm`, and so on. Figure 20.3 shows a report in Access, and Figure 20.4 shows the HTML page generated.

This series of HTML documents is based on the report's underlying table or query, including the current `OrderBy` or `Filter` property settings of the table or query. They also approximate the proportions and layout of the actual report and the page orientation and margins set for the report. To change the page orientation and margins, open the report in Print Preview, and then use the Page Setup command to change settings before you save the report as HTML documents. These settings are saved from session to session for reports, so if you change them once, they will be used the next time you save the form or report as HTML documents.

Publishing Live Data: FTP and HTML Servers

Publishing static HTML data pages is fine for some applications, but in many cases you'll want to present the latest, up-to-date data at any given moment. For example, if Elgin Enterprises is a large real estate office with many properties being sold and listed every day, you'll want to get the data from the database at the time the user does a search. Otherwise, the data will be outdated. To do this, the Web server will dynamically create HTML pages in response to user requests.

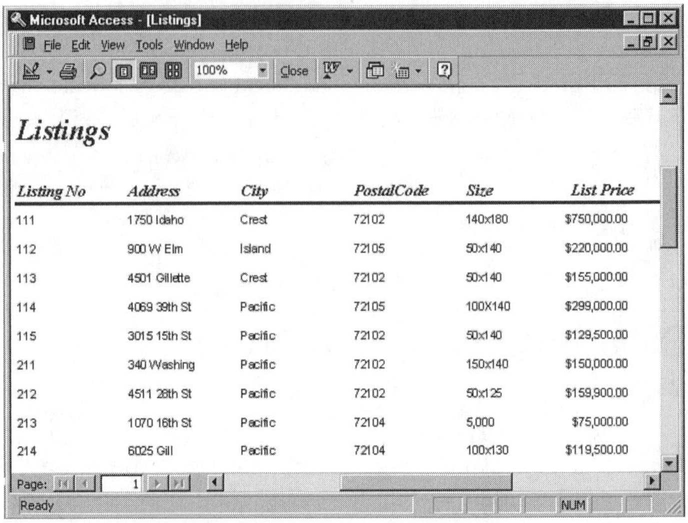

Figure 20.3.

Elgin's Listings table as a report in Access.

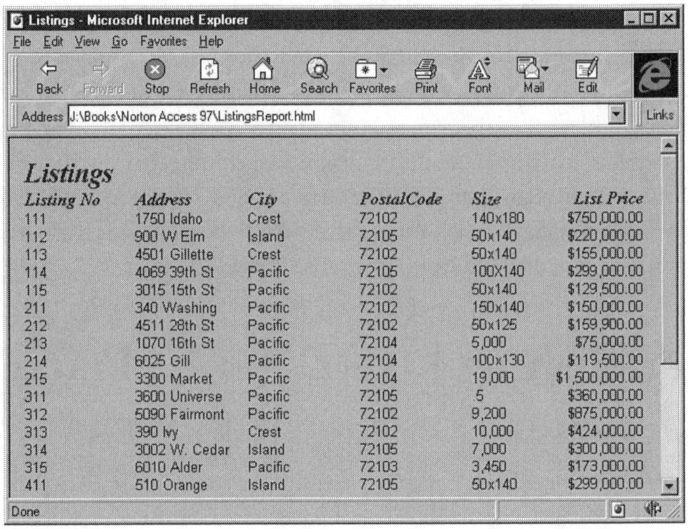

Figure 20.4.

Elgin's Listings table as an HTML page.

It is important, however, to understand that the data presented is the latest at the time the HTML page is created but is not automatically updated to reflect changes. Therefore, the data is more like a snapshot recordset than a dynaset. If you connect to a Web site and request data, you'll get data current as of that moment. Only by refreshing the page will you get any updates to the data. You can also use HTML META tags to automatically refresh the data at some interval, but this is just the same as if the user clicked the Refresh or Reload buttons in the Web browser.

Access supports two ways of publishing live data: Internet Database Connector and Active Server Pages. Both methods require that the pages be hosted on Microsoft's Internet Information Server (IIS).

Internet Database Connector

Access lets you save a table, query, or form datasheet as Internet Database Connector/HTML extension (IDC/HTX) files that generate HTML documents by querying your database located on a Web server.

Here's how to save a table, query, or form datasheet as an IDC/HTX file:

1. In the Database window, select the table, query, or form you want to save.

2. On the File menu, select Save As/Export.

3. In the Save As dialog box, click the To An External File Or Database radio button, and then click OK.

4. In the Save As Type combo box, select Microsoft IIS 1-2 (*.htx/*.idc). The file extension will change to .htx.

5. Enter the filename and directory location where you want to save the file, and then click Export.

6. In the HTML Output Options dialog box, specify the following:

    • The data source name that will be used for a copy of the current database.

    • A user name and password, if required to open the database.

    • An HTML template, if you want Microsoft Access to merge one with the HTML extension (.HTX) file. (See the "Using an HTML Template for Customization" section for more information about using templates.)

    • You can specify any of these items later, except the HTML template, by editing the resulting IDC file in a text editor such as Notepad.

7. Click OK.

When you save Internet Connector files, Access creates two files: an Internet Database Connector (.IDC) file and HTML extension (.HTX) file. These files are used to generate a Web page that displays current data from your database.

An .IDC file contains the necessary information to connect to the Open Database Connectivity (ODBC) data source you entered in the HTML Output Options dialog box and to run an SQL statement that queries the database. When you save the Listings datasheet from the Elgin real-estate database as .IDC/.HTX files, Access creates the following .IDC file:

```
Datasource:Listings DSN
Template:Listings.htx
SQLStatement:SELECT * FROM [Listings]
Password:
Username:
```

Because this .IDC file was created from a table, the SQLStatement entry is a simple SQL statement that selects all the records and fields in the table. Had this been created from an existing Access QueryDef, this entry would contain the full SQL statement underlying the query. Note, however, that because the SQL statement is specified in this file, any user who opens this Web page will receive the results of the same query, reflecting the current recordset that meets the query's specifications. The ODBC "Listings DSN" data source name must exist on the Web server running IIS, allowing an ODBC connection to the listings database.

An .IDC file also contains the name and location of an HTML extension (.HTX) file. The .HTX file is a template for the HTML document; it contains field merge codes that indicate where the values returned by the SQL statement should be inserted. For the Listings table, Access creates the following .HTX file (to save space here, some repetitive lines have been deleted, indicated by an ellipsis):

```
<HTML>
<HEAD>
<META HTTP-EQUIV="Content-Type" CONTENT="text/html;charset=windows-1252">
<TITLE>Listings</TITLE>
</HEAD>
<BODY>
<TABLE BORDER=1 BGCOLOR=#ffffff CELLSPACING=0><FONT FACE="Arial" COLOR=#000000>
<CAPTION><B>Listings</B></CAPTION>

<THEAD>
<TR>
<TH BGCOLOR=#c0c0c0 BORDERCOLOR=#000000 ><FONT SIZE=2 FACE="Arial"
COLOR=#000000>Listing No</FONT></TH>

<TH BGCOLOR=#c0c0c0 BORDERCOLOR=#000000 ><FONT SIZE=2 FACE="Arial"
COLOR=#000000>Type Code</FONT></TH>

<TH BGCOLOR=#c0c0c0 BORDERCOLOR=#000000 ><FONT SIZE=2 FACE="Arial"
COLOR=#000000>Definition</FONT></TH>

...

</TR>
</THEAD>
<TBODY>
<%BeginDetail%>
<TR VALIGN=TOP>
<TD BORDERCOLOR=#c0c0c0 ><FONT SIZE=2 FACE="Arial" COLOR=#000000><%Listing No%>
<BR></FONT></TD>

<TD BORDERCOLOR=#c0c0c0 ><FONT SIZE=2 FACE="Arial" COLOR=#000000><%Type Code%>
<BR></FONT></TD>

<TD BORDERCOLOR=#c0c0c0 ><FONT SIZE=2 FACE="Arial" COLOR=#000000><%Definition%>
<BR></FONT></TD>
```

```
...
</TR>
<%EndDetail%>
</TBODY>
<TFOOT></TFOOT>
</TABLE>
</BODY>
</HTML>
```

The lines in the .HTX file that use the <TH> and <TD> HTML tags format the data in the resulting HTML page sent to the user. The <TH> tag contains the field names for the column headings; you can edit the .HTX file to customize these headings. The <TD> tag contains placeholders for the actual data in the resulting recordset, forming the body of the table in the HTML page.

Microsoft Access saves the .HTX file to be used with an .IDC file with the same name as the .IDC file, except with .HTX and .IDC filename extensions. When a user requests the page from the server, IIS merges the database information into the HTML document and returns it to the user's Web browser. The appearance of the HTML page will be the same as a static page.

To use .IDC/.HTX files, your database and the .IDC/.HTX files must reside on a Microsoft Windows NT Server running Microsoft Internet Information Server or on a computer running Windows 95 or Windows NT Workstation and Personal Web Server. Microsoft Internet Information Server and Personal Web Server use a component called the Internet Database Connector (Httpodbc.dll) to generate Web pages from .IDC/.HTX files.

Internet Database Connector requires ODBC drivers to access a database. To access an Access database, the Microsoft Access Desktop driver (Odbcjt32.dll) must be installed on your Web server. This driver is installed when you install Microsoft Internet Information Server if you select the ODBC Drivers And Administration check box during setup (but it isn't installed with Personal Web Server). If Access is installed on the computer you are using to run Personal Web Server, and if you selected the driver when you installed Microsoft Access, the driver is already available.

After the Access Desktop driver is installed, you must create either a system DSN or a user DSN that specifies the name and connection information for each database you want to use on the server. You then specify that DSN when you generate the .IDC/.HTX files. See the Microsoft Office documentation for more information about ODBC.

Active Server Pages

With Access, you can save a form as an Active Server page that acts much like your form, displaying controls and enabling the user to navigate through the recordset. Access saves most, but not all, controls on the form as ActiveX controls that perform the same or similar functions. Microsoft Access doesn't save or run Visual Basic code behind the form or controls. If you need to duplicate the features of VBA code, you'll need to edit the resulting .ASP file using VBScript. VBScript is a subset of Visual Basic that lets you embed code in a Web page to control how the page is displayed and the data it shows. You can find more information about VBScript at http://www.microsoft.com/vbscript.

To copy the layout of your form as closely as possible, Microsoft Access uses the Microsoft HTML Layout control to position the controls on Active Server pages. (The HTML Layout control is typically installed with Microsoft Internet Explorer.) The resulting page uses a feature of Active Server called *server-side scripting* to connect to a copy of your database on an Internet server.

Users who open a form saved as an Active Server page can browse records, update or delete existing records, and add new records. Figure 20.5 shows an Access form and the equivalent ASP displayed in Internet Explorer. The figure doesn't show it, but Access automatically added navigation, Commit, Delete, and Refresh buttons to the bottom of the HTML page in Figure 20.6.

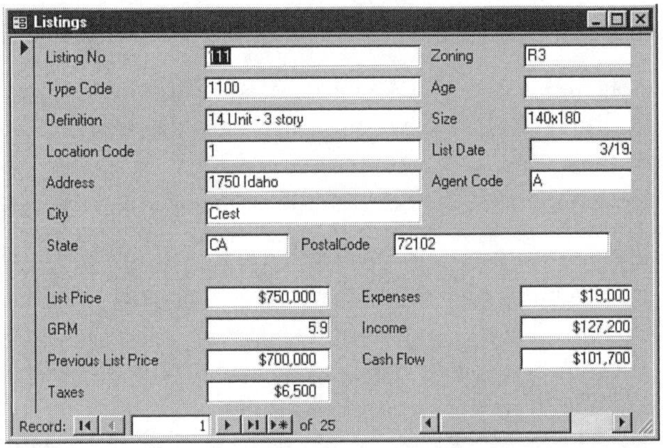

Figure 20.5.
A regular Access form shown in Access.

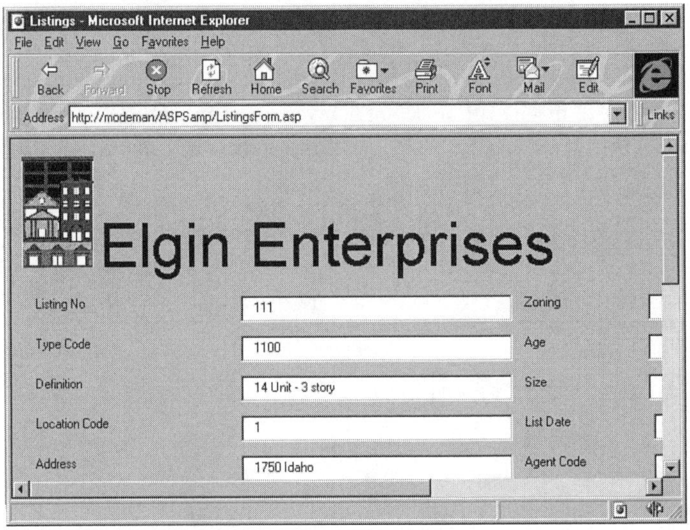

Figure 20.6.
A regular Access form shown as an Active Server Page.

You can also save table, query, and form datasheets as Active Server pages. When you open a datasheet saved as an Active Server page, Microsoft Access displays current data from a copy of your database located on an Internet server, much like .IDC/.HTX files do. However, unlike .IDC/.HTX files, Active Server pages require only one file per datasheet. The ASP file uses AVScript to establish a connection to the database on the server and contains information that it uses to format the datasheet. Unlike a form saved as an Active Server page, users can't update existing records in or add new records to a datasheet saved as an Active Server page.

Here's how to save a form or datasheet as an Active Server page:

1. In the Database window, select the form or datasheet you want to save.

2. On the File menu, select Save As/Export.

3. In the Save As dialog box, click the To An External File Or Database radio button, and then click OK.

4. In the Save As Type box, select Microsoft Active Server (*.asp). The file extension will change to .asp.

5. Enter the filename and directory location where you want to save the file, and then click Export.

6. In the HTML Output Options dialog box, specify the following:

   • The data source name that will be used for a copy of the current database.

   • A user name and password, if required to open the database.

   • An HTML template, if you want Microsoft Access to merge one with the Active Server page.

   • The URL for the server where the Active Server page will reside.

   • The Session Timeout setting, which determines how long a connection to the server is maintained after the user stops working with the Active Server page.

7. Click OK.

This process creates two files, with filenames *YourName*.ASP and *YourNamealx*.ASP. The first file contains the information the Web server needs to display the page and the server-side VBScript code to populate the fields on the form. The second file, with alx added to the filename, contains the code and control information that you'd find in a typical Access form, adapted to VBScript, and use in an HTML page. Both these files, like most Web pages, are text files. You can open them up and see exactly what Access has done.

> **Note:** If the form you save as an Active Server page has its `DefaultView` property set to Single Form or Continuous Forms, the Active Server page displays as a single form, unless it is open in Datasheet view when you use the Save As/Export command. If the form has its `DefaultView` property set to Datasheet, the Active Server page displays as a datasheet. Subforms always display as datasheets, regardless of their `DefaultView` property setting. All field data types are saved unformatted; that is, `Format` and `InputMask` property settings aren't saved.

When Microsoft Access saves a form as an Active Server page, it replaces Microsoft Access controls with ActiveX controls, as described in Table 20.1.

Table 20.1. Controls supported on Active Server pages.

Access Control	ActiveX Control
Text box	Text box.
Text box control bound to a Hyperlink field	Text box that displays the hyperlink text, but the hyperlink can't be followed.
List box	List box (single-column only).
Combo box	Combo box.
Label	Label. If the label has `HyperlinkAddress` and/or `HyperlinkSubAddress` properties set, a hyperlink is created for the label.
Command button	Command button, but any code behind the button isn't saved. If the command button has `HyperlinkAddress` and/or `HyperlinkSubAddress` properties set, a hyperlink is created for the button.
Option group	Option group, but without a group frame.
Option button	Option button.
Check box	Check box.
Toggle button	Toggle button.
ActiveX control	ActiveX control, but any code behind the control isn't saved.

Access doesn't support the following form elements when you save an Access form as an Active Server page:

- Tab controls

- Rectangles

- Lines

- Page breaks

- Unbound object frames

- Bound object frames

- Image controls

- The background of a form set with the `Picture` property

You can, however, edit the resulting `.ASP` file to include the HTML equivalents to these elements. Just remember that you'll have to add them again if you regenerate the HTML code from Access.

To display and use an Active Server page, a copy of your database and Active Server page must reside on a Microsoft Windows NT Server running Microsoft Internet Information Server version 3.0 and Active Server. Active Server pages require the Microsoft Access Desktop driver and a valid DSN to access a database.

Using the Publish to the Web Wizard

Now that you've looked at all the different ways that you can use Access to create HTML pages to publish your data, look at a wizard that makes it easier to do the work. The Publish to the Web Wizard included with Microsoft Office lets you create several HTML pages from the contents of your Access files all at once, saving you the trouble of creating each page individually. The wizard is shown in Figure 20.7.

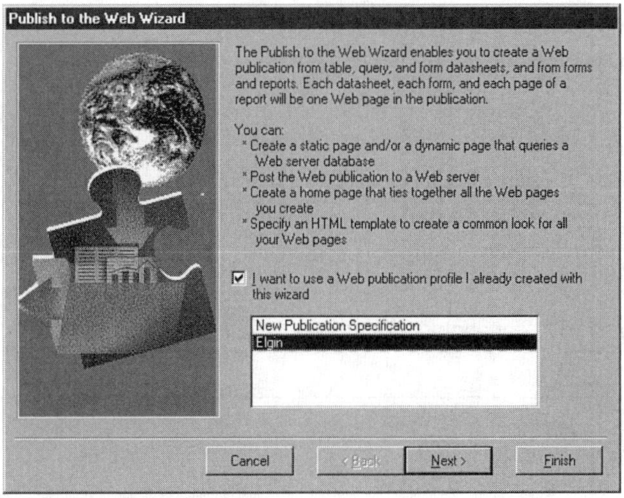

Figure 20.7.
The Microsoft Access 97 Publish to the Web Wizard.

You start the wizard from the File | Save as HTML selection from the Access main menu. If this menu item doesn't appear, you can install the wizard from the `\ValuPack\WebPost` directory on the Office 97 installation CD or download it from Microsoft's Web site.

The wizard has several features that simplify your work:

- Create a Web publication profile to save the selections you make for a particular set of Web pages.
- Pick any combination of tables, queries, forms, or reports to publish.
- Specify an HTML template to use for the selected objects. You can also opt to use different template files for different objects.
- Select to publish the pages as any combination of static HTML documents, `.IDC/.HTX` files, or Active Server pages.
- Create a default home page with links to all the pages you create.
- Automatically move the files that were created by the wizard to a Web server.

Using an HTML Template for Customization

Frankly, the HTML pages produced using any of the preceding methods produce pages that are rather unattractive. However, you can use an HTML template to customize the resulting pages' appearance and give them a consistent look. For example, you can include standard information in a page's header and use a custom background—anything that you can do with a regular HTML page.

You can use an HTML template when you save data as static HTML documents, when you save datasheets as `.IDC/.HTX` files, when you save a form or datasheet as an Active Server page, and when you use the Publish to the Web Wizard.

The HTML template can be any HTML document, a text file that includes HTML tags, and user-specified text and references. The template should include placeholders that tell Microsoft Access where to insert certain pieces of data in the HTML documents. Then, when data is saved as HTML documents, the placeholders are replaced with data. Table 20.2 describes each of the placeholders that you can use in an HTML template.

Table 20.2. Placeholders for Access data in an HTML template.

Placeholder	Location	Description
`<!--AccessTemplate_Title-->`	Between `<TITLE>` and `</TITLE>`	The name of the object being saved

Placeholder	Location	Description
`<!--AccessTemplate_Body-->`	Between `<BODY>` and `</BODY>`	The data or object being saved
`<!--AccessTemplate_FirstPage-->`	Between `<BODY>` and `</BODY>` or after `</BODY>`	An anchor tag to the first page
`<!--AccessTemplate_PreviousPage-->`	Between `<BODY>` and `</BODY>` or after `</BODY>`	An anchor tag to the previous page
`<!--AccessTemplate_NextPage-->`	Between `<BODY>` and `</BODY>` or after `</BODY>`	An anchor tag to the next page
`<!--AccessTemplate_LastPage-->`	Between `<BODY>` and `</BODY>` or after `</BODY>`	An anchor tag to the last page
`<!--AccessTemplate_PageNumber-->`	Between `<BODY>` and `</BODY>` or after `</BODY>`	The current page number

Only the first two placeholders, `<!--AccessTemplate_Title-->` and `<!--AccessTemplate_Body-->`, are used with table, query, and form datasheets. The other placeholders are used with the multiple HTML pages created with multipage reports. If you specify an HTML template that contains placeholders for navigation controls when you save a report as multiple HTML documents, Microsoft Access creates hyperlinks that the user can use to navigate to the first, previous, next, and last pages in the publication. Where Access places the hyperlinks depends on where you locate the placeholders in the HTML template.

Figure 20.8 shows the same static HTML page as Figure 20.1, but using the HTML template `Elgin.htm`. The code in this template controls how the page appears, adding logos and a heading, so that all pages you create using the template will have a similar appearance.

```
<HTML>

<TITLE><!--ACCESSTEMPLATE_TITLE--></TITLE>

<BODY background = sky.jpg>

<IMG SRC = "logor.gif" height=100>
<font FACE="ARIAL,HELVETICA"><font size=10>
Elgin Enterprises<font>

<!--ACCESSTEMPLATE_BODY-->
```

```
</BODY>

<BR><BR>

<IMG SRC = "msaccess.jpg">

</HTML>
```

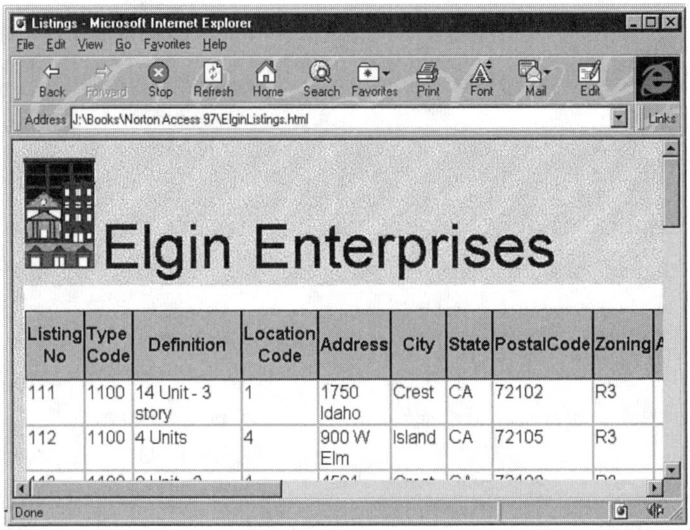

Figure 20.8.
*Elgin's Listings table as a
static HTML page using the*
`Elgin.htm` *template.*

Listing No	Type Code	Definition	Location Code	Address	City	State	PostalCode	Zoning
111	1100	14 Unit - 3 story	1	1750 Idaho	Crest	CA	72102	R3
112	1100	4 Units	4	900 W Elm	Island	CA	72105	R3

When you install Microsoft Access, sample HTML template files and graphics files are installed in the Access subfolder of the Templates folder (by default, at `C:\Program Files\Microsoft Office\Office\Templates\Access`). Looking at these templates is a good way to get a feel for what you can do with templates. You'll also find several `.JPG` image files that you can use for backgrounds, along with the requisite Created with Microsoft Access logo.

Importing and Exporting to HTML

Access 97 expanded its links to the Web by treating HTML pages as just another data source so that you can import and export data. This means that you can treat HTML pages that contain data the same way you treat dBASE, Oracle, or any other data source that you can open directly in Access or through ODBC. This gives you even more ways to obtain and use data over a network.

Importing and Linking Data from HTML

You can import or link data formatted as an HTML table to a Microsoft Access database the same as you can from any database. Because of the nature of HTML files, there are a few differences from using other conventional databases. In order to use the data, Access copies it into the local cache—an area of memory where Windows and applications store data for intermediate use. Whenever you open a linked table, Microsoft Access makes a local copy from the original on the Internet or an intranet before opening it. The data in the table, therefore, is read-only, because there is no mechanism for moving changed data from the cache to the original HTML files. Similarly, if you export the linked HTML table to an HTML file, Microsoft Access exports it to a local file, not the original file on the Internet.

Importing data stores the actual data in the Access database, whereas linking leaves the data where it is but saves information in Access where it can find the data when needed. The steps used to import or link data from HTML tables are similar to those used for other database types:

1. On the Access File menu, select Get External Data, and then click either Import or Link Tables.

2. In the Files Of Type list, select HTML Documents (`*.htm; *.html`).

3. Select the file to import or link from:

    - Use the Look In box and the list of files below it to browse through the file system on your local hard drive or network.

    - In the File Name box, type a valid Internet `http://` or `ftp://` URL. (`http:` searches the Web, and `ftp:` uses the Internet's File Transport Protocol.)

    - In the Look In box, click Internet Locations (FTP) and select a previously defined FTP site. Any FTP site you define here will be available the next time you use this method.

    - In the Look In box, click Add/Modify FTP Locations, and then specify a new FTP site and browse its files.

4. Click Import or Link.

5. Access launches the Import HTML Wizard, using the first table it finds in the HTML file. The rest of the steps in this wizard use the same techniques as importing other types of files, letting you specify whether the first row contains field names, refine the data types of each column, and add a primary key (or let Access do it). You can also opt to append the data to an existing table or create a new table.

When you import or link data from an HTML table, Microsoft Access parses the information contained within standard HTML tag pairs:

- `<TABLE>...</TABLE>`

- `<TH...>...</TH>`

- `<TR...>...</TR>`

- `<TD...>...</TD>`

- `<CAPTION...>...</CAPTION>`

You might have a problem if a table's cell contains anything other than text or an HTML hyperlink. An embedded graphic file uses an HTML <IMG SRC...> tag to identify the image file displayed. This tag may or may not have additional text that would be displayed, such as if the server can't find the file or the user clicks the browser's Stop button before the image is downloaded. If additional text is present, Microsoft Access imports it as the contents of the field, but doesn't import the embedded graphic and the tag that defines it. Access imports anchor tags <A HREF> as hyperlink fields. (See the following sections on hyperlinks for more information.)

HTML tables can contain lists that are embedded within a table cell. Lists in an HTML table cell are formatted with the <LI> and </LI> tags. Microsoft Access inserts a carriage return and line feed (<CR><LF>) after each list item and imports each item in the list as a separate field for that record.

HTML tables can also contain tables that are embedded within a table cell. You can import these as separate tables.

Exporting Data to Locations on the Network or Internet

You can also export Access data directly to an FTP server using Save As/Export from the Access File menu, saving the data as any file type. Note that this is similar to saving the data as HTML files, described earlier in this chapter, but you can put it anywhere on the network or Internet where you have write permission.

Here's how to export data from external data sources on an Internet FTP server:

1. On the File menu, select Save As/Export.

2. In the Save As dialog box, click the To An External File Or Database radio button, and then click OK.

3. In the Save As Type combo box, select the type of file you want to export. Depending on your selection, the Save Formatted and Autostart check boxes may or may not be enabled.

4. To export files on an FTP server, use any of the following methods:

    • In the File Name box, type a valid ftp:// URL.

    • In the Save In box, click Internet Locations (FTP) and select a previously defined FTP site.

    • In the Save In box, click Add/Modify FTP Locations, and then specify a new FTP site and browse its files.

5. Click Export.

Hyperlinks to Web Documents

Access 97 introduced a new data type you can include in any table, Hyperlinks, which lets the user of your application jump to other objects or locations on the network. Hyperlinks can jump to two kinds of objects: a Web page or other content on the Internet or an intranet, or to a Microsoft Office document, such as a Word document, an Excel worksheet, a PowerPoint slideshow, or an Access database stored on a local hard disk or the local network.

> **Tip:** You can create a field with the Hyperlink data type to store hyperlink addresses in a table and then bind that field to a text box on a form. This is useful when you have several different hyperlinks associated with different records in the database. Like other bound fields, as the user moves from record to record, the value in the text box changes to display the current record's hyperlink value. For example, you can use hyperlinks in this way to create an application in which users can jump to Web pages or to other content on the Internet or an intranet from a predefined list of addresses. You can also use hyperlinks in this way to create an application that displays and manages Microsoft Office documents.

If you need to simply provide a way for a user to jump to another location, you can create a label, image control, or command button on a form that references a specified hyperlink address. In this case, the hyperlink doesn't change as you move from record to record. For example, you can use hyperlinks in this way to navigate to other database objects within the same database or to open a Web page on an intranet that contains updated information on how to use your application.

When you include hyperlinks in your applications, you can use the Web toolbar available in all the Office applications to navigate between hyperlinks, just like when you are surfing the Web. Therefore, if the user follows a hyperlink from a Microsoft Access form to open a Microsoft Word document, he or she can click the Back button on the Web toolbar in Microsoft Word to return to the Access form.

The Hyperlinks Data Type

Access 97 introduced Hyperlinks as a native data type so that you can create a field in a table to store hyperlinks as data. To create a Hyperlink field, add a field in the table's Design View and set its DataType property to Hyperlink, just as you add any other new field to a table. Then you can follow a hyperlink stored in a table by clicking it in the table or when it appears in a control on a form.

A Hyperlink field stores up to three pieces of information: the *displaytext*, the *address*, and the *subaddress*. Each piece is separated by the pound sign (#), in the following format:

displaytext#address#subaddress

The *displaytext* portion of the hyperlink is optional. It contains the text the user sees in the Hyperlink field in a table or in a text box bound to the Hyperlink field. This string is typically used as a descriptive name for the Web site or object specified by the address and subaddress. If you do not specify display text, Microsoft Access displays the value of *address* instead.

The *address* is a valid URL that points to a page or file on the Internet or an intranet, or the path to a file on a local hard drive or network. If you enter a path on a network, you can omit a mapped drive letter and use the universal naming convention (UNC) format: \\server\path\filename. (See your network documentation for more information about UNC paths.) This item is required unless the subaddress points to an object in the current Access database file.

A *subaddress* specifies the location within a file or document, such as a form or report in a database. When referring to a database object, the name of the object should be preceded by its type: Table, Query, Form, Report, Macro, or Module. You can also specify a bookmark in a Microsoft Word document, an anchor in an HTML document, a Microsoft PowerPoint slide, or a cell or range in a Microsoft Excel worksheet. This is an optional part of the hyperlink.

Each piece of the Hyperlink field storage format can be up to 2,000 characters. The maximum length of the entire Hyperlink field value is 6,000 characters.

Table 20.3 gives a few examples of valid Hyperlink field values.

Table 20.3. Examples of valid Hyperlink values.

Hyperlink Value	Action When Clicked
#http://www.microsoft.com#	Jumps to the Microsoft home page. Because the display text field isn't used, http://www.microsoft.com appears in the field or text box.

Hyperlink Value	Action When Clicked
`Search Using Excite#http://www.excite.com/#`	Jumps to the Excite search engine. The text `Search Using Excite` appears in the field or text box.
`1996 Sales Report#\\BINKY\Reports\1996Sales.Doc#West`	Opens a Word document, `1996Sales.doc`, located on the local server BINKY, and jumps to the `West` bookmark in the document.
`#j:\Office\samples\northwind.mdb#Form Products`	Opens the Northwind database that ships with Access, located on the `J:` drive, and opens the Products form.
`Products Form##Form Products`	Opens the Products form in the current database, displaying `Products Form` in the field or text box.
`Mortgage Rates#d:\MyDocuments\Rates.xls#[Current Rates]!E15`	Opens the Rates Excel workbook located in the `D:` drive, opens the Current Rates worksheet, and makes E15 the current cell.

Protocols Supported by Access

Access supports an amazing number of protocols in hyperlinks, letting the user jump to almost any location on the local computer, network, or the Internet and opening any kind of file installed in the local Windows Registry. Most hyperlink URLs have to be in the following format:

```
Protocol://Serveraddress/Path
```

Protocol specifies the Internet protocol used to establish the connection to the server and is generally followed by a colon and two slash marks, such as http:// for Web URLs. *Serveraddress* specifies the domain name of the Internet server or the name of the drive containing the desired file. *Path* specifies the location and name of the page or file. Table 20.3 shows several examples.

You can jump to Web pages using http://, FTP file sites with ftp://, CompuServe with cid://, and you can start a Telnet connection with telnet://, and many others. Some of the protocols, such as nntp:// for Internet news and the Telnet protocol, automatically start the client software needed to read newsgroups or use a Telnet connection. For a current list of protocols, search Access Help under "protocols for hyperlinks." This list will no doubt expand over time.

Using Access Hyperlinks

Several of the Access custom controls have HyperlinkAddress and HyperlinkSubAddress properties you can use to specify where to jump or which document to open. These correspond to the address and subaddress elements discussed earlier. When you move the cursor over a command button, image control, or label control whose HyperlinkAddress property is set, the cursor changes to an upward-pointing hand. Clicking the control displays the object or Web page specified by the link. To open objects in the current database, leave the HyperlinkAddress property blank and specify the object type and object name you want to open in the HyperlinkSubAddress property.

Access also provides several other methods and properties for working with hyperlinks in your applications, as listed in Table 20.4.

Table 20.4. Hyperlink methods and properties.

Item	Description
AddToFavorites method	When applied to the Application object, the AddToFavorites method adds a hyperlink address for the current database to the Favorites folder on the local machine. When applied to a Control object, the AddToFavorites method adds the hyperlink address contained in a control.

Item	Description
`Follow` method	Opens the document or Web page specified by a hyperlink address associated with a control on a form or report. It has the same effect as clicking a hyperlink. You don't have to specify the hyperlink as long as the control has the `HyperlinkAddress` or `HyperlinkSubAddress` property set.
`FollowHyperlink` method	Opens the document or Web page specified by a hyperlink address. This is a method of the Access `Application` object, letting you specify a URL to open in code, which doesn't have to be set in a control.
`Hyperlink` property	Returns a reference to the `Hyperlink` object so that you can access the properties and methods of a control that contains a hyperlink.
`HyperlinkPart` function	Returns information about data stored as a Hyperlink data type. Depending on the value you set for the *part* argument in the function, `HyperlinkPart` returns the displayed value, display text, address, or subaddress of the hyperlink.

Summary

This chapter has only touched the surface of all the options that you have to publish your data to the World Wide Web. The good news is that Access 97 provides many options and wizards, freeing you from the drudgery of writing HTML code by hand. At worst, you can fine tune the HTML in the pages that Access generates.

Static Web pages are fine for data that rarely, if ever, changes, and can be displayed on virtually any Web server. But you'll need to use more complex methods if the data changes frequently and the user needs the most up-to-date data available. Publishing live data, however, means that you must use a Web server, such as Microsoft's Internet Information Server, to dynamically generate pages with your data.

VII

Appendixes

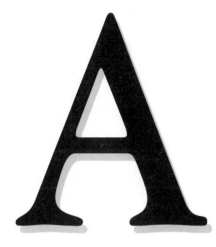

A

What's New in Programming Access 97?

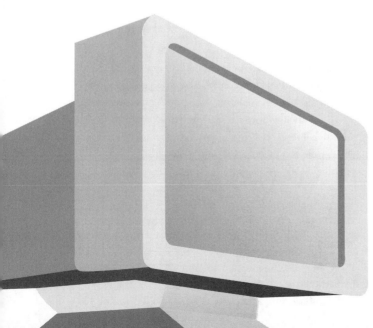

This appendix describes the changes Microsoft has made in the Access programming environment. Improvements in both Access 95 and 97 are discussed. Improvements made to the Access user environment are not addressed in this appendix. It is assumed that readers of this book are already familiar with Access databases and how to create and use them.

What's New for the Programmer?

Access continues to make the development process easier and more fool-proof. With Version 97, new language elements are introduced and others are more uniformly named. Many new features in the module and Debug windows also smooth the way for code generation.

New Language Elements

The following sections describe the new and modified VBA language elements.

New Data Types

Three new VBA data types were introduced in Access 95 for use in declaration statements:

- The *Boolean* data type stores variables as 16-bit (2-byte) numbers but can contain only True (-1) or False (0) values. A Boolean value displays as True or False. When you convert other numeric types to Boolean, a variable with a 0 value converts to False, and all other values convert to True.

- The *Byte* data type stores a single, unsigned 8-bit (1-byte) number between 0 and 255. It is used to store binary data.

- The *Date* data type stores IEEE 64-bit (8-byte) floating-point numbers representing dates. The values can range from 1 January 100 to 31 December 9999. The Time portion of the new Date data type can store times from 0:00:00 to 23:59:59. When you convert other data types to the Date type, values to the left of the decimal are interpreted as date information and values on the right are time values. A 0 represents midnight and .5 translates to noon. Dates before 30 December 1899 are represented by negative whole numbers.

New Events

Four new events were added to Access 95 and an additional four are included in Access 97. The new events from Access 97 are the following:

- The Initialize event applies to a class module and occurs when you create a new instance of that module directly by using the New keyword. It also occurs when you create a new instance of a class indirectly by setting or returning a property or by applying a method defined in a class module.

- The `ItemAdded` event applies to a `References` collection rather than to a form, control, or report. It occurs when a reference is added to the project by VBA, not when you check a reference in the References dialog box. The `ItemAdded` event can run only an event procedure, not a macro.

- The `ItemRemoved` event is similar to the `ItemAdded` event and occurs when a reference is deleted from the `References` collection by a VBA procedure, not by removing it from the list in the References dialog box.

- The `Terminate` event applies to a class module and occurs when all references to an instance of that class are removed from memory. Place the code you want to run when the event occurs in the `Terminate` event procedure for the class module.

The four new events that were introduced in Access 95 are the following:

- The `ApplyFilter` event applies to forms and occurs when the user applies or removes a filter by choosing from a menu or clicking a toolbar button. To respond to the event, run a macro or event procedure attached to the `OnApplyFilter` property. The actions occur before the filter is applied or removed, so this event offers a good way to make sure the filter is correct in time to make changes if it isn't.

- The `Filter` event also applies to forms and occurs when the user opens the Filter By Form or the Advanced Filter/Sort window to create a new filter. Set the `OnFilter` property to run a macro or event procedure when the `Filter` event occurs. The `Filter` event is useful for removing a previous filter or for entering default filter settings.

- The `NoData` event occurs after Access has formatted a report for printing that contains no records (that is, it is bound to an empty recordset). Attach a macro or event procedure to the `OnNoData` property to cancel printing a blank report. The event occurs before the first `Print` and first `Page` events.

- The `Page` event occurs after a page of a report is formatted but before it is printed. It occurs after all the `Format` events for the report have occurred and before the `Print` events begin for the page. You can use this event to run a macro or event procedure that adds a graphic element or border to the page just before printing rather than storing it with the report design.

Changed Property Names

A few properties have new names or different functionality than in previous versions. Although the properties are still accepted for backward compatibility, it is recommended that you use the current properties in your code. The following properties have been changed:

- `AllowEditing` and `DefaultEditing` have been changed to the more specific properties `AllowAdditions`, `AllowDeletions`, `AllowEdits`, and `DataEntry`.

- `MaxButton` and `MinButton` have been combined into `MinMaxButtons`.

- `BorderLineStyle` is now called `BorderStyle`.
- `AllowUpdating` has been changed to `RecordsetType`.
- `Dynaset` is now `RecordsetClone`.
- `ShowGrid` is now `DatasheetGridlinesBehavior`.

Enumerated Constants

Many of the intrinsic constants have been changed or added to create the lists of *enumerated constants* that display in the Auto List Members list. This list is very helpful for selecting arguments for Access methods, functions, and properties as you write code in the module window. You don't have to remember which ones are valid and how to spell them; you can just select from the list.

Each method, function, or property argument has a set of enumerated constants. The name of the set is displayed in the syntax line for the method, function, or property when Auto Quick Info is activated. For example, if you are typing the `OpenReport` method of the `DoCmd` object, the syntax line shows `[View as AcReportView=acViewNormal]` for the `View` argument of the `OpenReport` method. `AcReportView` is the name of the set of enumerated constants, and `acViewNormal` is the default setting for the argument.

The old constants still work. For example, if you used `acNormal` instead of `acViewNormal`, the result would be the same. However, it is good practice to use the most recent names and terminology.

In previous versions, you could leave many arguments blank and Access would insert the default argument. This is still true, but many of the default constants have changed. The exception to this is when you run code from a previous version by using Automation. Arguments left blank will cause an error if they have new default constants.

Table A.1 lists the intrinsic constants that have been added or changed to create the enumerated constants lists. The name of the method, object, or property that includes the argument is shown in the list as well as the name of the argument itself.

Table A.1. New and changed intrinsic constants.

Language Element	Argument	Old Constant	New Constant
Close method	save	acPrompt	acSavePrompt
Close method	objecttype	(none)	acDefault
CopyObject method	sourceobjecttype	(none)	acDefault
DeleteObject method	objecttype	(none)	acDefault
GoToRecord method	objecttype	acTable	acDataTable
GoToRecord method	objecttype	acQuery	acDataQuery

Language Element	Argument	Old Constant	New Constant
GoToRecord method	objecttype	acForm	acDataForm
GoToRecord method	objecttype	(none)	acActiveDataObject
OpenForm method	datamode	acAdd	acFormAdd
OpenForm method	datamode	acEdit	acFormEdit
OpenForm method	datamode	acReadOnly	acFormReadOnly
OpenForm method	datamode	(none)	acFormProperty Settings
OpenForm method	windowmode	acNormal	acWindowNormal
OpenQuery method	view	acNormal	acViewNormal
OpenQuery method	view	acDesign	acViewDesign
OpenQuery method	view	acPreview	acViewPreview
OpenReport method	view	acNormal	acViewNormal
OpenReport method	view	acDesign	acViewDesign
OpenReport method	view	acPreview	acViewPreview
OpenTable method	view	acNormal	acViewNormal
OpenTable method	view	acDesign	acViewDesign
OpenTable method	view	acPreview	acViewPreview
OutputTo method	objecttype	acTable	acOutputTable
OutputTo method	objecttype	acQuery	acOutputQuery
OutputTo method	objecttype	acForm	acOutputForm
OutputTo method	objecttype	acReport	acOutputReport
OutputTo method	objecttype	acModule	acOutputModule
Quit method (DoCmd)	options	acPrompt	acQuitPrompt
Quit method (DoCmd)	options	acSaveYes or acSave	acQuitSaveAll
Quit method (DoCmd)	options	acSaveNo or acExit	acQuitSaveNone
Quit method (Application)	options	acPrompt	acQuitPrompt
Quit method (Application)	options	acSaveYes or acSave	acQuitSaveAll
Quit method (Application)	options	acExit	acQuitSaveNone

continues

Table A.1. continued

Language Element	Argument	Old Constant	New Constant
Rename method	objecttype	(none)	acDefault
RepaintObject method	objecttype	(none)	acDefault
Save method	objecttype	(none)	acDefault
SendObject method	objecttype	acTable	acSendTable
SendObject method	objecttype	acQuery	acSendQuery
SendObject method	objecttype	acForm	acSendForm
SendObject method	objecttype	acReport	acSendReport
SendObject method	objecttype	acModule	acSendModule
SendObject method	objecttype	(none)	acSendNoObject
TransferSpreadsheet method	spreadsheettype	(none)	acSpreadsheetTypeExcel3
TransferSpreadsheet method	spreadsheettype	(none)	acSpreadSheetTypeExcel4
TransferSpreadsheet method	spreadsheettype	(none)	acSpreadsheetTypeExcel5
TransferSpreadsheet method	spreadsheettype	(none)	acSpreadsheetTypeExcel7
TransferSpreadsheet method	spreadsheettype	(none)	acSpreadsheetTypeExcel97
TransferSpreadsheet method	spreadsheettype	(none)	acSpreadsheetTypeLotusWK1
TransferSpreadsheet method	spreadsheettype	(none)	acSpreadsheetTypeLotusWK3
TransferSpreadsheet method	spreadsheettype	(none)	acSpreadsheetTypeLotusWJ2 (Japanese version only)
TransferSpreadsheet method	spreadsheettype	(none)	acSpreadsheetTypeLotusWK4
TransferText method	transfertype	(none)	acImportHTML
TransferText method	transfertype	(none)	acExportHTML
TransferText method	transfertype	(none)	acLinkHTML

Language Element	Argument	Old Constant	New Constant
HyperlinkPart function	part	(none)	acAddress
HyperlinkPart function	part	(none)	acDisplayedValue
HyperlinkPart function	part	(none)	acDisplayName
HyperlinkPart function	part	(none)	acSubAddress
Type property	[setting]	(none)	acClassModule
Type property	[setting]	(none)	acStandardModule

Automation

What was formerly known as OLE Automation is now called simply Automation. Access is an *ActiveX component*, an application that can use objects supplied by another component and can make its own objects available to another. These applications were previously called OLE Automation servers and controllers.

In Access, you can set a reference to another component's type library to view the objects from that library in the Object Browser. You can also view the objects' methods and properties. This improves performance when working with objects in another application. Conversely, the other ActiveX component can also view the objects in the Access type library.

See Chapter 17, "Linking with Other Office Applications," for more information on working with Access objects through Automation and ActiveX controls.

Writing and Debugging VBA Code

The programming environment is a critical factor in successfully creating complete and accurate VBA code. Improvements in the design windows and the Object Browser go a long way in assisting the developer with code generation.

The Module Window

Several new module window improvements were introduced in Access 95 and still more in Access 97, including new debugging options, new menu items, and code options such as color-coding and text formatting.

The Module tab of the Options dialog box contains the following new options added in Access 97 (see Figure A.1):

- *Auto List Members*, which displays a list of valid choices as you enter a statement. As you type the name of the object, Access automatically tries to fill in the complete word for you by displaying a list of objects, methods, or properties that could follow the name of the object you have already entered.

- *Auto Quick Info*, which displays syntax information when you type a procedure or method name. The current element you are entering appears in bold in the syntax statement.

- *Auto Data Tips*, which shows the current value of a variable when you pause the mouse pointer on the variable name. Procedure must be in the break mode to see it.

- Choosing the *Drag-And-Drop Text Editing* option lets you use that technique to move selected text to a new location.

- With the *Debug Window on Top* option set, the Debug window remains on top of all open windows in the current session. This is useful for watching how the values of the variables and expressions change as you step through code.

- The *Margin Indicator Bar* shows symbols in the left margin that mark the line of code as a breakpoint or a bookmark.

Figure A.1.
New options have been added to the Module tab of the Options dialog box.

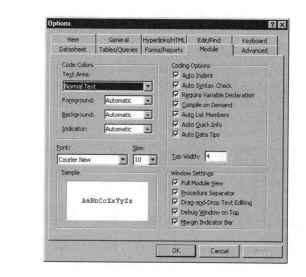

The Advanced tab of the Options dialog box has a new group of options for error trapping (see Figure A.2). Most of them are new in Access 97, but one of them, Break on All Errors, was included in the Module tab in Version 95 and was moved to the Advanced tab for Access 97. These new options determine how VBA enters break mode when an error occurs. The options are as follows:

- *Break on All Errors* does just what it says: it breaks on all handled and unhandled errors in all modules, either class or standard. The module that contains the error appears in the Debug window with the offending line highlighted.

- *Break in Class Module* is useful for debugging class modules. This option breaks on all unhandled errors in both class and standard modules. If the error is in a class module, the module becomes active in the Debug window, and the line with the error is highlighted in the module window.

- *Break on Unhandled Errors* breaks on unhandled errors in a standard module. If the error is in a class module, VBA breaks on the line that called the class module containing the error rather than on the line in the class module that contains the error.

- The *Project Name* option lets you assign a name to the current project other than the database name. The project name can be used to reference the application.

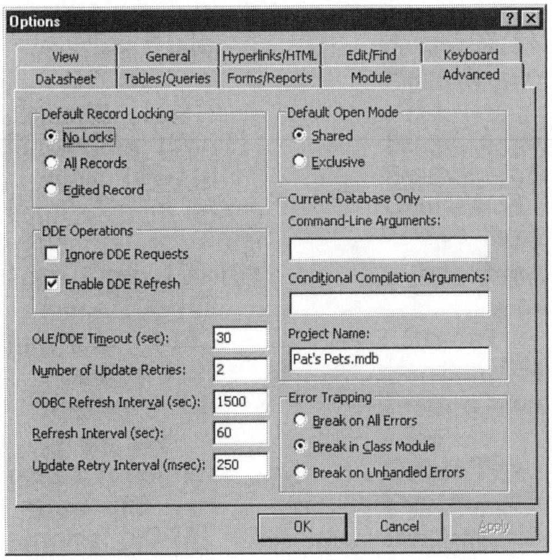

Figure A.2.
New options have been added to the Advanced tab of the Options dialog box.

The new Debug menu, available when you are in module design view, contains some of the items that were on the Run menu or the Tools menu in Access 95 as well as the following three new commands:

- The *Compile And Save All Modules* command compiles all the modules in the current project and saves them as compiled code.

- The *Step Into* command lets you step through the current procedure in the module window without suspending execution.

- The *Step Out* command quickly runs all the code in procedures that are nested within the calling procedure. Then it returns to the next higher procedure, the one that called the procedure containing the Step Out command. This command saves time if you don't need to step through a group of nested procedures that are already checked out.

Other menu additions in Access 97 include the following:

- The *Select All* command (Edit menu) selects all the text in the current procedure, or in the current module if you are in full module view. This is handy for copying a procedure to the Clipboard to paste the code into another procedure or module.

- You can use the *Find Next* command (Edit menu) to locate the next occurrence of the string you specified in the Find command.

- Choosing *Complete Word* (Edit menu) displays a list of functions, methods, and properties that you can choose from to complete a word of code.

- Choosing *Definition* (View menu) after selecting a keyword in the module window opens the Object Browser to show the definition of the keyword.

- With the *Go/Continue* command (Run menu) you can run a procedure from the module window instead of having to enter the procedure name in the Debug window.

Note: Module window improvements include Access 95 customized color-coded syntax and formatting options that were added to the Module tab of the Options dialog box. The *line continuation character* has also been added so that you can indicate that a long line of code continues on the next line in the window by entering a space followed by the underscore character.

Other options new with Access 95 are the following:

- *Full Module View*, which allows you to view an entire module instead of a single procedure. This is set in the Module tab.

- *Require Variable Declaration*, when set, requires that you explicitly declare all variables used in the module. This is also set in the Module tab.

- You can type the value you want the `Command` function to return by typing the arguments in the *Command-Line Arguments* line in the Advanced tab. This has the same effect as a `/Cmd` command-line option.

- Another option on the Advanced tab of the Options dialog box is the *Conditional Compilation Arguments* line in which you specify which parts of the module you want to include in the compilation and which to ignore.

New menu items were also available in the Access 95 module design window:

- The *Quick Watch* feature, available from the Debug menu, opens a dialog box that displays the current value of the selected variable or expression.

- *Show Next Statement* and *Show Previous Statement* are new Debug menu items available when execution is suspended. The two commands allow you to back up and run a line of code again or to skip over parts of the code.

- The *Last Position* command on the View menu lets you return the cursor to the previous position in the previous procedure.

- With the *References* command on the Tools menu, you can make procedures available to other databases by establishing a reference to them in the References dialog box.

- *End*, *Reset*, and *Go/Continue* are available as buttons on the Visual Basic toolbar as well as on the Run menu.

Other improvements to the module window include the Objects and Procedures boxes. The Objects pull-down list displays all the objects in the current database, and the Procedures list shows all the procedures that can be or have been created to the selected object. Existing procedures appear in bold in the list.

The Debug Window

The Access 97 Debug window has a new pane: the Locals pane, which alternates with the Watch pane while the Immediate pane remains visible. The Locals pane displays a list of variables such as user-defined types, arrays, and objects. In addition to the variable name or expression, the Locals pane shows its current value and type. The variables that contain hierarchical information appear with an expand/collapse button (+) to the left of the name that you can click to see the full tree.

The values in the Locals pane are automatically updated when you change the execution mode from run to break, such as when the code reaches a breakpoint or when you start a step-through.

The Watch and Immediate panes were introduced in Access 95. You can use the Watch pane to see the value of a variable or an expression while code is running. You can edit values in place in either the Locals or Watch pane. The Immediate pane is used to run sub or function procedures. Unless you are in break mode, you must fully qualify the procedure with the name of the class module that contains it.

The Object Browser

The Object Browser, new with Access 95, is used to display information about the objects, methods, and constants in the current project and in any referenced object libraries (see Figure A.3). The information includes definitions of the objects and their properties, methods, events, and constants, in addition to information about related functions and statements. The information is grouped into class modules and standard modules, which are listed in the Classes box. The related methods, properties, events, and constants of each object are listed in the Members Of box.

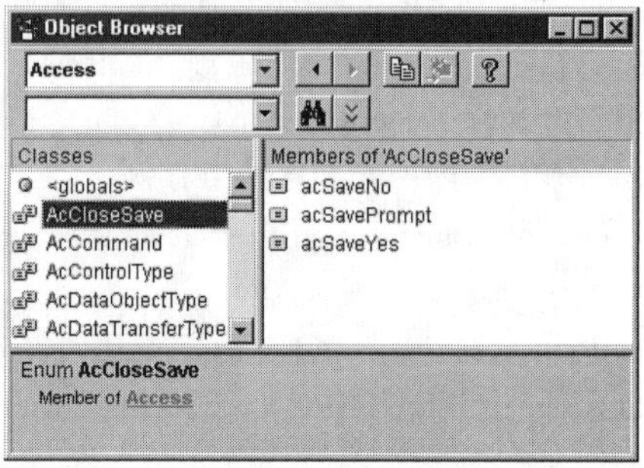

Figure A.3.
The Object Browser has new features.

New features that were added to the Object Browser for Access 97 include the following:

- The special <globals> item appears at the top of the Classes list for each library. When selected, the Members Of box shows all the members that can be accessed globally, including constants.

- A new search feature allows you to search a library for any class or member. Type the text to search for in the Search Text box then click the Search button. After the search is completed, click the two downward chevrons to see the results.

- The Object Browser toolbar includes a new Copy To Clipboard button that you can use to paste code into your module. Select the method or property and click the button; then switch to the module window, position the cursor, and click Paste on the Visual Basic toolbar in the module window.

- To get help with any object, method, property, or event in the Object Browser, select the name and then click the Help button on the Object Browser toolbar, or press F1.

- To see the definition of a user-defined procedure, select the name of the project that contains the procedure from the Project/Library list. Then select the module name from the Classes box and the procedure name from the Members Of list. Finally, click the View Definition button on the Object Browser toolbar. The module window opens, displaying the procedure showing the insertion point in the procedure.

- Two other buttons on the Object Browser toolbar let you navigate through the elements you have previously viewed. Go Back takes you to the previous element; Go Forward returns you to the element you just came from.

The enumerated constants are grouped in the Classes list and appear right after the <globals> item. The names of the enumerated constants all begin with Ac, and the constants that are members of that class all begin with ac. You can also tell what kind of element you are looking at by the icon that appears just to the left of the name. Enumerated constants are marked with a pair of overlapping yellow rectangles, and constants have a single gray rectangle.

Arguments and Parameters

When you pass arguments to a sub or function procedure, you have a choice between passing them by position or by name. Before Access 95, you could only pass the arguments in the order they appeared in the procedure definition. If you chose not to pass optional arguments, you still had to include the comma separators so that Access would know the argument was missing.

The new option of passing arguments by name eliminates the need for the extra commas. For example, the sub procedure CallCust uses four arguments: strArg1, intArg2, dteArg3, and blnArg4:

```
Sub CallCust(strArg1 As String, intArg2 As Integer, dteArg3 As Date, blnArg4 As Boolean)
```

You can call the CallCust procedure by passing the arguments positionally with the following statement typed in the Debug window:

```
CallCust "George Beckman", 54, #10/25/97#, True
```

Or by name as in this statement:

```
CallCust intArg2:=54, dteArg3:=#10/25/97#, blnArg4:=True, strArg1:="George Beckman"
```

> **Tip:** Optional arguments are preceded by the keyword Optional in the procedure statement. Using named arguments also helps you keep track of which arguments you have passed and which optional arguments you skipped.

You can pass an array of arguments to a procedure by using the keyword ParamArray. You don't have to know how many elements are in the array when you define the procedure. The array must be the last argument in the series and must be declared as Variant data type. The following statements show an example of passing a parameter array as an argument and using a For...Next loop to print each element until the upper bound is reached:

```
Sub GameScores(strTeam As String, ParamArray varFinal() As Variant)
Dim intN As Integer
Debug.Print strTeam, "Final"
For intN = 0 To Ubound(varFinal())
    Debug.Print " "; varFinal(intN)
Next intN
End Sub
```

You can call this procedure with either of the following statements:

```
GameScores "USC", 24, 16, 43, 79, 36
GameScores "USC", "Great", "Mediocre", "Strong", "Dismal", "Improving"
```

Developer Edition Tools

The Access Source Code Control component of the Office 97 Developer Edition (ODE) is a tool for developing an application in a team environment. When several programmers are working on the same project, confusion can set in if the code is not strictly managed. The source code control program can keep track of and store changes to the programs during development.

The key feature of a source code control program is the check out process. When a programmer wants to make a change to one of the application objects, she must check it out from the source code control project.

The source code control project is not the same as the development project. The source code control project is a collection of files and objects stored centrally in the source code control program. When you check an object out to work on it, it is not removed from the source code control project. The development project is a copy of the object in your local workstation that you can change. The object in the source code control project is locked and not available to others until you check it back in. When you do check it back in, the changes you have made are copied to the object stored in the source code control project.

The Microsoft Visual SourceSafe is one of the source code control providers available on the market. The basic process of developing an application in a multideveloper atmosphere is as follows:

1. Create the new Access 97 database.

2. Create the forms, reports, queries, modules, and other objects for the new database. As you save each one, the source code control provider asks if you want to add it to the source code control project.

3. After the objects are checked into the source code control project, a programmer must check them in and out from within Access.

4. To change an object, check it out of the source code control, make the changes in Access, and then check it back in to copy the changes to the source code control project. While you have it in your local project, no one else can make any changes to it.

Improvements in Runtime Performance

Many new features have been added to both Access 95 and 97 that speed up loading, compiling, and running a database. Improvements have also been made in the Jet database engine Version 3.5 and the DAO connection that optimize the performance of your Access projects.

Loading and Compilation

Forms and reports open much faster in Access 97 because they no longer load the associated class module unless it contains event procedures for the form or report. When you create a new form or report, it doesn't automatically have a module associated with it. As a result, your project may have fewer modules to compile, and each form or report without a module will load more quickly than those with modules.

In addition, Access doesn't load a form or report module until the VBA code in the module is executed. This also improves project performance. In Access 95, when you ran a procedure in one module, all the modules that could be called by a procedure in the first module were loaded but not compiled until a procedure within them was called. Access 97 loads modules only when needed. For this reason, you can help improve your database performance by grouping procedures in modules with other procedures that they call instead of having them call procedures in unrelated modules.

Access 97 does a better job of managing the compiled state of your database modules. All code is kept compiled unless you make a change in the module. Then, only the code you have changed and any code that depends on it is uncompiled. The rest remains compiled.

The new Compile On Demand option, available in the Module tab of the Options dialog box, can improve performance. When this option is selected, Access doesn't compile a module until it is loaded for execution. If this option is not selected, an uncompiled module is compiled when a module that contains a procedure that calls one in the uncompiled module is loaded, whether the call is ever made or not. You can improve performance by keeping the Compile On Demand option selected. Better yet, keep all your modules stored in a compiled state by using the new Compile And Save All Modules option in the Debug menu.

Also, Access no longer loads software components such as VBA and DAO until the database needs them. As a result, your database loads quicker and its overall performance is improved.

Processing Speed

The performance of several controls has been improved in both Access 95 and 97. Embedded ActiveX controls and combo boxes work much faster in Access 97 than in earlier versions. You can now display unbound pictures in forms and reports much faster as image controls instead of unbound object frames. Report previewing also goes faster because the Error, Focus, Print, and Window events are triggered only the first time you page through the report.

The Performance Analyzer, introduced in Access 95, is a wizard that looks over your database objects and makes suggestions as to how you can speed up your processing. You can select any or all of the database objects you want to optimize. To use the Performance Analyzer, follow these steps:

1. Choose Tools | Analyze | Performance. The Performance Analyzer dialog box opens showing eight tabs: one for each type of database object and one for all objects (see Figure A.4).

2. Click the tab of the type of object you want to optimize, or click All.

3. Select the names of the objects you want the Analyzer to examine and click Select or click Select All.

4. Open another tab to select from other object lists and click OK. After a few moments, the Performance Analyzer results dialog box opens.

Figure A.4.

Choose the objects you want analyzed in the Performance Analyzer dialog box.

Figure A.5 shows the results of analyzing all objects in the Pat's Pets database. The Analyzer displays four categories of results: Recommendation, Suggestion, Idea, and Fixed. When you select one in the list, information about it is displayed in the Analysis Notes box below the list. The Performance Analyzer can perform a Recommendation or Suggestion optimization if you select it and click Optimize. You have to carry out the Idea optimizations yourself. These optimization suggestions apply only to your database, not to Access itself or your system.

Figure A.5.

The Performance Analyzer offers optimization tips.

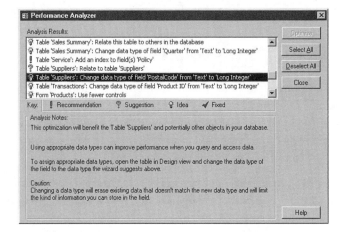

You can run bulk update or delete queries against an Object Database Connectivity (ODBC) source such as the SQL Server, which processes all the appropriate records at once instead of one at a time. The new FailOnError property specifies whether to stop processing if an error occurs.

With the property set to Yes, the query will be sent to the server if it executes against a single table and doesn't contain any expression that the server can't evaluate. An error terminates the query, and the table is rolled back to its original state. If FailOnError is set to No, the query runs against local data and works the same as in earlier versions. Errors don't stop the query; when the query is completed, the reason for any error is displayed with the number of records that are affected. You can then accept the query results or roll back any changes.

Database Replication

Database replication was introduced in Access 95 and provides a method of enabling users in different physical locations to share a database. Each user works on his or her own copy of the database and shares or synchronizes the changes he or she makes with the other users.

Partial replicas are special copies of the database that contain only a subset of records from the full replica. There are several advantages to using partial replicas. They make your local database effectively smaller because you need only those portions you work with frequently. It also takes less time to synchronize a partial replica, and less disk space is required. Partial replicas can also improve security in a database by excluding sensitive information from the replica.

See Chapter 18, "Working in a Multiuser Environment," for more information about creating and using database replicas.

Jet Database Engine Improvements

The Jet database engine version 3.5 contains many improvements over version 3.0, which is used with Access 95, and over the version used with Access 1.x and 2.0. Some of the enhancements over the 3.0 version that improve performance are the following:

- Large queries run faster because of new Registry settings and improvements in the SQL statements. The MaxLocksPerFile setting forces transactions to commit when the lock threshold is reached. Use the SetOption DAO method to override the setting at runtime and improve performance in NetWare and Windows NT–based server environments.

- The engine now allows users to create partial replications of tables by placing row restrictions on the table. Partial replication uses two types of filters: Boolean and relationship. A Boolean filter selects only those rows that meet the criteria and is represented by the ReplicaFilter property of a table definition. The relationship filter applies to related tables and enforces a relationship between two partially replicated tables. Setting the PartialReplica property of a relation object allows that relation to be used in partial replication.

- Indexed table field columns improve multiuser access to a table. More users can update indexed columns and avoid locking conflicts.

- The Jet database engine can now allocate up to 64KB of disk space at a time, which speeds up sequential read operations.

- Temporary queries and queries that contain an inequality operator (<>) in a criterion run faster.

Some improvements over the version 1.x and 2.0 environments are as follows:

- The new index structure requires less storage space and lessens the time required to create indexes on two or more fields. When a database is compacted, the indexes are updated and optimized for better performance. Compact the database regularly to take advantage of this optimization.

- When you use a `Delete` operation, portions of the page are removed all at once instead of a row at a time.

- Improvements in the engine's page allocation algorithm makes it more likely that data from the same table will be stored in adjacent pages.

- The engine is multithreaded so that one thread reads ahead while another writes behind. In addition, a dynamically configured cache is included that bases the size of the cache depending on the amount of memory available at startup.

- The Jet database engine has built-in implicit transactions that take the place of the explicit `BeginTrans` and `CommitTrans` methods. This can speed up transaction processing. Revert to the explicit methods when writing data to disk so that you have control over the write operation.

- A new sorting mechanism improves sorting performance.

DAO Connection and ODBCDirect

The new version of DAO Version 3.5 includes a new client/server connection mode that establishes a connection with an ODBC data source without using the Jet database engine. ODBCDirect is helpful when you need to use specific ODBC features.

ODBCDirect offers several advantages for ODBC operations:

- The direct access to ODBC data sources makes your code run faster and more efficiently because it does not need to load the Jet database engine.

- You have improved access to server-specific features, such as cursor specification, as well as improved interaction with stored procedures at the server level.

- You can run asynchronous queries and also run other operations without waiting for the query to finish.

- With batch updating, changes are cached locally and then sent to the server in a single batch.

- You can create simple result sets or more complex cursors for running queries. You can create a query to return any number of result sets and limit the number of rows to be returned.

The `Connection` object is the connection to an ODBC database, and it contains information about the connection to an ODBC data source. It is similar to a database object on an ODBC data source; both represent different references to the same object. The new properties of both let you have a reference to the other object, which simplifies converting existing client applications from the Jet engine to the ODBCDirect server.

A new batch update cursor can be used by client applications. This allows them to store update information on many records in a batch and update them all at once instead of updating each record one at a time. Collisions can occur during the time lag between opening a recordset for updating and sending the updates back to the server. Other users can get in and change the original data before the changes are received by the server, so your changes collide with those of other users. Some new features help identify where collisions have occurred and help you resolve them.

The `dbRunAsync` option, which can be used with the `Execute`, `MoveLast`, `OpenConnection`, and `OpenRecordset` methods, allows the client to run the update in the background while carrying out other tasks.

Table A.2 describes the new methods and properties included in the new DAO 3.5 interface with ODBCDirect.

Table A.2. New interfaces with ODBCDirect.

Method or Property	Applies To	Description
`Cancel` method	Connection QueryDef Recordset	Cancels execution of an asynchronous operation.
`NextRecordset` method	Recordset	Retrieves next set of records returned by a query that resulted in multiple sets of records and indicates whether it was successful.
`OpenConnection` method	Workspace	Opens connection object on an ODBC data source.
`BatchCollisionCount` property	Recordset	Returns the number of records that were not completed during the last batch update.
`BatchCollisions` property	Recordset	Returns an array of bookmarks showing the rows that caused collisions during last batch update.

continues

Table A.2. continued

Method or Property	Applies To	Description
BatchSize property	Recordset	Sets or returns the number of statements sent back to the server in each batch.
Connection property	Recordset	Returns the connection object that corresponds to the database or owns the recordset.
Database property	Connection	Returns the name of the database object corresponding to the connection.
DefaultCursorDriver property	Workspace	Sets or returns the type of cursor driver used for recordset objects.
DefaultType property	DBEngine	Shows what type of workspace will be created by the next CreateWorkspace method call.
Direction property	Parameter	Indicates whether a parameter object is input, output, or both, or if it is returned from a stored procedure.
MaxRecords property	QueryDef	Sets or returns the maximum number of records to return from the query.
OriginalValue property	Field	Returns the value of a field that existed when the last batch update began.
Prepare property	QueryDef	Returns a value that indicates whether a query is to be prepared and stored or executed directly.
RecordStatus property	Recordset	Returns the update status of the current record if it is part of the batch update.
StillExecuting property	Connection	Returns a value that indicates whether the asynchronous operation is finished.
UpdateOptions property	Recordset	Returns a value that indicates how the WHERE clause is defined and how the update is to be executed.
VisibleValue property	Recordset	Returns a value in the database that is newer than the OriginalValue, as compared by a batch update conflict.

DAO 3.5 also has new interfaces with the Jet database engine, as described in Table A.3.

Table A.3. New interfaces with the Jet database engine.

Method or Property	Applies To	Description
`PopulatePartial` method	Database	Synchronizes changes in a partial replica with the full replica. Clears the partial replica and repopulates the partial replica based on the current replica filters.
`SetOption` method	DBEngine	Overrides Registry values for the duration of the current instance of DAO.
`FieldSize` property	Field	Replaces the `FieldSize` method.
`MaxRecords` property	QueryDef	Sets or returns maximum number of records to return from query.
`ReplicaFilter` property	TableDef	Returns a value that indicates which subset of records is replicated in this partial replica from a full replica.
`PartialReplica` property	Relation	Indicates which relation object is to be used when populating a partial replica from a full replica.

The ODBCDirect to Jet engine interface is necessary for several reasons. They provide different but complimentary functionality. To access `.mdb` files and ISAM data formats, you must use a Jet workspace. The Jet engine also has some unique capabilities that ODBCDirect does not have. For example, if you have recordset objects based on multiple-table joins or joins from different data sources, you must update them in a Jet workspace. All DDL operations using DAO must also be performed in a Jet workspace. In addition, if any of your forms or controls are bound to data in an ODBC data source, you must use Jet to access them.

You can mix and match Jet and ODBCDirect workspaces in your application and use the capabilities of both as necessary.

More New Developer Tools in Access 95 and 97

Several new tools have broadened Access's development capabilities. Class modules are no longer exclusively associated with a form or report. They can be used to define new classes of objects. Forms can now contain several tabs by means of the new tab control. Access 97 includes command bars that are programmable toolbars and menu bars you can design for an application.

Class Modules

In previous versions, class modules existed only in association with a form or report. In Access 97, you can create a new class module that defines a custom object. The module name you assign when you save the module becomes the name of the new object. The public sub and function procedures in the module become the methods of the object and the public `PropertyLet`, `PropertyGet`, and `PropertySet` procedures become the object's properties.

After defining the procedures in the new class module, you can create a new instance of the object by declaring a variable of the type defined by the class. For example, suppose you have created a new class named `FirstClass`. You can create a new instance of it with the following statement using the `New` keyword:

```
Dim fst As New FirstClass
```

This code creates a new instance of the `FirstClass` class object, whose methods and properties you can apply by using the `fst` variable.

In Access 95, you are able to create a default instance of a form class object. The *default instance* is a memory location where the object exists and from which you can call its methods and set or return its properties. When you work with a form, you are usually working with its default instance. If you create multiple instances of the form's class, these are nondefault instances. A form's class has only one default instance.

You would create multiple nondefault instances of a form's class if you needed to display more than one instance of the form at a time (perhaps showing different areas of the form in separate windows). A nondefault instance of a form is not visible until you set its `Visible` property to `Yes`. A nondefault instance of a form cannot be referred to by name; you must use its index number.

Tabbed Forms

Adding a tab control to a form design lets you group related sets of controls together on a single page. The individual pages in the tab control are the page objects in the pages collection. Each page in turn has its own set of controls that are contained in the controls collection. See Chapter 12, "Customizing Data Entry," for an example of using a tab control to create a three-page form.

Command Bars

With the new programmable command bars, you can create special toolbars and menu bars for your application. Before you can program with command bars, you must set a reference to the Microsoft Office 8.0 object library in the References dialog box (Tools | References).

All the existing command bars are included in the command bar collection. Each command bar has, in turn, a set of controls in a controls collection. These controls differ from those you add to forms. They include buttons, combo boxes, and pop-up boxes that can be combined on a single command bar.

The code in Listing A.1 creates a new command bar named CommandBar and sets its Visible property to True so you can see it. Next, the code creates a single button named Button1 and attaches a MsgBox function to the OnAction property of the new button.

Listing A.1. Creating a command bar with code.

```
Sub BuildBar()
Dim cmb As CommandBar
Dim cbc As CommandBarControl

Set cmb = Application.CommandBars.Add("CommandBar")
cmb.Visible = True
Set cbc = cmb.Controls.Add(msoControlButton)
cbc.Caption = "Button1"
cbc.Style = msoButtonCaption

CommandBars("CommandBar").Controls("Button1").OnAction = _
    "=MsgBox(""Good Job!"")"

End Sub
```

Figure A.6 shows the results of running the procedure and clicking the command button.

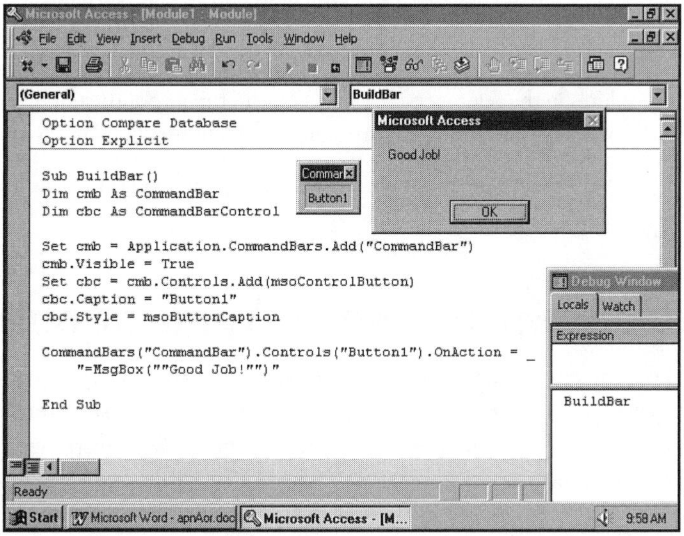

Figure A.6.
Creating a new command bar.

You can add custom captions to both the command bar and the controls in it to accommodate the activities of your application.

New Outside Connections

When you want to use objects from another application, you set a reference to that application's type library. You can set references to a project in another Access database or to a type library in another Office application such as Excel or Word.

Many new features in Access give you an entry into the Internet where you can publish your own Web page, import or link information from an HTML file, and export datasheets and forms to HTML format.

References to Type Libraries

To set a reference from Access, choose Tools | References and set the reference in the References dialog box. To set a reference from VBA code, you create a new `Reference` object by using the `AddFromFile` or `AddFromGUID` method of the `References` collection. If you want to remove a reference that is no longer useful, use the `Remove` method.

There are many advantages to setting references, including faster execution of your Automation code.

You can set a reference to a VBA project in another Access database. The VBA project is the set of all the modules, both class and standard, in the project. When you set a reference from one project to a project in an Access database, a library database, or an add-in in an `.mde` file, you can run the procedures in the referenced project. You can run any of the public procedures contained in a standard module. You cannot run procedures in a class module or any that are labeled `Private`.

If you want to set a reference to a project created with an earlier version of Access, you must convert it to Access 97 first.

Connect to Other Applications

Even though you can work with objects from another application without setting a reference to that application's type library, your code will run faster if you first set the reference. For example, you can simply declare an object variable that represents an Excel worksheet as a specific type, as in the following declaration statement:

```
Dim appExl As New Excel.Application
```

Tip: Another advantage of using references to type libraries is that all of the objects along with their methods and properties will appear in the Object Browser. This makes it easy to see what is available and how to spell them.

Here are other new features in Access that can help you work with other applications:

- The new Office Assistant offers help for all the Office applications. You can ask specific questions or choose from the list of Help topics the Assistant displays.
- You can track database activity with the Outlook Journal, the desktop information management program that comes with Office 97. You can use Outlook to manage e-mail messages, appointments, contacts, tasks, and files in addition to keeping track of when your database was opened or closed and which report was printed. You can import and export data to and from Outlook.

The following features were introduced in Access 95:

- The text formatting is retained when you copy or cut data from Access and paste it in an Excel spreadsheet.
- When you save a report to a `.txt`, `.rtf`, or `.xls` file format, and it includes a subreport, the subreport is output as well.
- You can activate the Access Report Wizard from Excel when you need to use the grouping and formatting features of Access. You also can convert an Excel spreadsheet to an Access database by choosing Convert To Access from the Excel Data menu.
- The new PivotTable control can be added to a form when you need to summarize a lot of data. A PivotTable resembles a crosstab query. When you use the PivotTable Wizard available from Excel, you can specify the format and calculations you need. You must have Excel installed to use the PivotTable Wizard.
- You can now link spreadsheet data from Excel or Lotus 1-2-3 to your database if the data is arranged in a suitable tabular format.
- With the new drag-and-drop capabilities, you can now do the following:

    Move database objects between open databases

    Move tables and queries to other applications

    Create a table by dragging and dropping a range of cells from an Excel spreadsheet

    Drag and drop OLE objects into an OLE Object field in a form in either form or design view as well as into a report in design view

See Chapter 17 for more information on exchanging data.

New Internet Features

The new hyperlinks in Access 97 can easily connect your application to the Internet or a local area network. The hyperlink can jump to another object in the database, a document in your system or in another system, or an Internet location.

Hyperlink is a new data type that contains the address information of the destination object. A table field can be defined as a hyperlink type, or you can include hyperlinks on a form or report in any of three kinds of controls: command buttons, labels, and image controls. These controls have `Hyperlink` properties, which return the name of the object representing the hyperlink in the control. Each control also has a `HyperlinkAddress` and a `HyperlinkSubAddress`, which can set or return the address and subaddress of the hyperlink.

The hyperlink can be a path to a file on your hard disk, a UNC (Universal Naming Convention) path, or a URL (Universal Resource Locator). When you click the hyperlink, Access jumps to the object, document, Web page, or some other specified destination.

Clicking a control containing a hyperlink triggers the `Click` event and follows the hyperlink to the document or object specified in the address properties. The `HyperlinkAddress` property can refer to a form in your database, a document on another computer, or an address on the Web. If it refers to a Word document on another computer on the network, Word is launched on that computer and the document is opened. If it refers to an address on the Web, your Web browser opens and displays the Web page.

To get the same effect in VBA as clicking on the hyperlink object, use the `Follow` method of the `Hyperlink` object or the `FollowHyperlink` method of the `Application` object.

The Save As HTML option on the File menu lets you export a table, query, form, or report to HTML format. Reports can only be exported to static HTML format, but forms and datasheets can be exported to either static or dynamic HTML format. The Save As HTML option also can open the new Publish to the Web Wizard, which can output one or more datasheets, forms, or reports to HTML format using one or more of the HTML templates. The templates can help create handsomer and more consistent Web pages.

The Web Wizard also creates a home page and stores all files in a specified folder as a Web publication, copies the files to the Web server, and saves the publication profile.

When you import or link HTML tables and lists into your application, they are read-only. Choose File | Get External Data and click either Import or Link Tables. Then, choose HTML documents (`*.html`, `*.htm`) in the File Of Type box and use the Look In list in the Import or Link dialog box to find the folder that contains the files you want. Repeat the process for each file you want to import or link. The Import HTML Wizard and Link HTML Wizard convert HTML links to a hyperlink field.

You can also import or link data on FTP or HTTP servers, or you can export an Access database object to an FTP server.

See Chapter 20, "Posting Your Database to the Web," for more information on hyperlinks and how to import and export information using the Internet.

B

Converting from Earlier Versions of Access

Although you can enable a database created in an earlier version of Access to run in Access 97 without converting it, most of the time you will want to convert it. Most conversions take place with little or no user involvement. However, there are some programming considerations to be taken into account. New features are added and others removed. This appendix discusses some of the concerns relating to converting Access objects. It also points out some changes to your code that you need to know about and other changes you need to make so that your application runs successfully in Access 97. After it is converted, the database can no longer be opened by the earlier version.

Code that you have used in earlier versions of Access is automatically converted to VBA with only a few details that need your attention. Some new key words must be avoided in the converted code and some data types have been changed. Some of the VBA functions behave differently and may cause run-time errors. The main difference is that VBA used by Access 97 operates in a 32-bit environment while the Access Basic code from previous versions runs in a 16-bit environment.

Converting Access Objects

Although you can run a database created in an earlier version of Access in Access 97, you will not be able to change any of the object designs or take advantage of any of the new features. It is better to convert the database to Access 97 and make any necessary changes to adapt to the new environment.

Databases

To convert a normal, single-user database from an earlier version of Access, perform the following steps:

1. Make a backup copy of the database as a safeguard, and then close the database.
2. In the blank Access 97 window, choose Tools | Database Utilities | Convert Database.
3. Select the database you want to convert in the Database To Convert From dialog box, and click Convert.
4. In the Convert Database Into dialog box, type a new name for the database if you want to convert it in place. If you want to put it in another location, choose the location and keep the same name or enter a new one.
5. Click Save.

Warning: If your database has linked tables, be sure that the external tables remain in the same folder that they were in when the database was created. You won't be able to use the converted database if Access can't find the linked tables. After you convert the database, you can move the linked tables and relink them with the Linked Table Manager. The linked tables are not converted with the database.

Access 97 uses a new style of toolbars and menu bars. When you convert a database, the custom toolbars are automatically converted to the new style along with the built-in toolbars. Custom menu bars created with the Menu Builder in Access 95 or with a macro are treated as new style menu bars but are not actually converted. You cannot use the Customize dialog box to edit them. If you create a new style menu bar from a macro with the Tools | Create Menu (or Shortcut Menu) From Macro command, the result is a new style menu that can be edited with the Customize dialog box.

You must take special measures if the database is shared with other users who might or might not be converting to Access 97 at the same time. Secured databases also present special problems.

Converting Shared Databases

When not all of the users who share a multiuser database can upgrade to Access 97 at the same time, you can upgrade part of the database and leave the original database as is. Users of all versions then share the same data whether the database is one file or split into a front-end/back-end application.

If your database is in one file, perform the following steps to convert it to Access 97:

1. Convert the database and give it a new name.
2. Choose Tools | Add-Ins | Database Splitter, and use the Database Splitter Wizard to split the newly converted database into a front-end/back-end application.
3. You want to use the original database as the back-end database so that all the users work with the same data. To do this, delete the back-end database that was created by the wizard.
4. Choose Tools | Add-Ins, and run the Linked Table Manager to link the new Access 97 front-end database to the original back-end database.

All the users still have access to the original data in the back-end database, and the Access 97 users can enhance their front-end database objects to take advantage of the new features.

If the database was already split, convert the front-end only and leave the back-end database alone. Then run the Linked Table Manager as before to link the new Access 97 front-end database to the original back-end database.

Converting Secured Databases

Some additional steps are required when the database you want to convert is a secured database. First, you must join the workgroup information file in which the user accounts are defined or the one that was in use when the database was secured. To join an Access workgroup, you must exit Access and open the Workgroup Administrator. The process then depends on your operating system. Refer to Chapter 19, "Adding Security to the Application," for information on working with secured databases.

Your user account must have the following permissions:

- Open/Run and Open Exclusive at the database level
- Modify Design or Administer for all the tables or be the owner of all the tables
- Read Design for all the database objects

If all the users are upgrading at once, convert the database and its workgroup information file to Access 97. If not, the users can share the database and the workgroup information file across the various versions of Access.

How you convert a secured database depends on which version of Access it is upgrading from. If you are converting from a version 1.x or 2.0 secured database, you convert both the database and the workgroup information file, usually named the default System.mda. Then, tell the users to join the converted workgroup information file, now named System.mdw, before opening the converted database.

If you are converting from Access 95, convert only the database. The workgroup information file can be used without converting, but it should be compacted before it is used with the converted database. To convert an Access 95 database, perform the following steps:

1. Convert the database.
2. Compact the database and exit Access.
3. Temporarily join another workgroup information file and restart Access without opening any database.
4. Compact the workgroup information file that was used with the secured database.
5. Tell users to join the newly compacted workgroup information file before opening the converted database.

See Chapter 18, "Working in a Multiuser Environment," for more information about workgroups and shared databases. See Chapter 19 for information about secured databases.

Tables, Forms, and Reports

There are several changes in Access 97 that might affect how your version 1.*x* or 2.0 applications operate. Many of the important changes that influence the behavior of your tables, forms, reports, and workspace are described in the following list:

- The Jet DBEngine 3.5 used in Access 97 creates indexes for tables on both sides of a relationship. An Access table is limited to 32 indexes, so if you have complex tables with many relationships, you might exceed this limit and the conversion will fail. If this happens, delete some of the relationships and try again.

- In version 2.0, a combo box whose LimitToList property was set to True would not accept a Null value unless it was included in the list. In Access 97, a combo box will accept a Null value when LimitToList is set to True whether it is in the list or not. Therefore, if you want to be sure the users do not enter a Null value, set the combo box Required property to Yes.

- In Access 97, you cannot use an expression to refer to a control on a read-only form that is bound to an empty record source. In earlier versions, the expression would return a Null value if the form was empty, but Access 97 displays an error message.

- In earlier versions, a form or report had a class module assigned to it even if there was no code associated with the object. If you are not planning to add any code to the class module, set the HasModule property to False. A form or report without an associated class module takes up less disk space and loads faster.

- If reports you created in version 2.0 do not print properly, the margins might be the problem. If the report had some margins set to 0, they are no longer set to 0 when the report is converted. They are set instead to the minimum margin that is acceptable to the default printer.

- If you used the version 2.0 or 7.0 Command Button Wizard to generate code used to call another application, you should replace the buttons in Access 97. Delete the buttons and use the Access 97 Command Button Wizard to replace them.

The SendKey statement or action might require recoding. With so many changes to the menus and submenus, all SendKey key combinations must be reviewed. Many of the submenus have moved to different menus, so the key combinations will be different. For example, the Add-Ins submenu has moved to the Tools menu (key combination TI) from the File menu (key combination FI). Many other menu items have been reworded. For example, the Import, Export, and Attach submenus on the File menu have been changed to Get External Data and Save As/Export.

It is better to avoid the very explicit SendKeys action and use some other method of carrying out commands or filling in dialog boxes. Some alternatives are the following:

- Use a macro action or VBA method.
- If no equivalent macro or method is available, use RunCommand, which has several arguments indicating the position of the item in the menu instead of specific key letters.

- Use the `GetOption` and `SetOption` methods to set options in the Options dialog box because the option text can change, which also changes the key combinations.

- If all else fails, define keystrokes as constants and then refer to them in the `SendKeys` statement. They are easier to update as constants than if scattered throughout your code.

Properties and Validation Rules

Several properties have different names or functions in Access 97 than in prior versions. They are still accepted in Access 97 for backward compatibility, but you should use the current properties instead. Table B.1 shows the changes in the properties.

Table B.1. Properties changed in Access 97.

Previous Property	Current Property	Applies To
AllowEditing, DefaultEditing	AllowAdditions, AllowDeletions, AllowEdits, DataEntry	Forms
MaxButton, MinButton	MinMaxButtons	Forms
BorderLineStyle	BorderStyle	Forms and controls
AllowUpdating	RecordsetType	Crosstab and select queries, forms
Dynaset	RecordsetClone	Forms
ShowGrid	DatasheetGridlinesBehavior	Forms, querydefs, tabledefs

If you want to see a list of the new properties added with Access 97, open the Properties Reference in the Help window. The properties marked with a single asterisk (*) were added in Access 95 and those marked with a double asterisk (**) were added in Access 97.

Some validation rules are not converted because they are invalid, and others because Access 97 has improved versions of the rules. When Access finds an invalid rule, it makes a table called ConvertErrors that contains specific information about the rules that failed. The table has the following fields:

- Error—Describes the error
- Field—Names the field in which the error occurred
- Property—Names the table property in which the error occurred

- Table—Names the table containing the error
- Unconvertible Value—Shows the property value that caused the error

Errors can occur in both field and record validation rules that contain any of the following elements:

- User-defined functions
- Domain aggregate functions
- Aggregate functions
- References to forms, queries, or tables
- References to other fields (in a field validation rule)

Use the ConvertErrors table to identify the rules that failed conversion and to add validation rules as necessary.

Convert Access Basic to VBA

Access 97 uses Visual Basic for Applications, which is the programming language shared by all Microsoft products. When you convert a database created by an earlier version of Access, your code is automatically converted to VBA. VBA is nearly identical to Access Basic, but there are a few things to watch out for. The conversion process changes some of the code automatically, and other changes you need to make yourself.

The New 32-Bit Environment

The main difference is that VBA is a 32-bit application that runs on the 32-bit version of Windows. Access Basic is a 16-bit application that runs on a 16-bit version of Windows.

When you convert forms and reports that contain ActiveX controls, check carefully to make sure they have been converted correctly. Access 2.0 supported OLE controls, whereas Access 97 supports only the new 32-bit ActiveX controls. If your system does not have the 32-bit version of the control you want to convert, you will get an error message. Then, you must get the 32-bit version of the control and register it in the Windows Registry. After updating the OLE control to the ActiveX control, close and reopen the database to complete the conversion.

Code That Calls a Dynamic Link Library

The Windows Application Programming Interface (API) is actually a group of dynamic link libraries (DLLs) that provide all the functions, data types and structures, messages and statements you use to create an application to run on a Windows 95 or Windows NT platform. Before you can call these procedures from VBA, you must declare them with a declaration statement.

You might need to make some changes in your code when you convert the database to Access 97. The following suggestions can help you find and fix problem areas:

- If a `Declare` statement calls a 16-bit Windows API, you must change the references to call the DLLs by their new 32-bit names:

    `User.dll` becomes `User32.dll`

    `Kernel.dll` becomes `Kernel32.dll`

    `GUI.dll` becomes `GUI32.dll`

- Check the names of the API functions your code calls. Some names have been changed, and all names are now case sensitive.

- Check for new parameter data types in function calls.

- Avoid having a 16-bit DLL with the same name as a 32-bit DLL. Access might try to call the wrong one.

- Some functions in 32-bit DLLs have two different versions to accommodate both ANSI and Unicode strings. A function name ending with an A is the ANSI version; a W indicates the Unicode version. If the function in your code takes string arguments, you should call the function with the trailing A.

If you get the message `Specified DLL function not found` when converting to 32-bit, add `32` to the end of the library name and `A` to the name of the routine you are calling. This will usually correct the error.

If your database calls procedures in DLLs other than the API, you must have the 32-bit versions and make the appropriate changes in your code when you convert. If you can't find the 32-bit versions, you might be able to convert the 16-bit DLL with the help of an intermediary DLL.

Microsoft provides several sources for more information about 32-bit API procedures, including the following:

- The Microsoft Office 97 Developer Edition Windows API Viewer contains information about the syntax for all the 32-bit declarations, data types, and constants.

- Information about porting a 16-bit, Office-based application to a 32-bit platform is contained in the Microsoft Office Resource Kit.

- For complete information about 32-bit API procedures, consult the Microsoft Win32 Software Development Kit.

Data Type

Some properties now return string variables that in previous versions returned Variant values. You must be sure that the converted code produces no data type–related errors. Some of the optional arguments that were Variant are now also strictly typed. Among those affected are the following:

- The `GoToPage` method of a form object
- The `OpenCurrentDatabase`, `Echo`, `Quit`, `CreateForm`, `CreateReport`, `CreateControl`, and `CreateReportControl` methods of the application object
- The `Column` property of a combo box or list box
- Domain aggregate functions such as `DAvg()`, `DCount`, `DMin`, and `DMax`

If your application includes any of these, you should check to make sure no errors occur after the conversion: first by compiling all the modules and then by running the application to catch runtime errors. Errors such as `Type mismatch` and `Invalid use of Null` are the most common runtime errors that occur because of the new strict data typing.

Other errors might occur that are not found at runtime. For example, using a record source property for a control that previously referred to a Variant value, which is now converted to a string. You might have included code to check for `Null` values in the field. A string value cannot be `Null`, so your code will not do what you intend. If you use the `IsNull()` function to test the value, it will never return `True`. Instead, change the code to test for a zero-length string by comparing the value returned by the `Len()` function.

OLE objects and other binary data should be converted to an array of bytes in VBA. In Access 1.*x* and 2.0, you assigned OLE objects and data returned by the `GetChunk` method to string variables when you needed to manipulate them in code. VBA now has a Byte data type, which is stored as an unsigned 8-bit number. In Access 97, store binary data in an array of bytes instead of a string variable and use byte functions to work with the data. For example, the byte version of the `Len()` function is `LenB()`.

When you declared a variable in Access 1.*x* and 2.0 to store the channel number for a DDE channel, you used an integer number. In Access 97, you can declare the channel number, which is a Long value, as either Long or Variant. Be sure to change the declaration statement to reflect the changed data type when you convert to Access 97.

You will have trouble if you try to convert a string containing a percent sign (`%`) to a variable or field of the number data type. For example, the first of the following statements will cause an error, whereas the second statement will convert properly:

```
Dim intNum1 As Double, intNum2 As Double
    intNum1 = "125%"     'Causes Run-time error #13, Type mismatch.
    IntNum2 = "125"      'Is correct.
```

The Time portion of Date/Time values have changed in Access 97. If you have any query criteria that depend on Date/Time values, they might return different results than did previous versions. You might also have trouble with this when you try to link tables from an earlier database with databases created in Access 97.

Formats

The Format() function works differently in Access 97 than in Access 2.0. In Access 2.0, you could use the Format() function to return one value if the argument contained a Null value and a different value if it was a zero-length string. The following Access 2.0 statement formats the string passed to it and displays the string if it contains characters, as specified by the @ character. The words, "Zero Length" are displayed if it contains a zero-length string, and "Null" is displayed if it is a Null value:

```
Dim varResult As Variant, strMsg As String
'Give the strMsg a value and pass to the Format() function.
varResult = Format(strMsg, "@;Zero Length;Null")
```

In Access 97, the string format expression in the Format() function has only two sections: one for the characters in the string and the second to be used if the string is either empty or Null. You must test separately for a Null value. One way to accomplish this is to change your code to test first for a Null value and then use the Format function to decide on the appropriate value to return based on the results of the IIf() function. The following statement will return the same result as the previous statement:

```
varResult = IIf(IsNull(strMsg), "Null", Format(strMsg, "@;Zero Length"))
```

You no longer can use the Format property in a table datasheet view to distinguish between Null values and zero-length strings. If you have depended on either of these uses of formatting, change the code or property settings accordingly.

Properties

The hWnd property determines the handle that is assigned by Windows to the current window. The property applies to forms and reports and is used when making calls to Windows API functions or other external routines. In Access 1.x and 2.0, the hWnd property value is an Integer value, while in Access 97 it is a Long value. For this reason, you should change your code to accept the new data type or pass the hWnd property directly to the routine rather than assign it to a variable.

The Parent property of a control in VBA code or in an expression usually returns the name of the form or report that contains the control. For example, in Access 97 the code, Forms!Transaction_Log!Transaction_ID.Parent would refer to the Transaction Log form. However, if the control is an attached label, it returns the name of the control to which it is attached. If the control is one of the options in an option group, the Parent property returns the name of the option group control.

The Category property is no longer supported for form, report, and control objects.

Access Modules

The modules containing procedures not specific to any form or report module were called *global modules* in Access 1.*x* and 2.0. Now they are called *standard modules*. Access 97 also includes *class modules* that can be used to create custom forms and reports. They can exist either in association with or independent of a specific form or report.

In Access 1.*x* and 2.0, you were limited to the procedures defined within a form or report and could not call routines from any other form or report module. In Access 97, you can call a public procedure in a form or report module from anywhere in the current database. You must, however, refer to it by the full class name of its source. For example, if you wanted to call the ShowCategories procedure from the Transactions Log form, you would use the following syntax:

```
Form_Transaction_Log.ShowCategories
```

It is better practice to place all the procedures you may call from an external source in a standard module. This way they are always available, even if you delete the form or report whose module contained the code.

Each form and report contains one module, and VBA limits the number of modules to 1024 per database. If you have more than that you will get an Out of memory error message when you try to convert the database to Access 97. To solve this problem, eliminate some of the objects or split the database into two or more separate databases. Another solution might be to store very large modules in a library database that does not count against the current database. Procedures in a library database can be accessed by any application after establishing a reference from the current database to the library database.

Sub and Function Procedure Behavior

To return a Database object variable that refers to the current database, use the CurrentDB function instead of DBengine(0)(0). The DBengine(0)(0) function refers only to the open copy of the current database, which limits your ability to use more than one variable to refer to the current database. The CurrentDB function creates another instance of the database, which enables you to refer to the database with more than one Database type variable. DBengine is still supported, but using CurrentDB instead might prevent conflicts if you should open the database for multiuser access.

The behavior of the CurDir function has changed in Access 97 because of the way applications interact in the Windows 95 environment. Each application has its own folder, and double-clicking a Windows 95 folder icon does not change the current folder in Access. CurDir always returns the current path.

Most functions can be used in expressions as well as VBA code. Six functions can no longer be used outside a user-defined procedure. They are EOF(), FileAttr(), FreeFile(), Loc(), LOF(), and Seek(). They can be indirectly used in an expression by calling the function from within a user-defined function procedure.

If any of the lines in your converted Access 1.*x* or 2.0 modules are assigned line numbers greater than 65,529, you must reassign them to lower numbers.

Debugging and Error Handling

VBA now lets ActiveX objects that support Automation return more specific error information. Automation was previously called OLE Automation servers. In Access 1.*x* and 2.0, only a single Automation error message was available. If your database includes error trapping based on that one error, you might want to expand the code to handle the more specific errors that are now reported.

The properties of the Err object in Access 97 give you information about the Access error that has occurred. Err.Number returns the error code number, and Err.Description returns its description. If you want information about Access, VBA, or DAO errors, you can use the AccessError method. An error need not occur before you can acquire information with the AccessError method.

ActiveX controls were formerly called OLE or custom controls. If your application contains any that were set up in Access 2.0, you might need to pass them to a procedure with the ByVal keyword. To find out if you need to add ByVal, choose Debug | Compile All Modules in the module design window. If you see the message Event procedure declaration doesn't match description of event having the same name, you need to insert the ByVal keyword in front of the argument. New procedures using ActiveX controls as arguments automatically include the ByVal keyword.

When you are testing new code, you must use full references to objects you want to see in the Debug window unless you have suspended execution. For example, to refer to the Type control in the Transaction Log form in form view, use the code Forms!Transaction_Log!Type. You may not use the Me keyword in the Debug window unless execution is suspended.

In Access 1.*x* and 2.0, the module toolbar included two buttons that are no longer available in Access 97: Next Procedure and Previous Procedure. If you have created a custom toolbar that included those buttons for your application and converted the application to Access 97, the buttons will still appear in the toolbar but they will have no effect when clicked.

Using References

If you enable a large database created in Access 1.*x* or 2.0 without converting it to Access 97, your default buffer size might be insufficient. To increase it, you need to open the Windows Registry. To do this, click Start and then Run. Next, type regedit in the Run dialog box and then click OK. In the Registry Editor dialog box, navigate to the following folder:

`\HKEY_LOCAL\MACHINE\SOFTWARE\Microsoft\Jet\3.0\Engines\Jet2.x`

Next, choose Edit | New | Key and add a new key named ISAM; then add a new DWORD value called MaxBufferSize. Enter 1024 (kilobytes) as the new value for MaxBufferSize. The buffer size can be set to a value between 9 and 4096 with the default value 512KB.

The new exclamation point (!) operator refers to user-named objects in Access 97. If you used the dot (.) operator exclusively in Access 1.x and 2.0, you must change those references to use the ! operator. If you don't want to modify the operators, you can establish a reference to the Microsoft DAO 2.5/3.5 compatibility library in the References dialog box. To open this dialog box, choose Tools | References while in the module window. Then, check the box next to the option in the Available References list and choose OK.

Access 2.0 made no distinction between wizards and libraries. All the public code contained in them was available to the current database. You could call procedures in a wizard just as easily as you could call one in a library. Access 97 no longer treats wizards as libraries, so after you convert the application, you must establish a reference from it to the wizard database where the procedures you need are stored. Wizards also add more and more capability with each version of Access, so you might need to redo the code to accommodate these changes.

Some code, such as AutoDialer, is no longer available from a wizard but has been added to the special library database named Utility.mda. A reference to the Utility.mda add-ins file is automatically added when you convert to Access 97 or you can add it yourself by opening the References Editor dialog box and choosing Browse. Next, use the Add Reference dialog box to search for the Utility.mda file. It is usually located in the Office subfolder of the Microsoft Office folder. After locating the file, click Add, and it is added to the Available References list where you can check to establish the reference.

You can rename a database, but when you do, all the code is decompiled and must be recompiled. You can wait until you want to run the application again or recompile immediately by opening a module in design view and choosing Debug | Compile and Save All Modules.

You cannot set a reference within Access 97 to a database from an earlier version without converting it first.

Scope and Object Name Compatibility

The naming rules in Access 97 forbid beginning a module name with the name of an Access or DAO object. When you try to convert the database, you will get a compilation error message and be asked to rename a module with such a name before the conversion is completed. For example, a module named Report_NewProduct would trigger an error. Rename the module and move on with the conversion.

VBA has added some new keywords that cannot be used as identifiers. If the database you want to convert uses any of the new keywords as identifiers, you will get a compile error. Here's a list of the new keywords:

AddressOf	Event
Assert	Friend
Decimal	Implements
DefDec	RaiseEvent
Enum	WithEvents

Rename the identifiers to complete the conversion.

In prior Access versions, the project name was simply the name of the database. In Access 97, a project name other than the database name is specified by the ProjectName property setting. The project name may not be the same as an object name. If your database has the same name as a class of objects, Access adds an underscore character to the project name to differentiate it from the corresponding object name.

Library Databases and Add-Ins

If you intend to use library databases and add-ins that you created in prior versions, you must first convert them to Access 97. You might also need to make some changes in the objects, procedures, and macros to make sure they work the way you want.

To use a converted library database, you must establish a reference to it for each of the applications that need it. Choose Tools | References while in the module window and check the desired library database.

Access 97 no longer allows circular references among libraries. That is, if Library A includes a reference to Library B, you cannot establish a reference from Library B to Library A.

In Access 97, you can see all the intrinsic constants in the type libraries in the Object Browser. The Microsoft Access, Data Access Objects, and Visual Basic libraries all include intrinsic constants. In the list of constants, some of the names are all uppercase and include the underscore character (for example, A_FORM). This is a constant held over from versions 1.x and 2.0. The new format is a combination of upper- and lowercase (for example, acForm). The old formats will still work and are not automatically converted to the new format.

Converting DAO Code

DAO code is backward compatible now but might not be in the future. You should use the new DAO objects, methods, and properties with new applications and change to them when you modify current applications. To keep using older DAO versions, establish a reference to the DAO 2.5/3.5 Compatibility library (choose Tools | References). This enables you to use DAO elements from versions 1.*x*, 2.0, and 95 (7.0).

The DAO 3.5 library doesn't include the older elements and is automatically selected for all new applications. If you don't use any of the old DAO elements, you don't need to include the DAO 2.5/3.5 Compatibility library when you distribute the application to the users, which saves disk space.

To check the dependency of an application on the DAO 2.5/3.5 Compatibility library, clear it in the References dialog box and recompile the application. If no errors occur, your application doesn't need the Compatibility library anymore.

To modify existing code to remove the need for the Compatibility library, change the functionality that doesn't appear in DAO 3.5 to the recommended replacement. Refer to the Access 97 Help topic "DAO Object Library Compatibility" for a list of things to change. The topic "Examples of Converting DAO Code" shows many helpful examples of converting code constructs from earlier versions to DAO 3.5.

Table B.2 lists the obsolete DAO features and their replacements.

Table B.2. Replacement features for DAO 3.5.

Obsolete Feature	Replacement Feature
CreateDynaset methods (all)	OpenRecordset method
CreateSnapshot methods (all)	OpenRecordset method
ListFields methods (all)	Fields collection
ListIndexes methods (all)	Indexes collection
CompactDatabase statement	DBEngine.CompactDatabase method
CreateDatabase statement	DBEngine.CreateDatabase method
DBEngine.FreeLocks method	DBEngine.Idle method
DBEngine.SetDefaultWorkspace method	DBEngine.DefaultUser and DBEngine.Password properties
DBEngine.SetDataAccessOption method	DBEngine.IniPath property
Database.BeginTrans method	Workspace.BeginTrans method
Database.CommitTrans method	Workspace.CommitTrans method
Database.Rollback method	Workspace.Rollback method
Database.DeleteQueryDef method	Delete method

continues

Table B.2. continued

Obsolete Feature	Replacement Feature
`Database.ExecuteSQL` method	`Execute` method
`Database.ListTables` method	`TableDefs` collection
`Database.OpenQueryDef` method	`QueryDefs` collection
`Database.OpenTable` method	`OpenRecordset` method
`FieldSize` method	`FieldSize` property
`Index.Fields` property	`Index.Fields` collection
`OpenDatabase` statement	`DBEngine.OpenDatabase` method
`QueryDef.ListParameters` method	`Parameters` collection
`Snapshot` object	`Recordset` object
`Dynaset` object	`Recordset` object
`Table` object	`Recordset` object

Other Considerations

The `/runtime` command-line switch is no longer supported in the stand-alone or the Office Professional version of Access 97. If you want to use `/runtime`, you must use the Office Developer Edition of Access 97.

If you need more help converting databases from other versions of Access, the Help topics, "Conversion and Compatibility Issues" and "Convert Access Basic Code to Visual Basic" contain a lot of information.

Index

CHECK OUT THE BOOKS IN THIS LIBRARY.

You'll find thousands of shareware files and over 1600 computer books designed for both technowizards and technophobes. You can browse through 700 sample chapters, get the latest news on the Net, and find just about anything using our massive search directories.

All Macmillan Computer Publishing books are available at your local bookstore.

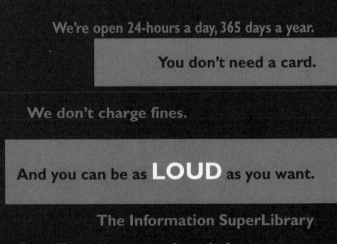

We're open 24-hours a day, 365 days a year.

You don't need a card.

We don't charge fines.

And you can be as **LOUD** as you want.

The Information SuperLibrary
http://www.mcp.com/mcp/   ftp.mcp.com

MACMILLAN COMPUTER PUBLISHING USA

A VIACOM COMPANY

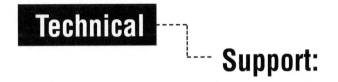

Support:

If you need assistance with the information in this book or with a CD/Disk accompanying the book, please access the Knowledge Base on our Web site at **http://www.superlibrary.com/general/support**. Our most Frequently Asked Questions are answered there. If you do not find the answer to your questions on our Web site, you may contact Macmillan Technical Support **(317) 581-3833** or e-mail us at **support@mcp.com**.

Access 97 Unleashed, Second Edition

Dwayne Gifford, et al.

Access, one of Microsoft's database managers for Windows, has become one of the most accepted standards of database management for personal computers. The *Unleashed* format for this book enables current and new users to quickly and easily find the information they need on the new features. It also serves as a complete reference for database programmers new to Access. Readers learn advanced techniques for working with tables, queries, forms, and data and how to program Access and integrate the database with the Internet.

Price: $49.99 USA/$70.95 CDN   *User level: Accomplished–Expert*
ISBN: 0-672-30983-1   *1,100 pages*

Access 97 Programming Unleashed

Scott Billings, Joe Rhemann, et al.

Access 97 solves all the development problems within Access 95, so more developers have been adopting Access 97 as their preferred database application development environment. Using hands-on, real-world examples, this book teaches users key programming and development concepts and provides extensive coverage of the most widely used topics in database programming. Covers key topics, including VBA, Active Data Objects, OLE DB, ODBCDirect, Jet replication, code libraries, performance optimization, security, Visual SourceSafe, and Web connectivity.

Price: $49.99 USA/$70.95 CAN   *User level: Accomplished–Expert*
ISBN: 0-672-31049-X   *1,000 pages*

Visual Basic 5 Developer's Guide

Anthony T. Mann

Visual Basic 5 Developer's Guide takes the programmer with a basic knowledge of Visual Basic programming to a higher skill level. Readers learn how to exploit the new features of the latest version of Visual Basic, in addition to implementing Visual Basic in a network setting and in conjunction with other technologies and software. Learn expert programming techniques and strategies to create better applications. The CD-ROM contains the complete source code for all of the programs in the book.

Price: $49.99 USA/$70.95 CAN   *User level: Accomplished–Expert*
ISBN: 0-672-31048-1   *1,000 pages*

ActiveX Programming Unleashed

Weiying Chen, et al.

ActiveX is Microsoft's core Internet communications technology. This book describes and details that technology, giving programmers the knowledge they need to create powerful ActiveX programs for the Web and beyond. Covers ActiveX controls—the full-featured components of the Internet—and teaches you how to use ActiveX documents, server framework, ISAPI, security, and more.

Price: $39.99 USA/$56.95 CDN   *User level: Accomplished–Expert*
ISBN: 1-57521-154-8   *700 pages*

Add to Your Sams Library Today with the Best Books for Programming, Operating Systems, and New Technologies

The easiest way to order is to pick up the phone and call

1-800-428-5331

between 9:00 a.m. and 5:00 p.m. EST.
For faster service please have your credit card available.

ISBN	Quantity	Description of Item	Unit Cost	Total Cost
0-672-30983-1		Access 97 Unleashed, Second Edition	$49.99	
0-672-31049-X		Access 97 Programming Unleashed	$49.99	
0-672-31048-1		Visual Basic 5 Developer's Guide	$49.99	
1-57521-154-8		ActiveX Programming Unleashed	$39.99	
❏ 3 ½" Disk		Shipping and Handling: See information below.		
❏ 5 ¼" Disk		TOTAL		

Shipping and Handling: $4.00 for the first book, and $1.75 for each additional book. Floppy disk: add $1.75 for shipping and handling. If you need to have it NOW, we can ship product to you in 24 hours for an additional charge of approximately $18.00, and you will receive your item overnight or in two days. Overseas shipping and handling adds $2.00 per book and $8.00 for up to three disks. Prices subject to change. Call for availability and pricing information on latest editions.

201 W. 103rd Street, Indianapolis, Indiana 46290

1-800-428-5331 — Orders   1-800-835-3202 — FAX   1-800-858-7674 — Customer Service

Book ISBN: 0-672-31050-3

What's on
the Disc

The companion CD-ROM contains all of the authors' source code and samples from the book and many third-party software products.

Windows NT Installation Instructions

1. Insert the CD-ROM disc into your CD-ROM drive.

2. From File Manager or Program Manager, choose Run from the File menu.

3. Type `<drive>\SETUP.EXE` and press Enter, where `<drive>` corresponds to the drive letter of your CD-ROM. For example, if your CD-ROM is drive `D:`, type `D:\SETUP.EXE`, and press Enter.

4. Installation creates a program named PN Access 97 Prog. This group will contain icons that enable you to browse the CD-ROM.

Windows 95 Installation Instructions

1. Insert the CD-ROM disc into your CD-ROM drive.

2. From the Windows 95 desktop, double-click the My Computer icon.

3. Double-click the icon representing your CD-ROM drive.

4. Double-click the icon titled SETUP.EXE to run the installation program.

5. Installation creates a program group named PN Access 97 Prog. This group will contain icons that enable you to browse the CD-ROM.

Note: If Windows 95 is installed on your computer and you have the AutoPlay feature enabled, the SETUP.EXE program starts automatically whenever you insert the disc into your CD-ROM drive.